To Make This Land Our Own

The Carolina Lowcountry and the Atlantic World
Sponsored by the Carolina Lowcountry and Atlantic World Program of the College of Charleston

Money, Trade, and Power
Edited by Jack P. Greene, Rosemary Brana-Shute, and Randy J. Sparks

The Impact of the Haitian Revolution in the Atlantic World
Edited by David P. Geggus

London Booksellers and American Customers
James Raven

Memory and Identity
Edited by Bertrand Van Ruymbeke and Randy J. Sparks

This Remote Part of the World
Bradford J. Wood

The Final Victims
James A. McMillin

The Atlantic Economy during the Seventeenth and Eighteenth Centuries
Edited by Peter A. Coclanis

From New Babylon to Eden
Bertrand Van Ruymbeke

Saints and Their Cults in the Atlantic World
Edited by Margaret Cormack

Who Shall Rule at Home?
Jonathan Mercantini

To Make This Land Our Own
Arlin C. Migliazzo

To Make This Land Our Own

Community, Identity, and Cultural Adaptation in Purrysburg Township, South Carolina, 1732–1865

Arlin C. Migliazzo

Foreword by Lawrence S. Rowland

The University of South Carolina Press

Published by the University of South Carolina Press
Columbia, South Carolina 29208

www.sc.edu/uscpress

Manufactured in the United States of America

16 15 14 13 12 11 10 09 08 07   10 9 8 7 6 5 4 3 2 1

Library of Congress Cataloging-in-Publication Data

Migliazzo, Arlin C., 1951–
To make this land our own : community, identity, and cultural adaptation in Purrysburg Township, South Carolina, 1732–1865 / Arlin C. Migliazzo ; foreword by Lawrence S. Rowland.
p. cm. — (The Carolina lowcountry and the Atlantic world)
Includes bibliographical references and index.
ISBN-13: 978-1-57003-682-8 (cloth : alk. paper)
ISBN-10: 1-57003-682-9 (cloth : alk. paper)
1. Purrysburg (S.C. : Township)—History 18th century. 2. Purrysburg (S.C. : Township)—History 19th century. 3. Purrysburg (S.C. : Township)—Social conditions. 4. Purrysburg (S.C. : Township)—Commerce—Social aspects—History. 5. Community life—South Carolina—Purrysburg (Township)—History. 6. Group identity—South Carolina—Purrysburg (Township)—History. 7. Ethnicity—South Carolina—Purrysburg (Township)—History. 8. Acculturation—South Carolina—Purrysburg (Township)—History. 9. Social networks—South Carolina—Purrysburg (Township)—History. I. Title.
F279.P87M54 2007
975.7'98—dc22

2006100450

This book was printed on Glatfelter Natures, a recycled paper with 50 percent postconsumer waste content.

To the settlers of Purrysburg Township
who created a new homeland in the Carolina wilderness
and to those who perpetuate their legacy of courage
in each generation

Contents

Illustrations

Following page 156

Foreword

Lawrence S. Rowland

From 1670, when the first English settlers of South Carolina sailed into Port Royal Sound, to 1733, when General James Oglethorpe led the first settlers of Georgia up the Savannah River to Yamacraw Bluff, the Savannah River boundary of South Carolina was also the southern boundary of British North America. From 1670 to 1733, South Carolina colonists maintained a beleaguered outpost of the British Empire. They were beset by hostile Creek Indians to the south and surrounded by powerful European rivals in Spanish Florida (1565–1763) and French Louisiana (1702–1763). In addition, Carolinians were increasingly worried by the threat to their domestic security posed by the increasing majority of African slaves. It was within this context of concern for the security, even the survival, of South Carolina that the political leaders of the province proposed plans to the British Board of Trade to populate the dangerous southern frontier with European immigrants. Colonel John "Tuscarora Jack" Barnwell of Beaufort proposed a ring of forts from the Altamaha River in Georgia to the mountains of Tennessee garrisoned by British redcoats. In 1723 he and his Carolina Scouts built the only one of these frontier forts at Darien, Georgia, but no settlers followed.

Governor Robert Johnson (1730–1735), South Carolina's first permanent royal governor, proposed a more practical plan. Johnson's "Township Plan" created spacious townships across the Carolina frontier and offered free land and agricultural assistance to any Protestant Europeans who would settle there. This was the beginning of the settlement of the South Carolina backcountry and the beginning of the movement that eventually led to British dominion of the American Southeast. Purrysburg was the very first of these frontier townships.

Purrysburg was not only the creation of British imperial and provincial policy, but also the realization of the dream of one of South Carolina's most visionary and enigmatic colonial entrepreneurs. The adventures of Jean Pierre Purry (1675–1736) led him about as far from his home in Neuchâtel, Switzerland, as the globe could accommodate. In 1713 he traveled to the Dutch East Indies (Indonesia) and from there perhaps to western Australia. He came to the curious belief that the ideal locations for human habitation on earth were at thirty-three degrees north or south latitude. This led him and six hundred Swiss colonists to the Great Yamassee Bluff on the banks of the Savannah River beginning in 1732.

The story that follows is the story of the French-speaking Swiss, the German-speaking Swiss, and a few Protestant families from the Italian Piedmont who populated South Carolina's first frontier township. While the location of the Purrysburg Township in the "pine barren" section of the Carolina low-country was not favorable for plantation agriculture, it was well situated to capture a fair share of the commerce between South Carolina and the new province of Georgia.

For nearly three decades following Purrysburg's founding in 1732, the little village was the principal crossing of the lower Savannah River on the "King's Highway" that connected Charleston to Savannah. During these years, a small collection of merchants and artisans, mostly original Swiss immigrants or their descendants, kept the village alive. In the 1760s, Charles and Jermyn Wright, brothers of Georgia governor Sir James Wright, built a three-mile causeway across the Savannah River marshes to the main river channel directly across from the Georgia capital. In 1762 the Wright brothers obtained a South Carolina charter for "Rochester Ferry" at that location. This soon became the preferred crossing for travelers going from South Carolina to Georgia. Purrysburg was bypassed, and the village began to decline.

Purrysburg played a small but strategic part in the Revolutionary War. The middle-class artisans, merchants, and yeoman farmers of Purrysburg contributed a sizable company of militia, commanded by Colonel John Lewis Bourquin, to the patriot forces in South Carolina. In 1779 the township hosted the encampment of Colonel William Moultrie's South Carolina militia guarding the Savannah River boundary against British-occupied Georgia. British general Augustine Prevost used unguarded landings in Purrysburg Township to launch his invasion of South Carolina in 1779, and the following year General James Patterson led three British regiments across the Savannah River just north of Purrysburg Township on his way to securing the envelopment and eventual surrender of Charleston in May 1780. At the end of the Revolutionary War, Purrysburg, like much of the South Carolina lowcountry, was "peeled, pillaged and plundered." During the next twenty years, many of the descendants of the original settlers moved out of the township to more promising agricultural areas or to nearby cities and towns. Purrysburg nearly disappeared.

The old river town experienced a revival of sorts in April 1816, when the S.S. *Enterprise*, the first steam paddle wheeler to ascend the Savannah River, stopped at the Purrysburg landing. For the next forty years, Purrysburg was a regular stop for the steamboats that plied the Savannah River between Savannah and Augusta.

In 1853 the South Carolina General Assembly issued a corporate charter for the Charleston and Savannah Railroad Company inaugurating the railroad era in the lowcountry. Between 1856 and 1860, the railroad line was surveyed, cleared, graded and constructed. The line of the new railroad passed two miles east of the old river town, and the whistle stop village of Hardeeville grew up at that location. The new mode of transportation once again bypassed Purrysburg.

The Charleston and Savannah Railroad was the great strategic prize of the Civil War campaigns in the lowcountry, and for three years (1861–1864) it enabled the Confederate garrisons in Savannah and Charleston to protect the hinterland of South Carolina from invasion. When William Tecumseh Sherman's Union army crossed into South Carolina in January 1865, Union gunboats ascended the Savannah River beyond Purrysburg to protect its crossing. Elements of the Union army actually camped at Purrysburg, but by then little was left of the old town. What little was there when the Union army arrived was a charred ruin when it left. Like much of the rest of the countryside between Savannah and Columbia, Purrysburg never recovered from the Civil War. Only a stone cross placed by the Huguenot Society of South Carolina marks the spot of old Purrysburg today. Although the old town has disappeared, the descendants of the Swiss, German and Piedmontese families who settled there in the 1730s have woven themselves thoroughly into the fabric of South Carolina history.

To Make This Land Our Own: Community, Identity, and Cultural Adaptation in Purrysburg Township, South Carolina, 1732–1865 is the most thorough and comprehensive study ever done on Purrysburg, and it is likewise one of the most comprehensive studies done for any community on the southern frontier. Like the old stone cross of the Huguenot Society on the banks of the Savannah River, this book will likely stand for generations as a monument to the memory of the intrepid pioneers of old Purrysburg and the talented and enterprising progeny that they contributed to the history of South Carolina.

PREFACE

I vividly recall my first visit to the Southeast in the torrid summer of 1980. It was during that Carolina sojourn when it dawned on me just how far removed I was from the subjects of my research. Land forms, the flora and fauna, climate, customs, institutions—all these features I knew would be quite different from the West I knew so well. But there was also much I did not know. As my family and I left behind salmon bakes, Rosauer's supermarkets, and wineries for grits, sweet tea, Piggly Wiggly, and Harris-Teeter, we also discovered a deeper history than we had ever known.

The evocative power of that history became apparent to me the day we visited the site of Purrysburg Township.[1] I had read about the cross placed by the Huguenot Society of South Carolina on the Great Yamassee Bluff in 1941, probably fairly close to where Jean Pierre Purry and his associates stood with Captain Evans of the Carolina Rangers during the summer of 1731. I knew about the old wharf on the Savannah River that once brought mail, news, products, and visitors—such as General James Oglethorpe, the Reverend John Wesley, and President George Washington—from up and down the Atlantic coast and Europe. I had also read about the overland road system connecting the township to Charleston, Coosawhatchie, Beaufort, Orangeburg, Augusta, and Savannah and had already become acquainted with some of the families that had immigrated there so many generations earlier. So Purrysburg was not unknown to me even before we stopped along the two-lane river highway that hot summer day.[2]

I took time to read the historical marker and examine the gravestones in the nearby cemetery, finding some familiar Purrysburg names and others of more recent demise that I did not recognize. As I thought about all that had happened in this place more than two centuries prior to my arrival, it struck me that the commuters and sightseers driving the highway flashed past the marker and the dilapidated graveyard perhaps never realizing on their way to Savannah or Augusta or Columbia that they had passed directly through the center of a frontier settlement. They were as far removed from the history of this place as was I. The lives and deaths, hopes and fears of the hundreds who lived in Purrysburg remained as foreign to them as South Carolina felt to me, for when it comes to the past, any past, we are all strangers in a strange land.

That realization became an encouraging epiphany for me because historians are, after all, committed to a discipline that requires of its partisans a practiced schizophrenia. We recognize that our vocation proceeds from a commitment to render faithfully an accurate understanding of the past. At the same time, we are fully cognizant of the fact that the same past we so much seek to know is gone forever along with the vast majority of the evidence verifying its existence. Nevertheless, while conceding the difficulty of our task, historians cannot succumb to the cultural currents swirling through our own time that would have us believe that there is no "true" history to discover. The distance between what actually occurred and why it did, on the one hand, and the fragmentary sources at our disposal to guide our attempts to recapture events none of us directly witnessed, on the other, is where the historian must travel. Some may choose not to follow certain routes of inquiry for the path is potholed, strewn with debris, and mucked up quite a little even where it is visible, but it does exist. Moreover, if historians make only provisional journeys of reconnaissance along parts of its length, others will follow and edge closer to that far country of historical truth. We may never "know" the subjects of our inquiry as fully as we would desire, but just because we cannot know all of what really was does not mean we cannot know some of what was and is no more.

Purrysburg Township, South Carolina, is located in that far country of verifiable reality. Unfortunately, the remaining recorded facts regarding it are scattered, incomplete, and inadequate. Of course, we could wish for more solid data upon which to hang reasonable suppositions. But no matter how much reliable information might be available, the whole story of hundreds of people from dozens of locales, over the span of more than a hundred years could never be told as historians would wish. No amount of theorizing about ethnic identity, community development, or adaptive strategies would be able to tell the complete saga of life in a place none of us has ever experienced in a time radically different than our own. In this regard, this study of Purrysburg Township is no different than any other work of historical scholarship, and, if the data sets are less than what social historians might hope for, they are sufficiently rich and varied to have provided me better than two decades of scholarly investigation. The decision has to be made at some point in any historical inquiry whether what records we do possess legitimate an effort to develop a narrative around them. Although I have believed for more than twenty years that we do not have enough of the right kinds of records relating to Purrysburg, I have simultaneously acted upon the conviction that what we have is enough to advance our understanding of the contours of life in the first South Carolina township and through it sharpen our perspectives on life in the colonial Southeast.

As I look back on my years of research and writing on Purrysburg Township, I am most amazed that what began as an exploration into a place so far removed from my own resulted in a deeper recognition of just how much we have in common with those long-ago immigrants to the southern frontier. For, after living with so many colonial pioneers for so many years, I believe that what we can learn of Purrysburg connects us in space and time not only to the township residents and our forebears, but also to the intrinsic humanness that binds us inextricably to them and to each other.

Acknowledgments

The publication of this volume marks the end of a twenty-five-year personal and professional odyssey for me. I began my study of Purrysburg as a relatively youthful, recently married graduate student at Washington State University in the early 1980s and now conclude it in the early twenty-first century as a professor of history at a respected church-related college in the Pacific Northwest not that far-removed from entertaining serious thoughts about retirement. Along the way, it seemed on more than one occasion that I had left Purrysburg and her people behind for one reason or another. Family commitments intervened. I pursued other research and teaching interests. Before I knew it, nearly seventeen years had elapsed between my first research trip to South Carolina and my second. Yet, even during those years, I could not really shake myself free of the questions that had piqued my initial curiosity in South Carolina's first township. They informed my teaching and provoked substantial self-reflection even as I studied, wrote, and spoke on other topics because at a very basic level they are questions that we as humans always ask: Who am I? Who are you? Why am I here? What am I to do with my life? Perhaps one of the reasons it has taken me more than two decades to answer these questions for the residents of Purrysburg Township proceeds from the recognition that it has taken me at least that long to begin to comprehend my own answers to them. Those answers have, at least in part been generated by the powerful influence my family has had upon my personal and professional development. My wife, Judi, has been along for this entire journey, and, though we have navigated some treacherous waters over the years, she has been and will continue to be the person to whom I most often look for support and encouragement. My thanks go above all to her, for all she means to me. Our daughter was barely a year old when we first traveled to South Carolina. She is today a woman of whom any father would be proud and one of the great joys of my life. Our son's birth came a few years after I began this project. Today I am grateful father to a young man whose most treasured gift to me is his presence in my life. I thank both Sara and Nathan for "dad time" with each of them as well as their forbearance when I had to spend "Purrysburg time" with those southerners always waiting for me downstairs in the basement. I have also been fortunate to have mentors, colleagues, and friends whose support helped me maintain the stamina needed to bring this project to completion. My undergraduate advisor from Biola University, the late Masakazu Iwata, and his wife, Doreen, never ceased to believe that this project had merit. David Coon, my mentor at Washington State University and fellow scholar of colonial South Carolina, helped move my formative research on Purrysburg in productive directions and saved me from significant egregious methodological faux pas during those early years. Other members of the history faculty at WSU, particularly my committee members Richard Hume, Thomas Kennedy, and Edwin Garretson, provided helpful suggestions and posed important questions for me to consider as did Fred Bohm, now director of the Michigan State University Press.

For most of my professional life I have been fortunate to live and work in engaging communities of scholar-teachers. My colleagues at Whitworth College have not only sustained me and listened to more Purrysburg stories than they would care to admit, but some have also graciously given of their time and expertise. Without the language skills of Corliss Slack, Pierrette Christianne-Lovrien, and 'BioDun Ogundayo in French and Elisabeth Buxton in German, my understanding of Purry's life and writings would have suffered appreciably. They spent hours translating text for me—a substantial amount of which was in eighteenth-century script. Their work makes this a much stronger manuscript than it otherwise would have been. The most practical help I have been given during my years of study on Purrysburg has come from Whitworth College administrators and granting committees. The Faculty Research and Development Committee supplied financial assistance during the summer of 1986 that allowed me to begin the first major revision of what had been a passable dissertation but a rather inadequate book. A research fellowship from the Weyerhaeuser Center for Christian Faith and Learning thirteen summers later provided research and travel funds that underwrote twelve weeks of research in South Carolina and writing back in Washington State. My work has also been greatly facilitated by study releases granted by the Office of the Academic Vice President. A January term study release in 1994 was especially helpful in continuing my investigation of Purry's geographical writings. Sabbatical leaves of absence granted for the fall and January terms of 1999–2000 and 2003–2004 enabled me to concentrate on the completion of this project. Travel funds provided by Dean Tammy Reid, gave me the opportunity to present a paper entitled "'To Serve and to Protect': Purryburg Township, South Carolina and the Defense of the Southern Frontier" at the annual meeting of the Southern Historical Association in November 2004, the gist of which has been incorporated herein. A number of professional staff members at Whitworth also contributed in their own ways to the present volume. Hans Bynagle, director of the Harriet Cheney Cowles Memorial Library, and librarians Bob Lacerte, Nancy Bunker, Tami Robinson, and Barbara Carden made much of my research work less burdensome thanks to their knowledge and efficiency. Interlibrary loan specialist Gail Fielding was of special assistance to me. Throughout nearly twenty years, she left no stone unturned and no repository uncontacted as she worked tirelessly to satisfy my repeated requests for research materials—often of a quite obscure nature. Ken Pecka, director of instructional resources, spent hours aligning my tables and manipulating the maps to gain the highest possible resolution. Academic program assistant Barbara Brodrick has lived with this project nearly as much as I have during the past seven years. Her technical expertise and careful supervision of student research assistants greatly expedited the design and formatting of the tables and procurement of appropriate maps. The hours of labor contributed by student assistants Lisa Picchinino, Michelle Pettitt, Matthew Kaemingk, Laura Thaut, and Laura Adams meant that I could attend to other matters with the knowledge that my data was in capable hands. In this regard I should also mention the critiques offered by my former student Ben Cassidy and the collaborative work initiated by my senior seminar students.

While Whitworth College colleagues and students have played a vital role in moving this monograph toward completion, without the aid of an international network of scholars, archivists, and genealogists, this volume would not have been possible. Some have changed positions, others have retired, and a few have passed away, but I would be remiss if their names did not appear as instrumental contributors to this project. Just as I began to entertain the idea of refocusing the manuscript, I had the good fortune to participate in a 1987 National Endowment for the Humanities summer seminar at the University of Michigan under the leadership of Maris Vinovskis. That summer what is now the introduction benefited from the constructive criticism of Maris and my fellow seminar members. C. C. Macknight, of the Australian National University, Tasmania, and I have never met, but through the wonders of electronic technology we have exchanged research and ideas about Purry and his exploits while with the Dutch East India Company. He graciously gave me access to his unpublished studies of Purry, which strengthened the biographical section of chapter 1. Likewise, I have not had the pleasure of meeting any of the de Pury family who still reside in Switzerland, but Albert supplied me with rare documents including a copy of the de Pury family history. Eason Cross and members of the Purysburg Preservation Foundation were most encouraging through the latter stages of research and writing. One of the members of the foundation, Albert Greer Albergotti III, provided me with his insights, as well as copies of his published work on the Albergottis of Purrysburg and later St. Helena's Parish. I also received a very complete genealogy of the Poyas family from Carolyn Holbrook. Thomas Wilkins not only gave me copies of his own research related to General James Oglethorpe's connections to Purry, but also sent a facsimile of the formal agreement between the two—a document I had been searching for in vain for nearly twenty years and had nearly decided references to it were spurious.

Over these many years I have become especially indebted to reference librarians and archivists upon whom I have depended for everything from the retrieval of documents and digitization of maps to the securing of permission to quote from sources or reproduce images in the text. Alexia Helsley, Charles Lesser, Steve Tuttle, and Bryan Collars, of the South Carolina Department of Archives and History were particularly helpful—Ms. Helsley at the beginning of my research and Mr. Lesser and his colleagues as I neared the end. I am deeply grateful for their work on my behalf and especially appreciated Mr. Lesser's unflagging persistence in securing the best possible maps for inclusion in the text. Likewise, I was the beneficiary in the early stages of my research of the efforts of Sallie Doscher and David Moltke-Hansen, during their tenure at the South Carolina Historical Society Library and Archives, and more recently from SCHS staff members Eric Emerson and Mike Coker. Martha Burns and Alice Burckett, of the Huguenot Society of South Carolina, were among the first people I met in Charleston, and their gracious ways and extensive knowledge of the French Protestant experience in South Carolina have never been forgotten. Reference librarians Alice Spitzer and CerciLee Anderson of the Holland Library at Washington State University were similarly accommodating to my specialized research needs, as were John Rhodehamel of the Huntington Library; Susan Stekel Rippley of the John Ford Bell Library, University of Minnesota; and Damian Cole of the National Library of Australia

I should also note with appreciation the assistance I received from anonymous staff members at the South Caroliniana Library and Thomas Cooper Library, University of South Carolina; the Library and Archives of the Georgia Historical Society, Savannah, Georgia; the Suzzallo Research Library and Condon Law Library, University of Washington; the Charles E. Young Research Library, University of California, Los Angeles; the Holland Library and Owens Science and Engineering Library, Washington State University; the Library of the Genealogical Society of the Church of Jesus Christ of Latter-Day Saints, Salt Lake City, Utah; and the Tacoma Public Library, Tacoma, Washington.

Over the years I have presented portions of my research on Jean Pierre Purry and Purrysburg Township at various conferences. Some of it has been published. I am grateful to Julien Yoseloff and the Associated University Presses for permission to reproduce sections from my edition of Purry's promotional pamphlets, *Lands of True and Certain Bounty: The Geographical Theories and Colonization Strategies of Jean Pierre Purry* (Susquehanna University Press, 2002) in chapter 1. That chapter also benefits from permission received from Eric Emerson and the South Carolina Historical Society to draw on material that originally appeared in the article "A Tarnished Legacy Revisited: Jean Pierre Purry and the Settlement of the Southern Frontier, 1718–1736" in the *South Carolina Historical Magazine* 92 (October 1991): 232–52.

Finally, I would like to conclude these acknowledgments with words of deep appreciation to three scholars whose support for this research sustained me through the years. Without the professional expertise and personal encouragement of George C. Rogers Jr. over nearly two decades, I doubt this project would have been completed. Although he did not live to see the publication of this book, he deserves much of the credit for its appearance. Lawrence S. Rowland's numerous scholarly publications, as well as his dissertation on Beaufort County, have served as a foundation for much of what appears herein. Yet just as significant to me has been his personal interest in my work. From telephone conversations and recommendation letters to a great dinner at one of his favorite Beaufort restaurants and his willingness to write the foreword, included here, Larry has given me not just the incentive to bring this project to completion, but also the passion to do so. If George and Larry prompted me to complete this study, Alexander Moore cultivated the audience for it. Since 1999 Alex has provided me with specific recommendations and wise counsel that ultimately resulted in a contract from the University of South Carolina Press. Without the influential support of these three scholars, this book would not be in your hands today. And, though they and the many others mentioned in these pages have truly made this volume a community effort, any errors of fact or interpretation are mine and mine alone.

To Make This Land Our Own

Introduction

Another South

Well over thirty-five years ago, a genre of historical writing pioneered by Europeans a generation earlier burst upon the American scholarly landscape, altering both conceptions of our past and assumptions about our future. Drawing on antecedents from such sources as the continental *Annales* school and the Cambridge Center for the Study of Population in History, what was christened the "new social history" crossed the Atlantic to the United States in the 1960s. This approach to historical inquiry passed through an adventurous adolescence in the 1970s and ripened into full, if somewhat fractious, maturity over the ensuing two decades. The new social historians mined sources, such as land, church, tax, court, birth, marriage, and death records, previously utilized almost exclusively by genealogists and legal professionals, to reveal the everyday lives of the heretofore invisible "plain folk" who lived as most of us do—without the blinding glare of fame or fortune illuminating each detail of our daily routines. In 1970 social history took center stage in the profession with the publication of four monographs that injected a new vitality into the discipline and opened the door to a more comprehensive understanding of the colonial American past. Philip Greven's painstaking study of land records and extant wills in Andover, Massachusetts, gave us a new sense of the timeless quality of generational tensions and the struggle for identity while other early American scholars such as Kenneth Lockridge, John Demos, and Michael Zuckerman painted for us a much more complex picture of the parameters of community and individuality in early America.[1] The monographs that followed have generally been meticulously researched, highly interdisciplinary, and illustrative of the tremendous contribution social science methodology and quantification can make to our understanding of the American past.

I

In the ensuing two decades, numerous fine local studies continued to roll off the presses, but because of the richness of the data sets most of the books focused upon colonial New England. Aside from Page Smith, it has only been in the comparatively recent past that historians have noted the need for comparable community research in other regions. Unfortunately, the dearth of extant sources when compared to New England seemed to make the endeavor somewhat problematic in the colonial South.[2] By the late 1970s and 1980s, a variety of studies began to appear that belied a universal document vacuum in the colonial and antebellum coastal Southeast. Exceptional research by Darrett and Anita Rutman on Middlesex County, Virginia, Orville Vernon Burton on Edgefield County, South Carolina, Robert C. Kenzer on Orange County, North Carolina, Robert D. Mitchell on the Shenandoah Valley, Carville V. Earle on All Hallow's Parish, Maryland, Richard Beeman on Lunenburg County, Virginia, and the various Chesapeake studies of Lorena Walsh, Russell Menard, Thomas Breen, Lois Green Carr, and Aubrey Land demonstrated the viability of conducting local social history in this region.[3] During the past fifteen years, social historians of the American South have combined sophisticated social science methodology with incisive historical narrative to illuminate the variegated textures of life for a number of the region's peoples and communities. Colonial and antebellum South Carolina has been the focus of many of the finest of these studies.[4] What is perhaps most encouraging about recent scholarly activity is that southern communities are increasingly being scrutinized, thereby allowing comparative analysis of common social processes. As a direct result, not only has our understanding of the formation and maintenance of individual and collective identity been enhanced, but we also have an increasingly better perspective on the relationship between identity development and the variables of class, race, gender, and ethnicity. It is this interrelationship between community and identity, and the social processes energizing both phenomena, that contemporary social historians of the American South are so skillfully revealing.

II

Yet, even in the midst of the reinterpretation of the southern experience engendered by social historians, a word of caution should be sounded, for there existed another South whose lineaments are still shrouded in relative obscurity. This is so because, just as it has been well said that the Puritan towns of Massachusetts are not necessarily archetypical of the northern community, nor is the tidewater Chesapeake, the Lunenburg or Edgefield backcountry, or even wealthy Georgetown necessarily representative of southern community life. There was, after all, another South, not of the Rutmans' freely mobile random settlers of the upper South or of Beeman's community of accumulation, predominantly built as time passed by the constant seepage of settlers into a common geographical locale.[5] This other South, as yet largely undisclosed, resembled very much in conception and intent Christopher Hill's covenanted community of English Puritans.[6] Transported across the Atlantic under contractual agreement, the settlers of this other South tried to establish the kind of communities in the southern colonies that Smith found in New England. The agreements that bound them were not necessarily strictly religious—in fact, they owed more to legal and military arrangements than they did to overtly religious issues in most cases. The contracts per se tended to mutate rather quickly in the suffocating heat and the miasmatic swamps of the Carolinas and Georgia, but contracted communities certainly were not as atypical a plan of southern settlement as we have been led to believe—even if boundaries defining the community varied from the northern model. Be that as it may, we know little of these communities.[7]

In addition to contractual southern communities, this other South bore a distinction about which we hear even less. This was the South of ethnic diversity. Certainly there has been abundant investigation of the peoples of color in the region. Historians of the African American and Native American experience have added immensely to our recognition of the complexity and ingenuity of these cultures in their forced confrontation with European colonists. We have also been apprised over the years of the contributions Scots-Irish, Germans, French Huguenots, Welsh, and others made in the Old South. More recently we have been alerted to the fact that ethnicity "certainly affected life-styles sometimes subtly, sometimes blatantly" in the colonies.[8] A number of other commentators have lately argued for the persistence of European ethnic identity in some recognizable form.[9] The logical assumption that follows from these observations is that some self-awareness of ethnic distinctiveness existed and could be a key variable for scholarly study of southern community life, but we have also been told repeatedly that white ethnic groups quickly adjusted to the exigencies of southern slave society and left the identities of their forebears to become daughters and sons of the monolithic Cavalier white culture that stood against the Union in 1861.[10] This supposed process of total cultural assimilation, however, has lacked systematic longitudinal analysis.[11] Scholars seem to have accepted as an article of faith southern white assimilation without ever having been shown empirically and conclusively that the Confederates who fell at Manassas or Antietam died southern whites first and last and that none of the maimed at Chancellorsville shed a drop of French or German or Scots-Irish blood.[12] The distinct possibility of white ethnic adaptation rather than obliteration in the southern colonial and antebellum environment has never been adequately explored.[13] Of the potential existence of this other South, we are almost completely unaware.

Finally, what of the South where both of the above variables were operative simultaneously? That is to say, by what set of adaptive cultural processes could an ethnically diverse group of strangers bound together only by their pledge to immigrate to a certain geographical location create a *community* in any sense of the term? Linguistically this would be problematic for the first generation—or so it would appear. Did ethnic identity fragment, or at least inhibit, a sense of community based in geographical proximity? Did ethnicity disappear in these diverse southern communities not just because of any threat from black slaves, but rather from the real necessity to turn ethnic strangers into a community of neighbors and friends in order to function in the New World context? Or did ethnic boundaries merely shift to accommodate ethnic self-awareness to altered social conditions? The answers to these and related questions about this other South have not been forthcoming because historians have not yet chosen to study them.[14]

III

At first glance, Purrysburg Township, South Carolina, would seem an unlikely community from which to seek answers to these questions for it no longer exists. Its people and their stories, however, provide us the clearest picture to date of the other South characterized above. For all three of the previously noted factors—the existence of a contracted population, ethnically diverse immigrants, and adaptive strategies for survival in the New World environment—converged in the first South Carolina township.

Purrysburg Township owed its existence to the French-Swiss explorer and colonial entrepreneur Jean Pierre Purry. It was because of his relentless efforts that the settlement became a reality. Purry persuaded imperial leaders to establish a contractual agreement with him for the purpose of populating the exposed southern flank of British North America. He promised to transport hundreds of European émigrés to the township where they would receive land and material support from South Carolina. For his part, the royal administration of the province granted Purry a large tract of land and the lion's share of civil, military, and legal authority in the township. The contract then was a three-way agreement between Purry, civil authorities, and the Europeans he transported to North America. As such, it became the source of both hope and despair for all concerned.

Purrysburg Township also furnishes a laboratory from which to examine ethnic phenomena in the colonial and antebellum South. Even as the earliest settlers arrived in 1732 and 1733, it became evident that the township would be populated by many different white ethnic groups, including French Huguenot, French-Swiss, Italian Piedmontese and Florentine, Salzburg German, German-Swiss, and English settlers. Families and individuals from these groups were more or less deposited by colonial authorities on the southern frontier and forced to create a functional community for themselves. The only initial common bond between the members of all the disparate ethnic groups who called Purrysburg home was their contractual agreement with Purry to settle with him in the township. As a result, the social processes cobbled together by the immigrants to create a workable sense of community and identity on the southern frontier had many origins. The cumulative impact of the cultural diversity of township inhabitants, which also must include the significant influence of Native Americans and African slaves upon the patterns of community life, allows some tentative conclusions regarding the character of ethnicity among whites in the pre–Civil War South.[15]

While Purrysburg Township therefore beckons us to learn of another South, there are constraints upon what this investigation might reveal. We are after all attempting to understand the lifeways of persons who died more than two centuries ago, never knowing they would be the objects of a social historian's scrutiny. There are no extant diaries of any of the residents of Purrysburg, and not many of them are mentioned in other sources. The most consistent commentator on life at the South Carolina township over the first thirty years of its existence was the Reverend Johann Martin Boltzius, leader of the nearby Salzburg Lutheran colony of Ebenezer, Georgia, and an implacable critic of the township and its people—not the most objective source for details on the nature of Purrysburg community life. It is important to note at the outset that my interpretations are based on a wide though fragmentary array of sources. What has been reconstructed here comes in the main from land, probate court, military, tax, death, inheritance records, travel accounts, and official correspondence. If the sources do not allow the historian to tell seamless stories of the families who lived and labored in Purrysburg Township, it is hoped that in order to further our comprehension of the colonial Southeast, half a loaf will be considered better than none at all, for, whereas others have put pen to paper about the township, past scholarship has not done justice to the records that are available or to the complexity of life on the southern colonial frontier.

IV

Purrysburg Township has been the subject of numerous minor studies over the years, but its evolution as an ethnically diverse southern community has never been systematically documented. In a very real sense scholars have treated Purrysburg much the same as did the Huguenot Society of South Carolina in 1939 when a plan for erecting a monument marking the site of the then abandoned town had to be postponed because other society projects were deemed more important.[16] What little we do know of the township and its French-Swiss founder has by and large come from popular fable, ethnic apologists, or clearly limited research.[17] Some of the works in these categories label the majority of Purrysburg settlers "Swiss"—which, indeed, most of them were—but without noting the turbulent, localist, and ethnically diverse nature of Switzerland in the seventeenth and eighteenth centuries or the fact that other ethnic groups were also resident in the township. Failure to account for these factors cloaks the fact that the designation "Swiss" delimited neither a national nor an ethnic collectivity in a pure sense during these centuries and so obscures the possibility of producing an ethnically sensitive study of Purrysburg.[18]

The tendency of those who have written on Purrysburg to concentrate on only one segment of the population, usually in connection with deferential studies of French Huguenots or German speakers in South Carolina, has effectively stifled consistent, systematic analysis of the social and ethnic dynamics within the township. Such an approach has obscured some of the very tensions that transformed it from essentially a settlement of strangers in 1732 into a multi-ethnic community by the latter third of the eighteenth century. The continued evolution of that community led many of its members into extensive participation in the plantation economy and adoption of the social values of the lower South between the Revolution and the nullification crisis, but insular studies of single ethnic groups in the township have failed to uncover and explain the factors internal to the township itself that contributed to the transformation of community life. Instead, most published scholarship on Purrysburg artificially isolates the ethnic group under study from the elaborate network of social and commercial relationships with the rest of the community and the region. As a matter of course, these studies have also often resulted in clearly exaggerated claims for the particular group under consideration.

In his otherwise notable research on the German-speaking peoples in South Carolina, Gilbert P. Voigt examines only the township's German and German-Swiss contingent, yielding an unbalanced perspective both of the German influence there and of the township itself.[19] Almost as if to rebut studies of the significant Germanic contribution to the life of Purrysburg, Harriet Dubose Kershaw Leiding overcompensated for Voigt's snubbing of the French-speaking population of the township with her 1934 article "Purrysburg: A Swiss-French Settlement of South Carolina, on the Savannah River." The necessity of chronicling the German, German-Swiss, Italian, or English presence at Purrysburg is rendered irrelevant by the unabashed claim of the title.[20] In perhaps the most conspicuous faux pas in the apologetic literature on the township, the distinguished German-American scholar Albert B. Faust determined that the Reverend Joseph Bugnion, a French Reformed turned Anglican pastor at Purrysburg, was really of German descent. He performed this redoubtable sleight of hand simply by adding an umlaut to the spelling of Bugnion's name.[21] Abundant evidence exists to prove conclusively that not only was Bugnion not German, but also that he conducted all services during his tenure at Purrysburg in his native tongue—French.[22] Even Jon Butler, in his finely crafted and definitive volume on the Huguenots in America, does not know quite what to do with Purrysburg. Rather than attempt to sort out the Huguenot population of the township, or at least to address the issue of the ethnic diversity of the township, Butler seems to take the path of least resistance for he dismisses the French Huguenot portion of the township and labels the settlement "Swiss." Hence, there is no need for him to include an analysis of the complex nature of Purrysburg in his volume—and he does not.[23]

V

If the need for comprehensive examination of the aggregate population of the township is rendered obvious by the above examples, the most appropriate method to animate such analysis is less apparent. The tendency of some scholars merely "to tell the story" of a given community without concern for wider social processes has brought the wrath of social scientists down upon them. Even among historians of the local community there is a heightened desire for more synthetic interpretations of the numerous studies that have emerged since the early 1970s. For although they have broadened our historical horizons, these local histories have simultaneously narrowed our focus, leaving us with more questions than they have purported to answer.[24] Anthropologist Anthony F. C. Wallace warned those engaged in local research more than twenty years ago to be sure to connect the local community "with the larger world, and to reveal in the detailed study of one small group of people social and cultural processes of theoretical interest to a discipline."[25] His plea for more relevance justifiably compels scholars to be more circumspect in probing for deeper meanings, but that such warnings should even be sounded demonstrated the vitality of community studies since the melding together of traditional genealogical-style local history and the new social history of the 1960s and 1970s.

If scholars are convinced of the need to ask large questions in small places, however, the thorny problem of how to go about doing so coherently and effectively remains. George A. Hillery Jr., in his encyclopedic overview of theoretical definitions of community published nearly fifty years ago, noted then a mind-boggling ninety-four different definitions.[26] And all of these definitions peppered the scholarly literature well before social history emerged from its infancy. With such a plethora of options from which to choose, systematic analysis of *community* proved little more scientific than the old saw about the three blind men and the elephant—each investigator finding an appropriate definition to fit the evidence. This sorry state of affairs led Margaret Stacey in 1969 to advocate blacklisting the term altogether in her provocatively titled article "The Myth of Community Studies."[27]

As social historians ventured into local community studies, other problems arose. One prominent historian of American religious life observed that "social and community studies have turned historians inward, or at least away from Europe. Community is equated with residence. It is defined too often by land deeds and town boundaries, too seldom by habits of mind and memorable tradition, even tradition that reaches back across the Atlantic."[28]

In a roundtable exchange in the mid-1990s, Harry S. Stout questioned the efficacy of any definition of community, no matter how rigorous or analytical its formulation, because the inherent human desire for connections to each other will cause the investigator always to find "declension and breakdown" of community over time. Finely crafted definitions, Stout argued, "cannot displace the common sense identification of community with home, family, and nurture with 'TRUE' or 'REAL' community. As individuals and as groups, we crave community. It captures our innermost yearnings and aspirations; its lack expresses the void we blame for depression, anomie, or most literally, alienation (the state of being strangers in our own land, bereft of community) . . . community is invariably a state we perpetually seek and perpetually find missing in our lives or the lives around us. . . . The fact is that no matter what period we look in American history, we find the absence of community."[29] He prudently suggested that following Thomas Bender's lead, historians of local communities should recognize that all societies contain elements of order and disorder, integration and disintegration. All communities carry within them these bifurcated tendencies, and each one should be envisioned "not as a peasant village but as an organization."[30] My understanding of the Purrysburg community proceeds from this perspective on the dialectics of its development.

There arises one further substantial roadblock for the historian engaged in local history. Most of the speculative thinking on communities has been done by sociologists, social anthropologists, and archaeologists. Consequently, much of the theoretical construction regarding the creation and maintenance of community life is more adaptable to the functionalist field-study methods of the social sciences. Problematic for the historian of the local community is the impossibility of securing interviews with populations long since departed, statistically significant random sample data, or consistent longitudinal information on individuals and families. Thus limited by the constraints of time, place, and appropriate sources, the approach most applicable to the secondary nature of historical research and the one most historians of the community are exploring with most satisfying results has been termed *social network* or simply *network* theory. The general approach has undergone refinements since its introduction, but network theory essentially renounces any value-laden interpretation of community as being the "true" or "real" local entity. It holds that there are different contexts of community and these contexts are dynamic, not static. Such contexts can be studied by analyzing the "horizontal" relationships (social, economic, religious, political, cultural) between individuals at the local level and the "vertical" relationships of those at the local level (either individuals or groups) with those in wider social or geographical contexts. This model assumes that community is present because people cluster in geographical space although the sense of community is not limited to geographic proximity.

Network theory lends itself to historical analysis because evidence exists that allows the scholar to follow, at least partially, the creation, maintenance, alteration, and decline of horizontal and vertical relationships as well as the interstices between them. As members of the local community become more culturally and economically enmeshed in the larger social context, we would expect to note more relationships with those outside the local community. These more complex and less geographically bound relationships do not signify the end of the local community, as has been assumed in the past, but rather its transformation. Network theory does not prescribe that the ratio of horizontal relationships to vertical ones must only continue in one direction as time passes, but merely attempts to demonstrate that individuals live in different levels of interaction and community given various factors. This aspect of the model allows for changes in the direction of relationships and is therefore aptly described by one of its prime proponents as an explanatory process theory. In his recent study of the lower Cape Fear area of North Carolina during the eighteenth century, Bradford J. Wood used network theory most effectively to delineate the community relationships constructed by residents of that border region.[31] In light of the kinds of sources at the disposal of historians regarding the Purrysburg population and what these sources tell us about the relationships of the inhabitants with each other and with those beyond the township limits, the network approach will constitute the preeminent method of analysis for the ensuing study.[32]

VI

The organizational framework of the chapters that follow reflects the centrality of this network approach. The chapters have been organized in a broadly topical rather than a strictly chronological order because the clusters of horizontal and vertical relationships that are the focus of the study cohere more clearly when discussing areas of human activity over time than to the passage of time itself. Within each chapter, however, the narrative proceeds chronologically. For the sake of clarity in understanding these relationships, separate chapters will examine those aspects of community life that most directly contributed to its character.

It was Jean Pierre Purry's colonial vision, juxtaposed with South Carolina's palpable fear of armed violence in the 1720s, that led to the creation of the township in 1732. Chapter 1 charts the independent trajectories of Purry's incessant ambition and Carolinian security concerns, each precipitating a chain of events that brought both together in Sir Robert Johnson's township plan of settlement. By 1731 Purry and the royal government of South Carolina reached a contractual agreement regarding the peopling of a township to be named in his honor on the Savannah River, and the French-Swiss adventurer returned to Switzerland to solicit willing emigrants.

Chapter 2 opens with a profile of the Europeans who agreed to emigrate with Purry, as well as the immediate problems they faced upon arrival at the township. The diverse ethnic backgrounds of the émigrés and the unstable socioeconomic environment of the Swiss cantons contributed to the overwhelming response Purry received for his venture. He departed for his township in 1732 with the first of the emigrants ready to begin life anew on the South Carolina frontier. Much to the chagrin of colonists and colonizer alike, all was not as promised by the authorities. Land fraud and inadequate supplies plagued the township through its early years and soured the colonists on Purry's leadership because they blamed him for their troubles. It goes without saying that the experience severely weakened Purry's faith in the promises of governmental bureaucrats.

Chapter 3 centers on a discussion of the most basic of all relational networks constructed by the Purrysburg settlers—the family. Purrysburg families experienced tremendous volatility from sickness, death, and the dangerous isolation of frontier life. The high mortality rate Purrysburg shared with other southern settlements appears to have fostered interethnic marriages rather quickly, with marriages outside the community also increasing over time. Such intermarriage patterns have been taken as a sign of the loss of ethnic loyalties in other contexts, but in Purrysburg this may not exclusively have been the case. As family plantation estates grew, paternal authority was challenged here as it was elsewhere in North America; yet, at the same time, the companionate marriage seems to have survived the rigors of township life.

If the family provided the primary network of relationships, the church traditionally furnished the second-most-powerful set of relationships. It is the cluster of relationships proceeding from religious sensibilities that constitutes chapter 4. Purrysburg settlers found that the Old World religious confessions in which they had been nurtured were not only next to impossible to maintain, they also tended to separate rather than unify township dwellers as adherents of both Lutheran and Reformed traditions resided there. To indicate that these Protestant groups were less than amicably inclined toward one another in the eighteenth century is to put the best face on a deeply antagonistic relationship. The proximity of the Salzburg Lutheran settlement of Ebenezer, Georgia, only compounded the problem. Township inhabitants therefore were forced to create a viable religious environment by the selective adaptation of traditional ethnic religious loyalties and substantial alteration of confessional rules promulgated by the South Carolina establishment—until linguistic barriers disappeared. Similar accommodations had to be made with regard to the education of the young. Even with the problems associated with religious expression and educational opportunities in the township, at least two of her own became renowned Christian ministers in the decades before the War of the Revolution. The founding of a Presbyterian church in Purrysburg during the revolutionary era permitted reconfigured religious loyalties to resurface forty years after they had supposedly been destroyed.

Chapters 5 and 6 are perhaps the most intricately constructed for they examine the initial structural, legal, and political impediments to diversified commercial activity, the creation and maintenance of the infrastructure developed to foster commercial relationships, the specific economic activities of Purrysburg landholders and the development of wide-ranging networks of commercial relationships between Purrysburg settlers and others in the colonial South. As a group, township inhabitants began from a position of intense privation in the 1730s, except for a few well-to-do residents. Political and legal machinations by the lowcountry elite, particularly regarding land acquisition and local government, served only to make their climb out of poverty more problematic. Many Purrysburg émigrés had been artisans in Europe, and when they found little market for their skills in the South Carolina wilderness, members of this potential craft sector of the population were forced to migrate elsewhere or turn to agricultural pursuits to provide for their families. By the 1750s the remaining township residents had overcome the dislocations of earlier years, and they began to build modest plantations. As they marketed their agricultural goods, relationships evolved with merchants in Savannah, Beaufort, and Charles Town. On the eve of the Revolutionary War, Purrysburg had developed distinct classes ranging from paupers to substantial planters. The township embraced the institution of slavery, which embedded racism into the warp and woof of township life, as much as any other lowcountry parish.

Defense of the lowcountry parishes against both domestic and foreign threats lay behind the creation of Purrysburg Township, so it should come as no surprise that, throughout the eighteenth century, wars and rumors of wars threatened to disrupt the process of community building in Purrysburg. Chapter 7 draws on the records of armed conflict predating the Stono Rebellion through the American Revolution to analyze the impact of war on the community. Purrysburg settlers found themselves in the unenviable position of serving as the first line of defense against foreign invasion and potential violence against whites by Carolinians of color while simultaneously attempting to build a stable community. Times of crisis exposed fissures in the community, and, especially in the case of the American Revolution, these fractures rent bonds of community that had been nurtured for nearly fifty years.

Chapter 8 surveys the continued evolution of Purrysburg from the Confederation to the nullification crisis and beyond. The aftermath of the War of the Revolution brought not only dislocation and privation, but also a resurgence of economic prosperity to the township that lasted well into the early national period. A statewide commitment to internal improvements and technological innovation accelerated the integration of Purrysburg Township into the fabric of southern culture between the 1780s and the 1820s. Although the town proper declined significantly in the first half of the nineteenth century, the township site continued to be occupied by wealthy Purrysburg landowners ever more committed to the plantation system and the institution of slavery upon which it rested.

The conclusion revisits the central concerns of community, identity, and cultural adaptation as illuminated by the narrative developed over the preceding chapters. It offers some tentative theses that link the Purrysburg experience to the broader milieu of early American social history while also generating questions in need of further comparative study by scholars of the American South before categorical pronouncements can be made.

VII

As the parameters of community, identity, and cultural adaptation at Purrysburg Township unfold in the pages that follow, it will be readily apparent that the colonists had to confront a world vastly different than the one they had left behind. In an era when the conventional wisdom of American immigration scholars of an earlier generation is increasingly being called into question, the history of Purrysburg Township and of the people who called it home serve to remind the contemporary reader of the wrenching dislocations of those who chose to immigrate to British North America. If the Purrysburg experience does not fit the well-known paradigm regarding the lack of relative hardships of New England Puritans or even certain other southern colonists, this only serves to reiterate the distinctiveness of the other South to be studied herein.[33] For traditions so familiar and appropriate for European social and religious stability failed horribly in the forbidding environment bounded by the lower Savannah River and the Coosawhatchie swamps. Community solidarity could not be achieved in the same manner, or sometimes even in the same form, in the Carolina wilderness as it had been in the Old World. A neighborhood of strangers had to be pieced together, refracted off the American experience as well as the ethnic diversity of the colonists themselves and refocused in ways that would meet needs—regardless of whether that refracted community looked anything like the world the immigrants had lost. Ethnicity, marriage, family, religious faith, friendship, vocation—in peace and at war, all had to be redefined for survival. The process took decades, but a functional community was hewed from the wilderness by a company of strangers who initially possessed little more in common than the land upon which they settled and a passion to make this land their own.

ONE

The Founding Vision

Advocates of New World colonization in the seventeenth and eighteenth centuries were notorious for their adamant refusal to consider the possibility of adapting their settlement plans to an environment in which the ratio of land to person was the inverse of the European experience. With the scarcity of land available for cultivation in the early modern period and a population boom underway, European village hamlets and commercial ports served as magnets to pull individuals into community with others. In British North America, however, the tables turned and a minuscule population scattered across a vast expanse of available land. Even after the failure of concentrated settlement was obvious in Virginia and Maryland, the cohesive village unit lived on as the ideal settlement system for human habitation in the New World. In a legacy stretching back nearly 400 years, contemporary Americans still tend to idealize small town life as the true expression of some ethereal communal spirit.

The propensity to cling to the small town as the "true" community perhaps owes as much to the early success of the Puritan communities of New England as it does to the traditions of Tudor-Stuart England. That success proceeded at least in part from the particular physical environment of New England, but it has been widely conceded that Puritanism, as epitomized in the idea of the social covenant or contract, provided the impetus for much of the vitality of New England in the seventeenth century. The social contract linked individuals to one another "uniting the classes and the society to God." This powerful bond sustained colonists in an environment that otherwise threatened to dissolve any sense of community. Members of the community also drew encouragement from the assurance that they were part of the divine plan to reconcile humans to each other and to God. The church nurtured and monitored relationships with others in the town and discouraged relationships with those outside the covenant. Ethnic as well as religious homogeneity contributed to the sense of solidarity evident in the New England towns.[1]

To be sure, the southern colonies never achieved the kind of communal ideology that so characterized early New England. For one thing, Puritanism never achieved the same strength in the South. For another, topographic and economic considerations militated against self-contained villages. Nevertheless, although the social contract based in Puritan theology never appeared, contractual southern communities did. From the very beginning of his attempt to establish a colony of his own, the founder of Purrysburg Township believed in the necessity of hierarchical leadership and mutual bonds of accountability. Purry's vision of community owed much to the legacy of medieval European assumptions about authority as well as to his own desire to achieve New World notoriety, but he nonetheless possessed a clear conception as to the form his community was to take and the role it would play in the ongoing rivalry between early modern Western imperial powers. He consistently pressed his ambitions for colonization upon some of the most powerful commercial and political leaders of his day for nearly fifteen years before his personal desires and the needs of the British Empire in North America coalesced into a shared vision for settlement on the southern flank of the eastern seaboard that became Purrysburg Township.[2]

I

Jean Pierre Purry, a colorful character by any measure, came from a prominent family of the French-speaking region of Neuchâtel, Switzerland. His lineage in the canton can be traced back to 1383, when the surname first appeared in public records. Many among his forebears held distinguished civil, military, and religious offices. Purry's father, Henry, was an innkeeper who also became a skilled pewter craftsman like his father and grandfather. He married Marie Hesler (also Ersel), and the couple had four children before Jean Pierre's birth in 1675. Young Purry never knew his biological father as Henry died the same year. Marie remarried in 1676, and her husband, Louis Quinche, raised the Purry siblings as his own children. Not much is known about his childhood or adolescence, but he seems to have had a solid and supportive upbringing. In 1693 at the age of eighteen, Purry received appointment as tax collector/customs agent of Boudry in east central Neuchâtel. He held the post only a short time for he was dismissed the following year, apparently never knowing the reason for his termination. It is not known whether he secured another post shortly thereafter, but whatever his circumstance, in 1695 Purry married Lucrèce (also Lucie, Louise) of the notable Chaillet family, also of Neuchâtel. Between 1696 and 1710 the couple had eight children, though only four of them survived to young adulthood. Charles, the firstborn (1696–1754), would eventually accompany his father to South Carolina and become a prominent lowcountry merchant. François-Louis (1697–1700) and Marie-Marguerite (1700–1706) died in childhood. Rose (1704–1731) lived to young adulthood. Lucrèce (1705–1708) and Jean-Henry (1706–1709) followed, and both succumbed before their fourth birthdays. David (1709–1786), the most successful, pursued a lucrative career in Lisbon and became a major benefactor of his native land. Marie, called Manon (1710–1764), was the youngest child and lived into her midfifties.[3]

Little else about Purry's life between 1695 and 1709 is known for certain, though highly plausible conjectures based on circumstantial evidence give some indication of at least some of his activities. It was during these years that he became involved in various commercial ventures, one of which was exporting wine to England. Louis-Edouard Roulet speculates that, in light of his subsequent service with the Dutch East India Company, Purry may have spent at least part of this time as a mercenary soldier or an officer in the Neuchâtel military establishment trying to support his large family. In any event, 1709 proved to be a turning point in Purry's life, for he accepted an appointment dated 7 May from Frederick I, King of Prussia and Prince of Neuchâtel, as mayor of Lignières in the northeastern part of the canton. The notice of his appointment, signed by the king himself, spoke highly of Purry's wisdom, loyalty, and work ethic, though the effusive tenor of the document may owe more to courtly ceremonialism than to the king's actual awareness of Purry's administrative gifts—especially in light of his short tenure at Boudry. In fact, the language and the appointment (as well as Purry's earlier loss of the civil post at Boudry in 1694) probably had more to do with the factional politics of early modern Neuchâtel than with either Purry's personal qualifications or the conventions of early eighteenth-century bureaucratic jargon.[4]

Regardless of the rationale for his appointment, this office provided thirty-four-year-old Purry elevated status in the ancien régime because he represented the king and, therefore, royal authority. As mayor, Purry became at least partially responsible for the administration of justice in Lignières and performed other civic duties as well. Thus, the young Swiss municipal leader emerged as one of the local officials of the upper bourgeoisie—but he had no feudal estate or title. Should he be able to fulfill his obligations adequately and the political climate remained favorable, Purry could rightly anticipate the possibility of further advancement in the future. Unfortunately, as one of his biographers wrote, "*la bonne fortune ne lui sourit guère*" ("good fortune did not much smile on him").[5]

Less is known about the quality of Purry's mayoral leadership between May 1709 and September 1711 than his very public personal affairs, which appear to have taken a disastrous turn during the same period. So desperate was his situation that on 17 September 1711 a delegation comprising Lucrèce, his brother-in-law David Chaillet, his stepbrothers Louis (Lewis) and David Quinche, and his advocate Mr. Martinet, *maître-bourgeois* and mayor of Côte, came before the council of state at Neuchâtel Castle requesting that Purry be released from his office. Martinet acquainted the magistrates of the severity of the mayor's circumstances, which included a fire that destroyed part of his home and commercial property and the demise of his wine-exporting business to England. He also presented the councilors a partial account of Purry's income and expenses and asked for their assistance in helping him put his financial affairs in order. Fortunately for the destitute mayor, the magistrates decided to allow Purry to resign and did not pursue any legal action against him for the debts he incurred while serving in that office. In the face of such devastating events in his native land, Purry decided to leave Neuchâtel hoping to recoup his losses elsewhere.

It is unclear whether Purry went directly to the United Provinces in 1711 or arrived there at some later date. What is certain is that Purry decided to affiliate himself with the Chamber of Amsterdam for the East Indies, better known as the Dutch East India Company by the spring of 1713. His contract with the company stipulated that he serve as one of two corporals under the command of a sergeant in charge of seventy men.[6] He and Anthony Mestersmit, the other corporal, were to be paid a monthly sum of fourteen Dutch guilders and fined if any of the men under their control deserted. As was customary, Purry drew two month's salary in advance, but it is not known whether this sum (minus the seven guilders he was fined for absenting himself from the muster roll call!) reached Lucrèce, who was soon to become single parent to four children under the age of eighteen. According to one account of this phase of his life, Purry did return to Neuchâtel—for the express purpose of procuring a wide variety of wine grape plants to cultivate at the Cape Colony.[7]

On 26 May 1713, Purry sailed from Texel Island near Amsterdam aboard the company ship *Prins Eugenius* for Batavia (modern day Jakarta). The *Prins Eugenius* made a three-day stop at the Cape Verde Islands in late July and then sailed on to the company's prosperous but small Cape Colony settlement in South Africa, arriving on 18 October. The ship remained in port at Cape Town until 20 November, when the crew weighed anchor, finally reaching Batavia on 2 February 1714.[8]

For a number of reasons, Purry's career in Batavia, between February 1714 and 11 December 1717, is difficult to follow. First, although he was hired in a military capacity, Purry does not appear regularly on the muster role of company employees. Second, in the "Advertisement" preceding the 1744 English translation of his first treatise on climatology, it is noted that Purry, "by his Plantations and by being Reader to the Reform'd Church in that City, . . . pretty well repair'd his Fortune."[9] C. C. Macknight's extensive study of the records of the company archives, however, has found neither reference to these plantations nor to any indication that Purry served as a salaried employee of the company for the Reformed Church in Batavia.[10] Although he could have been paid by the congregation itself (at a much lower salary than would be provided by the company), the status, compensation, and duration of his service to the Reformed of the city is ambiguous at best and could not have been the source of his renewed prosperity.

It is also somewhat unclear how Purry could have "pretty well Repair'd his fortune" in the company's employ, because his salary remained far from generous throughout his more than four and a half years on Java. According to Macknight's analysis of his account, Purry built up a credit balance of approximately twelve guilders per month from February to mid-April 1714 that rose to nearly twenty guilders per month until the books closed for the fiscal year on 31 August 1714. During the two ensuing years, however, he seems to have earned credit of only three guilders, five stuivers per annum. If the entire period from 10 February 1714 to 31 August 1716 is examined, it appears the company never paid Purry his contracted amount. Over the next year, the company credited a single stuiver to his account. From 31 August 1717 onward, his credited account rose back to about twenty guilders per month, though there seems to have been a minor error in the calculation so that the account lost some value just prior to his departure. His assignment changed on 15 November, and he earned credit of nearly twenty-three guilders per month until 19 July. The final pay out by the company amounted to 315 guilders, 5 stuiver, 2 pfenning—not a large sum for better than four years of service. Because there does not appear any indication in company records that Purry was able to make private investments in Batavia during this time, it is difficult to imagine that his time in Batavia could have resulted in any great accumulation of wealth.[11] It would seem the only plausible explanations for the fact that Purry's financial situation improved during his sojourn in Indonesia would be that he did indeed successfully import viniculture to the Cape Colony and received remuneration for the productivity of the vineyards or that he somehow engaged in some type of unrecorded agricultural pursuit (other than wine grapes) while in Batavia that proved lucrative. In either case, given his dire financial situation just prior to his employment with the company, Purry would have required significant assistance from well-heeled relations in Neuchâtel to undertake either project.

A final mystery surrounding his time in the East Indies pertains to whether he ventured from Java to explore other regions of New Holland. There is some indication that he at least pondered the possibility of a reconnaissance voyage along the southern coast of Australia, but there is no evidence in company archives that Purry actually took part in such an expedition. While his absence from the records does not prove he did not do so, it does make the possibility seem quite unlikely. Yet the authoritative manner with which he later speaks of the southern coast of Australia would seem to indicate not only a familiarity with relevant geographical sources of information about the territory, but perhaps also a firsthand knowledge of the terrain.[12]

The region he would have visited, *la terre de Nuyts* (Nuyt's Land) included the cluster of islands just off the Eyre Peninsula of south-central Australia as well as the coastline ringing the Great Australian Bight. Pieter Nuyts, a rising employee of the Dutch East India Company and member of the Dutch Indian Council with his son Laurens, left the Dutch Republic for Batavia on

22 May 1626 aboard the *Gulden Seepaert* commanded by François Thijssen. After being blown off course by contrary winds, the ship made landfall on the uncharted southwestern coast of Australia near present-day Cape Leeuwin on 26 January 1627. Proceeding eastward for more than 1,500 kilometers, the crew reconnoitered the region for the company and, in the process, made the first reliable map of what had been known as *Terra Australis Incognita* (The Unknown South Land). Because Nuyts was the highest-ranking company official aboard ship, Thijssen named the coast and one of the islands after him.[13]

Regardless of whether Purry visited the area, he did have extensive knowledge of it and also of the company's claim to it as part of New Holland. It made a lasting impression on him and seems to have further stimulated his thinking concerning a linkage between successful colonization and meteorology that began after his first visit to southern Africa in 1713. Shortly thereafter, perhaps in 1716 or early 1717, he began to theorize about the linkage between sunlight, climate, and soil productivity. Well past forty years of age by the spring of 1717, Purry decided to organize his thoughts on the causal interrelationship between these topics, which culminated in an empirically based theory of climatology.[14]

Predicated upon his own travels and the best geographical knowledge of the day, Purry formulated what he believed to be a scientifically verifiable theory that determined where colonies could be most successfully planted worldwide. The core of his argument centered on his belief in the existence of ideal climates for human ecology. Purry defined such climates in terms of agricultural productivity and amount of sunlight as well as precipitation and temperature. According to his research, there were a total of twenty-four climate zones on the earth from North Pole to South Pole, with twelve in each hemisphere. The prevailing conditions in the fifth of these zones in both hemispheres made it the most conducive to sustained bounty. This best of all possible climates existed at or near the thirty-third degree of latitude in both hemispheres. From his computations he believed that the climate at that latitude would yield a rich agricultural bonanza of products without much labor. Seizing the opportunity to achieve a level of notoriety and success that had eluded him in feudal Europe, Purry decided to offer his theory and supporting evidence to stimulate colonization by the Dutch East India Company of the Terre de Nuyts and the southeastern region of southern Africa near the Cape Colony.[15] Because these areas were located geographically at or near the optimal climate zone of the earth, they could not help but bring certain bounty to the company and, he hoped, to its faithful employee.[16]

Purry put his scientific theory and personal ambitions in Australia and South Africa to the test by approaching Christophel van Swol, resident governor-general of the Dutch East India Company's operation in Batavia, with his findings.[17] He prepared a manuscript for van Swol's consideration and presented it to him on 20 May 1717. Purry addressed it directly to van Swol, though it also seems to have circulated to some extent in Batavia. His expressed purpose in petitioning the governor-general was to aid in the extension of profits and influence of the company. Purry, of course, was not purely altruistic. In his desire to look out for the interests of the company, he hoped for some reward for his efforts. Unfortunately, the governor-general was unmoved by the elaborate scientific proofs and historical arguments of the treatise and remained patently unimpressed.[18] The author offered to reply to van Swol's objections in writing, though he refused even to discuss Purry's proposals with the governing board of the company. Van Swol did grant him permission to approach company authorities in Europe with his ideas if he so desired, but the ridicule he endured as his proposals became known to a wider audience in Batavia did not bode well for his future with the company.[19] At this point Purry's quest for land and title might have ended had he been less forceful or van Swol more patient, but his adamant refusal to accept van Swol's rejection of his proposal and the governor-general's stolid opposition to it led to Purry's rather hasty departure from the East Indies.

It is difficult to ascertain exactly what triggered the ensuing chain of events, but we do know that Purry fell out of favor rather quickly in Batavia, suffered the loss of 1,000 crowns,[20] and forfeited his position with the company. Whether Governor-General van Swol severed his affiliation with the company, his economic hardships (perpetrated by nature or the governing authorities) prompted him to leave, or he merely decided to cut his losses and take van Swol's suggestion to argue his case at the "home office" is unknown. Most likely, because Purry would not take no for an answer and became such a nuisance to van Swol, the governor-general decided to terminate the relationship between Purry and the Dutch East India Company, giving the Swiss little recourse but to leave. Whatever the reason, Purry found his circumstances in Batavia untenable and determined to travel to Holland to present his ideas to van Swol's superiors. A sympathetic company official identified by Purry only as Counselor Faas, secured him a position as bookkeeper aboard the *Hogermeer,* which sailed for Texel on 11 December 1717, arriving there on 17 July 1718 after a six-week stop in Cape Town (22 February–7 April).

Almost immediately upon his arrival in Amsterdam, Purry published a revision of the ideas he had presented to van Swol. An introductory preface dated 25 July 1718 explained his rationale for approaching the directors of the company with propositions that had already been dismissed by one of their lieutenants in the field. Realizing also that the directors had received van Swol's enumerated objections to the colonization plan described in the now-published essay, Purry set to work crafting a second to answer these concerns. He addressed this second pamphlet, dated 1 September 1718, directly to "The Deputies to the Assembly of the Seventeen Who Represent the General Company of the Dutch East Indies."[21] This treatise was Purry's attempt to nullify van Swol's decision by taking his case directly to those who had ultimate authority over company decisions. Its more strident tone and acerbic references to van Swol's leadership give the reader some sense of the betrayal Purry must have felt at his curt dismissal by the governor-general.

This time Purry succeeded in getting the company's attention, and on 3 October 1718 the directors found his proposals of sufficient merit to refer the matter to the Amsterdam chamber of the company. The chamber interviewed the author and reported back to the directors. The directors received the chamber's favorable report and on 11 March 1719 decided to try to verify Purry's theoretical conclusions. The directors left it to the Amsterdam chamber to see to the arrangements and provide ships for the venture. After nearly two years of sustained effort, Purry was within sight of at least partially realizing his vision, when, on 17 April 1719, the Amsterdam chamber met—and decided to do nothing.[22] Spurned by company officials and apparently blacklisted in the Dutch Republic,[23] Purry returned to Neuchâtel, where, once again, it becomes difficult to separate reality from legend surrounding the peripatetic Swiss.

He evidently spent a very short time in his homeland, choosing instead to pursue other colonial and financial prospects. Though defeated in his negotiations with Dutch officials and seemingly without much in the way of financial resources, the indefatigable Purry lost neither his resolve nor his confidence. Purry, in fact, seemed all the more convinced of his cause for the troubles it brought him. He turned next to France and traveled at least twice to Paris and once back to Switzerland in an effort to secure French support for a reworked colonial plan specially tailored to complement that empire's imperial strategy. The plan of settlement he proposed to French royal authorities was based on his climatological theory and fashioned upon the feudal model already in use throughout the empire. It also, no doubt, provided material benefits to the Swiss entrepreneur as well as to the international mercantile bureaucracy of the French monarchy. The royal ministers to whom he first presented his proposal referred it to the Académie Royale des Sciences for an assessment of its virtues. The *Journal des Sçavans* took note of his proposition and fairly represented it to the public, but it never received official sanction. The Académie Royale reported back through Mr. Fontenelle that "they could not pass a Judgment on a Country which they had never seen, and that therefore it would not be advisable to make expensive Settlements in Places they were unacquainted with."[24] Purry, however, must have been highly respected by French officials and especially well thought of by French commercial interests as he became a director-general of the Compagnie des Indes en France.[25] Most likely another major reason for its rejection had to do with the economic chaos surrounding the collapse of the Mississippi Company, which not only caused further financial hardship for Purry and for his prospective imperial benefactors, but also occurred at roughly the same time that he was lobbying French authorities vis-à-vis his colonial ambitions.

Like many others, it appears that Purry saw an opportunity for significant financial gain in one of the most brazen speculative ventures of the eighteenth century, promoted by Scottish financier John Law. Law founded both the Bank of France and the Compagnie des Indes en France based in Paris. To take full financial advantage of the French Empire's North American territories, he created the Mississippi Company in 1717 as a subordinate enterprise under the auspices of the Compagnie des Indes. Fueled by the Scotsman's machinations over the next three years a stupendous windfall for investors occurred as speculation in Louisiana land reached fever pitch.[26] After leaving Amsterdam for Neuchâtel, presumably sometime in the late spring of 1719, Purry apparently moved to Paris in 1720 to participate in Law's dangerous scheme and may have even allowed himself to be appointed a director-general of Law's Compagnie des Indes at this time. Such an appointment might have added legitimacy to the enterprise because of his experience with the Dutch East India Company. At one point Purry's holdings were reported to have amounted to 600,000 francs. When his friend (and subsequent Prussian minister to Paris) Jean Chambrier attempted to cool his enthusiasm for greater profits, he supposedly replied, "Here everybody speaks of millions. Once I have a few millions, I'll cash out."[27] He never got the chance, for the Mississippi bubble burst in 1720 and destroyed him financially, completely eradicating any profits remaining from his commercial activities while in the East Indies.

Because surviving sources concerning this period of Purry's career are so imprecise, it is extremely difficult to construct accurately a clear chronological picture of either his involvement in the Mississippi bubble debacle or his discussions with French authorities regarding his proposed colonial settlement. Contemporary scholarship casts some doubt on earlier accounts of this French interlude—particularly the personal financial implications of Law's scheme for the Swiss theorist—for his own fiscal situation before his initial trip to Paris in 1720 is far from clear.[28] As previously noted, Purry opted for employment with the Dutch East India Company for monetary reasons in light of the personal and professional misfortunes he suffered between 1709 and 1711. It is also quite obvious that his known income while under contract with the Dutch East India Company was anything but exorbitant. These factors, when coupled with Purry's stated losses of a thousand crowns just prior to his departure from Batavia, would seem to indicate that he was not in the best financial position of his life in 1718. In addition, the stories that have circulated for well over two centuries about his supposed profits from undisclosed Batavian plantations have not been substantiated by recent research in the company archives.[29]

Nevertheless, Purry could not have been completely destitute because within a week of his return to Holland he had his first memorial published, followed the next year by his second. Perhaps this money came from profits from the vineyards that Purry may have established in Kaffraria in 1713 before he even arrived in Indonesia. This reinterpretation of the source of whatever profits he realized while a company employee could explain the references to his mysterious plantations that scholars have always assumed were in Batavia by recognizing that the vineyards were "plantations" and they were functioning when he was in Batavia. They were just not located there.[30]

It is difficult to estimate what his profits might have been from wine production in Kaffraria, because no source provides any clear details on the size of the vineyards he supposedly planted, only on the numerous varieties of wine grapes he brought with him from Neuchâtel. It is unlikely, however, that his monetary gains could have been significant enough to produce the massive accumulation of wealth that has been attributed to his Mississippi investments—especially since he could not have been able even to purchase shares until sometime after the late spring of 1719. By this late date, his investment had only a little over a year to mature. It should be recalled, however, that Purry returned to Neuchâtel sometime after mid-April before traveling to Paris in 1720. If he did have respectable profits from a South African vineyard, he may have been able to induce family and friends to pool their resources so that he could invest it with the Mississippi Company. The resulting capital accumulation might indeed have generated quite a return in the year before the bubble burst. If Purry did take extensive capital resources to Paris in 1720, he might have caught the attention of not only Law, but also crown officials intent on reinforcing France's imperial position with new colonists. Whatever economic reverses Purry experienced in 1720, they did not dissuade him from his determination to plant a colony somewhere for someone in the fifth climate zone.

The task of untangling the chronology and intent of Purry's time in Paris gets even more complicated when considering the rationale for his appointment as a director-general of the Compagnie des Indes en France. He could have been offered the post in late 1719 or early 1720 as an enticement to persuade him to invest in its subsidiary, the Mississippi Company. By the same token, Law and his compatriots might have wanted Purry to serve in this capacity because his nearly five years as a field employee of the Dutch East India Company would lend an air of legitimacy to the Compagnie's commercial offspring whose profits seemed perhaps too good to be true. On the basis of subsequent events, however, there is the possibility that Purry's appointment came after the collapse of 1720 in an attempt by those in charge of the reorganization of the Compagnie des Indes to reaffirm the legitimacy of the Mississippi Company's parent firm. His willingness to accept the office even after losing money in the Mississippi bubble fiasco might have been a strategic move on Purry's part also for it demonstrated his willingness to support French commercial interests tied closely to the monarchy at the same time that he was proposing the crown support his geographical theory and colonial plan. Although the Académie Royale ultimately decided against Purry's proposal, French commercial interests must have valued his contribution to the country's quest for financial stability for his treatise on European economic policy with a focus on Parisian fiscal matters found a publisher in the capital in 1726.[31] Regardless of the esteem in which he was held by the French in the mid-1720s, Purry's resolute focus on his vision to build a successful colony in the New World meant that he had to continue his search for a willing partner. His rebuff by two global imperial powers of the eighteenth century allowed him to turn his attention to the greatest empire of them all.

When it became obvious to Purry that his hopes for French support of his colonial enterprise were misplaced, he turned in short order to the English. He contacted Horatio (Horace) Walpole, the English ambassador at Paris, and presented him with a three-and-one-half-page proposal written in French and addressed to the king, reprising his theory and settlement plans, set now in a British imperial context. In this initial petition to English authorities Purry proposed to plant a colony of Swiss immigrants in South Carolina provided that (1) the king grant him four square leagues (approximately twelve square miles) of land, (2) he raise the men of his colony into a Swiss military regiment of which he would receive the commission as colonel and the right to nominate his officers, (3) he would be appointed judge of the colony, and (4) the emigrants would be transported to the colony by the king from one of the English ports to the site of the projected colony at no expense either to Purry or to the colonists.[32]

The ambassador found enough value in the proposal to forward it to London. It appears that Purry followed the petition there, where his plan received a rather distinguished, albeit qualified, reception. The Duke of Newcastle first received the proposal while walking the grounds of Kensington Palace with the king in 1721. Shortly thereafter it was called to the attention of Sir Isaac Newton, who—while urging exploration of the territories before settlement began—generally agreed with Purry's theory and settlement proposition. It would be another three years, however, before conditions on the southern frontier of British settlement in North America pressed imperial authorities to consider more seriously Purry's settlement idea. By letter from Whitehall dated 5 June 1724, the king via the secretary of state, the Duke of Newcastle, requested the Lords Commissioners of Trade look into the feasibility and legality of Purry's proposal. Particular attention was to be paid to "how far it may consist with His Majesty's Service and the publick good."[33] The Board of Trade took up the matter on 9 June and ordered Mr. Shelton, secretary to the Lords Proprietors of South Carolina, to appear before them on 11 June to discuss the settlement proposal. Shelton asked for and received from the board an extract of Purry's petition so that he might better inform the Lords Proprietors regarding its provisions. Surely aware of the heightened interest in his proposal—especially as it might augment settlement in South Carolina—Purry followed up the brief document first delivered to Walpole in Paris with an extended discussion of the applicability of his theory of climates and productivity focused upon the region of primary interest to the British Empire—the southern frontier of their southernmost colony in North America. He completed the French manuscript on 18 July 1724 and had it published in London. His *Mémoire Presenté à Sa*

Gr. My Lord Duc de Newcastle drew on the same climatological theory he propounded in his previous two tracts, but the specifics of settlement differed from them because of the imperial priorities and colonial needs of his new audience. The *Mémoire* demonstrated his belief in the bountiful possibilities of planting a settlement of Protestant European émigrés in South Carolina. Purry also outlined explicit reasons for such a settlement as well as the hopes he entertained for his role in it.[34] In light of Purry's proposition, on 23 July 1724, Secretary Shelton reported back to the Board of Trade that, although the Lords Proprietors usually sold land for twenty pounds per thousand acres with quitrent payments of a penny an acre, they would be willing to alter these arrangements to encourage settlement of South Carolina. They proposed to the board that they would offer the land if the grantees would agree to pay two cents per acre quitrent after three years.[35]

Purry's third published pamphlet clearly illustrates his desire to gather all political, civil, and military authority to himself as befitting the rank of a feudal lord. His would be the responsibility of adjudicating internal conflicts and repelling external enemies. He would demand allegiance from his colonists, but he would play the benevolent lord watching over and nurturing his community. Perhaps it was this vision of a closely knit village community thriving on the edge of the Carolina wilderness that gave the British pause to contemplate Purry's ambitious proposition. For all was not well in South Carolina in the 1720s, nor had it been since the devastating Yamassee War of 1715.

II

The young colony of South Carolina passed through a tumultuous adolescence during the decade and a half from 1715 to 1730. These volatile years were laced with Indian warfare, foreign intrigues, and the eventual overthrow of the proprietary government because of its slipshod handling of colonial affairs.[36] As the eighteenth century progressed, South Carolinians relied more heavily on profitable rice and indigo cultivation even though naval stores production continued to be an important commercial activity despite the disruptions of the early years of the century.[37] The concomitant rise in the black slave population in the colony bred fear and distrust among white planters and merchants. By 1729 white settlement constituted only one-third of the total population of 30,000. The dangerous racial imbalance, coupled with a burgeoning and agriculturally expansive plantation system, triggered crucial alterations in English policy toward South Carolina.[38]

Prior to the Yamassee Indian War of 1715, the Lords Proprietors had encouraged settlement in Carolina primarily out of mercantilist necessity. Defense of the colony against Indian and foreign attack was definitely an issue, but the larger concern for English self-sufficiency and private profit overshadowed the strategic importance of colonial defense. Immigration policies favored those émigrés who, like the French Huguenots, possessed skills necessary for the advancement of the English mercantilist system. But beginning with the Church Acts of 1704 and 1706 and culminating in the Yamassee War and its aftermath, policies that excluded or sidestepped the issue of colonial defense were called into question.[39]

In the wake of the war's devastation, Sir Robert Montgomery of Skelmorly and two associates advanced a plan in 1717 to establish a frontier colony on the Savannah River modeled on medieval precedent. The proposed margravate of Azila provided Montgomery with feudal privileges and served simultaneously as a buffer colony for the protection of established populations to the north and east. As margrave, Montgomery would preside as governor over the several fortified towns surrounding his palace. An upper class of proprietors and gentry would be supported by a more substantial population of servants whose labor would produce raisins, olives, wines, and other exotic staples prized by British mercantilists. Both the Lords Proprietors and the Board of Trade looked favorably upon Montgomery's plan, and the former granted him land between the Savannah and Altamaha Rivers as the site of the margravate. Unfortunately for Montgomery and his partners, however, the proprietors' stake in Carolina became increasingly tenuous. In 1720 the Board of Trade refused to approve the plan until proprietary interest in the region ended. Although the board's action ultimately doomed Montgomery's venture, the fact that it received initial sanction demonstrates a heightened emphasis upon colonial security. On the other hand, a continued ambivalence regarding the highest priority for the colony—profit or security—is evident as Azila advocates made little effort to emphasize the strategic importance of the colony as a buffer against foreign aggression. It does appear that the Lords Proprietors viewed the margravate as an opportunity to meet both commercial and military objectives, but their days of administering Carolina were numbered.[40]

The Revolution of 1719, which marked the beginning of the end of the proprietary government, set in motion a process that reoriented English and colonial settlement strategy in South Carolina.[41] After years of uncertainty, a royal policy emerged in 1730 that concentrated on colonial defense but also continued to make allowances for skilled white immigrants, whose labors would contribute to colonial economic diversification and English self-sufficiency while reducing the colony's reliance on slave labor.

For more than a decade prior to 1730, English authorities considered various proposals to secure the southern frontier from enemy attack. Before the outbreak of war with the Yamassee people, the colonial government had reserved the land between the Combahee and Savannah Rivers for them and their allies. After their defeat in 1716, the South Carolina Commons House of Assembly and the proprietors planned to redistribute confiscated Yamassee land to new settlers. The Commons House passed legislation granting 300–400 acres to emigrants from Ireland, Great Britain, or the northern colonies. Prospective settlers had to be resident on the land for ten months of every twelve and pay yearly quitrent, but the purchase price of three pounds could be deferred for four years to attract poorer immigrants. The colony paid special bounties as inducements to import white Protestant servants. Black slaves were expressly forbidden. The public dissemination of these laws in England drew 500 prospective Irish Protestant émigrés. But, ostensibly because of a dispute between the proprietors and the Commons House over land allotments for the settlers, the proprietors altered their settlement strategy in 1718. Instead of parceling out small tracts to many, they decided to create large feudal-style baronies—sixteen in all—of 12,000 acres each. Three years later, the proprietors quashed a second plan of settlement.

Perhaps frustrated by proprietary neglect, John Barnwell, a Beaufort planter and veteran of numerous conflicts with native populations, proposed a strategy for the defense of South Carolina's exposed frontiers in 1720. This original plan borrowed heavily from Virginia and New England defensive schemes and paid homage to the French method of empire building that had proved so successful in the New World. On a trip to London in 1720, Barnwell suggested that a line of fortifications be erected on the frontier to secure English territory against attack. The lands surrounding the forts were to be reserved for the use of officers, troops, and other prospective settlers who might take up residence near the garrisons free of quitrent payments. Barnwell believed that this policy, though involving substantial initial outlays of capital, would best protect the Carolina frontier from enemy invasion. He held also that the forts would guarantee the maintenance of friendly and lucrative trade relations with the Indians. His plan received critical acclaim from many British officials and was endorsed almost immediately by the influential Board of Trade. The Lords Proprietors, however, who had lost their power to govern Carolina but not their land claims in the colony, balked at the tremendous effort and capital it would take to institute Barnwell's proposal. Over the ensuing nine years, French movement in the Carolina backcountry continued to threaten the British position, but the proprietors steadfastly refused to allocate funds to implement the fortifications system. When the land claims of the proprietors were finally extinguished in 1728 and royal authority encompassed all facets of life in South Carolina, the colony desperately needed a coherent blueprint for frontier defense.[42]

The troubled 1720s convinced South Carolinians of the need for a cordon sanitaire on their southern flank. In the early years of the decade, the Commons House of Assembly, presumably drawing upon Barnwell's scheme, proposed what would eventually become the township plan of settlement. But, because of the problems faced by the colony over the course of the decade, no concrete action could be taken.[43] By 1729 the entrepreneur Joshua Gee offered a similar plan for colonial defense. Engaged in the West Indian trade, Gee in 1718 had been one of the promoters of a project for settling soldiers in Nova Scotia to raise hemp and produce naval stores.[44] In his widely read tract *The Trade and*

Navigation of Great Britain Considered, Gee reaffirmed the economic potential of South Carolina but feared that it was "liable to be overrun by the French, Spaniards, and Indians for want of sufficient protection." Gee proposed a line of defensive fortifications and a more liberal land policy, which would enable more immigrants to settle in frontier areas to secure the western flank of the colony. He noted that the piedmont was a country "large enough to canton out into distinct lots" for settlement and that "all the inhabitants we shall be capable of sending" would constitute a further defense perimeter. Gee suggested that land be granted to immigrants free of quitrent payments for a number of years. This granted piedmont land, now more attractive to prospective settlers, would be populated and therefore defended from enemy attack. Immigrants would make economic contributions to the colony while simultaneously policing the colonial frontier.[45]

III

It was into the midst of this precipitous state of affairs that Purry injected his memorial of 18 July 1724 to the Duke of Newcastle.[46] This pamphlet laid down in specific terms Purry's reasons for seeking a plantation in South Carolina—most especially because of its proximity to the thirty-third parallel. He demonstrated how other geographers had failed to discover the truth of his theory. In so doing he "proved" his contention that Carolina was capable of producing abundant wealth from agriculture and from silk manufacture, citing the adverse French experience in the far Canadian north, and the riches he found in his own travels at or near the fifth climate zone.[47] The following year Purry and several Swiss associates pressed the advantage by appearing before royal officials in London. Purry requested that the Lords Commissioners of Trade transport 600 Swiss immigrants to South Carolina as per his initial proposal to Ambassador Walpole. Both the Duke of Newcastle and the Board of Trade reacted favorably to Purry's planned settlement, especially because the immigrants could contribute to the economic vitality of the province while providing necessary guard duty along the frontier. Purry's petition for 48,000 acres of land did not strike them as excessive. And the prospect of white settlers on the frontier producing needed materials, such as silk, for the economy of the empire would aid in giving England a favorable balance of payments with her international trading partners. The proprietors, however, who still held title to South Carolina lands, balked at the cost of transporting such a large group to a colony in which they had progressively fewer rights. Consequently, in the late spring of 1725 the proprietors reworked Purry's original proposal to suit their needs. They agreed to grant him a barony of 12,000 acres in South Carolina on or near the Savannah River on the condition that he transport 300 immigrants to the province at his own expense within one year of the date of the patent. The proprietors promised him an additional barony of 12,000 acres when he had built a settlement 1,200 strong at the site. By mid-June Purry seems to have acceded to these new conditions as he understood them and agreed to conduct 1,200 immigrants to South Carolina. For its part, the Board of Trade appears to have concurred with the new arrangement. Convinced that the necessary negotiations were complete, a triumphant Purry departed for Switzerland to enlist recruits for the adventure.[48]

On his return to Neuchâtel, Purry founded a company (Purry et Cie) with the help of his Swiss friends to oversee the recruiting and transportation of the émigrés. He also procured the services of Jean Vat(t) [also John Watt] of Biel (Bienne) as an immigration agent whose function it was to assist Purry in his future communications with English authorities.[49] Because of the social and economic dislocations rending the fabric of Swiss society in the opening decades of the eighteenth century, Purry and Vat found no lack of applicants ready to leave the cantons for South Carolina. It should be noted that Swiss cantons had ceased to offer welcome to religious dissenters and that vexed municipal magistrates desired to rid themselves of as many unwanted refugees as possible so that exploding relief roles might be cut back. Seen in this light, Purry's solicitation for adventurous souls to join him in South Carolina actually dovetailed nicely with the desires of Swiss officials—as long as only refugees and not Swiss citizens quit the state.[50]

From all over the Swiss Confederation, prospective emigrants flocked to Neuchâtel, which served as the rendezvous for departure to the New World. Vat memorialized the Duke of Newcastle concerning "the six hundred Swiss designing to settle in South Carolina."[51] Like those who preceded them and those who would follow, many of these tentative Carolinians were in desperate straits and perceived the English province as an opportunity for a fresh start. M. Vernett, one of Purry's financial associates, raised at least a hundred would-be colonists in Geneva alone. Popular interest continued to mount, and the enterprise appeared headed for imminent success. Emigrants gathered at Neuchâtel in September 1726 and remained there for nearly a month while final preparations for their departure were arranged. Then, inexplicably at this late date, the proprietors reneged on the agreement of June 1725 with Purry and sought redress on key provisions. They renounced their pledge to aid in the financial burden of transporting some of the immigrants—Purry had contracted to transport 300 settlers at his expense, but more than 300 awaited departure. The proprietors also backed down on the 12,000-acre barony promised to Purry. They opted now to place the land in a trust held by Stephen Godin and Jacob Satur, their agents in South Carolina. The land would not be conferred to him until it could be verified that he had transported 200 immigrants at his own expense to the colony. Although this latter alteration would have actually saved Purry from having to underwrite the passage of the additional hundred persons had it arrived earlier, the news came too late, for now he and Neuchâtel were forced to contend with hundreds of anxious émigrés. When word of this new codicil reached Neuchâtel, Purry's financial partners, fearing the worst was yet to come, immediately withdrew their support. Vernett disappeared, cutting those of his party adrift on the streets of Neuchâtel. And Purry found himself alone and constrained to answer questions that had no satisfactory answers. In the face of insurmountable problems and a progressively more restive mob, he fled on the evening of 30 October "to avoid the fury of the People, who having spent their money, wander up and down the Streets not knowing where to find a Dinner nor a bed to lie down upon at night." It was left to hapless municipal authorities to mitigate the impact of the debacle on hundreds of disgruntled and hungry would-be emigrants. Vilified by both emigrants and cantonal officials alike as the perpetrator of a cruel hoax, Purry became associated with charges of fraud and deceit, which shredded his reputation and followed him to the end of his days.[52]

On 31 October 1726 Vat wrote to English authorities (presumably from a safe place) about the turn of events precipitated by the proprietors' disregard for the original agreement reached with Purry. He recounted the miserable condition of the now deserted emigrants and could not imagine "what will be the Issue of this which will make much noise in the World." Vat firmly believed that more than 600 persons would have gone to South Carolina if funds had been available because "so many People offered themselves on the sight of the Vessel prepared." The immigration agent could barely contain his frustration with the Lords Proprietors and argued that their mismanagement "hath been the Principal Cause of the Miscarrying of the Undertaking by the Alteration of their Pattent and refusing to fullfill the Agreement for the Transportation of 600 Persons from England to Carolina." Vat concluded his letter by asking to be remembered to Dr. Bray among others "and all our friends," saddened that the current situation "quite overturns the design of our good friend Mounr. Pury."[53]

Out of the entire party that had assembled at Neuchâtel in the early fall of 1726, only twenty-four—undoubtedly the most wealthy of the group—secured passage to the colony, and this on their own initiative and at their own expense. Among those who arrived in Charles Town in December 1726 were members of the Zubly and Desaussure families. Both families were destined to receive land in the township eventually planted by Purry on the South Carolina frontier. But, for their immediate succor and in what probably remained a futile effort, Vat petitioned the English government and proprietors on behalf of the twenty-four men, women, and children to reimburse them for the cost of their passage and aid them in the hardships, which they would invariably encounter during their initial period of adjustment in the New World.[54]

Fortunately for the hundreds who because of financial or other reasons could not join this small cohort, authorities in Neuchâtel undertook to provide for them as best they could, but the proprietor-instigated demise of Purry's planned settlement bred contempt for the rising frenzy of "emigration fever" affecting more and more Swiss inhabitants.[55] Arthur Henry Hirsch has speculated that Purry's difficulties might have been caused by South Carolina governor Francis Nicholson. His distinctly anti-Calvinist predilections had surfaced in the Anglican-Dissenter struggles over the issues of Commons House representation and paper money in the early 1720s and may have played some role in the reversal of proprietary policy toward the Calvinist Purry and his like-minded émigrés.[56] Corroboration for Hirsch's claim might be construed from an enigmatic passage in a letter written by Nicholson on 23 July 1726, fully two months before the debacle in Neuchâtel. The letter appears to have been written from London and includes information about unnamed policies of the Lords Proprietors. Regarding Purry's venture, Nicholson wrote, "by Mr. Peter John Purry's Papers you will see what Contrivances there are about the Swiss And I conceive that the Assembly ought to take that matter into their Serious Consideration and Enquire of Mr. Vernod the Minister whether he received the Letter mentioned in the paper and what he has done upon it, at present I find they are at a Stand in that affair."[57] The content of the papers to which Nicholson refers is unknown as is that of the letter apparently sent to the Reverend Francis Varnod (also Vernod). But his extremely unusual inversion of Purry's Anglicized given and middle names and his use of the pejorative term *contrivance* in connection with arrangements for the Swiss could hint at Nicholson's disposition toward Purry and his plans. His notation that "they are at a Stand in that affair" might signal Nicholson's awareness in July that the proprietors were on the verge of altering their agreement with Purry or had already done so. Perhaps it is for that reason that Vat implored an English official to present his letter of 31 October to "General Nicholson" and why Nicholson in late November 1726 sent some unidentified papers to President Middleton of the South Carolina Assembly informing him of the present state of the "Neufchatelus."[58] Although none of these incidents indicate Nicholson's direct involvement in the ill-starred affair, taken together they do raise some questions about Governor Nicholson's level of commitment to the settlement of non-Anglican immigrants in his province.

If prospective colonists and Swiss civic leaders suffered because of the duplicity of the Lords Proprietors, at least their reputations were intact. Purry's fared far worse. Ruined financially for the third time and with his credibility obliterated, Purry appears to have gone into hiding by the end of 1726. His family sequestered him—probably for his own protection—on a mountain farm across Lake Neuchâtel in the Payerne district of Vaud within, or at least very near, the commune of Cerniaz. He wrote periodically to his two stepbrothers Quinche asking for small amounts of money for postage and tobacco. For the better part of two years Purry lived in relative obscurity. Yet, even after many family crises, three separate financial disasters, and four failed attempts to apply practically his scientific theory to the needs of three of the most powerful empires of his era, Purry's confidence in his vision remained unshakable. When the possibility of another opportunity to implement it appeared in 1730, he rose to the occasion once more.[59]

IV

Ironically, the denouement of Purry's first attempt to establish a colony in South Carolina may have actually spurred positive reactions to his subsequent proposals by directing royal attention again to the exposed southern flank of English settlement in North America. Perhaps because of the fiasco of 1726, the proprietors lost even more of their credibility, resulting in the absolute end of proprietary influence in South Carolina in 1728. As royally appointed officials grasped the reins of power falling from the hands of the proprietors, they also turned their attention to the plight of the frontier.[60]

Robert Johnson, South Carolina's second royal governor, quickly realized the necessity of securing the frontier and moved toward implementing a comprehensive policy for colonial defense. In the same year that Gee's pamphlet was published, Johnson noted the dire need to augment the white population to make the colony safe from any potential enemies—foreign, Native American, or black. The governor believed the best strategy to ensure the security of the colony lay in enticing poor foreign Protestants by providing special inducements, such as limitations on quitrents. These immigrants would then take up small landholdings in frontier regions of the province.[61] Three times in early 1730 Johnson contacted the Board of Trade concerning his ideas for encouraging immigration to the colony.[62] Partially because of his efforts, the board became convinced of the urgency of revising colonial settlement policies. In a communiqué to the Privy Council in 1732, the board stated that "an accession of New Inhabitants in ye Plantations cannot fail to increase the Trade and Commerce of this Kingdom, whilst It creates an Augmentation of His Majesty's Revenues in his Quit Rents. . . . As It is Our Frontier to ye Spanish and French Settlements, and is surrounded by a great number of Indian Nations, the well peopling of this Province Seems to be a very necessary Measure for the Defense and Security of all Our Plantations on the Continent of America."[63]

This document vividly indicates the reordered priorities of English immigration strategy after 1730. Henceforth, immigration incentives would emphasize the necessity of population growth for defensive purposes above economically discerned mercantilist reasons. European immigrants who had been courted prior to 1730 primarily for the contributions they could make to the colonial economy were to be recruited after 1730 primarily to augment the white population and defend the colony from prospective enemies. From this vantage point, subsequent laws and bounties concerning immigration and economic development may be perceived essentially as inducements to fortify the frontier while simultaneously encouraging the expansion of the colonial economy. The provisions of many of these laws committed citizens to near total subsidy of white immigrants and gave greater support to those newcomers settling in the frontier areas.[64] Bounties on such commercial endeavors as wine, hemp, and silk existed as much to draw those skilled in their cultivation to South Carolina as they did to encourage economic development. Instead of spreading the plantation system so heavily dependent upon the importation of increasing numbers of black slaves, the poorer Protestant immigrants would aid in the diversification of the provincial economy on smaller plots of land ringing the lowcountry with a band of white small farmers and craftspeople. Their expertise in the protected industries held out the promise of economic gain, and the promise of gain accelerated immigration, ensuring a larger white population and more effective defense against foreign and domestic enemies.[65] Joyce Chaplin's analysis of what would become the township plan advances an even more comprehensive interpretation of the settlement strategy: "People who settled in the townships . . . fulfilled several expectations drawn from mercantilism and the moral tradition. They produced commodities Britain would otherwise have to buy from foreigners and were (supposedly) better able to resist military threat. Without slaves and plantation-sized tracts, settlers worked more for a common benefit than for individual gain and could not display the laziness and luxury common to people free from labor."[66]

Johnson's blueprint for immigration called his township plan or "scheme," as amended by the Board of Trade and launched as royal law in 1730 stipulated that eleven townships in remote and underdefended locations would be laid out: two on the Altamaha River, two on the Savannah River, one at the head of the Pon Pon River, two on the Santee River, and one each on the Wateree, Black, Pee Dee, and Waccamaw rivers. River systems were logical sites for the townships because of their strategic importance as defensible transportation and communication links with Charles Town. Each township consisted of a square 20,000-acre tract with 250–300 acres reserved for a formal town that would be divided into 200 lots. Each lot was to be no more than a quarter acre in size. In addition to the town core, another fifty acres were reserved for a schoolhouse, churches, craft industries, and other civic amenities. Authorities provided the settlers of each township "a right of Common and Herbage" on all lands "as shall not be taken up by particular Grants made to said inhabitants" and set aside "a quantity of land not exceeding 300 acres contiguous to the said town . . . for a Common in perpetuity, to each of the said Towns, free from Quit Rent." Remaining acreage in the township was to be carved into 200 parcels for distribution to town residents. Only those living in the town were to be allowed land in the outlying areas, which also included a six-square-mile buffer zone erected between the frontier townships and the nearest legal land grants of nontownship settlers.[67]

Each resident family member was allowed fifty acres of land. Fifty additional acres were provided the household for each white servant and black slave. Residents could accumulate more land at any time provided the family or individual could bring the additional land under cultivation. Such land grants were free of quitrent payments (set at no less than four shillings proclamation money per 100 acres) for a period of ten years, after which the settlers would be liable for the yearly quitrent payment to colonial officers.[68] The first settlers of each township received grants closest to the town proper. The plan did not limit township grants to foreign immigrants, but extended the right of ownership to His Majesty's subjects as well—the only condition being that grantees live in the township and cultivate the granted land within a certain period of time or forfeit the grant. In an effort to offset the black majority in the province, white servants, once their terms of service expired, could receive fifty acres in their own right—an inducement to keep them in South Carolina and augment the white minority population. Persons already possessing title to land elsewhere in the province could not receive any more land in the township unless they settled there within one year's time. No one was to be allowed more than one lot in the township, nor could anyone's granted land front on any river by more than one-quarter its depth. Johnson's plan also stipulated that each township with its six-mile extended boundary should be established into a separate parish. When any of the parishes so constituted attained a population of 100 heads of household, it would be entitled to send two representatives to the Commons House of Assembly—foreigners and free-born subjects sharing equal voting rights.[69]

At this point the township parish was also to be conferred all the rights of existing parishes, thereby placing it on an equitable footing with the other parishes in the province. Theoretically this status would allow the frontier parishes to enter the mainstream of colonial political and economic life while maintaining the defensive chain of settlements ringing the prosperous lowcountry. The Board of Trade empowered Governor Johnson to earmark colonial funds for the surveys of the townships and for the purchase of tools, provisions, and other incidentals for any poor Protestants who might wish to settle in any of them. The South Carolina Assembly fully supported the plan of settlement and made overtures to undertake the financial task of providing European émigrés with the means to sustain themselves until they could clear land and harvest crops. The assembly imposed a further duty on imported slaves and set aside 5,000 pounds current money for the laying out and surveying of the townships and for the needs of the prospective settlers. To those immigrants from commercial centers, this subsidy, christened the township or settlement fund, was particularly important because of their initial unfamiliarity with rural life, much less life on the southern frontier. By 1731 the township plan, sites for the proposed settlements, and incentives for enticing Europeans to immigrate to South Carolina were in place. The colony eagerly awaited the influx of whites who would essentially serve as frontier sentinels for the defense of lowcountry merchants, planters, and financiers.

V

As Governor Johnson and other royal authorities busied themselves reassessing and reworking Barnwell's strategy, Purry departed his rural Swiss hideaway to reintroduce himself to the well-placed English friends he had made earlier, hoping their advocacy might persuade the right people to support his renewed interest in South Carolina. Among his most significant friendships were those he sustained with the notable group of philanthropic and reform-minded clergymen and secular leaders in the circle of Dr. Thomas Bray, which included James Oglethorpe. Instrumental in the future founding of Georgia, these "Associates of Dr. Bray," as they were called, looked with favor upon Purry's colonial vision. On at least one occasion, the associates invited him to speak before them. He must have been quite convincing for they subscribed more than 200 pounds sterling to assist him in his colonial quest. After Bray's death the associates donated part of his library to Purry. Using these and other contacts, the determined Swiss planned to approach royal leaders.[70]

Purry's resolve quickened with the ultimate demise of the proprietors. He drafted a new settlement proposal to the royal administration of the colony even as Johnson's township plan worked its way toward approval. He first memorialized the Lords Commissioners of Trade and Plantations through his son Charles on 24 March 1730, reacquainting them the specifics of the events and agreements of 1725 and 1726. At the end of the short petition, Purry expressed his continued interest in planting a colony of Swiss immigrants in South Carolina. The Board of Trade heard the report the following day and intended to consider Purry's colonial ambitions "at another opportunity,"[71] but the petition languished for the next three months. By midsummer it appears that Purry was cognizant of Johnson's township plan and strategized accordingly. In July he decided to take matters into his own hands and approached the authorities with more specifics. This document, written in French and dated 9 July 1730, resurrected some of his proposals from the previous decade. He agreed to transport a colony of 600 Swiss Protestants within six years to South Carolina with the proviso that he be granted 12,000 acres gratis and that no quitrent payments would be required of the émigrés for some years after their arrival. Leaving nothing to chance this time, Purry briefed Governor Johnson on his new plan. Less than two weeks after his petition arrived, a letter from Johnson appealed to the Lords Commissioners on his behalf. In his letter of 20 July 1730, the governor noted the "great Expence and trouble" Purry had already faced trying to settle Swiss in South Carolina. He also appealed to the fact that "as nothing is so much wanted as White Inhabitants for the Security and improvement of that Frontier Colony," Purry's proposal was well worth their consideration. Johnson then specifically suggested that Purry's immigrants be settled together in one of the new townships on the Savannah River "[n]ear the Palachuccola Fort or any other part (upon that River) where Conveniency can be found at the Discretion of the Governor and Council." Johnson concluded by requesting that the crown give "an immediate Conditional Instruction to the Governor for the time being" so that arrangements could proceed. With proof that Purry fulfilled his responsibilities, the governor would grant his 12,000-acre barony for which he would pay a token five shilling annual quitrent.[72]

With Johnson's endorsement and with its not coincidental similarity to the governor's own township scheme for settlement of the South Carolina frontier, Purry's proposal seemed assured of success. The Lords Commissioners appeared equally enthusiastic, for they read Johnson's letter on 22 July and the next day "represented to His Majesty that during His Royal Father's reign Mr. Jean Pierre Purry was recommended by His Majesty's Ministers at Paris as a person well qualified to make a settlement of Swiss Protestants in South Carolina."[73] In early September, board members ordered a draft of instructions prepared for Governor Johnson informing him that Purry's proposal had been accepted with only minor conditions, such as the required oath of allegiance, being added. After reviewing these instructions, however, the board "thought proper not to grant any Land in Carolina, without a Reservation of Qt. Rents to His Majesty." Unfortunately for all concerned, the issue of quitrent payments became a major impediment to further progress on a satisfactory accord. Revised instructions regarding the proposed settlement did not reach Governor Johnson until 30 November 1731. These directives stipulated the conditions under which Purry's colony was to proceed and included a problematic modification from Johnson's recommendation of the previous year. Now it was understood that Purry would "settle Six Hundred Swiss Protestants in Carolina, including Women and Children at their own Expence, within the space of Six Years to commence from Christmas next." The immigrants "of competent age" were to take the usual oath of allegiance to the crown upon their arrival and all were to receive rights equal to the rest of his majesty's subjects in the province. After the oath of allegiance had been administered, Governor Johnson was to "grant them Lands and Settle them in such Place and in such manner as you shall Judge most conducive to the Interest and Security of said Province." Purry was not to receive his land until one or more customs officials could certify that he fulfilled this agreement. More ominously, however, the instructions amended Purry's proposal requiring him to pay quitrent on his 12,000-acre barony beginning ten years after he received the land.[74]

Regrettably, Purry was initially unaware of this development. Buoyed by the support of Governor Johnson and the apparent enthusiasm of British officials for his plan as he proposed it, he decided to visit South Carolina for the first time to select a proper tract for his township settlement. He arrived in May 1731, accompanied by fellow emigration enthusiasts James Richard of Geneva and Abraham Meuron and Henry Raimond (Raymond) of St. Sulpy (also St. Sulpice).[75] The provincial legislature allowed the party 150 pounds of South Carolina current money for traveling and provisioning expenses for the trip to the Savannah River to locate a suitable habitation. Captain Rowland

Evans, whose militia unit of the Carolina Rangers patrolled the region from Fort Palachuccola southeastward along the Savannah River, met Purry and his colleagues at Port Royal and conducted them to the southern frontier. The French-speaking Anglican pastor the Reverend Francis Varnod traveled with them, presumably to serve as interpreter. With mandatory "assistance" from Evans, Purry selected the Great Yamassee Bluff as the site for the settlement and marked a tree in what was to become the center of town.

Purry's group returned to Charles Town in the late summer. By September 1731, several significant steps had been taken to ensure that the southern frontier would soon be populated with white Swiss Protestants. First, in late August, the South Carolina General Assembly came to an agreement with Purry, which granted him 600 pounds sterling for every 100 men he persuaded to reside in his township. In the same act, ratified on 20 August, provincial authorities also set aside funds for land surveys, tools, and provisions for the use of 300 persons, provided the settlers were Protestants of good reputation. Finally, by official proclamation on 1 September, Governor Johnson set aside 20,000 acres for the first South Carolina township at the place selected a few weeks earlier to be called Purrysburg in Purry's honor.[76]

To the delight of royal authorities, and perhaps in response to their legal and monetary commitments to him, Purry completed two related documents in Charles Town on 23 September 1731. The shorter of the two set forth qualifications for prospective émigrés to the township. Purry's vision for the new community is clear from this brief text. It will be composed of both "persons who go to settle on their own Account" and servants. Servants must be skilled in at least one profession (agriculture, carpentry, and viniculture are specifically mentioned) or good laborers. They must not be completely destitute. Servants will have a three-year contract to fulfill but must be paid a fair wage. They have the right to hold the "Fruits of their Labour" as security for the wages that will be paid at the end of each year and have the right to ask for an advance on wages to purchase clothing and other "Necessaries." When overcome by sickness, they shall be cared for without charge but will be liable to make up the time lost to their masters. Finally, "Victuals and Lodgings from the Day of their Imbarkation . . . and their Passage by Sea" will not be charged to them. The only directive addressed to nonservants regards the fact that they must have "at least 50 Crowns each."[77] In this document, Purry moves beyond the general structure of the contractual community to demonstrate specifically the division of labor, class distinctions, and the concept of mutuality that were to motivate life in the township.

The longer document, *Description abrégée de l'état présent de la Caroline Meridionale,* has been his best-known, and also his most disparaged, treatise.[78] This excellent example of promotional tract literature of the age exalted the superior merits of South Carolina over any other place in the world. It made extensive use of his theory of optimal climates, reaffirmed the need for skilled craftsmen in the colony, and heralded the tremendous material progress possible for those in South Carolina. Since an English translation appeared in a popular Charles Town journal the following year just as the first immigrants to Purrysburg were set to arrive, the tract served as much to encourage South Carolinians as it did to draw Swiss families to his colonial experiment. As both French and English versions appeared within a few months of each other on opposite sides of the Atlantic (and in German a short while later), it easily achieved both goals in due course.

From shortly after its initial publication to the present day, Purry's tract has been denounced for flagrantly misrepresenting South Carolina to advance the author's own purposes. While Purry certainly was not above self-promotion, it is difficult to sustain the charges of fraud and deceit from which his reputation still suffers. After enumerating the vast wealth of goods and livestock produced by the colony, Purry then spends the better part of three pages explaining the dangers of living in Carolina. He meets each of the problems directly (climate, sickness, mosquitoes, rattlesnakes) and, though perhaps dismissing the issue of ill health a bit too blithely from a contemporary vantage point, Purry's explanations and "remedies" were no different than those of his contemporaries. In short, nearly every topic he addresses in the pamphlet has a much stronger measure of truth to it than has been previously assumed.[79] From the kinds of crops he mentions and the increasing wealth of the colonists to his examination of disease, the author remains truthful throughout.[80] Purry surmises that the death and disease many had experienced in Carolina came not so much from the climate as from the reaction of the inhabitants to it in terms of their habits of eating and drinking. He was not alone in his assessment of the cause of the problem.[81] In addition, recall that Purry had served in the tropics for a number of years prior to his initial visit to South Carolina and may have been somewhat acclimatized to the humid mesothermal climate of the province.

Finally, it should also be observed that Purry and his friends visited the future site of Purrysburg during the most disagreeable season of the year, when heat, humidity, pathogens, and predators were most conspicuous. Their fifteen-day sojourn in the wilderness of South Carolina, probably during late July and August 1731, does not seem to have adversely affected their health. They were not even troubled by venomous snakes as they traversed the high grasses and sandy bluffs. If their journey had been fraught with grave sickness and an overtly hostile environment, they would have no reason to continue to pursue colonizing plans. Who would desire to live in such an inhospitable place even if the land was free? Remember that Purry had also been impressed with southern Africa and southern Australia, which also lay in the fifth climate zone. His theory of optimal climates coupled with his own reconnaissance as an employee of the Dutch East India Company offered convincing proof of the bounty of South Carolina—even if he had yet to experience that bounty firsthand. The blame for what exaggeration of the economic data is evident must be laid at the doorstep of colonial officials who had access to that information—and the ability to stretch the truth if it meant the difference between new white settlers or none.[82]

Purry and his friends must have left for Europe directly after he completed the documents because his *Description abrégée de l'état présent de la Caroline Meridionale* was published in Neuchâtel in December 1731. Booksellers in both Neuchâtel and in St. Sulpy carried the popularly received essay. Those companions who had traveled to the province with him signed the document, attesting to the accuracy of Purry's depiction of South Carolina.[83] The ubiquitous but confused excitement it immediately generated, including a host of questions and objections, led the author to publish a revised and expanded edition in March 1732 under the full title *Description abrégée de l'état présent de la Caroline Meridionale, nouvelle edition, avec des eclaircissemens, les actes des concessions faites à ce suject à l'auteur, tant pour luy que pour ceux qui voudront predre parti avec luy, Et enfin une instruction qui contient les conditions, sous lesquelles on pourra l'accompagner.* In this *nouvelle edition,* Purry included vital details not present in the first, which he believed prospective emigrants needed to make informed decisions about whether to join his colony. After the *Description* proper, which remained fundamentally unchanged, Purry added an entirely new section of *eclaircissemens* (clarifications) designed to answer concerns raised by curious, but cautious, potential emigrants. Purry also included the text of an act passed 20 August 1731 by the South Carolina General Assembly regarding the arrangements for him and his colonists, a proclamation about Purrysburg from Governor Johnson dated 1 September 1731, and an affidavit attesting to the veracity of the arrangements dated 14 September 1731. The inclusion of these documents served further to legitimize Purry's undertaking in the eyes of potential émigrés since it was apparent from them that he had the support of the governing authorities in South Carolina. He then appended his *Instruction* regarding the qualifications cited earlier for those desirous of going with him to South Carolina, but he added a coda publicizing the date of departure for the next trip to Purrysburg and listing necessities for the journey.[84]

The publication of the *Description* and its dissemination throughout the region set off what distraught Swiss officials derisively labeled the "Rabies Carolinae." In short order, 170 Swiss residents made application to leave for Purrysburg in spite of the widely known failure of Purry's earlier attempt to found a colony in South Carolina. Local magistrates took every precaution to stop native Swiss from joining expatriate émigrés, but even legal restrictions failed to discourage citizens from doing so.[85] At this point, General James Oglethorpe, soon to be a trustee of Georgia and cognizant of the imminent success of Purry's project, opened negotiations with the Swiss and by a secret agreement of 4 December 1731 bought a quarter interest in the colonial venture. For a total of fifty pounds sterling, Purry ceded 3,000 of his initial 12,000 acres to Oglethorpe. The two also appear to have reached an accord on the transfer of 20,000 acres of Oglethorpe's land in South Carolina to Purry for the latter's pledge to transport religious refugees from Salzburg to Savannah at some time in the future.[86]

Purry and his associates had no trouble raising emigrants for transport to South Carolina, but financing their passage became a major obstacle when Purry discovered how the Lords Commissioners had changed his original proposal of July 1730. It should be recalled that after Johnson's letter to the Board of Trade on his behalf and the initial draft instructions to Johnson, Purry mistakenly believed that the board would approve his proposal as written. His overconfidence led him to depart for South Carolina in 1731 before the Lords Commissioners had solidified their consent to the colonial plan. He had begun the process of recruiting settlers for his township on the assumption that he would be granted 12,000 acres free of quitrent payments. Purry secured the financial backing of "several Gentlemen in London" on the basis of this false assumption. Once they discovered that Purry would have to pay quitrent on the land, however, they refused to advance him the funds necessary to finance the passage of the Swiss to Purrysburg. Undaunted by this setback, Purry decided to proceed with his colonial plans sometime before early March 1731, leaving his agent Jean Vat to iron out the difficulties. Vat directed a petition for redress directly to the lord president of the Privy Council dated 7 March 1731/32. In it he asked the king to increase Purry's land grant to "48,000 acres subject to Quit Rents in Lieu of the 12,000 acres clear of Quit Rents." Perhaps summoning the specter of a repeat of the chaos of 1726, Vat raised the possibility that the whole enterprise would be "rendered abortive unless His Majesty shall be graciously pleased to grant him" this request. The clever agent noted that Purry "thinks he is more justified in this proposal since the Grant of 12,000 acres clear of Quit Rents was in lieu of 48,000 acres formerly granted him by the Lords Proprietors for that purpose and without that quantity of Land he hath no hope of raising a sum of Money sufficient to carry out this undertaking." This request did not seem an unreasonable one to the petitioners for Purry demonstrated that the cost to his estate of transporting 600 Swiss Protestants to the province would be nearly 2,400 pounds sterling.[87]

Officials apparently conceded the point and in "Additional Instructions" for Governor Johnson dated 12 March 1732 stated, "We do grant to the said Purry and his Heirs in consideration of his trouble labor and expence Twelve thousand acres of Land in that province free from Quit Rent." But confusion remained for the document ended by reaffirming that the land was "subject to the Quit Rent reserved by Your Instructions after the expiration of the first ten years from the date of His Grant."[88] To resolve the matter, the Board of Trade summoned Vat to appear before the Lords Commissioners on 25 April 1732. They asked him whether Purry planned to settle his 600 immigrants on the 48,000 acres he had requested. He assured them that that was not the case and that Purry desired to use the land as security. He "intended to borrow the Money that was necessary to defray the charge of transporting the said Swiss—that he could not raise a sufficient sum upon a less quantity of Land." Two days later the Lords Commissioners took up issue again and instructed that an investigative report be prepared.[89]

The scrupulous investigation involving a committee of five took nearly a month. The Lords of the Committee of the Privy Council received the eight-page report dated 26 May 1732 detailing the history of the government's dealings with Purry from 1724 to the present. The authors of the report argued that Purry's projected colony would bring a large number of new white inhabitants to a colony badly in need of settlers to protect it from foreign and domestic threats, which was a long-standing concern of the Board of Trade. They wrote, "In all probability one great Reason why South Carolina has not hitherto been peopled in the same proportion with other parts of His Majesty's Dominions in America, has been that a considerable number of People have never before made an offer of Settling together in one place." Purry's township settlement could therefore provide South Carolina with exactly what was needed. The authors believed that he would eventually sell some of the land to other settlers thereby further augmenting the white population of the southern frontier and increasing the commerce of the colony. The report concluded by recommending that the 48,000 acres be granted to Purry free of quitrents for ten years as long as he fulfilled his pledge to people the township with 600 Protestants.[90] On 6 June 1732, the Committee of the Privy Council directed the Board of Trade to prepare a draft of instructions to Governor Johnson for a grant of 48,000 acres to Purry for the settlement of Swiss families in South Carolina. The Lords Commissioners agreed, and it was so ordered on 15 June. The "Additional Instructions" were drawn up the following day, and Johnson received them in July. These instructions authorized him to grant the land to Purry with the stipulation that he settle 600 Swiss Protestant men, women, and children in the colony within six years from Christmas 1731. The 48,000-acre grant was to be laid out in the "buffer zone" immediately surrounding the township and would not be granted to Purry until customs officials could verify all 600 Swiss Protestants had arrived.[91]

Even before the arrival of the first group of Swiss émigrés, colonial leaders made provision for their sustenance as agreed. In early October the Provincial Council ordered three months of provisions for each settler as well as transportation to the township. A few days later six cannon from Port Royal and other tools and necessaries were ordered to Purrysburg. Each person over twelve years of age was entitled to eight bushels of corn and peas, three hundredweight of beef, fiftyweight of pork, two hundredweight of rice, one bushel of salt, one axe, one broad hoe, and one narrow hoe. One cow, one calf, and one young sow were appropriated for every five persons and also some shot and powder. Succeeding transports of Swiss for the township were also to be aided with provisions set aside by the colony for their use.[92]

VI

After nearly fifteen years of relentless effort, Jean Pierre Purry stood on the verge of success in the summer of 1732. To this point in his life he had attained status as a civic official, a military officer, a wealthy merchant, an agent of well-established international trading companies, a world traveler, a geographical theorist, and in some circles an unscrupulous opportunist. He had been ruined financially three times and had petitioned, prodded, and pestered some of the most powerful figures in three of the great world empires on five different occasions. As the aging adventurer approached his fifty-seventh birthday, however, the one prize that had eluded him throughout his life, the one vocation that defined success and achievement for all societies of the ancien régime enticed him again across the Atlantic. For he was now to take his place as the baronial lord of hundreds of immigrants he would transport to his contractual community—Purrysburg Township, South Carolina. Vested with civil and military authority from Carolina officials desperate to populate their vulnerable frontiers as insurance against foreign and domestic enemies, Purry stood ready to lead his people like an early modern Moses to a new promised land of plenty and opportunity. He and the colonists who contracted to settle with him on the southern frontier anticipated the challenge of forging new relationships into a village community, but unfortunately neither the land, the leader, nor the colonists could ensure a future that resembled either their ideals or their European past.

Two

The Precarious Contexts of Settlement

Although Jean Pierre Purry and royal authorities brought quite different perspetives to the establishment of Purrysburg Township, all had reason to believe in midsummer 1732 that its imminent settlement would satisfy the expectations of all parties. Like the plans of Thomas Dale at Henrico and the Lords Baltimore in Maryland, however, visions of a tightly knit self-sufficient village community vanished abruptly in the New World wilderness.[1] In Virginia and Maryland alike, the common forces of ethnic homogeneity and civil law could not counteract the lure of land and prosperity, especially because most early colonists had no families to bind their interests to a particular locality. Their dispersal caused officials to fear for the future of New World white civilization because there was no precedent for such a phenomenon in England.[2] Even the village communities of colonial New England experienced "hivings out" as community became too confining for some of the freer spirits of that region. Seen in this context and coupled with the fact that the township served as prototype for an entirely new approach to augment the white population of South Carolina, the beginning of settlement at Purrysburg may not appear so very different from other colonial plantations at first glance.

And yet there were variables operative in the peopling of the township that failed to materialize in these earlier efforts in Virginia and Maryland and that set the Purrysburg experience apart from them. The entrenched power of a colonial elite, while evident in both Virginia and Maryland, did not play such a disruptive and debilitating role as it did in the township. Because the provincial aristocracy worked hand in glove with crown officials, township colonists had to contend with an intrusive bureaucracy that had grown in strength and insularity since the seventeenth century. The complex cultural history of the Purrysburg émigrés further complicated township community life because the multivariant contexts of settlement on the southern frontier skewed their European religious, political, and socioeconomic heritage. The heterogeneity of the township certainly created tensions neither Virginia, Maryland, nor New England faced in the colonial era. Ironically, however, although the township's ethnic diversity gave it more commonality with Pennsylvania or New York, the policies of both crown and colony attempted to reinforce a cultural conformity more characteristic of New England or other regions of the coastal Southeast.

In light of such ambiguity, it should come as no surprise that the township got off to a less than auspicious start in the early years. These immediate problems were aggravated by Purry's unshakable faith in the veracity of his scientific theory. Taken together, these issues impeded the cultivation of relationships that would foster the development of the cohesive community of artisans and yeoman farmers envisioned by Purry and royal officials alike. In fact, the trials faced by Purrysburg inhabitants in the early years of settlement contributed to a climate of instability and disarray that seemed to preclude the possibility of ever creating such relationships.

I

Perhaps more so in South Carolina than in any other North American colony, the government exercised extensive control over who should settle where on how much land and with what privileges. And as a provincial commercial elite began to assert its power by the turn of the eighteenth century, it became obvious that regardless of whether the Lords Proprietors or the crown ultimately owned the colony, local interests would take precedence in those decisions. This was especially true with regard to the development of towns. As early as 1705 planter aristocrats along the western branch of the Cooper River used their resources and influence on the General Assembly to secure funding for the construction of Strawberry Ferry. Two years later their concerted efforts resulted in the founding of Childsbury Towne Landing. According to William S. Barr, "The ferry and Town represent power, control, and dominance by the white elite over local populations, indigenous natural resources, and routes of trade."[3] Twenty years later, when Purry fixed his colonial vision on British interests in North America, the melding of local elite interests with political power was nearly complete. Governor Johnson's township plan demonstrated just how powerfully the two were fused.

South Carolina tidewater planters, cognizant of the surging imbalance between white and black inhabitants of the colony, desired significant growth of the white population, but they wanted more than numbers. They hoped to surround the plantation belt with an underdeveloped band of white settlements free of slavery. Intentionally small land grants in outlying (and less fertile) areas and officially sanctioned bounties on key commodities militated against the expansion of the plantation system and the institution of chattel slavery. Because poor Protestant immigrants would be freed from the religious persecution and economic privation of their European homelands, the provincial aristocracy reasoned that they would be compliant partners in this complex plan. Their gratitude would preclude any desire to compete directly with those to whom they were so indebted.[4]

The location and physical configuration of the townships confirm the blended interests of the government and the provincial aristocracy. Their strategic placement on river systems facilitated military preparedness and provided necessary transportation and communication linkages with the prosperous lowcountry. The detailed layout of the townships attempted to reproduce European life ways and therefore Old World commercial pursuits. In a very real sense, the townships of South Carolina transferred the tradition of city planning evident in Europe to the colonial frontier to defend the lowcountry against potential threats and to fulfill their ordained commercial role. And Purrysburg Township became the archetype. Unfortunately for the architects of the elaborate scheme, but especially for those who would flock to the first township, the physical environment of settlement drastically transformed the context of life on the southern frontier.[5]

Although South Carolina welcomed Purry and his associates in 1731, the Swiss theorist did not choose the site for the township that bore his name. Nothing in his petitions and memorials in the 1720s or 1730s stipulated a location for the settlement he proposed. But, in keeping with his theory of optimal climates, Purry did specifically mention that "the best countries of the world ought to be on or about the 33rd degree of latitude" in his memorial to the Duke of Newcastle in 1724.[6] The fact that royal officials disregarded Purry's theoretical conclusions highlighted their ambivalence with regard to his science and their determination to bend his ambition to their designs. Had provincial authorities or aristocrats been more interested in facilitating the greatest measure of success for Purrysburg than in securing their own objectives, the entire enterprise might have had a completely different outcome.[7] Nevertheless, in his letter of 20 July 1730, Johnson recommended that Purry's colony "be upon the Savana River, Near the Palachuccola Fort or any other part (upon that River) where Conveniency can be found at the Discretion of the Governor and Council." With sabers rattling in Spanish Florida to the south, as well as in the French trans-Appalachian interior, and with tensions mounting among numerous Native American groups throughout the region, it was no coincidence that Captain Evans of the Carolina Rangers led Purry to the exact location noted by Johnson as the best site for the settlement. He and his men were charged with patrolling the vulnerable frontier between Fort Palachuccola to the northwest and McPherson's Cowpen at Yamassee to the southeast. The supposed joint selection of the Great Yamassee Bluff by Purry and Evans as the center of the township (just above the thirty-second degree of north latitude) had little to do with Purry's complex theory and everything to do with the protection of lowcountry planters from threats real and imagined. The site lay a scant thirty miles from Indian territory to the north and west, thereby protecting the rising tidewater aristocracy from Native American or French attack. Purrysburg also guarded the overland invasion route from Spanish Florida. Because of the innumerable rivers, creeks, and swamps intersecting the coast, enemies attempting to invade the lowcountry from the south had to advance inland along the Savannah River to the vicinity of the Great Yamassee Bluff. As direct evidence of the strategic import of this location, when the township became populated and the local militia firmly established by the mid-1730s, Fort Palachuccola was decommissioned by the Commons House of Assembly.[8]

The calculated selection of the Great Yamassee Bluff as the township site also virtually guaranteed that the vast majority of Purrysburg settlers would be relegated to the yeoman class of small farmers and ranchers, unable to break into the ranks of the planter gentry. The land on which the township grew ensured their status and anchored the southern frontier with precisely the type of settlement most desired by the lowcountry provincial elite, for authorities located Purrysburg Township almost exclusively on the most infertile land available.[9]

Thirty miles or so upriver from the mouth of the Savannah River on its east bank, Purrysburg lay squarely in the coastal plain that stretches from the seaboard inland for at least 120 miles, ending at the Sandhills region of the middle country. In specific geological terms it existed in the Sea Island complex of the coastal zone on the lower or outer coastal plain of South Carolina. Geomorphically a young environment, the coastal plain was formed by sedimentary deposition. Consisting mainly of particles deposited by river systems into the Atlantic Ocean salt-water ecosystem, the region is underlain with muds, silts, sands, clays, and marls of marine origin. Some materials have been compacted to form sandstones, shales, conglomerates, and coquinas, whereas much of the region's sedimentary materials exist as soft layers strewn with unconsolidated rocks. The sedimentary layer, which is only a few feet deep at the fall line, reaches a thickness of nearly two-thirds of a mile at the coastline. Topographically the outer coastal plain is nearly flat, with an almost undetectable declension to sea level. Identifiable characteristics include broad flood plains and cut-off lakes or bays created by meandering rivers, lowland swamp vegetation, open canebrake savannahs, and forested areas of both hardwoods and pines. Dominant tree types include both deciduous and evergreens, such as sweet gum, water hickory, laurel and overcup oak, cypress, tupelo, and pine.

Just south of the township, wide flood plains were blessed with nutrient-rich alluvial soils. It was upon these organic sediments called *inceptisols* that plantation rice culture developed. North and east of the township a relatively fertile band of soils stretches across present-day Colleton and Hampton Counties. The sandy and loamy coastal plain sediments are the parent of these *entisols,* which support truck farming and melons as well as forest vegetation. The township and its immediate environs, however, contained none of these profitable soils except in its most inaccessible reaches—the forks between creeks and their attendant swamps, which were subject to inundation at high tide. Cultivation of this scarce land was impossible without exhaustive, labor-intensive modification of the local topography (draining, banking, diking, and so forth). The vast majority of land in and around Purrysburg Township consisted of soils descriptively labeled the pine barrens, for it was heavily forested and only marginally suited for any cultivation whatsoever. The mostly poor sandy soil is best suited for free-range livestock, some provision crops, and low-yield short-staple cotton.

Lumber products could also be harvested. A Scotch visitor to South Carolina in the early national period perhaps described this region most graphically, albeit somewhat inelegantly: "The Last class of Land takes the name of Pine Barren from its inadequacy to produce any thing but the Pine tree and on that account are [*sic*] quite invaluable unless they are [*sic*] situated near a river, by which its produce might be brought to market at little expense. The Lands are quite sandy and the surface seems bare of all vegetation and one is amased [*sic*] at the innumerable quantity of fine majestic trees with which it abounds."[10]

Widely known among Carolinians as the least productive soil, pine barren land was ignored by all but the poorest settlers, and, it should be added, Swiss theorists convinced of their own ingenuity. From every vantage point it is apparent that the creation of Purrysburg Township served the interests of entrenched provincial elites at the expense of the colonists to be. By design, strategic military concerns located the township on high ground at the nexus of the most logical invasion routes from the north, west, and south into the vulnerable lowcountry. With deliberate intent authorities denied township residents access to agriculturally productive land, thereby relegating them to a subsistence standard of living from the land complemented by intensive labor in craft pursuits such as silk or wine production so desired by colonial aristocrats. Joyce Chaplin is certainly correct in asserting that provincial leaders encouraged township residents to grow crops such as cotton, flax, and foodstuffs and not commercial staples of the era, but, because of self-serving advance planning in the case of Purrysburg, little encouragement was necessary for there were few options.[11] Purry's visions, both theoretical and practical, had been preempted by the grand schemes of lowcountry planters and their allies. He and his settlers were to pay a dear price to preserve the continued security and accelerating prosperity of their tidewater neighbors. At the commencement of his long-anticipated colonial enterprise, however, the Swiss adventurer had no reason to doubt the success of his township or the truth of his climatological theory. For although Purrysburg did not sit astride the thirty-third degree of north latitude, it was still close enough to effect sufficient levels of abundance for all comers under his watchful eye as their feudal lord—and there turned out to be plenty of comers.

II

As Purry debarked with his first colonists in 1732, he probably had little idea and less concern regarding the impact European cultural traditions would have on the life of his New World township. His interests turned toward the more immediate and concrete objectives of getting the immigrants to the township in numbers sizable enough to receive his land grant from the crown. Besides, he also had been born and bred in Europe and had adapted to radically different physical environments with but a modicum of trauma. French-Swiss by birth, he had lived and worked in many European countries and, in doing so, had made quite a name for himself. His colonists would be no different. But in his consuming desire to people his South Carolina barony, Purry minimized the intricate nature of historical relationships animating the Swiss Confederation and its neighbors to the west and north. The cultural power of these relationships would serve as a source of contention for years in Purrysburg Township, stunting the development of relationships crucial to the creation of a viable community settlement.

The unique cultural composition of the Swiss Confederation proceeded from central Europe's medieval past. For centuries its strategic geopolitical location in the heart of Europe left the tiny collection of cantons open to outside influences and invasion from numerous sources. The migration of the Germanic Alemanni supplanted the customs and language of the Romanized Celtic population of the region except in isolated areas where the old Latin dialect of Romansh survived. A threat from the House of Hapsburg centuries later prompted formation of the Perpetual Union by the three forest cantons of Uri, Schwyz, and Unterwalden in 1291. This defensive alliance became the basis of the Eidgenossen, or Swiss Confederation. When the Confederation achieved independence from the Holy Roman Empire in 1499, there were thirteen members, but even before the religious zeal of Alpine reformers split the cantons into armed camps, the members had fallen into intense rivalries bordering on civil war. The Confederation for the most part escaped the ravages of the Thirty Years' War (1618–1649), though Swiss religious refugees did immigrate to regions such as the Kraichgau and the Palatinate. The loose alliance system buckled, however, under pressures generated by religious and ethnic diversity as well as economic and political antagonism such as the War of the League of Augsburg (1688–1697) and the War of the Spanish Succession (1701–1714). By 1700 the spirit of liberty and equality, which had spurred the formation of the Eidgenossen in the thirteenth century, had dissolved into a series of petty squabbles among unequal members of a nondemocratic collection of quasi-sovereign ethnic regions. In the words of one noted Swiss scholar, the Confederation in the eighteenth century was "the most fragmented nation imaginable."[12]

The imperatives imposed upon the Swiss Confederation because of its geographic condition exacerbated and in some cases caused the aforementioned problems. Fully three-fifths of the land area of the member cantons is mountainous. The only relatively level region is the plateau extending from Geneva to Constance, which contains the major urban centers. Deeply slashed Alpine valleys and towering mountains ensured the isolation of those settling in the area, which fact was made all the more apparent by the existence of four major languages (French, German, Italian, and Romansh) in the Confederation. In the wake of the Reformation, Catholicism ruled in the east central cantons while the followers of Calvin and Zwingli predominated elsewhere. Needless to say, the religious rift was not only between Catholic and Protestant, but also between competing Protestant confessions.[13]

The perpetuation of cultural diversity was both a cause and a consequence of the structure of the Swiss Confederation. The close proximity of French-Swiss to German-Swiss served as a basis for periodic mutual distrust firmly rooted in the historical conflicts between the Frankish and Teutonic kingdoms dating from the medieval past. In addition, the spirit of nationalism percolating throughout Europe in the eighteenth century stressed ethnic and cultural homogeneity as the focus for nationhood. In such an exclusive context, the Swiss Confederation appeared an anomaly ripe for dismemberment. Culturally located international alliances caused no less a concern. The close relationship between France and the Confederation in the seventeenth and eighteenth centuries troubled French-Swiss, as well as the French Calvinist refugees who had fled the repressive French Catholic regime. In these settings, it was next to impossible for citizens of the Confederation to call themselves "Swiss." They were, rather, "French-Swiss" or "German-Swiss."[14]

Cultural and geographical issues aside, the cantons faced political and social crises of significant proportions as early as the mid–seventeenth century. The federal connection virtually disappeared because the diet did not even meet for well over a century (1663–1776). Republican virtues were still upheld, but, in the eighteenth century, cities maintained control over the outlying countryside without providing any representation to the rural districts. Rural communities did exercise a large degree of self-government in their own internal affairs, but only the propertied classes exercised voting rights—and only over local matters. In the cities a coterie of oligarchic rulers in nearly all member cantons subverted republican ideals by consolidating power among themselves. It was said that Neuchâtel (known as Neuenburg among German speakers) possessed the most equitable system of government, and it was administered by the king of Prussia! Drawn by the pomp and pageantry of the court of Louis XIV, many leaders in the cantons flirted with the spirit of French absolutism while Swiss mercenaries fought in foreign armies and served foreign authorities for financial gain. As the political gulf widened, so also did social and economic distinctions. Irregularities appeared not only in the federal fabric of the Confederation but also among social classes within each canton. As the Swiss historian George Thürer observed, such a state of affairs "was a betrayal of the original ideals of self-government in the Confederation, which was now rent not only by religious divisions, but by an ever-deepening social gulf. It was only a question of time before this split between rulers and subjects would paralyze the Confederation if not break it up altogether."[15] Especially during the tumultuous eighteenth century there existed little if any hope for upward social mobility. In the words of one scholar, "even though Switzerland was a republic, it was not yet a democracy; many a poor man saw that his only hope lay in the New World."[16]

The nature of the federal relationship lay at the heart of the Swiss condition, and its nature in the eighteenth century was clearly characterized by an ethnocentric localism. Traveling in the Confederation in 1764, James Boswell noted that Swiss allegiances often went no further than the city limits of one's birthplace.[17] No effective central authority existed. No federal army, treasury, laws, or constitution served all members of the union. The members abandoned neither their right to make war nor their right to enter alliances without mutual consultation. Except in times of crisis, each canton considered itself sovereign and independent. Individuals fancied themselves citizens of their particular canton or of a Protestant or Catholic faction. This graphic demonstration of *Kantönligeist* (narrow cantonal spirit, little canton-mindedness) was so pervasive in the eighteenth century that a Swiss resettling in a neighboring canton was considered a foreigner for all intents and purposes by the native-born of that locality. Perhaps more than in most European geopolitical entities it could well be said that "there is little congruence between significant social and national boundaries. In the early modern period, it is more useful to think in terms of regional entities." Walter Sorell recognized that perhaps the major distinction of the Swiss has been their ability to maintain the vibrancy of four separate linguistic, religious, cultural, and ethnographic traditions throughout more than three and a half centuries of living together in a federal republic. Although it must be noted that the Confederation was from the beginning more a federation of states than a federal state, it is obvious that the entity that passed for a union of cantons faced a number of serious difficulties in the seventeenth and eighteenth centuries. The final variable to be factored into this complex human equation was the influx of thousands of refugees who poured across Swiss borders to escape religious persecution.[18]

The first great exodus of Protestants fleeing to the Swiss cantons began during the French religious wars of the sixteenth century, but by far the largest number immigrated there during the years just prior to and just after Louis XIV revoked the Edict of Nantes in 1685.[19] His action coincided with the resumption of the Duke of Savoy's persecution of Piedmontese Waldensians, and many of them joined the French Huguenot refugees in exile.[20] By the 1690s the western canton of Vaud, then under the domination of Berne, provided haven for an estimated 6,000 Dissenters. Refugee Protestants comprised fully one-fifth of the population of Berne itself. One-quarter of Geneva's populace was Huguenot, as were between a quarter and a half of the populations of Vevey and Lausanne.[21]

Despite close spiritual ties between the Swiss Reformed and French Reformed confessions, Swiss cantons exhibited a distinct ambivalence regarding the immigrants spilling across their borders. Many of the refugees were urged to travel through the Confederation and settle in the German states. Geneva, though the spiritual home of Calvinism, had grave reservations concerning the ability of its citizens to absorb so many new refugees into its churches and economy. Pressure exerted by Louis XIV also prevented Genevans from welcoming the émigrés too quickly or too warmly. At one point the Sun King directly threatened the city with economic and military reprisals should more Huguenots receive haven there. Tension ran so high the government officially requested that the Huguenots leave, though this action turned out to be merely a diplomatic and symbolic gesture. The Protestants were, however, denied the citizenship that would have allowed them possible admission to the Swiss guild system, and only a minority were granted inhabitant status (a type of halfway citizenship) because of the pressure on local magistrates of native-born skilled artisans and craftsmen seeking to protect their livelihood. Hard times after the War of the League of Augsburg caused many Swiss to blame the refugees. Bernese workers in particular were quick to point to the thousands of unemployed émigrés as blights upon the canton.[22]

By 1700, Reformed Protestants who had fled to the Swiss Confederation were becoming increasingly restive. Some who had been able to liquidate their assets before leaving France did well to the point of setting up their own financial houses in exile. Neuchâtel became a thriving center of commerce largely because of Huguenot capital and merchant traders. Some refugees found financial success in the lucrative smuggling business, while others sought reward in the Swiss linen and silk industries. By and large, however, life in the heartland of Calvinism was not kind to the exiled shopkeepers and artisans. Hardest hit were the Piedmont's Waldensian émigrés, who had no skills outside agriculture. With land scarce and money tight, the Piedmontese became added burdens on relief rolls. Reports from French and Swiss officials emphasized the discouragement of refugees, who endured social as well as economic discrimination. In this context it is easy to understand the mounting spirit of democratic activism espoused by many of the émigrés in Geneva. Exiled Francophone Protestants added to the problem by clinging tenaciously to French culture. As long as the refugees continued such an allegiance, the resulting clannishness engendered ill will between host cantons and émigrés.[23]

Throughout the opening decades of the eighteenth century, social and economic problems worsened in the region. Even apart from the refugees, by the middle decades of the century the native-born population of the southwest German states and the Swiss Confederation reached record levels threatening traditional village life and vocations. The practice of partible inheritance in rural areas meant that, by midcentury, the landholdings of many families could not provide an adequate sustainable standard of living. As early as 1724 the government of Karlsruhe forbade in-migration, proscribed marriage for those under the age of twenty-five, and outlawed some partible inheritance practices. In Basel by the 1730s, land accumulation and field consolidation by the wealthy deprived peasants of their sustenance. A higher fixed rate of interest, which went into effect by mandate in January 1735, made it virtually illegal to lend money at less than 5 percent interest. Though affecting all segments of Basel's population, higher interest rates hit day laborers especially hard. Population increases and unemployment in Basel led to heightened social discontent. Berne,

Geneva, and Zurich confronted similar dilemmas. These less than ideal political and socioeconomic dislocations led hundreds of native Swiss and refugees to consider emigration as a means to escape the deteriorating situation in the Swiss Confederation. Purry's colonial plans were not the first, nor the best, but perhaps only among the most publicized and available.[24]

III

Purry may have aroused the ire of Swiss officials when he began soliciting recruits for his township in late 1731, but the emigrants who chose to go with him left with hope, for he furnished them a way to escape an environment of diminishing opportunities. The first transport of emigrants, including the four principals from the trip to South Carolina in 1731, departed sometime during the early summer of 1732. After a brief stay in London, the party left for Charles Town on 1 August and arrived in the provincial capital in November. The departure from Charles Town of the first township's first settlers was a festive occasion for they were saluted with seven cannon shots as they began the last leg of their journey. It appears that the group subsequently became temporarily divided—all too symbolic of the separations that were to come. Governor Johnson noted that sixty-seven immigrants left for the township on 18 November 1732. About seventy others, including Purry, departed with the former group but were forced back by a leaky vessel.[25]

Numerous transports of colonists followed these first immigrants, swelling the number of settlers at the township. In an affidavit signed in March 1733, Purry claimed to have transported sixty-one men, women, and children to Charles Town on 1 November 1732; forty-two additional émigrés on 13 December 1732; and forty-nine more on 15 December 1732.[26] A list of prospective settlers qualifying before Governor Johnson on 22 and 23 December 1732, the only such document extant, illustrates two key characteristics of the settlement. First, the vast majority of township residents were to be from French- or German-speaking backgrounds. As table 1 demonstrates, the ethnic composition of immigrants to the township was fairly evenly split between French-surnamed (forty-seven) and German-surnamed (forty-five) individuals. A second key characteristic was the preponderance of families. Family groups of five to seven were average, and those of eight to nine were not uncommon. Many of the immigrants had very young children, and heads of household tended to be quite elderly for the time. Single passengers proved to be in the exceptional minority, and even some among these (Andriane Richard, for example) were meeting family members already at the township. Unlike the early Chesapeake plantations, the Purrysburg Township community evolved primarily as a settlement of immigrant families not of single adventurers or malcontents.[27] These characteristics remained part of the demography of Purrysburg throughout the eighteenth century.[28]

TABLE 1: Prospective Purrysburg Settlers Qualifying before Governor Robert Johnson, 22 and 23 December 1732

French Surnamed	(Age)	No. in Family	German Surnamed	(Age)	No. in Family
David Huguenin	(60)	6	Jaque Winckler	(?)	8
Susanna Jacot	(47)		Anna Catarina	(43)	
Daniel	(14)		Jaque	(19)	
David	(18)		Nicolas	(16)	
Abraham	(10)		Jen Jaque	(9)	
Marguerite	(12)		Luis	(6)	
Josue Robert	(56)	3	Frederick	(3)	
Joshue Robert	(21)		Eva Elisabeth	(12)	
Mary Madeleine	(29)		Theobald Kuffer	(49)	9
Anne Valloton,	(49)	6	Anna Margarita	(40)	
widow of Pierre			Jaque	(16)	
Henry	(19)		Theobald	(13)	
Jacques Abram	(17)		Margaritt	(14)	
Jean Pierre	(14)		Elizabeht Margaritt	(11)	
Maria	(21)		Elizabeht Catarina	(9)	
Rose Marie	(9)		Maria Ottillia	(4)	
François Buche	(46)	6	Barbara	(2)	
Margarette	(50)		Luis Kohl	(45)	8
Jean Pierre	(4)		Anna Barbara	(40)	
Daniel Henry	(1)		Jen Nicolas	(11)	
Abram	(2)		Jen Laguer	(5)	
Susanne	(8)	5	Nicolas	(3)	
Henry Girardin	(32)		Margaritha	(13)	
Marguerite	(32)		Anna Marill	(8)	
David	(7)		Maria Margaritha	(1)	
Henry	(4)		Nicolus Riger	(46)	5
Anne	(2)	5	Anna Barbara	(36)	
François Bouchelois	(46)		Jen Michael	(13)	
Madeleine	(36)		Janett Ottalia	(18)	
Batiste	(6)		Catarina Barbara	(4)	
Françoise	(3.5)		Heinrich Cronenberger	(40)	5
Maria	(4.5)	2	Elizabeht	(35)	
the widow Breton	(55)		Nicolas	(15)	
Jean Pierre	(17)	1	Gertrues	(5)	
Ulric Bac	(50)	1	Anna Catharina	(2)	
Jacob Calame	(56)	1	Jorg Mengersdorff	(28)	4
Abram Marte	(60)	1	Anna Sibilla	(26)	
David Giroud	(18)	1	Jen Hendrick	(3)	
Jacob Henry Meuron	(19)		Elizabeht	(2)	
Madame Varnod	(?)	5	Andres Winckler	(23)	2

French Surnamed	(Age)	No. in Family	German Surnamed	(Age)	No. in Family
Abram	(?)		Anna Susan	(23)	
François	(?)		Leonards Franck	(50)	3
Frantions	(?)		Anna Susana	(48)	
Mariane	(?)		Danl	(8)	
Andriane Richard	(?)	1	Christian T(F)icus	(32)	1
Monsieur Purry	(?)	1			
Monsieur buttot	(?)	1			
Monsieur Flar	(?)	1			

Source: Miscellaneous Records, 20:3–6, "Commissions and Instructions, 1732–1742," South Carolina Department of Archives and History.

Purry returned to Europe in 1733 armed with the letters of immigrants reporting favorably on their new lives in Carolina. He published these letters in Berne the following year, together with some other reports under the title "The Contented and Homesickless Swiss Settlers in the New World." He also had an abridged German version of his *Description abrégée de l'état présent de la Caroline Meridionale* prepared. It was published in Leipzig, also in 1734.[29] His success in enticing more immigrants to South Carolina was matched only by the disdain with which he was regarded by Swiss officials who were fearful of losing their most productive citizens to the emigration frenzy gripping south central Europe. In 1734, by which time Purry's exploits had become so noted in the popular mythology of the day that an English transport ship was named after his frontier colony, he secured another 260–280 settlers for Purrysburg. His stepbrother in Neuchâtel, Captain Louis Quinche, registered those ready to go to the township and was able to recruit craftspeople and servants for the trip. In late March the following year, Quinche reported that officials in Berne and Schaffhausen refused to publish the good reports from South Carolina. To counter the good reports, livid government authorities published a patriotic tract listing the negatives of emigrating: the dangerous voyage, certain slavery upon arrival, and lack of tools to harvest crops even if the land was fertile. Quinche observed, "The desire to go to Carolina was so strong among our Swiss, if the king or some lord would be willing to advance their transportation, I am persuaded that in ten years all . . . uncultivated lands of this country would be inhabited." King George II must have been duly impressed for he subscribed 574 pounds sterling specifically for assisting emigrants destined for Purrysburg and Savannah. In the spring of 1735 another 230 or so immigrants were said to be destined for the township.[30] In a petition dated 18 May 1738, Purry's son Charles stated that there were 600 residents in Purrysburg. Although it is highly doubtful that all these individuals ended up in Purry's barony and that others not associated with these major transports found their way to the settlement, by the closing months of 1735 Purrysburg was no mean colony. From contemporary accounts, it boasted as many as 100 dwellings.[31]

Estimates of the aggregate Purrysburg population in the early years of settlement have ranged from 360 to 800 according to various writers on the subject.[32] Because of the nature of records available, an exact tabulation of the township population by the mid-1730s is not possible, but an educated estimate for the size of the settlement using the information we do have can be made on the basis of statistical principles used by historical demographers of early America and by analyzing land plats recorded in the township.[33] The prosperous merchant Samuel Eveleigh witnessed a muster of the Purrysburg militia in May 1735 and placed its strength at 120 men. Colonel Purry informed Eveleigh that many of the men were away for one reason or another. He estimated the effective size of the regiment to be 250 men. Using these numbers and Evarts B. Greene and Virginia Harrington's ratio of militia strength to total population of five to one, the maximum population of the township would be somewhat higher than earlier estimates—between 600 and 1250 colonists. If Greene and Harrington's ratio of houses to population of at least seven to one is used, a figure of 700 results. Taking into consideration the rather large size of family groups living in each house, the probability is that, although Purry's estimate of 250 militiamen is high, the smaller number of 120 is just as probably too low; and taking into account that some settlers never reached the township while others settled there illegally, the probable total maximum population of Purrysburg approached 900 in its early years of existence.[34]

Most of the Purrysburg colonists were French Huguenot refugees and French and German Reformed inhabitants of various Swiss cantons, but parties of other groups made it their home also.[35] A small group of twenty-five Lutherans, fleeing the tyranny of Leopold Anton Eleutherius von Firmian, the Catholic archbishop of Salzburg in 1731, found their way to the township.[36] A much larger contingent of these Pietists, also known as Evangelical Lutherans, found haven only a few miles from Purrysburg in the Ebenezer settlement of Georgia. Led by their pastors, the Reverend Johann Martin Boltzius and the Reverend Israel Gronau, these Salzburg refugees were among the earliest settlers to establish lasting social, economic, and religious ties with Purrysburg though these relationships had the dual effect of linking some German speakers of Purrysburg more closely to Ebenezer than to their own township and of disrupting Salzburg Lutheran norms. In addition to these Salzburgers, about forty Piedmontese Waldensians terrorized by intermittent religious persecutions by the Dukes of Savoy also settled in the township. Finally, small groups from Württemberg, as well as a few English immigrants and even some of noble repute such as the Brandenburg Prussian army doctor John Frederick Holzendorf and the Frenchman Hector Berenger de Beaufin, who claimed English Queen Caroline as family, resided at least for a time in the frontier township. As the first of the South Carolina townships, Purrysburg seemed an appropriate model for those to follow for it was contractually founded, strategically located, heavily populated, and boasted a potpourri of ethnic groups and nationalities.[37]

IV

This model, however, proved to be deeply flawed and perpetuated a host of interconnected problems that threatened the viability of the township from the initial years of colonization.[38] In spite of the detailed plan for township settlement and supposed strict controls over the survey and distribution of land and provisions to Purrysburg immigrants, major irregularities occurred in land disbursement, provisioning, and actual settlement. Less than three months before the arrival of the first émigrés, Governor Johnson, in consultation with a committee of the Assembly, decided that the township surveys ordered by the crown should be delayed for a variety of reasons. A compromise appears to have been worked out in fairly short order, but any postponement in the laying out of Purrysburg township could have potentially devastating effects upon the settlers already in transit to South Carolina.[39]

Even this brief delay in surveying the township probably exacerbated a controversy involving rival land claims in Purrysburg and its environs. Soon after the first colonists arrived, it was discovered that a number of illegal grants had been made within the township limits and the six-square-mile buffer zone ringing the settlement, which was to have been reserved only for township citizens. During the spring of 1734 Charles Purry, writing on behalf of his father, noted among other concerns the fact that "several Persons . . . had under divers Pretences caused to be Surveyed all or most of the South and East Sides of the Lands adjoining and contiguous to the said 20,000 acres laid out for the said Township which are the best and most valuable Lands." The petition reached the Privy Council on 11 May and was read on 20 June, but no action appears to have been taken at that time. Growing more and more disenchanted, the elder Purry fired off a blistering memorial in French on 13 July 1734, complaining of an assortment of deleterious circumstances overtaking the Purrysburg settlers because of bureaucratic bungling and neglect. The land issue was only one of his concerns but, nonetheless, a crucial one. After months of acrimony and an official investigation, the Board of Trade and the Privy Council agreed that all grants made under proprietary leadership or illegally in Purrysburg Township or the six-mile buffer zone were invalid—including an 8,000-acre tract surveyed for Governor Johnson. It appeared that at least the land title issue was moving toward resolution.[40]

In an attempt to resolve most expeditiously the land question, however, Governor Johnson decided to move the township upriver from its original location. In a letter to the Board of Trade dated 9 November 1734, Johnson wrote that as soon as Purry and his associates had chosen the site for the center of town he had issued the proclamation prohibiting anyone but Purry's colonists from possessing land in the township or the six-mile buffer zone. Nevertheless, because of inclement weather, he failed to order an immediate survey of the land. When the weather improved, Johnson dispatched Colonel Bull to conduct the survey. Bull soon discovered that influential individuals held title to several tracts within the six-mile limit.[41] He dutifully reported the aberrations to the council and suggested that "it would be more advantageous to the Township to have what was wanting below the Town, laid out above." Bull said he believed that acreage above the town would better serve the township inhabitants, but he probably suggested this to protect the interests of the elite in the richer alluvial tidewater land below the town. Consequently, the council ordered Bull "to give double the Quantity above the town instead of below." According to Johnson's letter, Purry "made no objection as Col. Bull told me, but afterwards he and the people of Purrisburgh altered their Sentiments, and he Petition'd the Council to have it altered." Purry's zealous reaction to what paternalistically must have seemed a generous settlement to the governor and his council caught Johnson completely by surprise. Upon hearing of the discontent of the settlers, he "refused Signing such Grants as I could discover were likely to be within the 6 miles Line." The delicate wording here lends credence to the possibility that Johnson did sign some grants within the original township site and six-mile buffer zone prior to learning of their frustration—not out of ignorance but out of his genuine belief that the council's solution to the land issue would be amenable to the township inhabitants and their leader. He went on to note that "since I have found such Mistakes have happened there is a Proviso in all Grants that they shall not be within the Six Miles Line of any Township." The governor assured Purry that the council would "do the Township Justice," but, wary of promises not kept, Johnson apprised the king's council of the matter. Johnson admitted that "the Township and 6 miles not being run out occasioned these surveys, for it is Impossible to Judge of distances in the Woods, for which reason we have had both the 20,000 Acres and 6 miles of the other Townships Surveyed and marked to prevent mistakes." Unfortunately, an admission that mistakes were made did not facilitate good fortune for the residents of South Carolina's first township.[42]

That part of the township's land troubles proceeded from political factionalism in the wake of the land hunger of the 1730s cannot be denied. Johnson's advocacy for the quitrent reform law of 1731 streamlined colonial land policy, and his township plan made room for small landowners, but redirecting South Carolina's land payment and allocation system brought him into conflict with powerful provincial special interests. Whether by fate, design, or unfortunate timing, Purry and his immigrant colony found themselves drawn into a power play between Johnson and two of his most bitter enemies, Surveyor General James St. John and his deputy Benjamin Whitaker, former attorney general of South Carolina. Purrysburg's very existence as the first township became a lightning rod that seemed to intensify radically differing views regarding land policy and the personal antagonisms that erupted because of them. Purry's priority was the welfare of the township that bore his name (and his legacy). His involvement had less to do with the personalities involved than with his desire to establish a secure foundation for his township. St. John and Whitaker seem to have persuaded an already irate Purry to dispute the compromise of moving the township limits north rather than extinguishing all invalid land claims within the original township and its six-mile limit. Purry's cry of fraud galvanized Johnson into action and resulted in his swift restoration of the original site as well as his decision to divest himself of his tract within the boundaries of the township without compensation. Even after these steps had been taken, the problem was not fully resolved until Johnson's successor, Thomas Broughton, took office in 1735. Broughton completed the resurvey of Purrysburg and forced all South Carolinians to take up land elsewhere, though his general administration of the townships was in other respects less than exemplary.[43]

If these problems were not enough, mismanagement by Carolina bureaucrats resulted in further hardship and confusion for Purrysburg settlers and their feudal baron. The final survey of the township and the granting of land to the original émigrés was not concluded for more than five years because of the lack of funds to pay for the surveyor's services. The precarious nature of land titles in the township and its six-mile buffer zone due to tenuous financial and legal arrangements as noted here animated Purry to try to protect his interests in the township. Alarmed at the problems already evident by early 1733, burdened by the expense of his efforts, and eager to secure his own rights, he petitioned royal authorities through his son and attorney Charles on 22 May 1733 to receive a proportionate amount of the promised 48,000 acres in direct relation to the number of colonists he had transported to the township. (Charles put the figure at 150 at the time of the petition—a quarter of the 600 his father promised to bring to the colony by Christmas 1737.) The elder Purry also asked that the entire 48,000 acres be set aside for him as he fulfilled his pledge to bring 600 Swiss to Purrysburg. In a letter to the Privy Council dated 19 June, the Board of Trade agreed to honor Purry's request to receive a proportion of the 48,000 acres. The rest of the land was to be "designed as ye future reward of Col. Purry's services when performed" and therefore was to "be forthwith marked out, in ye lands most contiguous to ye Swiss Townships, and that no part of ye said 48,000 should be granted to any Person except ye said Col. Purry, nor any part of the said Township to other Persons except ye Swiss Protestants, intended to be settled there." The Privy Council concurred, but nearly five years later, and almost two years after Purry's death, his son was still petitioning royal authorities for the rest of the land the province owed his father.[44]

The problems of land conveyance necessarily worked a long-term hardship on the early vitality of the settlement and militated against the development of a positive community environment. Even more serious than the land issue for the Purrysburg settlers, however, was the crisis precipitated by the lack of promised provisions from the government of South Carolina.[45] Prior to June 1732, before any immigrants had arrived in Purrysburg, Governor Johnson received directives from London that appeared to threaten the import duty on Africans, which was to be partially appropriated for township surveys and the initial sustenance of township residents. The governor argued that 5,000 pounds per year for the next six years should be set aside from the import tax exclusively for these purposes. Two years later Purry had to petition the Privy Council to keep the township settlement fund intact when the Lords Commissioners of Trade recommended its liquidation. Shortly thereafter, on 13 July 1734, Purry wrote a strongly worded letter explaining the serious adversity faced by his colonists because of the lack of promised support from provincial authorities, for although the township fund had been established to provide for the material needs of new immigrants, the South Carolina Commons House of Assembly disregarded the stipulated use of the fund, subsequently draining its resources to pay a mounting provincial debt so that no new taxes would have to be levied. Ten days later London officials received notification of Purry's unequivocal support for the original allocation of more than 104,700 pounds sterling raised by the appropriations act of 20 August 1731, which included assistance for his settlers. In his continuing efforts to exercise whatever power he had on behalf of the struggling colonists, Purry waded into the rancorous debate over payment of the public debt of South Carolina. In so doing, he sided with Governor Johnson, the Council, and the Commons House against an array of London and Bristol merchants who opposed the stipulations of the appropriations law of 1731.

His efforts, however, could not prevent the near-total depletion of the township fund by 1735. The Commons House hastily passed a revenue law on 8 May 1735 raising the duty on imported Africans to replenish its coffers. The proceeds were earmarked exclusively "for the support and maintenance of the poor Protestants settled in Purrysburg, the money arising by the propriation law not being sufficient for their support." To make sure that all the money went to the immigrants and none of it as payment of fees and commissions to provincial officials associated with the process of granting township lands to the settlers, the Commons House worded the law to restrict such payments to revenue drawn from other duties. Unfortunately, the executive claimed final authority in managing disbursements from the tax on slaves, which did not resolve the problem. Until at least 1750 a significant portion of the monies raised lined the pockets of government bureaucrats. A Charles Town merchant, who was certainly not alone in his assessment, remarked in May 1735 that the duty was extremely odious but also noted that the "heavy tax" did not stop the sale of blacks at the Charles Town slave market and did help in securing an abundance of white colonists. In addition to the new tax, the council appointed stewards for Purrysburg and the three more recently established townships of Orangeburg, Amelia, and Saxe Gotha in the same year. The stewards were to oversee distribution of allotted provisions, hopefully ending any possible graft or misallocation of goods designated for township residents. But Broughton did not help matters by allowing some merchants to put off payment of import duties. By March 1737 the township settlement fund faced a 12,000 pound deficit. Stopgap measures propped up the fund again; however, serious financial troubles continued to compromise its security and so perpetuated instability in the Purrysburg community.[46] With all these outstanding problems it is not surprising that the immigrants struggled through the first years of settlement on the frontier, never receiving the levels of promised support from the provincial government. While Purry may have been blamed for these problems by his disheartened colonists, it is clear that the land baron lost control of Purrysburg's destiny to royal authorities, who backed out of their contractual agreements with him and his émigrés.

More problems appeared when Purrysburg land finally was surveyed and granted.[47] In direct violation of the township plan, numerous individuals, mostly of English descent, received land in Purrysburg or in the lands reserved for township settlers as demonstrated by map 6, though they never resided within the boundaries of the township. Prominent lowcountry planters, including Miles Brewton, Arthur, Henry, and William Middleton of Charles Town, John and Colonel Daniel Heyward of Beaufort, and William Williamson, received land in Purrysburg, though they were at best absentee landlords. Charles Town and Beaufort merchants such as Rice Price and Jemmitt Cobley, as well as entrepreneurs from Savannah such as Robert Williams, accepted land patents in the township. Peter (Pierre) Simond, a wealthy London merchant of Huguenot descent who maintained financial ties with Charles Purry and was related to Purry's business partner Samuel Montaigut, received 12,350 acres of Purrysburg land. His Majesty's surveyor Hugh Rose was granted 550 acres. David Rumpf and James Stobo received land in the township though both of them resided in other parishes. John Delagaye, a French religious refugee living in Beaufort temporarily before his return to Nimes, France, got land in the township. The Reverend Francis Varnod, the Anglican French minister from St. George's Parish, received a warrant for a thousand acres of land in Purrysburg. He died before the land officially passed to him, but his wife was in the process of conveying the tract to Englishman John Hammerton when she died. Among others with illegal land acquisitions in Purrysburg were a former London merchant residing in St. Helena's Parish and living in Beaufort (Joseph Edward Flower), a military officer stationed at Fort Johnson who then deeded his Purrysburg land to his son John in Ireland (Capt. John Pennefather), a mariner who probably never saw Purrysburg but did know Charles Purry (Isaac Overy), and a well-to-do French Huguenot (Daniel Vernezobre).[48] Even the evangelist the Reverend George Whitefield reportedly purchased "a large plantation in Purrysburg."[49]

The actual transfer of title to the township immigrants was problematic at a variety of levels. The three-stage process of acquiring ownership of land in colonial South Carolina was perhaps only tedious to those conversant with English land law. To non-English immigrants such as the Purrysburg colonists, the procedure had to have been onerous, convoluted, and mystifying. Provincial officials provided some assistance to township settlers, but in light of the exigencies of Purrysburg life and the distance from the township to Charles Town, it is small wonder that so few complete land records (warrant, plat, and grant) exist for them. The expensive and bureaucratic procedure often discouraged land seekers from securing legal title to the land they settled.[50] Even when the process was followed, it often took so long to complete that petitioners sometimes remained legally uncertain of the status of their claim for years.[51] Such uncertainty could be exacerbated by bureaucratic bungling as was the case when Purrysburg inhabitants were erroneously informed that they had to pay the fees for having their lands platted. In April 1739 "John Linder on behalf of himself and the rest of the poor Protestants now settled in Purrysburg" petitioned the council for "such relief as may prevent delay in obtaining their grants." The ruling of the council to live up to its obligations to the Purryburg immigrants also redounded to the benefit of the residents of the other South Carolina townships.[52] Some faced more than apprehension and uncertainty from official negligence. On 28 January 1735/36 the council considered a petition from a number of Purrysburg settlers who had arrived in October 1734, but whose lot lines had still not been run by the surveyor's office. Because they did not hold legal title to land, these immigrants had been unable to raise any crops and the allowance of provisions for their initial sustenance in the colony had run out. Without the council's affirmative action, which extended the allowance for another six months, these township inhabitants might not have survived the winter.[53]

Although some land transactions for township residents were completed within a year or two,[54] most took between two and four years. Gaps of five to seven years between the platting of land and the certification of the grant were not uncommon. Others had to wait far longer. Jean Rodolph Grand was one of the earliest settlers in Purrysburg and followed the appropriate procedure for obtaining legal title to his land beginning in 1733. More than a decade later, Grand still had not received his legitimate grant for 350 acres of land in the township. Hans Conrade Verley appeared before the council in October 1744 to certify that he had come to settle in Purrysburg with his father some years previous but had not yet received his land in the township.[55] In April 1753, nearly twenty years after his arrival in Purrysburg, Jonas Pelot, father of the Reverend Francis Pelot, had still not received the land he had been entitled to according to the stipulations of the township plan of settlement.[56]

If Purrysburg settlers were fortunate enough to secure legal title to the acreage they deserved, the location of the grant—something over which the immigrants had little control—could be challenging.[57] Low-lying land was subject to frequent freshets, and the pine barrens that dominated the topography of the township made productive farming even at a subsistence level impossible for some. Theobald (also Devald) and Jacob Kieffer did not wait for their warrant to be executed when they realized that they had been platted 200 acres of swampland. They petitioned the council successfully in December 1737 to exchange that acreage and another fifty in the township for 250 acres in a more suitable location.[58] Unfortunately, George Talebach (Telback) did not find the council quite so understanding in his case. Talebach had come to Purrysburg with Purry and was one of those settlers who discovered that "having had lots of land run out without regard either to goodness or Conveniency the Petitioner fell on a lot of 250 acres of entire pine-barren, so that your Petitioner is not able to get bread thereon." He had lived for nearly twenty years on the land, making his living as a stonecutter but, because of his age, was forced to "depend on his provision in house." He hoped to exchange his unproductive Purrysburg land for fertile land between the Broad and Saluda Rivers, which would enable the petitioner "to pay his Taxes as a good subject." The council thought otherwise and denied his petition of May 1751.[59] Jonas Pelot confronted a similar situation in August 1735, when he received a warrant from Lieutenant Governor Thomas Broughton directing Surveyor-General James St. John to lay out 250 acres in Purrysburg. On examination, a tract "suitable for Culture" in the township could not be found until the early 1750s. That these were not isolated cases is illustrated by the fact that in 1751 twenty-five Purrysburg residents formally declared that their lots were worthless and they had been obliged to abandon them.[60]

A discussion of the problems inherent in the process of land acquisition in Purrysburg reveals a myriad of ways in which township inhabitants were denied the expeditious disbursement of land due them but leaves untouched the hardships created by the actual physical arrangement of the surveyed township.[61] Map 7 is an idealized rendering of the 20,000-acre township plat with the 800-acre town site and glebe lands clearly labeled. Map 9 is the plat of the town proper with all town lots numbered. Both maps locate the town of Purrysburg fronting the Savannah River on the west. The town proper contained 455 town lots. As platted, the town was 1.325 miles (6,996 feet) long from north to south. Because of the course of the river, it was 0.85 miles (4,488 feet) long from the northwest to northeast boundary but only 0.625 miles (3,300 feet) on the southwest to southeast line. Lots were one acre and square or rhombus shaped, except for five rather irregular lots on or near the eastern town line. The square lots measured 208.7052 feet (3.1622 chains) while the rhomboid lots running 5 degrees east were 209.9988 feet (3.1818 chains). The rhomboid lots, which ran 17 degress east were 210.87 feet (3.195 chains) front and rear.[62] Nine streets, each sixty-six feet wide, divided the town as evenly as possible from west to east; and sixteen from north to south.[63] Individual town lots were numbered consecutively from the northwest to the southwest (lots 1–58) along the river in blocks of four (two lots long and two lots wide).[64] The most southerly lots (57–58) were only grouped in pairs, for they abutted the town boundary. Subsequently, lot blocks ran roughly parallel to the first row (59–116, 117–174, and so on). The most easterly lots also had the most irregular shapes. Although the town common is not specifically labeled on the plat, unnumbered but surveyed land on the eastern edge of town, and the absence of a street marking its eastern perimeter probably indicates its location.[65] The numbering system used and the irregularities on the southern and eastern borders of Purrysburg would suggest that the town's most northwest boundary served as the point of origin for the survey.

The roughly rectangular shape of the town reproduced in theory the ideal of a nucleated village. Had provincial authorities decided to build on this precedent, they could have placed the church in the center of the town, granting land from that center outward that clustered linguistically related settlers together. This practice would have undoubtedly benefited the immigrants and could have fostered a more cohesive community, but the township did not exist primarily for the benefit of its citizens. Consequently, although the physical structure of the town might facilitate at least an attempt to create a European-style town, the South Carolina gentry made sure that did not happen. Instead of placing the church in the center of the town, it was located on lot 32. This site did place the church in the center of town north to south, but it was also at the extreme western fringe of the town and very close to low-lying Savannah River swampland.

An analysis of the town lots platted for Purrysburg residents indicates that rather than construct the town outward from the church north, south, and east in a relatively equitable disbursement pattern, lots were allocated along the length of the town from north to south and along the narrow western perimeter fronting on the Savannah River. Most of the earliest platted lots dating from 1733 and 1734 occur along the entire length of the town in the first two rows of lots (1–58 and 59–116). The first row had only seven vacant lots by the end of 1738 (1–4, 6, 40, 57), but the second row, which includes plats from 1733–1737 had twenty-one (65–66, 76, 81–82, 83, 85–90, 93–94, 101, 104, 106–107, 111, 113, 114). The third row (117–74), made up of plats from 1733–1738, had thirty-two (120–21, 125–35, 139, 142–44, 146, 148–51, 155–57, 159–60, 163–66, 172). The fourth row (175–232), including plats from 1733–1737, had twenty-five (177–79, 186, 192, 195–96, 198–202, 204, 207, 211, 213–14, 216–19, 221–23, 225). The fifth and sixth rows contain so many lots that were still vacant after 1738 that it is easier to list those occupied. In row 5 (233–90), platted between 1735 and 1737, nineteen were taken (241–42, 244–47, 249–51, 254–55, 261–62, 265–66, 272, 287–88, 290). Row 6 (291–348), surveyed from 1736 and 1737, had only six allocated (299, 312, 340, 344, 347–48). None of the town lots in rows 7, 8, or 9 (349–455) were ever owned by any original Purrysburg settler and do not appear in any subsequent land records.

The distribution pattern of town lots to the residents of the township reveals clearly that protection of lowcountry interests superseded the needs of the immigrants. By stringing the settlers' town lots along the entire nearly mile and one-third length of Purrysburg, the colonial leadership ensured that the longest possible expanse of the Savannah River was under close observation. A similar argument could be made for the nearly solid line of occupied sites along the southern boundary of the town.[66] Proceeding eastward past the first two rows of town lots, settlers became increasingly isolated from each other. David Buech (1736, no. 299), Gasper Myer (1736, no. 312), Maria Bourguin (1737, no. 212), Anna Maria Viellers (1737, no. 215), and Lewis Mitchell (1737, no. 220) had only one neighbor whose lot could be considered adjoining theirs. George Taleback (1736, no. 272) had no contiguous neighbors. The isolation of these and other Purrysburg settlers most likely occurred because the gentry elite worried more about enemies approaching from the west, south, and north since areas east of the township were more heavily settled and therefore the eastern approach to the town did not require as much surveillance. At least in the case of Purrysburg (though the same might be said of all the South Carolina townships), the town proper conformed less "to the lay of the land and its proximity to transportation routes" than it did to the machinations of lowcountry politicians. The reason that Purrysburg initially developed as Kaylene Richardson's elongated "street village" had to do with colonial security priorities, not necessarily the predilections of its families.[67]

To make matters worse, although much of the town proper existed on land high enough off the Savannah River to preclude the possibility of flooding during storms or excessively high tides, a significant number of lots fronting on the river and granted for the most part to French-surnamed families were in a low, swampy section. Purry, represented again by his son Charles, petitioned the Privy Council in the spring of 1734 asking the council to double the town lots of the unfortunates granted swampy land. He reasoned that doubling the lot size would offset the added labor and expense the immigrants faced in draining their original grants. The Lords of the Committee of the Privy Council in 1734 decided to follow Purry's suggestion and granted double town lots to those with low-lying land.[68]

The granting of town lots also paid little or no heed to cultural barriers that may have existed among settlement groups. Although map 10 demonstrates that mostly French-surnamed individuals acquired the greatest number of town lots along the Savannah River, isolated German-surnamed settlers were intermingled with the French in this riverfront area. Throughout the entire town, the same practice of granting French-surnamed and German-surnamed settlers land next to each other without concern for cultural and/or linguistic barriers continued. Sociolinguist Einar Haugen has noted that ethnic groups in contact will reach a point of linguistic accommodation, but this shortsighted provincial policy certainly did nothing to foster community cohesion and may have contributed to the township's loss of population in the 1730s and 1740s.[69]

Little is known of the physical composition and dimensions of homes built on the Purrysburg site. Larry Lepionka's archaeological survey of 1979 found no indication of the use of tabby, a compound of oyster shell and lime widely used in areas closer to the coast. Stone, which also might have been used, was not available in the region. The survey did discover numerous brick scatters that date from the early period when a short-lived brick-making industry began in the township during the first decade of settlement. The high cost of labor, however, coupled with the fact that the bricks were "full of sand and not much better than bricks dried in the sun because they are fired in open air without an oven," ended the enterprise before the mid-1740s. Archaeological evidence (or lack thereof) from this survey as well as a more comprehensive reconnaissance conducted by Daniel Elliot for Garrow & Associates in January 1985 lead to the conclusion that the homes of eighteenth-century Purrysburg settlers were constructed primarily, if not entirely, of wood. Lepionka surmised that "it is likely that all early construction was limited to log and frame dwellings set on cypress pilings." The use of perishable timber for construction would also explain the lack of structural evidence from the initial decades of settlement. Elliot's survey did discover the apparent footprint of a probable early Purrysburg home that had burned down prior to the late eighteenth century. Ebenezer Lutheran pastor the Reverend Boltzius mentioned in his journal that, already by late winter 1739, in Purrysburg "whole huts have burned down on several occasions because few people or none come to help, since they all live so far apart." In April 1741 Purrysburg cobbler John Jacob Reck and his wife lost their home (lot 169) and belongings in a fire that ignited while they were away. Two years later a fire destroyed some recently cut lumber but spared the home of Theobald Kieffer Sr.[70]

The earliest description of a Purrysburg home dates from late winter 1736, when township blacksmith John Dominique Audet (Dominic Andallo) sold a portion of his town lot (lot 266) and buildings to his immediate neighbor to the north (lot 265) Joseph Barraguy (Barrakey, Barroquier), a Purrysburg laborer. Audet's home had two rooms with oven and chimney. The sale also included a detached blacksmith shop. It is likely that most Purrysburg homes were somewhat similar in construction with the possible exception that craftspeople with less volatile professions probably carried on their work from within the confines of their homes. The fact that the cobbler Reck lost "much leather, shoes, boots, and tools" in the fire that consumed his home would seem to lend credence to the existence of combination homes/workshops—at least during the early years of settlement.[71]

V

These initial contexts of settlement at Purrysburg Township reveal just how tenuous life must have been for Purry and his immigrants in the mid-1730s. Their physical needs for sustenance and shelter, as well as their psychological needs for stability and community, were either paternalistically minimized or blatantly sidestepped by English and South Carolina authorities alike.[72] Oblivious to the basic human necessities of those whose presence was calculated to further their designs, many of the wealthier element of the colony used the founding of Purrysburg to augment further their massive accumulations of land and capital. Even the Reverend Boltzius, one of the township's harshest critics, observed in June 1740 that Purrysburg settlers suffered grievously because of the flawed land allotment system. He noted that many of the immigrants had no agricultural background and that they could not choose their neighbors as land was assigned to them. Thousands of acres of Purrysburg land had been taken by wealthy South Carolinians and Europeans. In light of these conditions, Boltzius wrote, "I do not see how the country of Purrysburg can be settled if the present arrangement stays the same."[73] When the provincial emphasis on the strategic importance of the township rather than on the well-being of its residents is coupled with the hardships and diseases associated with life on the frontier, it is no wonder that many of the settlers blamed Purry for their misfortunes and resolved to leave the township. Some of the original grantees either never reached Purrysburg, left the settlement at an early date, or decided to sell their grants illegally to nonqualified buyers—sometimes before they legally had full title to the land. It also appears that a few returned to Europe. Some, including Hector Berenger de Beaufin and Tisley Rechillon, met with General Oglethorpe on one of his visits to Georgia to acquaint him with the serious problems facing the township's settlers. Oglethorpe returned the call and lodged with Purry, presumably to discuss the problems raised, but they continued unabated. By the time of his death, Purry was reviled on both sides of the Atlantic and blamed as the sole source of the adversities faced by those who had once looked to him as deliverer.[74]

One former citizen of Berne wrote from London in February 1735 that "Mr. Pury treats the German Swiss very badly"; making them "work for him half a year before he assigns their land to them." The settlers are not only "taken to the hottest part and to the borderlands of Carolina, but Mr. Pury requires of them a threefold ground-rent, and as I have said, makes them agree to pay over a sixth of the produce of the land to him." The anonymous writer also accused Purry of selling rum to colonists, "for which they must work his land for him." His 1731 pamphlet came under attack "in which Carolina is represented as much better than it is and no mention is made of the difficulties, expenses, nor of how to plan for the journey, so that they are forced to accept any conditions, however hard they may be, in order to reach Carolina." The letter was written "only from pity of these poor people, in order that they may not be led on to their destruction." In December 1737, writing to friends and family in Switzerland from Charles Town after visiting Purrysburg, Samuel Dyssli echoed similar sentiments, opining that "I ought to answer Puri's mendacious booklet paragraph by paragraph" but could not find the time to do so. Nonetheless, he concluded, "all citizens be kindly warned" of the true state of affairs in the province.[75]

There can be little doubt that Purry deserved some of the vitriol he received. From the perspective of Purrysburg Township residents, his culpability is understandable—especially because he explicitly received from the British crown exactly what he desired for so long, all-encompassing authority within his colony. Civil and military power in feudal Europe comparable to that held by Purry in South Carolina meant that the bearer of such power was directly responsible for the welfare of those over whom power was exerted. Neither his colonists nor European observers could possibly fathom that, rather than being the lord of all he surveyed, Purry's position was more akin to the ham in a ham sandwich—pressed upon by both sides and powerless to escape unscathed. The Bernese letter writer could not have known Purry had nothing to do with the actual granting of land or its location. It should also be recalled that the new land baron had been careful to speak to the dangers of life in Carolina in his pamphlet and that he did set out very specific conditions for traveling to the province. There must, however, be some element of truth in the other charges against Purry, even though this letter was reproduced in the newspaper *Bernische Avis-Blättlein* and served the purposes of the anti-immigration Bernese Bureau of Information. There is also more than meets the eye in the Dyssli letter. While being quite dismissive of Purry's efforts, it is intriguing to observe that Dyssli commented upon the high cost of living and the lack of provisions granted to newcomers—two issues completely out of Purry's control. Even so, he made sure to write extensively of his considerable success in the colony. Other correspondents from the mid-1730s attest to this more positive side of life in the province and at the township.[76] Some prospered in the environment, but many did not.

The precarious contexts of settlement at Purrysburg Township, the effects of which will be examined in subsequent chapters, led to significant attrition during the first decade and a half of its existence. The Bernese gentleman, Samuel Auspourger (Augspurger) departed for Frederica, Georgia, in the mid-1730s and became a surveyor and immigration agent for that colony. John Frederick Holzendorf also left Purrysburg as a recruiter for James Oglethorpe and maintained plantations at Frederica. Peter Dupra advertised a "dwelling house, a lot on the river, and a tanyard together with a bark mill" for sale in Purrysburg in 1739. Three years later John Rodolf Grand offered "a plantation containing 350 acres choice rice and corn land in Purrysburg township fronting the Savannah River," together with "a good dwelling house and other commodious buildings thereon—also some choice cattle and a good negro slave." Hector Berenger de Beaufin removed to Charles Town, where he became His Majesty's collector of customs in 1746.[77]

Other Purrysburg citizens moved to Georgia locations, including Ebenezer and Savannah. Still more were to be found in and around the Orangeburg and Beaufort Districts of South Carolina, but a significant and substantial core of French Reformed, German Reformed, German Lutheran, and Piedmontese Waldensians, as well as a few English settlers, continued to reside in the township into the late colonial period and beyond. This core of settlement at Purrysburg was not only the first large group of French-speaking Reformed Protestants to settle in South Carolina since 1687 and the first group of them to settle in the southern districts, but also included the first major influx of Germanic peoples into the province.[78] According to M. Eugene Sirmans, this multiethnic frontier enclave became the most prosperous of all the South Carolina townships.[79] But it was not easy. Together the Purrysburg immigrants defended the frontier and built the economy of the southernmost parish of the province. They forged a culturally diverse community, which—in order to form—had to be refracted off a sometimes hostile and always bewildering New World environment. In so doing, they created an amalgamated society in a region where relationships and ethnicity had to take new forms if the residents were to survive. Purrysburg Township then, by and large left to fend for itself, navigated the rocky 1730s and 1740s and experienced a great rise in living standards and extension of community networks after 1750, which made it progressively more a part of the surging social and economic prosperity of colonial South Carolina.

The contract that brought the immigrants to Purrysburg largely disintegrated in the confusion and animosities of the early years of settlement, but it had served one of its purposes—the township was populated. The indomitable Swiss author of the contract and guiding force of colonization was also gone. Purry died on 17 August 1736, just as some of the problems that had plagued the early years moved toward resolution. With the contract that brought them across the Atlantic a memory and its architect buried in the soil he so coveted, it fell to the residents themselves to create community out of geographical proximity—to make of unknown neighbors, friends.

THREE

A Neighborhood of Families

Just a year after the first immigrants journeyed up the Savannah River to begin their new life in Purrysburg Township, a young Englishman recorded his impressions of the growing settlement when he arrived on 16 January 1734:

> Purrysburg is a very pleasant place, being situate [*sic*] on the north side of the Savannah river, on a very pleasant bluff, about 20 feet high. The land thereabouts is generally speaking very good, but the poor people have been unjustly cheated of the best part of it; I mean that part lying between them and Savannah. It is judged not to be above 14 miles on a direct line from thence, and it is supposed will not be long ere they have a road cut: it is judged to be upwards of 200 miles at present by land from Charles Town and not above 160 by water, but when the roads are made passable, which they propose this next spring, it will then not exceed an 120 at most; they have already built, at their own expense, a very pretty fort, and can mount on occasion 24 guns. The town is at least one mile and a quarter long, but they have, at present, only barracks to lie in; but the people seem to be very industrious, and had they but some small supply from England, it would shortly become a flourishing place.[1]

A return visit three months later left the anonymous traveler impressed by the work that had been accomplished since January: "The next morning I took a second view of the town (Purrysburg), but it was surprising to see the improvement those poor people had made, in such a short time; there was several families that had begun to make improvements on their plantations; I understand they intend speedily to build another fort at the upper end of the town, which will be a great security to it."[2]

These candid observations, among the earliest recorded by an impartial visitor, bear witness to many of the problematic issues that would afflict the frontier township from the inception of its settlement: the paucity of productive land, the distance from other urban centers, the difficulty of overland transport to those centers, the pervasive influence of its military function, the longitudinal sprawl of the town proper, and the lack of support from colonial authorities. If the young traveler in all innocence was able to enumerate most of the obstacles Purrysburg residents would have to overcome, he also recognized the single greatest asset of the township and the central source of its measure of success—the industry of its families. The most intimate relationships binding individuals together have always been those of family, in whatever fashion family may be defined in a given context. It is, therefore, at this most basic level of commitment and support that the creation of community life at Purrysburg Township had to begin. But, whereas the creation of community life begins with the attachments of blood and kin, it would be erroneous to equate family networks with community building for family ties address solely those horizontal webs of relationships originating in the accidents of birth and marriage, which only partially describe the intricacies of community life. The formation of community relationships include family linkages yet are not fully described by them.[3] More than other groups studied in South Carolina, Virginia, or Maryland, however, the family is a logical starting point for the discovery of the parameters of community life at Purrysburg simply because the barriers of language and culture severely limited, at least initially, the construction of relational networks with others whether they were from another ethnic group within the township or from outside it.

Even so, to tease out the webs of family relationships from others that obviously developed in the township is tacitly to imply that Purrysburg settlers lived in layers of relationships—the religious network on top of the family network, the commercial network on top of that. Such, of course, was not the case. Purrysburg community relationships were a vast array of interconnected strands streaming in all directions from the individuals who lived in the township and conditioned by a confluence of factors from the confrontation between Old World assumptions and the colonial frontier environment to the occupational and spiritual choices forced upon each inhabitant. The following discussion of family networks in Purrysburg Township does not presume to be an exercise in collective genealogy, though genealogical research plays a central role in our understanding of family life in the township. Nor is it a heavily quantified aggregate portrait of Purrysburg families, for the available records will not allow such calculations. It will be instead a series of highly focused and fragmentary glimpses into the intimate lives of families touched by the same rhythms of life and death that have affected families in every age. These glimpses will illuminate the impact of disease and death upon those who survived as well as the suffering of those who did not. They will demonstrate that family relationships in Purrysburg became more intricately interwoven and expansive as time passed, radiating progressively outward from the township but never exclusively so. Much as the Rutmans found the nexus of relationships that shaped Middlesex society rooted in the institution of the family and from thence spiraling "upward and outward" as an expanding helix, so too will be the case in Purrysburg.[4] Finally, these focused glimpses will furnish at least some contours of the complex, even confounding construction of ethnicity and the evolution of family life in the frontier township.

I

Although it has been possible to compile a comprehensive list of original landholders in Purrysburg Township in table 2,[5] the listing does not allow an accurate assessment of the composition of families, because of the intricacies of the headright system, which included servants and slaves in the allocation of land.[6] As a result, the exact nature and size of Purrysburg families cannot be ascertained. Nevertheless, it is obvious from all extant sources that the township was settled primarily by family units—most of them probably with multiple children. There were some single individuals who chose to make their homes in the township, and a few retained servants who themselves had families. There were also a few cases of unmarried family arrangements. For example, Jean Pierre Purry was joined by one son, two stepbrothers, and a distant cousin (Jean-Rodolphe [John Rodolph] Purry). Elias Kohler successfully petitioned for 350 acres of land in Purrysburg based upon the fact that he came with his wife, his wife's father, two of her brothers, and two of her sisters. Adam Cuillat and Peter Netman held 300 acres in joint tenancy. The Huguenin siblings—David, Abraham, and Margaret—were also granted land jointly. Township carpenter Hans Krüsy lived with his son Adrian, his widowed niece Engel Koller, and her sickly young daughter, at least temporarily. His wife and other children remained in Appenzell. These examples demonstrate the variety of family groups that settled in Purrysburg, but they tend to be the exception rather than the rule.[7]

TABLE 2: Original Landholders of Purrysburg Township

Date of Plat/Grant	Town Lot No.	No. of Acres	Name	Source
12/5/1734	80	200	Ageron (Agernon), Anthony	township grants, 41 #4
Mid 1730s		550	Albergotti, Ulisse Antoine	*Albergotti Creek*, 14
9/3/1736	266	0	Andallo, John Dominic	plat vol 03: 405
1/22/1735	0	600	Ausbourger, Samuel	plat vol 02: 170
9/16/1738	123		Ausbourger, Samuel (.5 acre)	LDS film 5342 pt. 2, 214–15
10/5/1733	7	0	Bache, Ulrick (heirs of) (.5 acre)	plat folder 057 / LDS film 5342 pt. 2, 162–63
1018/1733	0	50	Bache, Ulrick (heirs of)	plat folder 058
10/12/1733	0	250	Bachelor, François	plat folder 058
10/6/1733	26	0	Bachelor, François (.5 acre)	plat folder 058 / LDS Film 5342 pt. 2, 154

Date of Plat/Grant	Town Lot No.	No. of Acres	Name	Source
4/20/1772	0	200	Baraquier, John	plat folder 073
9/3/1736	265	0	Baroquier, Joseph	plat folder 073
5/18/1757	0	250	Barrakey, John (part in/ part out of Purrysburg)	plat vol 06: 341
1/24/1735/6	0	250	Barrakey, Joseph	plat folder royal plat index, vol. 1:51
1/24/1735/6	0	500	Barraquin, John	plat vol 06: 428
6/1/1764	0	400	Barton, Thomas	plat vol 08: 230*
6/1/1764	0	400	Barton, Thomas	plat vol 08: 023*
4/10/1733	0	50	Bartoun, Augustus	plat folder 083
3/1/1736/7	0	50	Bear, John	plat folder 093
4/4/1736	249	0	Bear, John	plat folder 093
12/16/1737	0	151	Bearnerd, Elias	plat folder 096
10/11/1735	0	100	Bernard, Elias	plat vol 06: 346*
5/10/1736	0	100	Bernard, Elias	plat vol 06: 346*
1/3/1765	0	100	Billau, Antoine	plat vol 08: 216
10/6/1733	105	0	Blanquhart (Blanquart), Stephen (.5 acre)	plat vol 21: 091 / LDS film 5342 pt. 2, 185
4/9/1736	18	0	Bonninguer, Abraham	plat folder 152
4/5/1736	0	200	Bonninger (Binninger, Pininger?), Abraham	plat folder 152
9/8/1736	0	150	Bonijoe (Bonyoe), Isaac	township grants 41 #284
3/23/1761	0	600	Bouche (Buche?), John	plat vol 07: 133
12/11/1737	212	0	Bourgin (Baquin), Maria	plat vol 13: 443
12/11/1735	0	100	Bourgin (Bourguin), Mary	plat vol 13: 442
9/14/1767	0	50	Bourguin, Capt. John	plat vol 13: 283
10/5/1733	17	0	Bourquin, Henry François (.5 acre)	plat folder 161 / LDS film 5342 pt. 2, 158–59
12/16/1735	208	0	Bourquin, Benedict	plat folder 161/ township grants 41 #282
1/3/1735/6	0	50	Bourquin, Henry	plat folder 161
4/12/1758	0	1000	Bourquin, Henry	plat vol 06: 343
4/14/1758	0	1000	Bourquin, Henry	plat vol 06: 342
5/17/1739	0	100	Bourquin, Henry	plat folder 161
10/6/1733	21?	0	Bourquin, John Baptiste (.5 acre)	plat folder 161 / LDS film 5342 pt. 2, 152–53

Date of Plat/Grant	Town Lot No.	No. of Acres	Name	Source
9/3/1737	0	100	Bourquin, John Baptiste	plat folder 162
4/7/1758	0	500	Bourquin, John Baptiste	plat vol 07: 142
11/11/1761	0	550	Bourquin, John Lewis	plat vol 07: 243
10/18/1765	0	50	Bourquin, John Lewis	plat vol 08: 173
5/28/1766	0	400	Bourquin, John Lewis	plat vol 08: 173
9/6/1769	0	100	Bourquin, John Lewis	plat folder 162
10/5/1733	19	0	Brabant, Dr. Daniel (.5 acre)	plat vol 13: 300 / LDS film 5342 pt. 2, 189
2/23/1732	0	500	Brabant, Dr. Daniel (John)	plat vol 13: 300
2/18/1735	0	100	Brace, John Peter	plat vol 13: 299
9/3/1736	109	0	Brace, John Peter	plat vol 13: 299
10/1/1733	103	0	Breton, Françoise (.5 acre)	plat vol 13: 325 / LDS film 5342 pt. 2, 183–84
10/15/1733	0	100	Breton, Françoise	plat vol 13: 329
9/23/1765	0	544	Brewton, Miles	plat vol 08: 053
10/15/1736	0	200	Brickell, Christopher	plat vol 13: 335
4/29/1736	193	0	Brickell, Christopher	plat vol 13: 335
9/1/1761	0	500	Britton, John Peter	plat vol 07: 225
5/5/1737	0	1225	Broughton, Andrew	plat vol 09: 368
9/4/1736	0	200	Buch, Francis	plat vol 04: 125
10/5/1733	34	0	Buche, François (.5 acre)	plat vol 13: 406 / LDS film 5342 pt. 2, 182–83
6/10/1733	0	200	Buche, François	plat vol 13: 405
1/14/1734/5	0	100	Buche, Francis	plat vol 13: 404
6/8/1774	0	550	Buche, John	plat vol 13: 404
9/9/1736	299	0	Buech, David	plat vol 13: 406
10/5/1733	5	0	Bugnion, The Reverend Mr. Joseph (.5 acre)	plat vol 13: p 415 / LDS film 5342 pt. 2, 181
10/15/1733	0	600	Bugnion, The Reverend Mr. Joseph	plat vol 13: p 414
7/16/1765	1	0	Bullock, James (purchase?)	LDS film, 5342 pt. 2, 385
10/6/1733	48	0	Bulot, Guillaume (.5 acre)	plat vol 13: p 418 / LDS film 5342 pt. 2, 154–55
6/8/1733	0	50	Bulot, Mon Guillaume	plat vol 13: 420

Date of Plat/Grant	Town Lot No.	No. of Acres	Name	Source
9/29/1764	0	200	Cail, George	plat vol 08: 334
4/8/1733	0	50	Calis, Benj.	plat vol 13: 487
10/6/1773	101	0	Calis, Benj. (.5 acre)	plat vol 13: 490 / LDS film 5342 pt. 2, 151
10/4/1733	25	0	Callume (Collume), Jacob (.5 acre)	plat vol 13: 492 / LDS film 5342 pt. 2, 179–80
6/7/1765	0	400	Camber, Thomas	plat vol 08: 035
7/?/1765	0	500	Camber, Thomas	plat vol 11: 132
12/22/1737	152	0	Cast (Coste), Isaac	plat vol 09: 390
1/24/1735/6	0	150	Caste, Isaac	plat vol 09: 391
1/10/1764	0	1000	Cater, Stephen	plat vol 08: 315
3/16/1764	0	350	Cater, Stephen	plat vol 07: 428
12/4/1737	287	0	Chardonie, Abraham	plat vol 09: 388
2/14/1735/6	0	300	Chardonnelle, Abraham	plat vol 09: 383
11/9/1742	0	450	Chiffelle, The Reverend Mr. Henrie	plat vol 04: 173
2/12/1755	0	700	Cheffele, The Reverend Mr. Henry	plat vol 09: 387
2/13/1755	0	400	Cheffille, The Reverend Mr. Henry	plat vol 09: 386
3/17/1735/6	0	100	Cheffile (Sheffile), The Reverend Mr. Henry (for himself and sister)	plat vol 09: 386
9/6/1736	115	0	Cheffile (Sheffile), The Reverend Henry (and his sister)	plat vol 09: 385
9/9/1736	58	0	Cheffile (Sheffele), The Reverend Henry (for himself and sister)	plat vol 09: 385
1/3/1735/6	0	450	Cheffele (or Scheffley), John Lewis	plat vol 09: 385
4/23/1736	119	0	Chiffele (or Schiffley), John Lewis	plat vol 09: 384
2/5/1734/5	73	100	Chermason, Peter	plat vol 09: 387
10/15/1736	0	450	Chevilette, John	plat vol 14: 074
4/10/1734	59	50	Chivellet, John	plat vol 14: 075
5/31/1737	0	50	Chipard (Shipard, Choupart), Daniel	plat vol 09: 384
9/3/1736	210	0	Choupart, Daniel	plat vol 09: 383
10/13/1736	0	250	Christian, David	plat vol 09: 382

Date of Plat/Grant	Town Lot No.	No. of Acres	Name	Source
7/13/1774	0	500	Christian, Philip	plat vol 14: 087
12/16/1735	0	100	Chupart, Daniel	plat vol 09: 382
10/6/1733	49	0	Cobley, Mr. Jamiett (.5 acre)	plat vol 09: 390 / LDS film 5342 pt. 2, 148–49
10/17/1733	0	50	Collume (Callume), Jacob (heirs of)	plat vol 13: 492
10/13/1767	0	143	Cronberger, Nicholas	plat vol 10: 092
11/20/1772	0	250	Cronburger, Nicholas	plat vol 14: 258
10/13/1733	0	250	Cuillat, Adam	plat vol 09: 402
?	0	250	Cuillat, Adam	plat vol 09: 403*
10/6/1733	45	0	Cuilliat (Cuillot), Adam (.5 acre)	plat vol 09: 403 / LDS film 5342 pt. 2, 164–65
10/5/1733	181	0	Cuillat, Wallier (.5 acre #18)	plat vol 09: 403 / LDS film 5342 pt. 2, 171–72
10/11/1733	0	50	Cuillat, Wallier	plat vol 09: 401
9/6/1736	206	0	Dallaner (Dallow), James	plat vol 09: 400
4/16/1736	0	450	Dallas, Peter	plat vol 02: 232
12/8/1737	73	0	Dallas, Peter	plat vol 09: 399
10/15/1736	0	300	Dallow (DeLas), James	plat vol 09: 400
5/8/1739	0	200	Dalmester (Delmestrie, Pierre), Peter	plat vol 09: 399
12/9/1735	0	50	Davison (Devision), Peter Abraham (alias Vauchers)	plat vol 09: 408
9/3/1736	153	0	de Beaufin, Hector Belenger (.5 acre)	plat vol 09: 404 / LDS film, 5342 pt. 2, 205
9/3/1737	0	850	de Beaufin, Hector Beringer	plat vol 16: 063*
9/3/1737	0	850	de Beaufin, Hector Beringer	plat vol 02: 213*
12/9/1735	0	800	de Beaufin, Hector Beringer	plat vol 20: 252*
5/7/1736	0	150	de Beaufin, Hector Berenger	plat vol 02: 042*
5/7/1736	0	200	de Beaufin, Hector Berenger	plat vol 02: 042*
12/9/1735	0	800	de Beaufin, Hector Berenger	plat vol 02: 041*
10/16/1733	0	50	De Gallier, Jean Pierre	plat vol 09: 405
10/6/1733	112	0	De Gallier, Jean Pierre (.5 acre)	plat vol 09: 406 / LDS film, 5342 pt. 2, 177–78
10/6/1733	71	0	Dejean, Capt. Frederick (.5 acre)	plat vol 09: 416 / LDS film, 5342 pt. 2, 161

Date of Plat/Grant	Town Lot No.	No. of Acres	Name	Source
1/24/1738/9	0	600	Dejean, Capt. Frederick	plat vol 06: 327
4/30/1734	0	450	Dejean, Frederick	plat vol 09: 416
2/8/1742/3	0	250	Delagage (Delagaye), John	plat vol 04: 240
4/23/1736	118	0	Delahere (Delasure), Henry (.5 acre)	plat vol 09: 415 (LDS film 5342 pt. 2, 219–20
10/23/1734	158	50	Delescate (Delescale), Vincent	plat vol 09: 415
10/6/1733	84	0	Delmestre (Dalmestre, Peter) (.5 acre), Pierre	plat vol 09: 415 / LDS film 5342 pt. 2, 147–48
4/26/1733	0	50	Del Pont, Jean	plat vol 09:414
10/6/1733	72	0	Demonclar, André Albalestier	plat vol 09: 413
4/3/1734	0	150	De Monclar, Andrew Albaterlier	plat vol 09: 414
9/29/1737	0	100	De Pea (De Pred, De Pia), Peter	plat vol 09: 414
12/8/1737	136	0	De Pred, Peter	plat vol 09: 413
6/7/1733	0	50	De Roach, Jean Henry	plat vol 09: 411
2/14/1735	0	50	Deroch, John Henry	plat vol 09: 413
2/2/1735/6	10	0	Deroche, Jean (sris)	LDS film, 5342 pt. 2, 169
4/1/1740	0	50	Desaure, Henry	plat vol 09: 412
2/3/1736	0	300	Desaussure, Henry	plat vol 09: 412
3/6/1753	0	240	Desaussure, Henry	plat vol 01: 277–8
6/4/1734	61	100	Destcher (Detscher)	plat vol 09: 409
4/23/1736	180	0	DeStriuis, Godfrey	plat vol 09: 411
3/29/1736	0	500	Detrieus, Godfrey	plat vol 07: 248
12/9/1735	0	50	Deville, Lewis	plat vol 09: 404
9/9/1736	98	0	Deville, Lewis	plat vol 09: 411
9/25/1742	0	400	Dimester (Delmostre, Dilmastre), Peter	plat vol 09: 407
9/5/1737	224	0	Disne, Samuel	plat vol 09: 407
10/14/1736	0	50	Dominic (Andallo?), John	plat vol 09: 418
4/31/1736 [*sic*]	0	50	Donnat, Abraham	plat vol 09: 417
5/2/1737	0	100	Duberdoffer (Duberdosser), Henry	plat vol 09: 421
6/8/1733	0	50	Ecolier, David	plat vol 09: 426
10/5/1733	20	0	Ecolier, David (.5 acre)	plat vol 09: 430 / LDS film 5342 pt. 2, 186–87
8/21/1764	0	200	Egar, Ulrick	plat vol 14: 541*
8/21/1764	0	200	Egar, Ulrick	plat vol 08: 343

Date of Plat/Grant	Town Lot No.	No. of Acres	Name	Source
5/31/1737	?	?	Egnier, Anne Marie (land stats. missing)	plat vol 09: 431
1/19/1745/6	0	800	Ehizhardt, Abraham	plat vol 02: 247
2/15/1758	?	?	Elbert William	plat vol 08: 535
1/19/1735/6	228	0	Elizard (Ehizhardt), Abraham	plat vol 09: 430 / township grants 41 #145
4/29/1736	255	0	Enderly, Henry	plat vol 09: 436
4/22/1736	183	0	Engler (Englier, Englerin?), Henry (.5 acre)	plat vol 09: 435 / LDS film 5342 pt. 2, 218–19
4/22/1736	185	0	Englerin, Anna	plat vol 09: 435
10/6/1766	0	400	Erhardt, Francis	plat vol 08: 509
1/15/1735/6	0	400	Fallet, Abraham	plat vol 09: 434
12/4/1737	230	0	Fallet, Abraham	plat vol 09: 437
9/20/1738	0	250	Fauconet, David	plat vol 09: 435
4/14/1761	0	800	Fesch, Andrew	plat vol 07: 158
10/23/1734	0	50	Ficus, Christian	plat vol 09: 383
5/3/1733	0	350	Flower, Joseph Edward & Cobley, Capt. Jemmit	plat vol 09: 442
10/6/1733	53	0	Flower, Col. Joseph Edward (.5 acre)	plat vol 09: 443 / LDS film 5342 pt. 2, 188–89
2/18/1736/7	0	150	Fountain, John	plat vol 09: 448/ township grants 41 #172
12/17/1737	91	0	Fountain, John (possibly lot #97)	plat vol 09: 448
10/5/1733	11	0	Fourqueran, Pierre (.5 acre)	plat vol 09: 448 / LDS film 5342 pt. 2, 162
10/18/1733	0	50	Fourqueran, Pierre	plat vol 09: 447
10/6/1733	23	0	Frank, Ann Barbara (.5 acre)	plat vol 09: 447 / LDS film 5342 pt. 2, 170
1/14/1734/5	0	50	Frank, Ann Barbara	plat vol 09: 446
4/18/1733	0	100	Frank, Ann Barbara	plat vol 09: 446
10/7/1767	0	50	Fulker, John Melchior	plat vol 10: 090
6/8/1733	0	350	Galache, Pierre	plat vol 09: 452
10/6/1733	161	0	Gallache, Pierre (.5 acre #116?)	plat vol 09: 452 / LDS film 5342 pt. 2, 155–56
3/18/1761	0	600	Garvey, John	plat vol 07: 129
4/23/1736	182	0	Gasman, Henry	plat vol 09: 459

Date of Plat/Grant	Town Lot No.	No. of Acres	Name	Source
4/4/1736	0	200	Gasmans, Henry	plat vol 09: 459
6/18/1767	0	300	Gauthier, John Babtist	plat vol 16: 054
4/27/1733	0	400	Gautier, David	plat vol 09: 457
10/6/1733	100	0	Gautier, David (.5 acre)	plat vol 09: 456 / LDS film 5342 pt. 2, 184–85
8/8/1734	12	200	Genbrets, John (alias Michael Gombre)	plat vol 16: 049
6/7/1733	0	50	Geroud (Giroud), David	plat vol 09: 464
10/5/1733	9	0	Geroud (Giroud), David (.5 acre)	plat vol 03: 307 / LDS film 5342 pt. 2, 159–60
2/13/1760	0	350	Geroud (Giroud), David	plat vol 07: 114
2/12/1773	0	100	Gigneliatt, Mary	plat vol 16: 075
5/2/1737	0	300	Ginger, David	plat vol 03: 478
12/4/1737	227	0	Ginger, David	plat vol 09: 464
10/6/1738	42	0	Girardin, George (.5 acre)	plat vol 09: 461 / LDS film 5342 pt. 2, 165
10/6/1733	99	0	Girardin, Henry (.5 acre)	plat vol 09: 462 / LDS film 5342 pt. 2, 193
10/17/1733	0	50	Girardin, Henry	plat vol 09: 460
6/8/1733	0	250	Girardin, Jean Henry	plat vol 09: 462
10/4/1733	30	0	Girardin, Jean Henry (.5 acre)	plat vol 09: 462 / LDS film 5342 pt. 2, 166–67
6/8/1733	0	100	Girardin, Joseph	plat vol 09: 463
10/6/1733	55	0	Girardin, Joseph (.5 acre)	plat vol 09: 463 / LDS film 5342 pt. 2, 173–74
11/30/1752	0	400	Giroud, David	plat vol 05: 287
1/29/1761	0	400	Giroud, David	plat vol 07: 218
3/2/1761	0	400	Giroud, David	plat vol 07: 131
8/17/1761	0	150	Giroud, David	plat vol 07: 240
11/9/1763	0	296	Giroud, David	plat vol 07: 426
3/12/1765	40	0	Giroud, David (purchase?)	LDS film 5342 pt. 2, 384–85
3/14/1765	0	187	Giroud, David	plat vol 07: 407
4/1/1740	0	50	Godet (Godel?), David	plat vol 09: 272
4/23/1736	175	0	Gotier (Goliere), Anthony	plat vol 16: 169
4/23/1733	0	350	Grand, Jean Rodolph (lost & certified 10/31/1744)	plat vol 09: 467
9/2/1736	0	350	Grand, John Rodolphe	plat vol 04: 240

Date of Plat/Grant	Town Lot No.	No. of Acres	Name	Source
10/5/1733	35	0	Grande, Jean Rodolph (.5 acre)	plat vol 09: 465 / LDS film 5342 pt.2, 175–76
10/4/1733	27	0	Graunemberg (Grovenemberg), Henry (.5 acre)	plat vol 09: 473 / LDS film 5342 pt. 2, 151–52
12/29/1735	0	400	Greneer, John	plat vol 09: 468
12/5/1737	167	0	Greneer (Grenier), John	plat vol 09: 467
5/30/1766	0	200	Griffin, Patrick	plat vol 08: 181
3/31/1736	0	50	Grob, Andeiltheil (Adelheith)	plat vol 16: 244
3/31/1736	0	50	Grob, Eliz.	plat vol 16: 245
12/16/1737	141	0	Grob, Elizabeth	plat vol 16: 246
12/17/1737	145	0	Grob(b), John (.5 acre)	plat vol 16: 247 / LDS film 5342 pt. 2, 212–13
3/31/1736	0	50	Grobs, John	plat vol 16: 246
2/20/1742/3	0	50	Grobs, John	plat vol 07: 035
6/7/1733	0	250	Grovenemberg (Graunemberg), Henry	plat vol 16: 249
12/4/1737	229	0	Haudliker (Kaudliker), Nicholas	plat vol 09: 476
9/9/1736	254	0	Helptad, Gaspard (.5 acre)	plat vol 15: 388 / LDS film 5342 pt. 2, 217–18
8/30/1765	0	500	Henderly (Enderly?), Henry	plat vol 08: 070
10/5/1733	38	0	Henrie (Henrion, Henriod), Benjamin (.5 acre)	plat vol 15: 405 / LDS film 5342 pt. 2, 175
6/21/1737	0	50	Henrie, John Francis (Jean François)	plat vol 15: 405
12/6/1737	52	0	Henrie, John Francis (Jean François)	plat vol 15: 404
6/24/1737	0	50	Henrie, Marie	plat vol 15: 409
6/7/1733	0	250	Henrioud (Henrie?), Benjamin	plat vol 15: 405
2/17/1741/2	0	100	Henry, John Francis (Jean François)	plat vol 04: 174*
2/17/1741/2	0	100	Henry, John Francis (Jean François)	plat vol 15: 408*
6/1/1767	58	0	Henry, Margaret	LDS film 5342 pt. 2, 398
4/4/1736	197	0	Herchnecht (Herenecht), George	plat vol 15: 415

Date of Plat/Grant	Town Lot No.	No. of Acres	Name	Source
2/2/1757	0	200	Herdstein (Hartstone?),	plat vol 06: 264
3/29/1736	0	50	Herenecht (Herchnecht), George	plat vol 15: 414
3/15/1763	0	272	Heyward, Daniel	plat vol 07: 328
5/7/1763	0	300	Heyward, Daniel	plat vol 07: 360
2/10/1764	0	200	Heyward, Daniel	plat vol 08: 374
3/13/1764	0	150	Heyward, Col. Daniel	plat vol 07: 480
3/20/1765	0	450	Heyward, Daniel	plat vol 08: 355
5/20/1766	0	188	Heyward, Daniel	plat vol 08: 185
6/4/1767	0	212	Heyward, Daniel	plat vol 09: 067
1/15/1773	0	122.5	Heyward, Daniel	plat vol 15: 429
4/9/1773	0	257	Heyward, Daniel	plat vol 15: 428
5/5/1773	0	238	Heyward, Daniel	plat vol 15: 429
11/14/1764	0	250	Heyward, John	plat vol 08: 352
4/9/1765	0	350	Heyward, John	plat vol 07: 399
5/24/1737	0	250	Hobzendorff (Holdzendorff), Capt. John Frederick	plat vol 09: 485
12/8/1737	62	0	Hobzendorff, Capt. John Frederick (.5 acre)	plat vol 09: 485 / LDS film 5342 pt. 2, 216–17
4/4/1734	60	200	Hobzendorff (Holzendorf), Jon Frederick	plat vol 09: 485
10/4/1733	29	0	Hugudneir (Huguneir), David (.5 acre)	plat vol 17: 168 / LDS film 5342 pt. 2, 168–69
1/14/1734/5	0	100	Huguneir (Huginier, Huquin), David	plat vol 17: 168
6/7/1733	0	200	Huguenin, Marguerite & Abraham, David: Minors	plat vol 17: 167
5/29/1739	0	200	Huguenin, Daniel/Abraham/ David/Margaret	plat vol 04: 174
10/13/1740	0	200	Humber (Humbert), David Pierre	plat vol 17: 161
2/2/1757	0	500	Humbert, David	plat vol 06: 219
8/18/1761	0	50	Humbert, David	plat vol 07: 226
2/28/1764	0	100	Imer, The Reverend Abraham	plat vol 08: 531
4/3/1736	0	250	Inglene (Ingler[ine]), Anna	plat vol 17: 270
5/28/1737	0	50	Isoug, Hans Ubuck	plat vol 17: 370
1/4/1765	0	250	Jacob (Jacot?), Abraham	plat vol 08: 532
09/15/1736	0	50	Jaton, Anthony	township grants 42 #163

Date of Plat/Grant	Town Lot No.	No. of Acres	Name	Source
06/06/1737	0	50	Jaton, Anthony	township grants 42 #63
10/5/1733	14	0	Jeanerett (Jeuneret), Ann (.5 acre)	plat vol 17: 246 / LDS film 5342 pt. 2, 191–92
2/19/1761	0	750	Jenerat (Jeanerett), Henry	plat vol 07: 127
2/20/1761	0	700	Jenerat (Jeanerett), Henry	plat vol 07: 149
6/4/1733	0	250	Jeuneret (Jeanerett), Anne	plat vol 17: 239
9/6/1736	203	0	Jindra (Gindrat), Abraham	plat vol 17: 255
9/27/1737	0	192	Jindra (Gindrat), Abraham	plat vol 17: 257
2/2/1735/6	95	0	Kail, Lovdwick (.5 acre)	LDS film 5342 pt. 2, 158
12/14/1739	0	300	Kaill, Lodovick	township grants 42 #59
4/12/1773	0	122	Keal, David	plat vol 17: 389
6/7/1733	0	450	Keuffer (Kieffer), Deval	plat vol 12: 055
10/5/1733	16	0	Keuffer (Kieffer), Theobold (.5 acre)	plat vol 12: 052 / LDS film 5342 pt. 2, 172–73
1/14/1734/5	0	50	Keuffer (Kieffer), Theobold	plat vol 12: 052
10/23/1734	0	100	Khell (Kaill, Kail, Kehl), Loudwick (Louis, Sadovick)	township grants 41 #291
1/18/1737/8	0	250	King, John	plat vol 10: 248
4/2/1736	0	150	Kreeps (Krip, Crip), John	plat vol 17: 527
12/16/1737	138	0	Krip (Kreeps), John	plat vol 17: 529
2/3/1738/9	0	450	Kueffer (Kieffer), Devill	plat vol 12: 053
7/7/1766	0	100	Kysell, Conrad	plat vol 08: 435
9/9/1736	348	0	Labord, John	plat vol 12: 050
7/14/1737	0	50	Labord, John	plat vol 12: 050
3/26/1740	0	150	Labord, John	plat vol 12: 051
4/23/1733	0	50	LaCroix, Alexander	plat vol 16: 268
10/6/1733	39	0	LaCroix, Alexander	plat vol 16: 266 / LDS film 5342 pt. 2, 187–88
7/16/1739	0	450	Laffete, Capt. Peter	plat vol 02: 432
2/2/1735/6	96	0	Laffitt, Pierre (.5 acre)	LDS film 5342 pt.2, 190
1/29/1735/6	0	150	Laffitte, Capt. Peter	plat vol 03: 385
1/29/1735/6	0	450	Laffitte, Capt. Peter	plat vol 03: 405
1/15/1738/9	0	225	Lafitte (Laffitte), Peter (224.74 acres)	plat vol 12: 049

Date of Plat/Grant	Town Lot No.	No. of Acres	Name	Source
12/20/1737	?	?	Lage (Laye), Joseph	plat vol. 12: 60
9/9/1736	262	0	Lainey, Lucey (Lucy) (.5 acre)	plat vol 16: 285 / LDS film 5342 pt. 2, 220–21
3/1/1740/1	0	250	Lameau, Jn. Martin	plat vol 05: 509
1/24/1735/6?	0	50	LaPierre, Mathieu (Matthew) (plat: 1735–8)	plat vol 05: 152
4/22/1736	189	0	LaPierre, Matthew	plat vol 05: 085
3/5/1740	0	250	Lasman (Gasman?), John Martin	township grants 42 #160
10/13/1765	0	100	LeBray (Bray), Francis	plat vol 10: 072
12/10/????	0	300	LeBray (LaBray), Francis	plat vol 12: 050
12/10/1737	0	300	Lebray (LaBray, Bray), widow Jane, Twinet Twinet & Fanshaw	township grants 41 #338
9/2/1738	0	50	Legare, John	township grants 41 #337
9/20/1738	0	100	Legare, John	township grants 41 #336
9/9/1736	231	0	Legaye (Lagayes, DeLaGaye), John	plat vol 05: 508
3/9/1761	0	350	Liechtensteiger, Melchion (Melchior)	plat vol 07: 165
3/10/1761	0	100	Liechtensteiger, Melchior	plat vol 07: 145
11/9/1764	0	100	Liechtensteiger, Melcher (Melchior)	plat vol 08: 498
11/19/1764	0	150	Liechtensteiger (Leictensteiger), Melchior	plat vol 08: 488
1/18/1765	76	0	Liechtensteiger, Mel chior (purchase?)	LDS film 5342 pt. 2, 375–76
1/31/1735/6	0	50	Lier(s), Rodolph (John Rodolff)	plat vol 16: 350
1/3/1737/8	0	450	Linder, John	plat vol 12: 064
6/9/1738	0	150	Linder, John	plat vol 12: 063
12/20/????	340	0	Linder, John	plat vol 12: 063
2/7/1755	0	300	Linder, John	plat vol 12: 063
10/22/1759	0	150	Loarman, Johannes	plat vol 07: 199
11/23/1764	0	100	Mallet, Daniel	plat vol 07: 499
6/9/1736	0	550	Mallet, Gideon	plat vol 12: 087
6/11/1737	0	50	Mallet, Gideon	plat vol 12: 085
12/4/1737	170	0	Mallet, Gideon (.5 acre)	plat vol 12: 085 / LDS film 5342 pt. 2, 210

Date of Plat/Grant	Town Lot No.	No. of Acres	Name	Source
10/6/1733	46	0	Mallier, Pierre (.5 acre)	plat vol 12: 086 / LDS film 5342 pt. 2, 174
3/31/1740	0	200	Mallier, Peter (Pierre)	plat vol 12: 086
12/6/1737	171	0	Martainang, Philip	plat vol 18: 043
11/29/1735	0	50	Mason, Mary	plat vol 12: 093
12/22/1737	64	0	Mason, Peter	plat vol 12: 091
4/22/1736	8	0	Masson (Mason), Mary	plat vol 12: 091
2/14/1735/6	0	50	Masson (Mason), Peter	plat vol 12: 092
3/12/1735/6	0	200	Mattey, Abraham	plat vol 18: 058
9/3/1736	140	0	Mattey, Abraham	plat vol 18: 059
3/5/1761	25	150	Mayer, Adrian	plat vol 07: 210
1/18/1765	20	0	Mayer, Adrian (purchase?)	LDS film 5342 pt. 2, 371
2/11/1765	0	183	Mayer, Adrian	plat vol 08: 397
4/29/1736	244	0	Mayerhoffer, (Mayerhaven) (Mayerheaven), (John) Henry	plat vol 18: 079
9/3/1736	242	0	Mayerhoffer(r) (Mayerhaven?), (John) Henry (.5 acre)	plat vol 18: 080 / LDS film 5342 pt. 2, 206–7
6/20/1737	0	100	Mayerhoffer (Mayerhaven?), (John) Henry	plat vol 12: 087
12/4/1737	288	0	Meret (Merret), John Philip	plat vol 18: 360
1/3/1735/6	0	150	Merot, John Philip	plat vol 18: 359
5/2/1737	0	50	Merratt (Merret), Daniel	plat vol 12: 083
12/8/1737	77	0	Merrett, Daniel	plat vol 12: 083
10/19/1764	0	313	Merron (Mevron?), Henry	plat vol 08: 406
10/5/1733	33	0	Merthe, Abraham (.5 acre)	plat vol 18: 451 / LDS film 5342 pt. 2, 163–64
10/9/1733	0	50	Merthe (Marthe), Abraham	plat vol 18: 447
8/8/1734	75	350	Metsger, Jacob	plat vol 18: 364
6/7/1733	0	100	Meuraw (Mevron), Abraham	plat vol 18: 362
10/6/1733	41	0	Meuron, Abraham (Muron) (.5 acre)	plat vol 18: 363 / LDS film 5342 pt. 2, 178–79
6/20/1737	0	100	Meyerhoffer (Mayerhoffer), Henry	plat vol 12: 085
6/20/1737	0	100	Meyerhoffer, John Henry	plat vol 12: 088
8/7/1741	0	47	Michall (Michele?), John (46.51 acres)	plat vol 18: 373

Date of Plat/Grant	Town Lot No.	No. of Acres	Name	Source
8/7/1740	0	23	Michele (Michell?), John (22.6 acres)	plat vol 18: 371
9/15/1736	0	50	Michele (Michall, Michell?), Lewis	plat vol 18: 371
8/7/1741	0	31	Michell (Michall), John (30.9 acres)	plat vol 18: 373
11/23/1732	0	4705	Middleton, Arthur	plat vol 05: 02
1/22/1757	0	585	Middleton, Henry	plat vol 06: 239
1/22/1757	0	448	Middleton, William	plat vol 06: 239
5/11/1761	0	43	Middleton, William	plat vol 07: 241
2/4/1735/6	0	100	Miller, John Jacob	plat vol. 18: 412
4/20/1733	0	100	Mingersdorf (Mingersdorffe), George	plat vol 18: 447
9/6/1734	0	100	Mingersdorf (Minguers Dorff), George	plat vol 08: 447
9/1/1740	0	50	Mingersdorff, George	plat vol 18: 446
3/30/1756	0	300	Mingersdorff, George	plat vol 06: 147
10/4/1733	28	0	Minguersdorf, George (.5 acre)	plat vol 18: 448 / LDS film 5342 pt. 2, 170–71
9/10/1764	0	200	Mingerstaff (Mingersdorf), George	plat vol 07: 441
12/20/1737	200	0	Mitchell (Michele? Michall?), Lewis	plat vol 18: 374
12/16/1737	78	0	Mongin, David	plat vol 18: 483
2/17/1735/6	0	650	Mongin (Mangin), David & Francis	plat vol 18: 487
9/5/1737	0	1100	Montagu (Montaigut), Col. Samuel	plat vol 03: 371
12/9/1735	0	700	Montague (Montaigut), Samuel	plat vol 02: 463
9/3/1736	154	0	Montague, Samuel (.5 acre)	plat vol 12: 109 / LDS film 5342 pt. 2, 204–5
4/24/1740	0	1250	Montague, Samuel (to the heirs of)	plat vol 02: 466
4/23/1736	184	0	Moor (Morr?, Moore?), John James	plat vol 18: 508
04/3/1736	0	200	Moore (Moor?, Mohr?) John James	plat vol 12: 112
2/18/1735/6	0	150	Moore (Moor?, Morr?), Matthew	plat vol 18: 517

Date of Plat/Grant	Town Lot No.	No. of Acres	Name	Source
12/5/1737	226	0	Moore, Matthew	plat vol 18: 518
2/10/1755	0	300	Morgantaller, Gasper	plat vol 12: 111
4/5/1735	31	50	Morreau, Joseph	plat vol 18: 552
4/9/1736	247	0	Moy (Mog), John	plat vol 21: 013
9/27/1735	0	150	Moy, John (no certification date)	plat vol 21: 013
??/??/1736	0	1130	Muddleton (Middleton), Arthur	plat vol 03: 369
9/9/1736	205	0	Muller (Miller), James (.5 acre)	plat vol 21: 019 / LDS film 5342 pt. 2, 221
9/9/1736	312	0	Myer (Myers), Gasper	plat vol 21: 026
1/3/1735/6	0	200	Myers, Gasper	plat vol 21: 027
9/16/1765	0	250	Neile, John	plat vol 08: 024
2/2/1735/6	44	0	Netman, Jean Rudolph	LDS film 5342 pt. 2, 149
10/12/1736	0	300	Netman, John Redolph & Cullet (Cuillat), Adam	plat vol 16: 481
9/29/1737	0	350	Netman (Nettmann, Nellman), John Rudolph	plat vol 16: 480
12/20/1733	0	450	Newall, Thomas	plat vol 03: 330
1/16/1736/7	0	50	Nichol(s), (Nichold), David	plat vol 16: 496
9/3/1736	290	0	Nichol, David	plat vol 16: 494
6/10/1765	0	150	Nicholas, Pierre	plat vol 10: 132
5/2/1737	0	100	Oavery (Overy), Esau	plat vol 19: 016
8/8/1734	69	100	Ortellier, Daniel Jacob	plat vol 19: 008
6/11/1742	0	200	Overy (Oavery), Isaac	plat vol 19: 010
4/22/1736	176	0	Pallon(s), (Patton), Anthony	plat vol 19: 034
4/2/1736	187	0	Parollet (Parrottet), John Peter	plat vol 19: 056
2/4/1735	0	100	Parrollet, John Peter	plat vol 19: 055
12/28/1735	0	200	Patton (Pallor), Anthony	plat vol 19: 033
6/28/1752	0	500	Pelot, The Reverend Mr. Francis	plat vol 05: 301
9/29/1752	0	250	Pelot, Francis	plat vol 05: 301
4/13/1759	0	250	Pelot, Francis	plat vol 07: 046
4/29/1736	241	0	Pelow (Pelot), Jonas	plat vol 19: 124
10/6/1733	162	0	Pennefather (Pennesather?), Capt. John	plat vol 19: 133
10/20/1733	0	150	Pennefather, Capt. John	plat vol 19: 135
10/18/1736	0	200	Pichard, Charles Jacob	plat vol 19: 173

Date of Plat/Grant	Town Lot No.	No. of Acres	Name	Source
12/12/1737	347	0	Pillet, Daniel	plat vol 19: 179
2/11/1738/9	0	100	Pillet, Daniel	plat vol 19: 182
2/3/1735/6	0	150	Pinnell, Abel	plat vol 19: 189
12/16/1737	147	0	Pinell, Abel(l)	plat vol 19: 189
9/8/1764	0	200	Pininger (Bonninger, Binninger?), John Rodolph	plat vol 08: 036
6/11/1737	0	50	Piosh, Huget	plat vol 19: 191
12/16/1737	344	0	Piosh, Huget	plat vol 19: 191
4/22/1736	246	0	Plier (Pleir, Plire, Lier?), John Redolph	plat vol 19: 201
3/29/1736	0	50	Plier, John Redolph (Radolph)	plat vol 19: 200
2/18/1735/6	0	350	Poyas, John Lewis	plat vol 19: 260
10/18/1733	0	100	Price, Rice	plat vol 19: 275
10/6/1733	68	0	Price, Mr. Rice	plat vol 19: 275
11/4/1736	56	0	Purry, Charles	plat vol 19: 298
11/4/1736	173	0	Purrie (Purry), John Rodolph	plat vol 19: 301
1/16/1736/7	0	600	Purre (Purry), Col. John Peter	plat vol 19: 299
3/3/1733/4	0	12000	Purry, John Peter	plat vol 01: 318–19
11/12/1736	0	6650	Purry, John Peter	plat vol 03: 304
9/2/1736	0	100	Purrie, Col. John Peter	plat vol 18: 73
10/6/1733	54	0	Purrie, Col. John Peter (.5 acre)	plat vol 19: 300 / LDS film 5342 pt. 2, 166
6/8/1733	0	100	Purry, Col. Pierre	plat vol 19: 299
3/18/1735/6	0	300	Purry, John Redolph (Rudolph)	plat vol 19: 300
9/9/1736	174	0	Quinch, Lewis	plat vol 20: 003
12/9/1763	0	500	Quinch, Luis	plat vol 08: 547
4/8/1771	64	0	Ravot, Abraham	plat vol 20: 030
4/8/1771	66	0	Ravot, Abraham	plat vol 20: 024
10/6/1733	47	0	Ravot, Francis Gabriel (.5 acre)	plat vol 20: 042 / LDS film 5342 pt. 2, 186
6/10/1733	0	50	Ravot (Ravout, Revout), Gabriel François	plat vol 20: 041
9/10/1764	0	650	Ravot, Gabriel	plat vol 08: 295
12/4/1737	169	0	Reck (Rack), John Jacob (.5 acre)	plat vol 20: 007 / LDS film 5342 pt. 2, 209–10
12/17/1737	0	227	Reck, (Roch, Roach), John Jacob (227.37)	plat vol 20: 170

Date of Plat/Grant	Town Lot No.	No. of Acres	Name	Source
9/27/1736	0	100	Recorden (Recorder), Francis Lewis	plat vol 20: 054
6/8/1733	0	150	Recordon (Recondon), Pierre Louis	plat vol 20: 055
10/5/1733	37	0	Recordon, Pierre Louis (.5 acre)	plat vol 20: 043 / LDS film 5342 pt. 2, 153
12/28/1735	0	200	Remond (Remound, Reymond?), Jaremiah	plat vol 20: 071
12/5/1737	168	0	Remond (Reymond), Jeramiah (Jeremiah)	plat vol 20: 071
8/22/1764	0	300	Rester, Frederick	plat vol 07: 465
6/8/1733	0	50	Reymond, Joseph	plat vol 20: 072
10/6/1733	43	0	Reymond, Joseph (.5 acre)	plat vol 20: 076 / LDS film 5342 pt. 2, 160–61
2/13/1755	0	100	Rhynover (Rhynower), Leonard	plat vol 06: 074
1/18/1738/9	0	400	Richard, James	plat vol 20: 082
10/6/1733	50	0	Richard, Maj. James (.5 acre)	plat vol 20: 095 / LDS film 5342 pt. 2, 181–82
6/8/1733	0	300	Richard, James	plat vol 20: 098
10/13/1733	?	?	Rigeur (Riguer), Jean Nicholas	plat vol 20: 113
10/6/1733	92	0	Rigour, John Nichalas (.5 acre)	plat vol 20: 111 / LDS film 5342 pt. 2, 176–77
1/18/1741	0	250	Ring, John	township grants 42 # 66
9/3/1736	209	0	Robert, David	plat vol 20: 119
10/11/1733	0	250	Robert, Josué	plat vol 20: 152
10/7/1737	0	300	Robert(s), David	plat vol 20: 118
10/5/1733	22	0	Robert(s), Josué (.5 acre)	plat vol 20: 137 / LDS film 5342 pt. 2, 157
2/23/1735/6	0	450	Robert(s), William	plat vol 20: 152
2/20/1742/3	0	150	Rorere, Michael	plat vol 07: 036
5/9/1737	0	150	Rose, Hugh	plat vol 03: 266*
5/9/1737	0	150	Rose, Hugh	plat vol 20: 195*
8/6/1741	0	50	Rose, Hugh	plat vol 20: 197
4/29/1761	0	200	Rose, Hugh	plat vol 07: 238

Date of Plat/Grant	Town Lot No.	No. of Acres	Name	Source
2/11/1755	0	400	Rumph, David	plat vol 06: 075
1/1/1735/6	0	50	Sauce (Sause, Sausse, Saussy), David	plat vol 19: 310
10/3/1764	0	100	Sause Jr., David	plat vol 08: 257
7/16/1765	15	0	Sause Jr., David (purchase?)	LDS film 5342 pt. 2, 386
10/1/1764	0	200	Sause Sr., David	plat vol 08: 255
10/21/1766	0	100	Sausse, Gabriel	plat vol 08: 464
10/12/1733	0	50	Saussy, David	plat vol 19: 311
2/13/1755	0	250	Saussy, David	plat vol 07: 010
10/5/1733	13	0	Saussy, David (.5 acre)	plat vol 19: 310 / LDS film 5342 pt. 2, 156–57
2/3/1735/6	0	50	Schönmannsgruber (Grobert), George Shonman	plat vol 16: 247
4/24/1736	124	0	Schönmannsgruber (Gravico, Grobert) George Schonman (.5 acre)	plat vol 16: 189 / LDS film 5342 pt. 2, 206
10/10/1733	0	50	Spach (Spack), Jonas	plat vol 12: 157
10/11/1733	91	0	Spack, Jonas (.5 acre)	plat vol 12: 161 / LDS film 5342 pt. 2, 180
6/5/1737	0	150	Sterchy, Peter	township grants 42 #68
9/16/1738	190	0	Sterchy, Peter (.5 acre)	LDS film 5342 pt. 2, 207–8
4/3/1736	0	250	Stersby (Sterchis), James	plat vol 21: 104
9/26/1736	0	100	Steples (Staples?), William	plat vol 21: 103
9/6/1737	0	1450	Stobo, James (S. side of Purrysburg Township)	plat vol 03: 092
8/9/1734	108	300	Stranblar (Stranblor), John	plat vol 21: 162
2/9/1760	0	600	Strobart (Strouper?), George	plat vol 07: 114
10/18/1760	0	343	Strobert (Strobart, Strobhar), Jacob	plat vol 07: 226
5/??/1757	0	450	Strouper, George (part in township & part outside)	plat vol 06: 324
5/28/1737	0	50	Sutie (Lutie?), Peter	plat vol 12: 066
9/4/1736	272	0	Talebach (Telebach), George	plat vol 20: 265
9/3/1734	0	50	Tanner, Jacob	plat vol 20: 263
8/7/1734	67	300	Tannor, Jacob	plat vol 20: 266
6/4/1737	0	250	Telebach (Talebach), George	plat vol 20: 264

Date of Plat/Grant	Town Lot No.	No. of Acres	Name	Source
4/21/1733	0	100	Thermin, Anthoine	plat vol 20: 297
10/5/1733	15	0	Thermin, Anthony (.5 acre)	plat vol 20: 294 / LDS film 5342 pt. 2, 193–94
8/30/1765	0	200	Tobishop (Tobyshop), John	plat vol 08: 524
5/16/1766	57	0	Tobyshop, John	LDS film 5342, pt. 2, 398
10/6/1733	70	0	Tullier(s) (Tullius), Joshua Daniel (.5 acre)	plat vol 20: 401 / LDS film 5342 pt. 2, 192–93
12/1/1737	0	100	Vallatan (Vollaton), Jeremiah Olivier	plat vol 20: 431
12/1/1737	0	50	Vallatan, Susanna	plat vol 20: 430
4/29/1736	251	0	Vallaton, Jeremiah Oliver (.5 acre)	plat vol 20: 431 / LDS film 5342 pt. 2, 211–12
12/16/1737	205	0	Vallours (Vellonirs), Jacques	plat vol 20: 429
12/28/1737	0	200	Valours (Villours), Jaques	plat vol 20: 430
6/5/1737	0	50	Vanay (Venney), John Francis	plat vol 20: 424
3/6/1734/5	0	500	Vanderheyde, Peter Garret	plat vol 20: 425
10/6/1733	102	0	Vanderstyde, Peter Ganet (Garret) (.5 acre)	plat vol 08: 633 / LDS film 5342 pt. 2, 194–95
12/22/1760	0	200	Vaucher (Vauchier?), John	plat vol 07: 227
3/11/1761	0	288	Vauchier, Francis	plat vol 07: 151
2/20/1761	0	300	Vauchier, John	plat vol 07: 167
5/26/1767	0	350	Vauchier, John	plat vol 09: 039
8/17/1736	0	2000	Venerabre (Vernezobre), Daniel	plat vol 03: 167
10/13/1736	0	50	Venney (Vernay), Francis	plat vol 20: 460
2/25/1735/6	0	500	Verdier, Andrew	plat vol 20: 457
12/5/1737	110	0	Verdier, Andrew	plat vol 20: 460
1/17/1737/8	0	1000	Varnod (Vernodivido), Mrs. Mary	plat vol 05: 508
12/22/1737	188	0	Vernay, Francis	plat vol 20: 462
8/17/1736	0	2000	Vernezobre, Daniel	township grants 41 #144
1/31/1733/4	0	100	Vignequ (Vigneu), Stephen	plat vol 20: 484
12/21/1737	215	0	Viellers (Villiers, Viller), Anna Maria	plat vol 20: 473
2/4/1735/6	0	100	Villars (Viellers), Mrs. Anne Mary	plat vol 20: 471

Date of Plat/Grant	Town Lot No.	No. of Acres	Name	Source
12/15/1735	0	300	Viller (Viellers), Anna Maria	plat vol 20: 472
9/6/1767	0	250	Vonalma, Ma(r)tha (Mathias Von Alma?)	plat vol 10: 96
4/24/1733	0	50	Voyer, Jeanne Verbaine	plat vol 20: 483
10/6/1733	36	0	Voyer(l), Jeanne Verbaine (.5 acre)	plat vol 20: 480 / LDS film 5342 pt. 2, 150
2/13/1768	104	0	Waldberger, Jacob	LDS film 5243 pt. 2, 402
2/13/1768	106	0	Waldberger, Jacob	LDS film 5243 pt. 2, 402
5/19/1762	0	100	Waldburger, Jacob	plat vol 07: 262
8/24/1767	0	700	Waldburger, Jacob	plat vol 10: 145
6/4/1765	0	100	Waldburger, Jacob	plat vol 16: 104
4/25/1735	245	0	Walker, Joseph (.5 acre)	plat vol 21: 273 / LDS film 5342 pt. 2, 211
5/25/1757	0	100	Walser, Andrew	plat vol 07: 100
11/13/1761	0	400	Wanderly, David	plat vol 15: 335
12/27/1737	137	0	Weff (Welf), Henrie (.5 acre)	plat vol 21: 377 / LDS film 5342 pt. 2, 213–14
3/31/1736	0	50	Weff(s), John	plat vol 21: 377
3/13/1735/6	0	150	Werlix, Jacob	plat vol 21: 325
4/24/1736	191	0	Werlix, James (Jacob?)	plat vol 21: 324
4/29/1736	250	0	Westneof, John	plat vol 21: 398
8/6/1737	0	1300	Williams, Robert	plat vol 08: 615
6/15/1762	0	126	Williams, Robert	plat vol 07: 271
11/6/1764	0	227	Williams, Robert	plat vol 08: 417
6/16/1767	0	889	Williamson, William	plat vol 10: 147
8/21/1764	0	300	Winglar (Winkler), Lewis	plat vol 08: 419
9/6/1734	0	50	Winkler, Andrew (Andrez)	plat vol 08: 611
1/31/1735/6	0	50	Winkler, Andrew	plat vol 21: 556
10/13/1733	0	100	Winkler, Andrez	plat vol 21: 554
10/5/1733	24	0	Winkler, Andrez (.5 acre)	plat vol 21: 556 / LDS film 5342 pt. 2, 190–91
10/6/1733	51	0	Winkler, Anne Catherine (.5 acre)	plat vol 21: 557 / LDS film 5742 pt. 2, 167–68
6/7/1773	0	350	Winkler (precept dated 2/23/1732–33), Jacob	plat vol 21: 553
11/19/1764	0	400	Winkler, Jacob	plat vol 08: 422

Date of Plat/Grant	Town Lot No.	No. of Acres	Name	Source
5/10/1772	0	256	Wright, Alen	plat vol 20: 508
8/7/1734	63	200	Wunderlick, John	plat vol 20: 522
11/28/1735	0	250	Yanam, Francis	plat vol 20: 532
4/22/1736	122	0	Yanam, Francis	plat vol 20: 532
9/24/1735	0	250	Yonam Yanam), Francis	plat vol 03: 237
12/9/1736	5	0	Yonam, Francis	plat vol 03: 237
12/8/1737	117	0	Zauberbuckler (Zouberbühler), Sebastain	plat vol 08: 608
5/5/1737	0	100	Zouberbukler, Sebastian	plat vol 12: 196
12/8/1737	74	0	Zublie, David (.5 acre)	plat vol 08: 609 / LDS film 5342 pt. 2, 215–16
10/25/1737	0	600	Zublie, David	plat vol 08: 608

Note: * Record may be a duplicate or is otherwise suspect.

The only document that provides unequivocal data on Purrysburg family size, ethnic character, gender balance, and ages of family members is the list of those qualifying before Governor Johnson in December 1732, as enumerated in table 1. Of the group of ninety-two people, the largest family contained nine members, two families had eight members, three had six members, five had five members, one had four, two had three, two had two members, and ten were traveling as singles (though at least three of this last group had families). The ratio of males to females in the sample varies widely within various age groups, but the overall proportion of males to females in the list is 59.8 percent to 40.2 percent. With regard to age, 32.6 percent were between forty and sixty-five years of age, 67.4 percent were younger than forty, and 53.3 percent below the age of twenty. It would be inappropriate to speculate too extensively on the basis of such a small sample—probably less than 10 percent of the total population of the township—but other data support the contention that Purrysburg remained a settlement of families that were fairly even split between French and German surnames with a minority of settlers of English and Italian extraction.[8]

Attempting to locate the original homelands for most of the families who lived in Purrysburg is just as difficult as it is to unravel the composition of the families themselves. The turmoil of early modern European life provides only some of the context for the complexity of this problem. Even if the homelands of some Purrysburg settlers cannot be determined, however, those township dwellers whose places of origin can be traced speak to the ethnic diversity of the township and to the necessity of blood and kin to forge the first bonds of intimacy on the South Carolina frontier.

For example, representatives from at least twelve families (Bourguin, Chaillet, Giroud, Henriod, Huguenin, Humbert, Jeanneret, Meuron, Purry, Reymond,

Richard, and Robert) came from Purry's home canton of Neuchâtel—at least in the generation that left for Purrysburg.[9] Jean François Bourguin was banished from France and left for the Swiss Confederation in the late seventeenth century. He died prior to 1730. His widow (Marie), their children (Jean Baptiste, Henri François, Ann Marie, and Benedict), and their families left for Purrysburg.[10] The Huguenin family had lived in Neuchâtel for three generations as refugees from France before David and his family immigrated to Purrysburg.[11] The Humbert family, or at least a branch of it, left Genoa for South Carolina.[12] The Gindrat (Jindra) family originated in Berne, whereas the Albergottis trace their ancestry to Ulisse Antoine (Ulysses Anthony), a native of Arezzo in Tuscany who forsook the Roman Catholic priesthood for Calvinist proclivities after sojourns in Paris and Geneva.[13] John Frederick Holzendorf was a native of Brandenburg, John Linder of Berlin, and Hector Berenger de Beaufin of Orange, France. The Uselts (Unselt) were Palatines; the Kieffers came from the southern German states, and the Winklers from Würtemberg.[14] The Mingersdorff (Mengersdorff) family may have originated in the Bamberg region of northern Bavaria.[15] The Mallets came from a long line of Rouen Calvinist cloth merchants who fled to Geneva in the sixteenth century.[16] Members of the Lafitte family fled to Switzerland from France (from the province of Guienne on the maternal side) soon after the revocation of the Edict of Nantes, while the Giroud family left earlier, residing as refugees in Neuchâtel for at least three generations prior to the 1730s.[17] André Verdier, the progenitor of the line in South Carolina, appears to have been born in France but removed to the Confederation before 1728. The origin of the Montaigut (Montague) family is even more nebulous, but its immigrant forebear seems to have been born in one of the cantons. The Desaussure family originated in Lorraine, but Antoine fled with his family to Lausaunne from which place Henry debarked for South Carolina in the mid-1720s.[18]

The puzzling heritage of the Poyas family illustrates the difficulty of uncovering the original domicile of many of the Purrysburg settlers. In the text of an act passed by the South Carolina General Assembly on 11 March 1737/38, John (Jean) Lewis (Louis) Poyas is described as "Piedmontese." Mabel Webber, however, claimed that Jean Louis and his brother John Ernest escaped France at the time of the revocation, domiciled in England, and then left for Purrysburg. Because the Piedmont shares borders with the Swiss Confederation and France—as well as sharing a less than completely independent history with its western neighbor—it is entirely possible that Poyas ancestors lived in southern France and then migrated to the Piedmont. It is just as plausible, however, that northwestern Italy was the family homeland and members converted to the Waldensian brand of Reformed Christianity, which made their continued safety in the region doubtful. Add to these issues the fact that John Lewis was fluent in French and the task of uncovering the true home of the Poyas family becomes nearly impossible. The same can be said for other Purrysburg families.[19] Whatever else might be discovered about the ancestral origins of other township families, it is apparent that they were drawn from the culturally and geographically diverse cockpit of central southwestern Europe. Thrown together on the southern frontier, they had to face a New World physical environment that forced them out of familiar relational patterns to, as Darrett and Anita Rutman discovered in their study of Virginia's Middlesex County settlers, order "themselves in their own fashion,"[20] for they labored to arrange their lives in ways that would allow them to construct some semblance of security and stability for their families in the midst of a hostile and even deadly new world.

Immigrants to Purrysburg quickly discovered that their preconceptions of South Carolina did not match the realities of life in the wilderness. Erroneous notions concerning the region were surely fueled by Purry's enthusiastic pamphleteering, but they also resulted from errors and misrepresentations by the world's most respected cartographers and geographers and were exacerbated by the fumbling provincial government.[21] As a result of mistakes and oversights, the location of the colony, the diverse ethnic nature of the settlement, and the lack of promised assistance, Purrysburg families suffered more than their share of tragedy.[22]

II

An astronomical mortality rate, characteristic of southern colonial settlements, was perhaps the most immediate fact of township life to confront the new residents. Forced to adapt to a humid subtropical climate, confronted with exotic diseases, and plagued by insufficient support from British officials, township residents sickened and died at an alarming rate, particularly in the first decades of settlement. Nothing better illustrates the capriciousness of health and life on the southern frontier than the fate of a nameless blacksmith at Purrysburg. The Reverend Johann Martin Boltzius, pastor of a the nearby settlement of Salzburg German Lutherans in Ebenezer, Georgia, observed sardonically in 1737 that the smith had expired because "believing that he was well accustomed to the heat, [he] had continued working despite the hot sun." While he may have felt that that would not hurt him, he must have experienced the contrary.[23] Although John Duffy contends that health conditions in the American colonies were as a whole better than in England during the eighteenth century, he concedes that such conditions were far from benign to the immigrants. More recent demographic research has uncovered an alarming disparity in life expectancy among colonists in the Chesapeake as opposed to New England. Russell Menard calculated that, throughout the seventeenth century, Maryland immigrants could expect to live an average of fifteen years fewer than their counterparts in New England. He also estimated that 40–45 percent of native-born children died before the age of twenty. Similarities between the physical environment and the pathogens in the Chesapeake and the lower South would lead one to expect corresponding patterns in Purrysburg.[24]

The humid mesothermal climate of coastal South Carolina and Georgia brings pleasant spring weather but also intense Caribbean summer heat and oppressive humidity. Abundant precipitation characterizes the lowcountry (close to fifty inches yearly in the vicinity of the township), and, although no distinctly dry or rainy seasons exist, much of the rain comes during the warmer months as the result of violent and recurrent thunderstorms. Mean summer temperatures range between 75 and 80 degrees, with average January temperatures at the Purrysburg site hovering near 49 degrees. Sir James Wright of neighboring Georgia proclaimed early spring very pleasant, but he characterized the weather from the end of May to the end of September as "clear but exceedingly hot." The torrid summers were caused by tropical southerly winds generated by the Bermuda High, an enormous high pressure cell over the Atlantic Ocean. It is little wonder that so many uninitiated European immigrants failed to survive. Indeed, the death toll reached such epidemic proportions that contemporary books on the South Carolina climate stressed a causal connection between climate and disease.[25]

Diseases linked to climate and human nutrition were widespread in the colonial Southeast and claimed victims from among Purrysburg families. Climate-related diseases such as various strains of malaria (called the ague, or "seasoning fever"), and diphtheria struck with a vengeance during the hot, humid months of June through October. Malaria posed a particular problem for, if it did not kill its victim, its debilitating effects promoted infection and death by other pathogens. Pregnant women and their unborn children were peculiarly susceptible to this syndrome. It has been estimated that for every death directly attributable to malaria, five more could be added, with malaria working in consort with other diseases. It is this "piggyback effect" that may partially explain the differing mortality rates between New England and the South. Nutritionally linked maladies such as beriberi and scurvy were not uncommon, even though sturgeon prevalent in southern river systems could supply enough thiamin to eradicate the former condition.

If untreated, beriberi, which attacked the nervous system, could lead to circulatory distress, neuritis, stiffness, and paralysis. Unchecked scurvy resulted in weakness, anemia, bleeding and spongy gums, loss of teeth, and muscular degeneration. Nearly all colonists suffered from at least one of these ailments. Many so afflicted died, and even those who survived the multiyear "seasoning" could be debilitated for life, leaving them susceptible to the ravages of other diseases. Women who contracted beriberi or scurvy ceased to ovulate. In such an environment, pregnancy itself presented grave dangers to both mother and fetus. In both the Chesapeake and the lower South, women in their childbearing years ran a high risk of death, and childhood deaths were all too common. Just across the Savannah River from Purrysburg in Georgia, nearly every pregnant woman died in childbirth during 1733, the first year of colonization. Nutritionally deprived mothers passed deficiencies on to their nursing children. The passive transmission of disease was so great that most infants born in the opening decades of Georgia settlement expired before reaching their first birthday. The infant mortality rate remained so high in the lowcountry until fairly recent times that African Americans on the Georgia coast called a newborn baby a "come see" because the child only came to see if it wanted to stay—and it often did not.[26]

The intestinal ailments of dysentery ("bloody flux") and typhoid fever also posed dire health risks for southern colonists and were linked to the water resources of the area. Repeated attacks could be common because there were no antibodies to ward off successive bouts with dysentery and only slight immunity existed to prevent recurring attacks of typhoid fever. Limiting contact with other colonists could ameliorate these conditions as demonstrated by the increased survival rate in Virginia after John Smith scattered the settlers. Salt intoxication was also possible in regions at or below the tidewater line, as Carville V. Earle has discovered in the early Chesapeake. River-borne pathogens tend to increase with the tidewater effect, so Purrysburg's location at the edge of the tidewater may have contributed to elevated mortality rates in the township. It may well be that as the township residents were able to move to their plantations when the surveys were completed by the late 1730s, their ability to survive followed the Jamestown pattern.[27]

Diseases linked to climate and nutrition were not the only threats to the health and vitality of Purrysburg settlers. Measles, smallpox, influenza, whooping cough, pleurisies, and other respiratory complaints such as colds and pneumonia took their toll on those who lived in the region.[28] Add to these maladies natural threats from poisonous snakes, alligators, wild animals, and the constant specter accidental death by drowning, food poisoning, or abduction by neighboring hostiles, and it becomes evident that frontier life in the township provided little in the way of external order or stability.

Perhaps as frightening as the pervasiveness of disease and the omnipresent possibility of accidental injury was the fact that often the treatment was as potentially injurious as the complaint itself—if treatment was even available. The southern frontier generally appears to have had a decided lack of trained doctors, and, although that cannot be said for Purrysburg residents, the treatments provided often reflected a level of medical knowledge that, in retrospect, may have more a part of the problem rather than its cure. As one historian of the South Carolina backcountry wrote with her tongue planted firmly in her cheek, the "harsh treatment of the professionals (blistering, bleeding, sweating, purging, and vomiting) of the era was not always conducive to recovery."[29] In summer 1741 John Linder (Lindner) suffered through a lengthy and painful illness. The treatment regimen prescribed by a Purrysburg doctor included induced vomiting and "six *sesicutoria* two hands wide and long." Each one was laid on different parts of Linder's body for several days at a time. An observer described the intensity of his stomach and breast pain as well as his weakness "in the head."[30] During the late summer of the following year, the wife of

Theobald Kieffer Sr., Anna Margarita, suffered a snakebite while digging turnips in her garden. The wound was lanced, covered with salt, and bound tightly. The bandage induced numbness in the affected finger and had to be loosened, but that action led to anxiety and sharp pain in the finger and other parts of her body. Finally, after they "administered theriac to her and placed a certain kind of plaster upon it, the pains subsided,"[31] and she apparently recovered.

The therapy a married Purrysburg woman received from a township doctor in the spring of 1743 was said to have ruined her. Two years later one of the Purrysburg doctors treated the eighteen-year-old daughter of Theobald Kieffer Sr. with a mercury preparation designed to stimulate her salivary glands but left her "badly harmed."[32] Most nonsurgical cures, whether prescribed by a trained physician, midwife, or the patient's family member, provided little protection against the deleterious effects of those conditions they were meant to ameliorate.[33] When Ruprecht Steiner of Ebenezer sustained a serious snakebite in April 1742, a Purrysburg cobbler advised burying the victim up to his neck so the earth could draw out the poison. His advice was followed to no apparent effect. Some folk remedies, however, did seem to have had some prophylactic result. Cinchona bark, otherwise known as fever, peruvian, or jesuit's bark, was used to ward off malaria and was among the most effective treatments because it contained quinine. Used by whites regularly in the summer months to guard against fevers of all kinds, it was chewed, taken as an extract added to rum, fruit juices, or milk, or mashed with onion or garlic to mask the bitter taste of the quinine. The cure was surely not as deadly as the disease, but its administration—especially when preceded by an emetic such as ipecac to speed its therapeutic effects—could not have been a cause for too much rejoicing. Even so, the cinchona bark cure remained more the exception than the rule.[34]

If surgical procedures or cures proved ineffective, death was the most probable outcome. Perhaps because death from disease was so commonplace among Purrysburg colonists, it is rare to uncover the specific cause. With the exception of Jacob Kieffer, who died of tuberculosis on 5 February 1747, no other specific cause of death is known among the recorded deaths from disease of Purrysburg residents.[35] Only the naked fact of death remains. Some families lost loved ones before a season had passed in their new home. Ulrick Bac(he), Leonard Francke, and Mr. Uselt (Unselt), Jacob Callume, Mr. Breton, and the Reverend Varnod succumbed before they had even received their allotted land in the township.[36] Purrysburg schoolmaster Uselt died soon after the family's arrival in Purrysburg in the early 1730s. He left a wife and four daughters. His wife died soon afterward. In November 1736 Thomas Causton, the bailiff and storekeeper of Savannah, reported to the Georgia trustees that sickness and death were rampant in Purrysburg. He had recently been informed by Jean Pierre Purry that because of "fever and agues upwards of 30 men able to bear arms" had died.[37] Anna Margaretha Rosch, who was born in the township, lost both her parents in the early 1750s and removed across the Savannah River to Ebenezer. Anna Margarita Kieffer died in January 1753 at her Purrysburg plantation after enduring nearly three months of a painful illness just shortly before her son-in-law, Mr. Schrempf, succumbed. Less than two months later, David Zubly (Zübli, Züblin) and his son Thomas died within weeks of each other, leaving David's widow, Helena, alone at Purrysburg. The Reverend Abraham Imer, who left his parish in Berne in 1760 to serve the township congregation as its third minister, lost two daughters on the journey to Purrysburg.[38] The effects of these deaths and dozens of others are much more obvious than the causes. Death left families fatherless and/or motherless; it took children; and, on extreme occasions, it nearly blotted out entire families.[39]

Disease remained the major factor in the high mortality rate of Purrysburg family members, but accidental deaths were also not uncommon. In fact, the township death toll from accidents was significantly higher than that recorded for the townships of Orangeburg and Amelia.[40] In January 1738/39, the body of the daughter of Major James Richard washed up on the shore near Tybee in Georgia. She had lived with her children and second husband in the township. A trip to Charles Town with two of her children ended in tragedy as bad weather caught them and five other travelers on the return trip to Purrysburg. The canoe capsized somewhere in Daufuskie Sound. No one survived.[41] A similar accident seems to have occurred shortly thereafter that claimed the lives of one of the Purrysburg doctors and his entire family. The Purrysburg tailor, (Johann) Jacob Metsger (Metzger), and his wife lost three of their children in the same calamity.[42] Sometime before November 1741 the husband one of Metsger's surviving daughters also drowned. In October 1749 a young Purrysburg man, returning with fresh ground meal from the Ebenezer mill, capsized his boat on a stretch of the Savannah River congested with logs and drowned. The following February a Purrysburg planter and merchant only recently returned from New York nearly lost his life on the river when the boat in which he was traveling overturned a short distance from Savannah. The accident was triggered when the merchant and some of his slaves caught a deer swimming in the river and attempted to cut its throat after hauling it aboard. Two of the slaves perished. A decade later, in perhaps the most bizarre recorded death at the township, a man participating in a game of ten pins at Purrysburg had the decided misfortune of having the skittle ball bounce off a tree and strike him on the knee. The blow incapacitated him so severely that he apparently fell into the Savannah River and drowned.[43] Snakebite injuries were not unknown but appear to have been rather rare and not fatal. At least one township resident, John Linder, appears to have been murdered by Native Americans, though little is known about this incident.[44]

III

That death could come at any time wearing any guise meant that Purrysburg inhabitants lived in a constant state of uncertainty about the future. Perhaps among all the early Purrysburg immigrants, the troubles of the Uselt family best illustrate the disruption of family relationships attributable to the ubiquitous presence of disease and death on the southern frontier. The untimely death of the patriarch, probably sometime in 1735, left his wife and four daughters in a desperate situation. The widow approached the Reverend Boltzius about relocating to Ebenezer, but he referred her to Georgia trustee General James Oglethorpe. Georg Schweiger of Ebenezer, who had only recently lost his first wife, Anna Hofer, married the oldest Uselt daughter, Eva Regina (Ephrosia Regula), prior to April 1736. Unable to provide for her family, Mrs. Uselt and two of the daughters became servants at a plantation near Savannah, while the fourth appears to have stayed in either Purrysburg or Ebenezer. A short while later the widow visited Charles Town with her youngest daughter, Eva Rosina. Mrs. Uselt died there, and Eva was taken briefly to Pennsylvania. The daughter left on the plantation worked there for another year, but the owners departed the country soon afterward and left her behind without any visible means of support. She eventually found her way back to Ebenezer, and the Salzburg pastors there agreed to provide for her as best they could since her sister and brother-in-law were unable to do so. Finally, by 1738, the sisters were reunited, but only for a short while. One of the unmarried three was employed by Boltzius, and the two youngest were accepted into the orphanage where the older of the two prepared for her first communion. The following year Anna Justina Uselt married Franz Heinberger (Hernberger). A few years later they left for Pennsylvania. Another daughter, Sibilla Frederica, married Henry Bishop (Heinrich Bischoff), the English servant of the Reverend Boltzius.[45]

The tragic pattern of death and family disruption repeated itself at an alarming rate in the frontier township. Nearly as moving as the fate of the Uselts was the plight of an unnamed native of the canton of Appenzell and his family. During July 1739 the Appenzeller traveled from Purrysburg to Ebenezer with his young son to speak with the pastors about the possibility of his moving to the Georgia town. Two of his daughters and their husbands had recently died, and he found little opportunity to use his skills as a barrel- and cabinetmaker in the township. All of the money he had brought with him disappeared within a year of his arrival on the frontier. His wife and six other children remained in Europe, and, because of his destitute circumstances, he could not raise enough money to return to them or to pay for their passage to South Carolina.[46]

No matter what the circumstance, a death in the family left no member untouched. In 1738 a young Purrysburg girl who had been placed in the Ebenezer school lost her father after a lengthy illness. The dead man left his daughter sole possession of a legacy that came from his first wife's estate. His second wife regrettably squandered the legacy. Fortunately, a Purrysburg judge was summoned before the entire estate could be spent. Marguerite, one of the surviving children of Jacob Metsger, married, gave birth to three children in Purrysburg, lost her husband, remarried, moved to Ebenezer, was widowed a second time, and then died leaving two minor children. Shortly after her death in 1750, a Purrysburg youth who had been apprenticed to the Ebenezer locksmith Schrempf returned to the township to visit his parents and died there.[47]

As these cases illustrate, the loss of either husband or wife, when coupled with the challenges of life in the wilderness, made multiple marriages and blended families common among frontier settlers whether in seventeenth-century Maryland or Virginia or eighteenth-century Purrysburg.[48] In addition, although few marriage records survive by which ages at marriage might be determined, orphaned adolescents undoubtedly perceived the institution as providing some semblance of emotional, social, and economic security. They may have married sooner than their counterparts in New England because in a very real sense they were forced to mature faster.[49]

If age at first marriage among township settlers remains difficult to determine, the value of the institution to them is not. Barely two years after the first immigrants stepped ashore, they faced the departure of their minister, the Reverend Joseph Bugnion, for St. James Santee, in January 1734. Purrysburg couples intending to marry had to travel outside the township to legitimate their intentions until the arrival of the Reverend Henri François Chiffelle in November. Sometime during the ministerial interregnum of 1734—perhaps as early as January—six Purrysburg couples decided to take river passage to Savannah to do so. They sailed down the river in a long procession of boats filled with numerous attendants and led by Major James Richard of the township militia. General Oglethorpe of Georgia greeted the party and even donated a hog for the wedding feast. Abundant supplies of beer, wine, rum, and punch sufficiently lubricated the festivities. Dancing and revelry continued throughout the evening. At dawn the newlyweds thanked Oglethorpe for his hospitality, and they and their entourage prepared to leave for Purrysburg. As the boats headed upstream, a volley from the cannon wished the travelers well. A short while thereafter, the *South Carolina Gazette* carried word of the merrymaking, wryly crediting the "noble effects of the climate" at Purrysburg for the multiple marriage celebration. The *Gazette* also noted that six more township couples hoped to duplicate the fete in the near future.[50] The elaborate pageantry of this celebration symbolically illustrates the embedded social, emotional, spiritual, and legal value of marriage for settlers on the southern frontier.

Marriage patterns among township residents demonstrate that the network of relationships for the immigrants began locally and then expanded outward rather quickly—particularly toward the German settlement of Ebenezer. In 1735 David Giroud married Jean Ann Marie Robert, granddaughter of the Reverend Pierre Robert, one of the first French Huguenots to arrive in South Carolina. The Yanam and Chevillette families were united before December 1736. By April 1742 the Forquerant and Reymond (Raimond, Raymond) families shared a marriage bond, as did the Lohrman and Humbert (Humbart) families in 1759. The Bournant and Pelot families were linked, probably earlier than the 1760s. Leonard Reinauer (Rhynower) married Catherina Riger no later than the spring of 1769. The Huguenin and Ravot families were joined by the 1760s, and the Keall (Kehl) and Rehm families by the 1770s.[51] These connections fit the expected pattern of conjugal alliances between ethnically/linguistically similar township families, but this is not the only pattern of family relationships revealed by extant records.

There is evidence early in the township's genealogical history that for a variety of probable reasons some residents chose to marry those who appeared to be quite different from themselves. Irregular clerical offices and the distance of Purrysburg from most other pockets of settlement led to a reordering of marital relationships among the ethnically diverse immigrants. After the first year of settlement, it was not uncommon to find French-surnamed residents married to German-surnamed residents. At least two of the prospective marriages reported in the *South Carolina Gazette* story in 1734 involved French- and German-surnamed residents of the township. Peter Roche planned to marry a fifteen-year-old German girl, and Francis Buche hoped to wed the widow Anna Barbara Francke. A few years later another Purrysburg German widow married a French resident of the township.[52]

These marriages in and of themselves are not surprising; interethnic unions existed throughout the colonies. It is significant, however, that among township settlers interethnic marriages took place not only within the first generation, where traditional ethnic identifiers of language and culture are assumed to be strongest and hence militate against unions with members of other ethnic groups, but also within the first five years of settlement. Although too much cannot be made of this phenomenon because of the complex boundaries of Swiss ethnicity in the eighteenth century and the lack of complete marriage records, it is perhaps at least suggestive of a perception that marriage rather than conventional ethnic/linguistic factors constituted a primary means of emotional and social stability in the hostile frontier environment.[53]

That the southern frontier experience reordered ethnically defined marriage patterns is illustrated even more graphically by the paradoxical relationship between Purrysburg and Ebenezer. The Georgia Salzburg Lutheran settlement shared linguistic ties with the German-Swiss of Purrysburg, but the Reformed bent of most of the Purrysburg immigrants, both German speakers and French speakers, posed a formidable barrier to mutual friendship and a conspicuous obstacle to romance. Yet within two years of initial settlement at Purrysburg (and much to the chagrin of the pastors at Ebenezer), the first of many marriages between Ebenezer Lutherans and Purrysburg Reformed was solemnized when Mr. Rauner of Ebenezer married an unidentified widow from Purrysburg. Typically before the Reverend Boltzius or his colleague the Reverend Gronau would allow a resident of Ebenezer to marry an outsider, the couple had to publish their notice of intent to marry (called banns) in the hometown of each individual for three consecutive weeks. After the banns had been thus displayed with no objections, the marriage took place.

From this time on a number of marriages between Germans of Ebenezer and Purrysburg citizens were proposed and most of them consummated. In fact, according to the Reverend Boltzius, as late as September 1739, six years after the first Ebenezer settlers arrived, Purrysburg was still the only place where its residents had found brides. The widowed mother of the Uselt daughters, at least three of whom married Ebenezer colonists, received a proposal of marriage from Ebenezer resident Ruprecht Zittrauer. The marriage had to be postponed for want of enough money to pay the debt she incurred in passage to Purrysburg, and the widow died before she could remarry.[54]

Other Ebenezer inhabitants claimed spouses from among Purrysburg families and vice versa. The Theobald Kieffer Sr. family of Purrysburg boasted at least six marriages in the second generation that linked the two towns. Christian Riedelsperger proposed to Mary (Margaritt), Kieffer's oldest daughter, but she spurned his offer and married a Purrysburg Reformed German named Gruber. The Ebenezer resident Thomas Pichler (Bichler) was more successful in his pursuit of Margaretha (Elizabeht Margaritt). They married in June 1740. A third daughter, Elisabetha Catherina (Elizabeht Catarina), eventually married Matthias Zettler in 1741, but not without more than a little prodding from her father and the Reverend Boltzius. The next-youngest daughter, Otellia (Maria Ottellia), accepted a marriage proposal from the Ebenezer locksmith Mr. Schrempf in 1743. Dorothea married Johann Flerl. Kieffer's oldest son, Jacob (Johann Jacob, Jaque), in 1740 wed a Reformed Palatine woman (Anna Elisabeth Depp) who had moved to Ebenezer after a time of domestic service in Charles Town. The other son (Theobald Jr.) married Maria Bacher, the widowed daughter of Mattäus in 1742.

That same year Gottfried Christ, a Jewish tailor from Ebenezer who converted to Lutheranism, married Marguerite, the widowed daughter of Purrysburg tailor Jacob Metsger. She and her three children had relocated to Ebenezer. One of the two brothers of David Zubly (Zübli, Züblin) from Purrysburg (either Ambrosius or Johann Jacob) married Christiana Häussler, servant of the Reverend Boltzius and his family. The Swiss Reformed widow Maria Ihler (Imsler) wed Michael Reiser of Ebenezer. She brought a young daughter into the marriage. Besides Ebenezer, the settlement of Abercorn, Georgia, a few miles down the Savannah River from Purrysburg, boasted at least one marriage between a German male resident of that town and a "Swiss girl" from the South Carolina township. The six-week visit to Purrysburg of a group of 170 Swiss travelers in 1733 resulted in marriage between a wealthy Purrysburg German widower with one child and a female member of the visiting group.[55]

It appears that some of these marriages were between individuals of different ethnic traditions. The "Swiss girl" who married the Abercorn gentleman and the description of Maria Ihler as Swiss Reformed give no definite indication as to the German or French background of these women, but the most intriguing cases are the marriages between Rauner and the Purrysburg widow, the township widower and the female traveler, and the three Purrysburg French-German surname matches because they seem to have involved partners of different linguistic traditions. All the couples were married so soon after arriving in North America that it would be highly unlikely they would have had opportunity to learn a second language if they did not have competence in the second language before arrival.

The intimate bond marriage fosters would appear to be rooted in a common linguistic heritage. Yet, regarding Rauner's wife, Boltzius noted that he and Gronau could not "help her too well with her preparation for Holy Communion because she has not learned to understand the German language well enough"—even though she pays good attention and "gives evidence of grasping the power of the Word in her heart."[56] From the context of Boltzius's words, it would seem that she could understand some German but that her proficiency in it was far from polished.

This unusual case may be explained in one of two ways. First, and most obvious but also most improbable, Rauner took a French-speaking wife, though there is no indication by the pastors as there usually is that she is anything but a German speaker. A second, more plausible possibility would be that the Purrysburg woman was indeed German Reformed and was fluent in a German dialect called *Schwyzertütsch* spoken in the Germanic cantons of the Confederation. The Germans of Purrysburg most likely spoke this dialect. Rauner was not a Salzburger and was probably also fluent in *Schwyzertütsch*. His wife would still have trouble with religious instruction, because the pastors most probably taught in standard or High German.[57]

Recent research by sociolinguists have revealed that Switzerland is largely bilingual and that such bilingualism cuts across other correlates of ethnicity. Consequently, the fact that Purrysburg German-Swiss married French-Swiss does not negate the continuity ethnic identity. It should also be noted that neither do the marriages validate such ethnic awareness, but French or German ethnicity in the Confederation was probably not linked prescriptively to linguistic affiliation. The apparent problems involved in the marriage between the Purrysburg German widower and the French-Swiss female may be explained in the same manner.[58]

Over the years, marriage patterns expanded beyond the immediate vicinity of the township to initiate relationships between Purrysburg families and those from other areas of the region. At the same time, local relational networks continued to extend to other families in the township well into the revolutionary era. Before the first decade of settlement ended, the Netman (Netteman) and Richard families had been joined through marriage as had the Metsgers and De Roches. The Greniere family and Godet family were related by 1745.

Andrew Greniere's widow, Margaret, married into the Rorere (Row) family in the early 1750s. By the 1760s the Purrys, Garveys, and Bulls had intermarried. During the same decade the Barraque (Barrakey) and Gallache families, the Pelot and Sealy families, the Humbert and Hartstone families, and the Mallet, Ravot, Erhart, and Jones families had done likewise. The Mongins married into the well-to-do Harvey and Middleton families, and the Greniere and Mallet families shared marital ties. Other families related by marriage before the Revolution include the Saussy and Kehl families, the Dupont and Flower families, the Donnom and Bourguin families, the Wanderly and Leichtensteiger families, the Bourguin and Chiffelle families, the Imer and Himeli families, and the Chiffelle and Dillon families.

These intermarriage patterns demonstrate that some individuals married outside their ethnic/linguistic group and community. Some also married into some of the most elite families of the colonial period, but the general marriage tendency appears to be within similar ethnic groups and/or within the greater Purrysburg community. Even matches such as the Saussy-Kehl and Mallet-Ravot-Erhart links do not necessarily indicate the loss of ethnic identification among members of these dissimilar but community-related families, as discussed earlier.[59] What may have been the preeminent concern of Purrysburg family members revealed by township marriage patterns was the quest for emotional and economic stability in a hostile environment. The uncertainty of life and the constant specter of death may have led to a tremendous reordering of family relationships and may have drastically reoriented traditional conceptions of intimacy and ethnic solidarity.

IV

The higher mortality rate for children and women during their childbearing years ensured that many Purrysburg families could expect to lose mothers and young children, but the death of husbands and fathers potentially left women and children in an unstable position both legally and emotionally. Faced with the somber realities of lowcountry life and death, South Carolina allowed women to exercise more control over their property than perhaps any other British mainland colony.[60] The effects of the most liberal property laws of the era allowed Purrysburg women a significant amount of autonomy. It is rather commonplace to find them called to bear witness to property transactions for example—whether or not they were literate. Women initiated legally binding transactions from the opening decade of township settlement. They could be single women seeking property in their own right or widowed Purrysburg settlers attempting to protect their family's interests.

Mary Philander, widow of Frederick, appeared before the council in May 1739 to surrender a warrant for 400 acres and a town lot in Purrysburg that her husband had received. She asked for a new one "for the like quantity of land

and lot in the aforesaid township in her own name and her children now living vizt Christian and Martin her sons and Mary her daughter and prays also for the Bounty not having one yet." The council found her request "reasonable" and ordered "that a warrant do issue as prayed for, and that the Bounty be allowed for four together with the charges of running the land." Maria Henry received fifty acres in the township in her own right in December 1739. In 1742, Swiss Protestant Frenetta Cast, a single woman who traveled to South Carolina with her father, mother, and six siblings, requested a warrant for fifty acres in Purrysburg and attested to the fact that no one in her family had yet received land from the province. Although she mentioned the landlessness of her family, her successful petition spoke only to her desire for acreage and it was granted to her on that basis.[61]

Mary Catherin Gebhard's husband, Jacob, arrived in South Carolina in July 1742 during the alarm precipitated by the War of the Austrian Succession (1740–1748) and so at that time could obtain neither land for his family nor the bounty granted to Protestant immigrants. He, Mary, and their children were obliged to go to the country to subsist until proper arrangements could be made. Jacob subsequently died, and in 1744 Mary, on behalf of herself and their five children, obtained an affidavit signed by Purrysburg justice of the peace John Linder in support of her petition to receive the appropriate grant of land and the provincial bounty for which her family was eligible. In the same year Mary Bear, whose husband had received fifty acres in Purrysburg in 1736, sought and received a warrant for 100 acres in Orangeburg for herself and her young child to which they removed in the wake of her husband's death. The widow Mary Magdalen Gignilliat bought 250 acres of Purrysburg land for 700 pounds current money in 1761. Mary Ann Vaigneur of Purrysburg paid John Audibert fifty pounds current money in 1774 for 100 acres in St. Peter's Parish butting land granted previously to Henry Gindrat that Mary Ann now possessed.[62] Richard David Brooks found a similar pattern of female ownership of land in the region extending from Purrysburg northwest up the Savannah River to Augusta in the middle decades of the eighteenth century.[63]

It should be noted that Purrysburg women were often on the other side of land transactions. There are numerous cases of township females selling land in their own right. In October 1752 Mrs. Margaret (Margaretta) Henry approved, with her "X," the sale of seventy-five acres of Purrysburg land to John Rolph Beuninger (John Roldolph Bininger) for fifty pounds current money. Fifteen years later, planter Margaret Henry sold town lot 58 to Purrysburg shoemaker Abraham Jacot. In 1769 Henry, "for the love and affection she bears towards Abraham Bininger son of John Roldolph Bininger," sold to John Rodolph "for 35 shillings and other reasons" seventy-five acres in Purrysburg with the stipulation that she be allowed to live on the land for the duration of her life. Jane Pelot a Purrysburg widow twice over, sold 100 acres of Purrysburg land granted originally to her first husband, Elias Bournant, to Adrian Mayer for 100 pounds current money in September 1767 by making her mark on the document of conveyance. Mayer bought another 150 acres in the township for ten pounds sterling in August 1768 from Elizabeth Nichola(s), widow of Pier(r)e and his only heir.[64]

In addition to being able to buy and sell property without male involvement, women also partnered with males, usually their husbands, in the acquisition and disposition of land. When South Carolina women entered marriage with a dowry that included real or personal property, their consent was often needed for the sale of the property to occur. Sarah Yanam's father, Francis, had received a warrant for 500 acres and a town lot in Purrysburg but died before the grant could be conveyed to him. Sarah married John Chevillette of Purrysburg sometime before December 1736, and together they applied successfully to the council to have the land pass to them. Because the land came through Sarah's father to her, Chevillette could not own the land outright. Their conjugal petition demonstrates the degree of legal autonomy even married women could exercise. When the Purrysburg tailor Jacob Metsger decided to sell Purrysburg town lot 10 to David Giroud in 1742, he did so in partnership with his daughter Marguerite. Giroud paid them fifty pounds current money for the one-acre plot. The following month Giroud purchased an adjacent lot (11) from Joseph Lewis Reymond, but the transaction could not have happened had Reymond's wife, Ann, not given her consent; the lot had fallen to her as part of the estate of her deceased husband, Peter Fourquerant. In like manner, Jann Judith (Judah) Bourguin's agreement to "Quit her Claim Right Title and Dower" of 300 acres of Purryburg land in the winter of 1752 allowed her husband, Benedict Bourguin, to sell the land to planter William Elbert. When David Gautier died, his 400 acres in Purrysburg descended to his only child and heiress, Mary. She married Charles Christopher Peter but retained the land, which they sold together in June 1761. Leonard Reinauer (Rhynower) of Purrysburg married Catherina, the daughter of Nicholas Riger also of Purrysburg. When Riger died, his 250 acres of land fell to her. When the land sold in May 1769, both Leonard and Catherina appeared on the deed of conveyance. So also did Mary Holzendorf when her husband, John Frederick, sold family land in July 1774.[65]

Certainly there were limitations on the property rights of Purrysburg women, just as there were on women throughout colonial South Carolina. One must wonder for example, if expediency rather than a legal commitment to equal protection operated in the province when the only time Purrysburg women appeared on deeds of conveyance other than as witnesses to property transactions occurred when land that had been inherited or conveyed to them was sold, not when property was purchased. Still, it is apparent that in the province, even in the immigrant townships, women enjoyed a greater measure of legal equity than in other colonies in British North America.

V

If the mortality rate in South Carolina contributed to a greater measure of legal autonomy for the women of Purrysburg, a question worth asking is how that mortality rate intersected with the frontier conditions in the township to affect the contours of family life. What did family relationships "look like" in that environment? Life and death on the southern frontier affected families in a host of ways. Some families nurtured relationships that included parents, children, and extended kin. Families also dissolved, some succumbing to pressures generated from without, others appear to have been eroded from within. There is evidence of patriarchal families and of more equitable companionate ones. Some children thrived even in the most desperate of circumstances, whereas others eschewed their families and their heritage. In short, the responses of Purrysburg family members to the situations they faced were as varied as any other place in colonial America.

Even before the accident that killed three of the Metsger children, township life weighed heavily upon the family. In the spring of 1737, an apparently distraught Mrs. Metsger left the township for Charles Town, absconding not only with most of the family's material wealth, but also with the youngest daughter. Through the intercession of the Ebenezer pastors Mrs. Metsger returned sometime later that year, but only for a short time. By midsummer 1738, however, disheartened by reverses the family had suffered, she abducted two of the children and abandoned her husband again during the harvest season. She ended up once more in Charles Town begging on the streets for sustenance. Desperate to unite his family, Jacob sent his nineteen-year-old son to bring them back from the provincial capital. Mrs. Metsger refused to return, but the two children—a ten-year-old girl and a thirteen-year-old boy—departed with their older brother on the ship that took them to their deaths. In the years before 1742, another of the Metsger children, Marguerite, had been married to John Henry De Roche of Purrysburg, had given birth to three children, and was widowed. She then lived in her parents' Purrysburg home but wearied of the arrangement. In February 1742 she married Gottfried Christ of Ebenezer and moved there. Her three children attended the Ebenezer school, and the oldest daughter, who walked on her knees apparently because of rickets, was allowed into the Ebenezer orphanage for better care. A few weeks after Marguerite's marriage, Jacob petitioned the Reverend Boltzius to allow his oldest son to marry an Ebenezer woman and move to the site. That December he asked Boltzius whether he could move to Ebenezer with his remaining children, but he did not say anything about his wife's joining them. By early 1747 he must have been reunited with her as they relocated to the Georgia town. Jacob died three years later, attended by Theobald Kieffer Sr. of Purrysburg, who had known him in Europe. The Reverend Boltzius appears never to have fully accepted either of the Metsgers blaming the faults of their marriage primarily on "that strong-willed and quarrelsome woman."[66]

The husband of an unnamed woman must have had some of the same misgivings about Purrysburg life as did Mrs. Metsger. Shortly after he and his wife arrived at the township, most likely sometime in the mid-1730s, he and another man ventured into the dense woods surrounding Purrysburg and vanished. After an extensive but futile search, both were presumed dead. The woman properly waited one year before accepting a proposal of marriage. Soon after her second marriage, she discovered that her first husband and the man with whom he had disappeared were very much alive and working on a plantation near Charles Town. Her first husband had inquired of her from a mutual acquaintance in Purrysburg, but he gave no indication that he wished her to join him or that he would soon be returning to her. In the midst of marital problems with her second husband, however, she hoped for a speedy reunion.[67] Most likely the first husband tired of the effort required to make a success of frontier living and "got lost in the woods" as a pretext for leaving the township—not to mention his familial responsibilities. His scheme served to dissolve one marriage and seriously weaken a second.

Perhaps Mrs. Reck of Purrysburg entertained some hope that her husband would "get lost in the woods," for his abusive behavior made her life miserable. John Jacob Reck worked a great deal of the time in Ebenezer making shoes for the German settlers while simultaneously making a nuisance of himself in their midst. On one occasion after Reck had offended the sensibilities of the Salzburg Lutherans, the Reverend Boltzius traveled to Purrysburg to confront him personally. The pastor failed to find Reck at home, but he met a disconsolate Mrs. Reck at the door of their home. She recounted the sad results of her husband's profligate ways upon their family life, most especially poverty so devastating that she and the children lacked adequate food, clothing, and other necessities. She concluded by confiding to Boltzius that Reck had threatened to beat her and then desert the family for the West Indies if she told the pastor about his exploits. He apparently made good his threat, at least temporarily relocating in Ebenezer and enrolling their son in the Ebenezer school. Although we have relatively few incidents of desertion among Purrysburg families, the equivalent paucity of available records suggests that this method of terminating, at least temporarily, an undesirable marriage when divorce was not an option was as prevalent for both sexes in the township as it was in the Chesapeake.[68]

Purrysburg families were also wrenched apart by the presence of grinding poverty. On one occasion a family from the township took drastic action. The husband could not earn enough to support the entire family, so while the father and his young son traveled to Old Ebenezer to find work (there were two Ebenezer settlements by 1736), the wife and mother hired herself out as a domestic servant. The daughter also had to be given into service for several years. By 1738 only the father and son lived together, and the father hoped that the boy would be accepted at the Ebenezer school so that he might at least receive an education, because he did not have a family to nurture him.[69]

Disciplinary troubles with children sometimes connected Purrysburg and Ebenezer Germans. The widow Anna Barbara Francke had behavioral problems with her fatherless son, Johann, who was taken in by the Ebenezer school and lodged there with a Salzburger family. Francke admonished the schoolmaster to be strict with her son so he might benefit from the experience. By the winter of 1737, however, Johann had already run away to his mother's home across the Savannah River three times. He left her to become an Indian trader, finally returning to settle in Ebenezer in 1750. The Purrysburg widow who married Mr. Rauner of Ebenezer had a son by her previous husband. By accounts the son could not be controlled. He ran away from a Savannah craftsman to whom he had been apprenticed, traveled by boat to Purrysburg, and then made his way back to his mother and stepfather. Neither Rauner nor his wife could discipline the boy, which doubtless caused family problems and also provided the pretext for Boltzius's condemnation of Rauner's "rash" marriage to an outlander in 1735.[70] Discipline served a public as well as private purpose in places such as Purrysburg, for when successfully achieved it strengthened communal bonds. As elsewhere in colonial America, however, when conflict arose it could disrupt family and wider community relationships.[71]

Perhaps it was a combination of pastoral exhortation and family difficulties that led Mrs. Rauner to the Purrysburg plantation of a French-speaking seller of wine and rum in 1738, where she proceeded to drink herself into a stupor. Her husband also began frequenting the place and created various disorders of his own. He eventually terminated his visits and resolved to stop selling bread in Ebenezer for the Purrysburg vendor. When war came to the province in 1740, Rauner took up arms for South Carolina. His wife planned to follow him with her now fourteen-year-old son in tow but hoped to leave her daughter behind in the Ebenezer orphanage. Michael Rieser, who married Maria Ihler, another Purrysburg German widow, became disillusioned with his life in Ebenezer, sold some of his cattle, and then abruptly hired himself out either as a rower on an English trading boat or as a soldier at Fort Augustine in 1738. Whatever his new vocation, his Purrysburg wife, left alone at Ebenezer, in a real sense became a widow for the second time. Drunkenness, disorderly conduct, unruly children, and desertion severely conditioned the possibilities for family intimacy in the township.[72]

Cordial, if less than equalitarian, family relationships were further disrupted when underlying tensions surfaced during times of crisis. Two husbands preceded Marguerite (Metsger) Christ in death, but when she approached the end of her life in the fall of 1750, she still had two underage children, who needed a stable upbringing and education. By this time most of her immediate family had moved from Purrysburg to Ebenezer, and she believed her siblings "would like to take them and use them in their households." Fearing that such an arrangement would not be to their benefit, Marguerite secured a pledge from the Reverend Boltzius to care for them. One can only imagine how her relatives received news of this agreement.[73] An even more complicated situation confronted two generations of the Kieffer and Pichler families the following year. It will be recalled that Thomas Pichler married Margaretha Kieffer in June 1740. They had a daughter together before Margaretha died. Pichler then married into an Ebenezer family, but he died in 1751, leaving behind the daughter, now nine years old. Theobald Sr.'s wife, the child's grandmother, wanted her to come live with her grandparents on their Purrysburg plantation. On his deathbed, however, Pichler requested that Boltzius intercede on behalf of his child to keep her in Ebenezer at all costs, even if it meant that she could not live with her stepmother and had to be given to the care of an Ebenezer couple. Such a circumstance was a distinct possibility; Pichler's second wife was impoverished and could not provide for her two other children. When Boltzius shared the situation with Theobald and his wife, a potentially nasty custody battle was averted. It appears that Pichler's wife's mother took in the widow and her children and was able to provide for them all.[74]

Children fortunate enough to have both birth parents alive at their majority could provide just as much cause for parental concern, though of a somewhat different nature. In the spring of 1741, Elisabetha Catherina Kieffer promised to marry Matthias Zettler of Ebenezer after he proposed to her one day at her parents' Purrysburg plantation while her parents were out. She consented, and later the couple went to Theobald Sr. and his wife for their approval. A short time later Elisabetha thought better of her decision and sought to break the engagement. Kieffer tried to convince his daughter that she had an obligation to keep her word. After his time with her, Theobald was sure that she would listen to reason and told the Reverend Boltzius she would honor her earlier pledge. He reckoned without Elisabetha's strong will, however, and in early May he appealed to the Reverend Boltzius to conduct a conversation with the entire family to convince Elisabetha of her duty. At this point Zettler appears to have had enough and called off the marriage. Boltzius counseled Kieffer to "perform his fatherly functions on her," because from his perspective Elisabetha was deserving of punishment for the disruptions she had caused. Whether it was the "deserving punishment" her father meted out, further "discussions" with her parents, or a sincere reconsideration of Zettler's proposal, Elisabetha subsequently consented to marry him and did so on 19 May. This episode, when coupled with disciplinary problems of younger adolescents discussed earlier, lends credence to the generalization that Purryburg parents shared some loss of authority, as did their compatriots in colonial Maryland and Virginia, both in terms of courting proprieties and disciplinary issues.[75]

While strong-willed children, multiple marriages, and wayward parents affected nuclear and extended family units, marital discord could also threaten extended family networks. Anna Elisabeth Depp(e) came from a Reformed family that resided in Orangeburg Township. She served an indenture in Charles Town and somehow became acquainted with Jacob Kieffer, perhaps through a mutual friend. When he asked for her hand in marriage, she accepted. The marriage took place in April 1740. In September Jacob hoped to bring his mother-in-law from Orangeburg to live in Ebenezer so she could be closer to her daughter just across the river in Purrysburg. That same month Anna secretly gave birth to a premature, stillborn infant. Soon afterward, she began to manifest troubling behavior that caught the attention of her new husband. By the following January, Anna's brother Valentin(e) Depp, a German shoemaker, appears to have moved to Purrysburg. In February 1741 Jacob became concerned enough about his wife's restless state to ask the Reverend Boltzius to intercede. Soon the source of her anxiety became clear. She admitted that while in Charles Town she had promised to marry a Reformed German tailor there. The marriage never took place, though the couple consummated their relationship. She also confessed to aborting the unwanted child. Kieffer evidently knew the tailor (the mutual friend?) and appears to have questioned Anna on numerous occasions about him. She repeatedly denied that she was acquainted with him. By March her psychological condition deteriorated and began to affect not only her relationship with Jacob, but also with the rest of her in-laws. In April she attempted to escape to Charles Town. At this point it appears that Boltzius shared with Kieffer the basis for her anxiety, which by the end of the month seems to have brought her to the brink of nervous collapse. On 2 May Theobald Sr., probably also reeling from the impasse with Elisabetha, asked the Reverend Boltzius to visit Jacob at his Purrysburg plantation to try to assist them in what had become an issue of concern for the entire family. The tensions involved in dealing with Anna's deception and subsequent mental condition strained Jacob's relationship with his siblings. By the summer of 1741 Jacob and Anna's marital stress may have begun to affect negatively the new marriage of Elisabetha and Matthias Zettler. Boltzius noted that there had been exchanges between the two couples and a discernible level of marital strife between the newlyweds. Jacob left Purrysburg on 5 July for Charles Town, ostensibly to negotiate a matter with provincial leaders. Kieffer, however, managed to visit the tailor, who boasted to him of sleeping with his wife. The tailor died a few days after Kieffer's visit. He then traveled to Orangeburg to visit Anna's mother. One can only surmise what he accomplished on the trip or what occurred between Jacob and Anna upon his return in mid-August. The Reverend Boltzius observed that by the late summer both Jacob and Anna exhibited a renewed spiritual vigor. After her repentance before the Ebenezer congregation—she was to be confirmed in the Lutheran Church—the indiscretions of the past were laid to rest, and harmony appears to have returned to the Kieffer families—at least for a season. She gave birth to their son in November.[76]

During that season the fledgling marriage of Elisabetha and Matthias Zettler got off to a less than auspicious start. From the beginning Boltzius believed there were problems with the union and tried to address them with Elisabetha in private conversations and sometimes with Matthias present. In his journal he wrote of "inconstancy" on both sides of the marriage, but his opprobrium was reserved almost exclusively for Elizabetha. It is impossible to tell whether the marital problems of her brother and sister-in-law had anything to do with Boltzius's assessment of Elisabetha's character or the state of the marriage. Perhaps it was a combination of Boltzius's admonitions, Jacob and Anna's marital struggles, and her own state of mind that contributed to a sickness that manifested itself in severe physical symptoms as well as acute homesickness. Her condition worsened so much over three week's time that she feared for her life and salvation. In early February 1742 Theobald Sr. took his daughter back to his Purrysburg plantation to recuperate, promising to return her to Matthias in a few days.[77]

Crises that reached into family and extended kin networks at Purrysburg could also be triggered by the accumulation and disposition of real or personal property. Most often the crisis became discernible at the time of death, when the disbursement of estates revealed vast inequities in the bequests of the decedent. Rifts could also develop over the ways funds were spent or land transactions managed.

David and Helena Zubly, from St. Gall in the Swiss Confederation, were among the few that arrived in South Carolina in the wake of Purry's ill-fated attempt at settlement in 1724. They and David's brothers Ambrosius (Ambrose) and Johann Jacob settled in the township by the mid-1730s. By 1739 Ambrosius and Johann appear to have acquired a small plantation in Georgia near Ebenezer and divided their time between it and their brother David's plantation in Purrysburg. David, the most prosperous of the three, alternated between supporting his brothers and tiring of their persistent requests for aid. By 1739 David seems to have had enough and stopped supporting them, though they appear to have remained on speaking terms. Ambrosius even stayed with David and his family for an extended period in 1740. The Reverend Boltzius indicated in 1741 that, from his perspective, the disparity in capital accumulation did not bother Ambrosius or Johann because of the spiritual benefits they gained from the Ebenezer clerics. Although one might like to take Boltzius's optimistic report at face value, the fact that one brother left the area before December 1742 and that David continued his entrepreneurial success at least until the late 1740s could certainly indicate at least some source of tension in the family.[78]

Resentment at the quality of life on the frontier could explode into bitterly contested battles over the validity of property transactions, a family member's will, or the disbursement of a legacy built upon the toil and sacrifice of all family members. Johann (John) James Mohr (Moore) had been granted 200 acres of land in Purrysburg in September 1738. When he died, his son Jacob was a child. Jacob's mother placed him in the care of the Ebenezer pastors and then sold some of Johann's land, perhaps to meet her son's expenses. Years later, when Jacob became a Georgia planter, he sold the entire 200-acre tract to Willoughby Pugh, arguing that the previous sale of a portion of the land was invalid because not only was he underage when his mother sold the parcel, but also payment for it was never received. Mohr's resentment toward his mother for selling the land without his consent, even though he was a minor at the time of sale, remained palpable even a quarter century after the fact.[79] When Andrew Hendrie of Purrysburg died in 1766, his wife, Jean Marie, through Charles Pinckney, her lawyer, legally blocked the probate of his estate by challenging his competence to author a valid will. The caveat against Hendrie's will forced the judge to call witnesses cited in the will to testify concerning Hendrie's faculties. Everything was found to be fully in order. The estate in question, valued at nearly 3,750 pounds consisted of various home furnishings, tools, and books as well as one house and two lots, presumably his Purrysburg property. His largest investment, however, was in fourteen black slaves valued at more than 3,200 pounds. Perhaps the slaves were what Mrs. Hendrie was attempting to secure for herself, because an inventory of her estate dated 24 August 1773 contained meager furnishings and only two slaves, one of which was claimed by her Purrysburg neighbor, David Saussy. The total estate carried an appraised value of only 1,772 pounds, less than one half of the total value of her husband's estate only six years earlier. Andrew had obviously decided against conveying his estate in its entirety to his wife.[80]

A similar case reached the Court of Ordinary in 1770 concerning the will of David Mongin. In this case both Mongin's wife, Mary Ann, and his son, David, in separate court actions contested the proving of the will. Mary Ann, represented by her Purrysburg neighbor Abraham Ravot, entered a caveat against the execution of the will until her case could be heard before the governor of the Court of Ordinary. A short time later David, represented by his kinsman Robert Harvey, contested the will. The court then issued a special citation to John Lewis Bourguin and William Mongin to testify as the named executors of Mongin's estate. Bourguin and William Mongin appeared before Governor Montagu on 15 February 1771. After testimony and close examination of all the evidence, the judge ruled that Mongin was in control of his faculties at the time he authored the will and that the document should stand as his final will and testament.

It is not stated explicitly why Mongin's wife and son would contest the disbursement of the estate. Closer examination of the will in question, however, discloses a probable motive. Mongin's total estate was appraised at well over 10,000 pounds—a substantial sum. The estate included thirty-eight black slaves, who appear to be in family groups and appraised at approximately 9,700 pounds. Among his other belongings were farm tools, two feather beds, china, fine walnut and mahogany furniture, and cooper's and watchmaker's implements. Of this large estate Mongin willed only 500 pounds to his son David for his education, to be paid three years after the elder Mongin's death. Mary Ann received a 1,000-pound stipend, also to be paid three years after Mongin's demise, one slave named Lizzet, and one of his feather beds. Mongin also willed that she could continue to reside at his plantation during her widowhood and receive a quarter of the crop produced on the land as long as the estate remained intact. Except for a few small bequests, Mongin gave the sizable remainder of his estate to his sons William and John and his daughter Jane. It appears that son David felt particularly dissatisfied because of the inconsequential amount of his legacy in light of the size of the total estate. To a lesser degree the same assessment led Mary Ann to persuade Abraham Ravot to enter a caveat on her behalf. Why Ravot chose to become involved cannot be ascertained, but Harvey's complicity with David's case probably issued from his desire to share in the disbursement should his kinsman receive a positive ruling from the judge. It does not appear that Mary Ann bore any ill will toward the executors of her husband's estate, for, upon her death in September 1771, the Court of Ordinary named John Lewis Bourguin as her closest friend to administer her estate. Mary Ann's entire estate consisted only of a few dishes, a spinning wheel, some livestock, a little silver, Lizzet, and the bed David willed to her. The entire value of her worldly possessions amounted to only 495 pounds. Why Mongin chose to dispose of his estate in such an inequitable manner is unknown, but the conduct of Mary Ann and David seems understandable in light of the fact that building the estate on the frontier was a family affair, yet the entire family did not share equally in its disbursement.[81] The cases also belie the findings of relatively equitable divisions of estates in Maryland and in Middlesex County, Virginia. Because of the fragmentary nature of the Purrysburg sources, we can only speculate as to the practice there of using unequal estate dispersal to control family members, a practice scholars have observed in Massachusetts, Virginia, Maryland, and other regions of South Carolina.[82]

In the cases cited above, the possession of wealth, as well as the fear of poverty, provided the context for less than sanguine family relationships. But Purrysburg families also exemplified the generous and gracious spirit that one would expect to find in truly companionate relationships that engendered respect and love among family members. Though entitled to at least 300 acres of Purrysburg land (owing to the size of his family), David Huguenin chose to claim only the headright alltoment for his wife, Susanna, and himself. Thus the couple's four children shared ownership of the remaining 200 acres, which was platted to them in June 1733. Immediately after the council granted him a warrant for 350 acres of land "in or near Purrysburg or about Indianfield Swamp" in November 1754, David Rumpf sought and gained a second warrant for 400 acres in Purrysburg. He received the first grant based upon the size of his nuclear family (himself, his wife, and five children) and the second because of his ownership of eight slaves. In the second petition Rumpf noted that he was "desirous of settling some of his family separate from his own plantation." Although he could have petitioned for one grant of 750 acres, Rumpf—like David Hugenin—chose to divide his headright acreage to care for other family members.[83] Mary Girardin of Purrysburg bequeathed her entire estate to her five children, four of whom (John, Henry, David, and Elizabeth) were the children of her deceased husband, David Giroud, and one, Ann Fulmer, from another marriage. She made no distinction between the children and stipulated specifically that "all needs to be equally shared among them."[84]

The affectionate bonds of kinship among Purrysburg families went beyond the nuclear ties of husbands, wives, and children to include extended family members. Lewis Winkler agreed to hold in trust for his nephew Nicholas Winkler Jr.'s sole use, 350 acres of Purrysburg land sold to him for 100 pounds current money by his brother, Nicholas Sr., in September 1768. The mutuality exhibited by his parents, David and Susanna, was mirrored by David Huguenin Jr., who moved to St. Philip's Parish, Georgia, and came into sole possession of his family's Purrysburg acreage. In 1770, "in consideration of the love and affection which he beareth and hath toward . . . Abraham Ravot his nephew," Huguenin conveyed the entire parcel to Ravot for a token ten pounds current money. A year later, in return only for unnamed "valuable considerations," David Raymond (Reymond) of Purrysburg conveyed town lot 112 jointly to his brothers John and Peter. Heirs of John Frederick Holzendorf (William Holzendorf and Mary, his wife) still lived in Purrysburg in 1774 and sold a portion of the land granted to their ancestor John Frederick Holzendorf to his namesake, a Purrysburg tavern-keeper, for ten pounds current money.[85]

Familylike relationships existed among some Purrysburg residents who were not related by blood or marriage. For some time prior to November 1751, Purrysburg tailor Etienn(e) (Stephen) Vaigneur and his wife had taken care of their neighbor Abraham Matthey during what must have been an extended illness and convalescence. In a conveyance written in French and unique in the records of the township, Matthey gave all his possessions to the couple, "En consideration et des peines que Mr. Vaigneur et sa femme sesont donnè et se donne encore en maladie" without restrictions. In June 1769, for the sum of "35 shillings and other reasons," Margaret (Margarita) Henry sold seventy-five acres in Purrysburg to John Rodolph Bininger in trust for his son Abraham. The only stipulation for her generous bequest to a young man that bore no direct relationship to her family was that John and Abraham allowed her to occupy the land during her lifetime.[86]

It is the relationship between Gideon Mallet and his family members that most clearly illustrates that, even amid the disruption and uncertainty of life on the southern frontier, there continued to exist those families who found contentment and stability. At Mallet's death in the early 1770s, his estate was appraised at just over 1,800 pounds and included considerable livestock, a modest home with furnishings, and four slaves. Unlike any other Purrysburg male decedent for whom records exist, Mallet gave his wife, Mary Lombard, his entire estate after debts were paid, excluding only a small bond due his granddaughter Priscilla Jones. He lovingly described "the perfect union which has subsisted between her and me now nigh fifty years that we have lived together to this day." In conveying all his estate to her, Mallet also released her from "having to make an inventory of it or render any account of it whatever." He also gave her full power to "sell anything she pleases of the premises." In addition, he freed her from having to take the counsel of her male children by stipulating that "she may take the advice of her children or not as she thinks proper." He did encourage her to allow their son Daniel some consideration as, for example, some of the produce of the land, but in this family it seems logical to assume that the son would play an integral role in the ongoing work of the Mallet plantation. To assure conveyance to his progeny should his wife decide to keep the land, Mallet provided that the children (one son and two daughters) would share equally in the estate after the death of their mother and after all debts were paid. Finally, in a generational passing of the mantle, Gideon desired that Daniel receive his "clothes, guns, and linens" immediately upon his death. The personal regard for each family member clearly demonstrated by Mallet's equal provision for all illustrates that although families in Purrysburg suffered hardships of all sorts, companionate familial bonds could still be nurtured.[87]

A tangible indication of the regard Purrysburg family members held for each other was the care they took in maintaining the township cemetery. More than two generations after the founding of Purrysburg, a surveyor of the post roads, Ebenezer Hazard, noted the unique character of the cemetery during a visit in 1778: "It is customary in North and South Carolina for those who can afford it to fix poles round the graves of their deceased relations; In Purrysburgh they have improved upon this custom and generally add a tree, which is planted within the poles. I observed among the rest a number of peach trees. I suppose this is an allusion of the yews and cypresses of the ancients."[88]

VI

For Purrysburg, community truly began with family for most of the immigrants. Because the people of the township essentially consisted of family groups, most of whom probably had little if any contact with each other before setting sail for South Carolina, families provided an instant community network. As in colonial Virginia, families were most often nuclear, though relatives might live close by and occupy an integral place in the hierarchy of community. Initially, relational webs existed only at this most local of levels, and even they were forced to accommodate to the high mortality rate in the South and the implications of that statistic for family life. Coping with death in Purrysburg was probably much less influenced by friendships outside the family, especially in the early years, than was the case in the Chesapeake because of ethnic insularity.[89]

By the mid-1730s family networks began to expand outward within the township and vertically beyond the township to nearby villages and plantations.

Some of the settlers apparently married beyond cultural boundaries while not necessarily erasing all ethnic lines of distinction. Even those Purrysburg family members who married into substantial English planting families, such as the Garveys, Bulls, Middletons, and Harveys, maintained linkages with families of similar ethnic or linguistic affinities. It might also be noted that it appears to have been the more up-and-coming township families (Purrys, Mongins, Chiffelles) who extended those marital networks to other ethnic groups, while most of the middling sort for whom records remain continued to maintain primary affiliations with families of similar ethnicity in the local area.[90]

Crises, in whatever form they appeared, severely tested the elasticity of these most intimate of all relationships. The extant evidence at least suggests that the decline in parental authority observed elsewhere in the southern colonies also existed to some extent in Purrysburg. It also appears that some patriarchal males in Purrysburg, like males elsewhere, may have used the disbursing of their estates as the ultimate power play to reward filial loyalty or punish disobedience.

On the other hand, there is ample evidence to buttress the contention that more equitable family arrangements and companionate marriages were not unknown in the township. In his study of Plymouth colony, John Demos found only one example of expressed affection in all the records he studied. Yet he concluded that, because he found so few cases of disharmony in such a large population, at least marital conflict appears to have been minimal, indicating a perceptible movement toward the companionate ideal. Lorena Walsh's study of seventeenth-century Maryland implies the same trend.[91] Might not the same be said of Purrysburg? Perhaps the companionate nature of marriage did exist on a continuum, becoming more visible as time progressed. Burton, for example, discovered nineteenth-century Edgefield County families to be very close and affectionate. He also found Edgefield parents generally unwilling to interfere in the marital choices of their children—another sign of the emergence of the affectionate family of the Victorian era.[92]

Whatever else might be said about Purrysburg family life, it is obvious that the transition from Old World to New, at the very least, reordered family values and traditions. When these values and traditions were inevitably refracted through the lens of the Purrysburg environment, they refocused in new forms that resulted in an expanding network of relationships unlike any these immigrant families had experienced before.

FOUR

The Search for a Sacred Community

If the family supplied the most intimate of relational clusters in the colonial period, the church served to weld the local community of families together in relationship to each other through its spiritual and secular agencies. Bernard Bailyn and Philip D. Morgan argue that "in the broader cultural realm there was no more significant sphere of contact than religion" during this formative period.[1] Rooted deeply in the particular sociocultural contexts of its practitioners, religious activity, no matter what its expression, embodied, reflected, and determined personal aspirations and community values. While shaping the social world in which they existed, colonial religious institutions were simultaneously altered by the New World environment in ways that rendered them barely recognizable to their European counterparts. Still, however much Christianity had to be refracted off the challenging physical and multicultural terrain of British North America, it gained power and exerted its vital influence well beyond the spiritual realm throughout the colonial era.[2] The historian of religion Erskine Clark reminds us that "religion is not an autonomous cultural phenomenon but is rooted in a particular social reality" and as such helps shape the social context in which a people live. Consequently, "religious symbols are both a model *of* reality and a model *for* reality."[3]

In colonial New England, the Puritan congregation was the very basis for the existence of the social covenant. Its doctrines and rituals affirmed and renewed the covenant relationship that existed between neighbors and friends. The church drew townspeople to each other in relational networks as they expressed their corporate desire to draw nearer to God. The powerful ability of the church to focus the lives of its communicants on community welfare meant that for all intents and purposes congregation and community were coterminous. The social contract was after all authored in heaven as well as in Massachusetts.[4] Southern Anglicanism may have been somewhat less aggressive in a spiritual sense than its New England counterpart, but the reach of its religious and secular functions inexorably pried busy agrarians from their plantations with amazing regularity. The southern parish church provided the nexus around which life revolved. Local government business was conducted there, and notices of social and cultural events might well be tacked to the door of the church and often took place there. The Anglican Church may not have formally composed a theological rationale for the necessity of community life, yet it was through the parish and the church that southern colonists forged the interpersonal connections by which they identified themselves as living common lives.[5]

Unfortunately for the immigrants of Purrysburg Township, the church establishment there differed markedly from either precedent. In fact, one could argue that the church in all its roles as spiritual guide, educator, civic political force, and socializing agent posed a most formidable barrier to the creation of the relational networks central to the development of a vibrant local community in Purrysburg. Because of the frontier setting and of the ethnic and confessional diversity of township citizens, the religious establishment in Purrysburg actually inhibited local community development for nearly thirty years. The nature of religious leadership forced the immigrants to decide between cultural or religious traditions. Their ethnic heritage had to be accommodated to a narrow range of expressions, effectively rending the fabric of both religious and cultural community life. The limited religious options available to Purry's colonists fractured the township as they led to the creation of relationships with settlers in surrounding towns and villages before relationships had opportunity to flourish with neighbors in Purrysburg. It is therefore the spiritual pilgrimage of Purrysburg immigrants and their descendants that most graphically portrays the selective reordering of relationships necessitated by the imperatives of life on the southern frontier made all the more onerous by Purry's shortsighted decisions and the vicissitudes of provincial leadership.

The multicultural context of Purrysburg as it evolved over time makes concrete determination of religious affinity as a determinant of ethnic consciousness and community identity more difficult than would be the case if the settlement were a more ethnically homogenous society. The ambiguous nature of what it meant to be Swiss compounds the problem. An institutional approach to the measurement of these factors (for example the assessment of ethnicity based on the existence or absence of certain social and/or cultural institutions) might be useful in other cases. Such a methodology, however, would be inappropriate in analyzing the Purrysburg community unless the peculiar circumstances surrounding both the immigrants who settled there and the environment in which they settled were examined. For example, the emphasis on the de jure existence of an Anglican church building at Purrysburg rather than the de facto functioning of religious practice in the township has completely skirted the issue of the social and educative tasks of the church as it actually functioned as well as religious practice's role in nurturing or rupturing the multiethnic community. It has also bypassed the crucial fact that a large percentage of Purrysburg settlers were of the Reformed confession. What then of their religious life? Thus, a central problem in examining the religious history of Purrysburg has been and remains that of a focus that remains too narrowly concerned with the presence or absence of major religious structures as well as an oversimplification of or disinterest in the significant functional modifications township colonists made to the exercise of religious faith over the course of the eighteenth century. The proclivity of scholars to focus upon the study of only one or the other of the two major cultural/linguistic groups that settled Purrysburg has led to more institutional rather than social analysis—that is more on the existence of institutional forms than on their social function. This tendency has served to obscure both the true nature of the settlement as a religious community and the individuals who populated it.[6]

I

Christianity exerted a powerful and highly complex influence in the multiethnic context of Purrysburg Township. Its influence in the lives of the settlers proceeded directly from their diverse European Protestant heritages. Although it is generally true that ethnically diverse groups sharing the same confession, whether Reformed or Lutheran, viewed each other as spiritual kin, the same cannot be said about the relationships between Reformed and Lutheran. Confessional religious animosity even among ethnically similar cultural and linguistic groups loosened the tie of blood and culture and, in some cases, rivaled and even surpassed the divisiveness of the Protestant-Catholic schism.[7]

As people of the Reformed tradition journeyed to North America, much of the religious nomenclature born of ethnic or national distinctions eventually lost its European meaning and was, by and large, subsumed under the general confessional title "Reformed." The parishioners of the French Huguenot Church of Charles Town had no qualms about calling the pastor of the Walloon Church of London to serve them. Nor did the members of the Independent Church of the same city face a problem by calling the Purrysburg-born German Reformed pastor the Reverend John (Johann) Joachim Zubly to assist them as an interim minister in 1750. He had been called on in 1748 to serve the Presbyterian Church of Cainhoy and was further involved with the Independent Church of Charles Town as well as other Reformed churches in South Carolina and Georgia into the 1770s. Thus, in the colonial experience of South Carolina, some indicators of community solidarity (linguistic and cultural commonality) were held in abeyance so that another (affinity with a particular religious confession) could continue.[8]

Excluding a minor influx of English settlers during the early years, the Purrysburg community consisted chiefly of German and French speakers of the Reformed confession, mostly from the Swiss Confederation, though the difficulty of determining which of them were Swiss citizens and which of them were members of the substantial Calvinist Huguenot refugee population from France has already been established. Two dozen or so of the township residents appear to have emigrated from the southern German states, perhaps some even from Salzburg, and were by confession Pietists, while a few others came from the Reformed area of Piedmont. When a much larger contingent of Salzburgers settled in Ebenezer, Georgia, about twelve miles from Purrysburg, the physical proximity of Ebenezer to Purrysburg, coupled with cultural and linguistic traditions shared by many of the German-speaking inhabitants of both communities, would seem to have portended a warm and mutual exchange between the two isolated islands of frontier settlement.[9]

But if the ethnic ties of common culture and language presaged the formation of a cohesive bond between these immigrants, religious tradition threatened any attempt to fashion such a connection, for the Pietists maintained a European-bred antipathy toward those of the Reformed fold.[10] While in Europe, the Salzburg Lutherans had on occasion experienced mistreatment by those of the German Reformed confession, and they naturally approached the Reformed Germans of Purrysburg with trepidation, perhaps fearing similar treatment. Aside from strained social relationships, numerous theological differences between the confessions were considered unbridgeable—at least by the Salzburg clergy. As Pietists the Salzburgers placed no value on rank, position, or appearance of upright living as evidence of a close relationship with Christ. For them the inner spirit and the subjective attitude of the heart toward God, which is objectively unknowable to others, governed the individual's relationship with God. To those of the Reformed confession, outward upright living at least *suggested* an inward conviction of salvation. In addition to this fundamental disagreement concerning the nature of salvation, the two confessions also differed theologically about God's sovereignty, humanity's free will, the nature of God's grace, and the celebration of Holy Communion (the Eucharist). Lutheran teaching on these doctrines was so central to the Pietist conception of "true Christianity" that any deviation signaled apostasy. Hence, any theological tenets shared with Calvinists were considered relatively inconsequential if they did not also include these doctrines.[11]

Such religious predispositions did not bode well for amicable relationships between Purrysburg neighbors. For example, in June 1742 some Reformed inhabitants of Purrysburg conveyed two English visitors to the Pietist settlement and returned on Sunday morning, perhaps to attend worship back in Purrysburg. The Reverend Boltzius, however, viewed their early departure quite differently. He noted that, "although they had the opportunity to celebrate Sunday with us here and to learn something from God's Word for the Salvation of their souls, they did not avail themselves of it." Boltzius concluded, "This downright despicable scorn of God's law and word cannot possibly drag on into the future without retribution."[12] A few years later a Reformed widow from Purrysburg visited Boltzius to speak about the state of her soul. Boltzius recounted in his journal that "she told me that she had resolved to talk to me regarding her soul's condition but was afraid she would be too ignorant for such a conversation because she was Reformed."[13]

If theological questions prompted the Salzburg Pietist pastors to keep their distance from Purrysburg, it would seem that shared theology between the French Reformed and German Reformed at the township might form the basis for a functional interethnic community, but existing British policy regarding religion in South Carolina complicated further the development of that community. Until 1704 religious parity existed in South Carolina as set forth in the Fundamental Constitutions. In May of that year, however, because it was observed that matters of religion in the Commons House "hath often caused great contentions and animosities in this Province and hath very much obstructed public business," legislators passed the Exclusion Act by a one-vote majority. This act barred non-Anglicans from serving in the Commons House. When the Establishment Act followed in November, the Anglican Church achieved status as the only recognized church in the colony. This discriminatory legislation froze all Dissenters out of full political participation and also threatened the existence of their churches. Perhaps because of the vehement opposition that immediately gripped the province, Parliament disallowed the Exclusion Act. Governor Johnson, as always sensing which way to jump and when, asked for and received the repeal of both acts by the Commons House. On the same day they were repealed (30 November 1706), however, the house passed another more tolerant act.[14]

The Church Act of 1706, though more conciliatory in tone than either of the acts of 1704, served essentially the same function as the act of establishment. It divided South Carolina into parishes, each of which was to be administered by Anglican priests reciting Anglican liturgy from Anglican prayer books and psalters performing the sacraments according to Anglican precedent. Nine church officers chosen annually on Easter Monday by Anglican freeholders assumed leadership in the parishes that elected them. Two churchwardens were charged with the maintenance of church property and the procurement of necessary supplies, such as bread and wine, for communion. They also enforced laws regarding the Sabbath and confiscated firearms from those entering the church. It fell to the churchwardens to keep the parish register and also to report to the vestry those communicants who entertained unorthodox theological views, exhibited immoral behavior, or failed to attend services regularly. Churchwardens also managed the conduct of elections for parish representation to the Commons House of Assembly. The seven-member vestry supervised the work of the churchwardens and held ultimate responsibility for keeping the register of parish births, marriages, and deaths. Vestry members were also charged with electing by majority vote a sexton and a clerk, who were paid a small stipend. The vestry exerted rather extensive authority over local affairs as the eighteenth century progressed. After 1712 it took over from commissions appointed by the Commons House the responsibility of caring for the parish poor, which included the raising of the poor tax and disbursement of the funds collected. Also after 1712 the vestries were given the added task of building parish schools with public monies and hiring schoolmasters. On occasion vestries exercised some judicial and policing powers although not specifically empowered to do so. The vestry was required by the Church

Act to meet at least four times per year—more if deemed necessary. Failure to appear resulted in a fine of ten shillings. All church officers were required to own taxable property in their own right in the parish from which they received election and to be members of the Church of England. The public treasury was to assume responsibility for payment of the priest's salary and for the construction of parish church buildings.[15]

The legal establishment of the Anglican Church under the Church Act of 1706 did not necessarily preclude the surreptitious continuation of rival Protestant creeds while simultaneously adhering to the forms of Anglicanism. This "double identity dissent" characterized the French Huguenots in South Carolina, but it also appeared elsewhere in colonial America, perhaps most notably among immigrant communities in Rowan, Guilford, and Mecklenburg Counties in North Carolina. Daniel Thorp, a historian of the Moravian usurpation of Anglican authority in Dobbs Parish, North Carolina, found that Presbyterian, Baptist, and various German sectarians, not only "frequently gained control of frontier vestries," but also "effectively disestablished the established church."[16] In South Carolina, according to the Church Act, the French-speaking residents of St. Denis and St. James could use a French translation of the Anglican prayer book as long as necessary because of the language barrier, but they were still bound by law to use *only* the translated Anglican prayer book. Although all Huguenot churches except the one in Charles Town were supposedly fully Anglicanized by the third decade of the eighteenth century, French Anglican ministers still maintained portions of the Huguenot Reformed confession even after 1730. Many French Reformed ministers took Anglican orders in light of the Church Act, but some of these Anglicanized Calvinists claimed the right to administer the sacraments according to the Huguenot polity and did so, often with the encouragement of their parishioners. Most notable among them during Commissary Gideon Johnston's tenure (1708–1716) were Claude Philippe de Richebourg and John La Pierre[17]

The Reverend Francis Guichard, pastor of the Huguenot Church of Charles Town in the mid-1730s, was perhaps the most notorious of the discontented Anglicized Huguenots. Guichard received Anglican orders from the bishop of London and was constrained by his ordination to officiate solely according to the rites of the Church of England. This he consistently refused to do, flouting the Church Act by reading the French Reformed liturgy.[18] On one occasion he casually mentioned to Commissary Alexander Garden that "it was usual among the French ministers to use the one or other liturgy as the people were minded." Guichard's may be the most sensational documented case of such a disruption in the Anglican ranks, but it is not an isolated one; relations between Anglicans and French Huguenots were by no means entirely cordial for much of the eighteenth century.[19]

The conflict between English Anglicans and French Huguenots was not only an issue of the submission of one ethnic group to the dictates of another;

it also proceeded from certain Calvinist perspectives. As Robert M. Kingdon has noted, "Ecclesiastical institutions were extremely important to all the churches which issued from the Calvinist movement. It can be argued, in fact, that their concern for institutions is the most important such attitude which distinguishes Calvinists from such other orthodox Protestants as Lutherans, Zwinglians, and Anglicans." These ecclesiastical institutions, such as the offices of pastors, elders, and deacons, helped distinguish the Calvinist churches from unorthodox sects and the Roman Catholic Church. Together with the two other major tenets of Protestantism—the true preaching of God's word and the proper administration of the sacraments—these doctrines represented the core of French Calvinism and as such became the center of contention between Anglicans and Huguenots.[20]

While liturgical and theological issues bulked large in the struggle between Anglicans and Dissenters, other circumstances served to weaken the power of the Church of England in colonial South Carolina. Because little episcopal authority existed in British North America, a French Calvinist (or a French- or German-Swiss of the Reformed fold for that matter) could find it quite possible to join the Anglican Church in the colonies without turning away from Calvinism. The absence of an American bishop and the similarity of Anglican church governance to the Calvinist Presbyterian model minimized the distance between the two confessions—especially given the latitude that developed in the wake of the Church Act of 1706. For example, though expressly proscribed by the act, Dissenters were regularly elected as parish vestrymen and churchwardens. If this well-known practice diluted the strength of South Carolina Anglicanism, the same might be said of the not uncommon reverse practice of highly placed Anglicans purchasing pews in Dissenting churches. Although these bait-and-switch tactics had more to do with political and social power than theological subtleties, they nonetheless demonstrate a rather fluid religious identity for Carolinians in the first third of the eighteenth century. Another aberration of American Anglicanism from its European counterpart was the former's tendency toward congregational control. In South Carolina throughout the eighteenth century, lay parishioners exerted significant power over their churches—particularly in their penchant for hiring and firing of the clergy that served them. Such local control over parish life meant that directives proceeding from either the Anglican establishment overseas or its counterpart in the province stood a good chance of being disregarded or redesigned to fit local parish needs without much fear of official censure.[21]

II

In spite of the somewhat ambiguous relationship between the provincial Anglican establishment and its significant Dissenter population, South Carolina law stipulated that Purrysburg Township secure the services of an Anglican priest. Without waiting for assistance from the Anglican mission agency (the Society for the Propagation of the Gospel in Foreign Parts), Jean Pierre Purry selected the Reverend Joseph Bugnion to serve his Purrysburg colonists. Purry's choice of Bugnion was as logical to him as it was shortsighted for the township. The founder's home canton in western Switzerland had been steeped in French language, culture, and Reformed theology, and he sought a kindred pastor to meet the spiritual needs of his immigrants. Although it is unclear whether the Reverend Bugnion called France or one of the French-speaking cantons of the Swiss Confederation his ancestral home, he was a Francophone Reformed theologian. The pastor arrived in London with the first party of immigrants destined for Purrysburg, where he received ordination by Dr. Clagett, bishop of St. David's as an Anglican deacon on 23 July 1732 and as an Anglican priest on 25 July. When the party landed at Charles Town in the fall, Bugnion exhibited his testimonials to Commissary Garden on 25 November and traveled to the township to begin his ministerial labors. He attained colonial naturalization on 23 February of the following year. The Anglican ordination of Bugnion was in no way unique; many Reformed pastors had undergone the ritual after the 1706 Church Act. What made Bugnion's case strikingly unusual was that he was to be the sole Anglican priest to a congregation that, though basically unified in its espousal of the Reformed confession, was split along linguistic and cultural lines between French-, German-, and perhaps even some Italian-speaking confessors—not to mention the fact that he had just recently officially renounced his Reformed faith.[22]

Almost immediately Bugnion locked horns with Purry and other members of the settlement over a variety of issues. In a letter to the bishop of London in June 1733, Bugnion charged Purry with fraud and misrepresentation over the matter of his salary. Bugnion argued that Purry had led him to believe that he would receive an annual salary of 500 pounds current money. When Bugnion presented his claim for payment to the Commons House, the legislators rejected it out of hand because, with only sixty men in the township, Purrysburg was not yet eligible for formal parish status and hence could not receive provincial support. The house did grant Bugnion fifty pounds sterling to recompense him for his travel expenses to the colony. After this unsatisfactory adjudication of his claim from the Commons House, Bugnion planned to return to Europe to expose Purry's failure to fulfill his obligations. Whether the quoted salary was a misunderstanding on Bugnion's part or a ruse by Purry to entice him to immigrate to the township is not clear. What becomes evident is that the salary question was only a small part of the problem.[23]

The greater conflict between Bugnion and his Purrysburg parishioners proceeded from the priest's insistence on abiding by the law. He took his Anglican ordination seriously enough and ministered to his congregation according to the Anglican liturgy, over their vigorous protests. Although Bugnion was obviously in the right from the perspective of provincial law, his intransigence on this issue definitely widened the breech between him and his congregants. Purry appears to have led the Reformed cause by appointing a layman to officiate according to the liturgy of Calvin. His authority undermined, Bugnion appealed again to colonial authorities. Both General Oglethorpe of Georgia and Governor Johnson of South Carolina interceded on Bugnion's behalf, but to no avail. The animosity on both sides mounted in intensity. Bugnion accused Purry of deception, while one Purrysburg settler characterized the minister as "base" and another said Bugnion "led a shameful life."[24]

If the problems over wages and religious confession were not enough, language caused even more troubles for the French-speaking minister. His knowledge of only one language in a settlement composed of two major tongues limited his usefulness to the township and magnified his already hostile relationship with the settlers. The German speakers of Purrysburg were so ill served by Bugnion that the Ebenezer pastors wrote to the leader of the Pietist church in Halle seeking a minister for Germans in the township—Lutheran and Reformed. The cumulative effect of these crises manifested itself in January 1734, when Bugnion left Purrysburg to minister at the heavily French settled parish of St. James, Santee. He purchased 850 acres of land in the county in the mid-1730s and also received a grant in Williamsburg Township. Unfortunately, the move to St. James Santee did not eradicate Bugnion's problems. His inability to communicate in any language but French continued to hamper his ministry. After years of frustration, Bugnion mortgaged his land in Craven County and Williamsburg Township and departed South Carolina for good by 1739. Meanwhile, close on the heels of Bugnion's flight to St. James Santee forty-two citizens of Purrysburg, relieved to be rid of Bugnion, petitioned the bishop of London for a replacement minister who could speak both French and German. The fact that the letter seeking a bilingual pastor was written in French foreshadowed further problems that would inhibit the free exercise of religious life in the township for at least another thirty years.[25]

Table 3: Undated Petition for a New Minister for Purrysburg Township, Signed by "Les habitants de Purrysbourg"

Jean Pierre Purry, Colonel and judge of the country	José Girardin
	Jans ris deroches
Jacques Richard, Major (and judge of the country)	George Girardin
	X (mark of de François Buchè)
Guillaume Bulot, Secretaire	Jacob Henri Meuron
Daniel Brabant	François Favre
André De Monclar	Loudwig Kehl
Jean Babtiste Bourquin	Drobold Küffer
Jean Rodolph Netteman	Jörg Mengersdorff
Henry François Bourquin	Andrez Winkler
Pierre Mallier	NR (marks of Nicolas Riguer)
Wallier Cuillat	Anthoine Theremin
iosuè Robert	Jean Pierre Dagallier

Adam Cuillat	HJ (marks of Jean Henry Jeanneret)
David Giroud	Henry Girardin
David Sausy	abram pa Cotton
David Gautier	David Sausy
François Gabriel Ravot	Miclansz Gronemberg
D. Ecollier	Jean Pierre Jeanneret
Joseph Reymond	Abraham Jeanneret
Jean Roudolphe Grand	Jacob Henri Meuron
H (mark of Jean Henry Jeanneret)	Abraham Meuron

Source: Fulham Palace Papers: Bishop of London—General Correspondence, 1709–1769.

Before Purry left South Carolina to conduct another group of immigrants to the township in 1733, the conflict with Bugnion had convinced him that Purrysburg had to procure the services of a new minister as soon as possible. Choosing to not wait for the bishop of London to respond to the petition of township residents, Purry took the initiative to locate an appropriate candidate. He selected another French-speaking Reformed minister, the Reverend Henri François Chiffelle. A native of the Swiss Confederation, Chiffelle received ordination from Dr. Gibson, the bishop of London, as an Anglican deacon on 14 July 1734 and as a priest on 21 July. After the salary fiasco with Bugnion (and probably because of it), the Reverend Chiffelle arrived in Purrysburg in November 1734 as a missionary from the Society for the Propagation of the Gospel in Foreign Parts (SPG), which guaranteed his salary. As it turned out, Purry did repeat one crucial mistake in his choice of Chiffelle. Whether it was because he was more concerned or acquainted with the spiritual needs of the French-speaking immigrants or because Chiffelle overstated his credentials, Purry had secured another French-speaking pastor for his bilingual township. The new minister apparently had aspirations to take up the study of German, for the Reverend Boltzius noted that "Mr. Pury brought over a French preacher for the Swiss, who intends to practice German as much as he can." More than four years after his arrival, however, Chiffelle still had made no progress in learning the language. He never did become proficient, though the pastor eventually could speak and understand some German. He does not appear, however, to have made any concerted attempt to meet the spiritual needs of the Purrysburg German Reformed or Lutheran community, probably because of his rudimentary knowledge of the language.[26]

Chiffelle served as pastor at Purrysburg until his death in 1758. He came to South Carolina as a single man, but the earliest plat for land in the township (besides a town lot) bearing his name is for 100 acres for him and his sister dated 17 March 1735/36. In addition to her, at least one other adult male relative apparently accompanied him to Purrysburg. Chiffelle married in 1738, and by the mid-1750s he and his wife, Margaret, had a family of at least four children.[27] His twenty-four-year ministry at the township was characterized by the twin but somewhat incompatible goals of fulfilling his extensive pastoral responsibilities and establishing his social and economic position—not an uncommon occurrence in the southern colonies. Needless to say, while he pursued one of these objectives, the other suffered. At any given time Chiffelle could be perceived as a dedicated minister of the Gospel or as a hard-working planter and slave owner. During the first year of his labors at Purrysburg, for example, he was away from the township for several months, not only denying the citizens spiritual guidance, but also inhibiting those who desired to marry. When he was present, Chiffelle at times exhibited little pastoral concern for his communicants. He sent a Purrysburg German-speaking couple who decided to wed to the Pietist pastors at Ebenezer because he refused to marry them in their native language. On another occasion the wife of a French-speaking resident of Purrysburg requested that Chiffelle come to her home to comfort and pray with her sick husband. The minister offered to visit the poor man, but only if he was paid beforehand for his efforts. At this unseemly display of his priorities, one of the other settlers remarked that Chiffelle was "not a preacher but an overseer of Negroes or Moorish slaves for he was keeping them hard at work on his plantation and did not trouble himself at all about his congregation."[28]

The Salzburg Lutheran pastors were particularly appalled at what they perceived to be Chiffelle's worldly behavior, but their criticism might be dismissed as a kind of spiritual one-upmanship. Still, some in Purrysburg must have been intensely dissatisfied with their minister for the pastors to react so unfavorably and so often. Theobald Kieffer, one of the few Purrysburg German Lutherans, reported to Boltzius and Gronau in January 1737 that "people find neither physical nor spiritual sustenance at Purrysburg" and that Chiffelle has many complaints against him because he is "quite careless in the exercise of his functions and much too interested in things of this world." After Gronau visited Purrysburg the next month, Boltzius wrote that "the preacher there is most negligent with respect to both his sermons and the performance of his other duties and causes much vexation to everybody by his conduct, which is quite obviously directed toward the matters of this world only." By October the pastors at Ebenezer despaired over the spiritual state of their South Carolina neighbors. "If there were a righteous preacher in Purrysburg a few more souls could be saved from confusion in which they are straying around like sheep without a shepherd." In 1738 when one of the Salzburg ministers had to travel to Purrysburg to speak with Chiffelle, the Purrysburg pastor could not be found in town even though the settlers had built a substantial house and church for him with funds collected in Charles Town. The Pietists sought Chiffelle at his plantation "from which he comes occasionally (not every Sunday) to read a sermon." Less than three years after Chiffelle's arrival in Purrysburg, many of the German-speaking Reformed and Lutheran residents, feeling his dereliction of duty more acutely than the French-speaking Reformed, implored the

Ebenezer ministers to report to both London and Germany their need for a proper preacher. It is surprising that, in light of their expressed antipathy for Chiffelle, the pastors rejected the request as inappropriate.[29]

Besides these complaints, Chiffelle appears to have ignored the pastoral proprieties of his day. His deviation from established principle turned other ministers in the region against him. The Ebenezer pastors were incensed when Chiffelle baptized the half-Indian child of an unmarried Englishman in 1736. They had previously refused to administer the sacrament, so the father and child went to Purrysburg, where Chiffelle performed the baptism with no apparent qualms. A more serious breach of pastoral decorum occurred when Mary Musgrove desired to marry. Boltzius and Gronau refused her their offices because their ecclesial authority did not extend to the English. Anglican law held that no ordained minister could marry anyone but his own parishioners. But Musgrove discovered in early 1737 that Chiffelle had married three other couples from Savannah who were not members of his Purrysburg congregation. She and her fiancée traveled to the township and were obligingly married by Chiffelle. In June 1740 William Stephens of Savannah reported the death of John West's widow and noted in his journal the rather ambiguous state of her marital status, to which the Reverend Chiffelle contributed, "Whether she was a widow or a wife, many people doubted; though she cohabited with Mr. William Kellaway, a trader and Freeholder in this town; and it was said they were privately married by the French minister at Purrysburg, which some questioned."[30] According to Boltzius, the murder of a German woman and her child by Native Americans during the hostilities with Spain in the early 1740s was directly attributable to her premarital sexual relationship with an Englishman she later married. Neither their affair nor the fact that they were not resident in Purrysburg seems to have deterred Chiffelle from officiating at their marriage. Boltzius also spoke disparagingly of Chiffelle's propensity to socialize with and serve Holy Communion to those deemed by Pietists to be unworthy.

In addition to the Pietist pastors, Chiffelle's behavior drew the attention of the Reverend John Wesley, who had been ministering to Savannah residents since early 1736. Perhaps seeking an ally in their crusade against the Purrysburg pastor, Boltzius and Gronau informed Wesley of Chiffelle's willingness to marry Musgrove and other non-Purrysburg couples. Wesley's antipathy did not need overly to be encouraged for he had personal experience with Chiffelle's propensity to marry those from outside his parish. Wesley had been one of at least three suitors of eighteen-year-old Sophy Hopkey, the niece of Savannah official Thomas Causton. On 8 March 1737 Wesley recorded in his journal that Hopkey told him she had decided against continuing her relationship with Mr. Mellichamp but that William Williamson was calling on her though she had no particular feeling for him. Wesley's love for her and her affection for him are obvious in Wesley's journal entries for this period, but he failed to act. Hopkey simultaneously endured a difficult living situation at the Causton home. She had a particularly trying time on the evening of the eighth that included her aunt ordering her out of the house. Mrs. Causton apparently suggested that Wesley take her in, which he agreed to do. Hopkey, in tears, said nothing in response, and Wesley left the Causton residence alone about ten in the evening. He went back to the Causton home about midmorning the next day and was greeted with the news that Hopkey had become engaged to Williamson the previous evening after Wesley had gone. Taken completely by surprise, Wesley struggled with his course of action. He and Hopkey had a number of conversations over the next few days, and she seemed to give every indication that she would forsake Williamson for Wesley if he would make some movement toward her, but he did not. Perhaps because of Williamson's jealousy of Wesley, on Friday, 11 March 1737, Hopkey and Williamson along with another couple traveled to Purrysburg to be married without banns ever being published for the former. On Saturday, one year to the day after Hopkey and Wesley first spoke, the Reverend Chiffelle married her to Williamson. Less than a week after the marriage Wesley wrote a strongly worded letter to Chiffelle, urging him "to abstain from such functions which are not properly part of his duties."[31] He also resolved to notify the bishop of London about Chiffelle's behavior. In mid-April Wesley left for Charles Town to confer with Commissary Garden regarding the minister's improprieties.[32] In addition to the many other problems associated with Chiffelle's officiating at the Hopkey-Williamson nuptials and others previously discussed was the fact that he performed the wedding ceremonies in question entirely in French, which none of the betrothed individuals could understand. The attempts by Wesley and the Pietists to censure Chiffelle had little lasting effect on his career, and he continued these practices into the 1740s. He was not alone. The frontier environment forced adaptation of Old World and even urban provincial religious norms.[33]

The Reverend Chiffelle does seem to have struggled between fulfilling his pastoral duties and extending his temporal influence and material position. From contemporary accounts, he appears to have conducted only one service with a proper sermon every other Sunday for the French Reformed of his congregation. On alternate Sundays he directed a prayer meeting for the Germans (Reformed and Lutheran) based on a German translation of the Anglican prayer book. He never preached in German except on High Holy days, when he would then read a sermon in that language. But because he never mastered German, this practice most assuredly proved insufficient for his German communicants.[34]

While providing pastoral services in Purrysburg, Chiffelle simultaneously pursued opportunities that would enhance his stature in the profession. As early as December 1736 the pastor petitioned the governor and council to establish Purrysburg as a separate parish.[35] His action may have been prompted by his desire to be supported by both the SPG and the South Carolina Assembly. The creation of a new parish with Purrysburg as its center would most likely make Chiffelle the parish minister. Once elected he could not be dismissed except by the bishop of London or an ecclesiastical court—at least in theory—and, although the duties and privileges of a parish minister and a missionary of the SPG were generally similar, as a member of the Anglican parish clergy Chiffelle stood to gain a certain amount of notoriety and prestige. In addition, prompt and regular payment for his parish responsibilities would be assured because the money would come from the colonial treasury and not from the London office of the SPG. Finally Chiffelle had a better than even chance of receiving a substantial boost in salary as a recognized parish clergyman rather than as a missionary for the SPG. Nearly ten years passed between the time of Chiffelle's first request for Purrysburg parish autonomy and the passage of the act creating St. Peter's Parish on 17 February 1746/47, which included the frontier township and other acreage carved out of the southwestern corner of St. Helena's Parish. The act stipulated that Chiffelle's church and house would serve as the parish church and rectory. The elected minister of the parish would receive 100 pounds current money per annum. Chiffelle served in this capacity from the date of incorporation to his death in 1758.[36]

In addition to his pastoral duties at Purrysburg, the Reverend Chiffelle found time for other ministerial responsibilities. Perhaps because of his new position as parish rector, at the annual meeting of the Anglican clergy of South Carolina on 17 April 1751 Chiffelle received appointment to officiate at the prestigious church of St. Helena's Parish in Beaufort as interim pastor "as often as convenient until a missionary should arrive from England." The SPG sent the Reverend William Peasley to St. Helena's later that same year, but Chiffelle continued to offer his assistance to the Beaufort church periodically, at least until the spring of 1753. While serving the main church in St. Helena's Parish, Chiffelle officiated at a number of functions including weddings and baptisms.[37]

The Purrysburg pastor's most intriguing and, for present considerations, most significant interparish activity was his ongoing exercise of the Reformed confession while posing as an Anglican priest. Boltzius and Gronau may not even have known that Chiffelle had taken Anglican orders for they consistently referred to him as a Reformed minister. On more than one occasion, the Pietist pastors became involved with those of the Reformed confession outside Purrysburg, and on these occasions Chiffelle was consulted because of his affiliation with that tradition. In June 1738, while preparing for her first Lutheran communion, a former Purrysburg settler of the Reformed faith who had married an Ebenezer German was encouraged by the Reformed citizens of the township "not to apostatize but to remain with the faith of her fathers." The Ebenezer clergy, wary of the brewing controversy, had no desire to cause the woman undue hardship and suggested that, if she wished, because Purrysburg was not far, she could go there to take Reformed communion. As Chiffelle was the only minister at Purrysburg, such communion must have been served by him—though expressly forbidden by the Church Act of 1706.[38]

An even more blatant example of Chiffelle's surreptitious adherence to Reformed theology is the fact that he often visited Savannah to minister to the French and German Reformed of that city. In late 1738 he traveled there to serve communion to the Reformed Germans. As was his custom in Purrysburg because of his inadequate knowledge of German, Chiffelle read out of a book (perhaps the German translation of the Anglican prayer book) for the preparation. He was called upon to officiate at the funeral of former Purrysburg merchant Samuel Montaigut in November 1739, as the Savannah pastor was out of town. Again in late 1741 Chiffelle was observed in Savannah preaching to the French and Swiss. In this instance he was specifically denoted "a Calvinist from Purrysburg." These were not isolated incidents for accounts note that Chiffelle conducted services for the French and German Reformed of Savannah throughout the 1730s and 1740s. The German Reformed of Vernonsburg, Georgia, near Savannah, also desired Chiffelle's services. In 1743 the French settlers of the Georgia town asked General Oglethorpe to reimburse Chiffelle for the charges he incurred in his journeys back and forth from Purrysburg to Savannah because of his services to them. Oglethorpe agreed to defray Chiffelle's expenses and then discovered, to his surprise, that Chiffelle had been traveling to Savannah for the benefit of the Reformed confessors there for half a decade. The general duly reported this to the trustees and added that he desired to pay Chiffelle twenty-one pounds sterling for his service over the preceding five years. Accompanying documents, including a petition to Oglethorpe from the Reformed of Savannah attesting to Chiffelle's diligent and pious instruction and exemplary character, demonstrate that his services in Georgia were regularly conducted and well attended by many French Reformed and even by some Germans of the Reformed fold. The petitioners defended the Purrysburg pastor from undisclosed attackers and solemnly challenged Oglethorpe to allow Chiffelle to continue his ministrations. Chiffelle did preach in Savannah on a fairly regular basis until 1745, when the Reformed pastor the Reverend Johann Joachim Zubly, formerly of Purrysburg, began ministering in the city. Zubly, unlike Chiffelle, was fluent in French, German, and English and could serve the Reformed Germans with greater felicity.[39]

If the extant evidence is to be believed, Chiffelle appears to have been more appreciated (and more accommodating) to those outside his parish than he was to those within it. Attacks upon the Purrysburg minister by the Ebenezer pastors lessened with the passing of time as they too found it difficult to carry on the conduct of their offices as they had in the European homeland. By the late 1740s he faced little direct calumny, though in a journal entry of December 1760 Boltzius still remembered the deceased Chiffelle as "miserable" in meeting his pastoral obligations.[40]

While his extraparish activities bolstered the Reverend Chiffelle's professional reputation, he must have also applied himself quite assiduously to the achievement of higher social status that came with the accumulation of land. Soon after his arrival in the township and in joint ownership with his sister, Chiffelle was platted two town lots and 100 acres in the township. In 1742 he added 450 acres and on 12 and 13 February 1755/56 received plats for 700 and 400 acres more, respectively. He retained sole ownership of all these latter three parcels.[41]

Regardless of the criticism leveled at the Reverend Chiffelle or the Reformed nature of the liturgy he used in Purrysburg and elsewhere, the structural integuments of a regular Anglican parish took shape in the township. On the town plat of Purrysburg, the one-acre town lot 32, between Bay (or Front) Street and Church Street, at the intersection of Church and Savannah Streets was set aside for the church building. Glebe lands were laid out abutting the northern tier of lots of the town proper. The town plat then placed the church almost at the center of town from north to south, but less than two town lots distant from the Savannah River on the extreme western perimeter of the town.[42] There is, however, some confusion regarding the actual location of the church building. According to the act that created St. Peter's Parish, it was determined that "the church or chapel and the dwelling house . . . wherein the Rev. Mr. Chiffelle had preached and dwelt for some years past shall be deemed and taken and they are hereby declared to be the Parish Church and parsonage house of the said Parish of St. Peter." But the only town lots Chiffelle held legal title to were numbers 58 and 115, which faced each other across Church Street on the extreme southwestern edge of the town. If the act of incorporation is to be believed, then one of those two lots must have become the rectory in 1747 and the other the parish church. Yet this would locate the church and rectory fully twelve one-acre parcel lots from lot number 32—a considerable distance and far removed from the center of town. If the map that appeared in H. A. M. Smith's article on Purrysburg in the *South Carolina Historical and Genealogical Magazine* in 1909 adapted from earlier maps done by Hugh Bryan and Robert Mills can be taken as somewhat authoritative, it does appear that St. Peter's Church was located at the southern end of the town. The initial church building appears to have been constructed by 1738 with money said to have been collected in Charles Town—nearly ten years before Purrysburg would achieve parish status. A new home for Chiffelle had also been built next to the church by that time. It is unknown whether this building was replaced at a later date, but the somewhat ambiguous evidence would seem to indicate that it was either enlarged or completely reconstructed by 1744, perhaps after one of the fires that seemed to afflict the township, and perhaps relocated on lot 32. In any event, the church was large enough to accommodate at least thirty-two pews that were bought and sold by communicants. Henry L. Beck inspected the remains of the church on the south side of the Purrysburg graveyard during his visit in the early 1930s and estimated that its footprint was approximately thirty feet by sixty feet. In the late 1750s, parish resident David Giroud spent considerable effort repairing extensive but undisclosed damage to the church for which he submitted a claim of more that 303 pounds current money. Although certified by the unnamed vestry and churchwardens[43] of St. Peter's Purrysburg, the Commons House disallowed the claim as it "was not brought in the usual manner."[44] Such bureaucratic nitpicking had to have been discouraging for Giroud and the parish leadership, but it does not seem to have diminished religious activity in the township. What did adversely affect the exercise of religious offices at Purrysburg came as a gesture of appreciation and goodwill from parish and provincial leadership to the Reverend Chiffelle for his years of ministry on the southern frontier.

On 14 January 1755, after nearly twenty years of continuous service, Chiffelle petitioned the Commons House for a year's leave of absence from his parish responsibilities. The pastor hoped to return to his native land to recoup his health and vitality, which had been on the decline since at least November of the previous year. He had the blessing of his Purrysburg congregants but lacked sufficient funds to underwrite his trip or support his family at the township in his absence. Chiffelle noted that, without his salary as parish minister, he had no income because the SPG did not support him and his poor parishioners "who were but just able to live themselves" could not afford to do so. He wrote that "his small income which for about ten years was even less by fifty pounds than the salary of other parishes (besides the rent of a house) was but barely sufficient to maintain himself, a wife, and four children and never enabled him to get anything before hand." In light of these extenuating circumstances, Chiffelle requested, not only that his salary be continued during his absence, but also that the House "advance him a year's salary before he leaves to defray costs of his journey and to support his family in his absence." Perhaps in a generous mood because of prosperous times, the House resolved to let the minister "depart this province for recovery of his health" and granted him the continuance of his salary provided his leave did not extend beyond twelve months. The Commons House also ordered that Chiffelle be advanced six months salary out of the public treasury to finance his trip. Nothing is known about Chiffelle's trip or how his parishioners (or his family) fared without clerical offices in his absence. What is apparent from this petition is the familiarity Chiffelle had with the workings of provincial government and his ability to use his understanding and position in ways that benefited both him and his family. The obvious support of his Purrysburg congregation would seem to indicate a mutually satisfying relationship between the pastor and at least a substantial portion of Purrysburg residents, in spite of earlier conflicts with fellow ministers. The affirmative ruling by the House on Chiffelle's petition remains one of the few examples of beneficence for its own sake from the provincial government to Purrysburg in the entire colonial history of the township.[45]

Aside from his numerous pastoral duties, or perhaps in some ways because of them, Chiffelle was able to build a modest estate for himself and his family. Most of his material wealth must have been accumulated after his marriage, which was performed by the Reverend Gronau in February 1738, though there is no evidence to suggest that he married a woman of wealth. In the fall of the following year Chiffelle bought 300 acres of land in Purrysburg from Jean Pierre Purry's distant cousin John Roldolph Purry for 182 pounds current money. By 1753 he had a large enough estate to loan 480 pounds South Carolina current money to Jean Baptiste Bourguin, a longtime resident of the township. The bond was sealed and delivered in the presence of two other French Reformed inhabitants of the township, Gabriel Ravot and Abraham Bourguin. Upon Chiffelle's death in 1758, his estate was inventoried and appraised at more than 2,100 pounds current money. Among his more conspicuous belongings were 40.5 ounces of silver, a library of mostly French books, twenty-three men's shirts, and nearly fifty head of cattle and sheep. As with so many other Purrysburg settlers after 1750, his single largest investment had been in five slaves appraised at almost 1,100 pounds current money. As his estate indicates, the Reverend Chiffelle had been pursuing secular activities as well as a wide array of both Anglican and Reformed pastoral duties, not unlike many of his clerical contemporaries.[46]

The real losers during Chiffelle's long tenure as Purrysburg pastor were the Reformed German speakers, for, although there are indications that Chiffelle was less than an ideal minister to the Purrysburg Reformed French speakers, they at least were able to hear sermons, however infrequent, in their own tongue and from all appearances after their own confession. Unfortunately the German Reformed could not make the same claim. Chiffelle's uneven record of spiritual care for his congregation and especially of its German contingent resulted in the migration of religious loyalty geographically from Purrysburg to Ebenezer and the Savannah area and theologically from Reformed to Lutheran confession. The migration logically began with the few German-speaking Lutheran Pietists living in the township in the early 1730s, for they had been deprived of not only religious services in their native tongue but also worship in their own confession.

The few Pietist families of Purrysburg initially met with Judge John Frederick Holzendorf from Berlin, who read passages from a book of family prayers. Purry soon realized, however, that his township needed a German-speaking Lutheran pastor. He expressed this need to Boltzius and Gronau when he met them in Dover. General Oglethorpe was also aware of the spiritual needs at the township after the departure of the Reverend Bugnion. He asked the Pietist pastors to visit the town and present a sermon. The service was well received, and many Purrysburg Lutherans resolved to travel often to Ebenezer to worship in their own confession and language. Thus began the long lasting religious interchange between Purrysburg and Ebenezer, which in effect skewed Purrysburg community life. The Lutheran pastors frequently made trips to the township to celebrate religious services and sacraments, often at the home of Theobald Kieffer Sr. Many Purrysburg German speakers visited the Salzburger settlement for the same reason. Before long, Reformed as well as Pietist Purrysburg

German speakers awaited visits from the Lutheran pastors, and many of them made the journey to Ebenezer for spiritual support as it was their only real opportunity to participate fully in worship.[47]

Some Purrysburg Germans were satisfied enough with the spiritual guidance provided by the Salzburg pastors that they hoped to move across the Savannah River to join the settlement. The ministers encouraged Pietists to settle in Ebenezer, but neither they nor their congregants were always willing to accept Reformed Germans into the Georgia fold. They did continue to exercise pastoral concern for the plight of the Purrysburg German Reformed and even secured copies of the Anglican Prayer Book translated into German for their use in 1737. They had the books delivered to Chiffelle, who in turn had them distributed among some of the German families. In 1741 the pastors lent some religious books to Theobald Kieffer Sr. for dissemination to the Reformed of the township. After Kieffer had requested the volumes, Boltzius cryptically remarked to his diary that the Purrysburg settlers "may be able to get more out of them than by the minister(s) of their church."[48] Kieffer even appears to have preached to Purrysburg settlers on at least one occasion in 1741. Three years later Boltzius supplied two unnamed Reformed brothers from Purrysburg, who were in all likelihood German speakers, with an old Bible and a prayer book and songbook because they had no devotional books. In 1754 another unnamed Reformed resident, undoubtedly also a German speaker asked Boltzius for a book of sermons so that "he might edify himself with his neighbors during their Sunday meetings."[49] In loaning books to Purrysburg settlers from his own library, Boltzius hoped to contribute to the spiritual life of a needy community. But he found it difficult to ask for the return of the volumes—even if a substantial period of time had elapsed.[50]

Although the Purrysburg German speakers could worship according to the Lutheran liturgy, they remained frustrated in the exercise of their chosen Reformed confession. Hopes for a resident German Reformed pastor rose momentarily in the spring of 1738 when the Reverend Sebastian Zouberbühler, a German-Swiss Reformed minister originally from Appenzell, left New Windsor Township and decided to relocate in Purrysburg with his wife and young daughter. Zouberbühler's son Bartholomew, a student of theology, and an older married daughter and her husband also made their way to the township. The Reverend Zouberbühler preached to the Purrysburg Germans in late May. They were much taken with his sermon and had reason to hope that they had found a pastor of their own confession and language. Such was not to be the case. By mid-July his wife, younger daughter, and son-in-law had died. Soon thereafter, when he and his son became ill, his widowed daughter tended to them. Bartholomew recovered, but the elder Zouberbühler succumbed to the fever before December of that year. Bartholomew preached for some time at Purrysburg but soon relocated to Palachuccola. He subsequently served the Reformed in

Savannah in 1739. Late that year Zouberbühler traveled from Purrysburg to Ebenezer accompanied by John Linder, seeking a recommendation from the Reverend Boltzius for a permanent pastorate in Savannah. When Boltzius refused, he turned to the Reverend Chiffelle, who also denied his request.

With the death of the Reverend Sebastian Zouberbühler and the relocation of his son, the hope for a German Reformed pastor for the large German-speaking population of Purrysburg Township disappeared. From 1739 forward, the Purrysburg German speakers had to make either confessional or linguistic compromises. Whatever choice they made affected adversely the quality and solidarity of township community life. Some chose Ebenezer and Lutheran Pietism. Some chose Savannah or Acton or Vernonsburg and the German Reformed tradition. Some remained at their Purrysburg homes and worked to find spiritual peace while worshipping in an Anglican parish according to the Reformed liturgy in the French language led by a French-Swiss theologian who had taken Anglican ordination.[51] Perhaps the German Reformed Purrysburg shoemaker Valentin Depp best illustrates the challenges faced by German-speaking Calvinists at Purrysburg. Depp moved to Purrysburg and subsequently married into the Purrysburg Pietist Kieffer family in 1743. His wife desired to maintain her confessional allegiance to the Lutheran Church after their marriage. The family no doubt worshipped at Ebenezer, but Depp continued to favor his Calvinistic heritage. He moved his family to Ebenezer in March 1745, which would appear to indicate his decision to adopt Lutheran ways. Barely a month later, however, Depp traveled to Purrysburg, possibly to receive Holy Communion according to the Reformed rite, albeit in the French language. The Reverend Boltzius wrote, "It appears he is not happy at our place and that is probably the reason he wished to move away again for some time to the sorrow of his wife and parents-in-law." In light of the religious choices that German-speaking Purryburg settlers were forced to make, Depp was most likely not alone in his inability to find a real spiritual home in either Purrysburg or Ebenezer.[52]

By the time of the Reverend Chiffelle's death in 1758, the township had survived for more than a quarter century on the southern frontier. The adult immigrants of the early 1730s had either died or reached old age, and the first generation of American-born Purrysburg settlers had begun to reach maturity. This crucial moment in the life of the colony offered an ideal opportunity for the township to call a minister who could meet the spiritual needs of both Germanic and Francophone residents. It would seem that, after twenty-five years in an English colony European, languages would have diminished in importance as both German and French speakers adopted English—particularly the second generation. Such was not necessarily the case in Purrysburg, however, because several European languages were still spoken there. In an attempt to cover all possible contingencies, the third pastor called to serve the Purrysburg congregation, the Reverend Abraham Imer, a Swiss of French extraction, was fluent in French, German, and Latin.[53]

Like Bugnion and Chiffelle before him, initial contact with Imer was through the personal efforts of township residents and not by Anglican authorities. A nephew to the Reverend Chiffelle, the Reverend Barthelemi H. Himeli, pastor of the Charles Town Huguenot Church, had been approached by members of the township soon after their minister's death to aid them in finding another pastor. At the time Himeli wrote to him about the vacant position in Purrysburg, the Reverend Imer was a deacon and master of Latin (1744–1759) in Neuchâtel. He appears to have served for some years prior as a pastor in the canton of Berne. Himeli's letter to Imer emphasized that the Swiss minister possessed the necessary qualifications for the Purrysburg congregation, especially because he was fluent in the languages of the township. Himeli subsequently sent Imer the pastoral call letter written by the church officers of St. Peter's Parish, Purrysburg. The letter stipulated that the called minister should pledge himself to the discharge of his responsibilities according to the Anglican Church of South Carolina. The letter further encouraged the bishop of London to ordain the minister, who would then be paid the allotted yearly salary by the inhabitants of St. Peter's. Parishioners Gabriel Ravot and David Saussy, church wardens, and David Giroud, John Bourguin Imer, John Burke, Solon Kealt, Isaac Brabant, and Melchior Auchensteiger (Leichtensteiger), vestrymen, signed the letter on 1 March 1759.[54] Himeli urged Imer to present the call letter to the bishop of London, who would then give the new minister twenty pounds for passage money to America. In addition, the Charles Town pastor told Imer to visit the members of the SPG, who would also provide him with financial assistance. By October 1759 Imer had decided to accept the call. Before he left, the Board of Freemen of Neuchâtel granted him funds for the journey and provided him with a letter of recommendation to the Purrysburg parishioners.[55]

Relatively little else is known about the Reverend Imer or his ministry in Purrysburg. He brought only four of his ten children to South Carolina, and two of them perished on the way to Purrysburg. His wife died by 1764. It is not clear whether she accompanied her husband to the township. Imer did not arrive in Purrysburg until the summer of 1760, so the congregation had been without a regular pastor for nearly two years. Upon beginning his ministerial duties at the township, Imer noted that the original settlers, many of whom were still living thirty years after the founding of Purrysburg, were well endowed with a "deep and solid sort of piety" and had "sufficiently ample knowledge." He failed to express similar sentiments regarding the younger second- and third-generation inhabitants and characterized them as "in the deepest darkness of ignorance, rarely show(ing) forth works from which true and wholesome faith is apparent." His commentary on the state of the young ended by acknowledging—perhaps because of the effects of Chiffelle's fragmented ministry and the realities of life on the frontier—that the state of the young could "not in any way be expected to be otherwise."[56] He believed that his proficiency in both French and German made him especially welcomed, particularly "to the Germans, who got nothing from my French predecessors." The Reverend Boltzius entertained the hope that Imer would succeed where, at least in his eyes, Chiffelle had failed but noted that the new minister faced "a wild and ignorant congregation."[57]

Unlike the previous two ministers, Imer provided full services in French and German. Nevertheless, he seems to have had a falling out with the Purrysburg settlers, which led to his temporary departure from the community. An itinerant Anglican minister, the Reverend Charles Woodmason, wrote in 1766 that Imer had arrived in South Carolina with a group of French Protestants. After an unknown period of time, however, he differed with the inhabitants for undisclosed reasons and journeyed by 1765 to live among those with whom he had traveled to the province and "Stumpels German" [*sic*]. The only major immigration of French Huguenots to South Carolina in the 1760s was the party under the Reverend Pierre Gibert that settled in New Bordeaux, Hillsborough Township. Woodmason's oblique reference to Imer's problems at Purrysburg may indicate his move to this backcountry township, but, if so, it was only a temporary relocation, for Imer ultimately returned to his duties in Purrysburg and served there until his death in the late 1760s. His only tangible contribution was the instrumental part he played as chief initiator and founding member of the Society for the Relief of Widows and Children of the Clergy of the Church of England in the Province of South Carolina, chartered in April 1762. His granddaughter, Jane Imer of Charleston, became one of the beneficiaries of the society in 1803.[58]

Perhaps Imer's financial and personal affairs tainted his relationships with township residents, for, though he remained a pastor of fairly modest means throughout his years of service at Purrysburg, he did become involved in a number of legal matters, including a Georgia Sea Island land scheme with the prominent Charles Town Huguenot Gabriel Manigault. As early as July 1763 the Reverend Imer bonded himself to members of the Bourguin family as administrator for John Lewis Dethridge to the tune of 250 pounds current money to be repaid by 1 January 1769. He used a Purrysburg town lot as collateral to secure the bond. The following September, Imer sold 334 acres in Purrysburg Township to Stono planter Champernoun Williamson for 1,800 pounds current money. The indenture of release was signed by Abraham Imer, V.D.M., and Ann Imer. He had been granted the land only six months prior to the sale. Two years later, in a Court of Common Pleas case, Imer was served a writ on 29 May 1766 by Margaret Henery (Henry) for repayment of an unpaid loan that amounted to 100 pounds current money. He died before making any restitution, though an inventory of Imer's estate points to the fact that he could have paid his debt as his total worth was upward of 669 pounds current money. His home furnishings were of a modest nature, encompassing a small collection of pewter plates and various other dishes and utensils as well as inexpensive pine tables. But, as with

Chiffelle, his largest investment, assessed at 520 pounds, was his four slaves, who appear to have been a family.[59]

In the most unusual case on record, Imer bound himself on 2 May 1764 to shopkeeper Francis Morand and Charles Town merchants Jonathan Scott and John Scott Jr. for the substantial sum of 8,400 pounds current money. This bond cemented a prenuptial agreement between Imer, who had lost his wife sometime after his arrival in Purrysburg, and Ann Mauroumet, widowed daughter of Francis Morand. Imer stood to gain "a considerable Personal Estate, consisting of Sundry Goods, chattles, Jewells and other effects as the marriage Portion of and belonging unto the said Ann." To insure that Ann, her son John Mauroumet, his children, and any possible children from her marriage to Imer would be taken care of in the event of the pastor's death, Imer agreed to apportion his estate to them through the three men to which he had bonded himself. According to the bond, within six months of his death Imer's executors were to pay to Morand and the two Scotts 600 pounds sterling to be used equally by Ann and their children. If Ann died, the money was to be divided equally among any children of their union. If Imer, Ann, and the children of their marriage expired, Imer's heirs were bound to pay Morand and the two Scotts 200 pounds sterling for the use of Ann's son from her prior marriage, John. In the event of his death, the money would be divided equally among his children. If there were no children, the 200 pounds sterling reverted to Morand and the others to use as they deemed appropriate. This complex arrangement paved the way for his marriage to Ann by assuring her father and his associates that the bulk of Ann's marriage portion would remain in their control. On the other hand, it excluded from the provisions of this covenant Imer's six surviving children by his first wife still living in the Swiss Confederation. They could, however, be held liable to enforce the disbursement of his estate as noted in the bond.[60]

Following the death of the Reverend Imer, which probably occurred in 1768, the parish church failed to receive another incumbent minister. An Anglican itinerant minister, the Reverend J. Adam de Martel, appears to have been assigned the Purrysburg church as part of his 200-mile circuit the following year, but little is known about either the duration or the character of his ministry among the township residents. The only direct reference to Purrysburg in his report to the bishop of London in 1769 noted terribly hot weather at the township. He concluded his assessment by observing that the "only food is as bad. The only liquor is rum for drinking," which if consumed in excess, he believed, could lead to death. In a more general statement about his circuit, the Reverend de Martel wrote that the houses were ten miles from each other so that the settlers in the region "seldom see anybody at their habitation: it is the cause they are almost savages. Some have but very little religion, some none at all, the most part are what is called Anabaptists."[61] From the context it is difficult to determine which of these latter distinctives could be applied to the immediate environs of the township, though certainly the Baptist persuasion had made significant inroads in the region by the 1760s, as had plantation agriculture. Aside from services conducted by the Pietists from Ebenezer, exercise of formal religious services in the township outside the Anglican edifice appears to have depended on one of two sources. The first was the itinerant preaching in the area associated with the Great Awakening. The second was the founding of a Presbyterian church in Purrysburg before the American Revolution.[62]

III

Recent scholarship on eighteenth-century religious life has provided historians with a much more nuanced understanding of the scope and influence of the phenomenon historians have called the First Great Awakening with regard, not only to religious practice, but also to its social, political, and ideological dimensions.[63] From the first stirring of religious enthusiasm in the southern colonies in the 1740s to the apogee of evangelical influence in the 1760s and early 1770s, itinerant evangelists criss-crossed the region, triggering momentous and deeply significant changes that continued to shape southern culture for generations. David T. Morgan argues that South Carolina was particularly receptive to the message of the evangelicals because of what the province had faced since the late 1730s. Fear of attack from Spain in 1737 and the ravages of smallpox and yellow fever in 1738 and 1739 exacted a terrible toll on the colony. The yellow fever epidemic of September and October of 1739 alone killed the provincial chief justice, a judge of the Vice-Admiralty Court, the surveyor of customs, the clerk of the Commons House of Assembly, and the clerk of the Court of Admiralty—not to mention significant numbers of colonists. Bracketing by a matter of months the visit of the Reverend George Whitefield in January 1740 were the Stono Rebellion, the failed British attack on St. Augustine, and the fire that swept through Charles Town in November 1740.[64] Even given such apparent psychological readiness for the evangelical message, earlier discussions of the Great Awakening in South Carolina in the 1740s spurred by Whitefield's ministrations, tended to minimize its impact on provincial culture.[65] Building on Eugene D. Genovese's argument that paternalism provided the key to understanding the ideology of the slaveholding elite of the antebellum South, however, scholarship in the 1980s and 1990s began to rethink the religious context of the mid–eighteenth century and the impact of that context upon subsequent southern life and culture. Historians such as Robert M. Calhoon, Alan Gallay, Rachel N. Klein, Stephanie McCurry, Robert Olwell, and Richard Waterhouse began to discover significant linkages between evangelical Christianity and race, gender, and class relationships in South Carolina.[66]

In some ways it is difficult to determine the extent to which the evangelical movement affected Purrysburg Township in the later colonial era. Consigned to the political and economic periphery by provincial policy, Purrysburg remained outside the mainstream for most of the era. Yet the religious and social upheavals of the middle third of the eighteenth century did play a discernible role in the evolution of the religious life of the township. Its strategic location and the Reformed religious commitments of most of its population meant that Purrysburg's inhabitants confronted many of the same spiritual, ideological, and cultural effects of the Great Awakening, as did colonists in other, more centrally located communities in South Carolina. From the late 1730s through the revolutionary era, for example, numerous itinerant evangelists and missionaries passed through the township on their way elsewhere because Purrysburg was situated on the major overland route between Charleston and Savannah until the opening of the Rochester Ferry and on the most convenient water and land routes from Savannah to Augusta. Bishop Francis Asbury, the Reverend Peter Böhler, the Reverend Joseph Pilmoor (Philmoor), the Reverend George Schulius, the Reverend Archibald Simpson, the Reverend John Wesley, the Reverend George Whitefield, David Zeisberger, Henry Melchior Mühlenberg, and Johann Ettwein among others knew of Purrysburg, passed through at one time or another, and many of them held services there. Ettwein, leader of all the Moravians in North Carolina, had first heard of Purrysburg more than twenty-five years before his trip took him through the township. He had heard of it "in the festival song of the single Brethren (*im led. Brueder Fest-Lied*)" and determined on that count to "take a good look around" when he traveled to the region in 1765, just after the township residents had parted company with the Reverend Imer. He had planned to stay for a few days and to visit with the Purrysburg German speakers and preach to them, but he "did not feel comfortable" and found it "very expensive." The Methodist missionary the Reverend Joseph Pilmoor visited in 1773 and preached before a "good congregation." After the service, Pilmoor "was invited to dine with a Frenchman, who was one of the principal inhabitants, and expressed a very great desire that I would stay and be their parish minister." But he refused as his vocational calling was in itinerant mission work and not parish ministry. Even the self-styled "Prince of Württemberg," one of the more nefarious clerical imposters of the colonial period, visited the township.[67]

The existence of chattel slavery in Purrysburg sparked the humanitarian interests of mission boards and missionaries. Dr. John Potter, archbishop of Canterbury in the late 1730s, sent Moravian missionaries to establish a school for blacks in South Carolina.[68] The Reverend Peter Böhler, an ordained officer of the Moravian Church and mentor to John Wesley, supervised this enterprise. Four Savannah Moravians guided the missionary and his colleagues soon after their arrival in Georgia and shortly before 13 October 1738 to Purrysburg to begin their work. They carried a letter of introduction from a former township schoolteacher named Müller to Theobald Kieffer Sr. Kieffer opened his home to the Moravians, who remained guarded about their purposes in Purrysburg, most likely because of the historic rift between those of competing Protestant confessions.[69]

The missionaries enthusiastically began their labors at Purrysburg, but discouragement soon set in after reconnoitering the township for they found "scarce three Negroes in the town and not a hundred within a circle of twelve miles." This disheartening discovery led to a conference with General Oglethorpe regarding their prospects in the area. Emerging from the meeting, they determined for some unknown reason to make Purrysburg the center of their missionary operations. They may have felt more comfortable with the Germans at the township even though most of them were of the Reformed tradition, or the missionaries may have desired to remain as close as possible to the substantial Moravian community in Savannah. A third possibility lay in the credence they might have attached to the Reverend John Wesley's supposed comments regarding the prevalence of slavery at Purrysburg. They may have alternatively concluded that there were more slaves in the township than they had yet seen.

With their course set, the missionaries recommitted themselves to the work before them. By early December, though, Böhler and his associates had made no progress in evangelizing blacks in and around Purrysburg. This lack of tangible results, coupled with the recognition that township children had no formal education, led to the missionaries' decision "to instruct children in Purrysburg and to preach to the people on Sundays" provided the settlers wished Böhler to do so. There is little doubt that they did for he required no remuneration for his services, the German speakers were without a minister, and the settlement was without a teacher. Böhler and the others appear to have continued their work until the summer of 1740 when Böhler suffered with "a violent ague, a tumour, and a terrible cough." He eventually recovered from the life-threatening illness, but one of his co-workers, George Schulius, succumbed to a similar malady. Sickness, despair, and other complications combined with the formal declaration of war between England and Spain to prompt Böhler and his surviving helpers to depart Purrysburg for Savannah. They took with them a small but loyal Purrysburg contingent of five men, one woman, and one male child, the members of which probably resettled in Savannah among that town's Moravian population.[70]

Not much else is known about the interstices between Christian humanitarianism and forced servitude in the immediate vicinity of Purrysburg Township, at least at the institutional level, although much has been written about their existence elsewhere in the colonial Southeast. It is intriguing to note, however, that, in the same year that the Moravians left, the evangelist George Whitefield reportedly bought a tract of land in Purrysburg, "where he wishes to establish a Negro school and to buy some young Negroes who will go to school and do their work on the side."[71] Little is known of this attempt by the evangelist to link chattel slavery and education. Whitefield's Bethesda orphanage and school in Savannah had just opened in 1739 to alleviate the suffering of white children, so perhaps this land purchase and the projected school was his way of trying to provide similar assistance to enslaved black children who lived just across the river. George Fenwick Jones contends, however, that the slaves Whitefield purchased worked to support the Bethesda orphanage. Whatever his intentions, the school remained an unfulfilled dream, but even its conception bears glaring witness to the tangled roots of evangelical religion and colonial slave societies.

Two of Purrysburg's own did contribute significantly to religious revival on the southern frontier and maintained some connections to the township facilitated by geographical proximity, family, and community relationships. The Reverend Francis Pelot came from one of the early families that settled in Purrysburg. He had been born in 1720 in Neuveville (Norville) in the Swiss Confederation and emigrated with his father, Jonas, his mother, Susanne Marie, and a brother and sister to British North America. The family traveled first to Pennsylvania and then moved to Purrysburg no later than 1735. It has been noted that he was baptized and raised Presbyterian, though Reformed might be a more accurate descriptor given his ancestral heritage and the exercise of religious worship at Purrysburg. He progressively moved toward Regular (Particular) Baptist preferences and became a denominational licentiate of Isaac Chandler. In 1744 Pelot joined Euhaw Baptist Church about twenty miles northeast of the township. Two years later he accepted a call to the pastorate and became a Baptist minister. He served Euhaw Baptist Church with distinction from 1746 to 1774, receiving ordination in 1752 by the prominent Regular Baptist ministers Oliver Hart and John Stevens. The Reverend George Whitefield periodically held services in Pelot's church, which was purported to be the center of the Great Awakening in the southern district of South Carolina. Whitefield even delivered the inaugural sermon in the newly completed church on 5 March 1751/52.[72]

The Reverend Pelot appears to have been a well-read educator and maintained a substantial library. He helped educate other early Baptist ministers, including the Reverends Evan Pugh and Edmund Botsford, and had a part in the founding of at least three daughter congregations and also a Regular Baptist congregation at Coosawhatchie. In addition to his pastoral responsibilities, Pelot amassed sizable landholdings and owned a number of slaves. He actively solicited funds for the construction of what became the first Baptist college in the North American colonies (today's Brown University) and was chosen as one of three advocates to address the Baptists of America in support of the project. He also carried the distinction of being the first Baptist preacher of record in the Pipe Creek area by virtue of his Christmas Day sermon at Black Swamp in 1762. It is entirely possible that Pelot chose to spend his professional life just a few miles from Purrysburg to maintain the network of relationships that had been nurtured in the township. His close proximity to his parent's home there certainly made it more feasible for him to petition successfully colonial authorities in 1752 and 1753 on behalf of his father Jonas for legal title to land that Jonas had been entitled to since his arrival at the township with his young family in 1735. Although the Reverend Pelot lived exclusively north and east of Purrysburg in the Euhaw area for most of his adult life, he did not sell his pew in the parish church of St. Peter's Purrysburg until late 1768 and retained possession of his town lot in Purrysburg until March 1770—just four years before his death. Pelot might also have continued to maintain some affinity for the Reformed tradition of his youth as his Regular Baptist proclivities comported well with aspects of his Calvinistic heritage unlike the General Baptist persuasion, which grew apace in the South Carolina backcountry during the evangelical revival.[73]

The Reverend John (Johann) Joachim Zubly enjoyed an even more illustrious career than did Pelot. He has been called the most well-known of all the German Reformed preachers of the colonial period.[74] Zubly was the son of David and Helena Zubly, early Purrysburg immigrants from St. Gall in the Swiss Confederation. John was born on 27 August 1724, and he and his family arrived in South Carolina in 1726 with the few others who were well-heeled enough to pay their own passage after the Lords Proprietors sabotaged Purry's first effort at colonization in South Carolina.[75] His father sent him to study theology at Tübingen and Halle in preparation for the Reformed ministry. He was ordained before the age of twenty at the German Reformed Church of London.[76] The elder Zubly entertained some hopes that his son would choose to minister to the Reformed Germans of Purrysburg upon the completion of his studies because he was fluent in German, French, and English. As the Reverend Boltzius wrote in November 1742, however, "because the German people are becoming fewer and fewer and he has no strong desire to remain there, he wishes that the Reformed Germans of Savannah might call him to be their preacher." The Georgia trustees turned down a request by citizens of Vernonsburg, Acton, and adjacent villages to have Zubly installed as their pastor, citing his youth and the financial implications of his appointment. He did preach in Vernonsburg, Acton, and Hampstead and was recommended by the trustees to assist the Reverend Bartholomew Zouberbühler in those hamlets close to Savannah, where he hoped to pastor the Reformed Germans. He returned to South Carolina for a short time by 1745, visited his parents in Purrysburg, and appears to have remained in the general area for some time preaching variously at Savannah, Acton, and Vernonsburg in Georgia and perhaps occasionally to the Germans at Purrysburg, even though the Reverend Chiffelle remained the minister of record for the township. Soon after his marriage to Ann, daughter of early Purrysburg settler John Tobler in 1746, Zubly relocated to Amelia Township, where he preached at the Lutheran church through much of 1747 and into 1748.

In 1748 he began a series of preaching assignments at Reformed churches in Charles Town, Cainhoy, Orangeburg, and Wando Neck. He turned down an opportunity to minister to a German Reformed congregation in Lancaster, Pennsylvania, but did travel extensively in the North. He met most of the region's renowned ministers, including many of the Awakeners, such as Gilbert Tennant and James Davenport. He returned to the South with definite Presbyterian sympathies and accepted a call to the Independent Church and Meeting House of Savannah in 1758 (later to be known as the Independent Presbyterian Church). He became the church's full-time minister in 1760 and remained in that pastorate until his death, though the American Revolution would disrupt his ministry for some time. He served the largest congregation in the colony during the revolutionary era and preached in German, English, or French, depending on his audience. Zubly also found time to preach at an unnamed French Reformed settlement, which may have been Purrysburg or perhaps New Bordeaux in Hillsborough Township. He established a ferry across the Savannah River near Purrysburg on his land (Middlesex Island) and preached in the area occasionally—including at Purrysburg and Black Swamp. After the death of his wife in July 1765, Zubly married Ann Pye of Purrysburg.

Zubly wrote several books and continued to be an important force for spiritual renewal in South Carolina and Georgia up to the Revolution. With the coming of the Revolution, Zubly represented Georgia in the First Continental Congress and was a delegate to the first meeting of the Georgia Provincial Congress, but his ultimate loyalty to Great Britain cost him dearly. He was taken into custody by the Georgia Council of Safety and later lost half his estate and endured banishment from the state. He took refuge in South Carolina and preached at various places in the state, including Purrysburg. He returned to Savannah in December 1778, after the British victory. He left for Charleston in November 1779, finally returning to Savannah in April 1781. He resumed his ministerial duties in Savannah and died there on 23 July 1781.

Although he probably could not preach often to the Reformed of Purrysburg after the 1740s, he was a frequent visitor and well known to them as he was the executor of at least four wills of Purrysburg settlers: those of David Zubly (his father), George Herchnecht, Jacob Waldburger, and Margaret Henry. In 1750 Zubly left his South Carolina parish to visit the Reformed congregations in and around Savannah and must have stopped in Purrysburg, at least briefly. Four years later, when the Reverend Chiffelle could not petition the council in person because of illness, Zubly supported his land claim via an affidavit. Even after he moved to the Independent Church in Savannah, Zubly knew about the arrival of the Reverend Imer in Purrysburg before the Ebenezer clergy did, which would indicate the maintenance of significant connection to the township. He also witnessed the transfer of land in Purrysburg for at least one local resident and in one year (1778) preached the funeral sermons for Jacob Winkler, the stillborn child of the Holzendorfs, and Adrian Mayer—the wealthiest resident of the township. He baptized a number of children of Purrysburg landowners, including members of the Humbert, Winkler, Ravot, Roberts, Raymond, Keal, and Martinangel families, and married John Mayerhoff to Mary Winkler and Charles Fousche to Mary Elizabeth Jeanerett. When the eminent Lutheran minister Henry Melchior Mühlenberg visited South Carolina and Georgia in 1774, Zubly visited his longtime friend on his return from a trip to Purrysburg. In January of the following year, Mühlenberg noted in his diary that Zubly "returned from Purisburg where he had preached in English." Zubly often visited the Reverend Pelot at his residence as the two continued to maintain the friendship they had shared growing up together in Purrysburg. He also became involved in a legal matter with Purrysburg landowner Melchior Leichtensteiger.[77] The Reverend Zubly may well have been instrumental in the founding of a Presbyterian church in Purrysburg.

The establishment of a Reformed congregation under the Presbyterian polity sometime during the later colonial period was perhaps another legacy of the Great Awakening in Purrysburg Township. Because of the nature of extant evidence, the founding date of the church cannot be precisely determined. The Reverend Boltzius provides the first clue to its origin when he noted in his journal for 7 May 1760 that "Peter Hammer of Ebenezer commanded his oldest daughter to marry a Reformed minister in Purrysburg." The marriage was performed prior to 10 October of that year, because Boltizius on that date observed that Hammer and the rest of his family would be moving the following week "to his son-in-law in Purrysburg."[78] This minister could not have been the Reverend Abraham Imer, who arrived in the township in 1760 to begin his parish ministry. In his 2 December 1760 entry Boltzius specifically mentioned that Imer "arrived last summer." The summer arrival of the Reverend Imer was confirmed by a letter written to the Pietist pastor by the Reverend Zubly and duly noted by Boltzius on 4 July. Also in the December notation Boltzius wrote that the new minister at Purrysburg "has a wife and children."[79]

The presence of this anonymous, newly married Reformed minister in the township remains baffling because he is completely absent from any denominational history of the region. It is unknown whether "Reformed" denotes Presbyterian in this case, though the only other local enclaves with Reformed tendencies were located in the Savannah area and in Hillsborough Township up the Savannah River from Purrysburg. It is, however, generally agreed that from the mid-1740s into the 1770s much of the expanding evangelization work associated with the religious awakenings in South Carolina had been done by itinerant evangelical Presbyterian ministers. Extensive Presbyterian involvement in the religious enthusiasm of the era provided opportunities for the denomination to augment its numbers. Perhaps this Purrysburg Reformed minister had been a Presbyterian itinerant who decided to marry and settle in the township.[80] The presence of a nameless, "Reformed" minister in Purrysburg does not necessarily correlate either directly or immediately with the founding of a Presbyterian church there in the early 1760s, but in all likelihood the church was established sometime between Imer's initial departure in 1765 and the outbreak of hostilities on the southern frontier in late 1775, because there is no evidence to indicate the presence of an Anglican or any other minister resident in the township for most of that period. Nevertheless, nothing is known of the church, its minister, or its congregation between the date of its founding and January 1789, when a petition reached the General Assembly from Purrysburg.

The petition presented to the House on 21 January 1789 from members of the Presbyterian Church at Purrysburg,[81] informed the legislators that their church had been destroyed by the British. "Since then the petitioners have been deprived of [the] privilege of attending divine services and procuring a minister to perform public worship therein according to the Rights and Ceremonies of our Church." The Purrysburg Presbyterians appear to have been keenly aware of the religious right of legal incorporation accorded South Carolina Dissenting congregations by the Constitution of 1778.[82] They continue, "Whereas the petitioners and many others in St. Peter's have by voluntary subscription provided for the maintenance of a minister Now think our intentions should be more effectually carried into execution were we incorporated and made one body politic and corporate in law and vested with all the powers, privileges, and immunities which any of our sister churches enjoy. And we your petitioners also pray, that the glebe land and lots thereunto belonging might be secured to use by an Act of Assembly."[83] The House referred the petition to the Committee on Religion, which on 14 February recommended that the Purrysburg Presbyterian Church be allowed to incorporate. The committee also recommended that such a bill be crafted and brought before the legislature for action. Over the next three weeks, the bill worked its way through the General Assembly and was ratified on 7 March.[84]

Aside from the petition, not much else is known of the Purrysburg Presbyterian Church in the eighteenth century, but a close analysis of the petition does provide important details about the church and its congregation—both in 1789 and during the late colonial era. The names appearing on the petition are mostly of German, French, or English extraction. If this characteristic of 1789 held true for the church before its destruction, and there is no reason to believe that it did not, the Presbyterian congregation was a multiethnic one. It was also a family church as was common for rural areas of the time. Four different families have two members represented among the signatories (Hezekiah and James Roberts, Jacob and Nicholas Winkler, Daniel and Lewis Giroud, Philip and [illegible] Mayer). Many of the families represented had lived in the township since well before 1760 (Roberts, Winkler, Giroud, Mayer, Hover, Strobhart, Humbert, Bininger). Also significant to note is the fact that the seventeen petitioners "and many others" sustained the church up to the time of its destruction by their own voluntary contributions. They must have consistently raised enough money to keep a minister, maintain (and perhaps purchase) a manse with glebe for him, and still have funds left over to purchase other land for use by the church. They also had sufficient education or at least enough political awareness to follow the correct procedures that could lead to incorporation. The exact date of the destruction of the Purrysburg Presbyterian Church is uncertain, but a reasonable assumption would place the event sometime in May 1779, when the township became the staging area for a British invasion of South Carolina.

This Presbyterian congregation obviously comprised descendants of some of the early French-, German-, and English-speaking inhabitants of the township and offers a tantalizing indication that Purrysburg communal spirit may have coalesced around the extension of common confessional traditions divorced from linguistic insularity by the late colonial period. In other words, because of considerations noted previously, the common Reformed tradition of most Purrysburg settlers could not serve as a unifying force in the early decades of township settlement. Consequently the German-speaking Reformed of Purrysburg forsook their religious confession for the ethnic bond of common linguistic and cultural traditions at places such as Ebenezer. This bond was perceived as more important than maintaining a Reformed confessional allegiance without the ability to participate in worship, because services were conducted in French according to the Reformed or Anglican rite. By the 1770s, however, it is very likely that the preeminent value placed on linguistic commonality by earlier generations had lessened because of increased utility of the English language by second- and third-generation Purrysburg settlers. As a result, when the French and German speakers could communicate with each other in a common language—English—the bond of shared religious confession reemerged in Purrysburg through the establishment of a Presbyterian congregation. At this point, and only at this point, could the church serve as that potent force for community solidarity in the township as it did elsewhere in the eighteenth century. In light of the fact that in the wake of the evangelical movement in South Carolina the number of Presbyterian churches grew from eight in 1740 to forty-eight in 1775, it is entirely conceivable that the initial organization of the Purrysburg Presbyterian Church signifies the strength of the evangelical movement among township residents.[85]

That community social and ideological beliefs evolved via an existential tug of war with the evangelical enthusiasm of the mid–eighteenth century has been one of the most significant discoveries of recent inquiry on southern colonial religious life.[86] Perhaps no other family has been offered as more archetypical of these tensions than the Bryans of South Carolina. The manifold activities and intrigues of various members of the family have been offered as evidence to illustrate both the general failure of religious enthusiasm in South Carolina and the expansion of South Carolina planter interests into neighboring Georgia. The same family, however, has also been touted as a prime example of the power of evangelical Christianity to alter normative social ideology, albeit within clearly prescribed limits.[87]

According to Leigh Eric Schmidt, one of the most significant features of the evangelical faith of Hugh and Jonathan Bryan proceeded from their conviction that slaves too should be allowed into the Christian fold and be treated with Christian charity. This belief, at least partially inspired by Whitefield's perspective on the relationship between slaves, slavery, and Christian faith, directly challenged the conventional wisdom of the time. For Whitefield, the Bryans, and like-minded evangelicals along the Savannah River believed that white charity toward slaves and genuine concern for their conversion to Christianity would strengthen, not weaken, the institution of slavery. The Bryans maintained plantations all along the lower Savannah River and facilitated close-knit fellowship between evangelical inhabitants of the area, who included the Lutherans of Ebenezer. Among the most productive plantations and cattle ranches in the South Carolina lowcountry were those of Hugh Bryan at Monmouth Point within the confines of Purrysburg Township and in the rich alluvial lands to its southeast. The spiritual kinship between the Salzburg émigrés, the Reverend Whitefield, and the Bryan brothers paid dividends beyond a sense of religious solidarity. It also resulted in the dissemination of the progressive social agenda of evangelicals regarding slavery and presented opportunities for the exercise of charitable giving without ever raising the specter of emancipation.

It is a difficult task to determine to what extent the evangelicalism of their neighbors to the northwest at Ebenezer and families such as the Bryans to the south had upon the treatment of slaves by their Purrysburg masters. Yet there are indications that some township masters did indeed care for their chattels in much the same humanitarian ways as did the Bryans, failing—as did the Bryans, Whitefield, and other evangelicals—to question the efficacy of the institution. Perhaps the best example of slavery under the influence of evangelicalism is the seemingly paradoxical behavior of the Kieffer family. As early as May 1739, one of Theobald Sr.'s sons, probably Theobald Jr., requested a primer from the Reverend Boltzius so that he "might be able to teach his father's two Negroes how to read." The Pietist pastor wrote that the younger Kieffer was "eager to give them some instruction both during work and on other occasions in the recognition of the Lord." One of the slaves seemed particularly desirous to receive such instruction. Their lack of much knowledge of German, however, limited what they could learn at that time.[88]

In April 1742 Theobald Kieffer Jr., who had moved from Purrysburg to Ebenezer but worked his plantation in Purrysburg, brought one of his slaves to church services in the Salzburger settlement for the first time. The timing was significant as the Bryans had been holding religious meetings for their slaves along the Savannah River for nearly two years. The African male knew some

German and conducted himself with modesty and rectitude during the service, according to the Reverend Boltzius. The younger Kieffer had actually called on Boltzius to secure the pastor's permission to bring both of his slaves to worship and prayer services "so that they might learn the German language and become aware of the doctrine of Christ." The Salzburg settlers were so greatly affected by the slave's demeanor that he "forced out many moving sighs and prayers from us on his behalf, even some tears from some among us, from which this Negro himself also profited, for he was given a shirt and one other gift, for which he showed himself very grateful and humble."[89] Five years later, Kieffer lent his father—Theobald Sr.—money to buy one male and one female slave. Theobald Sr., who lived in Purrysburg but traveled regularly to Ebenezer to participate in worship and fellowship with other German-speaking Lutherans, had experienced financial reverses including the deaths of at least two of his own slaves. The two purchased slaves worked both the elder and younger Theobalds' plantations in Purrysburg Township. The slave couple eventually had a son together, and both the Kieffer males asked Boltzius to baptize the child. Though clearly an action for which he and others had earlier reproached the Reverend Chiffelle, Boltzius acceded to the request, with the Kieffer males and Theobald Jr.'s wife attended as witnesses. The father and son then took the highly unusual step of seeking permission of the boy's father to adopt him and raise him as their own "in a true Christian manner." The father agreed "on the condition that the Kieffers promise that the child would not change hands and would be raised Christian."[90] Although it cannot be known how widespread these responses to chattel slavery in Purrysburg were, at least the Zublys and a few other township families exhibited similar sentiments.[91]

Whatever the extent of a more humane approach to slavery among the Purrysburg residents, the Kieffer family's attempt to mitigate the institution's effects clearly illustrates the paradoxes embodied in the evangelical response to slavery in the mid–eighteenth century: a deep and genuine concern for the salvation of Africans, a humane regard for the physical well-being of individual slaves coupled with a disregard for black family life, a polite civility toward enslaved Africans, and a simultaneous and unwavering commitment to the unimpeded and continued expansion of the institution of slavery. If the Kieffers are at all indicative of the ways in which Purrysburg families understood slavery, Gallay's thesis that "evangelical religion helped white southerners adapt to the frontier conditions of loneliness, hardship, and noninstitutional support while alleviating the guilt that arose from the inhumane treatment of Indians and blacks" would fit the immigrant township as well as it seems to explain the Bryan family.[92]

IV

The multiple effects of evangelical piety upon the spiritual and social fabric of Purrysburg life should not obscure the educational impact of Christianity on the frontier township, for, in addition to offering spiritual guidance and ideological grounding, eighteenth-century Christianity championed education for the young. Schooling not only equipped young people for service in this world. It also prepared them for full church membership and responsibility. In early modern Protestant Europe, the most important educational agency had been the family. By its very structure and function in society, the family served to reinforce social authority and to train children for their proper role in society. The church also exercised educative functions, as did the local community. The pressures of life in British America, however, irreparably altered these Old World priorities and displaced the family as the primary educator of the young. Formal educational institutions were founded to undertake the training of children. The southern colonial experience was even more destructive of traditional European educational strategies than was that of New England. The desire to establish effective town and church institutions to rescue children from savagery took many forms in the southern provinces—hiring servant teachers, founding local or parish schools, and, most often, allocating money in parental wills for the education of children. Unfortunately for the Purrysburg immigrants and their descendants, South Carolina, not unlike the South in general, subordinated education and intellectual pursuits to social and economic gain. The Commons House of Assembly was notorious for its unwillingness to spend money on education, and its members repeatedly refused to establish schools in the province. As a result, most children living in rural parishes such as St. Peter's, could not read or write. Education, when it was available in Purrysburg, had to come from sources other than the colonial government. The relative scarcity of information on educational opportunities for Purrysburg Township residents is more indicative of the sorry state of intellectual exercise in the settlement than of the dearth of sources on the subject.[93]

Although the unusual religious situation of Purrysburg redounded to the benefit of the township's French speakers, the German speakers received to a greater extent the benefit of the educative role of the church, and many took advantage of their opportunities.[94] Indeed, although there is no indication that the French-speaking children of the township had any opportunity to attend school in their own language, if at all, the German-speaking children had two educational possibilities until at least 1736—one in Purrysburg and another in Ebenezer.[95] Purrysburg German speakers were fortunate to have had access to three schoolmasters within the first five years of settlement. Sometime in 1734 the Germanic schoolmaster Mr. Uselt arrived in Purrysburg with his family to begin a school. Upon Uselt's untimely demise, the position of schoolmaster remained open until the following year. As early as 22 April 1734 many of the German-speaking townspeople petitioned the pastors at Ebenezer to have their children accepted into the thriving Pietist school served by both pastors and a schoolteacher named Mr. Ortmann. Instruction at the school was heavily religious, and the pastors undoubtedly trained the children in the catechism and their religious duties. Because of the factors of distance, finances, and the unstable condition of the recently settled Salzburg refugees, Purrysburg children did not attend school there at this early time.[96]

By September 1735, through the efforts of Boltzius and Gronau, Purrysburg was temporarily provided with another schoolmaster. On one of his frequent trips to the township early that month, Boltzius listened as the German-speaking residents elaborated on the plight of their unschooled children. He ultimately agreed to support a Purrysburg weaver, George Schönmannsgruber, for one quarter as a schoolmaster at two pounds sterling. This stipend from Boltzius, made possible by a European supporter of the Ebenezer Lutherans, allowed poor parents in the township to give only what they could afford and still send their children to school. During the trial period, Schönmannsgruber was to take his directives from the Ebenezer pastors, and they exercised the right to visit him on their trips to Purrysburg to check on the execution of his teaching responsibilities. Less than two weeks into the school term, the schoolmaster traveled to Ebenezer to acquire some primers and catechetical texts and also to ask the advice of the pastors as to the conduct of his school. He accepted their admonitions and agreed not to allow the children to take home the loaned books. Schönmannsgruber expressed the wish, echoed by many in Purrysburg, that the pastors would take over the school entirely. For undetermined reasons, the Pietists refused to do so and also admonished the teacher to take into the school Reformed orphan children who had no place to go if such a request was made by Purrysburg residents.[97]

By October both teacher and students were hard at work. Even though he had to put up with parental faultfinding, Schönmannsgruber appeared to be an effective teacher. Unfortunately the probationary quarter ended in December and so did the Purrysburg school. The Ebenezer pastors could not continue to support it, and township residents were in no position to assume financial responsibility for its operation. Schönmannsgruber may have persevered without stipend for a brief time into 1736, but he resolved by April to venture northward to seek better employment opportunities. Sadly, he never reached his destination, for, although his family did leave Purrysburg for Pennsylvania, Schönmannsgruber was overcome by a fever and died while on route in January 1737.

A Mr. Müller also appears to have instructed Purrysburg children, but only for a short time during the 1730s. Another effort to establish a school in the township was begun in late 1738 by Moravian missionaries, but this enterprise headed by the Reverend Peter Böhler expired shortly after its inception. A further attempt to secure a schoolmaster for Purrysburg ended in failure when a Mr. Falk from Pennsylvania refused the position in January 1739. Over the next decade and a half, as the struggling Purrysburg economy began to prosper, education became less important than tending plantations and livestock. Under the twenty-four-year ministry of the Reverend Chiffelle, there are no indications that he conducted schooling for any of his Purrysburg congregants. Lewis Netman (Nettman) provided education for Purrysburg children for some time in the 1750s and may have continued to do so into the 1760s, but nothing is known of his efforts. Just prior to the Reverend Imer's arrival in 1760, an itinerant schoolmaster taught in the township for eight or nine months, charging twelve pounds current money per student. Imer noted upon his arrival that "a few of the French or English and none of the German youths" were able to read. The new minister resolved to reverse this state of affairs by teaching the children three times weekly. Imer's commitment to the young impressed the Reverend Boltzius, who noted after an extended meeting with him in early December 1760 that he desired to fulfill his spiritual vocation in the township, which included attention to the educational needs of the younger generation. That Imer required material assistance for his educative work became obvious when he observed that "Bibles are scarce. French or German ones would be preferred." Just what the Reverend Imer contributed to the education of Purrysburg's youth is uncertain, but between at least 1760 and 1765 Purryburg resident John Lester appears to have conducted some educational activities. After Imer's death in 1768 formal schooling in the township must have been sporadic at best unless it was conducted by the unnamed Presbyterian minister(s) who served that congregation after its founding. It would be logical to assume that periodic, but temporary, instruction may have been supplied by itinerant schoolmasters. Just at the beginning of the constitutional period in 1787, Purrysburg did secure the services of George Fisher, who continued to teach township children until at least 1790.[98]

Even before the brief episode with Schönmannsgruber, Purrysburg German speakers had already begun entering their children in the Ebenezer school, encouraged by the religious interchange between Germanic inhabitants of the two settlements and by the stability of the school. Though Ebenezer suffered as much privation as did Purrysburg in the early years, the Pietists were able to offer aid to indigent township children because of the financial support they received from the SPG and from other sources in Europe. Nearly contemporaneous with the opening of the school at the township under Schönmannsgruber, Purrysburg tailor Jacob Metsger enrolled his teen-aged son in its Ebenezer counterpart. While the Pietist pastors considered the seventeen-year-old Metsger "right stupid to be sure," he remained industrious and attentive and so stayed at the school until he was prepared for his first communion.[99]

As the decade of the 1730s progressed the bonds formed between the Salzburg Germans in Ebenezer and Purrysburg German speakers were strengthened by the number of township children cared for in the Georgia town. Both Purrysburg Lutheran and Reformed families took advantage of the opportunities afforded the young across the Savannah River. By 1740 children from the Kieffer, Waldburger

(Wallpurger), Metsger, Uselt, Reck, Mohr, Krüsy, and Francke families, as well as others, had spent time there. In August 1744, for example, two apparently orphaned Reformed Purrysburg brothers brought their ten-year-old sister to enroll at the Ebenezer school. She lodged with a Salzburger family (the Brückners) that received monthly payments for looking after her. Fees for enrollment, room, and board meant that Purrysburg families had to make difficult decisions about the allocation of sometimes scarce resources. When such decisions led to the removal of Purrysburg children from the Ebenezer school, the Reverend Boltzius was less than understanding. In 1737 Mrs. Waldburger (Wallpurger) placed her two fatherless children at Ebenezer "for which she was to pay just a tolerable sum." She decided to take her children back to Purrysburg a few months later but continued to pay on what she owed into the early 1740s for the time they were enrolled. By September 1742 her second husband, "a Frenchman," died. She wrote to Boltzius, explaining her situation and that she desired to pay off the debt as soon as possible. He, however, took the occasion to assess the commitment Purrysburg parents had to the education of their children:

> Some few people from Purrysburg have had their children here and had them boarded in the orphanage, but soon the small boarding fee would become too high for them, hence, they took them home, and would rather let them go astray and grow up wild than apply a few monies to them. The great bulk of people care only for their own and their children's bellies; little or nothing is applied to church, school, and proper raising. Even if there are some who are poor who otherwise might have been able to send their children to school, they prefer to use them for herding cattle, in tilling the soil, at fishing, hunting, or supervising blacks.[100]

More children replaced these, many of their names never appearing in Boltzius's otherwise meticulous observations of life in Ebenezer. With the reception of a gift from European supporters, the Pietists built an orphanage that eventually housed many Purrysburg children. Unfortunately the need continually outpaced the facilities, and all needy children from the township could not be accommodated. Orphaned Purrysburg children were provided clothing and food by their relatives, and many were placed in the homes of pious Salzburgers for care and supervision. At the completion of the orphanage, most of the children were housed there. Many of the poor German speakers of Purrysburg could not pay the required school dues in currency, so arrangements were made for payment in kind when crops were harvested or in cash when possible. The Ebenezer pastors demonstrated their compassion for Purrysburg orphans by interceding for one of them in court. One former Purrysburg couple (Theobald Kieffer Jr. and his wife) even considered sending their son to Europe with Boltzius for a proper education at Halle. On occasion, the Salzburg pastors received totally indigent children of Purrysburg and undertook their sole support while they remained in school. Yet they were not afraid to punish what they determined to be lax or unbecoming behavior.[101]

The evangelist George Whitefield provided another opportunity for Purrysburg children to receive an education in 1739 when he opened the Bethesda orphanage a few miles north of Savannah. The orphanage quickly became a regional center of social welfare and education, for as early as September 1741 only one half the children at Bethesda were from Georgia. Less than six months later, only fourteen of sixty at the institution were from the colony. Even with the large number of children at the orphanage from outside Georgia, only one reference makes note of Purrysburg children there. In this singular reference the child in question had contracted smallpox at the orphanage but recovered and was doing well in September 1740.[102] Whitefield also entertained the thought of establishing a public school and college in Georgia for he believed that these institutions were needed by children in the surrounding countryside, including Purrysburg. He wrote in March 1746 that "if there should be peace, it is certain that such a school would be exceedingly useful not only for those northern parts of the colony, but also for the more southern parts of Carolina, and for Purrysburg and Frederica, where are many fine youths. I have been prevailed upon to take one from Frederica and another from Purrysburg, and it may be I shall admit more."[103] Although he received some encouragement in these plans and even grants of land for the college he envisioned, the orphanage school remained his only real educational accomplishment and the only other option for the children of Purrysburg until the Reverend Imer's arrival in 1760.[104]

V

It is difficult to determine accurately how many Purrysburg children were educated at Ebenezer and Bethesda or how long families continued sending their children to board elsewhere for educational purposes. Whatever the number or however long these educational practices continued, their significance lies in the fact that the greater educative opportunities for German speakers, Reformed or Lutheran, in Ebenezer meshed with greater spiritual opportunities there, so that the Purrysburg immigrants experienced a schism along distinctly linguistic lines that lasted from the 1730s well into the 1760s and contributed heavily to the siphoning off of Purrysburg settlers of Germanic linguistic heritage across the Savannah River into Georgia. Although French speakers were somewhat better serviced by the resident ministers of the township, they also experienced uneven exercise of their faith. Consequently, where Robert Mitchell found a lessening of ethnic consciousness among some groups in the Shenandoah Valley in the wake of the religious enthusiasm of the 1750s and the revivals of the revolutionary era, the exact opposite effect seems to have characterized Purryburg. The Reverend Chiffelle's proclamation of the Reformed liturgy in French not only perpetuated the religious predilections of nearly one half the population of the township, but also served to alienate the other half, who sought other avenues to satisfy their spiritual needs. The proximity of Ebenezer only exacerbated the chasm between the French and German speakers and drained Purrysburg of communal vitality. In Germantown, Pennsylvania, the degree of religious assimilation paralleled the extent of cultural assimilation. In nearby Reading, Michael Zuckerman argues, ethnicity and religious life were not conflated, and choices were made by settlers to jettison either their religious heritage or their ethnic traditions. Unfortunately the Purrysburg case is far more complex than the Pennsylvania examples, for in the township, language, religious expression, and colonial policy forced the settlers to chose *between* the ethnic markers of language or religious faith—but both choices tore at the fabric of the Purrysburg community and conditioned the viability both of that community and of the religious expression of its inhabitants.[105]

What becomes clear is that Purrysburg settlers, whether French or German speakers, labored under adversity that inhibited the free and continuous exercise of religious and educational proclivities. Whereas in most other American contexts the church "operated as a center of cultural life among the Reformed and Lutherans," the ethnic boundaries of language and religious confession in the frontier township could not exist simultaneously for all the immigrants and therefore that centrality was severely tested.[106] Not until the Reverend Imer's arrival in the 1760s did both French and Germans in the township have the opportunity to worship in Purrysburg. The founding of a Purrysburg Presbyterian congregation at roughly the same time signifies a vital and ongoing link to the Reformed confession by English-speaking descendants of the original settlers of the township. The emergence of a viable community-based Reformed congregation in the late colonial period speaks directly to the ability of second- and third-generation Purrysburg settlers to coalesce around the historic confession of their parents and grandparents, thereby reconstituting an important aspect of ethnicity adapted to the altered linguistic environment of the 1770s. The religious history of Purrysburg Township provides an example of the dynamic relationship between ethnicity and denominational affiliation, as well as a case study with regard to under "what conditions immigrants adhered to their ethnic communities or abandoned them and in what circumstances settlers stayed within their religious traditions or strayed from them."[107] In their reordering of ethnic priorities Purrysburg Township inhabitants were not unique, but the perseverance and ingenuity of its citizens are instructive.[108] The adaptability of its community members during this reorientation of religious life illustrates the existence of flexible ethnic boundaries, as well as a dynamic network of vertical and horizontal relationships.

The Purrysburg Presbyterian Church served both a communal and ethnic function. Frederik Barth, who has written extensively the phenomena of ethnic boundaries, contends that boundaries that set off one group from another are not fixed and so can change over time. The priority of various ethnic boundaries or markers can change (as in the religious life of Purrysburg) without being eradicated over time. Boundaries are thus permeable and fluid, shifting as demanded by the wider cultural environment.[109] The exigencies of frontier life in Purrysburg Township forced its inhabitants to choose among linguistic, religious, and communal boundaries because, given the peculiar circumstances the immigrants discovered upon their arrival, all ethnic and communal traits could not exist in harmony with each other. Perhaps their remarkable ability to adapt confessional allegiances and to refocus both their sense of ethnicity and community proceeded at least in part from a religious enthusiasm that grew in power and strength even as Purrysburg itself matured.[110]

MEMOIRE
SUR
LE PAIS DES CAFRES,
ET
LA TERRE DE NUYTS.
Par raport à l'utilité que la Compagnie des INDES ORIENTALES en pourroit retirer pour ſon Commerce.

A AMSTERDAM,
Chez PIERRE HUMBERT.
M DCC XVIII.

Title page from Purry's first published tract, *Memoire*, explaining his theory of optimal climates and his plan for the Dutch East India Company's colonization of portions of southern Africa and Australia.

SECOND
MEMOIRE
SUR
LE PAIS DES CAFRES,
ET
LA TERRE DE NUYTS.
Servant d'éclairciſſement aux propoſitions faites dans le premier, pour l'utilité de la Compagnie des INDES ORIENTALES.

A AMSTERDAM,
Chez PIERRE HUMBERT
M DCC XVIII.

Title page from Purry's second attempt to convince officials of the Dutch East India Company to support his colonization plans for the company's claimed territory in southern Africa and southern Australia.

MEMOIRE

Presenté à Sa Gr.

MYLORD DUC de *NEWCASTLE*,

Chambellan de S. M. le Roi GEORGE, &c.
& Secretaire d'Etat:

Sur l'état présent de la CAROLINE & sur les moyens de l'améliorer;

Par JEAN PIERRE PURRY, de Neufchâtel de Suisse.

Title page from Purry's memorial to the Duke of Newcastle. It was widely reported that Sir Issac Newton, while urging further investigation, generally supported Purry's climatological theory and colonization plans.

DESCRIPTION ABREGEE

De l'Etat présent de la

CAROLINE

MERIDIONALE,

NOUVELLE EDITION,

Avec des

ECLAIRCISSEMENS,

les

ACTES

des

CONCESSIONS

Faites à ce sujet à l'Auteur, tant pour luy que pour ceux qui voudront prendre parti avec luy.

Et enfin une

INSTRUCTION

qui contient les

Conditions, sous lesquelles on pourra l'accompagner.

A NEUFCHATEL.

Se vend chez le Sr. Jacob Boyve à Neufchatel;
Et chez le Sr. Sécretaire Du Bois à St. Sulpy.

Title page from the original French language version of Purry's "brief description of Carolina, new edition with clarifications." No copy of the French version of the initial edition has been found.

Detail from *Novissima et perfectissima Africae descriptio* (1696) by Carel Allard. Purry believed that the region called Caffaria (Kaffraria in his tracts), just inland from the southeastern coast of Africa, would yield a rich bounty to the country that chose to colonize it because it existed in the optimal fifth climate zone, as explained in his climatological theory. Reproduced by permission of the John Ford Bell Library, University of Minnesota

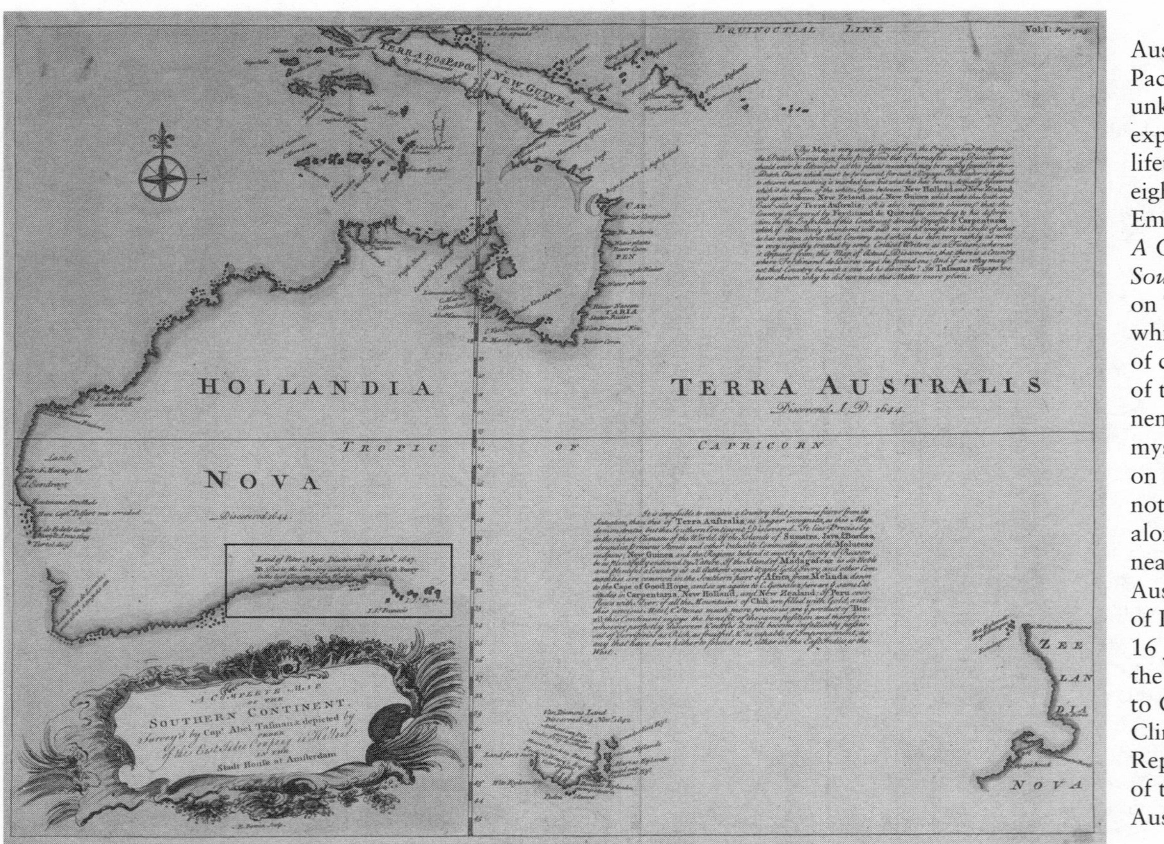

Australia and the South Pacific were still relatively unknown to western explorers during Purry's lifetime and well into the eighteenth century. In 1744 Emanuel Bowen published *A Complete Map of the Southern Continent*, based on Thevenot's map of 1663, which illustrates the extent of cartographic knowledge of the era. While the continent of Australia was still mysterious, Purry's designs on its southern region were not. The notation in the box along the Nullarbor Plain near the head of the Great Australian Bight reads "Land of Peter Nuyts Discovered 16 Jan'y 1627. NB. This is the Country seated according to Coll. Purry in the best Climate, in the World." Reproduced by permission of the National Library of Australia

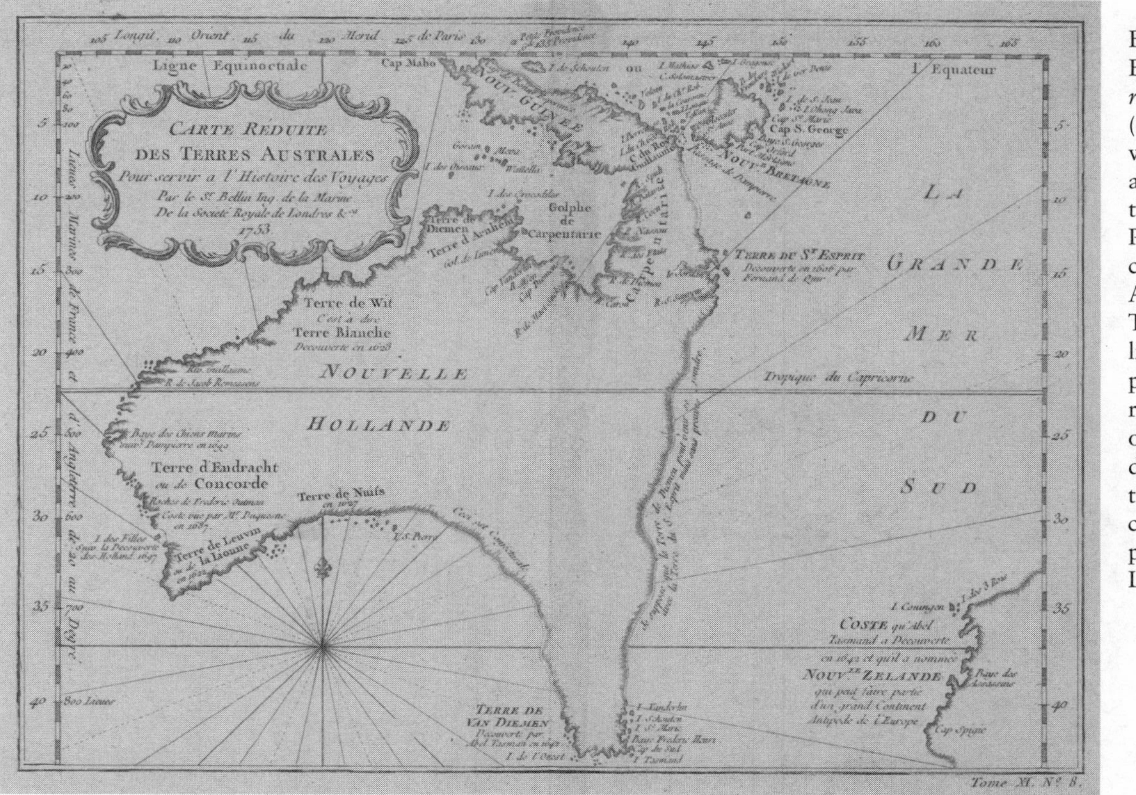

By the time that Jacques Bellin published his *Carte réduite des terres australes* (Paris: Chez Didot, 1753), western mapmakers were able to add some features to the landforms in the South Pacific although accurate cartographic knowledge of Australia, New Zealand, and Tasmania was still rather limited at midcentury. Bellin presented a more detailed rendering of the coastline of the Terre de Nuits [Terre de Nuyts] but also noted that his depiction of it was conjectural. Reproduced by permission of the National Library of Australia

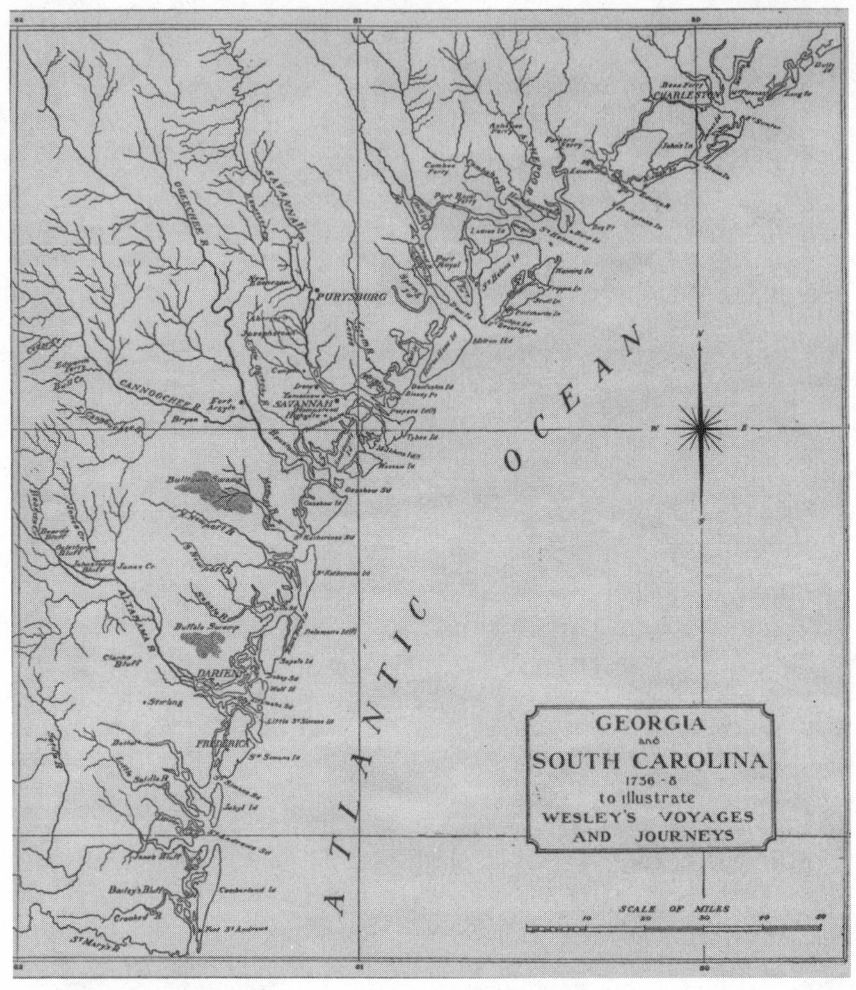

The colonial Southeast in 1738, with "Purysburg" prominently displayed. Reproduced from Nehemiah Curnock, *The Journal of John Wesley, A.M.*, standard edition, vol. 1 (New York: Eaton and Mains, 1909)

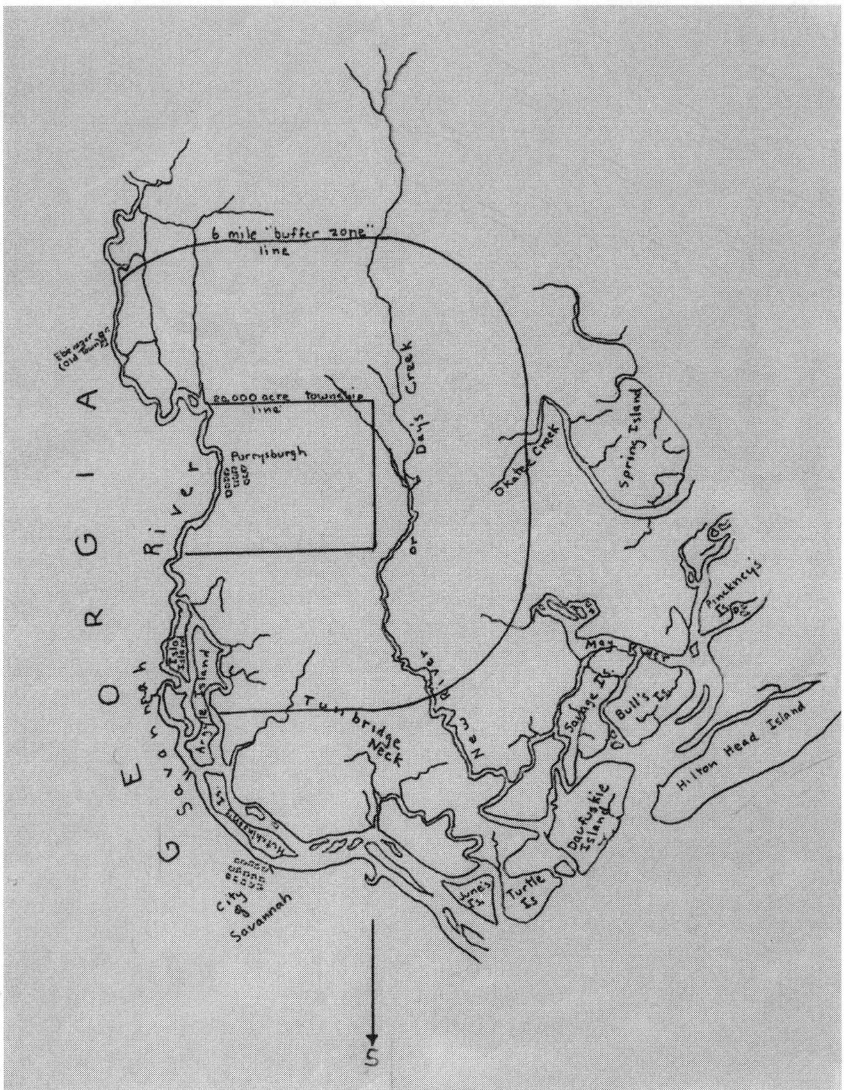

"Purrysburgh" Township and its immediate environs with the six-mile boundary line. Adapted from the map that accompanied H. A. M. Smith's article on Purrysburg in the *South Carolina Historical and Genealogical Magazine* 10 (October 1909): facing page 187

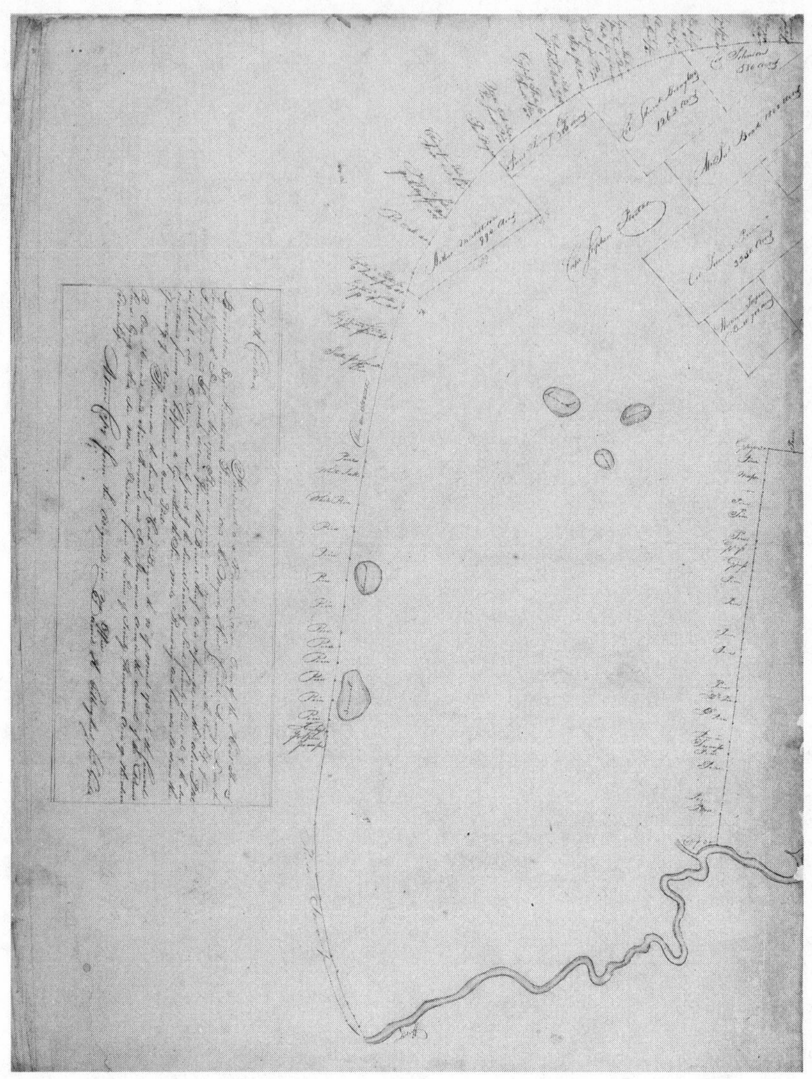

Above and facing: Surveyor General Daniel H. Tillinghast supervised the completion of this 1820–1821 copy of Hugh Bryan's original 1735 map of Purrysburg Township. It includes the site of the roughly rectangular eight-hundred-acre town proper enclosed by the twenty-thousand-acre township boundary, both of which were surrounded by a six-mile line ringing the township, within which only Purrysburg residents were to hold land titles. Notice the number of grants to nonresidents, including one to Robert Thorpe that intrudes directly onto township land. Reproduced courtesy of the South Carolina Department of Archives and History

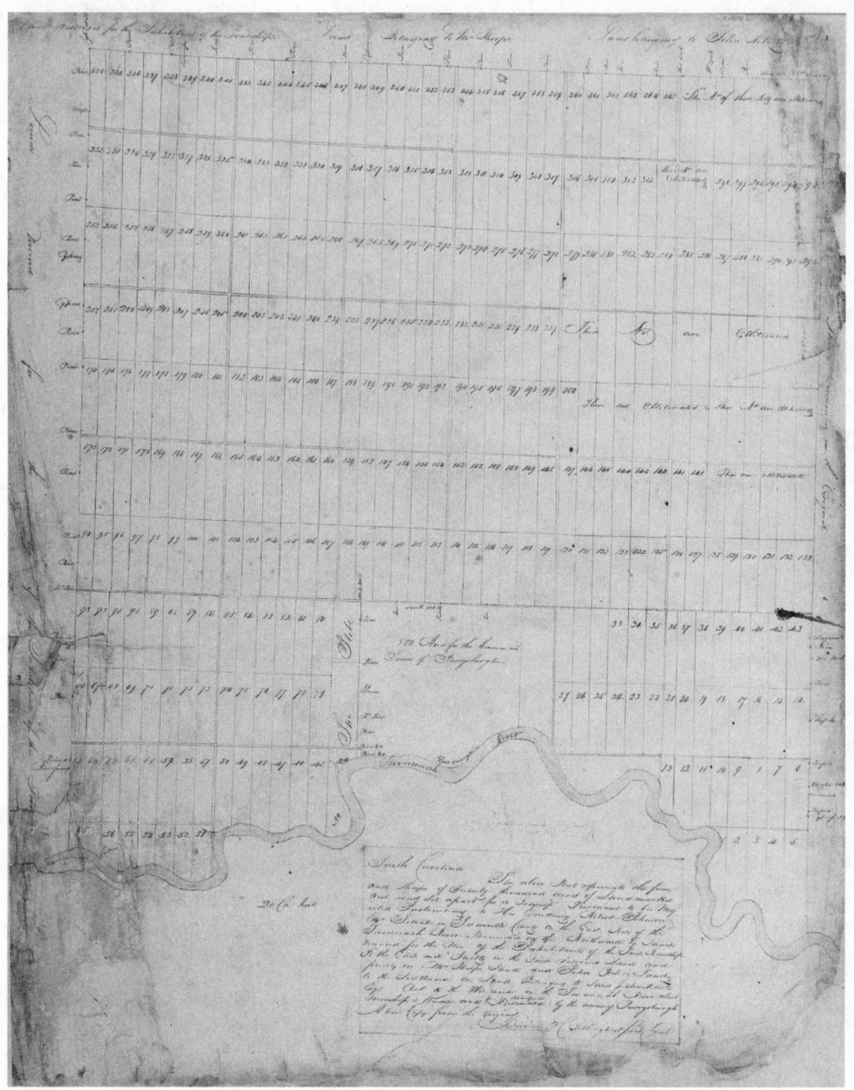

Undated plat of "Purrysbourg" Township showing symmetrically sized plots of land, the eight-hundred-acre Purrysburg town site, and the location of glebe lands. This is most likely an idealized rendering of the township site from the early 1730s. Reproduced courtesy of the South Carolina Department of Archives and History

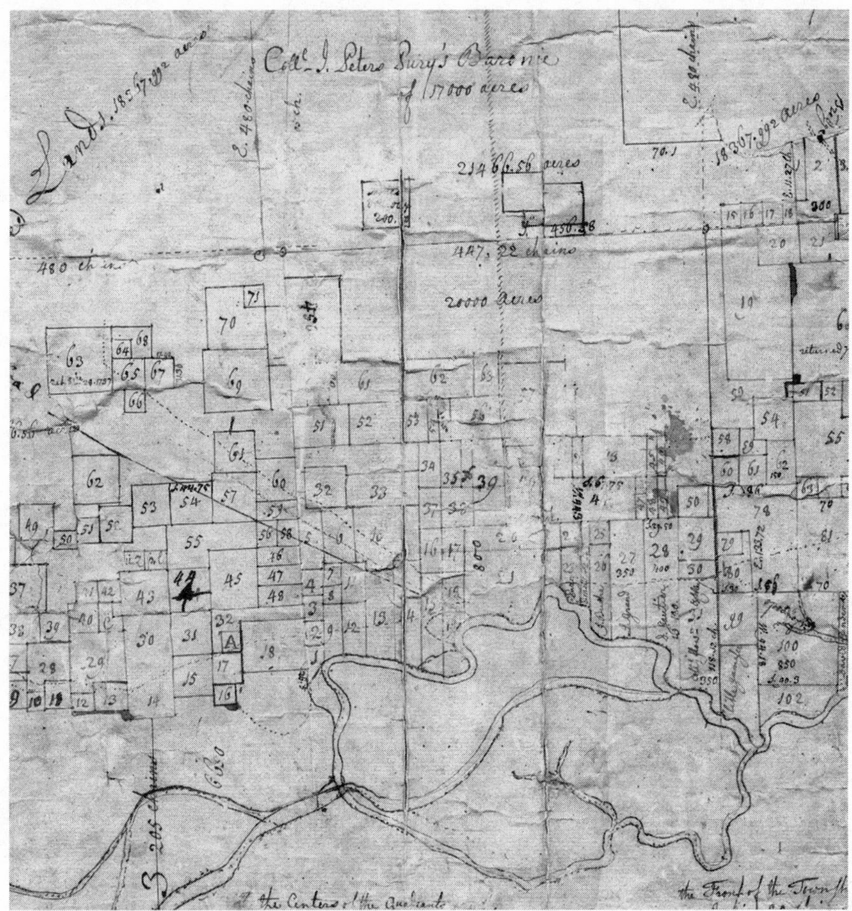

In this portion of the *Map showing subdivisions of Col. Purry's barony, c. 1735*, all that remains identifiable of the rendering of Purrysburg Township from map 7 are the eight-hundred-acre town site at the center right and the glebe lands just to the left of the town site. The headright system of granting land quickly destroyed the idealized symmetry of township development evident in the previous map. Reproduced by permission from the collections of the South Carolina Historical Society

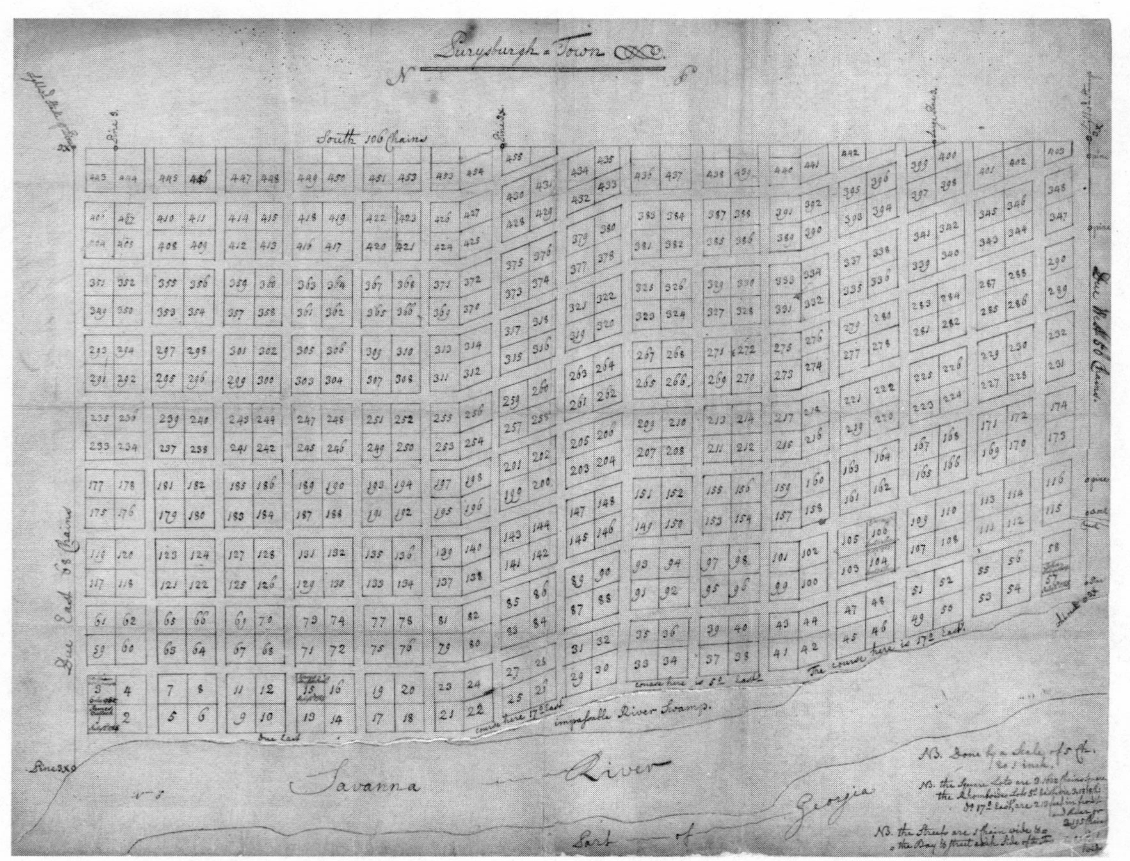

Plat map of "Purysburgh= Town" ca. 1765. Lots 21 through approximately 42 lie along what is noted on the map as "impassable River Swamp." Reproduced courtesy of the South Carolina Department of Archives and History

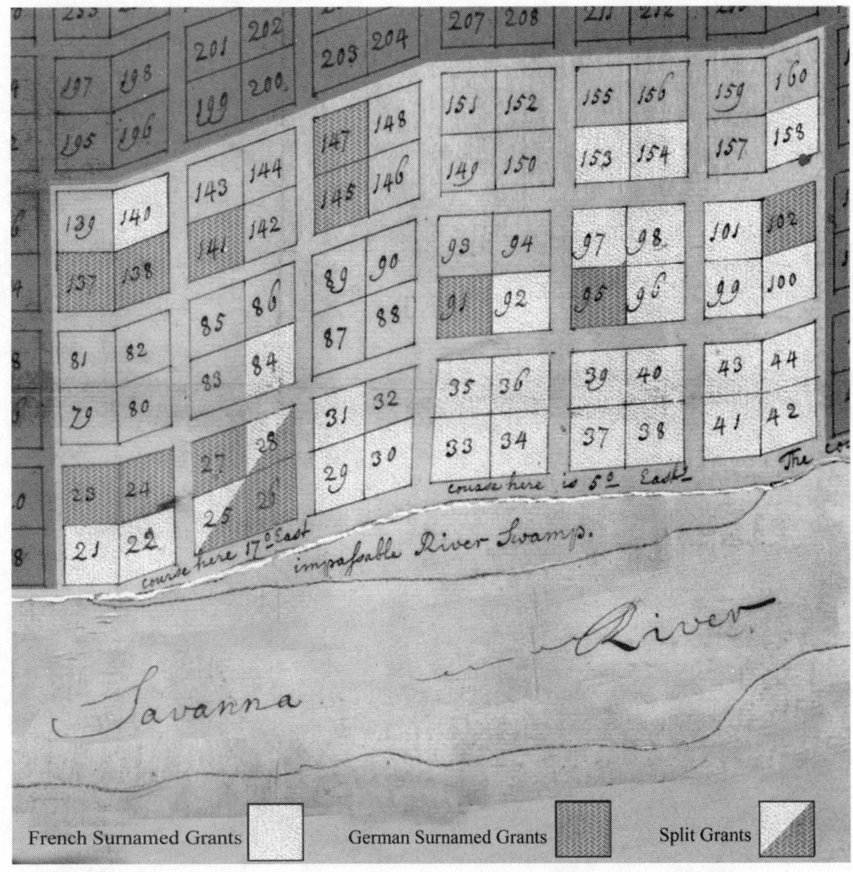

Detail from the plat of "Purysburgh=Town" ca. 1765 showing granted lots to French- and German-speaking residents. Adapted from the plat of "Purysburgh=Town." Courtesy of the South Carolina Department of Archives and History

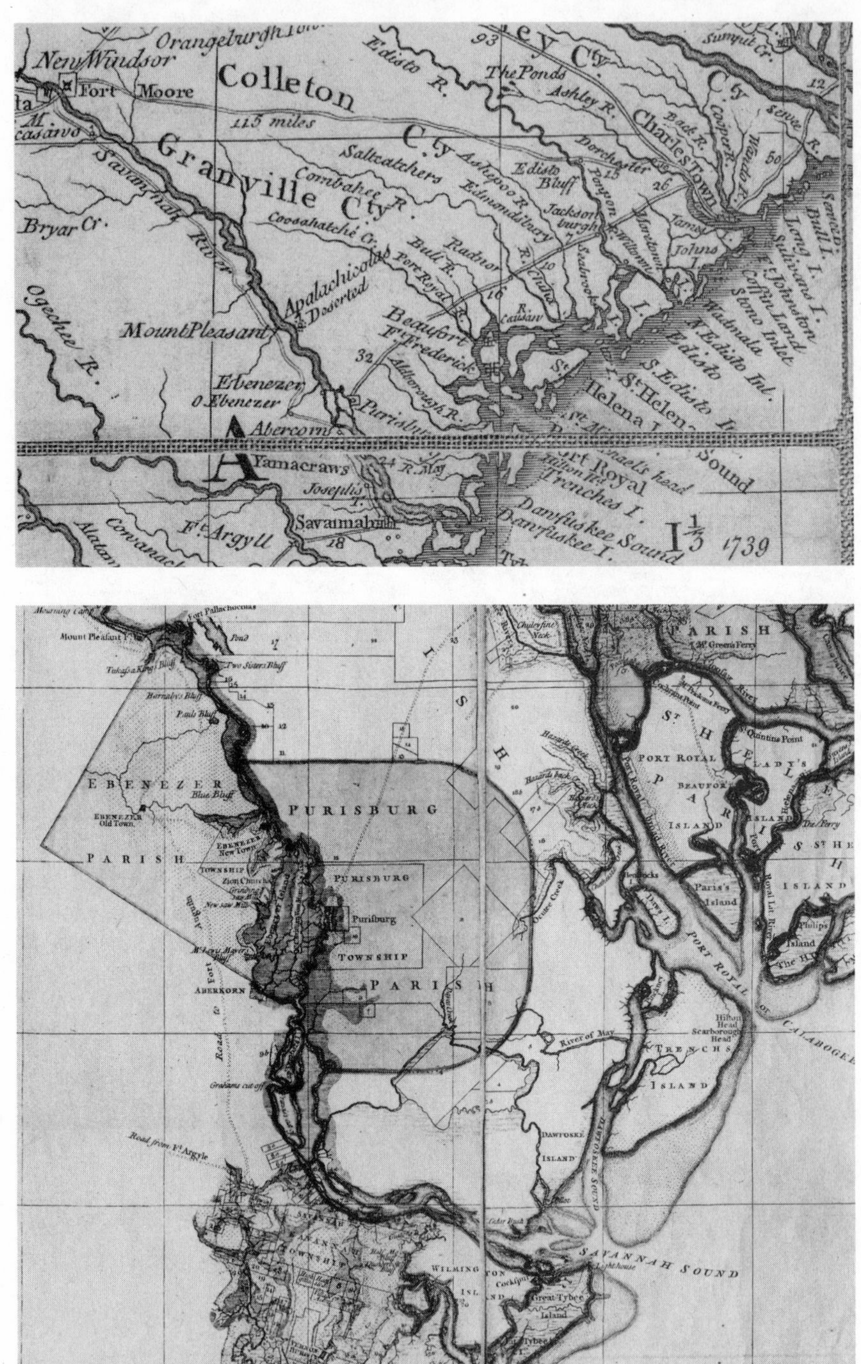

New Windsor
Fort Moore
Orangeburgh
Colleton
Granville Cty
115 miles
Edisto R.
The Ponds
Ashley R.
Charles Town
Dorchester
Saltcatchers
Ashepoo R.
Combahee R.
Edisto Bluff
Edmondsbury
Jacksonburgh
Coosahatche Cr.
Bryar Cr.
Savannah River
Apalachicola Deserted
Port Royal R.
Bull R.
Radnor
Mount Pleasant
Beaufort
Ft. Frederick
Ogechee R.
Ebenezer
O Ebenezer
Purisburg
Abercorn
Yamacraws
Josephs I.
Savannah
Ft. Argyll
Port Royal
Trenches I.
Danfuskee Sound
Danfuskee I.
S. Edisto
N. Edisto
Stono Inlet
Long I.
Sullivans I.
1739
EBENEZER
PARISH
Blue Bluff
EBENEZER Old Town
EBENEZER New Town
PURISBURG
PURISBURG TOWNSHIP
Purisburg
ABERKORN
PARISH
Two Sisters Bluff
Road from Ft. Argyle
Grahams cut off
SAVANNAH TOWNSHIP
WILMINGTON ISLAND
Cockspur
Great Tybee Island
Lighthouse
SAVANNAH SOUND
DAWFOSKE ISLAND
DAWFOSKEE SOUND
TRENCHS ISLAND
Hilton Head
Scarborough Head
River of May
PORT ROYAL
PORT ROYAL ISLAND
BEAUFORT
Paris's Island
Philips Island
LADY'S ISLAND
Quintins Point
ST. HELENA PARISH
PARISH

Above: Detail from James Cook's *A Map of the Province of South Carolina* (1773). The number of roadways connecting Purrysburg to backcountry and lowcountry destinations multiplied after midcentury. The Rochester Ferry route is marked across the river from the city of Savannah. The dotted line is the parish boundary between St. Peter's and St. Luke's. Reproduced courtesy of the David Rumsey Map Collection

Facing top: The King's Highway, or High Road, from "Purisburg" to Charles Town, detail from John Mitchell's *Map of the British and French Dominions in North America* (1757). His map reflects the route's alteration because of frequent flooding. Reproduced courtesy of the David Rumsey Map Collection

Facing bottom: By the late 1750s Purrysburg Township had become more deeply integrated into the lower southeast and was served by both overland and maritime transportation routes. This detail from *A Map of South Carolina and a Part of Georgia* by William De Brahm (1757) illustrates the contiguity of Purrysburg to other population centers. The cartographer mistakenly identified St. Peter's Parish as "Purisburg" Parish, a not uncommon occurrence in maps of the period. As drawn, the boundary line of this parish appears to coincide with the six-mile line that was to separate the land of Purrysburg residents from nonresidents. Reproduced by permission from the collections of the South Carolina Historical Society

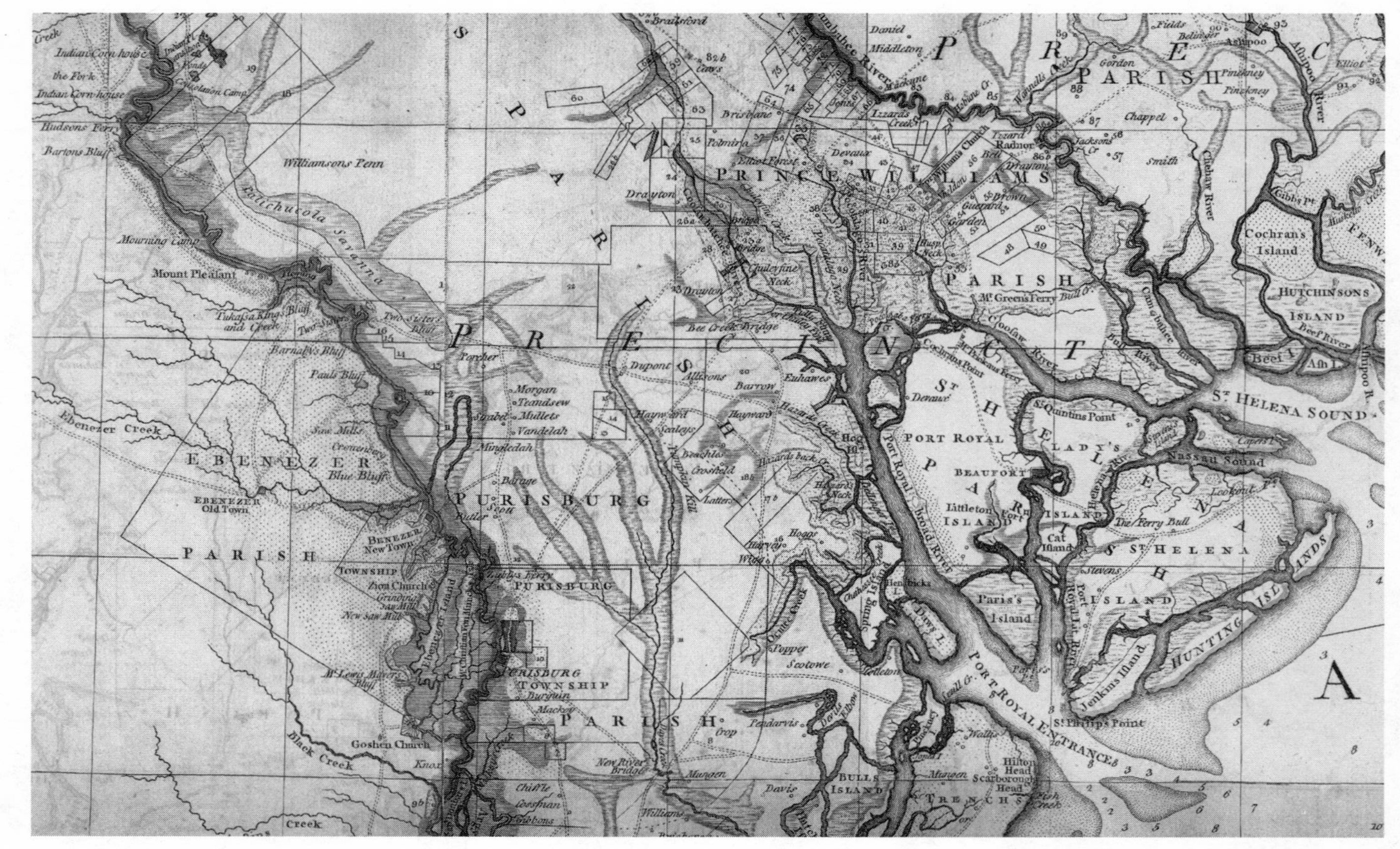

PRINCE WILLIAMS
PARISH
ST HELENA SOUND
PORT ROYAL ENTRANCES
PORT ROYAL
BEAUFORT
LADY'S
ISLAND
ST HELENA
Paris's Island
HUNTING ISLANDS
Jenkins Island
St. Philip's Point
Hilton Head
BULLS ISLAND
PURISBURG
PURISBURG TOWNSHIP
EBENEZER
EBENEZER Old Town
Ebenezer Creek
Mount Pleasant
Williamsons Penn
Cochrans Island
HUTCHINSONS ISLAND
Chehaw River
Ashipoo River
Coosaw River
Port Royal
Broad River
Bee Creek Bridge
Goshen Church
Black Creek
Hudsons Ferry
Bartons Bluff
Indian Corn house
Mourning Camp
Two Sisters Bluff
Littleton ISLAND
Cat Island
Daws I.
Nassau Sound
New River Bridge
Scotowe
Pendarvis

Facing: Detail from *A Map of South Carolina and a Part of Georgia*, from the surveys of William Bull, Wiliam De Brahm, and John Stuart (1780), showing the overland transportation system intersecting Purrysburg during the late Revolutionary period. Reproduced with permission from the collections of the South Carolina Historical Society

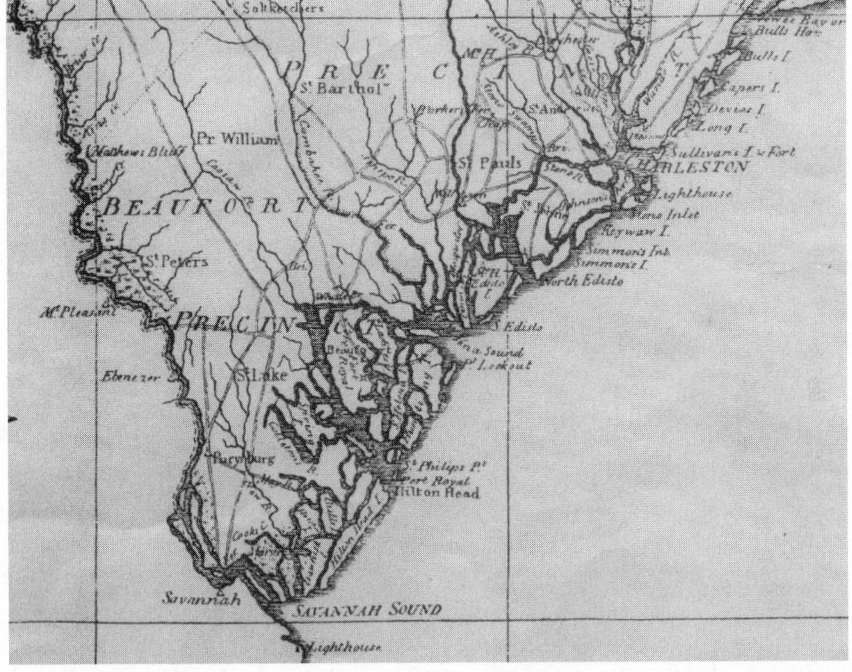

A view of southeastern South Carolina in the mid-1790s, as rendered in this detail from *The State of South Carolina from the Best Authorities* (1796), Andrew B. Graham Company, Lithographers. More than a decade after the end of the War of the Revolution, a number of roads intersected at or very near Purrysburg, illustrating its viability well into the early national period.

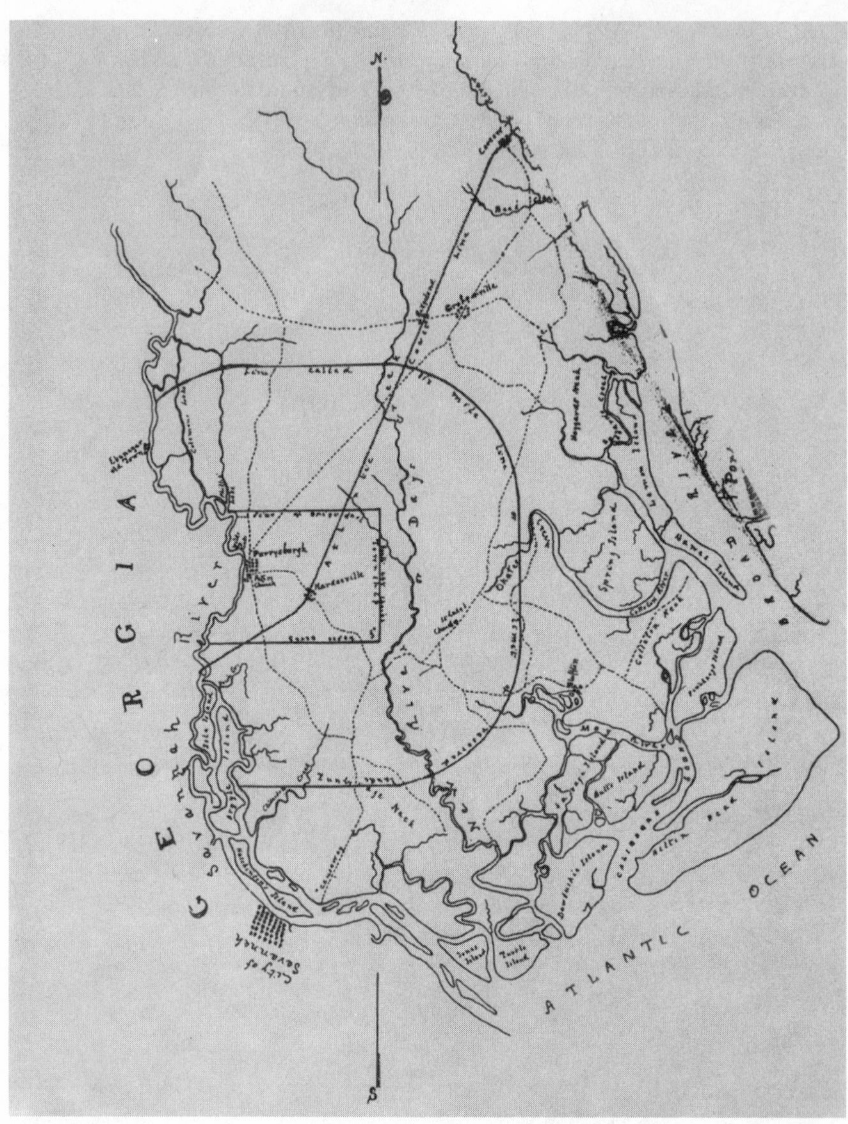

Composite map of "Purrysburgh" Township derived from Hugh Bryan's 1735 map and Mills's 1825 atlas. The railway lines were probably added by H. A. M. Smith, who included this map with his 1909 article on Purrysburg in the *South Carolina Historical Magazine*. The dotted lines designate prominent regional transportation routes.

Five

The Lineaments of Commercial Life

The limitations on family life and religious expression in Purrysburg hint at wider relational patterns that township residents, left by and large to fend for themselves, created for their own survival. The forging of such relationships indicate that far from evolving as a "communal society" characterized by lengthy and intimate relationships and slowly changing social and cultural morays, the contractual nature of Purrysburg's genesis and the diversity of its inhabitants meant that entrenched connections to traditional folkways and kin could not be maintained. In the "associational society" that resulted, individualistic and competitive socioeconomic connections supplanted gemeinschaft-based personal connections—at least structurally—and more formalized control mechanisms "furnished the substitutes for the bonds of solidarity that are relied upon to hold a folk society together."[1] It is entirely possible therefore to conceive of the commercial development of Purrysburg Township as an alternative method of community organization. Viewed in this context, the economic evolution of the township had distinct social consequences and built networks of commercial relationships radiating outward from Purrysburg that drew township dwellers closer to Ebenezer, Savannah, and the South Carolina lowcountry, as well as to each other.

The cultural and environmental constraints with which Purrysburg settlers had to contend from their first days on the southern frontier proved to be formidable. They lived lives of relentless adaptation to alien physiographic, political, and religious norms that, if not overtly hostile to them, were at the very least disruptive to the creation and maintenance of a cohesive community. These same constraints cradled and ultimately conditioned the economic development of the township. Yet for all the obstacles they faced, the first months of settlement gave evidence of a prosperous future for the frontier township. The Reverend Boltzius noted in the spring of 1734, "This town of Purrysburg is built up high on the bank of the river and since a good many people of means are living here it is hoped that it will become a fine city in a short time. The people here tend to their fields and gardens with much diligence and you can already buy meat, eggs, and garden vegetables here more easily than in Savannah. People here were very friendly toward us."[2]

A year later the merchant Samuel Eveleigh wrote to General Oglethorpe that "the people [at Purrysburg] appear to be very industrious and have their gardens pretty well improved." Already at this early date crops included flax, wheat, barley, oats, buckwheat, Indian corn, potatoes, and rice. Purrysburg rice especially drew Eveleigh's attention, and he described it as better than any he had previously seen in the province.[3]

The colonists, trained in a variety of occupations, were originally chosen by Purry (and welcomed by the provincial elite) precisely for their industry and expertise. They were as prepared as any uninitiated group could be to meet the challenges of frontier living, for Purrysburg landowners possessed the necessary commercial expertise to fulfill both the hopes of South Carolina authorities and their own aspirations. The township included farmers, as well as those who participated in stock raising, shipbuilding, silk manufacture, fruit tree husbandry, tavern keeping, and viniculture.[4] There were professionals and skilled craftspeople, retailers and merchants, members of the eighteenth-century service sector, and those aspiring to planter status. Such a diversity of skills and talents boded well for the development of a frontier commercial entrepôt—or so it appeared in 1735.[5]

As it matured, Purrysburg in no way approached the importance of other centers of southern colonial settlement such as Charles Town or Beaufort or Savannah. Nor did it participate in the process of urban and commercial expansion (population growth and economic productivity) at anywhere near the level of Georgetown, Fredericksburg, or Williamsburg. Indeed, rather than taking part in the general trend toward urbanization that characterized these other localities during the eighteenth century, the town proper appears to have consistently lost population. But, as Kenneth E. Lewis, Kaylene Hughes, William B. Barr, Joseph Ernst, and H. Roy Merrens, among others, have observed, even the smallest of urban centers in the colonial South provided the same functions of exchange, collection, storage, and distribution of commodities and manufactures as did major commercial centers. Frontier towns such as Purrysburg contributed to colonial commercial life in ways that often had relatively little to do with population or the aggregate wealth of their citizens.[6] The fact that Purrysburg lost population while other settlements gained inhabitants does not detract significantly from its function as a viable nexus of commercial exchange. It does, however, speak eloquently to the lack of opportunities for culturally or vocationally defined activities as the township environs became progressively drawn into the staple crop, slave-based plantation economy that dominated the other lowcountry parishes. The general trend over the course of the eighteenth century toward greater wealth and social status among Purrysburg planters and ranchers, while relatively minor when compared to the explosion of prosperity among those in the parishes surrounding Beaufort, Charles Town, and Georgetown, nonetheless demonstrates that Purrysburg became increasingly connected to a colonial social and commercial network involving neighboring urban centers via an intricate and elastic network of socioeconomic relationships that linked township residents with each other and with those around them.[7] Before that network could be constructed, however, township settlers had to grapple with the ramifications of their inferior position vis-à-vis the entrenched South Carolina lowcountry gentry. That secondary status created an environmental and political context for economic development that directly affected three of the most important preconditions for commercial exchange—a viable transportation infrastructure, a geographic location secure enough to foster economic productivity, and appropriate legal and political institutions for the promotion of social order.

I

The general decision regarding the location of Purrysburg Township had been made before Purry and his colleagues set foot on the Great Yamassee Bluff in the summer of 1731. The site selected for the first South Carolina township reflected the best guess of colonial authorities as to what strategic location would provide the highest level of security for the lowcountry parishes, the greatest possibility for economic diversification, and the most alluring inducement to potential white immigrants. Of the three factors, the first was obviously of utmost concern given the recent depredations of the Yamassee War, but the success of all three factors hinged on establishing a functional transportation matrix. Riverine thoroughfares, the least expensive mode of transport, and the creation and maintenance of a reliable overland transportation system were considered fundamental to the vitality of any frontier town.[8]

During the first few years Purrysburg settlers and those associated with them had access only to water transport, but even then the site of the township at the inland terminus of the tidewater region ensured its usefulness as a transportation center. Regular intercourse with other settlements was primarily facilitated by small ships, pirogues, and canoes as travel along Indian paths in the area was deemed imprudent. The earliest immigrants were conveyed up the Savannah River to the township. When Governor Johnson, Captain Massy, Major Barnwell, and General Oglethorpe paid a visit to Purrysburg in November of 1733, the trip from Savannah via the river took two days.[9] In subsequent years the town's role as a debarkation point for travelers venturing further into the backcountry and as a provisioning depot for those journeying inland from the Savannah River on either its Georgia or Carolina shore remained significant although not always appreciated.

One deleterious side effect of the efficiency of early riverine transport, at least from the perspective of the Georgia authorities attempting to enforce prohibition, was the easy availability of liquor from South Carolina suppliers. By the mid-1730s, the issue threatened relations between the two colonies. Oglethorpe wanted to take drastic action by requesting an adjustment of the Georgia–South Carolina boundary line. He planned to write his fellow Georgia trustees in England in April 1736 to persuade them to address Parliament so it would act to "enlarge the Bounds of his Government so far Northerly as Bloody Point up a straight Line in order to take in Purrysburgh and so up Back River, that he might command all that Part of the Country."[10] The situation became more volatile by mid-December, after Georgians at Bloody Point seized rum destined for South Carolinians. For its part, the South Carolina Commons House of Assembly investigated the rum-running controversy by hearing testimony from deposed witnesses. It became apparent that Georgia officials did not even want liquor to "pass by destined for Purrysburgh or other stores or plantations" on the Savannah River.[11] Shifting the boundary between the two colonies northeastward would give Oglethorpe control of both sides of the river as far as Purrysburg, thereby eradicating not only the illegal trade across the border, but also any liquor traffic on the river at all. Although there is no indication that Purrysburg Township settlers participated in the trade across the Savannah, rum was sold in the township legally and often to visitors from Georgia. The availability of liquor there and its location on the river made the township one of the foci of the boundary dispute. South Carolina authorities realized that, if Georgia gained the right to stop traffic on the Savannah River, residents of Purrysburg Township and New Windsor Township, who used the waterway as their principal means of transportation, might leave. If they deserted the frontier townships, lowcountry parishes would be as vulnerable to attack as they had been prior to 1732. This recognition led to a resolution of the crisis that, though not completely satisfactory to the Georgia trustees, who continued to fight a losing battle to keep the colony dry, did maintain the Savannah River boundary and preserved the free navigation of the Savannah for settlers in both townships.[12]

Water transit expedited the early settlement of the frontier township, but it could not long serve as the only mode of transportation and communication between Purrysburg and other colonial settlements. The construction of an overland route between the township and Savannah appears to have been planned by the end of 1733, though the fate of this road is unclear. It was hoped that a land route from Charles Town would be made passable by the spring of 1734. Work on the Purrysburg–Charles Town road had progressed far enough in December of that year for Savannah interests to establish a messenger service between Savannah and Charles Town at their own expense that would "secure a communication not easily cut off."[13] The high road from Charles Town was completed in the mid-1730s with Purrysburg its southern overland terminus. From Prince William's Parish, the King's Highway, as it was called, crossed the Coosawhatchie River and then veered sharply south to Day's (Daws) Creek before turning northwest to Purrysburg a few miles north of Cook's Cut. Travelers completed their journey to Savannah via water transport from the township. This road provided the primary land connection between Charles Town, Purrysburg, and Savannah for the next decade and a half, but keeping it open must have been problematic because of the many bridges that had to be maintained over swampy or frequently inundated areas. By the end of May 1750 the Commons House responded affirmatively to a petition for another bridge along the road over the Coosawhatchie River because the difficulty of fording it made passage between Savannah, Purrysburg, and Charles Town quite difficult.[14] Maintenance of the road proved an ongoing source of frustration, however, and in March 1753 the Commissioners of the High Roads and the "rest of the inhabitants of St. Peter's, Purrysburg" petitioned the Commons House for a new road. The petition noted that the road "by way of Daws Creek was incapable of ever being made good or even passable, by reason of the frequent return of great Freshes and Floods in the said creek which carried away the Bridges and causey, and had rendered all the work that had hitherto been done on it ineffectual." The petitioners continued that the road was "useless and likely never to be otherwise," and even if the route was salvageable, "it would be eighteen miles round about and out of the way of the petitioners and all other persons traveling to and from the Southward." They asked that the road be discontinued and another one constructed "in the most convenient and direct way from Purrysburg to Bee's Creek and thence to Coosawhatchie as the road already laid out runs (from Bee's Creek to Coosawhatchie) by which course the road would be shortened at least eighteen miles and the ground being better it would be much easier made and kept in repair." The Commons House appointed a committee to consider the petition—and failed to take any action. Two years later an identical petition came before the legislators (5 March 1755), who again appointed a committee. This time the committee took only a day to decide that the new road was needed and the Commons House only six weeks to pass the bill, which was ratified by the governor on 12 April 1755.[15] The new road was subsequently built, but even its completion did not end the debate over the best route.

A petition for another road from Ned's Bluff to Pocotaligo for the benefit of the outer settlements, such as Purrysburg, was introduced in the Commons House in May 1743. The same body proposed a spur line to improve travel to and from St. George's Parish, Dorchester, and the upper part of St. Paul's Parish to Combee, Port Royal, and Purrysburg in the spring of 1749. It was to be laid out from the Combahee River Ferry to Purrysburg and the Port Royal Ferry.[16] Another thoroughfare connecting the township and Coosawhatchie somewhat to the northwest of the Bee's Creek to Purrysburg road appears to have been completed in the fall of 1770. Because maintenance of the colonial roads was the domain of the citizens serviced by them, Purrysburg residents provided the labor to keep the roads in good repair and also served as commissioners of the roads leading to and from the township. In fact, despite the condition of some of them, M. Eugene Sirmans has characterized these roads as among the best in the colonies.[17] Although some of the roadways proved unsatisfactory and the Commons House somewhat slow in responding to the needs of the township settlers, the fact that so many overland routes and spur lines fused Purrysburg to other regional destinations is indicative of not merely the township's strategic location, but also its important role as a secondary center of colonial commerce.

Ferries also played a vital role in the colonial South Carolina transportation and communication grid. Depending upon where they ran, ferries on the Savannah River either contributed to Purrysburg's gradual incorporation into the greater commercial and social networks of the Southeast or reinforced its isolation and secondary economic importance. For nearly thirty years no formal vested ferry service across the Savannah River appears to have existed in the vicinity of Purrysburg. Private boats moored at the township site and at Savannah, however, did carry travelers and goods between the two towns. This arrangement assured Purrysburg boat owners a living wage because of the volume of transport on the river, which only grew over time. Ironically, the establishment of the first vested ferry in the area offering transport directly across the river actually threatened, not only the livelihoods of private Purrysburg entrepreneurs, but also the viability of the town proper.

The vesting of the Rochester Ferry in 1762 to Charles and Jermyn Wright, the largest rice planters on the lower Savannah drainage, resulted from a petition to the Commons House by the Wrights and a number of other lowcountry planters in the late 1750s.[18] They hoped to persuade the provincial legislature to restore the old road from Coosawhatchie to Purrysburg over Day's Creek. The planters desired a more direct route that would expedite lowcountry commercial exchange with Georgia and create a river crossing south of Purrysburg and more convenient to their interests. They believed that the section of road from Coosawhatchie to Day's Creek, which would then be continued southward to the Wright's rice plantation and connect to the road being constructed as part of the Rochester Causeway just across the Savannah River from Jonathan Bryan's Walnut Hill plantation near Savannah, Georgia, would serve their purposes well. Township settlers, who had petitioned successfully in 1755 for the construction of the new road from Bee's Creek to Purrysburg, submitted their own petition in January 1759 opposing the restoration of the former road. Ostensibly they were concerned that the road would not benefit them and those "that live within ten miles of the same old new Road, that is to say almost the whole township of Purrysburg should be compelled to work thereon." They clearly believed that the Wrights' petition was an example of their mistreatment by the lowcountry elite. The petition argued that if the Commons House ruled affirmatively on it the result would

> make your petitioners fall again a Sacrifice to the most sordid most glaring and most palpable self interest, to which for want of public spirited men among them that understood thoroughly the Laws and Language of the country and the Liberties of the subject according to our happy form of Government they

have ever been an easy Prey wanting even that commonly remaining and last Comfort of an injured and distressed people, i.e.[,] the means and capacity of seeking redress to their sufferings and Grievances: It would throw your petitioners into the old dilemma again, either to have no road at all to the Capitol or only a very bad one that leads seventeen miles round about, out of which they have been so lately delivered.[19]

The township petitioners reminded the Commons House that the act that created the new, straighter, and shorter road also exempted them from "ever working on said road again." After reiterating that the new road from Bee's Creek to Purrysburg was considerably shorter than the old road via Day's Creek and that they had been working to keep it in good repair since it was laid out four years prior, the petition concluded that "for these reasons and many more the petitioners might justly add (if this was the place to expose all the Variety of their distresses from the first settling the Township beyond and above what any other community of this flourishing Province ever did, which has reduced this, at first so populous a settlement to a handful of poor people) and praying the House maintain the Petitioners in all and every Appointment of the above mentioned act."[20]

The legislators referred the petition to the same committee charged with examining the Wrights' petition. Sir Egerton Leigh, representative from St. Peter's Parish to the Commons House, spoke for the petition on behalf of the township residents, but the lowcountry elite supported the Wrights. By 1762 the old road reopened from Coosawhatchie to Day's Creek, it was extended to the Wrights' plantation, and the Rochester Ferry began operation. What benefited lowcountry planters and merchants in both South Carolina and Georgia, however, had the opposite effect on the inhabitants of Purrysburg Township.[21]

Fortunately the other ferries established in St. Peter's Parish helped to maintain linkages between Charles Town, Savannah, the township, and the burgeoning backcountry settlements in both South Carolina and Georgia rather than disrupt them. Township resident John Vauchier initiated a private ferry service down the Savannah River from Purrysburg to Abercorn and Savannah only two years after the Rochester Ferry began operation. He maintained "at his own expense a ferry with proper boats and hands for the purpose of conveying and transporting passengers with their horses and carriages." In a petition of September 1776 seeking official vesting of the ferry by the new state of South Carolina, Vauchier wrote that he "has used every dispatch and given every necessary attendance that could be expected from a man in his slender circumstances and for the same received certain rates of ferriage as have been paid and given for a number of years." Vauchier argued that "great advantage" would result from "a quick communication between the States of South Carolina and Georgia," so he requested the passage of an act that would make the ferry a public one vested to him and his assigns for a period of years so that the ferry might be eligible to charge rates regulated by the House of Representatives. He believed that his ferry "may be the most convenient to travelers." A certificate attached to his petition signed by thirteen residents affirmed that a public ferry from Purrysburg "would be of great service,"[22] but a letter dated 17 September 1776 addressed to Philotheus Chiffelle, eldest son of the former Purrysburg minister, and signed by thirty-five residents of St. Peter's Parish opposed the idea. All documents were referred to committee members, who reported on 1 October 1776 "that quick connection between South Carolina and Georgia will be of great utility to both countries. And as a ferry fixed at Purrysburg from thence to Savannah and Abercorn in Georgia may be one means to procure dispatch to travelers, are of the opinion that a public ferry should be established at Purrysburg from thence to Abercorn and Savannah." The House agreed, and the ferry was accordingly vested to him and his assigns for seven years.[23]

A few years after Vauchier began his ferry service, residents of St. Peter's Parish petitioned the Commons House for a service across the Savannah River at Two Sisters Bluff, about fifteen miles upriver from the town of Purrysburg. The same petition requested that a road from the ferry be cut to connect the crossing to the Purrysburg–Coosawhatchie road. The Commons House passed the act establishing both the ferry and the connecting road on 23 August 1769. The ferry was vested to William Williamson, who also served St. Peter's Parish in the Commons House from 1768 to 1777.[24] In February 1770 the Reverend John J. Zubly, who maintained landholdings in Purrysburg even after he was called to serve the Independent Church of Savannah, petitioned the Georgia Commons House for permission to operate a public ferry across the river from his Georgia land just north of the town of Purrysburg near Ebenezer. Zubly had previously built a bridge over a creek on his Georgia property and procured a boat. He had been operating a private ferry from his Georgia acreage to his land in Purrysburg Township since July of the previous year and stated in his petition that, because the Georgia Commons House had recently mandated a public Savannah River crossing in the vicinity, his ferry was the natural choice for it. The petition also set forth prospective rates and described the operation. The Georgia Commons House passed the act establishing Zubly's Ferry also called Middlesex Island Ferry on 24 January 1771. The legislators passed a companion act on 29 September 1773 that mandated the laying out of a public road to Middlesex Island Ferry. The ferry road on the South Carolina side intersected the Charles Town road just three miles from Purrysburg. On the Georgia side, it joined the public road from Ebenezer to Savannah. It appears that another ferry in the township area was operated by Martin Dasher in the early 1770s.[25]

These roads and waterways made Purrysburg a convenient stop for travelers in the southern region. In light of the strategic importance attached to the township by royal authorities and its location at a nexus of the dendritic colonial transportation network, it is not surprising to discover that the township attained an early reputation as a cosmopolitan frontier town. After a visit to Purrysburg in 1735, Samuel Eveleigh of Savannah wrote about the presence of almost all European nationalities, such "as English, French, Dutch, High German, Prussians, Russians, Switzers, Savoyards, and Italians." Though specie was generally quite rare, particularly outside Charles Town, a frequent visitor to Purrysburg noticed in 1751 that, besides colonial currency and British sterling, Spanish silver and Spanish, Portuguese, Dutch, and French gold circulated in the region. Although these claims may be somewhat misleading, they do reflect social and economic activity characteristic of a locality linked soundly to surrounding settlements by a developed system of water and overland transport.

Even after the Rochester Ferry siphoned off a significant portion of lowcountry commercial traffic from the township after 1762, Purrysburg continued to serve as a commercial outpost. When the surveyor of the post roads for North America, Hugh Finlay, visited the township in early 1774 on his southern tour to assess the feasibility of establishing an overland postal route between Charles Town and Savannah, he believed that John Buche of Purrysburg, "who keeps Tavern here wou'd be a proper person to take charge of an office in this place if it shall be found necessary to have a house of receipt and delivery in Purrysburg."[26] Soon after Finlay's appointment to succeed Benjamin Franklin as deputy postmaster general later that same year, Purrysburg was made a post office with Buche as postmaster.[27] William Mylne, who lived seven miles upriver from Augusta, Georgia, by Stephen's Creek on the South Carolina side of the river, wrote in May 1774 about the significant amount of backcountry produce that traveled downriver to Charles Town or Savannah, much if not most of it passing by or through Purrysburg.[28] Though a secondary village by the 1770s, the township's multiethnic population successfully forged links with other colonial centers of population and commerce.[29] The formal creation of roads and the regulation of ferries could occur only with the support of the colonial legislature, and in most cases South Carolina and Georgia legislators enacted laws that enhanced transportation and communication between the township and other colonial settlements in the Southeast, thereby providing valuable support for commercial and social development. But in the one case when Purrysburg commercial interests came in direct conflict with the wishes of the lowcountry elite in the Rochester Ferry controversy, Purrysburg settlers lost. When the interests of township residents converged with those of the gentry, as in the boundary dispute with Georgia, Purrsyburg settlers won. The economic and social evolution of the township could only occur within these constraints.

II

That the transportation and communications network connecting the township to other destinations in the colonial Southeast served preeminently strategic purposes is readily apparent in the location of Purrysburg on the frontier between

European and Native American populations. Township social and economic life through the 1750s was deeply affected by the proximity of township whites to indigenous peoples, and, as with the development of the colonial transportation system that enhanced or impaired Purrysburg's commercial development depending on the whims of the provincial leadership, contact with Native Americans brought the possibility of both benefit and also great danger. The guiding rationale for the township scheme of settlement assured substantial intercultural exchange for the first generation of settlers for it located Purrysburg near a major Indian trading path.[30] By the time of the Cherokee War in 1760, however, the depletion of fur-bearing animals in the area and the westward advancement of the frontier line largely ended ongoing contact between Purrysburg inhabitants and southeastern Native American peoples.

Archaeological evidence indicates that the trading path was probably quite old. Native Americans inhabited the township site as early as the Late Archaic-Stallings period (circa 2500 B.C.E.), though a 1985 survey uncovered a chert fragment that resembled to some extent an Early Archaic point type. Occupation by indigenous peoples appears to have been continuous from the Late Archaic period forward through the Woodland, Mississippian, and eighteenth-century historic eras.[31] Luigi Castiglioni, who visited Purrysburg in March 1786, observed a Native American mound at the northwestern edge of the town overgrown with oak trees. He described it as "a hill artificially made of oyster and clam shells and located near the river." Two decades later John Lambert wrote that he saw "the tumuli of an Indian nation, which formerly resided here." These were probably the most obvious examples of prior occupation at the Purrysburg site before European intrusion, but it is unknown in which era the mounds originated, what people left them, or how extensive actual Indian habitation on the Purrysburg site might have been.[32] The Muskhogean-speaking Cusabo peoples, most notably the Yamassee and Euchee, lived in the region just prior to the founding of Purrysburg. There were also bands of their powerful cousins, the Creeks, nearby. Important Native American towns existed quite close to the site of the future township, including Pocotaligo, the chief council town of the Yamassee, a few miles to the east, and Palachuccola Town, upriver from the Great Yamassee Bluff.[33]

Probably the most consistent contact with Native Americans came from Purrysburg's participation in the lucrative Indian trade. South Carolina had the most elaborate Indian trading network of all the American colonies because of its economic priorities and international position. The trade, essentially an exchange of native deerskins and furs for colonial rice, rum, woolen cloth, farm tools, kitchen utensils, and trinkets, began in the late seventeenth century. As the Carolina trade grew, whites encroached on Native American land, and what good will had existed disappeared with the expansion of Indian slavery and abuses by white traders. Indian commerce, however, remained a proven way to achieve success in South Carolina and contributed to the growth and southwestward expansion of the province. At the same time Native Americans became increasingly enamored of white goods and spirits, ensuring an uneasy continuation of the trade. Provincial attempts at regulating the trade failed, and further abuses ultimately led to the banding together of Yamassee, Catawba, and Creek people and the outbreak of war in April 1715. At the conclusion of the Yamassee War, the trade resumed, albeit on a somewhat different footing and with more effective colonial regulation. It continued to be the one sector of the South Carolina economy that prospered during the otherwise stagnant 1720s and early 1730s. Since Purrysburg at that time was about as far southwest as one could get and still claim to be on South Carolina soil, the Indian trade played a substantial role in the early economy of the township. A witness to Purrysburg entrepreneurship in 1734 exclaimed that "the people [of Purrysburg] . . . have been all Indian traders."[34]

Although this bold assertion is obviously exaggerated, Purrysburg immigrants did achieve such great success that they diverted some of the commerce from their understandably irate Georgia competitors. If Native Americans had trouble selling their skins in Georgia, as they did in December 1734 when Robert Parker was under orders not to trade with them, they had only to visit the township, where there were few if any impediments to trade. The legality of liquor across the Savannah River probably contributed appreciably to the preference of Native Americans for South Carolina traders as the Georgia trustees prohibited trading in alcohol. In 1736 a party of Indians that had deposited their skins at a Georgia trading station quickly repacked their trade goods and headed for Purrysburg after discovering that the township had a plentiful supply of rum. Lobbying by furious Georgia commercial interests failed to alter South Carolina policy, much to the benefit of Purrysburg Indian traders.[35]

Although most of the Purrysburg settlers involved in the Indian trade remain nameless, the career of Johann Paul Francke is fairly well documented. Francke had come to Purrysburg with his father and mother in the early 1730s, perhaps with the first contingent of settlers qualifying before Governor Johnson in December 1732. His father died before any land could be conveyed to him. His mother, Anna Barbara, received the half-acre town lot number 23 in Purrysburg in 1733 and 150 acres of land in the township but found herself and her son in difficult circumstances from the beginning of their residence in the township. She contacted the Reverend Boltzius and gained his permission to enroll Johann in the Ebenezer school at some sacrifice to her own financial position. Young Francke had a checkered history at the school. He did well academically but often left, without permission, to go home. He finally decided to strike out on his own and ended up living with Native Americans, much to the dismay of his mother. He established himself in the lucrative Indian trade, probably as a teamster. After twelve years Francke returned to the area in 1750, but without much memory of his former life. He lodged in Purrysburg with Theobald Kieffer Sr.'s family to relearn his native German tongue and, as

Boltzius hoped, "to use the means of salvation," which he had also forgotten. Francke eventually moved to Ebenezer, married, and seems to have succeeded in spite of some initial discouragement with agricultural life, for he lived out the rest of his days as a valued member of the Ebenezer community. The decisive sign of his reintegration came in March 1753, when the Reverend Boltzius admitted him to communion for the first time.[36]

The trading connection with Purrysburg—as well as its proximity to the frontier—meant that the neighborhood around the township remained open to Native American influences well into the mid–eighteenth century. There were even attempts to found schools and initiate mission activities in Purrysburg for the benefit of Indian children. Natives traveled freely on the Savannah River and established what were called "sentry towns" near the township to facilitate trade with the whites. Palachuccola Town, for example, was located just north of Purrysburg, close to the site of Fort Palachuccola, and had been a Creek town until they abandoned it during the Yamassee War. A band of Euchee people resettled it from 1725 until the 1740s and were therefore among Purrysburg's closest neighbors. In 1737 the South Carolina Commons House commanded that the Euchees and some Creeks in the vicinity of Palachuccola Town be brought to Purrysburg to serve as scouts for white reprisals against natives. By April of that year reports indicated that close to 300 Indians had assembled in the township. Although the estimate was later scaled back by two-thirds, Purrysburg saw its share of Native Americans during this exercise. Two years later an attack by the French and their Native American allies on other Indians led to a successful attempt by General Oglethorpe to ransom a French prisoner, who was transported via Purrysburg to Savannah. After 1739, as war created shifting alliances among native populations, Europeans, and colonists, fear of Indian attack increased—especially after Indians allied with Spain captured Fort Venture on the Savannah River. The Euchees migrated toward Purrysburg and Savannah because of the war. In the process, some of them drove off horses from a Purrysburg plantation and committed other offenses against township settlers. When bands of Creeks and Euchees began killing each other near Ebenezer, whites and Indians on both sides of the river faced an uncertain future. At least one family of Euchees intended to escape the violence by departing for Purrysburg by March 1741.[37]

The rest of the decade passed without further incident, but in the mid-1750s Indian raiding parties committed various depredations upon white settlers near Purrysburg, including the murder of township resident John Linder at Palachuccola Town. Captain John Bourguin mustered the Purrysburg Company of militia and pursued Linder's attackers. Although the outcome of the search is unknown, the militia company was quite persistent, as Bourguin filed two orders on the pubic treasury to reimburse individuals for provisions supplied to the company, including one from an African American. It does not appear that widespread violence extended to the township residents at this time.[38]

Aside from these examples, as threatening as they were, the majority of contact experiences between Purrysburg settlers and the Indian peoples that lived near and even among them were relatively amicable. Throughout the 1730s and into at least the early 1740s, Native Americans traveled to Purrysburg frequently. Often their visits included a stop for rum purchased from a French-speaking township resident. When the Reverend Boltzius discovered in March 1741 that the vendor planned to move to Charles Town or Holland, he expressed relief, because the man's rum sales "attracted bad people like Indians and other rabble who afterwards cause us trouble in their drunkenness."[39] The Pietist pastor may have disapproved of his trade in spirits and those to whom he sold, but there is no indication that the Native Americans that he sold to ever caused a problem for those who lived in the township. Relations between Purrysburg whites and Indians seem eventually to have reached a relative state of equanimity that stimulated consistent, though not necessarily equitable, intercultural contacts. As late as 1752 Jonas Pelot, through his son, the Reverend Francis Pelot, petitioned the council for a total of 250 acres of land in Purrysburg Township that was also known to be claimed by Native Americans.[40]

Most Native Americans preferred to live in their own communities separate from whites, but some chose to build their bark and skin homes in places such as Purrysburg and live among whites. One such Indian made himself especially useful to the township by providing undisclosed services to his white neighbors prior to his untimely death from a rattlesnake bite in August 1734. Several natives assembled at Purrysburg to inter him in the tribal manner. They buried him in a sitting position with the most prized possessions he had collected and used during his lifetime—his hunting weapons, household tools, and clothes.[41]

As in other areas where Native Americans and whites lived in close proximity to each other, cultural exchange occurred in both directions. Indians and European immigrants residing at Purrysburg lived on the edge of two cultures, pulling aspects of both white and native societies together, which included intermarriage and language acquisition, among other cultural adaptations. The native man noted above, though buried according to ancient tribal custom, seems to have been buried in the European style of dress, which he had adopted. Another Indian male decided to take up residence in Purrysburg but still resorted to the tribal punishment of cutting off both ears and the hair of a native widow (also living in Purrysburg), whom he accused of "sitting with a white man" and becoming "too familiar in her conduct with him." The man bowed to white patriarchal sensibilities by not punishing the white male, which was also required by tribal law. The woman had grown her hair in response to historic tribal custom regarding widowhood, yet she lived in a white settlement and developed a rather ambiguous relationship with a white male. The nature of the relationship between these two individuals is unknown, but there were numerous cases of native–white sexual relationships. The exact number of mixed-race children in and around Purrysburg cannot be determined, but there were enough of them for other pastors to note that township minister the Reverend Chiffelle administered the sacraments to them. Chiffelle's actions illustrate as much the social impact of Native American–white relations as they do the breakdown of traditional church discipline on the frontier.[42]

Whether manifested in the Indian trade, the threat of conflict, or the vagaries of coexistence, Purrysburg Township and its first-generation immigrant colonists had to order their lives predicated upon the reality that they constituted an intrusive presence to indigenous peoples that existed at or very close to their own level of sociocultural integration. The relative parity between whites and Native Americans in and around Purrysburg not only conditioned social and economic opportunities for the settlers, but also threatened successful frontier colonization of the township.[43] To ensure that Purrysburg could meet the challenges posed by its location, its residents required the protection afforded others in South Carolina by provincial legal and political institutions, but the South Carolinians who could guarantee township residents equal access to those institutions were the same leaders who put their lives at risk in the first place.

III

If the location of the township and development of the provincial transportation network illustrate at least partially the primacy of Purrysburg's military rather than its commercial function, the unwillingness of the provincial legislature to endow the settlers in a timely manner with the legal and political rights to which they were entitled makes the designs of the lowcountry elite more explicit and leaves no doubt as to the secondary importance of the social and commercial interests of township settlers. An important provision of Governor Johnson's township plan of settlement stipulated that, when any township contained 100 heads of household, that township and the land within the six-mile buffer zone around it would be established as a parish with all the rights and privileges parish status entailed, including two representatives to the provincial legislature. As formally organized parishes, the frontier townships would then exist on an equal basis with all other South Carolina parishes. Parity included not only representation in the Commons House of Assembly but also the ability to promote social order through the parish vestry, which was the "center of such local government as existed" in the province, exerting both administrative and legal authority due to the absence of a viable system of county courts. As such "the parish acting through the vestry became the only unit of local government to acquire any significant authority in South Carolina before the Revolution." Consequently, until a township attained designation as a parish, it remained largely unable to wield legitimate authority and lacked a voice in legislative affairs that affected its citizens.[44]

The problems associated with the granting of land in Purrysburg Township provided the pretext for the denial of parish status for Purrysburg in the Reverend Chiffelle's petition of 1736. By the end of 1735, however, nearly seventy lots in the town proper had been platted or granted. The number almost doubled to at least 130 lots at the end of the following year. Just under 170 town lots had been claimed by the end of 1738. Clearly the township merited parish status well before 1737.[45] Why then did Purrysburg have to wait more than a decade before it was granted parish status?

Three possible explanations exist. First, because of the exigencies and uncertainties of the immigration process, especially in frontier areas, there were not one hundred eligible heads of household in the township until the late 1740s. Problems immigrant settlers faced in the granting of land in colonial South Carolina were matched by aberrations in the settling of lands so granted and could result in a lower de facto population than official records might indicate.[46] Although the drawing off of prospective Purrysburg settlers to other locales after they had applied for and received land in the township is possible, the loss of better than 40 percent of the heads of household by 1738 is unlikely. It is even more improbable when it is remembered that the mid- and late 1730s have been considered by many as the years when the population peaked at close to 800 persons.[47]

A second reason Purrysburg may have failed to achieve parish designation in the 1730s proceeds from the electoral laws of the colony and the concessions granted to those who immigrated to the township. By 1721 South Carolina electoral legislation allowed all white male freeholders with a minimum of fifty acres to vote, provided that they paid at least twenty shillings in taxes. Because the headright of each free white male who resided in the colony was at least fifty acres, and, since the provincial government collected a twenty-shilling tax on all applicants for land, all white male freeholders were therefore eligible to vote in elections for the Commons House. It must be recalled, however, that all fees related to land acquisition were paid out of the public treasury for the Purrysburg immigrants. In addition, the township residents were not required to remit quitrent payments for ten years. A quitrent is not a tax, but, coupled with the other financial incentives to encourage immigration to Purrysburg, the moratorium on rent payments during a decade in which the colony faced its share of challenges, economic and otherwise, may have encouraged the royal government to turn a deaf ear to the township's desire for elevation to parish status.[48]

There is some merit in this second explanation—particularly when linked to the most plausible reason for Purrysburg's decade without formal parish organization—the preemptive prerogatives of lowcountry interests. Had tidewater planters and merchants been as concerned about the full political and economic integration of Purrysburg and other township settlers into provincial life as they were about the protection of their own socioeconomic status and political power, Johnson's township plan of settlement might in reality have resulted in the type of quasi-democratic commercial networks that it promised in theory. In reality, Purrysburg and other frontier outposts had to wait years to achieve the parity that could ensure the order and stability necessary to establish robust commercial relationships.

Dissatisfaction with provincial policies toward Purrysburg seems to have peaked in November 1746, when township inhabitants signed and forwarded another petition to the South Carolina General Assembly outlining what they believed was an ongoing legislative injustice. After the expiration of the ten-year moratorium on quitrent payments for township settlers, the residents had been paying "for about four or five years last past their quota of the general tax of this Province in the same manner as the several other parts of the said Province had done," but they were still deprived of the "benefit of Parochial Government and Discipline." Because the township suffered "for want of church wardens or other proper parish officers many lewd women had and did come there to be delivered of their bastard children." The petition also notified the commission of other "irregularities" because Purrysburg had no legal status by virtue of not being included in any parish. The signatories requested that Purrysburg be erected into a parish with full rights and offices. The legislature dragged its heels but responded favorably to the petition by creating the rural Parish of St. Peter's on 17 February 1746/47 composed largely of Purrysburg Township and its attendant lands. The parish took its name from the Purrysburg church, St. Peter's.[49]

From this time forward, Purrysburg appears to have become more fully integrated into the legal and judicial system of South Carolina, though residents were still denied their full rights of representation for another decade. Contrary to the royal directives that established the townships, St. Peter's Parish was allowed only one member in the Commons House of Assembly—effectively cutting by 50 percent its representation and voice in Charles Town until 1757, when the second delegate was finally approved. In addition, St. Peter's Parish included a significant portion of affluent St. Helena's Parish—not just the township and its six-mile buffer zone as previously stipulated.[50] The inclusion of so much acreage outside that owned by Purrysburg settlers meant that there was a greater chance that the elected representative from the parish would not be an actual settler from Purrysburg but, rather, a landowner from another part of the parish—possibly one that did not even reside in the parish at all. And, indeed, this is exactly what happened.

The township freeholders and other inhabitants of St. Peter's Parish, Purrysburg met to elect their delegate to the Commons House, but Patrick McKay refused to serve. Not only did his refusal cause repercussions for township residents, but the failure of the parish to return the writ of election in the wake of McKay's decision also may have helped precipitate a conflict between Governor James

Glen and the Commons House. The parish had to wait until the following year before it could elect Thomas Dale, who consented to serve and was duly seated in the Commons House. In the years that followed, such notables as Henry Laurens, who bought a plantation in the parish in 1766 and received election to serve in the Commons House in 1773, were returned by St. Peter's freeholders.[51] Voting patterns in the parish demonstrate the propensity of township freeholders to elect their social betters to provincial office, but Laurens's election does hint at the possibility that ethnic heritage may have played some role also. This "deference syndrome" appears to have been as common in multiethnic Purrysburg as in other regions of the British North American colonies, which were more ethnically homogenous. Township citizens did serve in a variety of local political posts including tax collectors, petit and grand jurors, and commissioners of roads. In addition, the Purrysburg company of the South Carolina militia provided a venue for elevated social status and continued to be a well staffed and vital part of the Granville County regiment.[52]

The unwillingness of the South Carolina lowcountry elite to share political power with Purrysburg township settlers until 1746/47 and the inability of the new parish to seat a representative from St. Peter's Purrysburg until March of 1749 meant that the only legal and judicial authority in the township for most of its first two decades rested first in the person of Jean Pierre Purry and, upon his death in 1736, on the justices named in the commission of the peace.

To aver that Purry had more important matters on his mind than maintaining civil peace in his township between 1732 and 1736 is to state the obvious. Because his baronial dreams hinged upon the rapid transport and settlement of immigrants in Purrysburg, his most pressing concern was their recruitment in Europe. As a result he was at best an absentee feudal lord who dabbled in administration when necessary to secure his colony and his ambitions. There is some evidence of Court of Chancery proceedings in the area between 1732 and 1735, but how often the court met under Purry's jurisdiction in the refurbished roomed rented out for that purpose by vintners Francis Yanam and Charles Shepherd is unknown.[53] Purry did function as an advocate for two immigrants in February 1735/36, when he and Attorney General James Abercromby certified that Jacob Bouet and another prospective Purrysburg settler named Madeleine were entitled to land in the township. The council accepted their affidavit and ordered that warrants be prepared.[54] The only other evidence of Purry's exercise of authority brought him into direct conflict with one of the families he seems to have personally persuaded to settle in the township.

Aware of his colony's vulnerability to attack, in late 1734 Purry determined that one fort was insufficient to protect it. As commanding officer of the Purrysburg militia company, he seized Ulisse Antoin Albergotti's already improved town lot, reasoning that it was the best site for a second fort. Albergotti might have been more accommodating had Purry offered another town lot to him as a substitute, but this he refused to do. The displaced settler challenged Purry's preemptive act, whereupon the colonel imprisoned him for insubordination in the fort already built, forbidding anyone from visiting him from six o'clock in the evening until eight o'clock the next morning. Albergotti petitioned the council for redress of his grievances, noting his willingness to give up the town lot he had owned because it was a likely place for a new fort. The council ordered that the lot in question be reserved for a second fort and that Albergotti "be allowed to run out any other lott not before run out," but deferred any judgment regarding his arrest and imprisonment by advising him that he had to "sue for redress in the Court of Justice in the ordinary course of law." It is not known whether Albergotti pursued his case against Purry, but he did sell his Purrysburg land to Richard Hazzard in 1739 and purchased land on Port Royal Island and in Beaufort.[55]

Because parish status had been denied in 1736, Purry's death that year left the frontier township without legislative representation or local civil authority. Justices of the peace served elsewhere in colonial South Carolina as the equivalent of modern-day police officers, but because of the contractual agreement between Purry and the royal government granting him full authority in the township, it appears that no justices were appointed in Purrysburg until after its founder died. The office of the commissioner of the peace was one of the few administrative positions in colonial South Carolina that fell completely under the purview of the governor, though he could consult with the council regarding appointments. Because there was no specified number of commissioners mandated, the governor could appoint as many justices of the peace as he desired. Appointees took five oaths, pledging to be loyal to the king and to conduct themselves appropriately as officers of the peace. Their appointments were typically for life or until the monarch died. They were usually reappointed automatically once they took the oath of loyalty to the new sovereign. Appointment to the office brought elevated social status as justices of the peace mediated between imperial and colonial policy and the local community. In this sense they could legitimately claim to hold a small portion of the king's power and so entered the select membership of the colonial ruling class (albeit at the lowest rung) and were recognized as such by their ability to use the honored title of esquire.

Though endowed with relatively minor legal power, in eighteenth-century South Carolina the justices of the peace carried significant responsibilities at the local jurisdictional level. For Purrysburg Township, justices of the peace, also known somewhat ironically as parish officers, constituted the only political and legal connection between the frontier settlers and the provincial government from 1736 to 1749. They were charged with keeping the peace, regulating markets, maintaining law and order, and imposing fines for legal infractions such as failing to attend militia musters or using inaccurate or false weights and measures. To protect the peace, justices could compel prospective offenders to swear not to cause trouble. They could rule in cases of debt involving as much as twenty pounds current money, issue warrants, bind accused criminals over for trial, and impose bails. They could license tavern keepers and peddlers, as well as deliver vagrants to militia recruiting officers. When acting in consort with one or more colleagues, justices could assert juridical authority as a magistrate court to prosecute minor offenses such as petty theft. These courts, or "petty sessions," were conducted without lawyers or juries and appear to have been convened only occasionally in South Carolina. A more widely used judicial function was the convening of the slave court. Slave courts consisted of two justices of the peace and three freeholders. Such courts were given the power to assess the guilt or innocence of any slave charged with a crime and to impose whatever sentence was deemed necessary, including capital punishment.[56]

The royal conferral of sufficient power upon the commissioners of the peace to perform a wide array of civil tasks did not necessarily translate into a body of active civil servants. Justices of the peace were not actually under obligation to exercise their authority, for time spent in the execution of their prerogatives as justices detracted from their pursuit of the ultimate indictor of status—the possession of land and slaves. Robert Olwell discovered that most often the commissioners operated more as notaries, "transcribing, witnessing, and validating a private deed or contract." He also found that a relatively small minority even did that. Furthermore, in 1767 74 (28 percent) of a total of 264 enrolled justices signed even one of the compiled miscellaneous records between 1765 and 1769. Thirty-five (13 percent) signed more than one. Of that number, nine (3 percent) signed more than half of the documents, and two of the nine signed nearly a third of total records between them.[57] Because Purrysburg Township was completely bereft of any civil authority after Jean Pierre's death, the justices appointed by provincial governors did not quite fit the pattern Olwell found for the colony at large.

Like other South Carolina commissioners, the men listed as Purrysburg justices of the peace in table 4 spent most of their time serving notary functions for township and parish residents. Unlike their peers elsewhere, however, the majority of Purrysburg justices, into the 1770s, witnessed and/or signed multiple documents. John Bourguin, David Saussy, Adrian Mayer, John Linder, David Giroud, and others on the list show up again and again in records of the period. It is difficult to account for this aberration from Olwell's norms until it is recalled that until relatively late in the colonial era Purrysburg settlers were denied full access to their political and legal rights vis-à-vis parish status and full representation in the Commons House. The Purrysburg justices, constituting an emerging township elite, exhibited the other side of the deferential model of colonial leadership—that of consistent service to constituents, who needed all the help they could get. Olwell found that half of all the commissioners served in the Commons House at some time in their lives. The same cannot be said for most Purrysburg justices, but this pattern may be linked to another of Olwell's findings—that a smaller share (eight of thirty-five) of those who signed multiple documents tended to go to the assembly than those who signed one or none. Finally, justices were exempted from military service so they did not have to face the uneasy situation of serving in a subordinate role to militia officers, thereby undermining their elevated social position.[58] But among the Purrysburg commissioners, Peter Lafitte, Samuel Montaigut, James Richard, Frederick DeJean, John Linder, John Bourguin, Abraham Ehrhardt, Adrian Mayer, David Giroud, David Saussy, and Cornelius Dupont served in the militia. Lafitte, Montaigut, Richard, DeJean, and John Bourguin held commissions, but the rest did not.[59]

With regard to the southern frontier, the protection of the entrenched economic power and class privilege of the lowcountry elite trumped the legal and political rights that guaranteed township settlers a semblance of order, security, and stability, which is exactly what Purrysburg Township needed to develop the social bonds of commerce that could sustain settlement and facilitate its integration into the wider socioeconomic networks spreading throughout the colonial Southeast.

TABLE 4: South Carolina Justices of the Peace from Purrysburg Township

Name*	Year†	Source
Peter Lafitte	1736	Holcomb, *Petitions for Land,* 1:43
Hector Berenger de Beaufin	1737	Holcomb, *Petitions for Land,* 1:86
Samuel Montaigut	1737	Davis, *Families of SC & Georgia* (1926), 35‡
James Richard	1737	Inventories 1736–39, J. P. Purry's inventory
Frederick DeJean	1739	RMC, 2P:442
John Lewis Bourguin	1742	RMC, 3E:86
Andrew Verdier	1751/52	RMC, 2N:211–13
John Linder	1752	Holcomb, *Petitions for Land,* 3:23
John Bourguin (Sr.?)	1753	Langley, *Deed Abstracts,* 3:351
John Baptist Bourguin	1756	*SCG,* 4 November 1756
Henry Dessausure	1756	*SCG,* 4 November 1756
Abraham Ehrhardt	1756	*SCG,* 4 November 1756
Daniel Heyward§	1756	*SCG,* 4 November 1756
Adrian Mayer	1760	RMC, 3H:89–90
David Montaigut	1760	Langley, *Deed Abstracts,* 3:132
Henry Bourguin	1761	Langley, *Deed Abstracts,* 3:251
Robert Williams	1764	Langley, *Deed Abstracts,* 3:235
David Giroud	1769	RMC, 3W: 207–9
David Saussy	1772	Langley, *Deed Abstracts,* 4:212
Hugh Rose	1775	*SCG,* 23 January 1775
Daniel Dessausure (Beau. Dist.)	1776	Hemphill , *J. of the Gen. Assem.& H. of Repres., 1776–1780,* 14–15

Name*	Year†	Source
Cornelius Dupont (Beau. Dist.)	1776	Hemphill, *J. of the Gen. Assem. & H. of Repres., 1776–1780,* 14–15
David Zubly Jr. (96 Dist.)	1776	Hemphill, *J. of the Gen. Assem. & H. of Repres., 1776–1780,* 14–15
Bellamy Crawford	1777	RMC, 4T: 279–80
Henry Gindrat	1777	Holcomb *Deed Abstracts, 1773–1778,* 206
David Keal	1777	RMC, 4V:253–54

Notes: *This table includes names of those who lived, maintained landholdings, or presided at the township.

†The year designated is the first year the name of the justice appears on an extant record. It is not the year of official appointment, with the possible exception of the four citations from the *South Carolina Gazette* for 4 November 1756.

‡Davis uses the variant spelling of Montague.

§Daniel Heyward did not receive land in Purrysburg Township until the 1760s.

Six

The Social Bonds of Commerce

The Protestant immigrants who made Purrysburg Township their adopted home were forced to live their lives constrained, not only by the forces of nature, but also by socioeconomic and geopolitical realities of which they were most certainly unaware. The proprietary period was filled with attempts by the Lords Proprietors to develop Carolina in ways that would bring them profit, including agricultural experimentation and the recruitment of poor foreign Protestants. From the 1680s to the outbreak of the Yamassee War, their policies resulted in an economy marked by the production of increasingly valuable staples (naval stores and rice) and the pursuit of more exotic goods not readily available elsewhere in the empire (silk, wine, and medicinal herbs). Both aspects of the provincial economy could profit producer and proprietor alike. The recruitment of French Huguenot, Swiss, and German immigrants was promoted, at least partially, to spur production of commodities that lay beyond the mercantile grasp of the British Empire. By 1720 however, influenced by factors such as profit margins, wartime uncertainties, labor problems, and the physical environment, planters had embraced plantation-based staple crop production dependent upon slave labor.[1]

When the crown assumed control of South Carolina in 1729, decisions regarding the colony, which had been to that point made primarily with the private interests of the proprietors in mind, began to reflect the best interests of an empire. That broader perspective reordered, but did not significantly change, most of the priorities established under proprietary rule. As David Coon noted, an imperial and provincial assessment of the strategic and economic implications of the colony's location "emphasized the expansion of British interests on the southern frontier and the production of commodities such as silk, wine, naval stores, potash, and dyes (as had the programs of the earlier regime), but they also focused on the composition of the colony's population and continued growth of South Carolina's economy."[2]

That these four goals might not be compatible with the socioeconomic, political, and international conditions operative in South Carolina after the Yamassee War or even attainable in light of the track record of the proprietors did not mitigate enthusiasm for them. And Sir Robert Johnson's township plan of settlement seemed the ideal way to achieve all four at the same time. The only real problem was that their achievement would come largely at the expense of the Protestant immigrants who settled at Purrysburg and the other townships, for they were to be the instruments of the expansion of British interests—and therefore the first to be threatened when such expansion antagonized Native Americans or European competitors. They were to increase significantly the colony's white population—but they were consistently denied rights promised to them as white settlers. They were to expand and diversify with their labor an economy that had created a slave labor force that dwarfed the lowcountry white überclass—but they were never meant to share the massive wealth generated by the plantation-based staple crop economy. In short, township residents served imperial and provincial purposes to the detriment of their own. Joyce Chaplin summarized the "bewildering series of roles" a township resident or an inhabitant of trustee Georgia was expected to fulfill: "yeoman soldier, diligent subsistence farmer, participant in a diversified artisanal economy, opponent of black slavery, teetotaler, converter of Indians, tolerant observer of alien religions and cultural beliefs." As she also noted, however, "this complicated list of goals did little to promote the settler's material interests."[3] It was only within this context and with this multiplicity of responsibilities that the immigrants to Purrysburg Township could determine and pursue their material interests.

I

It should come as no surprise that those material interests should be so closely bound to the same networks of relationships that linked Purrysburg socially and religiously to other islands of frontier settlement in the colonial South. Because the residents came from such diverse backgrounds and were bound by their contract with Purry and the Carolina government rather than being allowed to choose for themselves, it was natural for them to reach beyond the township seeking social and commercial connections that they found lacking in Purrysburg. These social and commercial bonds were conditioned by geography, regulated by mutual necessity, and grew incrementally more complex as the eighteenth century progressed. They radiated outward from the township across the Savannah River to Georgia and ultimately to Beaufort and Charles Town.

The near simultaneous founding of Savannah, Georgia, and Purrysburg Township less than twenty-five miles from each other on the southern fringe of British settlement provided each population with important social and commercial outlets. Relationships between inhabitants of the two frontier towns began to form almost immediately upon the founding of the South Carolina immigrant community. The first recorded contact came on 24 May 1733, when Lord Carpenter, Mr. Vernon, and James Oglethorpe gave the laborers/vinedressers Jacob Winkler, Theobald Kieffer, Ludwig Keal, Henric Cronenberger, George Mingersdorff, Andrew Winkler, and Nicolas Riger "three guineas towards furnishing them with working tools; they with their families being the first Germans that are to establish the Town of Purrysburg."[4] In April 1734 a Savannah observer wrote, "There are several poor people from Purrysburg here who come down and earn two shillings a day, and go back up to their wives every Saturday night."[5]

Township founder Jean Pierre Purry paid a courtesy visit to Savannah in February 1733/34. Bailiff Peter Gordon was ordered to place a detachment of four of his guards at Purry's disposal during his stay. Upon his arrival the whole of the guard was ordered under arms and saluted the colonel with a firing of its guns. In November Oglethorpe and a number of South Carolina dignitaries, including Governor Robert Johnson, Captain Massy, and Major Barnwell, returned Purry's visit. Oglethorpe made several subsequent journeys to the township and on these occasions met with the immigrants and their leader. On one visit in February 1735/36 after he and Commissary Von Reck had toured the site that would be New Ebenezer, Oglethorpe was received in Purrysburg with a salute from several of the cannon. The township's founder and "the chief people of the city" welcomed him. When the Purrysburg Germans heard of his arrival, they "gathered in a large crowd and sought out Mr. Oglethorpe, each for his own purpose." Afterward, Oglethorpe and Von Reck dined with Purry and spent the evening in his home.[6]

The Savannah entrepreneur Robert Parker visited Purrysburg prior to the end of December 1734 and expressed his gratitude for its presence to the trustees. He planned to return for a social call, writing, "If I have time to spare I can go up to Purrysburg and spend a day or two with Mr. Beaufin and other good company agreeably," but he may not have been able to do so until June 1735, when he chose the site for a sawmill he planned to build three miles from Purrysburg. He hoped to supply lumber for the township, as well as Savannah, other settlements, and the Sugar Islands.[7] Savannah bailiff Thomas Causton, along with Mr. Lacy and Mr. Vanderplank, hired "some of the poor people at Purrysburg who were in a very low condition" to load 700 barrels of pitch and tar for Captain Dunbar in mid-January 1735/36. The following month Frederica storekeeper Francis Moore met a boat full of laborers on their way to Savannah, most of whom were from the township.[8]

Other notables—such as Georgia president and the trustees' secretary in the colony, Colonel William Stephens, the prosperous merchant Samuel Eveleigh, and Captain Thompson—traveled to the township during its first decade. A group of Moravian expatriates appears to have enjoyed Purrysburg hospitality in the winter of 1735 before moving on to their ultimate destination. The Savannah gardener, a French-speaking Piedmontese Waldensian named Paul Amatis, visited the township many times and entertained some hope of settling there because he was at odds with his superiors in the Georgia city in early 1735 over his agrarian policies as well as his tendency to take servants with him on his trips to Purrysburg. Amatis contracted with settlers there to supply mulberry leaves for the trustees' silk endeavor over the course of many trips to the township but apparently never stayed for extended periods. When his brother Nicholas came to join him in Savannah in the silk works, he brought Anthony (Jacob) Camuse (Camuso), his wife, Mary (Maria), and their three children as servants. The Camuses became proficient in sericulture. Anthony and his children left Savannah for Purrysburg to work in the industry, although they moved back to Georgia sometime in January 1750/51.[9]

Social and commercial intercourse between Purrysburg and Savannah happened in both directions. Charles Purry rented a house in the Georgia settlement and with Samuel Montaigut established a store in Savannah soon after the founding of Purrysburg. It was reported that the store took in more revenue than any other there. The two conducted business in both towns until the end of the 1730s. When Savannah needed provisions in June 1737, Purry proposed hiring a ship at his own expense to bring supplies down from New York or Philadelphia. A Purrysburg cooper traveled downriver to the Georgia town sometime before early April of 1739, apparently to find work. When Savannah residents had problems with their butcher in 1740, Johannes Altherr, a German-speaking butcher from Purrysburg, agreed to supply their needs. Georgia president William Stephens reported that Altherr's labor saved the colonists from significant difficulties. Altherr seems to have remained in Georgia for at least a year, providing the town less expensive meat than the previous vendor. He maintained a herd of cattle at Purrysburg for the future needs of Savannah. Savannah resident and member of the white laboring class Anthione Gautier (Gotier) owned property in Purrysburg at his death, perhaps signifying his move into the lower middle class. Theobald Kieffer's son Jacob traveled from the township to Savannah with the Reverend Boltzius in the spring of 1741 to have his wounded foot treated, by which time the Reverend Chiffelle had already been preaching regularly to the Reformed of the Georgia town for nearly three years. Stephens paid some indigent Purrysburg workers to help with the harvest in September 1738. At the request of Georgia authorities in Savannah, John (Johann) Frederick Holzendorf of the township agreed to accompany the surveyors charged with running out lots at New Ebenezer. By March 1745/46, members of the Savannah Reformed community had petitioned authorities to secure the services of three different ministers associated with Purrysburg—Henry Chiffelle, Bartholemew Zouberbühler, and John J. Zubly. When Colonel Heron requested a meeting with the Reverend Boltzius in the summer of 1750, he planned to travel from Savannah and rendezvous with Boltzius in Purrysburg. Helena Zubly visited Savannah shortly after the death of her husband and son in early 1753, perhaps to be consoled by members of the German-speaking community there. Isaac Brabant also appears to have conducted business in Savannah sometime before the late 1760s and may have taken up residence there by 1767. The relationships between Purrysburg and Savannah residents that originated during the early years of settlement grew more complex as the silk industry became established and the ministries of the Reverend Chiffelle and later the Reverend John J. Zubly continued to link Purrysburg and Savannah By the time of the smallpox epidemic in Charles Town and Santee in 1763, Georgia officials issued a proclamation of quarantine to the Purrysburg justices of the peace because of the frequency of contact between the two settlements.[10]

II

As important as the social and commercial linkages that tied Purrysburg and Savannah together were, they could not match those that developed between the township and Ebenezer. The journal the Reverend Boltzius kept for almost thirty years discloses his unremitting disapproval of most township citizens and nearly all their activities, but it also reveals a multilayered and intricate web of relationships that would not have existed had they not been in the best interests of both frontier towns. However complex or problematic the social, religious, and commercial connections may have been from the pastor's perspective, they were essential—especially from the 1730s to the 1750s as immigrants on both sides of the Savannah River struggled to adapt to life on the southeastern frontier.

Prior to the arrival of the Salzburg immigrants in British North America, connections between the two immigrant groups had already been established. The Reverends Boltzius and Gronau initially met Jean Pierre Purry in Dover before the pastors left for Georgia with the first transport of refugees aboard the *Purisburg* in December 1733. Purry communicated to them the needs of the Germanic residents of his township, who were already struggling with the religious context of life in Purrysburg. The Lutherans employed Jean Vat, who had collaborated closely with Purry in his colonizing efforts, to lead the second transport of Salzburgers to Ebenezer. He became the Savannah storekeeper in 1736. Upon his arrival in Ebenezer, Vat lost no time in renewing his friendship with Purry on an extended visit to the township. Vat seems also to have been on quite friendly terms with the Reverend Henry Chiffelle. Once the Salzburg immigrants arrived in Georgia, their journey upriver to Ebenezer brought them into direct association with Purrysburg before they had ever seen their new home because of the riverine transportation system. At least one member of the second transport (Sebastian Glantz) never left the South Carolina township, dying there before reaching the new Georgia settlement.[11]

The mutual necessity of working cooperatively in a hostile frontier environment bound the welfare of the two settlements together, even though antagonisms mounted as the connections deepened. The physical geography of the lower Southeast was one factor that bound the settlers together whether they liked it or not. Purrysburg quickly became an important link in the communication between the Reverend Boltzius, Oglethorpe, and Colonel Stephens.[12] In addition the Ebenezer immigrants most urgently required the continued shipment of promised provisions from the Savannah storehouse to see them through their first year in Georgia. Dense undergrowth and swampy conditions made Ebenezer Creek unnavigable, rendering water transport of the provisions directly to Ebenezer impossible. Purrysburg, however, maintained a wharf and could easily be reached from Savannah. After some discussion Savannah stores manager Thomas Causton agreed in 1734 to send supplies for the Salzburgers as far as Purrysburg. From there Ebenezer settlers would be responsible for packing the goods across the river to their own homes. Thereafter Purrysburg served as a provisioning depot for the Salzburgers on many an occasion. Lack of a direct route between the Lutheran settlement and Savannah or Charles Town meant that Purrysburg also served the Salzburgers as a communications outpost and a repository for their parcels. Meteorological realities encouraged Ebenezer travelers to use Purrysburg as a rest stop, especially in the searing heat and oppressive humidity of the summer months. The thick forests of the frontier Southeast inadvertently brought some residents of the two settlements together, for individuals lost in the woods periodically turned up haggard and hungry at their neighbors' homes. In each case, they were nursed back to health and conducted back across the Savannah River to their homes. Even after the Ebenezer settlers began their move to the more hospitable site of New Ebenezer in 1736, Purrysburg retained its importance to them as a transportation, communication, and supply station. For example, when the Reverend Boltzius experienced some difficulty with the unproven oarsman rowing his boat from Ebenezer to Purrysburg in the spring of 1743, he chose not to continue with him to Savannah. He later wrote, "Our Father granted me in Purrysburg a large boat laden with meat. I boarded it at about eleven o'clock and continued my journey quite comfortably and safely with my small boat following behind." These nearly continuous, though tentative, contacts led progressively to more sustained social and commercial relations between the communities. One set of those relationships proceeded from the medical needs of settlers on both sides of the Savannah River.[13]

Appropriate treatment of various of the maladies afflicting settlers in the colonial Southeast may have been a point of debate between Purrysburg doctors and the Ebenezer pastors, but residents of both settlements entrusted themselves to the ministrations those who embraced a worldview in which physical well-being was linked inexorably to much greater cosmic and spiritual truths. The desire to comprehend the complex intertwining of human vitality and the physical environment explains, not only why medical remedies of the era were so violent, but also why mystical incantations were perceived as viable treatments and why such close attention was paid to diet and climatological conditions.[14] It is within this context that medical diagnoses and treatments in the colonial Southeast need to be understood.

For example, Dr. John Frederick Holzendorf of Purrysburg offered numerous times to go to Ebenezer to bleed Salzburgers prior to his first visit in the spring of 1737. Medicinal bleeding was one way to purge the body of sickness by restoring the balance of the bodily humors. Holzendorf had been a captain in the Prussian military as well as a recognized surgeon who appears to have practiced only occasionally in the South Carolina township. When Holzendorf was invited to bleed several ill Salzburgers in May, Boltzius wrote that he had asked for nothing in payment and even offered to return when "we thought it necessary." In addition to performing the service, Holzendorf taught one of the pastors the technique. Boltzius was genuinely grateful for his expertise, noting, "We consider his willingness and kindness a great material blessing."[15] Holzendorf did return on 4 June 1740, not to treat Ebenezer settlers, but to request medicines necessary for his work among Purrysburg residents. His request appears to have been honored, but he did not receive enough, for he wrote to ask for more on 5 June.[16]

Whereas the Reverend Boltzius had nothing but praise for the German-speaking Holzendorf, he appears to have borne little but contempt for French-speaking Dr. Jean Baptiste Bourguin. Bourguin had served nine years in the Duke of Marlborough's army before immigrating to Purrysburg with other members of his family. In late July 1741 Bourguin apparently treated the German-speaking township shopkeeper John Linder for a long-standing ailment. His treatment consisted of a regimen of purging and the use of "six *sesicutoria* two hands wide," which were laid on different parts of Linder's body for several days. Boltzius reported when he visited Linder on 30 July that "not only did he suffer indescribable pain in his torture but he was extremely weakened and has severe stomach and breast pains and is weak in the head."[17] The next afternoon Linder felt well enough to travel to Ebenezer "seeking some peace and quiet medical attention." He made the boat trip with Christian Ernst Thilo, the Ebenezer physician from Halle, who had also gone to Purrysburg to sit with Linder. Boltzius cared for him until Linder returned to Purrysburg on 2 August with medicines given to him by Thilo.[18] Little more than two and one-half months later, Linder went through another purging because of a fever, probably administered by Bourguin. As a result of the procedure, however, Linder suffered gastrointestinal difficulties producing "many inconveniences." His distress was great enough that he wrote the Reverend Boltzius, seeking medicine to alleviate his symptoms and "offering . . . many favors in return." The medicines relieved Linder, and their effectiveness prompted a letter of gratitude, which Boltzius received by courier on 15 November.[19] Linder procured more medicines from Halle via Ebenezer in January 1742/43 and wrote then that "I will be beholden to you forever for the medicines we received. I can say with truth that God's blessing is in everything they have sent me. Everything has taken effect immediately. I thank your Reverence heartily for all such kindnesses."[20]

Bourguin's treatment of other patients led Boltzius to moderate to some extent his negative view of the Purrysburg surgeon's abilities, but only slightly. In late February 1740/41, Salzburger Joseph Ernst received treatment by Bourguin in Purrysburg for a hand injury, most likely a dislocated thumb. It seems not to have healed correctly, and, apparently after efforts by Thilo to treat it, Ernst returned to Bourguin in Purrysburg for more attention on 21 August 1741. Bourguin took one look at the injury and informed Ernst that the hand could not be saved. While Ernst decided for the surgery, Boltzius was not so sure. He confided to his journal that "in Purrysburg they like to use all sorts of violent Negro cures before necessity demands, and I advised him to seek better advice first."[21] By the twenty-fourth, Ernst made his final decision. Boltzius accompanied him to Purrysburg that day, but Bourguin did not know they were coming and had to put the operation off until the following day. On the twenty-fifth, David Zubly went with Boltzius and Ernst to Bourguin's home, where the surgeon performed the amputation. Once Bourguin realized the extent of the damage, he had to remove all but a few inches of the arm, which he subsequently showed Boltzius for his inspection. Zubly promised to offer spiritual support to Ernst during his convalescence in Purrysburg, for which Bourguin charged Ernst a shilling a day for board. For the next two months Boltzius looked in on Ernst at Bourguin's home as often as he could given his other responsibilities. Ernst returned to Ebenezer by 20 October 1741 with some medicine from Bourguin, but he was still quite ill.[22]

Seventeen forty-one was a trying year in Ebenezer, for in addition to those suffering from lesser health problems that visited Bourguin, two more severely injured Ebenezer settlers turned to him for medical help. On 2 October the Reverend Boltzius took both Maria Maurer and Peter Reiter to him for treatment. Maurer had been suffering from an abscess or ulceration of the uvula for fifteen months by the time Boltzius took her to Purrysburg. Bourguin examined her and believed the best course of action was to operate on the affected area. He used an instrument called a "Stone of Hell" to sear the infected/necrotic flesh in her mouth. In keeping with the mystical spirit of the age, the stone in the instrument was believed to be a type that possessed curative powers. After the operation, Bourguin prescribed medicines that contributed to her recovery. She was well enough by 16 October to be taken back to Ebenezer by her husband and the Reverend Gronau. Bourguin gave her medicines to take with her that he believed would result in a full recovery as long as she took them regularly.[23] Peter Reiter's injury proved to be more problematic. He had shot a bear out of a tree, and the animal, unfortunately, landed on him and dislocated his leg. Bourguin initially reset his femur in the socket in early October, and the patient appeared to be progressing though he remained unsteady and weak, but by 30 October Bourguin had reset it twice more with "cords and great force." Reiter was still convalescing in Purrysburg in early November, more than a month after his arrival. His wife paid him a visit there on 19 November. When Reiter was finally able to go home on 2 December 1741, he needed crutches, but Bourguin let him return to Ebenezer "with certain hope that in some time he will be able to use his injured leg as well as formerly."[24]

Bourguin's treatment of these three severely injured Pietists built a reservoir of good will between the French-speaking surgeon and the German speakers of Ebenezer, but it did not eliminate a recurring skepticism regarding his integrity and his skills, though they were in all likelihood commensurate with Holzendorf's. The Reverend Boltzius expressed his ambivalence regarding Bourguin's abilities when he visited a perilously ill Purrysburg woman in May 1741. After observing that "the doctor has probably ruined her even more," Boltzius left her with some medicine and scripture passages.[25] The pastor's attitude softened later in the year when he heard a good report from his colleague the Reverend Gronau. He admitted that Bourguin's "activity and willingness to serve has given me quite another concept of him than I had before." As Boltzius saw the Purrysburg doctor treat Ernst, Maurer, and Reiter he began to believe that he "serves for the sake of the patients."[26] By late October he wrote that, since Bourguin's treatment of the three, "he has now a good reputation among the Salzburgers and they would entrust themselves to him in all sorts of cases were he closer." Boltzius withheld his unqualified support, though, and did not encourage the Salzburgers to go to him, believing that the "surgeon has little medical understanding."[27] His assessment of Bourguin quickly deteriorated when Ernst died, probably of pneumonia, and Boltzius received a bill from the physician for eleven pounds sterling, which the Pietist denounced as exorbitant. At roughly the same time an Ebenezer master took his servant girl, who had injured her eye, to Bourguin for treatment. She stayed in the township for several weeks recovering, and when she returned to Ebenezer, her eyesight was still not totally restored. Boltzius found Bourguin's bill for twenty shillings sterling completely inappropriate under these circumstances. When Reiter returned in early December, Boltzius made a special notation in his diary that "the cost for his care is not yet known." In a mid-January entry still uncertain as to Reiter's bill because Bourguin had not been able to calculate it, Boltzius opined cryptically, "Doubtless it will amount to a great deal."[28] His negative appraisal of Bourguin and his township neighbors seemed to be reinforced when he recorded in his journal that "Reiter said he would rather be ill in Ebenezer than healthy in Purrysburg amongst the course folk. Catherina (Maria) Maurer said the same thing."[29] Final confirmation for the Reverend Boltzius of Bourguin's medical incompetence came in the mid-1740s. In May 1743 a small group of Purrysburg residents traveled to Ebenezer for assistance. The married woman, her mother, and two brothers were all quite ill. When the woman expired in late June, Boltzius placed all the blame on Bourguin, writing, "She had already been ruined fundamentally in Purrysburg by a local doctor." Nearly two years later, after Bourguin had treated an eighteen-year-old member of the Kieffer extended family for an oral malady, Boltzius believed she was harmed severely because of the physician's "inappropriate salivation."[30]

It is ironic to note that, although the Reverend Boltzius held Holzendorf in high regard and consistently maintained a skeptical attitude toward Bourguin, it is apparent from the pastor's journal that Ebenezer settlers relied much more often on Bourguin for their medical care than on Holdzendorf during the early years of settlement. Ethnic animosity may be ruled out because Boltzius also turned, on at least two different occasions in 1739, to the wife of a French-speaking township resident who assisted in Ebenezer births. In both cases the Reverend Boltzius spoke very highly of her skills. By contrast, in October 1760 it appears that Boltzius refused to provide medicines from the Ebenezer store to the German doctor George Friedrich Meissner, who probably arrived in Purrysburg sometime in the later 1750s after serving the people of Savannah, though there is some confusion on this point. The antipathy of the Pietist for Bourguin also does not seem to have been precipitated directly by what Boltzius perceived as outlandish treatment regimens. It is obvious that he believed Bourguin used more invasive procedures than were sometimes necessary, but Boltzius seems otherwise to have believed in the efficacy of mystical treatments that Bourguin too might have used, including the Purrysburg curative baths and folk remedies. Most likely it was Bourguin's religious leanings and secondarily his Purrysburg address that prompted Boltzius to regard him with such enduring suspicion.[31] But whatever the depth of his antipathy toward Bourguin and his Purrysburg neighbors, the fundamental need for access to health care bridged the religious gap, at least partially. The abilities of Purrysburg surgeons and a capable midwife were complemented by the availability of medicine at Ebenezer and initiated an important network of relationships between the two frontier towns.

III

A similar complementarity typified the exchange of commercial products and services between the settlements and presented opportunities for them to construct a different set of relationships. These economic relationships, like so many others forged between Ebenezer Lutherans and the Purrysburg Reformed, proved to be both mutually beneficial and often quite problematic. Shoemaker John Jacob Reck appears to have been the first township craftsperson called upon to meet the needs of Ebenezer. Although the Georgia colony had at least one cobbler of its own in the first years of settlement (Mr. Reidelsperger), he proved inadequate. In keeping with the Old World sensibilities of the Salzburg pastors, Ebenezer parishioners were admonished to maintain appropriate attire for Sundays and Holy Days, which included appropriate footwear. Children at the orphanage were particularly in need. First called upon to make shoes for the Ebenezer settlers in the spring of 1735, Reck continued periodically to do so until the Pietist pastors secured the services of a shoemaker more to their liking.

But Andreas Lorentz Arnsdorff drowned in July 1737, and the replacement shoemaker, who arrived in October 1738, did not meet expectations. After a second replacement cobbler died in August 1739, Reck was rehired by early October. Ebenezer resident Matthias Zettler moved to Purrysburg to become Reck's apprentice shortly thereafter.[32]

The Purrysburg shoemaker was appreciated for his craft but proved to be a less than stellar citizen. He frequented the Purrysburg tavern and overworked Zettler while feeding him unpalatable food. When war came, Reck persuaded Zettler to enlist—and reportedly kept half of his wages during his term of service. After Zettler had established his own business in Ebenezer by early 1741, he complained to Boltzius that Reck spread lies about him in Purrysburg, telling township inhabitants that his former apprentice had stolen leather from him. Reck left Purrysburg temporarily for a short stay in Port Royal in 1742 but returned within a few months, only to rent out his Purrysburg plantation to the Ebenezer orphanage in 1744. Zettler continued his trade in Ebenezer. Ironically the Salzburgers might have saved themselves from Reck's antics had Boltzius acted affirmatively upon the request of another Purrysburg shoemaker who sought his permission to move his family to Ebenezer in August 1739 and again in 1740. Boltzius noted that he made fine shoes and "he and his God-fearing wife are not concerned with making a living which they can also find in Purrysburg," but they were Reformed, not Lutheran.

Another Purrysburg artisan early employed by the Salzburgers was the mason Joshua Daniel Tullius. He accepted employment in Ebenezer to construct a fireplace in the fall of 1735. Aided by Salzburg volunteers, Tullius completed work on the project in short order. In the process of the masonry construction Tullius also let it be known that he knew how to make tar and pitch. He lengthened his stay for a few days to instruct the inhabitants in the production of these naval stores. Township resident Hans Krüsy possessed a number of skills—all of which were used on behalf of the Salzburg settlers. He fixed wagon and cart wheels, constructed the orphanage rice stamp in 1738,[33] and helped build the Reverend Boltzius's house in 1739. Marguerite, the widowed daughter of Jacob Metsger, and her three children relocated to Ebenezer in 1741 so that she could use her skill as a tailor there.

The Kieffer family supplied a number of services to Ebenezer. The Salzburgers relied often on the family's knowledge of the southeastern waterways and their expertise as mariners. In May 1735 Theobald Kieffer Sr. gave the Salzburgers a substantial number of fish his sons caught in the Savannah River. The following year the Kieffers sold a large transport boat they had built to the Ebenezer settlement for eighteen pounds sterling, dropping their price by two pounds out of consideration for the Georgians. In October 1738, when the Ebenezer boat sank with valuables aboard, the Reverend Boltzius employed the young brothers Jacob and Theobald Jr. as divers in an attempt to recover the lost cargo. Over the next few years members of the Kieffer family assisted the Salzburgers in various ways. One of the Kieffers allowed Ebenezer settlers to accompany him on a trip to Port Royal in July 1740 so that they could pick up linens purchased from the merchant Charles Purry. In December a Savannah merchant sent sackcloth for Ebenezer via one of the sons. The following fall both Jacob and Theobald Jr. helped some of the Pietists navigate the water route to Charles Town to purchase winter supplies. In 1742 Jacob sailed to Port Royal to ensure that horses and cattle promised the settlers would arrive. Two months later, in May, Jacob and Theobald Jr. went to Savannah in an Ebenezer boat to get supplies that had arrived there for the Pietists. In April 1744 Theobald Sr. and Jacob sold another large boat to Boltzius for sixteen pounds sterling for use by the Ebenezer orphanage.[34]

By 1737 commercial relationships were broadening between the two frontier settlements. In that year alone, Ebenezer employed twice as many Purrysburg craftsmen and laborers as it had in the previous four years combined. Because of a partial crop failure, the Salzburgers were forced to augment their provisions from the Georgia trustees in the late 1730s with supplies from the Purrysburg merchant and planter Samuel Montaigut. Montaigut initially sold them forty bushels of "Indian beans" in 1737. Boltzius and Gronau purchased twenty barrels of rice from the merchant in 1738 for distribution to the colonists. Three years later they bought ten bushels of corn for twenty shillings sterling from the French-speaking vendor at Purrysburg.[35]

Workers from the township whose names and occupations are unrecorded provided services at both Old and at New Ebenezer on a regular, though intermittent, basis. Purrysburg carpenters helped the Salzburgers build the only gristmill in colonial Georgia in 1740. Many of these construction workers remained on site for extended periods, leaving wives and children behind in Purrysburg. When the Ebenezer widow Mrs. Rauner had received no payment for her husband's service in the military expedition to St. Augustine, a French-speaking township resident agreed in late March 1741 to take the letter she wrote to the proper authorities in Charles Town for redress. A German-speaking orchardist from Purrysburg visited the Salzburgers in 1737 and sold them a number of peach trees, thus helping diversify the agricultural production of the colony. Plum trees from Purrysburg sold to them at roughly the same time grew well and produced fruit by 1739. A Purrysburg resident found honey pears and sweet grapes growing in the wild and harvested them for the Reverend Boltzius in August 1741. When the pastor expressed a desire in early 1742 to begin cultivation of wine grapes at Ebenezer, even though it was difficult to procure cuttings unless they were gotten from a friend, a Purrysburg vinedresser offered him some vines. Oglethorpe had purchased some from the same man the year before, but Boltzius turned him down because of the cost. A French-speaking township sericulturist provided Ebenezer with a number of white mulberry trees requested by Boltzius in early 1747, and at least two varieties of wheat, including the Sicilian strain, were provided to the Ebenezer settlers by township agriculturalists before June 1749. When Boltzius explored developing a tannery in Ebenezer in 1750, a French-speaking Purrysburg tanner (probably Abraham Ravot) agreed to teach the skill to two Ebenezer inhabitants, but Boltzius found the fee and the time commitment necessary to learn the trade too excessive and decided against employing him. A Purrysburg youth became an apprentice to the Ebenezer locksmith Schrempf but died on a visit to his parents in the township sometime before late March 1753. Purrysburg men assisted the royal surveyor as he platted land in Ebenezer, and township herdsmen tended the livestock of Ebenezer settlers. Purrysburg may have even played a central role in bringing blacksmithing to the Salzburgers as Boltzius advanced an Ebenezer man three pounds sterling in 1738 to purchase a Purrysburg smithy so the profession could be practiced in the settlement. Often after work on various projects had been completed by Purrysburg workers, township residents would take advantage of the services provided by the finished project. Especially noteworthy in this regard was the use by Purrysburg citizens of the Ebenezer saw- and gristmills.[36]

So useful were these mills, particularly the gristmill, that in August 1748 a number of French-speaking residents of the township offered to dam the waterway making the mill functional for most of the year. For reasons known only to him, Boltzius turned down their offer, noting that "we do not accept work from outsiders since we can pay cash for these and other expenditures." Later the same month a Purrysburg area planter and merchant told the pastor that several planters in the vicinity "would like to bring their European and local grains" to the Ebenezer mill. Because they believed that the way to Ebenezer via Purrysburg was too far, they wanted to construct a bridge "across an unpassable spot to the Savannah River about six English miles from us." Boltzius denied their request for carpentry help in constructing the bridge while at the same time inexplicably contending that he "would like to improve communication between us and Purrysburg and areas there."[37]

The initiation and expansion of socioeconomic relationships between Purrysburg Township settlers and their Georgia neighbors in Savannah and Ebenezer from the early 1730s to the mid-1750s, however problematic they might have been for various parties involved, occurred in certain ways to meet specific needs. The relational networks so established both proceeded from and contributed to the contours of township's evolution on the southern frontier—an evolution that moved its citizens progressively away from the township vision of Governor Johnson and toward expansive plantation agriculture that he had so hoped to counter.

IV

The conversion of the South Carolina wilderness that had been chosen as the site of the first township into an economically productive frontier community required long years of toil, wrenched children out of what little educational opportunities might have been afforded them, and left skilled artisans without much chance to practice their trades even if they had occasion to do so. An inadequate money supply and perpetual turmoil regarding everything from land titles and township security to weather-related crop damage made it extremely difficult for craftspeople and service professionals to stay in Purrysburg and still use their abilities to make a living. The circumstances of the early years of township settlement thus militated against diversified economic development. As a result, Purrysburg could not support a skilled craft sector and was located too far from any town that could for many artisans to remain there. Members of the service and craft sector who lived in the township were obliged to go elsewhere for employment, even if it meant hiring themselves out as laborers, leaving families for weeks at a time, or pulling up stakes completely and moving to another region more conducive to their economic health.[38]

From the first weeks of settlement, a large number of artisans and professionals immigrated to Purrysburg. They were exactly the type of settlers desired by the South Carolina authorities and the very people that the township plan was implemented to attract. Unfortunately, the expertise to practice a trade or profession in Purrysburg did not correlate significantly with the opportunity to earn a living by doing so in the township. Although many of the extant sources are somewhat skewed toward Georgia residents, it becomes quite obvious that there was a greater possibility for Purrysburg colonists to find employment in Savannah or Ebenezer than in the township. It is often difficult to ascertain whether the type of work township residents did for their employers matched their training, if they learned other skills "on the fly" to support their families, or if those who worked as unskilled laborers were, in fact, unskilled laborers when they arrived in South Carolina.[39] Nevertheless, the fact that a significant number of Purrysburg landowners could not find work in the township meant that the opportunity structure for the skilled craft/professional and service sectors of its economy contracted severely from the beginning of settlement in 1732.[40]

A barrel- and cabinetmaker left Purrysburg because he had "no opportunity to earn anything." Another township inhabitant unable to find work discovered that the only recourse left open to him was to oversee the dissolution of his family in order to save the individual members from starvation. Even the cobbler Reck found it next to impossible to collect payment in currency from Purrysburg customers. The tailor Marguerite (née Metsger) left Purrysburg for financial reasons as much as personal ones. Township weaver and temporary schoolmaster George Schönmannsgruber could not make a living and knew nothing about agriculture. He planned to move north with his family in hopes of finding better employment opportunities. The misfortunes of these craftspeople and professionals created significant strains on family life, which radiated outward to affect in one way or another township community life. Boltzius wrote in November 1737 that both French- and German-speaking

Purrysburg settlers "are suffering much want, and others are forced to work elsewhere for wages." Even Charles Purry reluctantly ended his association with his London Huguenot supplier Peter Simond, as well as his commercial endeavors in Purrysburg, because he could not find buyers for his merchandise unless he sold on credit since the citizens had so little currency. Farmers and their families could continue to live from the land in times of crisis, but artisans, professionals, and day laborers unaccustomed to agrarian pursuits were at the mercy of the marketplace during Purrysburg's early years. The departure of the underemployed from Purrysburg, some probably never again able to find steady work in their chosen professions, signaled a reduction in options for the future commercial direction of the township. With the craft sector depleted within the first decade, the opportunity structure pointed increasingly to the expansive plantation system and chattel slavery, which in turn may have pushed yeoman farmers off the land as well.[41]

Compounding the blight of underemployment, if not at least partially causing it, was lack of money in the township and its immediate environs. Specie from Spain, Portugal, France, and Holland may have circulated in the region in 1751, complementing British sterling and colonial currency, but not much of it stayed in Purrysburg.[42] When a South Carolina Englishman sold livestock to Purrysburg settlers prior to mid-August 1737, he was "obliged to give credit for long periods of time which causes him many losses."[43] Because of "the dearth of small change" on the frontier, merchants Purry and Montaigut resorted to issuing their own notes from the store in Savannah and then redeeming them with sterling. The Reverend Boltzius initiated a similar practice at Ebenezer by 1742 after earlier boasting that the Salzburgers could pay for their needs in cash. These strategies designed to lessen the negative consequences of a constricted money supply, however, came with their own risks, which Boltzius discovered when he received counterfeit notes from Montaigut. This lack of currency also affected the lives of Purrysburg's children. In an attempt to meet the educational needs of the Theobald Kieffer family, in 1739 Boltzius agreed to let three of the children board at the Ebenezer orphanage and attend the school without payment, based on Theobald Sr.'s pledge to repay all they owed. Boltzius made good on his offer even though Kieffer "has not been able to pay back all of what was previously paid out for maintenance and some clothing; but we are overlooking this and not pushing him because the money is not there." The Pietists contributed to the lack of circulating currency as they had been extended a line of credit in both Purrysburg and Savannah by June of 1739, and at least one Ebenezer family, the Ortmanns, appears to have incurred debts soon thereafter with at least three creditors, who may all have been Purrysburg residents. The Lutheran ministers were also indebted to Charles Purry, who worked with Simond to pay them their salaries on the strength of a promissory note delivered to Purry in May 1739.[44]

Triggered by the War of Jenkins' Ear (1739–1743) and King George's War (1743–1748), the recession of the 1740s made matters worse. The loss of men to the war effort drove wages higher, which had a similar effect on prices. In November 1741 Boltzius wrote that "the tradesmen in Purrysburg and Savannah seek very great profits. War is making everything expensive."[45] After a trip to Charles Town the following month, Boltzius discovered that what had been purchased there would have cost twice as much at Purrysburg or Savannah. It was also reported that a wealthy Purrysburg inhabitant was willing to lend his stallion out for stud service in the spring of 1744, but charged thirty shillings sterling to do so, which, as Boltzius observed "is difficult for poor people."[46] Without a diversified workforce paid in regular monetary wages, Purrysburg settlers had few options if they hoped to survive on the southern frontier. By the end of the decade it became apparent that their greatest chance for success would come from the land, not the skills and professions they brought to Purrysburg.

But if the 1740s proved to be pivotal for the future economic direction the township was to take, those years also revealed the difficulties inherent in establishing an agrarian economic base in the pine barrens. For Purrysburg craftspeople and professionals with no experience in agricultural production, the occupational leap they had to make constituted a major obstacle to efficient and profitable land use management. Their unfamiliarity with rural life would have been problematic no matter where they settled. For those in Purrysburg who had been farmers, vintners, sericulturalists, or tenders of livestock, the land itself presented the greatest challenge. The infertility of most of the township and the delay in gaining title to it were two major problems. A third proceeded from the proximity of many grants to the Savannah River, which overflowed its banks and destroyed crops on numerous occasions.[47]

Two other impediments to the development of agricultural production in Purrysburg were closely related. The first proceeded from Purry's intricate plan to finance the transportation and settlement of his colonists in South Carolina. He had requested 48,000 acres from the royal government as recompense for peopling the southern frontier with 600 colonists. But to ensure the success of his efforts he needed the assistance of well-placed supporters. In return for their backing, financial and otherwise, Purry promised them sizable grants within the land set aside for his settlement—the 20,000-acre township proper or the six-mile buffer zone that separated the immigrants from their nearest neighbors. This arrangement would be legal under the stipulations of the township plan endorsed by South Carolina authorities only if the grantees lived on the land they were granted. In the cases that can be documented, however, this does not seem to have been the case. Two of Purry's patrons, the wealthy Huguenot and London merchant Peter Simond and Georgia trustee James Oglethorpe, appear to have secured grants in exchange for their support, but there is no evidence that either of them lived on the grants they received.[48] In November 1734 the

South Carolina Gazette reported the arrival of 260 more émigrés bound for Purrysburg and noted that Oglethorpe, "the Duc de Montague[,] and several other Persons of distinction" had contributed financially to the enterprise.[49] The following July, Daniel Vernezobre petitioned the Board of Trade seeking land in Purrysburg. A year or so prior to his petition, Vernezobre had "given to a gentleman who was about to settle at Purrysburgh several of his people on condition that a proportion of the lands should be assigned over to him." He had assisted in transporting "people tools implements ironwork trees Negroes &c &c" by advancing them more than 1,000 pounds sterling and therefore held that the land requested should be his. The board disallowed this claim because he was not an inhabitant, but he did receive 2,000 acres in the township via his agent James Delas in 1736. Three years later Benjamin Whitaker, on behalf of John Roberts, assignee of former proprietor Lord Carteret, was able to block temporarily the transfer of the massive land grant to Purry's son Charles following Purry's death.[50] The Reverend Boltzius observed in 1740 that wealthy people from "England and Charles Town have many thousands of acres in Purrysburg." So much land had been taken that the pastor could "not see how the country of Purrysburg can be settled if the present arrangement stays the same" since "rich people have the most land."[51] These illegal grants not only took out of production some of the best land in the areas reserved for Purrysburg inhabitants, but also disrupted land claims of those who thought their titles once finally received were valid. Simond's low-lying land, located both above and below Ebenezer, was said to be "excellent for all kinds of fruit."[52] Perhaps because of influence peddling, but at least due to poor surveying work, the land supposedly granted to Purrysburg settlers Theobald Kieffer Sr., Jacob Reck, and the Reverend Chiffelle was determined in 1740 to be actually owned by Simond or Hector Berenger de Beaufin—the former never having lived in Purrysburg and the latter, gone from the township probably before 1742. Simond's extensive landholdings in Purrysburg also frustrated John Frederick Holzendorf because the land to which he hoped to gain title already belonged to Simond."[53] Others facing significant title problems included the Albergottis, Brabants, the Reverend Henry Chiffelle, Captain Frederick Dejean, the DeSaussures, Grands, Linders, the Morgantallers, Isaiah Overy, the Pelots, Hugh Rose, and the Reverend John J. Zubly.[54]

Mismanagement by the colonial administration made it difficult, if not impossible, for those who could not find work in their prior professions to make the transition to farming. A key provision in Purry's contract with South Carolina officials at the founding of the township was the promise of a generous allotment of provisions and tools for the settlers. Unfortunately, some immigrants never received the promised amounts of supplies from royal authorities or were forced to remain dependent on government provisions because of the delay in securing title to their own land. Purrysburg immigrants naturally, though erroneously (at least on this count), blamed Purry for their predicament. The inability of provincial leadership to fulfill its obligations of tools, provisions, and an expeditious transfer of land to the Purrysburg inhabitants contributed to severe privation in the first years of colonization as crop failures and related natural disasters precipitated financial and physical suffering that might have been somewhat mitigated had the colony lived up to its end of the township bargain. During the first five years of colonization, Purrysburg residents faced acute shortages of corn, sweet potatoes, poultry feed, and other necessities. Perhaps even the effects of the cattle plague, which began affecting Purrysburg herds in 1741, might have been lessened if the initial encouragement for economic diversification at the township been managed more systematically in the 1730s. Fortunately, during the early years of settlement even the poorest residents could be supplied with food, though not without duress to the rest of the settlers. At least one good harvest brightened these dark times.[55]

V

In spite of the obstacles to economic development, a nascent agrarian economy had begun to emerge in the frontier settlement by the 1740s. Although there is no evidence to indicate that Purrysburg was the locus of any wide-ranging commercial farming or ranching network at this early date, there are indications that the settlement, centered originally in the town proper, had begun to expand outward into the surrounding township lands and to spread out along the Savannah River in the traditional fashion of plantation economies elsewhere in the colonial South. The Reverend Boltzius lent credence to this hypothesis when he observed, as early as November 1737, that in Purrysburg, "the Lutherans there are no longer so close together as previously, but are scattered here and there on their plantations or in other occupations." The relocation of township citizens to their plantations left the town in less than a proper state. Two years later Boltzius wrote that "Purrysburg looks more like a forest than a town." He observed that even the Reverend Henry Chiffelle spent more time on his plantation attending to his commercial affairs than he did in town tending to the spiritual needs of his flock.[56] In early 1739 Boltzius documented the dispersal of residents to their township lands: "the people in Purrysburg, . . . do not live close together as neighbors but are spread far apart because of the wide tracts of land that each of them owns, particularly the so-called squires among them."[57] In December of the following year, the pastor heard of "the poor accommodations in the households even of the so-called gentlemen, although they have many Negroes."[58] A German-speaking Purrysburg resident complained to Boltzius in August 1741 of "the poor situation of the Purrysburg plantations which lie so dispersed that much . . . harm is caused."[59] The Ebenezer minister's depiction of Purrysburg in 1751 bears further witness to the maturation of an agrarian economy in the township and the dispersed settlement pattern characteristic of a plantation economy: "As far as I know there are no formal towns yet in Carolina except Charlestown and Port Royal, for Purrysburg resembles a long-drawn out village rather than a town. People live on their plantations, everyone almost in a private forest, as is the case in several colonies."[60] Twenty-three years later the plantation building process fully dominated the township as Surveyor of the Post Roads Hugh Finlay noted that homes of numerous farmers dotted the riverbank.[61]

But if Purrysburg Township made the transition to an increasingly staple crop/livestock plantation economy by the 1760s, it did so without many of its initial surviving members, who decided to cut their losses. Constrained socially and commercially during the initial years of settlement, some—such as Daniel Merratt (Marette) and Lewis (Louis) Deville—chose to sell their acreage in the township before their grants were even officially registered. On 19 March 1734/35 Merratt sold his fifty acres to Major James Richard. In August 1735 Deville deeded his acreage to Colonel Peter Lafitte.[62] Ludwig Kehl (Kail) sold his 300 acres to Major Richard in April 1736, while Abraham Chardonet (Chardonnelle) released his 300 acres to Benedict Bourguin for 100 pounds current money in December 1737. Purrysburg shoe mason Isaac Coste (Caste) and his wife, Magdalena, sold their 150 acres to Purrysburg doctor Peter Delmestre in November 1738, by which time Delmestre had relocated to Charles Town. The following month, François Buche (Buech) received 250 pounds current money for his 200 acres in the township from Abraham Ehrhard (Ehizhardt).[63] In January 1738/39 Ulisse Antoine Albergotti sold his 550 acres in Purrysburg to Richard Hazzard of Granville County. Six months later David Fauccunet (Fauconet) and his wife, Judith, sold 250 acres to deputy surveyor and Purrysburg resident Hugh Rose. Then, in October 1739, the Reverend Henry Chiffelle bought John Rodolph Purry's 300 acres for 182 pounds current money.[64] In each of these early land sales, with the exception of the Albergotti transaction, the buyer was a fellow Purrysburg settler. Most of the sellers seem to have kept title to their town lots, which could indicate both an unfamiliarity with agriculture and an attempt to generate a cash reserve to supplement meager income from the exercise of their crafts or professions.

During the next decade, the sale of land in the township, while still primarily exchanges between residents of Purrysburg, involved more town lots than agricultural acreage. In March 1741/42 Purrysburg carpenter David Giroud paid fifty pounds current money to John Jacob Metsger and his daughter Marguerite for town lot number 10, which had been granted to Marguerite's recently deceased husband, Jean Deroche. Joseph Reymond, with the consent of his wife, Ann, sold Giroud lot number 11 for thirty-five pounds current money in April 1742. In May of the following year, John Chevillette sold his 450 acres to John Baptist Bourguin. William Hamilton, who had previously bought town lot number 71 from its original grantee Captain Frederick Dejean, sold it to fellow Purrysburg resident Michael Peaset for 100 pounds current money on 2 March 1743/44. Hamilton also sold Peaset lot number 75, which he had previously acquired from Metsger. Later that month Purrysburg storekeeper

Charles Purry contracted with Peter Simond, to sell 12,350 acres of his deceased father's original grant to the London Huguenot merchant for 300 pounds sterling. In mid-November 1744, township settler Henry Desaussure sold his town lot number 113 to David Giroud.[65] It appears that, even as Purrysburg began its second decade of existence, there is evidence of some land consolidation both within the town limits and in the surrounding township acreage lands. These trends were to continue as economic options narrowed in the 1750s and 1760s. In the vast majority of these land transactions, it is impossible to determine whether the Purrysburg sellers remained in the township for any appreciable amount of time either on their town lots, if they sold their acreage, or on their plantations, if they sold their town lots. At the very least, however, the land transactions of the 1730s and 1740s indicate a level of activity that would seem to reflect a rather high degree of economic instability.

Although it is apparent that some members of the Purrysburg community chose to sell to their neighbors and pursue other options, as early as 1735 Purrysburg residents of Germanic descent began to explore the possibility of relocating with their ethnic cousins in Ebenezer. Barely seven years later, the first of a number of township settlers applied for resettlement grants in Ebenezer or surrounding areas of Georgia, citing the poor quality of their land at Purrysburg as the reason for their desire to leave. The seepage of the township's population into surrounding parishes in South Carolina and Georgia continued at least into the decade of the 1760s.[66]

Wherever frontier settlers moved in the lower Southeast in the middle decades of the eighteenth century, the towns and villages of the region needed each other, whether they welcomed or resisted that need. We have already noted that the conduct of Reck left much to be desired. Nor did the artisan Tullius measure up to Salzburger standards of behavior. Both received the opprobrium of the Reverend Boltzius while Ebenezer received the fruits of their labor. A Purrysburg cooper was convicted of stealing pipe staves in Savannah, but presumably he was there in the first place to provide needed services. Boltzius may have condemned the "Negro cures" and exorbitant prices of Dr. Bourguin, but the Salzburgers kept returning for treatment of various ailments. The pastor railed at the price Charles Purry wanted for two millstones, but he had no option other than to purchase them. Purry and his business associate Samuel Montaigut also aided Boltzius in making good his drafts from European contributors and procuring goods for Ebenezer, though these procedures were often involved and time consuming.

There were other points of tension between Purrysburg residents and Georgia authorities. In 1739 Hector Berenger de Beaufin and Samuel Montaigut threatened Georgia official Thomas Jones for not buying corn from them even though their price was six pence higher than what Jones paid. After Montaigut's death in November, Beaufin continued to harass Georgia dignitaries by scheming with the Malcontents to overthrow the trustees in favor of the crown. The

Purrysburg planter and merchant went so far as to address a petition to the king, imploring him to take over the colony. Beaufin even traveled to England to defend his petition, doing so while dining with the Georgia trustees. Another source of contention between Georgians and Purrysburg, as previously noted, was the supply of liquor at the South Carolina township. There are indications that part of Paul Amatis's problem with Georgia authorities stemmed from his sale of rum and wine in Savannah, which he may well have procured on his frequent travels to Purrysburg. By the summer of 1736, bootlegging was so rampant that Oglethorpe ordered that all boats sailing up the Savannah River to Purrysburg and Savannah Town (across the river from Augusta, Georgia) would be required to travel with a trustee-mandated inspector to enforce prohibition.[67]

To the dismay of trustees and ministers alike, even these stringent measures failed to alleviate the drinking problems in Georgia. Purry himself was reported to sell rum to all comers, making no distinction between Carolina and Georgia citizens. The Salzburg pastors found it impossible to enforce the ideal of temperance among their colonists and repeatedly reprimanded Ebenezer revelers for their raucous behavior. Ruprecht Zittrauer, for example, was a regular customer in Purrysburg taverns and was not the only one who found drinking partners in the township. On one occasion in April 1736, Mr. Spielbiegler, Mr. Rheinlander, and Mr. Arnsdorff got drunk in the township and suffered the wrath of Boltzius for their indiscretion. Tragedy sometimes resulted from overindulgence. In July 1737 Mr. Rothenberger accompanied Arnsdorff to Purrysburg to sample the spirits. On the return trip to Ebenezer, a drunken Arnsdorff tumbled out of the boat and drowned. Nearly thirteen years later, a drinking companion of one of the Ebenezer settlers formerly of Purrysburg who had moved to Savannah Town drank himself into a stupor and froze to death in the snow. Even the Salzburg schoolmaster, Mr. Ortmann, resorted to clandestine forays across the river, as Boltzius discovered by way of a letter sent from a Purrysburg "dealer in rum and tea" seeking payment of an unpaid drinking bill.

When Boltzius and Gronau learned that a French-speaking resident of Purrysburg was building a tavern and store directly across the Savannah River from Ebenezer, they threatened the proprietor with sanctions and complained to Thomas Causton, the Savannah bailiff. Already beleaguered by the demands of his office, Causton offered the pastors no relief and blamed the move to New Ebenezer for the liquor problems as that move brought the Georgia immigrants closer to Purrysburg and therefore closer to what Causton warned would be "a lot of strange people" who travel by and who "will infect our place with rum drinking; bad talk, and bad examples." The real issue of course was less the drunken infestation of others than the intemperance of Ebenezer citizens such as Mrs. Rauner, whom Boltzius suspected of getting drunk at the plantation of the French-speaking township resident in the spring of 1738. Both Mr. and Mrs. Rauner procured brandy and rum from the above-mentioned vendor. In

December of the same year, the Ebenezer shoemaker Solomon Adde drank enough Purrysburg liquor to make him ill. When the French-speaking supplier moved from the township in 1741, the new renter promised not to sell rum. Reports from Boltzius regarding Ebenezer residents who crossed the river to Purrysburg for liquor declined after this time but still appear in his journal, including the 1744 disruption in the township caused by the shoemaker Peter Kohleisen. It was obvious that neither pastoral condemnation nor ethnic dissimilarity dissuaded Georgia settlers from acquiring their liquor from the South Carolina township. Georgia trustees, if not the Reverend Boltzius, acknowledged the inevitable and allowed rum into the colony from the spring of 1747. Three years later Boltzius confessed to his journal that he had stopped Kohleisen from getting drunk in Ebenezer, but he more than made up for it when he ventured to Purrysburg or Savannah—which he did as often as he could.[68]

Causton believed that proximity of New Ebenezer to the major transportation route from Savannah to Purrysburg and from there to Beaufort, Port Royal, and Charles Town contributed to public drunkenness. His assessment illustrates the potential difficulties associated with the major overland road that cut directly through Purrysburg. The fact that this route became the most reliable roadway and quickest overland transit between Savannah and Charles Town until the 1760s meant that it would be used by travelers of all kinds—sometimes to the greater social and commercial benefit of the region and other times to its detriment. In the spring of 1733, the Swiss Anthony Gondy brought a group of 170 travelers with him from Virginia to the township. For six weeks Gondy and his people enjoyed the hospitality of Purrysburg settlers, by the end of which time his cousin Marianne had married Purrysburg widower Thomas Baumgartner, a Palatine from Speier worth 50,000 thalers.[69]

Within the space of three weeks in July 1737, one Purrysburg settler died on a trip to Savannah and another, Pierre Maillet, was able to inform Savannah authorities that a boat bound from Augusta to Savannah had been delayed, thereby allaying fears of a major mishap on the river.[70] It was the route that took John Wesley from Savannah to Purrysburg and Charles Town in April 1737 to report the Reverend Chiffelle's marriage of Sophy Hopkey to William Williamson, and it was the same route that took Wesley out of the colonies in December following Williamson's filing suit against him for his refusal to offer his wife the Eucharist.[71] It was the road that, in July 1739, took a Spanish spy from Purrysburg to Savannah, where he was arrested with two servants just as he was about to return to Purrysburg. The route also allowed sympathetic township settlers to assist many a Georgia indentured servant to escape the confines of servitude.[72]

One particularly noteworthy escape occurred on 9 July 1738, when three Savannah servants fled. Since many others had escaped to Purrysburg, Georgia authorities were convinced that the three had followed a similar course. A search party left immediately for the township and overtook the runaways twelve miles above Purrysburg on their way to Charles Town. On their way back to Savannah via the Charles Town–Purrysburg road with the recovered servants, the search party confronted a Purrysburg mob protesting their capture. The crowd's hostility so threatened the Georgians that they appealed to local justice of the peace Peter Lafitte for assistance. Lafitte dismissed the party's letter of authorization from Causton, declaring that the searchers had no power in South Carolina and that he would not be bound by it. This was not the last time that Georgia would have trouble reclaiming servants from South Carolina. Later that same year, more runaways were tracked through Purrysburg. As late as 1750 indentured servants used Purrysburg as a way station to freedom, sometimes with the direct assistance of township residents.[73]

Servants intent on escape were not the only fugitives the King's Highway brought to Purrysburg. In early December 1742 a man styling himself Carl Rudolph, Prince of Württemberg, and an ordained Lutheran pastor made his way to the township and was taken in by Theobald Kieffer Sr. He claimed to have been imprisoned in Corsica and Turkey and ultimately kidnapped in London and sold as an indentured servant in Frederica. He sought passage to Savannah Town to make his way to either the Spanish or French. Kieffer seems to have believed him, but the Reverend Boltzius had heard other reports. Rudolph apparently had preached to a number of Lutheran congregations in Virginia and Maryland posing as a minister—at least until his seduction of the daughters of parishioners was discovered. He made his way south and added to his reputation as a troublemaker by causing problems all over South Carolina. Kieffer's advocacy saved him from the Georgia Rangers who had been pursuing him, but had no authority in South Carolina. Boltzius, under orders to get him across the river into Georgia, summoned Kieffer to his home and admonished him to follow Scripture and stop harboring the fugitive. After their conversation Kieffer persuaded Rudolph to go to Boltzius's home but insisted that Boltzius do his best to see whether the man's claims were true. He confessed to the Pietist pastor that he had "stirred up no good everywhere." Rudolph seems to have been afflicted with a fever soon thereafter, and Kieffer stood guard while he recovered—either at the pastor's home or his own. After his recovery he must have been turned over to the authorities, but one source in 1750 claimed that he had joined the military in Boston, then deserted and made his way to Maryland posing again as a minister and up to his old tricks with female parishioners. In 1757 a man matching his description was accepted by a Lutheran and Reformed congregation at Vernonsburg.[74]

The Ebenezer pastors were no less disturbed by the number of their flock that quit the colony by way of Purrysburg. Mr. Volmar, a carpenter, fled the town by traveling to Purrysburg and from there via the overland route to Charles Town. Mrs. Ortmann, wife of the Ebenezer schoolmaster, allowed Volmar to lodge with her overnight before he left for South Carolina. Upon his departure, she deserted her sick husband to follow the carpenter to Charles Town. The dual "escape" from Ebenezer brought scandal to the settlement and enraged the pastors. Unfortunately, this was not to be the last time Mrs. Ortmann caused problems because of her liaisons and connections in Purrysburg. The Ortmanns also had harbored a man in their home, who had disguised a girl (probably an indentured servant) in man's clothing in Savannah and had aided her escape to Purrysburg and beyond. Another Ebenezer undesirable, the Austrian Mr. Grimminger, suspected of numerous thefts, removed to Purrysburg to evade condemnation. The Purrysburg cobbler Reck helped the Reidelspergers from Ebenezer to leave. They too departed via Purrysburg. Many others, including Mrs. Rheinlander, who stayed six days in the South Carolina township before returning to Ebenezer, used Purrysburg as a sanctuary of sorts.[75]

From the perspective of the Reverends Boltzius and Gronau, the Salzburg immigrants were also not particularly well served by Purrysburg merchants. One of the earliest economic problems faced by the Salzburgers was their inability to comprehend the provincial currency system. When traveling to Purrysburg in May 1735, many of the new colonists did not realize the monetary differences between the various denominations of current money or that Purrysburg merchants manipulated their ignorance by shortchanging them. When Rheinlander incurred a debt on the Reverend Boltzius's account in Charles Town, the pastor received word of the charge through a Purrysburg associate of the merchant, who also doubled as the collection agent.[76]

At times the pastors hesitated in going to Purrysburg to provide religious services because they believed the German speakers of the township failed to appreciate their efforts. They conducted worship services specifically for the German-speaking population but found themselves slandered by some of the same individuals who participated in worship. At one point, one of the pastors wrote that "we are sick and tired and fearful of conducting Holy Communion there. Nevertheless, there are still some good people at Purrysburg whom we shall not forget." Less than a week later, again serving the communicants at the South Carolina township, the Pietist pastor spoke of his ambivalent feelings: "To be sure, the many disorders that are the fashion among the people there hold us back, but the desire to gain something with them even once drives us back there again." As Christian ministers, Boltzius and Gronau denounced the perceived sinfulness of Purrysburg settlers yet desired to lead them to their definition of true Christian faith. As leaders of the settlement of Ebenezer, the pastors detested the influence of Purrysburg workers such as Reck and Tullius in their midst, but lack of options on the frontier forced frequent contact and forged links of commercial necessity, if not community solidarity, across the Savannah River. The same dilemma might have been indicative of the entire young colony of Georgia.[77]

VI

Unlike the grudgingly interdependent and ambivalent relationship between Purrysburg and neighboring Georgia settlements, most of the recorded transactions between township inhabitants and other citizens of South Carolina, though essentially legal and/or economic in nature, were not centered as much on mutual benefit as on the dictates of provincial law and the aspirations of Purrysburg residents for financial stability. As early as 1739 Charles Purry, trapped by the decreasing opportunity structure of the township's first years, traveled to Charles Town to present his views and proposals on the appropriate backing for bills of credit—an issue dear to any colonial merchant's heart—but his rather complex scheme did not elicit any widespread comment or support. Purry's partnership with Samuel Montaigut dissolved before the end of the year.[78] Three years later several Purrysburg Germans journeyed to the capital for an undisclosed purpose (most probably some legal matter) but seem to have met with recalcitrant authorities there who treated them quite badly.[79]

The elevated political status of Purrysburg Township after 1746 and its concomitant growing socioeconomic engagement with the broader contours of southern commercial life corresponded closely with the township's expanding participation in a plantation-based economy characterized by both white and black labor. The institutions of indentured servitude and slavery provide a window through which to observe the transformation of the frontier township from poverty to relative affluence.

From all indications white servitude existed at Purrysburg from its founding, but, as in the province of South Carolina generally, there is uncertainty as to the number of white servants at the township. Andrew and Barbara Walser of Neuchâtel, along with their children John and Martin, became indentured to Jean Pierre Purry for four years of service in South Carolina. It is unclear whether their terms were satisfied before his death in 1736, but the family relocated temporarily with John Holzendorf after his move to Frederica. In February 1742/43 they applied for and received their headright for land in Purrysburg. John Bear, a Swiss immigrant and his wife, Mary, could not pay their passage to South Carolina, so Purry also engaged their services for four years in the mid-1730s. John received both a town lot and acreage in Purrysburg by 1737 but died soon thereafter. Elizabeth Kese came to South Carolina with one of Purry's first transports and served an indenture, perhaps for some time to Purry himself. By mid-1739 Kese had completed her term of service and requested fifty acres of land, a town lot in Orangeburg, and the allotted allowance of provisions. John Martin Lasman sought similar benefits after his indenture was satisfied by early July 1739. John (Johann) Ring and his son served their indentures in Georgia and received land in Purrysburg by early 1741. John Koos completed five years of service to John Chevillette of Purrysburg (and later Orangeburg) by early January 1749/50. Magdalene Eiriston, who arrived in 1737, had been an indentured servant and continued to hire herself out to others, including Holzendorf, after her initial term expired. The Purrysburg doctor also bought the time of Michael Clatissen prior to July 1752. In the same year Henry Desaussure, "a long settler in Purisburgh Township," petitioned for land there, claiming two indentured servants among other members of his family. John William Lizard bound himself to Purrysburg watchmaker David Mongin sometime prior to 1752, but his relationship with Mongin deteriorated to the extent that John Ulrich Tobler picked up his contract. When seeking to establish his claim to Purrysburg land his father David had improved but to which he had never received title because the plat had been lost, the Reverend John Joachim Zubly buttressed his case in April 1753 by noting that, because he had two white servants for whom he had never received land, the 100-acre plot could be conveyed to him. One of these servants might have been Leonard Rhynower, whose contract passed to Zubly from Austin and Laurens. Rhynower married, and when his term of service expired in 1754, he received 100 acres in Purrysburg. The previous year longtime Purrysburg resident Jonas Pelot appealed for 250 acres of land in Purrysburg, claiming among his headright "a man servant that he keeps who is an Idiot out of charity." Purrysburg minister the Reverend Henry Chiffelle in a land-related affidavit delivered by Zubly referred to his retaining one white servant in late 1754.[80]

The elder Kieffers were indentured when they arrived in Purrysburg, but it is unknown who held their contract. Samuel Montaigut was said to have had an indentured boy as well as other white servants. Hector Berenger de Beaufin also appears to have retained some white servants. To pay her passage money to the colony, the daughter of the Ebenezer shoemaker Andreas Arnsdorff bound herself in service to an English resident of Purrysburg sometime before July 1737. One of the persons who drowned in a boating accident in 1739 was apparently a servant of the family of James Richard. A German-speaking blacksmith who was redeemed from his master by someone in Purrysburg took up residence in the township the same year. Sibylla Friederica Uselt served one of the Ebenezer ministers for some time prior to April 1740. In January 1750/51 the Ebenezer community bought the service of a young Lutheran man who was said to have been mistreated by his Purrysburg master. He was contracted to assist the town's miller. The only other known case of servanthood in Purrysburg was that of an English boy named Simon Barker (or Harper) brought to Purrysburg by the missionaries Böhler and Schulius. According to the Reverend Boltzius, he had been treated quite badly by the two, including being whipped for wetting his bed. Barker escaped to the home of a French-speaking resident. He soon left there to lodge with a German-speaking township citizen with whom he fared no better than when he was with the missionaries. A Purrysburg shoemaker finally took Barker in and nursed him back to health. From extant records, it appears as if the boy's parents in London probably had him indentured for service in Georgia, and the missionaries most likely escorted him across the ocean and paid for his passage themselves. In addition to these references to white service in Purrysburg Township, there were also a few tragic cases where free but destitute residents of the township sold themselves into service as a mode of self-preservation.[81]

Although these cases clearly demonstrate the presence of white servants in Purrysburg from the founding of the township, servitude in the township, as in other South Carolina parishes, was progressively more dependent upon the institution of black chattel slavery as the eighteenth century unfolded. The presence of slaves in the township coincided precisely with the advent of white settlement and their influence profoundly shaped the commercial and social contours of the immigrant enclave while substantiating the reality of slow but steady economic growth and prosperity among its inhabitants. The earliest extant will for an individual granted land in Purryburg Township, that of Thomas Newall in January 1736, included references to the disposition of an unnumbered company of slaves among his heirs. Little more than a year and a half later, the Reverend Boltzius encountered slaves on a visit to the Kieffer's plantation in the township. At the time of his death in 1736, Jean Pierre Purry owned six slaves, and Isaac Bonijoe left five at his death in 1742. Envious Georgia colonists, who could not own slaves legally until 1749, noted the success of Purrysburg as early as 1737 and attributed much of it to slave labor. Depending on the correspondent, the existence of black chattel slavery at the township could be used to demonstrate prosperity and hence the necessity for Georgia to allow slavery or to illustrate the debilitating effects of slave labor financed on credit and the beneficent results of honest hard work without slaves.[82]

Of the 101 petitions for land and/or provisions in the township during the formative period from the 1730s to the mid-1750s, nearly 20 percent of them (eighteen) included the enumeration of slaves in the household for purposes of headright land acquisition. Only one of the fifty-nine petitions from the 1730s included mention of black household members. This number tripled in the 1740s (three of twelve) even though these were years of war and economic recession. During the opening six years of the 1750s, the number almost quintupled again (fourteen of thirty). The rapid increase is all the more striking when the number of slaveholding households is compared to the total number of petitions by chronological period. By this measure, fully one-quarter of the petitions from the 1740s and just under half of those from 1750 to 1756 included slaves. Finally, it is quite apparent that over time Purrysburg landowners acquired increasing numbers of Africans or African Americans. The greater number of slaves per household by the mid-1750s, evident in the petitions for land as well as the increased number of those claiming slave ownership, indicates both the township's progressive dependence upon slave labor and an emerging economic prosperity among Purrysburg landholders.[83]

Although it is a relatively straightforward matter to document the growing number of slaves in the township over the first two decades of its existence, the actual social ramifications of chattel slavery are much more difficult to determine. The Reverend Boltzius's 29 August 1740 observation that South

Carolina slaves are "kept everywhere very harshly" would be more instructive if he had provided specific details from his direct observation of the treatment of slaves in Purrysburg.[84] The pastor did report in late December that a visitor to a plantation just above Purrysburg observed the "poor accommodations in the households even of the so-called gentlemen, although they have many Negroes or slaves."[85] Nearly two years later, Boltzius lamented the lack of attention Purrysburg settlers gave to the education of their children, preferring instead "to use them for herding cattle, in tilling the soil, at fishing, hunting, or supervising blacks."[86]

The pastor's more specific commentary on the Kieffer family's experience as slaveholders does point out the socioeconomic complexities of the peculiar institution. Sometime prior to May 1741 Theobald Sr. bought three male slaves. The expense of their purchase saddled him with a substantial debt that he carried for some years. Shortly after their arrival in Purrysburg, one of the slaves ran away. He was captured, but either because of the cold or because his feet were bound too tightly, both feet had to be amputated. In early May 1741 another of the three, who had been quite dependable to that time, escaped. Although he returned before the end of the month, the slave ran away again on 31 May and appears to have died. The third slave committed suicide by drowning sometime after 27 August 1741. Keiffer then sold the disabled slave for the price of a cow. Theobald Jr., who lived in Ebenezer by the early 1740s, loaned his father money to purchase two field slaves, a male and female. They worked the Purrysburg plantations of both men. In 1744 the elder Keiffer's cumulative indebtedness caused him to consider selling his slaves, who may have included others besides the two purchased with money borrowed from his son, but he seems to have maintained his ownership of most if not all his chattels, some of whom rowed him to Ebenezer and even attended church with him there. Circumstantial evidence is quite strong that at some later date Kieffer sold the female—pregnant at the time—to an Ebenezer shoemaker. It was probably this child who was baptized by Boltzius sometime before May 1747. Both Kieffers, father and son, adopted the boy, pledged to raise him as their own, and provide him a Christian upbringing. Before the boy's father would allow the adoption to take place, he exacted a promise from the Kieffers that the child would not be sold, thereby guaranteeing that what happened to the mother would not happen to the son. When slavery was allowed in Georgia, Theobald Jr. and his brother-in-law (Cronberger) kept slaves in Ebenezer.[87] While singular among Purrysburg township inhabitants for its detail, the experiences of the Kieffers and their slaves lay bare the tensions between the hope of gain and the risks of indebtedness, of financial exigencies and human compassion, which were common to all who staked their futures to an economic system centered in human exploitation.

As in other slaveholding regions, the dual specters of fear and prejudice increased proportionally with the black population. In February 1738/39, nearly seven months before the outbreak of the Stono Rebellion, Hector Berenger de

Beaufin and Samuel Montaigut were said to be in grave danger "by a conspiracy of their Negro slaves whereof they have got a great number upon a very large plantation . . . within the district of Purrysburgh." According to an informant, the blacks planned "to cut off their masters and families and all the white people that belonged to them . . . and to make their way as fast as they could to [St.] Augustine either by land or by water after furnishing themselves first with arms out of their masters' houses when plundered." Unlike the Stono Rebellion, this plot was uncovered before it could be carried out, but, in the wake of the September 1739 revolt, suspicion mounted as to which slaves might be threats to public safety. The Reverend Boltzius wrote in mid-July 1740 that "Kieffer from Purrysburg and a Frenchman almost directly across from us in Carolina, each have such a black man. They are said to have been secretly at our place a few times and to have stolen all kinds of things, although the broad Savannah is between them and us."[88]

There were enough black slaves in the area in 1751 for Boltzius to write overseas concerning sexual liaisons between blacks and whites, which he believed were rampant in South Carolina. He knew of white men in Carolina who carried on sexual relationships with black women, as well as "two white women, one French and one German" who had "secretly disgraced themselves with Negroes and have borne black children." Although it cannot be known for certain, it is likely that the pastor drew these examples from his intimate knowledge of Purrysburg as the specific notation of "French" and "German" fits the ethnic character of the township. Accounts of interracial sexual activity are characteristic of areas with rising black populations. As such, the pastor's observation probably indicates a fear of the expanding black presence that signaled the establishment of an expansive plantation economy in Purrysburg Township more than a widespread social phenomenon.[89]

Another measure of the integration of Purrysburg Township into the agrarian, slave-based plantation economy of the lower South by 1760 is the purchase of additional lands by township landowners and the concomitant rise in absentee landlordism. The process began slowly in the 1730s. Major James Richard added to his 400-acre grant by purchasing Daniel Marette's (Merrett) fifty acres in March 1734/35 and Ludwig Kehl's 150 acres. Charles Town resident and doctor Peter Delmestre appears to have become among the township's first multiple grant absentee landholders when he augmented his town lot number 84 with the 150 acres he bought from Purrysburg shoemaker Isaac Coste (Caste) and his wife, Magdalena, in November 1738. Seven other land transfers occurred in the 1730s, but the only one that involved an individual with no land in the township was the sale of Ulisse Albergotti's land, including 550 acres in the township to Richard Hazzard.[90] The character of land transfers in the recession filled 1740s differed little from the previous decade, though there were fewer conveyances of all types during the decade. In a case unique in the township, the widow Anna Maria Bourguin Viellers (Ann Mary Viller) in 1744 conveyed her entire Purrysburg estate and personal property to her children prior to her remarriage. While intratownship transfers of title continued, ownership of land outside the township began, with some residents physically leaving for other locations, though most of them remained fairly close to Purrysburg. Some—such as Jacob Tanner, Joseph Edward Flower, Gabriel Ravot, Nicholas Winkler, and members of the Bourguin and Jeanerett families—made formal applications for land in Georgia (see table 5). Others moved northwest to the region near Palachuccola called Oglethorpe's Barony, which had been surveyed late in 1739, or southeast toward Port Royal and St. Helena's Parish. [91]

Land transactions in the 1750s, though not numerous, illustrate the further emergence of multistranded sociocommercial relationships between Purrysburg landholders and inhabitants of other areas of the colonial Southeast. There were a number of intratownship conveyances, as in the previous two decades, demonstrating continued accumulation of property by certain landholders, such as John Linder, Jacob Stroubhart, Gabriel Ravot, and John Baptist Bourquin. Henry Desaussure expanded his real estate beyond Purrysburg by acquiring 584 acres from Morgan Sabb just outside the township boundary.[92] But during this decade conveyances also allowed nonimmigrants to purchase land in Purrysburg. Peter Mason (Masson), who was platted land in the 1730s but never received title until 1758, exchanged fifty acres with Joseph Girardin, who then conveyed the land to Jacob Henry Meuron (Merron, Murow). To this point the property stayed in the hands of township immigrants, but when Meuron then sold it to Hannah Elbert of Granville County in 1759, ownership passed to someone who lived outside the township.[93] At least two others, Nicholas Cronenberger of Ebenezer and Purrysburg shoemaker John Vauchier, both of whom would receive land in the township by headright petition in the future, secured their first direct ownership of acreage in Purrysburg by outright purchase. In February 1757, for the first time, Purrysburg land was offered at public auction to pay the deceased Hugh Bryan's debts. Charles Lowndes sold 1,100 acres to Charles Town merchant William Brisbane for 605 pounds current money.[94] The first of many transfers of Purrysburg land inherited by the second generation who had left the township also occurred in mid-decade, when Savannah tailor Peter Francis Grenier sold the 400 acres of land originally granted to his father John in 1738 to Savannah silversmith Adrian Loyer for five shillings sterling.[95] In another conveyance that stretched beyond township boundaries, Purrysburg landowner, the watchmaker and planter David Mongin, divested himself of property in Ansonborough. He also carried on other business transactions beyond the confines of the township.[96]

More individuals/families with Purrysburg land requested land in Georgia during the 1750s, as noted in table 5. Benedict Bourguin, for example applied for 800 acres of land in Georgia during the decade while selling the 300 acres of Purrysburg land he bought from Abraham Chardonnelle in 1747. He eventually became a resident of Georgia, as did his brother Henry, who practiced medicine in Savannah by 1763.[97] Their brother, John (Lewis) Sr., petitioned for land in Georgia on 5 March 1750/51. John's petition noted that he had for some years been cultivating a quite unproductive tract in Purrysburg. He also apparently requested additional land for Abraham and John, Benedict's sons. John Sr. told the Georgia authorities that he would relocate to Georgia in the fall with his entire family. All three requests for land were approved, but John Sr. remained in Purrysburg.[98]

TABLE 5: Application for Grants in Georgia by Purrysburg Landholders

Year of Application	Applicant	Land Requested (acres)	District, if Known
1741	Jacob Tanner	50	
1747	Joseph Edward Flower	500	Midway
1748	Benedict Bourguin	500	
1748	Henry Bourguin	500	
1748	John Bourguin	500	
1748	Abraham Jeanerett*	500	Midway
1748	Gabriel Ravot	500	Savannah/Ogeechee
1748	Nicholas Winkler	300	Savannah/Ogeechee
1749	Henry Bourguin	500	
1749	Benedict Bourguin	350	
1750	Abraham Bourguin	150	
1750	John Bourguin Sr.	250	
1750	John Bourguin Jr.	100	
1752	Benedict Bourguin	300	
1752	Donnam (Donnat) family*	1,000	
1752	Jacob Waldburger	100	
1754	David Humbert	300	Savannah/Ogeechee
1754	John Rudolph Purry	500	Savannah/Ogeechee
1754	Joseph Reymond	300	Savannah/Ogeechee
1754	George Winkler*	50	
1757	Henry Bourguin	500	Little Ogeechee
1757	Henry Bourguin	500	Little Ogeechee
1757	Henry Bourguin	500	Little Ogeechee
1757	Nicholas Cronenberger	200 and town lot	Ebenezer
1757	John Jacob Metsger	50 and 2 town lots	Ebenezer
1758	Benedict Bourguin	500	Little Ogeechee
1760	Samuel Augsperger	500	St. James' Parish
1760	Nicholas Cronenberger	200	St. Matthew's Parish

Year of Application	Applicant	Land Requested (acres)	District, if Known
1760	Theobald Kieffer	Town and garden lot	Ebenezer
1760	Jacob Metsger	250	St. Matthew's Parish
1761	Joachim Hartstone	400	St. Matthew's Parish
1762	Frederick Holzendorff	50	St. John's Parish
1762	David Huguenin	450	St. Philip's Parish
1763	John Walser	50 and town lot	Frederica Township

Note: *Applicant's family member(s) had land in Purrysburg, though he (they) did not.

Source: Compiled from Kenneth Coleman and Milton Ready, eds., *The Colonial Records of the State of Georgia*, vols. 27–28, pt. 1 (Athens: University of Georgia Press, 1976–1977); David Rogers Chestnutt, "South Carolina's Expansion into Georgia, 1720–1765" (Ph.D. dissertation, University of Georgia, 1973), 216–30.

VII

By the 1760s the economic prosperity of South Carolina, centered in the cultivation of rice and indigo, was unrivaled in the North American colonies of Great Britain. The province not only had the highest per capita wealth and income, but, also, its economic growth rate near midcentury was certainly the highest in the entire British Empire and, by some estimates, the highest in the world.[99] Both staples could only be produced in quantities sufficiently large for substantial profit on plantations dependent upon slave labor. Between 1768 and 1772 rice and indigo accounted for nearly 90 percent of South Carolina exports. In the late colonial period, indigo exports ranked fifth in value among exports from all the mainland colonies and rice third. Taken together, these two South Carolina plantation staples accounted for nearly 15 percent of exports from all thirteen mainland colonies.[100]

In addition to fueling a voracious appetite for land and forced labor from 1720s into the 1770s, the structure of the provincial economy in the decades after 1740 had significant ramifications for the colony in general that is reflected in trends evident in Purrysburg Township. First and foremost, even though the landholders of Purrysburg were denied access to the most productive tidewater land, many of them participated in the mounting affluence associated with the slave-based, staple crop plantation system. David R. Chestnutt's study of South Carolinians receiving land in Georgia between the 1740s and 1760s revealed that the out-migration to Georgia coincided with the development of the lucrative rice culture in that colony. He found that grantees, like the Purrys-burg landholders listed in table 5, almost universally chose areas conducive to rice cultivation, though the development of the crop did not occur until after the coming of the Carolinians.[101] In a sense, the Bourguins, Winklers, Humberts, Huguenins, and others became agricultural entrepreneurs. Finding their way to economic growth blocked by the South Carolina lowcountry gentry, they shifted their attention to the rich unclaimed soil of Georgia upon which to build prosperity. By 1768 so many South Carolinians had taken up lands in Georgia and had also transported their slaves across the Savannah that John Lewis Bourguin, the tax collector at Purrysburg, posted public notice of their South Carolina tax liability in the 24 August issue of the *Georgia Gazette.* He planned to be at John Buche's home in Purrysburg on 1 September to take sworn statements.[102]

That landholders in the township also experienced a significant rise in living standards during the late colonial period, which can be determined quantitatively by examining the aggregate estate values and slave ownership of Purrysburg families in table 6.[103] In roughly the first quarter century of Purrysburg settlement (1733–1760), relatively few slaves labored for township residents. Of the sixteen individuals with land in Purrysburg who died and whose wills or inventories are extant, only five owned any slaves at all. Of these five, two owned five, one owned six, and two owned an undisclosed number of blacks. During the next twenty-five years (1760–1785), however, Purrysburg slaveholding increased dramatically. Of the twenty-three township landholders who died during this period and whose wills survive, only one, Andrew Walser, owned no slaves whatsoever. Most slaveholders in this latter era owned between one and five slaves, with many claiming what seem to be family groups. A few individuals owned sizable numbers of blacks: Henry Jeanerett owned eleven, Andrew Hendrie fourteen, Thomas Camber eighteen, Jacob Waldburger twenty-one, David Humbert, Lewis Quinche, and Jacob Stroubhart twenty-two each. Among the largest slaveholders was David Mongin with thirty-eight. Henry Desaussure, who had earlier moved his place of residence to Pocotaligo while maintaining his land in Purrysburg, had thirty-nine slaves. As slave numbers increased in the township, so also did advertisements for the return of runaways in the 1760s and 1770s, especially in the Savannah press. Purrysburg slaveholders, like masters elsewhere, were quite aware of the ethnic background of their chattels and offered generous rewards for their return.[104]

TABLE 6: Aggregate Estate Values and Slave Ownership

Name	Date of Death (approximate)	Estate Value (pounds, approximate)	No. of Slaves
1733–60			
T. Newall	1735/36	?	?
J. P. Purry	1736	3,612	6
W. Staples	1737	24	None
I. Bonijoe	1742	714	5
J. Detrick	1739–43	140	None
J. Pennefather	1745	?	Unknown
J. Richard	1745	?	None
I. Overy	1745	?	?

Name	Date of Death (approximate)	Estate Value (pounds, approximate)	No. of Slaves
D. Godet	1746	?	None
A. Chardonnet	1746–48	175	None
A. Greniere	1752	177	None
D. Zubly	1753	?	None
H. Girardin	1753–56	100	None
A. Ehrhard	1755	?	Unknown
M Roro (Rorere)	1755	60	None
H. Chiffelle	1758	2,101	5
1760–85			
A. Walser	1761	?	None
H. Desaussure	1762	10,000	39
P. Lafitte	1762	?	Unknown
L. Ouinche	1764	4,687	At least 22
H. Jeanerett	1765	5,872	11
A. Hendrie	1766	3,743	14
A. Imer	1766	669	4
J. Barraque	1765–69	590	1
J. Stroubhart	1767	13,059	22
A. Jindra	1767	1,610	5
J. Pelot	1768	396	2
F. G. Ravot	1769	?	At least 4
D. Humbert	1769	7,039	22
J. Waldburger	1770	8,567	21
G. Mallett	1771	1,818	4
D. Mongin	1769–71	10,544	38
M. Mongin	1772	495	1
M. J. Henry (Hendrie)	1773	772	2
T. Camber	1774	8,886	18+
D. Mallett	1775	1,847	4
J. Pelot	1776	8,909	At least 4
F. Erhardt	1766–76	?	Unknown
H. Meuron	1784	95	3

Source: Data are derived from an analysis of microfilmed copies of the CWA will transcripts and handwritten inventories, Library of the Genealogical Society, Church of Jesus Christ of Latter Day Saints, Salt Lake City.

It is not surprising that total appraised estate values rose proportionately over time, generally following the trends in slave ownership. Between 1733 and 1760 only two estates, those of township founder Jean Pierre Purry and the Reverend Henry Chiffelle, were appraised at more than 1,000 pounds. The value of Purry's estate was fixed at 3,612 pounds and Chiffelle's at 2,101 pounds. Most of the other estates were appraised at between twenty-four pounds (William Staples) and 177 pounds (Andrew Greniere). Isaac Bonijoe's estate fell somewhere between the high and average figures with a total assessed value of 714 pounds. During the second quarter century of settlement, values skyrocketed. The smallest estate, so minuscule that it was not even appraised, belonged to Andrew Walser. The smallest appraised estate was the ninety-five-pound holding of Henry Meuron, but the next smallest jumped to 396 pounds. In all, only seven estates in this category were valued at less than 1,000 pounds. Three were appraised between 1,000 and 2,000 pounds, two between 2,000 and 5,000, six between 5,000 and 10,000, and two over 10,000 pounds. These wealthiest of Purrysburg landowners were David Mongin (10,544 pounds) and Jacob Stroubhart (13,059 pounds).

The systematic identification of estate property also serves to illustrate the steady rise in wealth and status of Purrysburg settlers over the course of the eighteenth century. In the estates of those who died in the first twenty-five years of settlement, only nine claimed any livestock. The largest stocks of animals were, of course, owned by the two men with the most sizable estates. Jean Pierre Purry claimed thirty head of cattle and three horses at his death. The Reverend Chiffelle owned forty-six head of stock, as well as a parcel of fowl, at his death in 1758. At the time of his death in 1762, Henry Desaussure claimed thirty-eight horses, forty head of cattle, and other animals. Other landholders owned stock, but documents fail to record either what kind or how many.[105]

In the second quarter century, the amount and value of Purrysburg planters' and ranchers' property escalated following the trends in total estate value and in the prevalence of slaveholding in the township. That a much more diversified economy had emerged by the end of the colonial era is also evident. The vast majority of those leaving estates in this period claimed varying amounts and kinds of livestock, demonstrating the appearance of a rather widespread ranching sector in the Purrysburg economy. Although few settlers in the early years showed ownership of any stock besides cattle or horses, many in this later period owned not just cattle and horses but also sheep and hogs. One planter even claimed rabbits and squirrels as part of his estate. The size of livestock holdings also increased in the second quarter century. Many of the estates contained between 50 and 150 head of livestock and David Humbert claimed a rather substantial 200 head of cattle, 125 hogs, and 20 to 25 horses. Some of the estates indicated that besides ranching Purrysburg produced plantation staples of the late colonial era, including rice, wheat, corn, potatoes, wool, and indigo. One township landholder even seems to have begun cotton production by the time of his death in 1776. The wider variety of commodities listed in the later period would seem to confirm the observation of John J. McCusker and Russell R. Menard that a relatively diversified economy continued to exist in South Carolina on the periphery of the rice belt. Unlike the plantation economy of the West Indies, where sugar cane production drove other agricultural production out of the immediate area, rice cultivation merely pushed such activities to the edges of the rice belt so that an intraregional diversity of production remained.

Purrysburg Township may have served as a resource for food and provisions for the great lowcountry planters on either side of the Savannah while also providing products for export from the region. In supplying foodstuffs that the lowcountry rice-growing elite needed and simultaneously contributing some export, the township served as an example of what McCusker and Menard called "colonies of colonies."[106]

Increasing wealth is also illustrated by the elegance of home furnishings. After the 1750s a number of families were able to afford not only fine walnut and/or mahogany furniture, but also elaborate table settings of silver utensils and China plate. Recall also that Purrysburg landholders continued to receive grants across the Savannah River to at least the early 1760s, further extending their economic power. From all the available economic indicators it is apparent that the widening inequalities of wealth evident throughout the province also characterized the realities of township life.[107]

A tabulation of the records of mesne conveyance for Purrysburg landholders from the 1730s through the 1780s presented in table 7 bears witness to explosive commercial activity in the township to which the wills and inventories of the period point.[108] The volume of transactions between 1760 and 1775 demonstrate extensive commercial activity when compared to the earlier period. Between the founding of the township in 1732 and 1759, a total of thirty-five conveyances were concluded involving at least one Purrysburg landholder. That number was surpassed in the five years between 1760 and 1764. During the decade of the 1760s, there were nearly three times as many transactions as there were during the previous twenty-seven years combined. Conveyances slowed in the 1770s and almost ceased during the 1780s, but if the two peak decades, 1760–1779, are taken as a percentage of all transactions between township landholders from 1732–1789, that twenty-year spike would include more than 80 percent (173 of 216) of the total.

TABLE 7: Records of Mesne Conveyance: Land, Bonds, Deeds of Gift Involving Purrysburg Township Property or Settlers

Years (Conveyances)						
1730–1739 (12):	1734 (1)	1735 (1)	1736 (2)	1737 (1)	1738 (2)	1739 (5)
1740–1749 (11):	1742 (2)	1743 (2)	1744 (3)	1745 (1)	1748 (3)	
1750–1759 (12):	1752 (6)	1754 (1)	1756 (1)	1757 (1)	1758 (1)	1759 (2)
1760–1769 (104):	1760 (5)	1761 (9)	1762 (3)	1763 (9)	1764 (10)	1765 (15)
	1766 (5)	1767 (19)	1768 (15)	1769 (14)		
1770–1779 (69):	1770 (9)	1771 (5)	1772(16)	1773 (8)	1774 (9)	1775 (14)
	1776 (2)	1777 (5)	1778 (1)			
1780–1789 (8):	1782 (2)	1783 (1)	1784 (1)	1785 (1)	1786 (3)	

Sources: Materials used in compiling this table include the Records of Mesne Conveyance volumes, Langley, *Deed Abstracts*, and Holcomb, *Deed Abstracts*.

As in the earlier period, the overwhelming majority of commercial transactions between 1760 and the Revolution involved the sale of town lots or acreage. Some stipulated the terms of monetary loans and a few others the sale of pews in the parish church of St. Peter's. The nature of these conveyances provide further insight into the complex socioeconomic development of the township during the prosperous era from the 1760s to the mid-1770s. Some of the deeds highlight the economic instability of the township during the formative period by listing all the landholders of a particular property. For example, in February 1762 the Purrysburg planter Jacob Waldburger bought town lot number 45 from Francis Erhard, a township cordwainer. Adam Cuillat had been the original owner of the lot in 1733, but he sold it to fellow Purrysburg settler Peter Maillier, who already owned lot number 46. Mallier subsequently sold the lot to David Godet, who conveyed it to Francis Henry. Henry passed it to the Reverend Chiffelle, who sold it to "Depont" (probably Jean Del Pont). It was he who then conveyed it to Erhard. The following year Waldburger sold two tracts of Purrysburg land to Stephen Cater of Dorchester. One tract for 350 acres had been initially granted to Michael Rorrer (Rorere), the other for fifty acres to John Grubb (Grob). Both Rorere and Grob conveyed the land to John Ulrich Zong (Hans Ubuck Isoug?), who then sold the acreage to Waldburger. Unique in all the land transactions are those of members of the Holzendorf family, for while the previous examples demonstrate the complexity of descent, the Holzendorf records of July 1774 illustrate complexity of allocation. Even though Captain John Frederick Holzendorf appears to have left Purrysburg for Georgia, he retained at least two tracts of Purrysburg land. Upon his death that land became part of his complicated estate. Holzendorf divided his township land into seven equal parcels for disbursement. The captain's namesake, a Purrysburg tavern keeper, paid William Holzendorf and his wife, Mary, also of the township, for the rights to one-seventh of both the 200-acre plot and the 250-acre tract. On the same day (1 July), John Frederick bought another seventh of both properties from John Postell and his wife, Rosina, of Purrysburg. On 18 July he purchased one-seventh of both tracts from John Russell and his wife, Elizabeth, of Prince William's Parish. The elder Holzendorf obviously intended that his heirs share equally in his Purrysburg landholdings, but it appears that only John Frederick had use for township land.[109]

The sale by second-generation Purrysburg landholders of township land, which first occurred in the mid-1750s, became a trend in this later period. Some time prior to late August 1764 Nicholas Grovenemberg (Graunemberg, Cronenberg) sold the 250 acres his father Henry had received in the early days of township settlement to a number of persons in portions. John Lewis Remond conveyed the 200 acres originally granted to his father Jeremiah in the mid-1730s to Andrew Hendrie and Hugh Bryan in August 1762. In June 1763 Adam Cuillat, planter and carpenter at Jacksonborough Pon Pon, sold 300 acres in Purrysburg that had been held in joint tenancy by his father,

Adam, and Peter Netman to John Graham of Savannah. Charles Town gentleman Philotheus Chiffelle, eldest son and heir of the Reverend Henry Chiffelle, sold 700 acres in Purrysburg originally granted his father to Daniel Heyward of St. Helena's Parish in April 1765. In the summer of the same year, Peter Albastestier de Monclair (Demonclar), also designated a gentleman of Charles Town, conveyed Purrysburg land that had been granted to his father Andrew in 1735 and also his town lot number 72 to township resident Adrian Mayer. Three years later George Lasman, a house carpenter in St. George's Dorchester, and son of John Martin Lasman, sold his father's land in Purrysburg to Philoman Waters of Charles Town. In early January 1770 Philotheus Chiffelle sold his younger brother Amadeus, of Savannah, 400 acres of township land that had been granted to their father. Two longtime township landholders divested themselves of acreage after more than thirty years of ownership. In May 1765 Monsieur Guillaume Boullot (Bulot), designated a gentleman of St. Peter's, sold the fifty acres in Purrysburg that had been platted to him in 1733. In July 1772 Anthony Gotier, then a baker in Savannah, sold fifty of 175 acres platted to him in Purrysburg in 1736 to John Lewis Bourguin.[110]

These conveyances also hint at two other dynamics of sociocommercial life in the township. First, the craft/nonagricultural portion of the population continued to erode. Skilled artisans and professionals had to relocate to find work as evident from the number of second-generation Purrysburg landholders selling their inherited land who listed professions or titles and another place of residence. Another option taken by a number of landholders by this time was to retrain for agricultural production. A review of table 8 illustrates the dramatic shift from artisan/professional designations dominant in the 1732–1759 period to planter/service sector designations from 1760 into the 1780s. It is likely that even those who had craft or professional designations in this later period still participated in the planting/ranching economy that progressively dominated South Carolina agriculture over the course of the eighteenth century.[111] David Mongin continued to practice his watchmaking business in Purrysburg as late as 1765, even as he became more connected to plantation economics. Adrian Mayer, the township's greatest landholder, was also a physician and merchant.[112] Second, although intratownship conveyances continued at a significant pace during the 1760s and 1770s, an increasing number of nontownship residents purchased land in the township. By the time of the Revolution, many of the most prominent families of the lower Southeast had become Purrysburg landowners either by direct headright grant or by purchase from earlier landowners. Miles Brewton, John Rutledge, Daniel and John Heyward, Robert Williams, William Williamson, and Henry Laurens were among the landowners in the township by the latter 1770s. Their collective influence, if not direct presence, in the township helped create wider networks of social and economic relationships into which the residents of Purrysburg were drawn.

TABLE 8: Occupations of Purrysburg Township Settlers-Landowners

Name*	Occupation	Year	Reference
Cronenberger, Henric	Laborer/ vinedresser	1733	Jones, *Georgia Dutch,* 33
Kieffer, Theobold	Laborer/ vinedresser	1733	Jones, *Georgia Dutch,* 33
Koel, Ludwig	Laborer/ vinedresser	1733	Jones, *Georgia Dutch,* 33
Mengersdorff, George	Laborer/ vinedresser	1733	Jones, *Georgia Dutch,* 33
Riger, Nicolas	Laborer/ vinedresser	1733	Jones, *Georgia Dutch,* 33
Winckler, Andreas	Laborer/ vinedresser	1733	Jones, *Georgia Dutch,* 33
Winckler, Jacob	Laborer/ vinedresser	1733	Jones, *Georgia Dutch,* 33
Metsger, Jacob	Tailor	1735	*Reports,* 2:166
Reck, Jacob	Shoemaker	1735	*Reports,* 2:172
Schönmannsgruber, George	Schoolmaster	1735	*Reports,* 2:218
Unselt, _____	Schoolteacher	1735	*Reports,* 4:142
Tullius, Joshua Daniel	Mason/naval stores processor	1735	*Reports,* 2:197, 199
Yanam, Francis	Vintner	1735	Gregorie, *Court of Chancery Papers,* 17
Mongin, David	Watchmaker	1735/6	Holcomb, *Pet. for Land,* 1:37
Audet (Oddet), John Dominique	Smith	1736	Langley, *Deed Abstracts,* 1:294
Barraquy, Joseph	Laborer	1736	Langley, *Deed Abstracts,* 1:294
Kehl, Ludwig	Planter	1736	Langley, *Deed Abstracts,* 2:357
Kieffer, Theobald	Herdsman	1736	*Reports,* 3:99
Müller, (James)	Servant/schoolteacher	1736	*Reports,* 3:239
Pelot, Jonas	Master shoemaker	1736	Tedcastle, "Testimonial," 61
Richard, Major James	Planter	1736	Langley, *Deed Abstracts,* 2:357
Schönmannsgruber, George	Carder/weaver	1736	*Reports,* 3:116
Bourguin, Benedict	Planter	1737	Langley, *Deed Abstracts,* 2:154

Name*	Occupation	Year	Reference
Chardonet, Abraham	Planter	1737	Langley, *Deed Abstracts*, 2:154
Holdzendorff, Frederick	Surgeon/captain	1737	*Reports*, 4:68
Augspourger, Samuel	Surveyor	1737/8	Stephens, *Journal of the Proceedings*, 1:94
Brabant, Daniel	Doctor	1738	Langley, *Deed Abstracts*, 3:183–84
Calis, ______	Tavernkeeper/baker	1738	*Reports*, 5:36, 182
Coste, Isaac	Shoemason	1738	RMC, S:390
Krüsy, Hans	Barrel- and cabinetmaker	1738	*Reports*, 5:171
Krüsy, Hans	Rice mill builder	1738	*Reports*, 5:196
Krüsy, Hans	Wheelwright	1738	*Reports*, 5:279
Poyas, John Lewis	Silk processor	1738	General Assembly Act, 11 March 1737/8
Dupra, Peter	Tanner/bark mill operator	1739	*SCG*, 8 September 1739
Fauccunet, David	Planter	1739	Langley *Deed Abstracts*, 1:365
"Frenchman's wife"	Midwife	1739	*Reports*, 6:23
Linder, John	Captain and judge	1739	*Reports*, 6:300
Montaigut, Samuel	Merchant	1739	Meriwether, *Expansion of SC*, 38, note 12
Purry, Charles	Merchant	1739	Meriwether, *Expansion of SC*, 38, note 12
______	Cooper	1739	Stephens, *Journal of the Proceedings*, 1:458
Telback, George	Stonecutter	1730s	Holcomb, *Pet. for Land*, 2:197
"German male" (Johann Alther?)	Butcher	1740	*CRG*, 22, pt. 2:447
Bourguin, Henry	Carpenter/joiner	1741	*SCG*, 11 June 1741
Delmester, Peter	Juice, vinegar, and wine vendor	1741	*SCG*, 11 June 1741
Kinder, David	Carpenter/joiner	1741	*SCG*, 11 June 1741
Metsger, Marguerite	Tailor	1741	*Reports*, 8:507

Name*	Occupation	Year	Reference
Truan, Jacob	Carpenter/joiner	1741	*SCG,* 11 June 1741
widow _____	Seamstress/knitter/ farmer	1741	*Reports,* 8:476
Lohrman, Johann Martin	Blacksmith	1741/2	*Reports,* 9:42, 18: 163
Giroud, David	Carpenter	1742	RMC, 3E:86
_________	Cobbler	1742	*Reports,* 9:94
_________	Brickmaker(s)	1742	*Reports,* 9:63
_________	Viniculturist	1742	*Reports,* 9:243
Delagaye, John	Vintner	1742/3	MR 2I, pt. 2:403–405
Albergotti, Ulisse Anthony	Planter	1743	Langley, *Deed Abstracts,* 2:90
Bourguin, John Baptiste	Surgeon	1743	RMC, 4O:200–204
Krüsy, Hans	Day laborer	1743	*Reports,* 10:37, 170
Barrakey, the widow	Silk processor	1744	Jones, *Georgia Dutch,* 221–22
Purry, Charles	Storekeeper	1744	RMC, 3H:226–28
Linder, John	Storekeeper	1745	Meriwether, *Expansion of SC,* 38, note 12
Mohr, Jacob	Blacksmith apprentice	1747	*Reports,* 11:94–95
Albergotti, Ulisse Anthony	Vintner	1748	RMC, 2F:209–10
Alther, Johann	Butcher	1748	Jones, *Georgia Dutch,* 154
Bourguin, Henry Lewis	Physician	1740s	Davis, *Some Families, Supp. 3,* 16
Mohr, _____	Knitter/weaver	1740s	*Reports,* 12:94–95
Kieffer, Theobold Jr.	Boatbuilder (in Ebenezer)	1750	*Reports,* 14:80
Zubly, David	Merchant	1750	*Reports,* 14:86
Depp, Valentin	Shoemaker	1751	*Reports,* 15:17
Vaigneur, Stephen	Tailor	1751	RMC, 3E:15–17
Brabant, Isaac	Merchant	1752	Meriwether, *Expansion of SC,* 38, note 12
Huguenin, David	Carpenter	1752	RMC, 2Y:603
Ravot, Abraham	Tanner	1752	RMC, 2Y:603

Name*	Occupation	Year	Reference
Stroubhart, Jacob	Planter	1752	RMC, 2P:180–81
________	Locksmith apprentice	1753	*Reports,* 16:50–51
Girardin, David	Shoemaker	1754	RMC, 2Q:297–302
Linder, John	Planter	1754	RMC, 2Q:297–302
Grenier, Peter Francis	Tailor (of Savannah)	1756	Langley, *Deed Abstracts,* 3:147
Jindra, Abraham, and Mary Margaret	Planters	1759	RMC, 2Z:198–207
Lohrman, Johann	Slave overseer	1759	*Reports,* 17:55, 297
Morgin, Catherine	Planter	1759	RMC, 2Z:198–207
Netman, Lewis	Schoolmaster	1759	Langley, *Deed Abstracts,* 3:110
Veigneur, Stephen, and Mary Ann	Planters	1759	RMC, 2Z:198–207
Bourguin, Henry Lewis	Surgeon	1760	CCPJR, 64A, 319A
Lester, John	schoolmaster	1760	RMC, 3H:89–90
Meissner, George Frederick	Doctor	1760	*Reports,* 17:261
Metsger, Jacob	Cobbler (Ebenezer)	1760	Jones, *Georgia Dutch,* 226
Pence, Andrew	Blacksmith	1760	RMC, 3H:89–90
Vaucher, John Henry	Shoemaker	1760	Langley, *Deed Abstracts,* 3:357
Hardstone, Joachim	Planter	1761	RMC, 2Y:187–90
Hendrie, Andrew	Planter (of Georgia)	1761	RMC, 2X:468–70
Humbert, David	Planter	1761	RMC, 2X:468–70
Mayerhoffer, Heinrich	Planter	1761	RMC, 3I:40–42
Reshter, Frederick	Planter	1761	Langley, *Deed Abstracts,* 3:158
Stierly, Gregory	Planter	1761	RMC, 3I:40–42
Stroubhart, Jacob	Planter	1761	RMC, 2Y:187–90
Erhard, Francis	Cordwainer†	1762	Langley, *Deed Abstracts,* 3:227
Waldburger, Jacob	Planter	1762	RMC, 3B:328–30
Giroud, David, Sr.	Planter (was carpenter)	1763	RMC, 3B:154–57
Hendrie, Andrew	Planter (of St. Peter's)	1763	RMC, 3B:154–57
Jeanerett, Henri	Planter	1763	RMC, 3E:239–41
Linder, John	Deputy surveyor	1763	MR, 2L, pt. 2:602
Mallet, Daniel	Planter	1763	Langley, *Deed Abstracts,* 3:357

Name*	Occupation	Year	Reference
Zubly, David	Planter	1763	Langley, *Deed Abstracts,* 3:357
Keall, George	Carpenter	1764	RMC, 3H:492–94
Marette, Daniel	Sexton	1764	RMC, 3B:756–58
Mayer, Adrian	Physician	1764	RMC, 3B:756–58
Stroubhart, Nicholas	Planter	1764	RMC, 3C:385–92
Vauchier, John	Ferryman	1764	*Journal of Gen. Assem. & House, 1776–1780,* 102
Wingler, Lewis	Planter	1764	Langley, *Deed Abstracts,* 3:239
Winkler, Nicholas	Planter	1764	RMC, 3D:273
Enderly, Henry	Planter	1765	Langley, *Deed Abstracts,* 3:285
Leichtensteiger, Melchior	Planter	1765	Langley, *Deed Abstracts,* 3:299
Mayer, Adrian	Planter	1765	RMC, 3E:567–69
Winkler, Jacob	Planter	1765	Langley, *Deed Abstracts,* 3:299
Buche, John	Innkeeper	1766	Langley, *Deed Abstracts,* 3:360
De Roche, Abraham Frederick	Cordwainer†	1766	Langley, *Deed Abstracts,* 3:311
Jacot, Abraham	Planter	1766	Langley, *Deed Abstracts,* 3:319
Reynover, Leonard	Planter	1766	RMC, 3Q:154–57
Billeau, Antoine	Freeholder	1767	Langley, *Deed Abstracts,* 3:357
Bourguin, John Lewis	Tax collector	1767	*Georgia Gazette,* 24 August 1768
Erhard, Francis	Planter (was cordwainer)	1767	Langley, *Deed Abstracts,* 3:337
Henderly, Catherin	Planter	1767	RMC, 3I:321–22
Henry, Margaretta (Johnhenry)	Planter	1767	Langley, *Deed Abstracts,* 3:352
Jacot, Abraham	Shoemaker (was planter)	1767	Langley, *Deed Abstracts,* 3:352
Linder, John	Tax collector	1767	Rowland, *Hist. of Beaufort Co.,* 180
Mayer, Adrian	Tax collector	1767	Rowland, *Hist. of Beaufort Co.,* 180
Meuron, Henry	Planter	1767	Langley, *Deed Abstracts,* 3:352–53

Name*	Occupation	Year	Reference
Ravot, Gabriel Francis	Tanner	1767	Langley, *Deed Abstracts,* 3:337
Raymond, Joseph	Retailer (of Savannah)	1767	RMC, 3H:494–95
Tobishop, John	Freeholder	1767	RMC, 3F:605
Fulker, (John) Melchior	Carpenter	1768	RMC, 3L:426–27
Keall, George	Tanner (earlier	1768	Langley, *Deed Abstracts,* 3:377
Long, James	Storekeeper	1768	*Court of Ordinary Abstracts, SCHGM* 30 (1929): 237–38
Vaucher, John	Shoemaker	1768	RMC, 3O:262–64
Walzer, Gabriel	Shoemaker	1768	RMC, 3K:344–46
Bininger, John Roldolph	Planter	1769	Langley, *Deed Abstracts,* 4:82
Kieffer, John Jacob	Boat builder (St. Matthew's Parish, Georgia)	1769	RMC, 30:478
Dupuis, William	Hatter	1770	RMC, 3Q:157
Giroud, Daniel	Shipwright	1770	Hawes, *Zubly's Journal,* 7
Peters, Christopher	Overseer	1770	*Court of Ordinary Abstracts, SCHGM* 42 (1941): 198
Reynower, Leonard	Laborer (was planter)	1770	RMC, 3Q:157
Callis, Benjamin‡	Storekeeper	1772	RMC, 3Z:315
Catterton, William	Planter	1772	Holcomb, *Deed Abstracts, 1773–78,* 98
Gotier, Anthony	Baker (in Savannah)	1772	RMC, 4F:40–44
Ravot, Abraham	Planter (earlier tanner)	1772	RMC, 3Z:313
Holbrook, Jacob	Bricklayer	1773	Holcomb, *Deed Abstracts, 1773–78,* 43
Strobhar, John	Planter	1773	RMC, 4E:60–61
Bourguin, John Lewis Jr.	Merchant and planter	1774	Rowland, *Hist. of Beaufort Co.,* 300
Buche, John	Tavernkeeper	1774	*Finley's Journal,* 60

Name*	Occupation	Year	Reference
Holzendorf, John Frederick	Tavernkeeper	1774	RMC, 4P:416–18
Humbert, Melcheor	Planter	1774	RMC, 4M:170
Postell, John	Planter	1774	RMC, 4P:418–19
Pugh, Willoughby	Planter	1774	RMC, 4M:172–74
Buche, John	Postmaster	1775	RMC, 4V:310–11
Mayer, Adrian	Merchant	1775	RMC, 4V:310–11
Rehm, Frederick	Doctor	1777	RMC, 4T:394–96
Buche, John	Innkeeper	1778	Forfeited Estates Claims on Estates, *Estate of John Buche v. John Linder Jr.*
Bourguin, John Lewis Jr.	Planter	1782	Holcomb, *Deed Abstracts, 1783–88, 56*

Notes: *This table includes only those individuals who were specifically noted in extant documents as practitioners of the vocations listed. In the vast majority of cases it is not possible to pinpoint the exact moment in time that each of the Purrysburg settler/landowners began the activity noted in this table. The years that appear correspond to the first mention of the individual's identification with the occupation designated, not necessarily the year of initial involvement with that endeavor. Several individuals were identified with more than one occupation. Separate entries are provided for each one.

†A cordwainer specialized in making shoes of Spanish cordovan leather.

‡This is the first indication that Callis had been a Purrysburg storekeeper. He arrived at the township by 1733 and had been deceased for some time by 1772. It is unknown when he died. He probably began his store within the first few years of his arrival.

Ultimately a few of Purrysburg's original settlers were able to make the leap to the planter/rancher class by owning more than one tract of land, and one, Adrian Mayer, deserves to be reckoned among the provincial landed elite. Joachim Hardstone (Hartstone, Herdstone, Herdstein) was platted 200 acres in Purrysburg Township in early February 1757. He soon acquired Georgia land and in the early 1770s became quite active in buying and selling real estate in the township. On one day (2 January 1772), Hardstone purchased a total of 400 acres from Henry Bourguin and fifty acres from Adrian Mayer—all located within the township. In May, Hardstone sold 295 of his Purrysburg acres to Abraham Jindrat, and in June of the following year, he and his wife sold 465.5 acres to Purrysburg bricklayer Jacob Holbrook. Hardstone bought another 450 acres in the township from Charles William Makinen of Savannah in November 1773. Although the text of the Makinen conveyance describes Hardstone as a planter of Purrysburg, in these land transactions he appears to be operating more as a speculator in township properties than strictly a planter.[113]

Melchior Leichtensteiger on the other hand, acquired township land for the purpose of agricultural production. His rather substantial headright land in Purrysburg amounted to 700 acres and town lot number 76 from five different plats—all of them executed between March 1761 and January 1765. In the fall of 1765, Leichtensteiger purchased an additional 400 acres from Jacob Winkler, which extended the former's land to the west. On 13 September 1766, Leichtensteiger bought 250 acres that abutted his land to the south. The owner, John Neile, acquired the parcel in 1765 but decided to leave Purrysburg for New Windsor Township. Purrysburg shoemaker Gabriel Walzer (Walser) sold Leichtensteiger 100 acres that had originally been the property of Henry Dubendosser (Duberdorffer) and had subsequently been purchased by Andrew Walser, Gabriel's father. Leichtensteiger further augmented his Purrysburg property in late May 1769 with the acquisition of 143 acres sold to him by boatbuilder Nicholas Cronenberg, who had moved to Ebenezer. That Leichtensteiger's accumulated Purrysburg estate must have provided him with some measure of commercial success is verified by his ability to loan fellow planter Richard Pendarvis more than 2,400 pounds current money the following month.[114]

George, Jacob, and John Stroubhart (Strobart) between them accounted for ten conveyances from 1752 to 1772. Jacob was by far the most acquisitive. In fact, he bought land in Purrysburg more than seven years before he received his headright allocation in the township. In December 1752 he purchased 150 acres from George Steerly and Henry Mayerhoffer's headright allotment of 100 acres. Then shortly after he received nearly 350 acres as his headright in the township, Jacob purchased town lot number 22 from Margaret Rhod (May 1761), 200 acres from Joachim Hardstone and his wife, Ann (June 1761), 150 acres from Frederick Rester (July 1761), and 700 acres from David Giroud (August 1761). George appears in the records only as a seller of Purrysburg land—one of his headright tracts of 600 acres to Stephen Bull of Sheldon in July 1770. In 1772 John appears to have purchased the 150-acre headright John Lowrman (Johannes Loarman) received in 1759. Loarman had moved to Christ Church Parish, Georgia. John sold the land less than eighteen months later to Adrian Mayer. Of the four male Stroubharts for whom records exist during this prerevolutionary era (George, Jacob, John, and Nicholas), Jacob clearly became the agricultural entrepreneur.[115]

There are numerous examples of Purrysburg landowners expanding their holdings in the township via the purchase of a few hundred acres or an extra town lot, but the above examples highlight the movement of some Purrysburg families into levels of economic prosperity, that, though not rivaling the great lowcountry planters, nonetheless illustrate the integration of at least a portion of the township landholders into the mainstream of provincial economic life. Two residents of Purrysburg, however, seem to have made the transition to a level of affluence unmatched in the township.

David Giroud was eighteen when he arrived in Purrysburg in late 1732. His father was a Neuchâtel carpenter and cabinetmaker, and Giroud learned the same profession. Although he was eligible for Purrysburg land, Giroud did not receive any until 1752, when in a petition dated 7 November he stated that though he was a township settler, he had not yet received any land from the authorities. The petition asked for 400 acres based on his headright for Jean (his wife), their four children, and three Africans. The council granted his request. No more Purrysburg land was platted to him until 1761, when he received three tracts comprising a total of 950 acres. Two years later an additional 296 acres were platted to him, with 187 more awarded in 1765. He also received town lot number 40 the same year.[116]

Giroud may have had to wait twenty years before receiving his headright in Purrysburg, but he had begun acquiring land through outright purchase in the township in the early 1740s. He first bought town lot number 10 from John Jacob Metsger and his daughter Marguerite in late March 1742 and the following month purchased lot number 11 from Joseph Lewis Reymond and his wife, Ann.[117] Two years later Henry Desaussure sold his headright, town lot number 118, to Giroud.[118]

By the mid-1740s Giroud owned four different Purrysburg town lots. Numbers 11 and 40 fronted on Church Street, which was the High Road from Charles Town through town; number 10 was on Bay or Front Street; and 118 was at the far northwestern edge of town. Two of his properties therefore lay on the major land route from Charles Town to Savannah, one a block from the road and the other along the Savannah River. The location of the purchased lots and his lack of any appreciable acreage, even fifteen years after his arrival in Purrysburg, would indicate that Giroud was attempting to use his woodworking skills and perhaps some mercantile knowledge to establish a small business in town. He seems to have played a role in the arrival in 1740 of Pierre Quinche in the township. Pierre, brother of Lewis and stepbrother to Jean Pierre Purry, had been a merchant in Neuchâtel. He stayed in Purrysburg for fourteen years, acting for at least a portion of that time as a special solicitor for Giroud. Pierre may have been Giroud's conduit, via his European contacts to market Giroud's products beyond the immediate region, thereby allowing him to achieve some level of economic stability while other township professionals were forced to yield to the flat local market and seek other opportunities.[119] Even moderate success by Giroud in his business ventures would explain why he delayed petitioning for his legal headright for twenty years. In this regard it is noteworthy to mention that Giroud's 1752 petition specifically stated that, although he was a settler in Purrysburg, he "desires to make a settlement for the benefit of his family"—a clear allusion to his felt need to provide for his wife and progeny.[120]

During the decade of the 1760s he provided quite well for all of them, apparently speculating in both town land and township acreage.[121] Purrysburg shoemaker John Henry Vauchier sold Giroud (still listed as "carpenter" on the deed) three tracts in early 1760: 100 acres that had been Lewis Kehl's, fifty acres (originally John Francis Henry's), and fifty acres that had been granted to Maria Henry. Three years later in September 1763, now designated a "Purrysburg Planter," Giroud acquired 200 acres in the township on the Savannah River originally granted to Jeremiah Reymond and sold by his son John Lewis to Andrew Hendrie and Hugh Burns from whom Giroud purchased the parcel. Two months later he bought 200 acres contiguous to the Hendrie-Burns property from Jonathan Belton. By the end of 1765, through headright grants and outright purchase, Giroud had increased his acreage to at least 1,800 acres of Purrysburg land and multiple town lots.[122]

Between 1766 and 1776, the spectrum of Giroud's commercial dealings broadened. In October 1766 he sold lot number 118 to Leonard Rhynower and lot 40 to John Buche a year later. In early February 1768 he loaned John Linder a total of 11,500 pounds current money. As security, Linder put up eleven black males, eight black females, five black children, and five tracts of Purrysburg land amounting to 1,700 acres. Two weeks later Giroud sold John Vauchier 500 acres in the township. In January 1769 Giroud purchased town lot number 99 from David Montaigut of Savannah, which had been originally granted to Henry Girardin. Not quite eighteen months later, in May 1770, Giroud sold the same lot to John Buche, who, it may be recalled, already owned lot number 40, which was just across Church Street from lot number 99. Because Giroud bought the lot from Montaigut for seven pounds sterling and sold it to Buche for eighty pounds current money, at a seven-to-one ratio of currency to sterling, he made a tidy profit of approximately 60 percent. In March 1771 Adrian Mayer bought 100 acres from Giroud. Giroud in November held the bond of Purrysburg tanner George Keal, who offered as security 296 acres in Purrysburg. Daniel Desaussure of St. Helena's Parish bought two adjoining 200 acre tracts from Giroud in October 1772. John Vauchier followed suit in June 1773 purchasing 450 acres from him. Giroud's interest returned to town land as the Revolution neared when he bought number 66 from Abraham Ravot of St. Matthew's Parish, Georgia, in December 1776.[123]

The number, variety, and timing of David Giroud's commercial dealings clearly illustrate both the attempt to establish a craft industry in the township and the inexorable lure of a slave-based plantation economy with its promise of greater return on investments. That Giroud appears to have also speculated in land and loaned some of his excess profits to other township residents demonstrates that successful Purrysburg planters exhibited the same entrepreneurial spirit that Weir observed in other lowcountry parishes.

If the commercial activities of David Giroud provide a sense of how and to what extent respectable economic prosperity could be achieved in Purrysburg, Adrian Mayer, more than any other township resident, deserves recognition as the most financially successful member of the community. Enticed by the inducements offered to foreign Protestants, Mayer and his brother arrived from the Swiss Confederation sometime before January 1756, because, on 6 January 1756, he petitioned for 100 acres and a town lot in Purrysburg as his headright. The council ruled affirmatively on the request, though there is no indication that he was actually platted the land until 1761 when he received 150 acres and town lot number 25, which lay in the area of the town subject to frequent freshets. Four years later he received town lot 20 and 183 more acres in the township. Sometime between early 1756 and February 1764, he met and married his wife, Barbara, but little is known about her. Mayer did not begin purchasing land until 1762, but between May of that year and September 1777, the Purrysburg settler was party to more than sixty-five different business transactions.[124] He purchased town lots 17, 19, 28, 30, 57, 58, 72 (twice), 74, 75, and 77 and sold lot number 35. In addition to his headright land in Purrysburg, he held the title to 8,653 acres in the township and another 18,500 acres in Granville County as far north as the Cherokee Line and Ninety-Six and as far east as St. Helena's Parish. Of the more than 27,000 acres and thirteen town lots he owned, Mayer sold only one lot and 100 acres of land prior to September 1777. He also owned pews 21 and 32 in the parish church of St. Peter's. He loaned Anderson Young of St. Helena's Parish 472 pounds current money in September 1774 and James Bullock of Savannah 1,750 pounds current money in April 1777.

All Mayer's acquisitions prior to April 1775 were in Purrysburg Township. Of the thirty-six transactions for acreage, six were for fifty acres, eight for 100 acres, three for 150 acres, one for 162 acres, five for 200 acres, five for 250, one for 313 acres, one for 350, one for 393, two for 400, one for 450, and two for 500. After April 1775 Mayer bought only five more parcels within the township for 150, 171, 214, 300, and 550 acres. The Purrysburg conveyances included land bought from original landholders or their heirs, a number of whom had left the township, but Mayer also bought Purrysburg land from many who had become township landowners via purchase and not initial settlement. The relatively small size of the purchases made and the large number of transactions bear witness to the fact that Purrysburg was no different than other South Carolina parishes where land consolidation in the hands of a small group often involved the decline of smaller, more diversified family farming.[125]

In contradistinction to his Purrysburg properties, the acquisitions Mayer began to make outside the confines of the township from April 1775 forward tended to be much larger tracts. His 18,500 acres outside Purrysburg were acquired in only eighteen transactions whereas his 8,653 acres within the boundaries of the township, excluding his headright grants and town lots, required forty-one conveyances. Of the former, only eight of the eighteen were under 500 acres—the smallest being for 200 acres. Three were for 500 acres, three for 1,000 acres, one for 2,000 acres, two for 3,000 acres, and one for 3,200 acres. The lower cost of backcountry land allowed Mayer to accumulate substantial acreage for speculative purposes. Mayer, like other large landowners, exhibited an entrepreneurial spirit that identified him not only as a planter in the records but also as a physician and a merchant. He also held office as a tax collector and juror for St. Peter's Parish.[126] If any Purrysburg settler aspired to commercial supremacy in Granville County, Adrian Mayer was the model to emulate.

VIII

However prominent Giroud or Mayer might have been in the region, Purrysburg was not known for its overwhelming contribution to the economy of the southern colonies. Indeed, St. Peter's Parish remained the least prosperous of the four parishes of the Beaufort District throughout the eighteenth century.[127] The parish and its immigrant township did nonetheless make use of the expanding commercial network of the late colonial Southeast, with many of its families achieving wealth commensurate with other secondary town centers in the region. The increase in the number of slaveholding residents, the growing number of slaves per household in the township, the progressively mounting valuation and composition of estates, the expansion of the township's economy, the emergence of an absentee landlord class, the consolidation of landholding, and the higher standard of living apparent by the 1760s and 1770s show clearly the rise of a planter-rancher class in Purrysburg by the beginning of the final third of the eighteenth century.

In 1764 Daniel Desaussure's 500-acre township plantation produced rice and corn, yielding "as good farming as any place about Purrysburg." The acreage had a house, barn, and a "great quantity of fine pine on it."[128] The following year a township property was described as having "a good barn, sundry good dwelling rooms at one end, a good rice machine, several Negro houses, and other convenient out buildings suitable for a good rice plantation." The waterfront land could accommodate a schooner carrying up to a hundred barrels of rice.[129] In advertising 450 acres of Purrysburg land for sale in January 1774, Adrian Loyer noted that the land had produced up to four and a half barrels of rice per acre and that enough of the land had been cleared for tidal rice culture that the site could employ more than fifty slaves. Corn produced on the property yielded seventy bushels per acre, and the land was suitable also for peas, potatoes, and other crops. Loyer's plantation included an overseer's home and slave quarters. Loyer concluded that the plantation "would suit a merchant that followed the West Indian trade."[130] From these examples it is apparent that, when Archibald Simpson wrote of Purrysburg as a "poor, deserted place" as he passed through the town proper in the 1760s, he failed to note significant economic expansion and prosperity for want of a thriving city to substantiate it.[131]

The new prosperity, the rise of a planter-rancher class, and the township's integration into the commercial network of the colonial Southeast transformed relationships among Purrysburg settlers and also provided the context for extending socioeconomic bonds beyond the township limits. Jacob Stroubhart alone held bonds from eight different individuals, only two of whom appear to have been residents of Purrysburg. Another member of the same family (George) maintained a partnership with Isaac McPherson, Foggison, and Anslea. Stroubhart must have begun to shift his financial affairs in April 1768 when he sold half of a cattle herd formerly belonging to the partnership to John Stroubhart for 2,127 pounds, 10 shillings current money. The following year George Stroubhart closed a deal with two Georgia cattlemen to sell another large herd of cattle for 5,250 pounds. David Giroud sold two slaves, a rowboat, and a wagon to Sutcliffe and Company in 1778. In the mid-1780s John Bourguin joined George Hooper and David Alexander in what may have been a business venture, because these three men held a bond for 2,333 pounds sterling on the Charles Town merchants Thomas Newall and Nathan Russell. Perhaps partly as a response to the increased commerce between Purrysburg and other regions of both South Carolina and Georgia, South Carolina governor Benjamin Guerard used a new law in July 1784 to appoint Joachim Hartstone (Hardstone) and John Buche, both of St. Peter's Purrysburg, along with two others from adjoining lands as commissioners of the Purrysburg–Euhaws road.[132]

Simultaneous with the rise of prosperity in Purrysburg was the rise in indebtedness among the emerging planter-rancher class in the township, which again resulted in tightening multiple bands of loyalties and affiliations both within and without the township. Members of the Bourguin, Buche, Camber, Giroud, Godet, Hendrie, Imer, Leichensteiger, Mayer, Pendarvis, Richard, Stroubhart, Vaigneur, Vauchier, Waldburger, Walser, Winkler, and Zubly families participated in various sorts of financial transactions, which were recorded in the Court of Common Pleas in Charles Town.[133] Most of these involved the borrowing or loaning of money to those of the township—presumably to augment landholding or to increase productivity. While the earliest of the bonds was signed in July 1732 by James Richard for 161 pounds, 2 pence, current money before he ever settled in the township, most of the transactions took place in the 1760s and 1770s for amounts between 100 and 1,000 pounds. A few of the bonds were for considerably larger amounts, such as Henry Lewis Bourguin's 1,500 pound bond, Richard Pendarvis's for 2,420, Thomas Camber's for 2,700, David Mongin's for nearly 3,100, and John Baptiste Bourguin's for 3,200 pounds.

Upon closer examination, these transactions appear to indicate a spreading network of relationships between Purrysburg residents and those of other urban centers of the Southeast. By the 1760s township citizens were engaging in financial dealings with both prestigious merchant combines and small-scale entrepreneurs in cities such as Charles Town, Savannah, and Beaufort. In November 1759 Andrew Walser borrowed 260 pounds from John Armbrister, a Charles Town baker. A year later Henry Lewis Bourguin and the widow Margaret Chiffelle bound themselves to the Charles Town merchant firm headed by Henry Laurens for 1,500 pounds. Jacob Waldburger bound himself to the merchant Francis Stuart of the same city for 1,510 pounds in April 1765. A few months later, in July, Andrew Hendrie signed a bond for 2,580 pounds with the firm of Samuel Brailsford and John Chapman based in Charles Town. The well-known Charles Town firm of James Bentham and John Sutcliffe did business with the Purrysburg landowner John Dupont, as did the lesser-known businessmen Henry Ellison and Richard Dickenson. David Mongin also had extensive contacts with Charles Town commercial leaders. John Vauchier signed a promissory note to John Simpson at Savannah in 1765. The Beaufort firm of Edward Fisher and Company took John L. Vaigneur of Purrysburg to court for defaulting on a loan of 1,360 pounds drawn in October 1773. David Zubly, son of the Reverend John J. Zubly, borrowed more than 317 pounds Georgia money from John Kean and Peter Lavien in 1777. Benjamin Carey accused John Buche of falsifying weights and measures at his Purrysburg store and took him to court in 1776 over the matter. Buche countersued for 1,000 pounds for damages to his reputation and received satisfaction, but not until 1795. Thomas Camber took the Savannah merchants Alexander Inglis and Nathaniel Hall to court to recover a debt of 2,700 pounds in South Carolina currency, and Jacob Winkler filed suit in Beaufort against Richard Keating in 1788 for recovery of a defaulted 112 pound debt.

The scramble for a share of the unprecedented affluence of South Carolina in the late colonial era provided the occasion for Purrysburg inhabitants to engage in various legal actions among themselves over matters of finance and property. Among the more complex of these legal maneuverings was the suit brought by Margaret Henery (Henrie) against the township pastor the Reverend Abraham Imer in May 1766. The Reverend Imer had borrowed twenty-nine pounds, two shillings, six pence from Henery the year before and failed to repay it. He then approached Henery for another twelve pounds, eight shillings, three pence. When Imer asked for a third loan without any payment on the other two, Henery had enough and sued for the outstanding debt plus punitive damages amounting to 100 pounds. Through his attorney, John Rutledge, Imer promised to make payment on the original loan and introduced as evidence a handwritten note in French to this effect dated January 1768. His abrupt death that year ended any possibility of Henery recovering her money.

Adrian Meyer loaned his Purrysburg neighbor Richard Pendarvis nearly 345 pounds, and, like Henery, found the only possible way to get back the money and accrued interest was to take Pendarvis to court, but Pendarvis's more serious financial problem lay with another township member, Melchior Leichtensteiger. For simultaneous with Mayer's suit against him, Leichtensteiger initiated litigation against the Englishman for recovery of a 2,420 pound past due note. John Vauchier's 181 pound, 19 shilling, 6 pence suit against John Linder originated in 1767 and 1768 when Vauchier provided shoemaking and associated services to Linder and his family on credit. Linder failed to begin payment of the debt and by August 1769 found himself in the Court of Common Pleas. These judgments all involve litigation regarding the rather mundane matters of personal and corporate finance. Multiple cases involving the Purrysburg storekeeper John Buche, however, are unique in surviving township records as they outline the only litigation pivoting around realty and personal property.

The first of these, brought by Buche against Thomas Barlow in April 1770, regarded Barlow's alleged trespass and desecration of Buche's property. According to the proceedings, Barlow broke into Buche's house, destroyed a fence enclosing the yard, and trampled some vegetation. There is no record of the defendant's testimony, so it is not known what might have triggered his behavior. Buche sued Barlow for 900 pounds, but there is no final judgment noted. Seventeen years later Buche's property was again subjected to criminal acts; this time by Francis Breen and Major John McPherson. They took Buche's horse, Davy, in 1786 and kept it for their own use in Purrysburg, eventually disposing of the animal in an unrevealed manner. Buche's lawyer, Henry William Desaussure, asked for forty-five pounds, plus eight pounds, fifteen shillings for incidental expenses associated with the theft, use, and disposal of the horse. Buche originally asked for 100 pounds, but settled the case for the reduced amount by 1795. The nature of these cases points toward the commission of property crimes in the township and the smooth, though somewhat protracted, functioning of legal institutions in Purrysburg by the end of the colonial era.

Another facet of Purrysburg life illustrated by these records is the intricate, interlocking webs of both horizontal (within Purrysburg) and vertical (outside Purrysburg) relationships that evolved in the township by the revolutionary period. Many Purrysburg individuals would not have been snared in litigation had they not served as administrators or executors of the wills and estates of friends and neighbors. David Giroud would never have been sued by the Charles Town trader William Yeomans had he not agreed to execute the will and estate of James Richard. John Lewis Bourguin and Jonathan Belton of Purrysburg found themselves party to a suit brought by Brailsford and Chapman because they had been named executors of Andrew Hendrie's will and estate. Belton died before the verdict was reached, and so Bourguin became solely responsible for the repayment of Hendrie's 2,580 pound debt with 44 pounds in assessed damages to the merchants tacked on for good measure.

Hendrie's death also worked hardship on David Giroud, who, with Hendrie, on 17 June 1765 had bound himself to James Watson for 610 pounds. Hendrie's death the following year made Giroud liable for the entire amount, for which suit was brought by Watson in July 1766. Perhaps because of the complexity of her husband's financial commitments, Hendrie's widow, Jean Marie, through her attorney Charles Pinckney, entered a caveat against the probate of his will and called witnesses to prove the validity of the will. When Belton died in 1767, Philotheus Chiffelle entered a caveat against "any pretended will" on behalf of Belton's widow, Henrietta. John Hollowell of Charles Town initially won the right to administer the estate of deceased Purrysburg resident Richard Booker

Coulthard in February 1768 as Coulthard's greatest creditor. John Linder challenged the probate of the estate on similar grounds. In August the Court of Ordinary awarded Linder the right to administer it because it was determined that he was Coulthard's principal creditor, but litigation in the case appears to have dragged on until at least November 1769.[134]

The proving of Purrysburg decedent Gideon Mallet's will in January 1771 would seem to have been a quite straightforward matter. His brother Daniel, also of Purrysburg, was granted administrative responsibilities as his next of kin. For some undisclosed reason, however, questions arose over the validity of the will. The Court of Ordinary issued a dedimus to Purrysburg justice of the peace Adrian Mayer to secure the sworn testimony of longtime Purrysburg resident William (Guillaume) Bulot as to the authenticity of the will. Henry Gendra (Gindrat, Jindra) was also called to testify that "he heard Gideon Mallet acknowledge that he had signed his name and also heard him publish that instrument to be his last will and testament and that he and his brother Abraham Gendra subscribed their names as witnesses to same."[135]

Family connections bound John Lewis Bourguin to Henry Laurens in 1764. A bond with Laurens for 1,500 pounds had been signed four years previous by Bourguin's kinsman Henry Lewis Bourguin and the widow Margaret Chiffelle. John Lewis Bourguin married Chiffelle in 1764, and the substantial debt, none of which had been repaid at the time of the marriage, became a family affair for which they were both held responsible. At practically the same time, Bourguin became enmeshed in another court case in which he was not even a litigant. It was discovered that title to a disputed tract of land in the case of *John Right vs. Thomas Thruston* belonged to Bourguin, even though Thruston had claimed it and yet another man attempted to lease it to a third (Right) for ten shillings per annum. Thruston wrote a hasty letter to Bourguin, informing him of the twisted proceedings, and warned him to defend his title to the land against Right because he (Thurston) refused to do so. It should also be recalled that Bourguin was party to the complicated adjudication of David Mongin's will in 1770 involving Abraham Ravot and Robert Harvey in addition to Mongin's wife and son. In much the same manner, David Giroud and John Buche were entangled in litigation regarding the validity of a land deed executed by their Purrysburg neighbor Daniel Merett.[136]

IX

Increased litigation, expanding commercial networking, and criminal activity came to Purrysburg as the development of a plantation economy proceeded through the course of the latter third of the eighteenth century. The state of the provincial economy in the 1730s and 1740s militated against the survival of a skilled craft sector in the township because of poverty, lack of circulating currency, and the wartime recession. In addition, the expanding plantation system discouraged skilled labor because of greater return on agricultural production. Such conditions, coupled with the commercial centrality of Charles Town, Savannah, and Beaufort, drew the labor of many of Purrysburg's skilled workers either away from the township or into plantation agriculture. One enterprise, however, did survive in Purrysburg throughout the colonial era and provided a crucial link between the European past of the colonists and their New World present. The silk industry remained a pursuit of township residents up to the revolutionary period and engaged the labors of sericulture specialists and agrarians, males and females, parents and children. Heavily subsidized by a government intent on attracting skilled white workers, the vitality of the industry at Purrysburg helped establish important connections with other immigrant communities and provided the settlers with opportunities to maintain expertise in a vocation directly related to their European heritage. The development of an indigenous silk industry also best embodied the desire of the South Carolina elite for economic diversification without the extension of the slave-based plantation system to white immigrants.

The widespread production of silk seemed entirely possible in South Carolina because the province was a native habitat for mulberry trees, the leaves of which were the main food for the grubs that spun cocoons of silk thread. The indigenous red mulberry grew wild, but it was early determined that the leaves of the white mulberry were favored by silkworms. The white mulberry was introduced in South Carolina as early as 1683 and flourished. Soon after the founding of Georgia, the trustees sent white mulberry seeds from the Chelsea Physic Garden to be planted in the Savannah experimental garden and distributed to settlers. Live silkworms were imported from Italy.[137]

The American silk industry took its technical cues from the Italians, who were recognized as producing the finest European product. Sheds containing numerous shelves were constructed to house and protect the worms as they fed on the mulberry leaves before spinning their cocoons. When the cocoons were completed, the shelving was removed and the cocoons gathered. The cocoons were then transported to a filature for the silk-spinning process. Inside the filature, fires were built over a series of metal basins. Placed in the heated basins, the cocoons became pliable, and their coils could be untangled and spun into usable thread. This was a time consuming, labor-intensive process and required constant vigilance by the sericulturalist at every stage from the raising of mulberry trees through the reeling of the silk thread. It took approximately sixteen pounds of cocoons to produce one pound of reeled silk thread.[138]

Spain, southern France, and the Piedmont region of northern Italy were the centers of sericulture in early modern Europe, and among the most skilled in the actual production of silk were said to be Italians, Swiss, Germans, Austrians, and the French. Warfare on the continent often threatened to disrupt the continental silk trade with Great Britain. Consequently, British mercantilists dreamed of a lucrative trade completely independent of sources outside the empire. In the meantime, however, they attempted to insure the supply of silk cloth during Queen Anne's War (1702–1713) via an alliance with Victor Amadeus II, the ruler of Savoy. The strategy may have benefited consumers, but business interests favored the importation of raw silk so that it could be processed by workers in London's Spitalfields district.[139] Jean Pierre Purry used the British desire to secure a regular source of silk to good advantage in both of his pamphlets written for British audiences. He ended his 1724 memorial to the Duke of Newcastle with a paragraph assuring the success of sericulture in South Carolina because of its "degree of heat and temperature." He boasted that within thirty years, "if certain sure and infallible methods for the cultivation of this article are put into general use (which the writer offers to indicate at any time)," South Carolina would be able to produce "a quantity of silk sufficient to supply the needs not only of her own subjects, but also if she found it necessary, of the rest of Europe."[140] His subsequent treatise on South Carolina made similar promises. Purry even took the time to address some concerns potential colonists had raised about the viability of silkworms in the Carolina environment in the "Clarifications" section he later added to this pamphlet. He referred to the "indifferent" silk of Provence and Languedoc and declared that the quality and profits of South Carolina silks would far exceed that product. Purry also mentioned the potential for wine making, but his emphasis on silk foreshadowed the preeminence given to this enterprise over the next forty-five years in the township that bore his name.[141]

News of the imminent arrival of the first Purrysburg colonists in late 1732 coincided with a flurry of excitement over sericulture in the region. The *South Carolina Gazette* featured a series of articles on all aspects of the silk industry, and the recently granted charter of Georgia spurred speculation that raw silk output from both colonies would approach 200,000 pounds, thereby ending the reliance of Great Britain on imported Piedmontese silk. In 1733 the trustees of Georgia fixed a bounty on silk cocoons, hoping to stimulate production in South Carolina as well as Georgia.[142] Bounty acts in 1736, 1738, and 1744 passed by the South Carolina General Assembly officially affirmed the importance of the silk industry to that colony. After Italy and Spain banned the exportation of raw silk in 1750, London mercantile interests petitioned Parliament for direct subsidization of the American silk enterprise. Expansion of the silk venture persuaded colonial authorities to appoint commissioners for the silk trade to promote even greater production. By 1739 the silk commission began buying advertisements in the *South Carolina Gazette* to encourage parents to have their children apprenticed to silk experts. That the entire cost of training children from frontier settlements came at public expense out of the provincial treasury illustrates the commitment of the colony to a prosperous silk industry that would keep immigrants away from the more profitable staples of rice and indigo and on the frontier. Throughout the 1740s and 1750s the silk enterprise remained much a part of South Carolina commerce, but the War of the Austrian Succession probably adversely affected production. The colony was said to have produced only 651 pounds of raw silk between 1742 and 1755. If that is the case, Purrysburg Township produced nearly a quarter of the total in 1749, for a correspondent known as R.T. reported seeing "above 1200 pounds of silk balls, made there this year, which will give 120 pounds of neat silk." In the year that the Treaty of Aix-la-Chapelle was signed ending the war, silk exports still accounted for just under 7 percent of the total aggregate value of all the naval stores exported during the same period. Through the 1740s, the South Carolina Commons House of Assembly exerted its influence upon the English Parliament to encourage further assistance for the silk venture. In 1755, acting as an agent for the Society for the Encouragement of Arts, Manufactures, and Commerce, Purrysburg landowner Hector Berenger de Beaufin offered prizes for the largest mulberry groves in the province. The following year Purrysburg landholder Benedict Bourguin and Theobald Kieffer Jr. of Georgia won second and third prize, respectively, from the society for the most mulberry trees planted before 1 March 1756. By 1759 South Carolina had increased its export of raw silk to 10,000 pounds.[143]

It is impossible to ascertain exactly how many township families became involved in the Purrysburg silk industry. The amount of silk produced in such a labor intensive pursuit indicates that participation, at least occasionally, was quite extensive. The Piedmontese Waldensians John Lewis Poyas and his wife, who arrived in Purryburg in 1734, were perhaps the most knowledgeable of the township residents in all aspects of sericulture. They shared their expertise with other Purrysburg families and provincial officials. By 1737 Poyas addressed the lieutenant governor and the council of South Carolina urging further support for the silk enterprise under his direction at the township. Perhaps favorably impressed with his gift of Purrysburg silks, officials voted Poyas fourteen pounds remuneration for it. More important for the industry, the assembly passed "An Act For encouraging the Manufacture of Silk in this Province, under the Direction of Mr. John Lewis Poyas, for Seven Years." The act appointed Thomas Waring, Ralph Izard, Benjamin Whitaker, Isaac Mazyck, and William Cattel as commissioners to carry out the terms of the act. They were charged with procuring for Poyas "at the publick Charge and expence, a Plantation in some convenient Place such as they shall think proper for carrying on a Silk Work." The commissioners were empowered to provide Poyas with up to six slaves and ten apprentices. All costs related to them were assumed by the colony. The province also paid all living expenses for Poyas and his family during the first year out of tax receipts. The act paid him 100 pounds sterling per year for the first three years. In exchange, Poyas promised to engage in "the Business of raising and cultivating Mulberry Trees and raising Worms and making Silk." He also agreed that he, his wife, "or any other person that he shall employ skilled in the said Work, shall be obliged to follow the Directions of the said Commissioners, in instructing the said Apprentices and other persons in the Drawing and Organzining [*sic*] Silk and all other Matters relating to the Silk

Work." Finally, Poyas committed to assist the commissioners in finding one or two people "more skillful in the Art of Drawing and Organzining Silk." Their expenses, including passage to South Carolina, would also be borne by the colony. To ensure his continuation in the project, the act stipulated that Poyas post a 500-pound sterling bond guaranteeing that he would remain the province for seven years. Unfortunately, four years into the joint project, the Commons House withdrew its support for lack of desired results. The House released Poyas, blaming him for the less-than-stellar return on the provincial investment, and decided to quit the silk industry. Though Poyas proved unsuccessful in securing government support after 1742, he continued to produce silk, advertising for silk products as late as 1752.[144]

Other township residents joined John Lewis Poyas and his wife in sericulture. In August 1744 the Reverend Boltzius hired the Purrysburg widow Mrs. Barrakey to instruct some of the Salzburg girls of Ebenezer in the enterprise. According to the pastor, however, Barrakey only let the prospective students watch her work because she preferred to keep the skill to herself. The Purrysburg widow's unwillingness actually to teach her charges and the price she charged persuaded Boltzius to look elsewhere for assistance in expanding Georgia's silk production. She called on him the following winter and wrote to him in 1745 to offer her expertise in silk reeling to the Georgia settlement, but under the same conditions. Boltzius wrote back in late March that her services would not be needed as some Ebenezer girls had just departed for Savannah to be taught the skill by Mary Camuse. There were said to be "several Italians" at Purrysburg who were involved in the industry prior to 1740, but their names are unrecorded. A decade later Boltzius heard from Purrysburg that, with the withdrawal of the silk subsidy, "an Italian is selling his cocoons a very low price" before leaving the township. It is also possible that the Piedmontese immigrant Mary Camuse of Savannah spent time in the South Carolina township attending to matters associated with the enterprise there prior to her death in late 1750. Her husband and their three children certainly did before their return to Savannah early that year. Their daughter was specifically mentioned as being directly involved in the spinning of silk with others in the township in July 1750.[145]

Purrysburg Italians were not the only ones associated with the silk industry in the township. In the spring of 1741 a French-speaking Purrysburg woman produced silk fine enough to be noticed by the Reverend Boltzius of Ebenezer. Boltzius approached her in May about teaching the craft to Salzburgers in the Georgia colony, and she consented to teach two Ebenezer girls, thereby beginning the silk industry there.[146] The Purrysburg cobbler Jacob Reck and his wife become quite involved in sericulture by the mid-1740s. The Reverend Boltzius recorded that the Recks produced about forty pounds of silk in 1743. Their output dropped drastically to only six pounds in 1744 because of an infestation that afflicted the silkworms. Early in that year, grateful for the assistance of Ebenezer settlers in rescuing their cattle during a flood, Mr. and Mrs. Reck instructed the Salzburgers in "the proper way to handle silkworms so they yield good and plentiful silk."[147] The only other named individual associated with silk production in Purrysburg was Paul Amatis, the Georgia trustees' gardener at Savannah. Amatis was blamed for problems that surfaced in the fledgling Georgia silk enterprise, including the lack of productivity of the mulberry trees under his care. In a letter written in the late 1730s to the trustees, Martha Causton accused Amatis and "the people of Purrysburg" of mismanaging the silk industry in the colony. Amatis contracted with an undisclosed number of Purrysburg inhabitants to provide Savannah a continuous supply of mulberry leaves, but the arrangement abruptly ended, which severely threatened efforts to stimulate production of silk there. Although the shortage of leaves for export may have exerted short-term hardships both in South Carolina and Georgia, production continued in both colonies through the 1760s, aided particularly in Georgia by the Ebenezer colonists, who established themselves as diligent workers in the enterprise without the widow Barrakey's help.[148]

Georgians in the silk trade continued to purchase cocoons from Purrysburg during most of these years, though competitive antagonisms threatened production in the 1740s. The rivalry surfaced soon after the Ebenezer silk enterprise began. In 1741 one-half of all the cocoons that arrived in Savannah came from Purrysburg. Boltzius reported in May 1742 that "people in Purrysburg and elsewhere in Carolina have been vaingloriously claiming that they alone, and not the inhabitants of Georgia have made silk, and that the silk sent annually to London shows only the industry of the inhabitants of Carolina." Georgia authorities apparently retaliated for this slight by refusing to accept Carolina silk at the Savannah storehouse. This caused sericulturists at Purrysburg, "who have drawn a fine sum of money from Savannah every year," to try "every idea they can to get their silk into the storehouse."[149] A low point came two years later, when the Georgia trustees paid only two shillings a pound for silk and refused to buy any Purrysburg silk.[150] The breech between Purrysburg silk producers and their Georgia counterparts started to heal when the Reverend Boltzius requested and received a substantial number of white mulberry trees from a French-speaking resident of the township in January 1747. In March 1749, just as recovery from King George's War began, an unknown malady struck the silkworms at Ebenezer. Boltzius hoped to get help from Purrysburg silk experts and even wrote former Purrysburg resident Hector Berenger de Beaufin to ask whether the latter could procure silkworms from Portugal for the Salzburgers. Neither source appears to have been able to provide assistance, so the trustees decided to pay the bounty for silk for one year, no matter where it had been produced.[151]

Fortunately, silk production in both colonies experienced a renascence by the 1750s.[152] The silk-spinning filature built in Georgia in 1751 processed a great deal of Purrysburg silk, though exact figures are unavailable.[153] In 1756 more silk cocoons were processed from South Carolina (most if not all of which were probably from the township) than from either Savannah or Ebenezer. Fully half the quantity of spun silk produced in Georgia in that year was contributed by Purrysburg settlers. The filature burned down during the summer of 1758 but was rebuilt shortly thereafter and accepted silk "from the entire colony, also from Purrysburg and other places in Carolina," though the trustees only paid half the three shilling bounty for South Carolina cocoons.[154] Aside from a poor year in 1760, sericulture appears to have experienced an expansion for much of the rest of the decade.[155] In the 1760s an observer commented that practically every family in Purrysburg Township raised silkworms. On a visit to the region in 1765 the Moravian Johann Ettewein wrote, "The Salzburgers, French Swiss, and other white people in the area around Purrysburg and Ebenezer keep many silkworms, which were alive everywhere just then. They told me that was the only way they could earn money. A good housewife with three or four children can get about three ounces of seed, and from that, if they are successful, they can get from twenty to thirty pounds sterling worth of cocoons, for which they receive cash money in Savannah at the filature."[156] In 1766 alone, one-third of the total production of spun silk from the filature came from the South Carolina township—some 300 pounds. Although the enterprise began to decline in Georgia after 1766, Purrysburg and other enclaves in Carolina, aided by the arrival of a considerable immigration of French Huguenots, produced significant amounts of silk well into the 1770s.[157]

These émigrés to New Bordeaux, Hillsborough Township, in the mid-1760s greatly expanded the silk venture in the late colonial period and are credited with developing sericulture to its highest level in South Carolina with the assistance of Gabriel Manigault. They were related linguistically—and to some extent culturally—to the Reformed in Purrysburg and joined their labors with those of Purrysburg residents to encourage greater production and increase popular support for the silk industry. Perhaps in some part because of their combined efforts, Parliament removed duties from silk and placed new bounties on its processing in the colonies. In 1766 the South Carolina Assembly appropriated 433 pounds to buy silk cocoons. By the spring of 1767 silk culture had been successfully planted in the backcountry, and its cultivation was widespread. During that year the construction of four filatures in South Carolina began. The Reverend Gibert of New Bordeaux was put in charge of the spinning facilities and carried the responsibility for supervising their operation. The provincial legislature set aside 1,000 pounds to subsidize the operation of the filatures opened at Charles Town and New Bordeaux. Purrysburg's ongoing importance to the expansion of the silk enterprise is indicated by the fact that the third filature erected in South Carolina was built in the township and began operation under Gibert's guidance in 1768.[158]

In 1769 Parliament passed another silk bounty bill to take full advantage of the resurging interest in silk production in South Carolina. Later that same year, Gibert hired Jean de la Bere, a French Protestant residing in London, to act as a silk broker for the South Carolina product. De la Bere received 300 pounds of silk from the colony in 1769 and sold it for more than 2,000 pounds sterling. In January 1770 de la Bere accepted 240 pounds of South Carolina silk. Purrysburg alone shipped 455 pounds of "exceedingly fine raw silk" and thirty-six pounds of "ordinary quality silk" from Charles Town aboard the *Beaufin* in January 1772. Robert Meriwether believed that in all likelihood the 592 pounds of silk exported the previous year came exclusively from the township. The coming of the Revolution, however, abruptly ended the sericulture experiment in South Carolina for it destroyed mercantilist price supports throughout the former colonial empire. When the subsidies ended, the provincial silk industry collapsed. Limited production did continue until just after the Revolutionary War but virtually disappeared soon thereafter. Georgia was said to have processed small amounts of the commodity as late as the 1840s, and in an 1804 letter Robert Mills wrote that, although rice and indigo cultivation characterized Purrysburg, which had about sixty buildings at the time, some silk was still produced by the inhabitants. The ultimate failure of the silk industry to remain a viable commercial force in South Carolina does not diminish the significant role Purrysburg residents played in the unsuccessful attempt to diversify the southeastern economy. Their long years of labor in sericulture demonstrate a determination to achieve economic stability but also illustrate the difficulty of finding it in an industry so labor intensive and dependent upon royal prerogatives. Once again, nonagricultural skills of Purrysburg settlers—skills closely linked to their European cultural heritage—were rendered useless. With vocational options so narrowed, it is smaller wonder that the slave-based plantation system exerted such a powerful attraction to Purrysburg inhabitants and served increasingly to shape the township's commercial future in the two decades before the War of the Revolution.[159]

X

Reflecting on the lives of nonelite whites in the antebellum years, Stephanie McCurry wrote, "Outside the household, lowcountry yeomen and their families were tied into complex social networks that extended from their own settlements of folk mostly like them and their few slaves to the neighborhoods beyond, with far more diverse populations of planter families and slaves, free blacks, poor whites of various kinds, and, of course, the merchants and tradesmen in whose establishments all the locals bumped elbows."[160]

Like the nineteenth-century yeoman families, Purrysburg landholders forged complex relational networks with people quite different from themselves. These networks carried both social and commercial significance and became essential for the vitality of township life. In addition, as the relational webs became more extensive, they served as the entrée through which Purrysburg settlers accessed the wider forces at work in the late colonial Southeast. Unlike

McCurry's families, however, the construction of these networks were not optional, for the contours of their creation and maintenance dictated whether Purrysburg Township would be able to provide the path to communal and commercial success for its immigrant population.

By the 1760s, with rising prosperity due to the expansion of plantation agriculture, Purrysburg landholders had clearly begun to establish multistranded vertical linkages to other regions within South Carolina and Georgia. Financial transactions predominated in the establishment of these interregional connections and bound township citizens to individuals and merchant houses in Charles Town, Savannah, and Beaufort. Legal and economic arrangements among Purrysburg settlers demonstrated, not only the increasing wealth of individuals after 1750, but also the intricate regional relational networks that were firmly established by the time of the Revolution. Some members of the Purrysburg community were able to make the leap to commercial success, and a few achieved a level of financial independence that rivaled the provincial elite.

A precise determination of the role ethnicity played in the maturation of township life is a more difficult matter than tracking Purrysburg's economic development. The current reassessment of white ethnic identity in early America led by scholars such as Bertrand Van Ruymbeke, John F. Bosher, and R. C. Nash has brought forward for reconsideration an issue thought settled decades ago.[161] Concentrating on the experiences of French Huguenot immigrants, a new generation of historians has raised questions and challenged the reigning assimilationist paradigm regarding them. Much of their work centers on what economic factors such as business partnerships and trading connections might reveal about the persistence of Huguenot ethnic identity when other more traditional indicators of ethnicity—such as linguistic fidelity, Calvinist religious affiliation, and endogamous marriage patterns—erode. Although the findings of these and other scholars working in the field are less than conclusive at this point in time, they have generated a renewed examination of strict assimilationist perspectives.[162]

The socioeconomic networks established by Purrysburg landowners provide further evidence of just how complex a matter it is to determine the ways in which white non-English immigrants to South Carolina established and maintained their identity. It is obvious that all Purrysburg Township families of German-speaking or French-speaking ancestry did not retain primary social and economic bonds with those of similar ethnic background over two and one-half generations. Individuals and some families did, however, remain connected in some ways to their European heritage even though the marriage patterns of many township families not uncommonly began to include other ethnic groups quite soon after arrival. The same ethnic affinity occurred in other realms of life, including business and finance, and cannot be overlooked or slighted. A number of families and individuals in Purrysburg appear to have maintained primary social and commercial relationships with those of their own or a closely affiliated ethnic group. The fact that several slaves that had run away from their masters in Purrysburg spoke French and German in addition to three other languages leads credence to the hypothesis that Purrysburg was still at least partially a multilingual community at midcentury.[163] Documents scattered through most of the later colonial period involving Purrysburg immigrants were written in or have notations in French, though the same cannot be said of Germanic township residents. Jacob Barraque, Abraham Jindra, Francis Gabriel Ravot, and Jacob Stroubhart in the 1760s and Margaret Jean Hendrie, Margaret Henrieu (Henriod), Gideon Mallet, and Hannah Mayerhoffer in the 1770s, all exhibited allegiance to their respective cultural traditions in various financial and social transactions. Not only did Henry Lewis Bourguin borrow money with Margaret Chiffelle from a Charles Town merchant company headed by Henry Laurens, but his kinsman John Lewis married the widow and borrowed money from another Charles Town financier, John Guerard, who also happened to be of French Huguenot descent. The business connections between Charles Purry, Samuel Montaigut, and Peter Simond, as well as Simond's sponsorship of Jean Pierre Purry, at least hint at the kinds of financial arrangements noted by Bosher that kept Huguenot refugees linked.[164] Is it more than coincidence that the Huguenot Andrew Fesch, who went into partnership with fellow Huguenot Peter Guinand, received a plat for 800 acres of land in Purrysburg in 1761 or that a large proportion of the intratownship land transfers were between members of the same linguistic groups?[165] And what are we to make of the long-standing professional relationship between David Giroud and Pierre Quinche?

Beyond these tantalizing indications that a European-born ethnicity could still have been operative in the identity formation of at least some of the Purrysburg landholders into the 1770s and 1780s, there are also the physical reminders. Sericulture that employed Purrysburg inhabitants from the early years of settlement and continued even into the early nineteenth century could well have been a material connection to a European heritage. The production of peach brandy in the township might have served a similar function.[166] The ship mill that David Zubly had built in the late 1740s on the Savannah River may have caused him undue economic hardship, but its construction was a direct link to his European homeland, as such mills were common on the Danube River.[167] Very little is known to this day about the brick-lined cistern near the Savannah River in Purrysburg, but, whatever its purpose, the "jugwell" appears to have been a contribution of the eighteenth-century immigrant settlers of the township. Did its construction and use also link the landowners to their heritage? Did the placing of poles in the township cemetery serve the same function?[168] In 1979 Larry Lepionka surmised that the lack of eighteenth-century artifacts at the township site could very well indicate that the Purrysburg settlers exhibited the "fixation on cleanliness, neatness, and order" characteristic of sites occupied by central Europeans but not by British settlers. If Lepionka is correct, the lacuna of physical evidence for the period of highest occupancy in the town of Purrysburg could be among the strongest indicators of an ongoing ethnic identification with the European traditions of the settlers.[169]

It would be careless to overstate the evidence on this point, yet that evidence does leave open the possibility that fluid and shifting ethnic boundaries were maintained among township landowners. Although the apparent existence of selective ethnic behaviors cannot be taken as conclusive, they may very well delineate tendencies evident in the Purrysburg community that merit further historical inquiry.

SEVEN

Wars and Rumors of Wars

The township plan for settlement of the South Carolina borderlands was always preeminently about provincial security, not the welfare of those who inhabited the frontier. Even as the frontier line moved toward the Appalachian Mountains in the 1750s and 1760s, Purrysburg Township continued to serve as a defensive garrison against potential attack from foreign or domestic threats. The paramilitary function of the township constantly reminded residents of their vulnerability on the exposed southern flank of British settlement and ultimately drove even women, children, and old men into a variant of conscripted military service merely because they lived there.

In a very real sense, the twentieth-century sobriquet "total war" describes with uncanny accuracy the nature of life in Purrysburg during the armed conflicts of the eighteenth century. Because colonial officials located the township on the farthest boundary of civilization, violence, or the constant threat of it, conditioned "normative" community life. On this disordered borderland, regular civil intercourse could degenerate into a destructive ferocity untethered to ordinary restraints of law and tradition.[1] Consequently, not only did Purrysburg neighbors suffer from the usual effects of warfare—family separation, death of community members in combat, military occupation, and forced requisition of supplies, but they suffered from them intermittently for the better part of three generations. The pervasive awareness of potential invasion and repeated military engagements contributed their own dynamic to the elastic contours of community life in Purrysburg Township.

A commanding view of the Savannah River from the Great Yamassee Bluff meant that the township could serve as both a surveillance and a naval post, because the river was navigable well past Purrysburg. In addition, the fact that the township existed so close to the edge of the lowcountry tidal zone meant that Purrysburg guarded the most accessible overland routes to and from Spanish Florida—the numerous swamps and inlets between Purrysburg and Savannah being less conducive to successful slave escapes and enemy troop movements than the better drained regions to the immediate north and west of the township.[2] Situated as it was between the major garrison at Savannah twenty-four miles downriver and Forts Palachuccola and Moore ten and sixty miles upriver, respectively, Purrysburg made the need for further fortifications along that stretch of the Savannah River unnecessary and Fort Palachuccola redundant. The Commons House of Assembly deactivated the lightly manned installation in March 1735 and removed its artillery and munitions to the township.[3]

Formation of the émigrés into a company of militia with Purry as colonel in command occurred promptly upon settlement of the township. All male township residents between the ages of sixteen and sixty granted land in Purrysburg were required to muster as members of their assigned company of the South Carolina Rangers at least four times a year. In the event that members of the company did not possess their own muskets, the crown provided arms at its expense and also planned to stockpile extra munitions at the township. The company was assigned regular patrol duty between the Salkehatchee River and Purrysburg.[4] Table 9, panel A, lists those males who received commissions in the militia company, with Purry maintaining command of the garrison until his death in 1736.[5] Panel B lists all the known members of the company in 1756.

TABLE 9: Purrysburg Township Military Personnel

Panel A: Commissioned Officers of the "Regiment of Switzers" at Purrysburg, 1732–41

Name	Date	Rank
Jean Pierre Purry	11 November 1732	Colonel
James Richard	before 11 November 1732	Major
Joseph Edward Flower	19 December 1732	Captain
John Savy (Lavy?)	19 December 1732	Lieutenant
Joseph Edward Flower	n.d. March 1732/33	Lieutenant Colonel
Jemmit Cobley	n.d. March 1732/33	Captain
Frederick (De)Jean	n.d. 1733/34	Brevet Captain
Peter Lafitte	n.d. 1733/34	Lieutenant
Andrew De Monclar	n.d. 1733/34	Lieutenant
Lewis Quinche	n.d. 1734	Undesignated militia commission
(Isaac) Bonijoe	n.d. 1734	Undesignated militia commission
Samuel Montaigut	1738*	Colonel
Frederick Icans (Icaris?)	29 June 1741†	Captain

Panel B: Muster Roll of the Purrysburg Militia Company, 1756[4]

Name	Rank/Function
Jacob Barakey	Militiaman
John. Barakey	Militiaman
Rodn. Bininger	Militiaman

Name	Rank/Function
Henry Lewis Bourguin	Militiaman
John Bourguin	Captain
John Bourguin (Junior?)	Ensn (Ensign?)
Abraham Boyd	Militiaman
Isaac Brabant	Lieutenant
Henry Brandley	Militiaman
John Buche[‡]	Militiaman
Gaspard Clogg	Militiaman
Cornelius Dupont	Militiaman
John Dupont	Militiaman
Anthony Dupres	Alarm man
Abraham Ehrhardt	Militiaman
Francis Ehrhardt	Militiaman
Matthew Fialman	Militiaman
Ulrich Fougg	Militiaman
Jacob Francke	Militiaman
Jacob Frigg	Militiaman
Abraham Gindrat	Alarm man
David Girardin	Militiaman
David Giroud	Militiaman
Jacob Gasman	Militiaman
Matthew Hanspack	Militiaman
David Humbert	Militiaman
John King	Alarm man
Frederick Kueffer	Militiaman
John Lastinger	Militiaman
Melchior Leichtensteiger	Militiaman
John Linder	Militiaman
Henry Henderly Dromer[§]	Militiaman
Daniel Mallett	Militiaman
Gideon Mallett	Alarm man
Daniel Marette	Militiaman
Adrian Mayer	Militiaman
Henry Mayerhoffer	Militiaman
Henry Meuron	Militiaman
George Mingersdorf	Militiaman
John George Mingersdorf	Militiaman
William Page	Militiaman
Andrew Pence	Militiaman
Charles Peters	Militiaman
Melchior Fulker	Militiaman
Mackr. Plowman	Militiaman
Gabriel Ravot	Militiaman

Name	Rank/Function
John Raylinder (John Ray Linder?)	Militiaman
Frederick Rester	Militiaman
Joseph Reymond	Militiaman
Leonard Reynower	Militiaman
Stephen Rhod	Militiaman
David Saussy	Alarm man
George Stroubhart	Militiaman
Nicholas Stroubhart	Militiaman
Stephen Vaigneur	Alarm man
Francis Vauchier	Militiaman
John Walser	Militiaman
Jacob Winkler	Militiaman
Lewis Winkler	Militiaman
Nicholas Winkler	Militiaman
David Wanderly	Militiaman
John Wanderly	Alarm man

Notes: *Montaigut (Montague) is not present on any extant list as an officer, but a land grant he received dated 1 June 1738 gives him the rank of colonel. Earlier grants do not note a military rank. Perhaps because of his business association with Charles Purry he received the rank after the death of the elder Purry in 1736. See Davis, *Some Families* (1926), 35.

†Icans's name was difficult to decipher. There is no record beyond this of a person of this name in the township. The date given is not the date of his commission—that is unknown. It is rather the first mention of his rank. Also by 1741 it appears that the "regiment of Switzers" previously under the command of Purry and then Montaigut had been renamed the Purrysburg Militia Company and came under the regimental command of Colonel H(ugh). Bryan.

‡John Buche became a captain of the militia company by 1765. See Jones, "Report of Mr. Ettewein's Journey," 251.

§Henry Henderly was most likely the *Drummer* for the company.

Sources: Panel A is derived from "The Public to John Hammerton, Esq.," Inventories 1732–1746, microfilm copies, LDS except as noted. Panel B is derived from Robert M. Weir, ed., "The Muster Roles of the South Carolina Granville and Colleton County Regiments of Militia, 1756," *SCHM* 70 (October 1971). In both panels some names have been altered to match their more common spellings.

While the formation of the Purrysburg militia company became the first line of township defense, appropriate fortifications were also of prime importance. By January 1734 the first garrison with twenty-four guns had been constructed, with a second planned by spring.[6] Purry's arbitrary acquisition of Ulisse Albergotti's land for the construction of this or perhaps even a third fort reflects an obvious desire to secure the township and its environs as quickly as possible and clearly indicates that the settlers were aware of their immediate need for military protection.

Unfortunately it was not until 1735 that the Commons House transferred cannons and munitions from Fort Palachuccola to Purrysburg. In a letter to a Swiss correspondent, Jean Baptist Bourguin provided the only physical description of township fortifications: "We have also built a fort of four bastions, with palisades made of trunks of trees, and six pieces of cannon which will enable us to defend ourselves against all those who should attack us."[7]

Bourguin's optimistic assessment of the township's ability to defend itself did not survive the following decade. Settlers lived in constant fear of attack from Spaniards to the south or Native Americans to the immediate north and west. The possibility of slaves escaping to Florida or fomenting insurrection augmented the tense military situation in Purrysburg. Finally in 1743, after an urgent petition of the township inhabitants spurred no doubt by the threat associated with King George's War, the Commons House of Assembly mandated the construction of another fort because the assembly conceded that Purrysburg was "more exposed than any other of the townships [and] deserved more particularly the consideration of the public." In light of the strategic purpose of the township, it is difficult to understand why the Commons House failed to consider it worthy enough to merit a fort funded by public monies before the outbreak of war. Surely Purrysburg's physical isolation could not have created much more anxiety than the realization that the inhabitants remained politically powerless to effect their own defense, even as they were charged with protecting the seat of that power in the lowcountry. It is unknown whether this infusion of provincial funds served to refurbish the fort built in 1734 or to build a second, third, or even a fourth one at another defensible location on the bluff, but, whatever its result, residents could at least take some comfort that their dangerous predicament had been officially recognized. When garrisoned with militiamen, the forts completed the transformation of the region from uninhabited frontier to a significant military outpost dedicated to the defense of South Carolina from all potential enemies.[8]

I

The first few years of Purrysburg's existence were filled with rumors of war with Spain over a variety of grievances. The immigrants spent the entire first decade in a nearly continuous state of alert because of the threats to colonial security posed by the possibility of war. As early as February 1733, Purrysburg served as a bivouac for a military force traveling through the township on its way to defend Georgia.[9] In the summer of 1733, when it was widely thought that the Spanish planned to launch a campaign against Savannah, Purrysburg residents took concrete steps to assist the colony by formally drilling the militia company. By May 1735 the company numbered between 120 and 250 men.[10]

As tensions mounted between Spain and England over boundary disputes and the Spanish charge that England encouraged Indian violence on Spanish colonists, the Duke of Newcastle sent his personal envoy Charles Dempsey as plenipotentiary to attempt a negotiated settlement of outstanding concerns. General Oglethorpe chose Major James Richard of Purrysburg to command the escort party traveling with Dempsey in February 1735/36. On 19 February they set out for St. Augustine, but the boat capsized just off shore before the party reached its destination. The men scrambled to shore through the breakers, saving the boat and some of the baggage. They walked along the beach toward St. Augustine until Captain Dom Pedro Lamberto met them with a detachment of his cavalry. Lamberto conducted Richard, Dempsey, and the rest to the governor, who received them civilly considering the circumstances. The Spaniards repaired the boat and sent the party back to Oglethorpe with letters from the Captain General of Florida Don Francisco del Moral Sanchez and the governor of St. Augustine. Upon his arrival back in Savannah in April 1736, Major Richard told Oglethorpe that the governor expected an answer to the letters within three weeks. Richard expressed his concern that the Spaniards might be plotting to arm the Florida and remaining Yamassee Indians in preparation for attacks on English settlements in the contested Altamaha country.

Oglethorpe sent Richard back to St. Augustine on 13 May with two boats, men, tools, and provisions for three months. Richard also carried Oglethorpe's response to the letters by the Spanish authorities. The arms and ammunition carried by Richard's party were ostensibly to assist the Spaniards in maintaining peace, appeasing the Indians, and suppressing troublemakers. To do so, Oglethorpe charged the group with patrolling the St. Johns River region. When Richard arrived at the agreed-upon rendezvous point no one met him. He waited for a few days, but wanting to convey Oglethorpe's response within the three week deadline, Richard and another member of the party (Horton, the second in command) worked out a plan for the latter officer to travel overland to St. Augustine to inform the governor of Richard's arrival. Two days later Richard crossed the river but found the Spaniards much less hospitable than they had been on his previous visit. They accompanied Richard to his destination while the rest of his party waited on the other side of the river. A few days later one of the English boats went across to the Spanish and returned with a message in German said by the Spaniards to have been written by Richard to Horton. The note contained nothing of importance, but the English surmised that both Richard and Horton been taken prisoner. At this point Oglethorpe left Savannah for St. Augustine after apprising Purrysburg landowner and engineer Samuel Augspourger (Augsperger) of his military responsibilities in Oglethorpe's absence.

Just as the situation appeared to be escalating out of control, Horton reappeared back at Frederica on 14 June. Horton declared that he and Richard had been received cordially by the governor of Florida and had presented Oglethorpe's reply to him. One evening, as they waited for the governor's response, Horton and Richard were invited to go dancing at the home of a Spanish official. They stayed until 3:00 A.M. and returned to their quarters. The next morning the pair was accused of taking a plan of St. Augustine and of its castle. They were placed under house arrest and interrogated by the governor. He questioned both men about the size of the garrison and strength of the fortifications at Frederica. He threatened Horton with banishment to the Spanish mines if he did not cooperate. In the meantime, Spanish soldiers reconnoitered the area and discovered that the English had fortified the nearby islands and populated them with armed men. Authorities called a council of war and resolved to send Richard, Horton, and the rest of the party back to Georgia with letters professing friendship and encouraging civil relations between the two countries. The release of Richard's party coincided with Spain's desire to reach a peaceful solution to this particular crisis. Prior to the men's return, however, Purrysburg citizens were pressed into service to help construct fortifications for Savannah in preparation for war between the two imperial powers.[11]

Ironically, after years of anticipating war with Spain, it was an internal revolt—the Stono Rebellion—that furnished the first real test of military preparedness for the Purrysburg militia company. The Spanish governor's promise of freedom to all slaves who escaped to Florida may have been the precipitating cause of the bloody insurrection given the debilitating character of chattel slavery. What excited township fears was the recognition that the main route to St. Augustine crossed the Savannah River very near Purrysburg. When word of the rebellion first reached Governor Stephens of Georgia on 13 September 1739, he immediately contacted Samuel Montaigut, a member of the Purrysburg militia, recommending that guards be posted at the site of old Fort Palachuccola and at all the passes in and around Purrysburg. The township militia company assembled and a contingent under the command of Captain John Frederick Holzendorf pursued runaway slaves. When Oglethorpe arrived at the fort less than a week later, he found thirty other Purrysburg militiamen standing watch to capture any slaves crossing the Savannah River. Though quickly suppressed, the slave revolt galvanized the white minority of South Carolina against the slave population. Member of the Commons House John Fenwicke supported the idea of giving cash rewards to those who helped quell the uprising. He proposed a fifty-pound bounty for each slave brought in alive and a twenty-five-pound bounty for each dead slave. Fenwicke hoped that these rewards would encourage the southern Indians and the people of Purrysburg, among others, to maintain their vigilance in apprehending escaped slaves. Perhaps as a reflection of the fear of a race war in the province, the Purrysburg militia remained on guard for an entire month after the end of the Stono Rebellion—which probably meant that families in the township lived in mortal fear of their own slaves. Although the Purrysburg militia saw only minor action during the crisis, the part it did play reinforced the strategic importance of the frontier settlement to South Carolina's internal defense network.[12]

The Stono Rebellion was inseparably linked in the minds of most to the Spanish threat, but Robert Walpole kept England out of war with Spain until 1739 and the War of Jenkins' Ear (1739–1748). When this conflict crossed the Atlantic as King George's War, Purrysburg experienced its first general alert as a frontier outpost against a foreign enemy. Even before the outbreak of formal hostilities, Purrysburg settlers assembled from their plantations to practice drilling and to hear orders for the township from Charles Town regarding preparations for an imminent Spanish attack. Georgia's General Oglethorpe called for volunteers to serve under him in a preemptive strike against the Spanish at St. Augustine in 1740. He was confident of securing "fifty very good men at Purrysburg" to augment his cavalry if South Carolina would consent to pay them. Captain John Linder and Sergeant Roech (Reck) of the township acted as recruiting officers for the operation.[13] In a letter to South Carolina officials from his camp before St. Augustine, Oglethorpe requested more troops for the siege and mentioned especially the Purrysburg settler Mr. [John Frederick] Holzendorf, who "has a very good interest, and is very proper to be employed" to raise more recruits. The Prussian immigrant Holzendorf had received a lieutenant's commission in the Purrysburg militia and commanded fifty South Carolina militiamen at Fort Palachuccola during the war.[14]

Purrysburg landowner Captain [Peter] Laffitte also recruited enlistees for the expedition from the township and adjacent areas. He commanded the whole company of the "Highland Foot" and a detachment of 250 private men of the Carolina regiment. Captain James Richard also led a company composed solely of Purrysburg recruits in the siege of St. Augustine. It was said that he found so many willing militiamen in Purrysburg that the whole town followed him "leaving only women and children with a few old men to keep possessions at home so that he had a surplus to spare towards forming the other [Laffitte's] company." Although there are no precise figures on total Purrysburg participation in King George's War, extant evidence including militia strength and arms shipments to the township indicates extensive involvement. Oglethorpe's ill-conceived foray into Spanish Florida failed in the wake of the debacle at Fort Moosa, but the South Carolina township plan of defense succeeded in barring any Spanish invasion of the colony from the south.[15]

Because community members left no record of personal response to the conflict, only general comments with regard to its effects are possible. Certainly the wartime recession adversely affected living standards in the township. Family structure and function were graphically rearranged as husbands and fathers, brothers and sons left for the war and mothers assumed the role of provider and protector, as well as the traditional role of nurturer. Young children, male and female, assumed adult roles in the crisis environment, which caused a significant reordering of traditional childhood activities. Older citizens filled positions of leadership in an attempt to carry on "business as usual" as much as that was possible in a potential combat zone.

The crisis also exacerbated tensions between Purrysburg and Ebenezer. Recruits to the expeditionary force, by one estimate reaching nearly 500 men, bivouacked at the township before leaving for Florida. Their presence contributed to "great disorder" according to one observer.[16] The redoubtable Jacob Reck, a noncommissioned officer and recruiter, enlisted at least ten Ebenezer Germans by April 1740, including Mr. Zant, who was almost completely blind, and the tubercular Johann Christ, but he was not the only township resident to pressure Ebenezer settlers to join the war effort. The Reverend Boltzius's patience began to wear thin by early May when a letter he wrote to Richard regarding what he believed had been the inappropriate recruitment of an Ebenezer herdsman remained unanswered. The pastor decided to contact Oglethorpe directly, who appears to have secured the herdsman's release. This incident, however, may have been the occasion for the attempted impressment by Richard and others of one of the Reverend Gronau's oarsmen. As they were tying him up, one of Richard's men was seized and declared a hostage until the rower was released. Savannah authorities interceded, and both men were freed. After a cluster of complaints, Oglethorpe expressed his frustration with the way Purrysburg recruiters went about their work. Their methods did nothing to facilitate amicable relationships with their neighbors in these Georgia towns.[17]

During the 1750s, Purrysburg continued to serve as a frontier outpost and maintained its militia company ready to meet internal or external threats to provincial security. In his March 1750/51 enumeration of armaments in South Carolina, Governor James Glen singled out only six sites for specific mention. He wrote to the Lords Commissioners of Trade and Plantations, "There are in Charles Town above 100 pieces of cannon 9, 12, and 18 pounders: about 36 at Ft. Johnson, 10 or 12 at Ft. Frederick, at Ft. Moore, Winyaw, Purrysburg, and the lookouts a few each."[18] Less than three months after Glen's survey and perhaps in response to it, the Commons House on 14 May authorized the establishment of a fourth troop of South Carolina Rangers "for the security of the Southern settlements about Purrysburg and the Salkeche's." The troop was to include twenty men besides the officers. The Commons House agreed to "make provision for defraying the cost of this troop" and sent the proposal up to the council, which it hoped would agree "to recommend it to the Governor."[19] The desire for an augmentation of troop strength on the southern frontier in all likelihood proceeded from the loss of Purrysburg militiamen through out-migration from the township and the high mortality rates apparent during the 1730s and 1740s. A petition bearing a 1743 date declared that the militia company stood at seventy men, a substantial decline in number since the mid-1730s. An enumeration of the company in 1756 listed only sixty-four members, less than half of its initial strength of two decades earlier. A quarter century after its founding, the township community still enclosed a significant population, but one that had seen its numbers decline precipitously.[20]

The Spanish defeat by 1748 greatly diminished the threat from that quarter. By midcentury, conventional wisdom among white South Carolinians regarded the internal dangers from their red and black neighbors a more immediate threat to provincial security than an attack from any external enemy, even though the French gained influence and courted allies from the indigenous population. For this and other reasons, Native Americans continued to excite fears as white encroachment pinned them against the piedmont. In 1750 and 1751 small bands of Shawnee, Iroquois, and Cherokee warriors initiated a series of strikes throughout the province, some of them taking place near Charles Town and Beaufort. It was most likely one of these raiding parties that killed Purrysburg resident John Linder at Palachuccola. Black slaves, particularly in the wake of the Stono Rebellion and because of their constantly mounting numbers in the colony, received considerable attention. Yet it was the imperial connection and international rivalries that ultimately plunged South Carolina into its next great armed conflict involving both foreign and domestic enemies.[21]

The French and Indian War (1754–1763) marked the culmination of French empire building in the New World. The general turmoil of the war was confined to areas far to the north of the Carolinas, but Purrysburg was again placed on alert when the Cherokee War ensued in 1759–1760. The township remained relatively distant from the fighting, but at least fifteen Purrysburg males participated in the expedition to Fort Prince George from October 1759 to January 1760 under Colonel Singleton and Captain MacPherson of the Granville County Regiment.[22] Purrysburg also experienced directly the dislocations of the war because it served as a refuge for those fleeing the upheavals in the middle and backcountry regions. Jacqueline Young notes that German-speaking refugees from Saxe-Gotha chose Purrysburg as one of their destinations and remained there until the cessation of hostilities.[23] The influx of refugees and troop movements along the Savannah River and via the overland routes, which passed through or near Purrysburg, brought the war home to residents of the township. In this conflict Purrysburg and the settlements even closer to the frontier continued to serve the purpose first envisioned for them in the 1730s. Kaylene Hughes may be overly generous to colonial authorities, but her observations accurately underscore the contexts of settlement in Purrysburg and other frontier habitations as they faced the coming revolutionary era:

> Unlike earlier attempts at expansion, the settlements established on the South Carolina frontier during the thirty years preceding the Cherokee War were able to withstand the upheaval and destruction in the 1760s because backcountry society (despite its lack of cohesiveness) was firmly entrenched before its troubles began. Provincial and royal officials had provided the necessary support to attract colonists to the backcountry while frontier residents had provided the fortitude, determination, and hard work necessary to ensure the success of their settlements. Even after the severe dislocations of the Indian War and its attendant problems, the backcountry basically remained the buffer zone envisioned by Robert Johnson and other colonial leaders.[24]

II

The 1763 Peace of Paris ended the French threat to colonial security but cast England in an adversarial role. Mutual recriminations and acts of violence that punctuated the ensuing twelve years intensified antagonisms and resulted in the severing of the bonds of empire in the War of the American Revolution, 1775–1783. Paradoxically, the township plan for colonial defense initiated by royal authorities to protect South Carolina as the king's possession now formed, at least partially, the basis of an American strategy for defending the Southeast against Great Britain. Because of its critical location, Purrysburg played a significant role as a defensive garrison against the very power that had brought it into being more than forty years earlier, but the nearly constant military activity in the township drastically altered township community life and ultimately turned neighbor against neighbor.

As soon as word of Lexington and Concord reached Charles Town, the colony took measures to break all ties with Great Britain and prepare for the coming conflagration. The South Carolina Association, the first independent, revolutionary government in the colonies, began functioning on 4 June 1775. Soon after, on 14 June 1775, the South Carolina Council of Safety was established and assumed control of all military matters serving as the de facto executive branch of government.[25] Because of the advance of the settlement line, Purrysburg in the 1770s was not the frontier outpost it had been at midcentury. Nonetheless, the same strategically significant geographical characteristics that determined its location in the 1730s were still operative during the revolutionary era and ensured that both the township and its people would play a pivotal role in the War. St. Peter's Parish sent six of its residents to the meetings of the Provincial Congress in Charles Town. Of the six elected to attend the First Congress on 11 January 1775, three (Cornelius Dupont, his son Gideon, and Philotheus Chiffelle) had close ties to Purrysburg. The other three members (Colonel Stephen Bull, William Williamson, and Thomas Middleton) were all members of the lowcountry elite with land in or near the township. Both Gideon Dupont and Philotheus Chiffelle were elected to the Second Provincial Congress from St. Peter's, which began its deliberations in Charles Town on 1 November 1775. Chiffelle was appointed a commissioner of the Congress on 16 November and assumed extensive authority with his fellow commissioners over the financial affairs of the province. The parish quickly organized its own committee of the Continental Association and carried on direct communication with the Council of Safety headquartered at Charles Town concerning matters of regional security. Members of the committee of the Continental Association for St. Peter's Purrysburg included Cornelius Dupont, John Lewis Bourguin, James Thompson, John Chisolme, Adrian Mayer, John Buche Sr., and Charles Dupont.[26]

Perhaps the most crucial function of the township's committee at this early stage of the Revolution proceeded from its surveillance of the Savannah River to seize contraband embargoed by the Continental Association. Citing the rise in illegal trade between colonies, the president of the Second Council of Safety at Charles Town, Henry Laurens, sternly charged the committee for St. Peter's (Purrysburg) to "watch for this illicit traffic and stop it if happening." Laurens further ordered the committee to seize the vessels, detain the culpable parties, and impound the cargoes until it received further instructions.[27] In another communiqué, he admonished Purrysburg settlers to do their best to thwart the efforts of enemy foraging parties seeking provisions for the British warships the *Tamar* and the *Cherokee* rumored to be upriver from Cockspur in the vicinity of the township. In the same letter, Laurens urged members of the Purrysburg committee to conduct Lord William Campbell, the fugitive royal governor of South Carolina, safely to Charles Town should he arrive at his plantation, assuring them that they would be indemnified by the council for their efforts.[28]

Besides functioning as an appendage of the central Council of Safety at Charles Town, the Purrysburg committee also initiated proceedings against those in its midst considered "bad risks" in a war with Great Britain. This duty, of course, drew the arc of community along strictly political lines and did not limit itself to overtly treasonous behavior. That the Purrysburg committee took its responsibilities seriously is borne out in a letter sent by the committee to the Charles Town Council of Safety dated 16 December 1775. The letter detailed the unseemly behavior of three residents of the neighborhood: Adrian Mayer, James Gignilliat, and James Brisbane. All three had been accused of "open and obstinate opposition to measures which we [the Council] are pursuing with a view to their interest in common with the interests of their fellow-subjects in America." This reference probably alludes to reluctance on the part of the trio to adhere to export restrictions. The letter appears to have asked for some direction as to the appropriate course of action toward the accused. The gravity of the situation in Purrysburg moved the council to forward the letter immediately to the highest executive body in the state for its deliberation. The General Committee was then summoned specifically to consider the matter. Brisbane had already run afoul of the committee at an earlier date and had been disciplined accordingly. Although his punishment is not mentioned, the Purrysburg committee was reminded that it would be indemnified "in all acts under the resolutions and orders of Congress," which probably signifies imprisonment. As to Mayer and Gignilliat, the Purrysburg authorities were directed to incarcerate them in the local jail or send them to Charles Town should they continue their suspicious conduct. The council entrusted "Mr. Dupont" (most likely Gideon Dupont of St. Peter's) with its reply to Purrysburg, but this communiqué was never delivered and may have been intercepted by the enemy. The second message did reach its destination, communicating both the council's ruling on the matter and its hope that the Purrysburg committee would diligently continue its patrol of the Savannah River guarding against any further traitorous incidents.[29]

Loyalist opposition remained a significant concern both in the township and throughout South Carolina. The province contained a large loyalist population, especially in the backcountry, from the onset of war in 1775. Loyalists in the state gave the revolution a distinctly partisan flavor and hampered the patriot cause throughout the war years. Numerous attempts were made to pacify loyalists, but they remained fifth columnists—even fighting for the Americans when faced with imprisonment. Loyalist participation in the war served to confuse the distinctions between friend and enemy, and Purrysburg was no less vulnerable to this disruption of community life than more populous areas. Loyalism stretched the web of community relationships to limits previously untested by two generations of township settlers.[30]

The first recorded contact between Purrysburg and a revolutionary military force other than the resident militia company occurred on or near 10 August 1775, when the Council of Safety ordered three companies of rangers and militia to march "by Orangeburgh to the Three Runs, thence down Savannah River to Purrysburg, thence to Pon Pon, and downward by the high Road." This early movement of troops was in all likelihood meant to be a demonstration of revolutionary power to discourage loyalist sentiment in the colony. It may have also been an attempt to reconnoiter strategic areas for defensive purposes as well as an opportunity to begin military maneuvers with South Carolina militia companies. Whatever its overt purposes, the sight of soldiers marching past their homes and plantations brought back memories of earlier conflicts to older Purrysburg settlers and must have created a sense of the imminence of the present conflict.[31]

Soon after the 10 August march through the township, the circumstances of war sent another military contingent to Purrysburg on a mission for the Council of Safety at Savannah. In a letter to its sister council in Charles Town, this body requested the immediate assistance of 200 men and repayment of some gunpowder loaned to Beaufort to meet an anticipated attack by the enemy. Laurens and the Charles Town Council responded quickly and ordered Colonel Bull to march with 200 men—more if possible—to Purrysburg and from there to cross the Savannah River to relieve the city. Further orders for the force were to be forwarded from the Savannah Council, which was to meet the detachment at Purrysburg. Sent by water from Beaufort to Brisbane's Landing on New River, the 2,000 pounds of gunpowder were loaded on wagons for the overland trip to the township. The successful relocation of this war material meant that, before the American Revolution was nine months old, Purrysburg had already been involved in military and civil matters upon which hinged the early security of the southern theater of war.[32] During the opening months of the War of the Revolution, Purrysburg functioned exactly as Gee, Barnwell, and Johnson envisioned it would nearly half a century before—as an outpost township guarding the southern flank of South Carolina—but it was not until major armies were committed to the defense of the southern region that the community was thrown fully into the eye of the revolutionary storm. As early as August 1776, a major army entered Purrysburg when General Charles Lee, then commanding the Southern Department of the Continental Army, encamped there on his return to Virginia in September after the failure of his attempt to dislodge the British under Major General Augustine Prevost from Florida.[33] After this brief encounter, Purrysburg and its immediate environs remained relatively free of major military operations for nearly three years, though troops did continue to march through St. Peter's Parish.

III

The northern states bore the brunt of British military power over the second and third years of war. By 1778, however, British strategy shifted from north to south. The British believed Georgia to be the "soft underbelly" of the colonies in rebellion. If Georgia's defenses could be overcome, it and neighboring South Carolina could be pacified. The recaptured colonies would then be able to supply the valuable West Indian sugar-producing islands with food and supplies. On 8 March 1778, British commander in chief Sir Henry Clinton received orders from King George III's secretary of war, Lord George Germain, to launch a southern offensive. Clinton's choice to spearhead the southern strategy with an invasion of Georgia at Savannah was Lieutenant Colonel Archibald Campbell. It took eight months for Clinton to dispatch Campbell from New York to Savannah with 3,000 men. In the meantime, American general Robert Howe, who had replaced Lee as the commander of the Southern Department, gathered intelligence that gauged Campbell's troop strength at 10,000. With his skeleton force of only 700, many of whom were untried militia recruits, Howe wrote to Brigadier General Moultrie from Zubly's Ferry, near Purrysburg Township, regarding his need for more troops and ammunition if Savannah was to be saved. Howe proceeded down the river to engage the British force hoping that reinforcements would reach him in time. They did not. After successfully crossing the Savannah River bar, the first British troops landed at the Girardeau plantation on the morning of 29 December. Rather than retreating back up the river toward Purrysburg to meet the forces gathering in South Carolina, Howe decided to engage Campbell. In the ensuing battle, more than three-quarters of the American force was killed or captured, and all artillery and support vehicles were lost. Savannah fell and, with Prevost's march northward from Florida in support of the Georgia campaign, Sunbury soon followed. Governor Houstoun, who had fled toward Purrysburg as Howe retreated, was captured just south of the township along with Jonathan Bryan at Bryan's South Carolina Union plantation. Georgia once more became part of the empire, and most in the Georgia lowcountry took the oath of allegiance to the king, with Georgia loyalists joining the British cause.[34] The loss of Georgia and the massive recruitment of loyalists meant that "South Carolina became an American march province with active enemies along its southern and western frontiers," much as it had been more than forty-five years earlier at the founding of the township that was destined to serve once again as a military outpost.[35]

As Howe and the remnant American force fled before the enemy advance, Purrysburg became a rallying point for troops. Close to 500 South Carolina regulars were stationed at or near the township by the fall of 1778. The British Georgia strategy incited fear of pending disaster among South Carolinians and generated a realignment in the upper echelons of military leadership. Congress relieved Howe of his command and, in his place, named Major General Benjamin Lincoln of Massachusetts as the chief Continental officer in the Southern Department.

Lincoln arrived at Charles Town on 19 December 1778—just ten days before the fall of Savannah—but found only 1,500 men ready to move southward. His army grew to 3,500 after the militia assembled. Lincoln then marched to Purrysburg to join troops already at that post. The township was to remain the headquarters of Lincoln's command from 3 January to late March 1779, and even later for his lieutenants. Quickly grasping the significance of Purrysburg's location and convinced of its utility as a center of operations, Lincoln encamped at the southeastern edge of town on the Great Yamassee Bluff and issued a series of orders immediately upon in his arrival meant to secure his command and protect Purrysburg citizens and their property.[36] Over the next few days, Lincoln had guards posted at the lower end of Purrysburg with orders to detain all boats traveling down the river without a pass from headquarters and ordered several detachments of troops to possible crossing sites up and down the Savannah near Purrysburg, including Zubly's Ferry, just north of the town proper and across from Abercorn, Georgia, four miles downriver from the town. With this deployment, Lincoln effectively "occupied" Purrysburg and, for all intents and purposes, turned the township into a military post from 3 January into early spring. Estimates of his total troop strength at Purrysburg headquarters at any one time vary from 1,200 to nearly 4,000, but, for the duration of his encampment at the township, the post probably contained 3,400–3,700 men. The troops bivouacked at the township included light horse, artillery, naval, and infantry units of the Continental line and militia companies of many states, including both the Carolinas. The army also maintained a "flying hospital" at Purrysburg. A "fixed hospital" was set up nearby at Heyward's plantation. In addition to the presence of such a large military force—by far the largest ever stationed at the township—Purrysburg families also had to confront the associated problems of Georgia refugees, camp followers, and the incursions of British spies and raiding parties based on the Georgia side of the Savannah River.[37]

Lincoln established his headquarters at Purrysburg because of its critical position. The river road from Purrysburg up the Savannah helped keep supply and communication lines open with the South Carolina backcountry, thereby lessening fear of Indian or loyalist attack in that isolated sector, and the position of the enemy in January 1779 indicated clearly that the Purrysburg–Charles Town road was the quickest, most direct route to the capital for the British armies. In addition to these factors, Purrysburg was located at a logical crossing point on the Savannah River. Moreover, as Lincoln entertained hopes of eventually mounting an offensive into Georgia to drive out the British, Purrysburg represented a defensible redoubt from which such an invasion could be successfully launched.[38]

The commander, however, remained continually frustrated in his desire to regain Georgia. The basic problems he faced in his drive to capture it for the United States—disregard for military discipline, lack of sufficient recruits and supplies, poor military intelligence, questionable field command decisions, and continued enemy harassment—adversely affected not just the American cause but also Purrysburg civilians, radically altering the context of their daily lives. In a very real sense, the entire township lost control of its collective destiny when Lincoln arrived.

No doubt the most traumatic immediate effect of so large a military force on the daily lives of Purrysburg settlers resulted from the widespread and flagrant disregard for military discipline displayed by the troops. Lincoln was regularly provoked by the careless attitudes of the soldiers stationed at Purrysburg and especially by the conduct of the South Carolina militia units. From the very beginning of his tenure as commander of the Southern Department, he complained of the militia's reluctance to take orders and its shoddy performance under fire.[39] Added to his frustration with the militia's caliber of service was his inability to discipline soldiers adequately. Supported by an earlier resolution of Congress, Lincoln had assumed that the militia was to be placed under his personal command. He soon discovered, however, that the South Carolina militia units not only refused to be put at his disposal, but also that the militia troops could not even be tried according to Continental Army procedures. Rather, the chief executive of South Carolina (John Rutledge) held sole authority in matters of military reprimand of the militia. Obviously perturbed by this situation Lincoln wrote bitterly, "Do the militia think that the continental officers have lost all ideas of the citizen—have a separate interest and therefore ought to be avoided?—or from what does this passion [illegible] spring? If I knew I would remove it if in my power for it does not require a prophetic mind to foretell that the worst consequences may ensue."[40] Even the Continental Congress failed to back Lincoln in this affair.[41] The disciplinary problems issuing from such dual jurisdiction severely hampered Lincoln's military authority and consequently weakened American defenses against the British. Needless to say, the command confusion carried with it some distinct implications for Purrysburg families.

The military courts-martial conducted while Lincoln encamped at Purrysburg illuminate both the magnitude of disciplinary problems and the variety of ways in which the lack of discipline threatened the security of the Purrysburg community. Of the nearly continuous string of courts-martial ordered by Lincoln during his stay at Purrysburg and at nearby Black Swamp, the vast majority involved charges of desertion, which remained the most serious problem throughout the war. Of these cases many of the alleged acts of desertion occurred while the defendants were intoxicated. Thirsty soldiers may have enriched the coffers of township innkeepers, but they undoubtedly also caused not a little concern for the rest of the population.[42]

Some of the courts-martial bore even more directly upon life in Purrysburg. Theft and fraud arrived via the military as illustrated by the case of Baswell Brown of Captain Smith's Company, Third South Carolina Regiment, and Matthew Griffin. Griffin, formerly of Georgia but then a refugee resident of Purrysburg, had engaged Brown to shave his beard and groom his hair. While Brown was doing so, Griffin produced a blue handkerchief containing a substantial amount of Georgia currency from which he paid Brown. Griffin alleged that, about half an hour after Brown had finished the job, he discovered that both the handkerchief and rest of the money were gone. He immediately went to the commander of Brown's regiment and asked that Brown be apprehended. Major Wise sent a contingent of men to search for the suspect. Members of this detachment testified that they found Brown, but he denied that he was the person they sought. As the soldiers were in the process of searching him, Brown suddenly bolted, dashed through a Purrysburg dwelling, and slipped away. Private John Priest of the search party reconnoitered the home through which Brown had fled and found "a sum of money tied up in a handkerchief." Griffin heard of the find and claimed it as his own. Other witnesses testified that Brown had paid them the same day as Griffin reported his money missing. At least one of the men was paid with Georgia money. Private William Courtney of the Third South Carolina Regiment stated that before Brown shaved Griffin he lamented that he "had not enough money to buy a dram [of spirits]." But two hours after Brown left Griffin, he had plenty of money. Ironically, it was Griffin who finally cornered Brown in "an old tavern in the town" at about eight in the evening. The court found Brown guilty of the charge and sentenced him to run the gauntlet twice through the brigade. In addition to this current charge, Brown, whose commanding officer described him as "indifferent," had been previously convicted and whipped for another theft.[43]

As the commanding officer of the post, General Lincoln reviewed Brown's case and sentence as he did all others and discovered an inescapable infraction of military law in the judgment. Though condemning Brown's actions as reprehensible, Lincoln could not approve the sentence, because it was "vague and uncertain and may greatly exceed 100 stripes, the highest corporal punishment allowed by the Rules and Articles for the better Government of the Army." He urged the court to reconsider the penalty, but the two parties deadlocked. The resulting impasse forced Lincoln's hand. Although he condemned Brown's criminal behavior, Lincoln also zealously guarded the rights of the troops under law. The general chose to return the convicted thief to duty.[44]

Failure of the military authorities to chastise Brown must have come as a rude awakening to Purrysburg civilians. If the military would not police itself, what further crimes against the landowners might go unpunished? Could this ruling—no matter how just it might be with regard to military jurisprudence—cause others to take advantage of the civilian population, which they so vastly outnumbered? Surely the heightened fear of theft, invasion of privacy, criminal trespass, and other crimes caused more than a little consternation among all but the innkeepers, who continued to do a banner business.

While the court-martial of Baswell Brown illustrates the economic and legal repercussions of military occupation (and the problem of refugees with money!), the curious trial of Sergeant Joseph Grimes of the light infantry demonstrates its social implications. On 24 February 1779 Grimes faced a general court-martial, accused of "dressing himself up like a girl and being out of camp after retreat beating." The court found Grimes guilty of both charges and sentenced him to "be reduced to the ranks and reprimanded at the head of the brigade to which he belongs."[45] One can only surmise the rationale for Grimes's behavior, but the possibility of a rendezvous with a female resident of Purrysburg lies not beyond the realm of possibility. (How else would he have occasion to procure female clothing on duty during wartime?) In any event, the reason for the act is not as compelling as the act itself, for—whether Grimes tried to sneak off for a romantic interlude with a Purrysburg woman or to desert in a novel manner—each possibility had ramifications for the social fabric of the Purrysburg community in ways that would not have been the case had it not been the scene of a major military encampment. Neither Grimes's motive nor the effect of this incident had on the community is recorded, but it does demonstrate another way the presence of the military affected the township.

Lincoln's problem with undisciplined conduct among the troops did not manifest itself solely in general courts-martial trials. From the beginning of his tenure at Purrysburg, the commander discovered a regular pattern of noncompliance with his directives, and, when his orders were disregarded by the soldiers, so also were the rights of civilians. The 3 January communiqué he issued to his officers, for example, clearly revealed his expectation that the protection of the lives and property of Purrysburg families was to be a high priority.[46] Lincoln's simultaneous order requiring the regimental quartermasters to supply wood to their respective detachments on a daily basis sought to alleviate the temptation for the men to demolish fences for firewood. A few days later, however, Lincoln discovered that his orders had been widely disregarded and that many Purrysburg families were without fences to pen their livestock. Once again, the general expressly forbade such destruction of private property and determined that "any person found sitting by a fire made of rails shall be answerable for the same punishment as the offender."[47] Perhaps this somewhat more pointed order had more the desired effect, for no further mention of this particular offense is noted. A more pessimistic but equally plausible interpretation, however, would be that no further infractions were reported because no fence posts or rails remained in the vicinity. In any event, serious damage had already been done to a number of Purrysburg residents. Losses of livestock and other property incurred in this manner remain uncounted in the records, but from the beginning Purrysburg families had reason to fear their own army as well as the enemy's.

Lincoln aimed another directive at the distinctly unmilitary practice of discharging firearms for no apparent reason.[48] But almost a month after issuing the order, nothing had changed.[49] It may have been disobedience of the order to cease firing weapons that caused the accidental shooting death of a soldier on 15 February. To make matters worse, hundreds of deserting militiamen took government issued ammunition with them, making a munitions shortage even more acute.[50] In this matter again, Lincoln's desire to keep the military from disrupting the civilian population of Purrysburg failed.[51]

His discouraging experience with the troops at this post moved Lincoln to admonish one of his lieutenants at another station not to let his troops mistreat the inhabitants. In an almost desperate tone he continued, "They must be prevented from plundering even the Tories for when permitted to plunder in any degree there is no restraining them."[52] The general's situation was so poor that many of his troops had to be bribed with rum to stay in camp.[53] In light of Lincoln's aggravation with the behavior of his troops, one can but guess at the unrecorded crimes against the citizens of Purrysburg committed by unruly patriots in their midst.

It should be noted, however, that General Lincoln also demonstrated that actions disruptive to Purrysburg community life were not only the domain of his subordinates. On one occasion he ordered that "all carcasses and filth in and about camp are to be thrown into the river or buried." This directive countermanded a Georgia law that prohibited the throwing of rubbish, ballast, or felled trees into the river because such materials might cause navigation hazards.[54]

Lincoln also regularly required the firing of all guns that could not be drawn in the evening before retreat beating. A few weeks prior to the waste disposal order, Lincoln precipitated perhaps the most extensive noncombat discharge of weapons in Purrysburg. On 26 January, after several days of rain and subsequent fire by British troops across the Savannah, the American troops were ordered to discharge all guns and cannon. In a letter to Colonel Pinckney, General Moultrie quipped, "I dare say the people within ten miles of this place, thought we were engaged."[55] It is certainly understandable that in these situations Lincoln acted in the best interests of the patriot cause. It is also granted that the demands of war create their own environments, which are often not subject to the norms of peace. Ridding the camp of rotting waste no doubt aided morale and impeded the outbreak of disease among the troops. The supervised firing weapons in camp kept them in good repair and assured the enemy that rain had not ruined either American gunpowder or resolve. Nonetheless, in creating these extraordinary environments, Lincoln further traumatized the civilian residents of Purrysburg Township, demonstrating just how powerless they were in time of war.

IV

If the most immediate psychosocial disruptions for Purrysburg settlers proceeded from the widespread lack of discipline among the soldiers, the most materially disturbing effects resulted from the number of soldiers garrisoned at the township and the lack of supplies afforded them. Lincoln was not only disappointed with the actions of his troops but was also exasperated by what he perceived to be their inadequate numbers and their lack of proper provisions and equipment. In a letter to General Washington, Lincoln wrote in early February that he had expected to have more than 7,000 men at his command. With only about half that number at Purrysburg, he believed that the size of his force actually jeopardized the safety of both the South Carolina backcountry and his supply and communications lines.[56] In an earlier message to Washington, sent just a few days after his arrival at Purrysburg, Lincoln expressed his frustration with the lack of munitions and military stores. Instead of the promised abundance of both, the general found "no field pieces, arms, tents, camp utensils, lead, and very little powder."[57] His requests for reinforcements and additional supplies went unanswered for weeks, and he received little support from suspicious South Carolina authorities.[58] Toward the end of January, a contingent of 1,100 North Carolina militiamen arrived under the command of General Ashe, but supplying the men at Purrysburg remained a major headache for Lincoln throughout the duration of his time at the township. The provisioning of troops proved to be such a burden that, when Lincoln heard of the intended resignation of Commissary General Valentine, he appealed directly to him not to leave the post at this critical moment. His personal appeal failed to keep Valentine in office.[59]

In light of the demands of the situation, General Lincoln moved to use the most easily accessible resources available for military use—the private property of the citizens of Purrysburg. By a resolution of Congress, military leaders were given the authority, if approved by state officials, to acquire "suitable supplies" if they were not readily available at reasonable prices.[60] Consequently, Lincoln and his subordinates impressed wagons, horses, cattle, sheep, hogs, grain, and any other necessary supplies from the surrounding settlers for the use of the armed forces. Even after the general moved his headquarters to defend Charles Town after the British invaded South Carolina, the practice of impressment continued so that, by the end of the war, numerous Purrysburg families filed claims to gain recompense for property that had been requisitioned by the army. An analysis of the audited accounts of these claims listed in table 10 illustrates the tangible ways in which Purrysburg citizens were called to sacrifice for the war effort and demonstrates the impact of warfare upon the economic life of the township. Signed depositions by the confiscating officers assured the owners that their losses would be reimbursed by the United States government. They could not, however, guarantee the existence of a United States government after the war. Nor could they guarantee that the reimbursement, if paid, would be paid at the prevailing market value of the commodities impressed, because as much as ten years elapsed between the time of the actual confiscation and filing of claims to the processing of the claims and final disbursement of funds.[61]

TABLE 10: Value of Revolutionary War Claims of Purrysburg Landowners

Panel A: French-Surnamed Claimants

Claimant	Approximate Value of Claims (pounds sterling)
David Giroud	2
Abraham Ravot	4
Jane Donnam Bourguin	9
Philip Christian	14
David Buche	16
Abraham Binninger	21
John L. and Benjamin Buche	32
Gideon Mallet	35
Abraham Gindrat	36
Henry Gindrat	80
John Baptiste Bourguin	84
David Saussy	105
David Mongin	139
Colonel John L. Bourguin	1,543
Cornelius Dupont	40,000 (current money, 3,000–5,000 pounds sterling)

Panel B: Germanic-Surnamed Claimants

Claimant	Approximate Value of Claims (pounds sterling)
Mr. Gasman	6
Elizabeth Winkler	15
Mary Winkler	21
Jacob Stroubhart	26
Lewis Winkler	35
Nicholas Winkler	52
Jacob Winkler	58
David Wanderly	135
John Stroubhart	500

Source: Comptroller General Accounts Audited: Revolutionary War Claims, SCDAH.

Twenty-five individuals owning property in Purrysburg Township filed claims through the state treasurer's office. Of these claimants, nine appear to have Germanic surnames and fifteen French surnames. (The numerical discrepancy proceeds from the fact that John L. and Benjamin Buche appear on the same claim indent). The relatively small number of claims audited may suggest the general poverty of the majority of the population, reticence to file a claim, ignorance of the right to file, or—perhaps more realistically in light of Lincoln's irritation with military conduct in South Carolina—the practice of confiscating supplies without informing the owners or without providing a written receipt for future reimbursement.[62] The approximate size of the claims submitted range from the modest 1 pound, 18 shilling, 3 pence, indent of David Giroud to the indent of John L. Bourguin, which amounted to well over 1,500 pounds. Cornelius Dupont's claim for more than 40,000 pounds current money was in a class by itself. Of the twenty-four accounts, eight were for 2 pounds or less, six for 25–50 pounds, four for 50–100 pounds, three for 100–500 pounds, and one each for 500–750, 750–1,200, and 1,200–2,000 pounds. Germanic-surnamed individuals account for eight of the twenty-one claims of 500 pounds or less and only one of the three accounts over 500 pounds. On the other hand, French-surnamed claimants represent a majority of both those under and over 500 pounds, with the two largest accounts, those of John L. Bourguin and Cornelius Dupont, easily equaling the combined total of all others. French-surnamed individuals exist at both extremes, whereas the Germanic claimants occur more toward the middle of the total value range of accounts.

Significantly, many family groups submitted multiple claims. The Stroubhart, Winkler, Buche, Bourguin, and Gindrat families each had more than one person filing claims. Five members of the Winkler family (including Elizabeth and Mary) filed claims; three members each from the Bourguin (including Jane Donnam Bourguin) and Buche families filed claims; and two claims each were filed by the Stroubhart and Gindrat families. Although these statistics are open to various interpretations, the significant discrepancies among claims may demonstrate the relative inequality of wealth among and between ethnic groups residing at or near Purrysburg—at least among those filing claims. The army was more likely to confiscate supplies where they were more readily abundant than to search for supplies on marginal homesteads.[63]

The accounts audited shed light on other aspects of life relative to the Purrysburg settlement during the 1770s and 1780s. When the size and composition of claims are compared, it becomes apparent that, as illustrated in the previous chapter for the 1760s and early 1770s, a few individuals and/or family groups had indeed made the transition from small immigrant farmers to substantial planters and ranchers. The increase in prosperity may not have been quite as spectacular as Richard Beeman has found during the same time in Lunenburg County, Virginia, but it is nonetheless instructive.[64] John Stroubhart, John L. Bourguin, and Cornelius Dupont seem to have come into great wealth through farming, ranching, and, in the case of Dupont, high finance and these vocations. The large quantity of rice, cattle, and swine enumerated point to the fact that the area around Purrysburg had been used as pasturage and that the swampy sections around the various rivers and streams had been turned into productive rice fields. In addition, because nearly all the claims included some kind of meat (usually beef or pork) and some type of grain (usually rice or corn) and/or vegetables (peas, potatoes), the economy appears to have been fairly diversified and possibly in certain instances, self-sufficient. David Saussy, for example claimed expenses from twenty-four head of cattle, 1,283 pounds of pork, and a quantity of rice. The Winkler provisioning claims were largely for beef and rice, whereas David Wanderly and Jacob Stroubhart contributed between them a wide array of staples including beef, pork, bacon, fowl, mutton, corn, peas, rice, and even potatoes. Jacob Stroubhart's account remains unique among those filed in that his contributions to the provisioning of troops included processed goods such as dressed meat (161 pounds of bacon) and refined corn flour. The flour and his indent for 100 bushels of corn (the largest enumeration of this grain among all claimants) probably indicate his possession of a gristmill and perhaps even his occupation as a local miller.

Although other claims were more diverse, none encompassed the quantity of goods supplied by John Stroubhart. His 500-pound claim is the third-largest of all accounts from the township and the largest among Germanic-surnamed residents. Among other goods, Stroubhart provided well over 160 bushels of rice, 50 bushels of corn, 80 head of cattle, 57 hogs, 2 sheep, and 170 pounds of pork. He also was one of three claimants to hire out one of his slaves for public service. The appropriated slave served eighteen days working on a boat, presumably on the Savannah River. The claim filed by Cornelius Dupont also included cattle and fodder, but his greatest contribution came from grains and vegetables. He filed claims for 15 bushels of corn, more than 220 bushels of rice, and a small quantity of potatoes. Seven of his slaves were impressed by the military. The number of slaves appropriated, coupled with his substantial contribution of rice (the most of any Purrysburg claimant), signifies the success of a Dupont rice plantation near the township.

The account filed by John L. Bourguin did not contain an enumeration of goods provided. His father's account, however, indicated that the family did hire out one slave for four days while another was pressed into service for more than two months as a military guide. The only other mention of slaves hired out is in John L. and Benjamin Buche's account. They provided a slave to the military for 122 days. Of all those from the township submitting accounts to the government for losses incurred during the war, John Stroubhart, John L. Bourguin, and Cornelius Dupont most deserve the designation as prosperous planters and ranchers.

One of the most intriguing facts about these indented claims is the number of times they passed from one person or family to another. David Wanderly's account claimed a loss on cattle presented to David Saussy. Abraham Binninger decided to turn over his indent to a Mr. Roberts. Jacob Stroubhart signed over various of his indents to Conrad Hover (dated 1 September 1785) and to David Saussy (dated 25 July 1787). But Saussy, who died soon afterward, signed over one of his claims to Hyan Levy (5 April 1791), who also received an account from Lewis Winkler by conveyance on the same day.

Others in the Winkler family followed suit. Elizabeth, in Camden District by 1783, conveyed her indent to Samuel Mathias (5 December 1783, 24 November 1785), while Mary passed her claim on to John Paisley. Jacob Winkler yielded his voucher to an unidentifiable party (18 January 1786). Lewis Winkler, by contrast, conveyed some of his accounts to Jacob his kinsman. Barbara Winkler even held a partial receipt on David Wanderly's account for rice and corn. Cornelius Dupont turned over his indent to the Charles Town Huguenot descendant Benjamin Villeponteaux.

Some of these internal transfers, particularly among Purrysburg residents, most probably were in payment for incurred debts from neighbors. But claims signed over to Hover, Paisley, Levy, and Mathias highlight either the upward mobility of the Purrysburg citizens or the involvement of these individuals in speculative activities in government securities and promissory notes. Joshua Loper, who bought indents from Henry Gindrat, was undoubtedly speculating in government debts. In any event, these external transfers provide further evidence of the extension of commercial activities beyond the township that had began to develop by midcentury.

Internal transfers were not merely limited to.monetary arrangements, for many Purrysburg inhabitants serving in the military were forced by circumstances to procure provisions for their troops. Continental officers of the line such as Lieutenant Colonel John Lewis Bourguin, as well as officers in the Purrysburg militia company, requisitioned supplies from their neighbors. Bourguin appropriated a steer from John Stroubhart and also fed some of his men from his father's provisions. Both Jacob Winkler and Joachim Hartstone, captains of the Purrysburg militia company, impressed supplies from their kinsman and neighbor Lewis Winkler. Jacob Winkler confiscated a substantial quantity of beef from John Stroubhart. Lieutenant Henry Gindrat went so far as to appropriate his own livestock while stationed at Palachuccola, just north of Purrysburg. Although it is difficult to interpret this information, it may suggest that the local officers of German descent were reluctant to confiscate the property of non-Germanic residents. Gindrat's action may signify the same for those officers of French or French-Swiss heritage. Bourguin's requisitioning of the steer from John Stroubhart would be the only exception to this phenomenon.

Nearly all the claims filed demonstrate continued military maneuvers near the township throughout the revolutionary era. Except for David Mongin's accounts, which stipulate that he supplied troops from Oakatee Creek and the May River (just south of the township line but still within the six-mile buffer zone), and possibly the accounts of Cornelius Dupont and the Gindrats, the claims are for supplies requisitioned by troops in the immediate area of

Purrysburg. From the claims, it is obvious that the township contributed not only a continuous supply of provisions, but also a significant number of men for military service. Jacob and John Stroubhart, Jacob and Nicholas Winkler, John and William Mongin, Henry and Abraham Gindrat, Gideon Mallett, Abraham Binninger, David Saussy, John L. Bourguin, Joachim Hartstone, John Barraque (Barrakey), Christopher Burgermeister, John Tobishop, James Garvey, and Peter Raymond served the state as military personnel. In addition, it appears that David Giroud functioned as a justice of the peace during the years of warfare. Major Peter Mallett, who may have been related to the Purrysburg Mallett family, served General Lincoln as a procurer of supplies.[65]

V

Records show that Purrysburg provided a strategically located encampment for the American cause, recruits for military service, and vital provisions during the conflict. But because Lincoln never received the number of reinforcements he desired to take the offensive against the enemy—or even to withstand a concerted attack from opposing forces across the Savannah River—his position remained constantly in jeopardy. And if his position remained precarious, so also did the welfare of the township. In the midst of his constant concern with reinforcements, Lincoln was plagued by officers who failed to assess intelligence and reconnaissance information adequately. Their mistaken judgments resulted in poor command decisions and costly defeats, further undermining the security of the Purrysburg garrison. Socially and economically disrupted by the consequences of military occupation, residents of the township also had to face an uncertain future because of the proximity of enemy troops and the relative weakness of Lincoln's forces. American military setbacks and constant British harassment from across the Savannah River served to multiply their fears. They could only wait and hope that, when the time arrived, their homes would be properly defended. Unhappily for township citizens, such was not to be the case.

The problem of poor intelligence and reconnaissance information resulted in large part from the fact that much of it was obtained from British deserters or loyalists, some of whom were brought directly to Purrysburg.[66] Lincoln distrusted deserters as "unprincipled and dangerous men and by no means to be trusted."[67] Yet he and others in his command used them to secure information about British troop movements and strength, much of it spurious or contradictory. Such a source in mid-January 1779 falsely reported imminent enemy troop movements toward Charles Town and Beaufort. In reality, after Prevost reinforced Campbell's position on the lower Savannah in early January, he sent the lieutenant colonel with a thousand British troops to secure Augusta on the Georgia side of the river and to solicit loyalist assistance. Campbell had posts both above and below Purrysburg at Zubly's Ferry, Abercorn, and Cherokee Hill and established his headquarters at Ebenezer as early as 8 January. A week later

General Moultrie reported that the British had even managed a beachhead on the South Carolina side of the river a scant four miles from Lincoln's position at Purrysburg but had deserted it by 16 January. By 20 January Campbell had added a Two Sisters redoubt. British spies sent to check Lincoln's encampment at Purrysburg reported to Campbell on 21 January. Their intelligence convinced the British commander that he could not move against the Purrysburg garrison with any guarantee of success. Instead he and Prevost planned a diversionary movement on Port Royal Island, hoping to pull Lincoln's force well south of the township, which would allow Campbell to occupy Augusta without American interference. He began his march to Augusta on 24 January. He reached Grenier's plantation twenty-three miles above Briar Creek on 27 January and secured Augusta on 31 January. The abortive Port Royal Island assault occurred on 3 February. Within a few days, Campbell enlisted nearly 1,400 loyalist militia in and around Augusta for the British cause, thanks to the advance work done by the loyalist colonel John Hamilton. He expected the arrival of more recruits from North and South Carolina momentarily. With these actions, Georgia fell fully under the British flag.[68]

In the meantime South Carolina patriots remained active in the backcountry. Colonel Andrew Pickens, with 500 militiamen from Georgia and Ninety-Six, met a North Carolina loyalist force under Colonel James Boyd marching to rendezvous with the British at Augusta. Pickens at first unsuccessfully engaged Hamilton and his 200 loyalists. Then they turned to face Boyd's 700 loyalists at Kettle Creek, about fifty miles northwest of Augusta. Pickens's men routed the loyalists and mortally wounded Boyd. At this point Lincoln, who did not take Campbell's Port Royal bait, peeled off about half his troops to join Pickens. Campbell did not relish the possibility of engaging nearly 4,000 patriots in the backcountry with recently recruited loyalist militiamen who seemed to be quickly losing their enthusiasm. By late February he abandoned Augusta to consolidate his position farther down the Savannah River.[69]

In light of Pickens's improbable victory, Lincoln decided in late February to go on the offensive to drive the British from the Georgia backcountry. One of the three columns he sent north under Brigadier General John Ashe's North Carolina militia, however, suffered heavy losses on 3 March 1779 at the Battle of Briar Creek. So convincing a British victory left the backcountry open to British overtures among the Indians and whites, which, fortunately for the patriot cause, they failed to make. The crushing defeat resulted in the possibility of a court-martial for the general and raised serious questions regarding his fitness for command. A subsequent court of inquiry, requested by him and conducted at Purrysburg beginning on 10 March, exonerated Ashe from charges of cowardice but challenged the efficacy of his security precautions and intelligence information. The Briar Creek debacle cast doubts on the ability of the militia to defend a post and upon Lincoln's ability to hold the southern flank.[70] In a letter of 4 March to his commander in chief in Savannah, Sir Henry Clinton, before he had word of the British victory at Briar Creek, Campbell confidently proclaimed, "We have nothing to fear at present from the Rebels of Carolina; they are creeping with cautious steps along the Frontiers, and we ought to encourage them to advance, for as we have already taken Care to eat up the Forage and Provisions in that Quarter, they will be under many Difficulties for a Supply of these Articles: When we can draw them nearer us, we may with a little good Management attack them with Advantage."[71]

Following Briar Creek, Lincoln called a general council of war to determine future strategy. The council, realizing the grave danger to the Purrysburg garrison, which was now clearly outnumbered by the enemy, decided that the entire force should be "collected to one point and no outpost should be held but such as can be supported by the main body but in case of surprise." The councilors agreed that the "one point" should remain Purrysburg.[72]

A second defeat less than a month later, this time a naval battle six miles downriver from Purrysburg, placed the township and the post in an even more vulnerable position. As early as 25 December 1778, in preparation for the assault on Savannah, more than twenty British vessels were anchored at the mouth of the Savannah River. By January 1779 both British and American forces were vying for control of the river. Early that month the British moved a galley, a sloop, and fourteen armed flatboats upriver to engage a small American naval force commanded by Colonel White in the vicinity of Purrysburg. Although White thought his position "tolerably secure" between Abercorn and Purrysburg, he lost three vessels in a move north and away from the enemy. The British outnumbered him two to one. With such a force, White was confident that the British would attack in the evening.[73]

Faced with what he took to be an imminent attack, White retreated upriver to the camp at Purrysburg, where his ships remained almost unmanned until March. The galleys *Congress* and *Lee* and the French sloop *Mary Magdalen,* evidently at port in Purrysburg for a considerable time, were combat readied by 19 March. Lincoln reoutfitted and remanned the vessels and placed them at White's disposal. On the evening of the nineteenth, the ships moved down the river to capture enemy raiding vessels about six miles below the Purrysburg post. A small militia force accompanied the galleys and sloop in small boats to take possession of a house opposite the British vessels in support of the attack. A few miles below Purrysburg, the French sloop and the *Congress* ran aground. This stalled the expedition until the 20 March. The following morning the *Congress* refloated, and the force continued toward Ramsey's Bluff. Just before the Americans could engage the British vessels the *Comet* and the *Hornet,* the *Congress* again ran aground and remained totally exposed to the fire of the British ships and support troops. The crew abandoned her. Additional British vessels suddenly appeared from farther downriver. In the confusion that followed, the crew of the *Lee* abandoned ship against orders from the captain, though the galley was still able to maneuver. Lincoln's "sure victory" ended in a rout of American personnel and the loss of both galleys. It proved to be an unmitigated disaster for the patriot cause as the potential for a viable American naval presence on the Savannah River vanished. Ironically Lincoln received a letter from Stephen Drayton three days after the decisive battle in which he and Governor Rutledge decided that the best way to get much needed arms to Lincoln's army was to send them by naval convoy up the Savannah River. Needless to say, that shipment of arms never arrived.[74]

VI

The stinging defeats at Briar Creek and Ramsey's Bluff convinced Lincoln of his deteriorating situation at Purrysburg. Again acting on sketchy intelligence wrung from deserters that enemy forces were ready to cross the Savannah River to the north, he quit the township in late March in a second attempt to secure the backcountry and foil any British bid to cross into South Carolina from the upper reaches of the Savannah. The general left approximately 1,200 men at Purrysburg under the command of General Moultrie. Lincoln reiterated the priority of the garrison to Moultrie and outlined options for its defense, but his departure, the recent British naval and land victories, and the truncated garrison left at Purrysburg resulted in the fall of the township and the march of the British toward Charles Town. Lincoln's questionable march toward Augusta allowed the British to move across the Savannah at Purrysburg from which place they launched operations culminating in their second attempt to take Charles Town.[75]

Lincoln and the main body of the army took post at Black Swamp, about ten miles from the township on 26 March. He left what he determined was a "strong command" at his former headquarters, but he also made contingency plans for its abandonment should the force be attacked in overwhelming numbers. The detachment left at Purrysburg had no baggage, and the men were advised as to their line of retreat. General Bull was called upon to cover the troops should the British move against them.[76] At five o'clock that evening Colonel Charles Cotesworth Pinckney, writing from Purrysburg, informed Lincoln that a Sebastian Awl, a Hessian drummer, had crossed the Savannah with information that placed the "chief part of the Enemy's force" at Two Sisters, three miles from Ebenezer, from which place they intended to cross into South Carolina. Pinckney surmised "the galleys will wash up and attempt to amuse us here while the enemy are crossing above as they do not yet know your march." After interrogating Awl, Pinckney sent the deserter off to Purrysburg in short order as "no stragler shall stay 5 minutes in *My Camp*."[77]

Little more than a week later, Lincoln ordered Colonel Saunders to detach 300 men from his brigade and march them to Barakee's (Barraque), two miles north of Zubly's Ferry, on the evening of 5 April. Colonel Armstrong, who expected an attack on the Purrysburg garrison on 6 April, could then look to the detachment occupying Barraque's land in the township for aid. Apparently Lincoln had other plans for Saunders's men as he ordered them back to the brigade if no attack broke by 10:00 A.M.[78] In a separate dispatch, Lincoln cautioned Armstrong against too great a sense of security simply because he believed that the field pieces at his disposal would dissuade British ships from landing troops at Purrysburg. Lincoln contended that if the enemy did bring ships up the river, "it will be rather to amuse you while they fall upon your rear, than attempting anything serious." Then, in a cryptic dispatch, the general revised his earlier conviction regarding the importance of the Purrysburg post: "I have only to add that we have no object at Purrysburg worth risquing the troops under your command; you will therefore, the moment you find they mean to attack you in force, take such ground, and make such a disposition of your few troops as will secure your retreat."[79]

Purrysburg never really acquired sufficient defense from either the Continental line or the militia rank and file, so residents of the community had to live with the constant fear of being overrun or raided by British troops. Residents had lived with the possibility of British invasion since the fall of Savannah, but their anxieties became more palpable as American morale (and troop strength) eroded by late March. Enemy victories at Briar Creek and Ramsey's Bluff further compromised their sense of security, while intermittent covert operations across the Savannah into the plantations surrounding Purrysburg throughout the winter of 1779 demonstrated just how vulnerable the township was to enemy attacks—even with the presence of a substantial American force.

The first such recorded incursion occurred on New Year's Day 1779, just as Lieutenant Colonel Campbell moved to secure a British outpost at Zubly's Ferry. Campbell's scouts discovered that Americans had penetrated Georgia for the purpose of removing loyalist slaves to Purrysburg. British light infantry troops pursued the Americans to the Savannah River, but the patriots escaped with the confiscated slaves via Zubly's Ferry before the British soldiers could catch them. Campbell stood on the Georgia side of the river observing the slaves less than a hundred yards from the South Carolina shore. He decided to rely on deception to regain the slaves for their Georgia owners. Campbell armed a mulatto loyalist and sent him with some blacks down to the riverbank. They hailed the Americans on the other side of the river and pleaded with them to save them from falling into British hands by sending over both the ferryboats. While American attention was drawn by the persistence of the actors, Campbell's light infantry made its way unseen down to the river. When the boats came across, the mulatto fired his musket as a signal to the light infantry to engage the Americans. The British were able to recapture eighty-three slaves without losing a man while a thousand American troops paraded within 800 yards of the ferry.[80]

Three weeks later, on 21 January 1779, Colonel John L. Bourguin received a message from Thomas Cater, a guard at Heyward's plantation not ten miles from Purrysburg. Cater warned that "two or three hundred of the enemy are almost within gunshot of our breastworks." They beat a hasty retreat to Mr. Bushe's (Buche), who resided in the township.[81] A month later one of Lincoln's subalterns saw "two enemy soldiers herding cattle in a swamp on this side of the river and a number of men supposed to be guarding on the other side 'til they drove the cattle over, which I will be glad of reinforcement."[82]

The British not only raided across the river, but also shelled the patriot positions in South Carolina. By March, British troops stationed across from Zubly's Ferry periodically fired over the river into Purrysburg (at 2:00 A.M.), which "alarmed our camp" as the general wryly noted. One must wonder how much more the exploding artillery shells did than alarm the terrified civilian population of the township wedged between the British and American lines.[83]

By the last week of March, with Lincoln and the main body of the army gone, the enemy became even bolder. Colonel Pinckney, who commanded a detachment of troops still at Purrysburg, discovered that a corps of British regulars, aided by the galleys *Snake* and *Hornet*, had made an abortive attempt to cross the Savannah at Patton's homestead. The only reason they failed was the timely sinking of a couple of field pieces in the river during the journey from Ebenezer. They doubtless would try again. Sources assured Pinckney that the British would move by the end of the month. The colonel relished the thought of engaging enemy troops in the coming battle and petitioned Lincoln that he might be allowed to remain at Purrysburg so that "with Colonel Armstrong's detachment and mine we shall play the Devil with them." Pinckney, unlike the township civilians, warmed to the occasion: "I would not ask you liberty to stay but I should like to have some hand in the drubbing of these damned rascals." He circulated false intelligence reports to the British that he had a ten-gun battery waiting for the British when they decided to cross the river.[84]

As it turned out, the British did not attempt a crossing at that time, but guerrilla activaties multiplied as tensions mounted. Sometime in April (the date cannot be clearly ascertained), some slaves belonging to David Raymond approached a guard near Purrysburg at 2:00 A.M. with news that some British troops in boats had come ashore a short distance away at Tunbridge Landing. The officer in charge sent out a reconnaissance party to verify this report. Shots were fired in the distance after the party had left. When the men returned at dawn, they told the officer that the raiders had slipped back across the river, firing as they retreated. This attack proved the final straw for at least two township households. Anthony Godfrey and Philip Martinangle gathered together their families, loaded as many of their possessions as they could carry on board a schooner, which met them just north of Purrysburg at Red Bluff, and fled the township. When informed by one of Godfrey's slaves that the families had left, the officers made the best of the situation by recommending that the stock of horses and cattle left behind by the refugees be confiscated for future public use.[85]

The most brazen attack upon Purrysburg settlers recorded before the fall of the township occurred on 22 April 1779 at the home of Joachim Hartstone, captain of the Purrysburg militia company. At midnight a raiding party of between twenty and forty Indians (or men dressed like Indians, as it appeared later because of the bayonets affixed to their guns) charged through the swamp at Yamassee. The terrorists proceeded to Hartstone's home and set it afire. His wife, daughter, and infant son narrowly escaped with their lives, but the home and all personal effects were lost. An elderly black woman, presumably a family slave, was not so fortunate. Stabbed multiple times, her scalped corpse was found sprawled near the blazing home. General Moultrie related to Lincoln the details of the grisly attack, conspicuously noting the fact that "neither the guard, which was posted at the entrance to the swamp, nor the party the guard had relieved, which was at Hartstone's house when the Indians appeared even fired a gun, by which means the alarm was not communicated in time to allow the party that was sent after them to impede their retreat." Moultrie responded to this attack upon Purrysburg women and children by requesting cavalry reinforcements and a contingent of Catawba Indians. General Casimir Pulaski's Light Horse arrived from the north in short order, and Moultrie's intelligence reports told him that there were about fifty Indians at British-held Abercorn six miles downriver.[86]

By mid-April Lincoln still hoped to secure the backcountry. He remained aware of the possibility of a major British move toward Charles Town should he not entice the redcoats to pursue him. Struggling with health problems, still without the promised supplies and reinforcements, disgusted with the deserting militia, and anticipating a British crossing of the Savannah thirty or forty miles above his camp at Black Swamp, Lincoln gave words to his true sentiments for the civilian population: "To see the distress of many of the good people of Georgia driven from their homes,—a state of influence to a state of real want,—wishing to return under that aid which is not in our power to grant,—and to observe the disquiet and anxiety of many of the inhabitants of this state from an expectation that their misfortunes will soon equal at least those of the Georgians—is misery indeed."[87] A short while later Lincoln ordered Bull to deploy a detachment of his troops south of Purrysburg on the neck between the Savannah and New Rivers. This detachment consisted of only eighty to a hundred men and was stationed too far from Purrysburg to blunt any concerted attack by the enemy from across the Savannah. The troops rather served as a token force stationed in southern St. Peter's Parish to provide minimal protection to inhabitants and their property. Lincoln's vulnerable position north of Black Swamp at Galphin's necessitated the recall to that post of many of the remaining military personnel still stationed at Purrysburg.

In a 22 April communiqué to General Moultrie headquartered at Black Swamp, Lincoln ordered all the Continental troops except the Second and Fifth Regiments of South Carolina to march northward with all artillery except the two pound guns and all supplies in the Purrysburg quartermaster's store not absolutely essential for the Second and Fifth. In this dispatch Lincoln made no mention of a possible attempt on Moultrie's part to defend the garrison or the town beyond "keeping a post at Purrysburg as long as you shall have it in your power." Lincoln feared that a successful enemy landing at Purrysburg could lead to a march to Charles Town but was not yet ready to abandon his backcountry strategy. He urged Moultrie to occupy several of the passes and delay as much as possible the advance of the British. By letter the following day, however, Moultrie was ordered to depart even the Black Swamp post. He withdrew his troops to the Tullifinny River northeast of Purrysburg. The final week of April opened with only a skeleton force left by Moultrie actually at post in the township while the majority of troops still stationed in the area bivouacked at Black Swamp with Lincoln.[88]

VII

The British invasion of South Carolina at Purrysburg began on 29 April 1779. Colonel McIntosh, commanding officer of the token patriot force left in the township, sent word to his superiors that more than 300 enemy troops had landed. That such a relatively small detachment compelled McIntosh to give ground toward Coosawhatchie confirmed that the township and its population were to be abandoned to the enemy without risking any loss of patriot life. Throughout 29 and 30 April, British troops swarmed across the river and completely overran the township. It was most likely during the initial hours of the assault that the British destroyed the Purrysburg Presbyterian Church equating as they did religious dissent with civil rebellion. By dusk on 30 April 1,500 men had crossed into South Carolina, and 500 more were expected to cross soon. On 2 May the invasion force began to advance deeper into South Carolina. Moultrie's desperate request for reinforcements to halt the British offensive failed to produce any additional manpower. Rather, even at this late date, Lincoln chose to believe that the British were not heading for Charles Town, and so, instead of marching to that city as Moultrie urged him, he crossed the Savannah River into Georgia and proceeded southward toward Ebenezer. The general hoped that such pressure on Prevost's former headquarters would constrain the enemy to fall back into Georgia.[89]

It did not. Little threatened by Moultrie's meager detachment, Prevost made directly for Charles Town. Had his troops been more enthusiastic about seizing Charles Town than about plundering the plantations that lay between Purrysburg and the capital, they might have had the advantage of surprise. By the time they arrived at the outskirts of the city on 14 May, Charles Town had time to ready its defenses and Lincoln, realizing his strategic error, had hastily recrossed the Savannah River and raced Prevost for the capital. The British commander called for the surrender of Charles Town. Governor Rutledge countered with an offer of neutrality, which was summarily rejected, but Prevost knew he had no time to lay siege to the city. Laden with booty and hundreds of confiscated slaves, his army began a retreat before Lincoln's advance. While the bulk of his forces lumbered toward Savannah via the coastal sea islands, Prevost detached

Lieutenant Colonel John Maitland's troops to fight a rearguard delaying action at Stono Ferry (20 June), which succeeded in halting the American pursuit. Prevost left a garrison under Maitland's command to hold Beaufort, while he continued his withdrawal from the state. At least one column of his army, perhaps the entire remaining force, moved from the immediate coastal region and reentered Purrysburg on the way back to Savannah.[90] Prevost's return set up the unsuccessful joint American and French siege of Savannah in September and October and guaranteed that Purrysburg, though never again the headquarters of a large British or American force, would continue to experience the privation and internecine violence that so characterized South Carolina's revolutionary experience in the early 1780s. It was also, on at least one more occasion in the late winter/early spring of 1780, directly in the path of an advancing British force under General Paterson. His foray toward the township coupled with the American expectation of enemy troop movement near Beaufort allowed British forces to land, untouched, to the rear of the American lines on Johns Island.[91] The final capitulation of Charles Town and the surrender of Lincoln's beleaguered army to General Clinton in May 1780 did little to quell the turmoil of a state at war with itself.

The final years of warfare in the southern theater brought continued hardships to most of the inhabitants of South Carolina because of the British strategy of "Americanizing" the war. The resulting partisan conflict during the last years of the Revolution became a ferocious civil war pitting neighbor against neighbor and infecting nearly the entire region.[92] The state endured more fighting and suffering than any other during the Revolution.[93] The devastation of Ninety-Six, Camden, and Georgetown Districts are well documented, but it should be remembered that the plundering and scorched-earth strategy employed by Prevost's army during its march through South Carolina in the spring and summer of 1779 began at Purrysburg.

The lowcountry parishes near Georgia, including St. Helena's and St. Peter's, were ransacked by the British. Edward Rutledge estimated that the Beaufort area had been stripped of property worth millions of pounds as Prevost made his way through southeastern South Carolina. Purrysburg property not expropriated by the Americans faced destruction or confiscation by the British; the population was forced to choose between living in a zone occupied by the enemy's army or fleeing as refugees to more secure locations. Its geographical position now became strategically important to the invaders, and the township had to tolerate the repeated movement of troops very near and even within its boundaries. From April 1779 into at least the spring of 1780, township roadways carried prisoners, confiscated goods, and enemy military personnel. Like much of the state, Purrysburg did not survive the war; it endured the war. So devastated was the population of St. Peter's Parish that when Governor John Rutledge called for elections to a new state legislature (the Jacksonborough Assembly) only thirteen voters cast ballots for six representatives and one senator.[94]

David Ramsay, an early historian of the Revolution in South Carolina, argued that the fall of Savannah provided the occasion for the fall of Charles Town. Ramsey's point is well taken, but speculation could also be offered with regard to the outcome of the war in South Carolina had more effort been extended to maintain the Purrysburg garrison. Certainly there are a host of factors to be considered in any reevaluation of Lincoln's strategies and tactics, and there is no question that the capture of Savannah permitted the enemy to envision the thrust into South Carolina. Yet the case might be made that the patriot evacuation of Purrysburg, ordered by Lincoln as a consequence of his desire to secure the backcountry, provided an open door for the initial British invasion of the state and from that perspective contributed ultimately to the fall of Charles Town. When Lincoln received word of the loss of Purrysburg, it seemed of no great importance to him and bore no relation to the fate of Charles Town: "It was not in my power to stop its [the British Army's] progress. There was nothing left for me to do but give it a just coloring; by which it appeared a very inconsiderable matter. I do not believe the enemy have it in their idea to march toward Charlestown at present."[95]

As a counterpoint to Lincoln's fatalistic assessment, Captain Johann Hinrichs, a Hessian officer in the British Army, noted succinctly the connection between the loss of Purrysburg and the patriot cause in South Carolina in 1779: "Major General Prevost advanced by land from St. Augustine to Purysburg. Having seized the latter, he joined Lieutenant Colonel Campbell, and before long the country was cleared of the enemy."[96] Had Lincoln been able to give the British a greater trial at Purrysburg, perhaps South Carolina might have been spared at least some of the depredations that followed. As it was, the township and the state endured foreign occupation and fratricidal guerrilla warfare for two more years. By 1782 Purrysburg and South Carolina began to emerge from the revolutionary carnage, but neither would soon recover the stability or the prosperity that had been consumed by the fires of war.

EIGHT

No Longer Strangers

The convening of the Jacksonborough Assembly in January 1782 symbolized the reestablishment of South Carolina state authority. Though skirmishes continued after the summer of 1781, their outcome never again threatened American control. The British occupied the capital until December 1782, but they were as much hostages to the rest of the state as Charles Town's citizens were to them. Most of the physical devastation of the War of the Revolution was behind South Carolinians by 1782, but the full impact of the conflict would continue to unfurl over the next few decades. Accommodation between the backcountry and the lowcountry, yeoman and planter, democratic theory and slavery, and the amalgamation of evangelical religious sentiment that would result in a unified political ideology upholding nullification and states' rights—all these developments lay still in the future.[1] What remained of immediate concern was the rebuilding of Carolina lives and fortunes. In Purrysburg Township, as elsewhere in the state, the task involved the sometimes contentious process of reconstructing the community and repairing social and economic relationships between the landowners and surrounding settlements in Georgia and South Carolina that had been severed or at least severely compromised by the war.

Charles Singer may be correct in his assertion that the War of the Revolution wrought greater economic hardship in South Carolina than in other states while producing fewer social changes, but the acquisition of land and property by Purrysburg citizens in the wake of the most destructive of all conflicts since the founding of the township surely contributed to a continued expansion of the wealthy planter and rancher class in St. Peter's Parish during the years after the Revolution. Much as in the upper South, as the disruptions of the Revolution passed into memory, the pursuit of prosperity and community in Purrysburg Township proceeded apace.[2] Purrysburg continued its progressive integration into the plantation economy and transportation infrastructure of other lowcountry regions during the 1790s and well into the nineteenth century.

Yet, twelve years of war or preparation for war had taken their toll on the township and its people. From early 1775 to as late as 3 May 1787, Purrysburg had served as a military command post, provisioning ground, point of march, potential battlefield, and refugee camp. Much if not all of the town proper had been destroyed, and injustice had been visited upon both enemy and friend.

Lives and property had been forfeited, and the contours of community had been radically altered. Still, Purrysburg and its people survived and helped rebuild the state of South Carolina under the federal regime while simultaneously salvaging what was left of their community.

The final military operation in the township related to the effects of the war came in 1787, long after the Treaty of Paris had been signed. During the war years thousands of slaves had been confiscated by the British, and many more had escaped to enlist in the Tory cause. After the war these former slaves, called maroons, remained fugitives. They established hidden communities along the Savannah River and survived for years, occasionally raiding nearby plantations for supplies. One such settlement was said to be a half mile long, containing upward of twenty houses and cultivated farmland.[3] In March 1787 John L. Bourguin Jr. described to Joachim Hartstone a particularly harrowing attack by some of the maroons in the Purrysburg neighborhood. "I make no doubt but that you have already heard of the many depredations that have been committed by the run-away Negroes about here. . . . They have in my hearing threatened the lives of many of the citizens amongst which I am included. Since your absence, they . . . paid a visit in our swamp plantation, and after some time they left us, with the loss of our driver fellow, ten barrels of clean rice and myself slightly wounded in the hip."[4]

Upon being informed of this attack and mindful that it was not a singular incident, Governor Thomas Pinckney apprised the South Carolina General Assembly of the situation. The legislature subsequently ordered "a company of minutemen, and a draft of the Granville County militia for the purpose of keeping the field 'til they are totally broken up.'" A number of Catawba Indians were included in the force. Under the command of Colonel Hutson, the force bivouacked at Purrysburg in April 1787 and requested support from Georgia officials for the operation. Hutson requisitioned supplies from Purrysburg landowners and called on township males to serve.[5] In late April Captain Winkler's troops engaged a detachment of the fugitives:

> Last Saturday evening the Col. detached Captain Winkler with three boats and about twenty-five men to waylay Collins Creek. About eight or nine o'clock one of Capt. Winkler's boats discovered four of their canoes full of men coming down the creek when a warm skirmish took place which ended in favour of the white people. Lewis (a black major) was killed and two others who fell overboard were supposed to have too as the canoes . . . fell into Capt. Winkler's hands, and the boat waited fifteen minutes without sign of their rising. Had not Capt. Winkler detached his other boats the whole of the Negro party must have been killed or taken. Two of the Carolinians were slightly wounded one in his hand and arm and the other in his face.[6]

The military apparently succeeded in killing a number of former slaves and perhaps in driving the rest away. Winkler received a ten pound bounty for killing the major. The Catawbas also were paid for the scalps they took.[7] It was only with the suppression of this threat that the Revolution finally ended for Purrysburg landowners, although postwar readjustments had begun with the initial legislative actions of the Jacksonborough Assembly in the early 1780s.

I

The first order of business for that body had both political and economic repercussions. The confiscation of loyalist estates, legalized by the legislation of 1782–1784, was motivated by a desire for revenge and in some ways exacerbated the tensions long evident between the lowcountry elite and backcountry inhabitants—to some extent a replay of the political intrigues that plagued first-generation Purrysburg settlers nearly fifty years earlier. At the same time, however, representatives from the backcountry and lowcountry parishes that had been ravaged by years of partisan warfare initially dominated the assembly and worked together to confiscate the estates of loyalists. In Purrysburg the sale of requisitioned estates brought the opportunity for some to augment their property holdings at the expense of British sympathizers who had been their neighbors. John Linder Sr. and John Linder Jr. were the only two Purrysburg residents convicted of loyalism and so forfeited their estates. The latter held a commission from the British government. Gideon Dupont was also convicted and lost his property, but he had since moved from the township. Robert Williams Sr. forfeited 1,480 acres in Purrysburg. The Reverend John Joachim Zubly, perhaps Georgia's most notable loyalist, actually spent much of the war on his plantation just north of Purrysburg and often provided services to his old family friends in the township.[8]

The Linder family set up as storekeepers in Purrysburg shortly after the founding of the township in 1732. By the 1770s the Linders had become heavily indebted to other Purrysburg residents as well as to some outside the township. When American authorities expropriated the Linders's estates, their creditors filed suit with the state for recovery of their debts. John Linder Sr. was named as the defendant in cases involving debts owed to David Saussy, George Keal, John Baptist Bourguin, Thomas Cooper, and Samuel Stirk of Georgia. Most of the claims against Linder's estate involved sums of money, but others pertained to more specific debts owed to neighbors and associates. Dr. John Baptist Bourguin treated Linder's family, his workers, and slaves for a series of ailments on a number of occasions between 1777 and 1780 and was never paid for these services. Bourguin brought suit against Linder's confiscated estate to recover his fee. Unfortunately, the doctor expired before the case was settled in his favor in 1785.[9]

Samuel Stirk's suit illuminates another aspect of Linder's character. A refugee Georgian, Stirk left many of his possessions with Linder in late March 1779 for safekeeping. These included furniture, food stuffs, and some liquor stores. As soon as General Prevost crossed the Savannah River at Purrysburg, Linder transported Stirk's goods (excluding the rum and a few other items) to Savannah and sold them, pocketing the profit. Stirk sued for 150 pounds and won the case in 1789. John Linder Jr. owed money to other members of the greater Purrysburg community, including John Buche, Adrian Mayer, John Stroubhart, Captain Thomas Budd, and Thomas Cooper. Each of them claimed portions of the younger Linder's confiscated property to cover his indebtedness to them.[10]

In addition to separate claims, father and son were named as codefendants in some cases. The most curious of these was suit brought by Colonel John L. Bourguin Sr. for repayment of 390 barrels of rice. From the witness affidavits of Philip Christian, John Buche, and Bourguin himself, it appears that John Linder Jr. had led a small British raiding party to Colonel Bourguin's plantation in July 1779. In December of the previous year, Philip Christian, one of Bourguin's Purrysburg neighbors, had left 400 bushels of rice at his plantation. Linder's party appropriated 390 barrels of the rice for use by British regulars. Although the commissioners of forfeited estates threw out Bourguin's claim because they believed that losses of this type were not covered by the confiscation fund, Bourguin's testimony illuminates the struggle of neighbor against neighbor that colored the later years of war.

When Bourguin asked the Linders how they could have stolen from him, they justified their actions by replying that he "well knew how they had been obliged to leave Purrisbourg in a hurry with their Negroes and had had no time to take provisions with them; that when they got in Savannah they had nothing for the Negroes to eat."[11] Perhaps the Linders hoped that their excuses softened the blow for their patriot friend, but they probably did not. Bourguin's personal sense of betrayal is almost palpable.

If warborne animosities strained the bonds of long standing friendships in Purrysburg, they also served as the source of new wealth. Township landowners purchased confiscated or abandoned land, stock, and property to augment their personal estates. Cornelius Dupont bought a parcel of land in Charleston (Charles Town prior to August 1783) previously owned by his loyalist relative Gideon Dupont Jr. Former Purrysburg landowner James Cuillat purchased 240 acres of Gideon's land. David Saussy bought 124 acres of John Linder Sr.'s land. More than one half of Robert Williams Sr.'s property went to David Villard (Villars?)—388 acres—and James Moore—406 acres. Other Purrysburg township landholders, including David Huguenin Sr. (554 acres of John Rose's land) and John Lewis Bourguin (250 acres of Richard Pendarvis's estate, 661 acres of Lieutenant Governor Irvine's land, and a colt and mare from John James Brisbane's estate) acquired holdings outside the township limits. In this way Purrysburg landowners and former residents continued to move out across the southeastern part of the state after the war while still maintaining land holdings in the township. At least two others—Glen Drayton and John McNish—became Purrysburg property owners by purchasing land that had been confiscated from Williams.[12]

Purrysburg landholders also acquired or sold property by regular conveyance during the 1780s. These transfers, though few in number, illustrate that exchanges continued to occur both internally between resident landholders and externally involving one or more parties who were nonresident in the township. John Lewis Bourguin and Henry Middleton, Thomas Lynch, and Robert Smith were involved in one such conveyance of 800 acres in December 1783. In October 1785 Nicholas Winkler Sr. purchased 275 acres that had been part of the estate of late township resident David Wanderly. In June 1786 Purrysburg landholder John Rutledge sold 200 Purrysburg acres to Gaspar Trotti. That same year Hezekiah Roberts of Purrysburg was involved in two different legal matters. The first pertained to the mortgage of a tract of land in Camden District, Richland County that also involved Benjamin Waller of Charleston. The second had to do with a bond agreement between Roberts and John Grive of Savannah. John Mongin of Hilton Head Island tentatively sold 500 acres of his land at Spanish Wells to Joseph Fickling in late 1788. Mongin still had an interest in Purrysburg property via his father David's legacy.[13] The two remaining cases of land disbursement among Purrysburg residents during this period illustrate many of the patterns regarding the complexities of family and commercial commitments as township residents intermarried, invested in the slave-based plantation system, and established socioeconomic relationships beyond the confines of Purrysburg.

By the mid-1770s David Keall of Purrysburg possessed a significant estate—and also a significant debt. Sometime before October 1776 Keall bonded himself to the Charles Town merchant house of Powell, Hopton & Co. for 3,008 pounds current money to secure payment of 1,504 pounds on or before 1 October 1776. Keall apparently had plenty of equity to settle the debt, but he died in early March 1784 without doing so. Keall's will of 14 November 1783 appointed his brother Lewis Bourguin Keall as his sole executor and bequeathed 500 pounds sterling to him. The remainder of his real and personal estate "(except his cattle, stores, household furniture, and 350 acres of land and 4½ plotts of land in Purrysburg), which he directed to be sold, he gave to be divided equally between his two sons, John Keall Jr. and David Washington Keall." On 25 April 1784 Lewis sold the 350 acres to Purrysburg landowner Joakim Harlston (Joachim Hartstone) for 995 pounds, 5 shillings sterling for debt service on his brother's estate just as his will stipulated, but Lewis failed to pay his brother's creditors with the proceeds of the land sale. He ultimately took charge of the entire estate, usurping what should have gone directly to David's sons, and sold a significant portion of it. David's creditors petitioned Lewis repeatedly and unsuccessfully for payment, arguing that the money from land and personal property sales, not to mention that the indigo crops Keall's slaves continued to cultivate and process after his death, should have been used to pay his debt. He told them that he did not have the resources to pay his brother's debt. Powell, Hopton & Co. finally took legal action against Lewis in 1793, requesting that the Court of Chancery issue a supeona to "Keall and his confederates when discovered." The merchants demanded an accounting of "if any what crop of indigo was remaining when he died and what crops have been raised since and how said crops were disposed. Names of Negroes left, how many and which of them were in the field capable of doing a whole or half task also which of the young Negroes have become taskable hands." They further wanted to know if Lewis had sold any of his brother's slaves. If so, they insisted that he provide their names, who bought them, and whether any of them were held in trust for David's sons. This convoluted case highlights the complex interplay between family commitments, the pursuit of prosperity, and the commercial connections between township landholders and financial capitalists elsewhere in the Southeast in the early national period.[14]

The situation of the extended Mongin family is even more indicative of the fact that by the revolutionary era, Purrysburg landowners were no longer strangers to each other or to others in the region. David Mongin had been a Charles Town watchmaker before moving to Purrysburg in the 1730s. His family became one of the more prominent and successful as the township moved toward productive plantation agriculture in the 1750s and 1760s. It should be recalled that by his will, dated 23 November 1770, Mongin chose two coexecutors—his son William and John Lewis Bourguin—to implement the provisions of his will. The inequitable distribution of Mongin's sizable estate caused his wife, Mary Ann, and son David to contest unsuccessfully the proving of the will. Within a few months of filing a caveat against the proving of the will, Mary Ann died in September 1771.[15]

Because William was an articled apprentice to Mr. Box of Savannah during the early 1770s, the execution of Mongin's will fell largely to John Lewis Bourguin, the coexecutor. Bourguin quickly discovered that David Sr.'s large estate owed creditors upward of 5,000 pounds current money. That amount, added to the legacies granted to family members, left Bourguin with a nearly 8,300-pound debt to pay out of the estate by 1774. This amount included neither the tripartite division of the estate willed to Jane, John, and William nor the one-quarter value of the rice crop of 1770 owed to Mary Ann. The plantation produced ninety-six barrels of rice in 1770 and only fifty-nine barrels in 1771. The decrease was attributed to the deaths of five of Mongin's thirty-eight slaves, the incapacity of others, and the location of the plantation in a narrow inland swamp choked with weeds. In the meantime daughter Jane became romantically involved with William Godfrey, also of St. Peter's Parish. If they married, Godfrey could claim Jane's third of her late father's estate. In late September 1771 Godfrey bound himself for 5,000 pounds Georgia money to William Brisbane of St. Peter's and William Mongin. As security on the debt, Godfrey promised to convey Jane's one-third interest in her father's estate to Brisbane and/or Mongin within six months of his marriage to her. They married and soon afterward insisted that the value of her one-third interest be released to them. This was done in early 1772. Bourguin turned to the sale of the estate's personal property at public auction to satisfy claims on it. William and Jane Godfrey purchased "Negroes and movables to a vast larger Sum than there [*sic*] dividend amounted to, say to the amount of 1881 pounds, 9 shillings, 2 pence more than there [*sic*] part." The two Williams appear to have reached some kind of compromise settlement, but Bourguin and William Mongin continued to act as trustees of Jane's actual portion of the estate till at least October of 1776—and Brisbane's name appears on financial records in 1776. According to William's deposition, in that year Jane and William Godfrey "by there [*sic*] misconduct was obliged to forsake it and leave it to be Done what could be thought best." During the Revolution, Godfrey remained loyal to Great Britain. On 18 October 1784 he wrote his brother-in-law William Mongin a letter explaining the necessity of his immediate departure for St. Mary's, Dominica, in the West Indies without Jane and their children. Godfrey expressed his thanks for all Mongin had done for him and his family:

> I beg that you will receive some part of my thanks and Mrs. Mongin, for the great care and pain that you have taken with my poor wife and little Ones—These favors cannot nor never will be forgot by me, and I have only to lament that it is not in my power to make you more greatfull acknowledgements at present than these few lines—I only beg to remind you that if ever I can serve you in any thing in our part of the world, that you will never be backward. I will always wish the Honour of Having it in my Power so to do—and should we continue at St. Mary's, I will always be Happy to see you and Mrs. Mongin at any time.

Godfrey also addressed the financial mess he left, which included a debt larger than anyone in the family realized in 1776. Some of his creditors held mortgages; others judgments against him. Godfrey even owed Mongin more than 600 pounds current money. Sheriff John Rhodes of Beaufort District levied all Godfrey's property late that year and had it sold to his creditors, whose bonds were then put into William's hands payable on 1 January 1777. William actually had to receive his own bond for 2,120 pounds, which included a female slave bought for Jane and another bought as room and board payment to Andrew Aggnew of Beaufort with whom John Mongin lodged while in school. Things got worse for William as "the rest of the Bonds I received when People chose to pay them a Considerable depreciation took place." Both he and John lost a significant amount of money in trying to secure the estate from the Godfreys's profligate ways. Now in 1784, preparing to leave South Carolina, Godfrey looked back on the grief he and Jane had caused William. He wrote that he wanted to make William "fully Satisfyed on the subject matter, that lay for so long a time in a Confused manner. I did not mean nor Neither had I any thought to have mentioned the matter, either directly or indirectly to You—and leave the whole to be finally determined between our selves in the *most amicable manner* . . . nor Neither would I ever wish to attempt any step, that would create the least Breach of friendship between us—your acquaintance and mine have been of so long a date." Godfrey asked for William's assistance in "Dispatching your Sister and the Children away as soon as the Sloop will arrive" and promised that, as soon as the ship arrived in St. Mary's carrying his family, he would "Transmit a special power of attorney" to William's older brother David and also "a final Discharge and acquittal" to William as executor of David Sr.'s estate. This vesting of both David and William with some authority to discharge the loyalist's remaining claim on their father's estate appears to have been an attempt to repair some of the damage he had inflicted on the family by facilitating a reconciliation between the brothers. Godfrey wrote of the "legal Clearance" that will be given up "to you by your Brother David, on your finally settling with him." Unfortunately his attempt to heal this rift did not sooth all the wounds opened over the disbursement of the estate. After Godfrey's death in the West Indies, Jane returned to South Carolina to file suit in 1796 against William for her share of her father's estate, which she claimed she never received in the nearly twenty-six years since David's death.[16]

II

Although its role as a military post ended with the Revolutionary War, Purrysburg continued to serve as an important link in the lower southeastern transportation and communication network well into the nineteenth century. The township lay directly on the regular postal route from Charleston and, though not the only route for travelers between that city, Augusta, and Savannah, it carried its share of passengers on the stage line that also stopped there. To ensure that passengers as well as the U.S. mail could be carried in a timely manner, appropriate maintenance of local roads was imperative. When Governor Benjamin Guerard and the Privy Council discovered in July 1784 that the freeholders of St. Peter's and St. Helena's had not been working to keep the road in good repair nor had they selected from their number anyone to oversee its maintenance, Judge Heyward suggested that Guerard appoint Joachim Hardstone, John Bush (Buche), James Brown, and Charles Dupont to serve as commissioners of the Purrysburg road. The freeholders appear to have taken their responsibilities more seriously after this incident, appointing their own commissioners in 1786.[17] The following year inhabitants and freeholders of Purrysburg Township and its environs, including John and Jacob Stroubhar (Stroubhart), Lewis and Nicholas Winkler, John Mirehover (Meyerhoffer), and John Gerardin (Girardin), petitioned the Senate and the House regarding the requirement that they maintain the high road from Bee's Creek to Purrysburg. The petitioners noted that the road was "not advantageous to them" and that because they had to service this road "the buy road from Quince's Mile to Purrysburg therefore becomes totally neglected . . . a road whereon all the inhabitants from the upper part of the Savannah River downwards carries their produce to Purrysburg their nearest marketplace the few inhabitants residing on the said road being insufficient to keep it in repair." They argued that the former road "in its present situation being highly inconvenient to your petitioners and travelers also: we therefore pray that the said road be removed from Baroquie's (Barrakey's) bridge so as to intersect Quince's Mile in the nearest most convenient way to establish the same as a publick highway and to appoint such persons to lay out and keep the same in repair."[18]

In January 1791, settlers in the New River neck area and others in Hilton County, including John L. Buche, John B. Waldburger, Frederick Rehm, Lewis B. Keale, John Keall, James Pelot, Joachim Hartstone, Philip Mayer, Hezekiah Roberts, Peter Raymond, John and Jacob Gasman, and David Erhart—all of whom were associated with Purrysburg, petitioned both houses of the assembly about local roadways. They wanted a road "leading from New River bridge, down to Tunbridge, and from thence the nearest and best route to the mouth of Savannah Back River, Including the road leading from Purrysburg lately laid out and worked upon, to continue on (the best and nearest way) and intersect into same." The road from Purrysburg to Dr. Channing's Back River plantation and the one from New River bridge "intersecting to the other leading from Purrysburg" granted the inhabitants a few years earlier had been found by the commissioners of these roads to be impossible to complete because of a "very deep swamp the distance at least three miles and subject to every high fresh." The petitioners wanted the road from Purrysburg to Dr. Channing's "disannulled and continue on with the road leading from Purrysburg, the best and nearest way to intersect the other road leading from New River bridge to Tunbridge." The petition concluded with an appeal both to convenience and commerce: "Your petitioners are also subject to great inconvenience for the want of a road at that place and would be highly beneficial to the country and the public in general and that from want of aforesaid road, your petitioners are deprived of that commercial intercourse that they ought to enjoy."[19] The fact that the residents of Lincoln County petitioned the assembly in May 1794 for a road leading from the Augusta road to intersect the Purrysburg road illustrates the continued importance of the township as a significant link in the regional transportation network.[20]

Located at the upper limits of the tidewater and accessible to South Carolinians and Georgians alike by water or road, the township not surprisingly continued to host a variety of notable visitors and regional travelers. The naturalist William Bartram surely passed by Purrysburg, if he did not lodge there, on his travels from Savannah to Augusta in the mid-1770s. In 1774 Hugh Finlay stopped there on an inspection tour for the postal service to secure a canoe and the aid of three blacks for his journey down the Savannah River. Four years later, in February 1778, Ebenezer Hazard, surveyor of the post roads, visited the township and stayed at Buche's Purrysburg inn on two separate occasions during his tour of southern postal routes. In 1784, after years of military activity in the area, the

Presbyterian minister the Reverend Archibald Simpson lodged for an evening at a home at the north end of town. The last leg of President Washington's southern tour in the spring of 1791 also included a stop in Purrysburg. He and his party, which included General Moultrie, left Judge Thomas Heyward Jr.'s White Hall plantation on Euhaw Creek at 5:00 A.M. on Thursday, 11 May, for the twenty-two-mile ride to the township before breakfast. At Purrysburg the president's party met Georgia dignitaries, including revolutionary patriots Noble Jones, Joseph Habersham, John Houstoun, Lachlan McIntosh, and Joseph Clay, who had traveled up from Savannah in an elaborately decorated boat to meet him. Township residents were said to have given the president a gold watch. By the late morning Washington and the Georgia entourage left Purrysburg landing for Savannah in the boat rowed by nine men "dressed in light blue jackets, black satin breeches, white silk stockings, and round hats with black ribbons bearing in letters of gold the device 'Long Live the President.'" Less than two years later, the Reverend Francis Asbury, whom John Wesley appointed general assistant superintendent, then bishop of the Methodist Societies in America, preached at Purrysburg during a visitation of Methodist activities in South Carolina and Georgia.[21] Other notable visitors who either passed through or lodged at Purrysburg over the next two decades included international travelers Luigi Castiglioni, the Duc de La Rochefoucauld Liancourt, John Davis, John Melish, and John Lambert. The English author Frank Silk Buckingham took note of the village of Purrysburg on his trip from Savannah to Augusta in February 1839. Notable travelers through Purrysburg were not always human, as the visit of an elephant and monkey in 1798—accompanied by their owner, of course—demonstrated.[22]

The advent of steamboat traffic on the Savannah River in 1816 did nothing to diminish Purrysburg's reputation as one of the more important boat landings on the river.[23] Georgia newspapers throughout the 1820s published the stage routes and carried advertisements for post, freight, and passengers. By the mid-1820s mail and passenger routes linking Savannah to Augusta and Charleston went through Purrysburg and ran three times a week, departing Savannah by steamboat at 6:00 A.M. for Purrysburg. At Purrysburg mail and passengers were transferred to four-horse stagecoaches for the rest of the journey if heading to Augusta or Charleston. The Charleston stage left daily at 2:00 A.M. for the overland journey to Purrysburg. The steamboats from Savannah spent the night at the Purrysburg landing to receive passengers arriving by coach from Charleston or Augusta at 7:00 A.M. for the trip back down the river. Separate portmanteaus were provided for mail service originating in Augusta and Charleston.[24]

The steamboat *Carolina* regularly made the run between Savannah and Purrysburg in the mid-1820s and was joined in July 1826 by the *Marion*. Mechanical problems with the stages, as well as the steamboats, inevitably delayed service, as did the weather on occasion, but human negligence could also be the culprit, as happened in November 1829 when the postal drivers, instead of exchanging stages at Purrysburg so their respective cargoes could proceed to the end of the line, somehow drove their own portmanteaus back, delaying the mail an entire day. Delays in mail service appear to have excited more passion than delays in passenger service, so important was the post at that time. Contracts were very clear about arrival and departure times.[25]

Detailed accounts of travel through Purrysburg during the steamboat era do not survive, but John Lambert's commentary on his journey from Charleston to Savannah in 1808 illustrates the character of travel in the region just before the age of the steamboat and provides further insight regarding Purrysburg's function in the transportation and communication network of the Southeast in the early national period. Lambert set out on foot from Charleston but decided to take the stage from Jacksonborough to Pocotaligo and, upon entering the vehicle, became convinced that one of his traveling companions was the French naturalist Michaud. Lambert went on to Coosawhatchie to spend the night. The next morning he awoke to rain. His stage left at 7:30 A.M. for Purrysburg. Along the way he saw a few plantations and "now and then a handsome house."[26] The causeways over the creeks and swamps he found quite dangerous, "being composed only of a few loose planks, with openings wide enough for a horse's leg to slip through." The rainstorm dissipated temporarily, but it became a heavy shower accompanied by deepening cold by the time he reached Purrysburg at 1:00 P.M. He discovered that the coach driver lived in Purrysburg. They took dinner at his house, where "his wife had everything ready for us upwards of two hours before our arrival."[27] He was not too taken with the town: "Purrysburgh is a paltry village, situated near the banks of the Savannah River, about 97 miles from Charleston and 25 from the town of Savannah. It contains scarcely a dozen houses, and they are occupied by the poorest sort of people. The tumuli of an Indian nation, which formerly resided here, are still visible, and carefully preserved by the inhabitants. . . . Mulberry trees grow spontaneously in various places and native silkworms, producing well formed cocoons, are often found in the woods."[28]

Lambert also described the mechanics of the transportation system:

> The stagecoach proceeds no farther than Purrysburgh, a boat being provided to carry the mail and passengers down the river to Savannah, a distance of twenty-five miles. The state pays $1,500 per annum for the carriage of the mail so that the comfort of the passengers is often less regarded by the proprietors, than the bag of letters. It happened unluckily for me, there were so many passengers, and so much baggage, that the usual covered boat was too small to hold us, and the conductor of the mail was obliged to procure a large canoe, but without any awning or shelter whatever. This was no very agreeable conveyance for twenty-five miles in rainy weather, and I was in doubt whether to go with them, or stay for a more favorable opportunity; but, having borrowed a great coat from the boatman, I embarked with the rest.[29]

His voyage down the river proved rather uncomfortable because of the weather, but also quite entertaining:

> We started from Purrysburgh about two o'clock and were rowed by four Negroes, for canoes are not paddled here as in Canada. They seemed to be jolly fellows, and rowed lustily to a boat song of their own composing. The words were given out by one of them, and the rest joined chorus at the end of every line. It began in the following manner:
>
> | | Chorus |
> |---|---|
> | "We are going down to Georgia, boys, | Aye, aye |
> | To see the pretty girls, boys, | Yoe, yoe |
> | We'll give 'em a pint of brandy, boys, | Aye, aye |
> | And a hearty kiss, besides, boys, | Yoe, yoe |
> | & c, & c, &c. | |
>
> The tune of this ditty was rather monotonous, but had a pleasing effect, as they kept time with it, at every stroke of their oars. The words were mere nonsense; anything, in fact, which came into their heads. I however remarked, that brandy was very frequently mentioned, and it was understood as a hint to the passengers to give them a dram. We had supplied ourselves with this article in Purrysburgh, and were not sparing of it to the Negroes, in order to encourage them to row quick. During the passage it rained incessantly, and prevented me from seeing the river to advantage.[30]

The party arrived in Savannah at dusk, though not without some excitement. Lambert reported that "our rowers, who were pretty far gone, in consequence of their frequent libations of brandy, had nearly upset the canoe, under the cable of a ship which was lying off the town."[31] On his return trip through Purrysburg and on to Charleston, Lambert remarked that "the road till within ten miles of Charleston, was so remarkably straight, smooth, and level, with scarcely a stone, rut, hole, or hillock to impede our progress, that walking, providing the weather were fair, would have been equally agreeable to riding."[32]

In addition to transporting passengers and the U.S. mail, the Savannah River also became increasingly congested with the transportation of cargo. To take advantage of closer commercial relations between Purrysburg and Savannah and the burgeoning freight traffic on the river, one township entrepreneur converted a large flatboat into a steamboat. He called it the *Cotton Plant* and ran the vessel for quite some time between Purrysburg and Savannah, making three round trips a week—down to Savannah one day and back to Purrysburg the next. The appearance of the converted boat must have been somewhat unique, for one historian of the region offered that, "if all the vessels of every description ever built, were molded into one and came flying into Charleston today, it would not create more wonder and amazement than the *Cotton Plant* did to the good people of Purrysburg and the surrounding country."[33]

III

The integration of Purrysburg Township into the greater political and economic forces operative in the Southeast also resumed after the war. Representation from St. Peter's Parish in the South Carolina legislature increased from one in 1775 to six by 1790 as it absorbed neighboring St. Luke's Parish, and, although township residents continued to elect their social betters to represent them, some of the lesser citizens among them served in minor offices such as commissioners of roads and parish election managers. For at least sixty years after the American Revolution, election managers continued to be selected to oversee the balloting at the town of Purrysburg and count the votes cast.[34] By 1795 the town proper had been rebuilt as the *U.S. Gazetteer* in that year called Purrysburg "a most handsome town in South Carolina . . . it contains forty to fifty dwellings and an Episcopalian Church." Robert Mills's letter of 1804 described Purrysburg as one of the six towns of note in the young state and indicated that the town proper included sixty dwellings with the main economic pursuits of township residents being the cultivation of rice and indigo, though the settlers still produced some silk. Purrysburg also had a resident doctor (Jeremiah Fickling) as late as the early 1820s.

The economic prosperity of Purrysburg, as well as its deepening commitment to the political economy of the plantation system, surged in the postwar decades, as illustrated by the dramatic expansion of slaveholding in the township. According to the 1790 census, a number of Purrysburg families had become major slaveholders. The Saussy family claimed fifteen slaves; the Waldburgers, twenty; the Winklers, twenty-one; the Humberts, thirty-seven; the Stroubharts, forty-three; Colonel John L. Bourguin, forty-five; Joachim Hartstone, forty-seven; the Buche, family fifty; Cornelius Dupont, sixty-two; and David Erhardt, 114. Only two Purrysburg families, the Fulkers and the Burgermeisters, claimed no slaves in 1790. By 1824 David Humbert alone claimed ten slaves, two members of the Winkler family claimed twenty, and two members of the Saussy family claimed a total of fifty-five slaves.[35]

The progressive increase in the number of slaves naturally intensified antipathy between blacks and whites in the region and excited recurring fears of slave rebellion. A slave named Stephen from the estate of Nicholas Winkler of Purrysburg was tried for planning an insurrection and sentenced to hang in May 1807. Only intervention by Governor Charles Pinckney granted the convicted slave a thirty-day stay of execution while further inquiry was made into his case. At roughly the same time, another slave conspiracy, centered near the Arm Oak neighborhood, a short distance from the township, was uncovered. The plot involved slaves from Euhaw plantations in the north to below Purrsyburg in the south and was reputed to have been activated by secret and quite volatile messages from Santo Domingo, which had experienced a successful slave revolt. The conspirators planned to fire the outbuildings of whites in the area and kill them as they emerged from their homes. A few attempted to test the plan a day early above Purrysburg, but they were dispersed by armed whites. The insurrection failed to materialize, as one of the conspirators betrayed his compatriots just hours before the appointed time. A trial held almost immediately at Purrysburg condemned at least ten slaves to death. After they were hanged, their heads were severed from the bodies and affixed to poles set up along the highway leading from Purrysburg to Coosawhatchie as a deterrent to further would-be rebels. The gruesome display so troubled some younger citizens that in defiance of the law the children removed and buried the heads.[36]

Another indication of the expansion of slaveholding in the township can be inferred from the appearance of newspaper advertisements regarding slaves. Practically nonexistent prior to the Revolution, between 1781 and 1810 a number of Purrysburg landholders advertised for the return of fugitive slaves or the sale of slaves. On 15 March 1781 John Stroubhar(t) of Purrysburg reported that Sarah, Renah, Rose, September (also called Jack), Butcher, Prince, and Monmouth had all gone missing. Rose and September had been branded with an "S" and Sarah had "country markings down her face." All of the slaves except September were from Guinea. Stroubhar offered three guineas reward for each if they were delivered to him in Purrysburg or one guinea if delivered to the Beaufort or Savannah jail, except for September, for whose return he offered two guineas. Stroubhar warned that he would prosecute any person harboring them. The sale of the personal estates of township residents David Giroud on 25 June 1783 and Captain David Keall on 25 March 1784 included slaves. A slave named Joe, said to be the property of John Cupper of Purrysburg, was turned into the Savannah workhouse in April 1797. In October of the following year a reward of ten dollars each was offered for the return of Brutus and Sam, who had run away three months earlier in July. They belonged to the estate of J. Waldburger. Henry Stroubhar offered twenty dollars in February 1811 for the return of York, who was well known in Purrysburg. In something of a turnabout, Jacob Winkler of the township placed an advertisement in May 1783 to find the owner of a slave named Sam whom Winker had apprehended.[37]

The available evidence points toward recovered prosperity for Purrysburg landholders in the decades after the Revolution. But, whereas social and economic development characterized the township except during the years of the Revolution and immediately thereafter, religious and educational opportunities remained as erratic after the conflict as before. The regular exercise of religious services was most likely not possible during the war years. The destruction of the Purrysburg Presbyterian Church by the British must have ended community worship services at least for the duration of the war; there is no evidence to suggest the existence of any other congregation after the 1760s. Without regular services of any confession, Purrysburg residents such as John and Ann Buche were forced to travel to Beaufort in 1783 to have their children baptized. After the Revolution, when the Anglican parishes lost their function as units of local civil government, there is no indication that an Anglican Church (after independence called the Protestant Episcopal Church) ever again served the community even though the parish contained 1,525 white inhabitants in 1819. The mention of an Episcopalian church in Purrysburg by the 1795 *U.S. Gazetter* in all probability referred to a building, not a denominational affiliation. Episcopal bishop the Right Reverend Theodore Dehon visited St. Peter's in 1816 on his statewide inspection tour of Episcopal parishes, but the yearly journals of the conventions of the Protestant Episcopal Church from 1785 through 1818 fail to note a representative from St. Peter's ever appearing at any of the meetings.[38]

Other religious groups were active in the area, but, with the exception of the Presbyterians, it is inconclusive as to how they were welcomed in the township. Adherence to the Reformed confession, however, continued strong among Purrysburg settlers. The petition of township residents for the rebuilding of their Presbyterian church was granted, and Reformed services continued there through at least the end of the century. There are no records to demonstrate that Purrysburg Presbyterians ever received a full-time Presbyterian minister, but at least two independent Presbyterian pastors, Mr. Beck and Mr. Crawford, alternately officiated without salary to the Reformed congregation until as late as 1807.[39] Mr. Beck eventually married one of his Purrysburg congregants. It is unclear whether the Great Revival of the early nineteenth century or the later Beaufort Revival of the early 1830s had an impact on township residents. It is known that the Baptist pastor of Pipe Creek, the Reverend Henry Holcombe, traveled with a Mr. Redding to Purrysburg in 1812 after he became "satisfied that a dispensation of the gospel" had been committed to him, but, though he may have held services there on this occasion or others, it is impossible to determine whether that was the case. Perhaps through the influence of the Pelot family in the area, there may have been some that turned to that persuasion, especially in the wake of the revivals.[40]

Educational opportunities were intermittent at best until the mid-1820s, when free school schoolmasters provided training until at least the late 1850s. Between 1787 and 1790, George Fisher taught school at Purrysburg, and advertised for students in the *Gazette of the State of Georgia* in May 1790: "George Fisher of Purysburg will open a school at his house near the Hon. John Houstoun's on Monday 24th instant where he will teach reading, writing, arithemetick [*sic*] and the useful branches of mathematics at his old price of four dollars per quarter. He hopes from his experience and assiduity to give satisfaction to those who may please to favor him with the education of their children; and as he taught the three preceding years in Purysburg, his character and abilities can easily be inquired into."[41] From this time until the Report of the Commissioners of Free Schools in 1825, which lists the first Purrysburg school, little is known about the extent or nature of educational opportunities. It is known that, even before 1790, Purrysburg children boarded in Beaufort to attend school there.[42]

Between 1825 and 1858 Purrysburg had free schools each year except 1827–1830, 1831–1834, 1835–1837, 1840–1843, 1846, and 1856–1857. In most years the school was served by a single teacher, but in 1825 there were two and in 1838–1839 perhaps three. Enrollment in any one year never exceeded twenty-one, and students often did not study for the entire year because fees were based on quarterly instruction. Still, in 1825 the eighteen students in the Purrysburg school constituted nearly 10 percent of the total parish enrollment, and the twenty-one students enrolled in 1847–1848 were the most in any free school in St. Peter's Parish. It is also worth noting that among the teachers in the parish was a Mr. Lafitte—a name long associated with the area. Beyond these statistics little else is known about schooling in Purrysburg in the antebellum decades.[43]

Under the dominant influence of slave-based plantation agriculture, however, the town of Purrysburg became less important in the decades after the Revolution, even as township landowners and St. Peter's Parish became more prosperous. The easy navigability of the Savannah River and the improvement in overland transportation routes drew Purrysburg Township closer to neighboring economic centers, which meant that the role of the town proper was probably reduced to the area close to the wharf and along the Savannah–Purrysburg–Charleston road. Its primary function after the Revolution was most likely as a service depot to off-load products or passengers at its busy docks or to carry the U.S. mail. The destruction brought on by the Revolution appears to have completely obliterated what little craft/artisan production remained prior to the late 1770s. Purrysburg rice, indigo, cotton, and other goods were off-loaded to the more populated and commercially more accessible urban centers of Savannah, Beaufort, and Charleston.

The town of Purrysburg appeared in Carey and Lea's 1822 "Geographical, Statistical, and Historical Map of South Carolina." Mills's 1825 atlas also included it. And, although it was reported to have virtually disappeared by the 1830s, Purrysburg was still designated a village in state land records of April 1852 and appeared on A. J. Johnson's maps of 1862. Certainly as railways supplanted stages as preferred modes of transportation and communication by the mid-1840s, the town's importance as a postal and passenger stop declined. This declension is perhaps best symbolized by the choice of nearby Hardeeville for the site of a railway station rather than Purrysburg. The ultimate demise of the village, however, can be attributed directly to its occupation and destruction during the Civil War.[44]

IV

Even prior to the outbreak of hostilities, General Robert E. Lee chose nearby Coosawhatchie as his headquarters when he bivouacked in the lowcountry. Once war was declared, the Confederacy operated regimental training camps, at least one of which was located at Purrysburg. The letters of Oliver P. Bostwick from his Purrysburg post to his relatives at Black Swamp in 1861 and 1862 speak about the nearly constant cannon fire from Union positions to the southeast, where Hilton Head Island was already in federal hands. Bostwick was also the first to mention the Purrysburg jugwell that may have at some point been used as a temporary restraining cell for prisoners.[45]

The presence of friendly troops in 1861 and 1862 probably affected the township residents in much the same way as Lincoln's presence did more than eighty years earlier. But it was General Sherman's advance from Savannah to Columbia in the winter of 1864–1865 that finally brought an end to the town of Purrysburg. According to John Bennett Walters, since the promulgation of Special Order 254 on 27 September 1862, the Union general had employed the strategy of totalizing warfare to intimidate noncombatants and demoralize the Confederacy.[46] By the time of his march to the sea, Sherman clearly subscribed to the theory of collective responsibility, which held noncombatants as culpable as the military and therefore as important to neutralize in any way possible as were soldiers of the line. When his 6,000-man army entered the birthplace of secession, the desire for vengeance animated officers and enlisted men alike and resulted in a ferocity directed against the civilian population unmatched even in Sherman's earlier campaigns.[47]

Sherman divided his army for the campaign. The left wing comprised the Army of the Cumberland under Major General H. W. Slocum—the Fourteenth Corps under General Jeff C. Davis taking the extreme left position on the Georgia side of the Savannah River, and the Twentieth Corps commanded by General A. S. Williams taking the left-center by crossing the Savannah at Union Causeway and proceeding upriver from there. General O. O. Howard led the Army of the Tennessee, whose Fifteenth and Seventeenth Corps under General John A. Logan and General Frank P. P. Blair, respectively, took the right wing and were transported from Savannah to Beaufort to take up their positions. Supporting the operation was the 4,000-man cavalry under General Judson Kilpatrick. Sherman's plan called for the right wing to "reestablish Port Royal Ferry, and mass the wing at or in the neighborhood of Pocotaligo." The left wing was charged "to work slowly across the causeway toward Hardeeville, to open a road by which wagons can reach their corps about Broad River: also, by a rapid movement of the left, to secure Sisters Ferry, and Augusta road out to Robertsville." Sherman hoped to have the whole army ready "to move with loaded wagons by the roads leading in the direction of Columbia, which afford the best chance of forage and provisions. Howard to be at Pocotaligo by the 15th January, and Slocum to be at Robertsville, and Kilpatrick at or near Coosawhatchie about the same date. General Foster's troops to occupy Savannah, and gunboats to protect the rivers as soon as Howard gets Pocotaligo."[48] All troops were reminded of their responsibilities not to enter buildings or commit trespass or destroy property except under orders from their commanding officers. Foraging parties under the leadership of at least one officer were to leave civilians sufficient supplies whenever possible. By early January the deployments had been made, and the operation commenced.[49]

Rainstorms, said to be the heaviest in two decades, drenched the region from 18 to 20 January and made roads impassable. The rain continued to fall almost without interruption through 23 January, by which time navigation by boat was the preferred mode of travel over roads submerged under nearly two feet of water. It was said that near "Purrysburg the only thing 'at home' were the alligators." The left wing alone had to construct 4,000 feet of pontoon bridges as it moved into the South Carolina lowcountry, and the combined armies built miles of corduroyed road to effect their passage.[50] In a tactic eerily reminiscent of Lincoln's withdrawal from the township in 1779, Confederate forces had constructed defensible redoubts (breastworks and roadblocks) near the river crossing that might have delayed Sherman's advance, but they provided little opposition and continued to fall back.[51] By 10 January Howard had begun his march from Beaufort, crossing to the mainland on 14 January. At roughly the same time, Slocum sent two divisions of the Twentieth across the Savannah River north of the city. After a laborious march the First Division occupied Purrysburg by 19 January, with a gunboat and two transports following. The other occupied nearby Hardeeville. Purrysburg served as the corps headquarters and supply depot. With both sites now in Union hands, Sherman's army "had effected a lodgement in South Carolina, and were ready to resume the march northward; but we had not yet accumulated enough provisions and forage to fill the wagons, and other causes of delay occurred."[52]

It was probably a combination of the terrible conditions under which the Union troops marched, a deep animosity toward South Carolina, and more than two years of waging total war that led to the final destruction of Purrysburg sometime between 19 January and 2 February 1865 and served as a precursor for the devastation to be replayed throughout the state over the next few weeks. Captain Conyngham, who also wrote as a war correspondent for the *New York Herald,* described what he heard and observed:

> There can be no denial of the assertion that the feeling among the troops was one of extreme bitterness towards the people of the state of South Carolina. It was freely expressed as the column hurried over the bridge at Sisters Ferry, eager to commence the punishment of "original secessionists." Threatening words were heard from soldiers who prided themselves in "conservatism in house-burning" while in Georgia, and officers openly confessed their fears that the coming campaign would be a wicked one. Just or unjust as this feeling was towards the country people of South Carolina, it was universal. . . .
>
> In Georgia a few houses were burned; here few escaped: and the country was converted into one vast bonfire. The pine forests were fired, the resin factories were fired, the public buildings and private dwellings were fired. The middle of the finest day looked black and gloomy, for a dense smoke arose on all sides, clouding the very heavens. At night the tall pine trees seemed so many huge pillars of fire. The flames hissed and screeched, as they fed on the fat resin and dry branches, imparting to the forests a most fearful appearance.

> Vandalism of this kind, though not encouraged, was seldom punished. . . . The ruined homesteads of the Palmetto State will long be remembered.[53]

Conyngham first experienced the indiscriminate destruction that was to characterize Sherman's march to Columbia at Purrysburg, which he mistakenly identified as Rarysburg: "I first saw its fruits at Rarysburg, where two or three piles of blackened brick and an acre or so of dying embers marked the site of an old revolutionary town; and this before the column had fairly got its 'hand in.'"[54] By 11 February much of the state had been reduced to smoldering ruins. In addition to Purrysburg, Hardeeville, McPhersonville, Grahamville, Gillisonville, Blackville, Midway, Hickory Hill, Brighton, Lawtonville, Robertsville, and Barnwell had been torched. Soon to follow were Orangeburg, Lexington, and ultimately Columbia on 17 February.[55] Much as had been the case after the initial burning of the town in 1779, for those living within the boundaries of the old township, the years following its second destruction in 1865 were laced with hostility and discord characteristic of the Reconstruction era.[56]

Although many of the other towns demolished in Sherman's march to Columbia were rebuilt after the war, Purrysburg had faced its last crisis. The town built to defend the colonial frontier in the 1730s passed into memory as did the southern socioeconomic culture it was created to preserve. The boat landing and wharves, however, remained useful. As late as 1879 significant quantities of "ranging lumber, steamboat wood, and turpentine" were still being shipped from the Purrysburg wharves. Perhaps because of the continued commercial importance of Purrysburg landing, it remained on the 1883 "Map of the State of South Carolina" issued by the Department of Agriculture of South Carolina, but the ruins of the town had not been cleared nor had new construction been initiated.[57] In an 1898 article, Dr. Muench reported that the town did not have "a toll gate, post office, or even a steamboat landing." Among the ruins left to mark the townsite, Muench could distinguish a silk mill, tavern site, the brick pillars of a house, the remnant of the oft-mentioned Indian mound, and the Purrysburg cemetery.[58]

V

The decline of the town, particularly after the 1820s, did not mean that the township was deserted, but it did symbolize the geographic, as well as the economic, mobility of Purrysburg landowners over the decades. The same plantation system that made Savannah and Beaufort more attractive as markets for the goods of Purrysburg planters also increased the wealth of township inhabitants. From the opening years of settlement and for a variety of reasons explored earlier, many Purrysburg families augmented their investments by acquiring lands in adjoining regions while maintaining their acreage in the township. Some chose to relocate to these new acquisitions. Some sold their lands in the township to provide them a stake for settlement elsewhere.

The mobility of the members of Jean Pierre Purry's own family who followed him to Purrysburg illustrates migration patterns that were reproduced over the course of next few township generations and well into the nineteenth century. After the demise of his business partnership with Samuel Montaigut in the late 1730s, Charles Purry moved to Beaufort, where he became a prominent member of that community. He operated two stores by the 1740s—one on Bay Street in Beaufort and a second at Okatee Bluff, called the "back door" to Purrysburg as it was the nearest tidewater landing to the township and allowed direct water passage to Beaufort and Charles Town. Purry's murder by one of his slaves on 21 July 1754 so galvanized the lowcountry that Governor James Glen issued a proclamation mobilizing "all officers, civil and military and all other His Majesty's subjects throughout this province to use their utmost endeavours for the discovery and detection of the persons concerned in committing the said murder." Glen offered to pardon any accomplice who came forward with the identity of the principal felon. The slave was soon found, tried, convicted, and his body gibbeted on Bay Street.[59] Purry's distant cousin John Rodolph received land across from Purrysburg in Georgia in the same year as Charles was murdered. He disappears from South Carolina records soon thereafter, which would indicate his possible move to his Georgia land. Of Purry's two stepbrothers Quinche, Lewis became a planter in St. Helena's Parish by the 1760s, and Pierre returned to Neuchâtel.[60]

By the 1750s the Desaussure and Verdier families moved closer to Beaufort, with Henry Desaussure established as a storekeeper and rice planter at Coosawhatchie and Verdiers at Okatee Bluff, where André managed Charles Purry's store in that decade. Jean De La Gaye left Purrysburg for Beaufort, where he became a successful merchant. When he sailed for Europe in 1769, he entrusted his business to Henry's son Daniel Desaussure of Beaufort. Members of the Bourguin family moved across the Savannah River into Georgia by the mid–eighteenth century, but John L. Bourguin remained a Purrysburg resident landholder, moving just outside the township to a plantation at Okatee Creek by 1790. David Mongin Jr. and John Mark Verdier became Sea Island planters, and John Mark, a Beaufort merchant, managed Daniel Desaussure's Beaufort store before the Revolution. The Marquis de Lafayette spoke from the portico of Verdier's elegant Beaufort home in 1825. The Huguenins had land in Georgia and in the Euhaws by 1790. Abraham Huguenin learned to build rice mills after the Revolution to recoup the family's fortune. His Roseland plantation became another source of prosperity for the family. The Huguenins also owned Spring Hill plantation, between Coosawatchie and Ridgeland. Together the family owned more than 25,000 acres in present-day Jasper County. Abraham went on to serve in the state legislature and also as a member of the Nullification Convention in 1832. A close relative, David Huguenin Beck, was killed in a duel on the streets of Coosawhatchie in 1826. Other families, such as the

Humberts, Mallets, Duponts, Stroubharts, Morgandollars (Morgantaller) and Ravots, received land in the adjacent areas of Effingham and Chatham counties in Georgia and the Euhaws (Grahamville) and Coosawhatchie districts of South Carolina. Purrysburg families that left Purrysburg for the Arm Oak area near Grahamville established productive rice plantations there. Chief among them were the Stoubharts and Humberts. The Stroubharts's Strawberry Hill plantation brought notoriety to the family but could not rival the Humberts'. In the antebellum years William Humbert owned 42,000 acres of land and more than a hundred slaves. The Saussys held land farther north in the Robertville area. The concentration of so many former Purrysburg families in this region ultimately led to the establishment of a village known as Switzerland. A few, including the sons of the Reverend Henry Chiffelle, ventured farther still from the township, with Philotheus removing to Charles Town and Amadeus to Savannah. John Chevillette chose to resettle in Orangeburg.[61]

Even as many acquired enough capital to leave the township and begin anew on lands more suitable to intensive plantation cultivation, it remained a viable entity, at least until the Civil War, and many continued to make it their primary place of residence—with a few, such as John Vauchier and Mrs. Sarah Baird, even moving into the township after the 1770s. William Williamson maintained his extensive Purrysburg acreage, including land that had been part of Purry's original barony, and died there in the late 1790s. Francis De La Croix of Purrysburg, perhaps a member of the third township generation of De La Croixs, offered for barter or sale "a two story house 32 feet long and 20 feet wide, with four fire rooms, well finished, having a shed room and a front piazza, with the necessary out buildings, a good orchard and so on in Purrysburg" in 1812. Well into the nineteenth century, settlers or their lineal heirs, such as George Herchnecht (1770), Daniel Mallett (1775), Adrian Mayer (1778), Dr. John Baptise Bourguin (1783), David Giroud (1783), Captain David Keall (1783), Henry Meuron (1784), and Major Philip Mayer (1817), died in the township and were interred there. Descendants of the families of Purrysburg kept up an attachment to the township by maintaining family burial plots in the Purrysburg cemetery at least as late as 1898.[62]

The Purrysburg Township community that faced the nullification crisis in 1828 was far removed from Purry's anxious frontier outpost of 1732. Long since incorporated into the social and economic patterns of the lower Southeast, those who remained in the township and others who relocated nearby were no longer strangers to each other or to the wider cultural consequences of increasingly strident political and ideological rhetoric. Relational networks continued to radiate outward toward Savannah, Charleston, Beaufort, Coosawhatchie, and beyond. These networks, more and more oriented vertically toward those individuals and issues outside the township though not forsaking local horizontal community connections, inexorably bound township landowners to the cause lost finally at Appomattox. The troubled times Purrysburg residents lived through brought tensions and uncertainties aplenty—sometimes with fellow members of the township—but there is little evidence to demonstrate the existence of long-standing animosity among the inhabitants. By the time storm clouds gathered for what was to be the township's final conflict, Purrysburg residents had developed communal networks, both within and without the township's boundaries, intricate enough to allow each citizen the luxury of forging a future without evoking the ghosts of a traumatic past.[63]

Conclusion

Long before Sherman's army laid waste to the village of Purrysburg, its raison d'être had been co-opted by the advance of the frontier line and the slave-based staple crop plantation political economy that it was founded in 1732 to protect. Purry's sudden death in August 1736, coupled with an array of difficulties during the early years of settlement, weakened and largely dissolved the quasi-legal bonds that tied the colonists to each other, to Purry, and to the provincial government. Left more or less to fend for themselves, the ethnically mixed population set about constructing relational networks that would meet their needs as traditional European lifeways, refracted through the lens of their South Carolina experience, were forced to adapt functionally to the New World environment. These adaptive relational networks—both horizontal ones with other members of the township, and vertical ones with those outside it—were conditioned by the personal, social, religious, economic, and military constraints under which the colonists operated as members of the township. The progressively more intricate relationships they established diverged from earlier conceptions of community and ethnic identity, but such divergence was more indicative of the pressures under which they had to live than it was of the disappearance of either community or ethnicity in the township.

If by the term *community* we refer to a set of social relations characterized by mutuality and interpersonal connections, then there is no doubt that Purrysburg residents and their descendants indeed created community in the wilderness.[1] But the idea of community involves a number of elements that go beyond social relations to include how those relationships are embedded in a geographic place and enfold both shared values and historical experience. And it was the manner in which the convergence of these factors had to occur that has led many to conclude that the township was a failure.[2]

One of the reasons for the assumption of Purrysburg's failure proceeds from the traditional conception of what a community should look like. The village ideal of early modern Europe as reproduced in Puritan New England became the accepted model for community in the New World. Where that model existed, so also did community. Where it did not, neither did community. Ferdinand Tönnies lent further credence to the dichotomy with his gemeinschaft and gesellschaft paradigm in the late nineteenth century. It is no wonder that historians practically defined the word *community* by the presence or absence of apparently transcendent New England traits.[3] Only recently have analysts begun to act on the realization that a community may take many structural forms. There is no one "true" community form.[4]

But while historians and social scientists have recognized the varieties of community organization, there is still the tendency to define a community in terms of geographic contiguity even though community networks can be forged between individuals otherwise separated by distance.[5] It is this tendency to equate proximity with community that leads to the second reason that Purrysburg has been considered a failure. For as has been demonstrated, when the immigrants first arrived at the township they may have been neighbors, but, in all likelihood, relatively few of them were emotionally linked to each other—especially considering their ethnic diversity. It would be more accurate then to designate the township a settlement system, which refers to the context of habitation, rather than to label Purrysburg a *community*, which refers to the network of relationships binding the immigrants together—particularly in the early months, perhaps years of its existence.[6] The sense of community at this early date most likely enclosed family members and existed only ephemerally or occasionally at any higher level of integration.

As the 1730s wore on, neighborhoods in the township developed centered in linguistic similarity, but, because of the provincial granting of adjoining town lots to speakers of different languages, such neighborhoods did not cluster in contiguous areas in Purrysburg. Rather, as the Rutmans found in Middlesex County, Virginia, these relational networks were structured around the individual homes of neighborhood community members, the religious meetings held in the Holzendorf home for German-speaking members of Purrysburg, for example.[7] There were then Purrysburg inhabitants living next to each other who remained, at least for a time, strangers because of ethno-cultural differences in the township.

Linguistic, religious, and commercial constraints inhibited a sense of community solidarity inside the township but promoted rapid construction of a host of vertical relationships (and hence community) with those outside Purrysburg. The presence of German-speaking Lutherans in Ebenezer and Reformed Germans in Savannah facilitated relationships with these towns, which became integral to the Purrysburg sense of community by the 1740s. The inability of the township to support a skilled craft sector in the early years also led to the migration of artisans from Purrysburg to other locales. This extended economic network pulled some permanently from the township and was undoubtedly one factor contributing to its population decline at least into the 1750s. But many stayed, content to maintain their physical residence in Purrysburg while simultaneously drawing emotional, economic, and affective support from outside it. As linguistic boundaries faded with the maturation of the native-born generation, Purrysburg families were finally able to strengthen horizontal relationships within the township itself.

In a very real sense the community networks some Purrysburg settlers had to fashion *began* vertically, with those outside the township, and only later did opportunities for horizontal relationships, with neighbors inside the township evolve. Just as these internal relationships became firmly established, Purrysburg faced the American Revolution, which further altered life and relational networks in the township. It was finally the growth of the state bureaucracy, an expansive plantation economy, and the melding of religious fervor with the institution of chattel slavery that cemented the planters and farmers of Purrysburg together and integrated them more fully into the wider social, political, and economic ideological assumptions of their fellow South Carolinians and ultimately the southern cause.[8]

A third reason for the supposed failure of Purrysburg Township was the reduction of the town proper, which began soon after its initial founding and continued at varying rates over the next three generations. But to label the township a failure based upon the population of the town of Purrysburg cannot account for the continued presence and progressive prosperity of township families. Purrysburg was never meant to become a central commercial community. Charles Town served that purpose and acted as a magnet to draw commerce from outlying regions to itself. Later Savannah, Beaufort, Columbia, and Augusta became the most important secondary urban centers in the lower Southeast. With commercial, religious, and legal authority centered in the capital and these nearby secondary commercial centers, it is no wonder that Purrysburg's status as a commercial agricultural community lessened over time even as prosperity continued to mount in South Carolina.[9] The loss of craftspeople and merchants in the first decade of settlement contributed to the decline of the town proper, but probably more significant was the progressive adoption of the slave-based plantation economy by township residents. The out-migration from the town proper to township plantations led to increased capital accumulation by Purrysburg planters while simultaneously depopulating the village at the heart of the township. The wharf continued to do brisk business as plantation commodities were sent down the Savannah to Charles Town. George C. Rogers Jr. observed a similar pattern, though not in as extreme a form, in the otherwise successful and quite wealthy city of Georgetown, South Carolina, by the 1840s.[10] In whatever ways the contractual and even theoretical basis of Purry's township may have been flawed, it was the ultimate success of his colonial vision based on the productive agricultural potential of South Carolina that contributed to the deurbanization of the township—not its failure.

The Purrysburg sense of community had to be created by individuals who initially had little in common with each other aside from their contractual agreement with Purry. The community they forged, though radically different structurally than the archetypical New England town, was nonetheless every bit as functional as that community model. But, as Thomas Bender has noted, constructing community in the South was very complicated business—and even more so in the multiethnic context of Purrysburg Township. Recovering the dynamics of ethnic identity formation and maintenance as well as reconstructing the creation and sustenance of the fluid and multilayered sense of community described in these chapters could become instructive for a reassessment of both in the antebellum South.[11]

Any precise determination of the extent of ethnic identity among and between French-, German-, and English-speaking Purrysburg settlers on the southern frontier is simply not possible because the "mix of assimilation and autonomy that characterized the response of peoples on the peripheries varied enormously. The combination is not easy to calculate in any mechanical fashion."[12] The inability of the historian to speak too authoritatively on this subject is, of course, an unfortunate consequence of the fact that ethnicity can only be most authentically studied when individuals can speak directly out of their own experiences. Consequently, it is upon social scientific field studies that the understanding of ethnicity is built, not on the secondary analysis of documentary evidence to which historians are so bound. This is not to say that social anthropology and sociology cannot aid the historian of ethnicity in assessing the past, merely that social science theory must be applied gingerly and with a healthy respect for the limitations inherent in the types of sources at the disposal of historians. Even so, failure to consider the implication of social scientific inquiry has led historians to investigate the concept of ethnicity as well as its presence or absence from faulty assumptions.

Because most historians have consistently assumed the existence or termination of what has been variously termed *ethnicity* or *ethnic identification,* they have seldom bothered to define exactly what is meant by the use of these terms. Although implicit definitions of the terms are taken for granted by the researcher, such definitions are rarely made explicit.[13] The tendency toward implicit definitions especially when dealing with white ethnic groups reveals severe weaknesses because it leaves critical and foundational issues untouched. Descriptive analysis of ethnic groups—the practice of describing behaviors and presuming such behaviors to be normative as though human beings exist in a steady-state world of equilibrium—proceeds directly from unexamined, implicit assumptions regarding the nature and content of ethnicity. Such analysis does not permit the scholar legitimately to advance any logically consistent and theoretically consonant definitions of ethnicity, which would be the determinative factors in any "we–they" dichotomy. In much the same manner as a botany student might lose sight of the diversity of vegetation in a given locale because she is too taken with studying one tree and then generalizing about the nature of the entire forest without ever recognizing her error, so also does descriptive analysis of ethnic groups merely describe "the correlates of ethnicity" without ever defining just what it is that the behaviors supposedly describe.[14]

Because of the traditional emphasis upon describing the phenomenon of ethnicity instead of examining the characteristics or behavior that prescribe ethnicity, historians have subscribed by default to what social scientists term the objective, structural, or etic definition of an ethnic group. This kind of definition delimits an ethnic group as a collectivity set off by race, religion, and (or) national origin and analyzes observed phenomena in terms of the values of the observer, not the observed.[15] As a direct result, historians of early America have made categorical statements, such as, "The French Huguenots, were, by contrast, so well assimilated by the time of the Revolution, that little remained to distinguish them from the rest of the colonial population except, perhaps, their surnames—and in many cases even these had become Americanized."[16] Or, "As a result of the resistant, undigested bits of foreign ways within the United States, American culture has been more colorful, more cosmopolitan, more diverse than any other people's since the days of Trajan and Hadrian and down until the creation of modern Israel. But as foreign newspapers die off one by one, as they have been doing, and the great tide of immigration lies increasingly farther in the past, the cultural diversity that has been one of the hallmarks of American civilization also begins to slide into homogeneity."[17]

Implicit reliance upon the objective, structural definition of ethnicity moved these historians to equate the disappearance of language, ecclesiastical ceremony, and cultural traditions with loss of ethnic group identity. Descriptive analysis after this fashion closes the door to an ethnically sensitive interpretation of white Euro-American colonial history and leaves inexplicable the subsequent behavioral phenomena of so-called Americanized white ethnic groups.

A much more appropriate methodology for the study of ethnicity proceeds from the subjective, phenomenological, or emic definition of ethnicity. Self-identification and identification by others illuminates the emic perspective. This approach is able to bypass potential errors by removing the perceptions of the observer from the analysis. As Wsevolod W. Isajiw notes, "In contrast to the objective approach by which ethnic groups are assumed to be existing as it were 'out there' as real phenomena, the subjective approach defines ethnicity as a process by which individuals either identify themselves as being different from others or belonging to a different group or are identified as different by others, or both identify themselves and are identified as different by others."[18]

The concept of ethnic identity or ethnicity then takes on psychological connotations and, as such, cannot be defined solely in terms of behavioral or structural indicators. What the individuals believe about themselves and what others believe about them in a social context, not by how they might appear to behave to an outside observer, must be taken into consideration. A deep psychological sense of belonging to a communal group in gemeinshaft terms underlies the emic perspective.[19] Amy Chua's enlightening study of contemporary ethnic conflict, *World on Fire,* uses this phenomenological perspective to great effect.[20]

A purely subjective model, however, cannot prove entirely satisfying to the historian, for there must be identifiable phenomena that can be objectively studied that define the boundaries between ethnic groups.[21] Therefore, the historian of ethnicity must analyze sources synthetically—drawing from both etic and emic perspectives. Isajiw's research has been predicated upon the necessity of determining a logically consistent and synthetic definition of ethnicity. His definition can be of significant assistance to social historians attempting to assess the persistence of white ethnicity in the antebellum South. Ethnicity, according to Isajiw, refers to "an involuntary group of people who share the same culture or descendants of such people who identify themselves and (or) are identified by others as belonging to the same involuntary group."[22]

Isajiw's definition allows for the analysis of subjectively based phenomena essential to a comprehensive understanding of ethnicity, even at the individual level, which social scientists have classified as symbolic ethnicity. David Schneider recognized that ethnic phenomena could be completely devoid of social content; yet such empty symbols could still function as ethnic "markers" as such signify identification with an ethnic entity.[23] Oscar Handlin hinted at this form of ethnicity without defining it when he noted that the offspring of immigrants maintained a continued patriotic tie with the old country, even though they had no affiliation with it.[24] Cultural symbols may vary from individual to individual and from ethnic group to ethnic group, but symbolic ethnicity tends to crystallize around cues or emblems carried over in some form from the Old World experience.[25] The cues may be rediscovered by individuals who have been socialized into the culture of the larger society but who then develop a symbolic attachment to the homeland of their forebears. There is great selectivity in the borrowing of cultural cues, but selectivity does not discount the validity or the evocative power of symbolic ethnicity. As may be readily concluded, only the subjective definition of ethnicity could adequately explore the psychocultural factors involved in the behavior of the rediscoverers.[26] Symbolic ethnicity most assuredly is not Clifford Geertz's primordial bond. Rather, the cultural symbols demonstrate that, while the host environment alters the conditions under which an individual may identify with her or his ethnic group of origin, continued links with the past of a visible ethnic collectivity are entirely possible.[27]

Although definitive answers concerning the extent of white ethnic identity and its effect on the contours of Purrysburg community life remain elusive, they do not remain completely obscured. For example, if Purrysburg ethnic lines were obliterated by the time of the American Revolution, as most have argued, why did the itinerant minister Joseph Pilmoor refer to Purrysburg as "a settlement of French refugees" on the occasion of his visit there in the winter of 1773?[28] Why then did Daniel Desaussure, whose father was one of the initial settlers of Purrysburg, continually assist John Mark Verdier, whose father was also a founding resident, even though the parents of these individuals left Purrysburg when their sons were still children?[29] Why did John Buche retain the services of his former Purrysburg neighbor Henry William Desaussure in his court case against Francis Breen and Major John McPherson even though Desaussure lived at Pocotaligo at the time? Why did the Reverend Zubly continue to remain involved in the lives of many Germanic residents of Purrysburg throughout his life even though he left the township before midcentury? Why did the Reformed confession in the form of the Purrysburg Presbyterian Church flourish at the township while the Anglican Church progressively lost what little influence it had? Why did the residents of the township address their petition for the rebuilding of their church in 1789 to Daniel Desaussure? Could not the continuation of the silk industry at Purrysburg even into the nineteenth century have something to do with the fact that sericulture was heavily practiced by French Huguenots and Piedmontese Waldensians as well as by the Reformed Swiss? Might not the skill have been passed down the generations as a sort of ethnic legacy? (There is evidence to suggest that at least one family with ancestral roots in the township [Malphrus] kept its connection to its Purrysburg and its commercial heritage by planting a mulberry tree wherever the family moved). How should we interpret David Giroud's nearly quarter-century association with Jean Pierre Purry's stepbrother Pierre, a Neuchâtel merchant who immigrated to Purrysburg in 1740, only to depart fourteen years later? What could be the significance, ethnically speaking, of David Zubly's ship mill, or the Purrysburg jugwell, or the fact that Gideon Mallet II, a third-generation Purrysburg settler, was fluent enough in French to serve as a translator during the Revolutionary War for General Francis Marion, who also happened to be descended from a French Reformed family. Why did Purrysburg descendants decorate the town cemetery with poles and retain family burial plots there? Why did the Stroubhart family go so far as to erect a memorial to its Purrysburg ancestors in the family cemetery near Purrysburg in 1887?[30]

At least partial answers to some of these questions can be found in the experience of a family that had linkages to Purrysburg and its surroundings. In 1788 Louise Gibert, daughter of the first Huguenot pastor of New Bordeaux in Hillsborough Township in the Savannah River backcountry married William Pettigrew. Pettigrew came from Scots-Irish stock in nearby Abbeville. Their first child, James Louis, was born in 1789. Louise named him after her father, Jean Louis. James was educated at Moses Waddell's academy and at South Carolina College. Shortly after he was admitted to the bar in 1812, James moved to Coosawhatchie to practice law. He also he altered the spelling of his last name to Petigru to reflect his mother's Huguenot heritage. All of his brothers and sisters followed his example. Jane and William Pease, biographers of the family, argue that the spelling change was far more than cosmetic: "More than a simple change in spelling, becoming a Petigru signaled the transformation of James's and his siblings' expectations and aspirations."[31]

Daniel Elliot Huger, member of another prominent Huguenot family, made Petigru his first law partner in Coosawhatchie. Huger had been mentored by Henry William Desaussure, whose father, Daniel, had also been helpful to him. In 1816 Petrgru married Jane Amelia Postell, daughter of a Purrysburg area landowner and whose mother also was of Huguenot ancestry. Their children were named for relatives and friends in three different Huguenot families—the

Porchers, Hugers, and Duponts. Naming patterns continued to reflect the Huguenot ancestry of the Petigrus, as well as their connections to other Huguenot descendants. His sister Adeline altered her name to Adelle as an adolescent and spelled it Adèle after she married. Another sister, Harriet, married into the prominent Huguenot Lesesne family in 1836.[32]

If all traces of white ethnic affinity in South Carolina were eradicated prior to the Civil War, what can explain such phenomena? What can explain Petigru's third anniversary address before the South Carolina Historical Society in 1858, which glorified his Huguenot ancestors?[33] How can the founding of the Huguenot Society of South Carolina in 1885 or Dr. George C. Rogers Jr.'s comments about the strength of the society in 1980 or the incorporation of the Purysburg Preservation Foundation in 1998 be explained without acknowledging the perseverance of an ethnic awareness that had supposedly expired well before the American Revolution? If Larry Lepionka is correct, the lack of eighteenth-century artifacts at the Purrysburg site reflects a recognized trait of central European immigrants and, as such, signals an ethnic characteristic. David Zubly's construction of the ship mill and the brick-lined jugwell could have served similar purposes. The historical understanding of ethnicity in Purrysburg clearly needs to be reconsidered, which in turn should reopen the question of the perseverance of white ethnicity in the nineteenth-century South. That process has begun with the work of scholars such as Amy E. Friedlander, Bertrand Van Ruymbeke, John F. Bosher, and R. C. Nash. Their research is illustrative of the new lines of inquiry possible with a broader conception of what constitutes ethnic association and identity.[34]

The immediate Swiss background of the majority of Purrysburg settlers renders questions of ethnicity even more complicated. For in the Swiss context even traditional ethnic markers such as language and religion might fail to delimit one ethnic group from another. Add this to the fact that it is nearly impossible to determine how many eventual Purrysburg immigrants were actually natives of the Swiss Confederation rather than refugees fleeing political and religious persecution and the ethnic picture becomes very complex indeed.[35]

Although most of them shared an affinity for the Reformed confession, linguistic and cultural barriers simultaneously separated them. To survive in Purrysburg, the immigrants were forced to choose among ethnic traits—either language, religion, or culture. The subsequent migration of Purrysburg German loyalties to Ebenezer and the drain of skilled artisans and craftspeople from the township, therefore, do not necessarily demonstrate a loss of all ethnic consciousness, merely a reordering of ethnic markers to cope with the realities of life in a new land. Even the early intermarriage of couples of apparently dissimilar ethnic groups in Purrysburg may only illustrate the strength of biculturalism as well as bilingualism among some of the residents. Another possibility is suggested by Charles Joyner's study of slavery in All Saint's Parish, South Carolina. His analysis of the slave community in this Georgetown District parish pivots around the selective adaptation of cultural elements of

African and European origin in the New World context. This cultural creolization manifested itself in numerous ways, only the most visible of which was language (Gullah).[36] Perhaps the same process of selective adaptation could help explain the Purrysburg experience—and the actions of descendants of the original township settlers in naming the locality to which they moved "Switzerland" after English became their lingua franca.

That the Reformed confession remained strong has been demonstrated by the actions of the settlers and by their supposedly Anglicanized ministers. The formal resurfacing of the Reformed confession in the 1770s with the founding of the Purrysburg Presbyterian Church and the apparent lack of enthusiasm for the Anglican Church indicate that the ethnic marker of Reformed religious conviction was in a real sense rediscovered in Purrysburg when linguistic division and colonial legislation were no longer impediments to that form of worship. In this case, it may well have been that while the presence of European-based languages initially served as identifiable links with the past, they also precluded the possibility of perpetuating ethnic identity based in religious confession and triggered an adaptive strategy of community formation by including relationships with similar speaking settlers in Georgia, though their religious expression was Evangelical Lutheran Pietism. The eventual acceptance of English by descendants of the original residents shifted the priority of ethnically defined religious behavior again and in a sense united the religious life of the township under the Reformed confession.

It is clear that these phenomena cannot be adequately explained by the reigning assimilationist paradigm of whiteness in the antebellum South. Another model is needed—one that can consistently interpret the evidence and simultaneously open new avenues of inquiry. Frederik Barth's theory of boundary maintenance is such a model.

Barth focuses on ethnicity as a form of social, not cultural, organization, which manifests itself in boundary maintenance between ethnic groups. Cultural parameters such as dress, food, language, religion, and marriage may be part of the boundary structure, but "these cultural features of significance are not the sum total of the objective differences between . . . groups."[37] To Barth the *maintenance* of social boundaries, not necessarily the *components* of the boundaries, are most significant because boundaries can change over time. These ethnic boundaries are not constants. They can be reconfigured to accommodate themselves to new circumstances. Malleable boundaries, no matter what form they may take, determine ethnicity in the Barthian model. His conviction that these subjectively determined ethnic boundaries may vary in cultural content and that even the cultural features that signal the boundaries may change seem to explain most accurately the complex Purrysburg findings. For though the boundaries between French, German, and English did vary with time, continued distinctions seem to have been made by some Purrysburg individuals and families. Those distinctions formed boundaries that perpetuated a sense of ethnic identity, which may have looked very different from European precedents but in effect served the same purpose. It is impossible to explain the naming of the region in upper St. Peter's Parish where a number of former Purrysburg families relocated in the nineteenth century Switzerland if all traces of ethnic identity with European homelands had been eradicated in the eighteenth.

Although Barth's paradigm generally explains the role of ethnicity, consideration must also be given to the role of David Schneider's observation that ethnic phenomena may be completely devoid of social content and yet still signify ethnic boundaries. "Symbolic ethnicity" may very well help to explain such varied phenomena as the continued ties between the Desaussures and the Verdiers, Buche's relationship with Henry William Desaussure, the persistence of the silk industry, the rebirth of the Reformed confession at Purrysburg in the 1770s, and a host of other phenomena described in this study. These are tentative observations open to further analysis and debate, and they have implications far beyond Purrysburg Township. The Petigru family's actions, such as James Louis's name change subsequently adopted by all his siblings, may well have signaled a collective psychological rediscovery of an ethnic link to the French Huguenots and as such marks a Barthian ethnic boundary. The founding of the Huguenot Society of South Carolina, the Purysburg Preservation Foundation, and other such organizations most assuredly says something about the existence of an ethnic boundary declared destroyed well over a century ago.

Perhaps this study has raised more questions than it has found evidence to answer. That would be a fine legacy. But it does seem that white identity formation and community development in Purrysburg and in the antebellum South generally are much more perplexing issues than previously thought. Both deserve closer scrutiny. Community life as it evolved in Purrysburg owed less to the contractual arrangement that first animated Purry to found the township and much more to the dogged determination of the settlers he recruited. Perhaps the contractual community ideal of Puritan New England could not be duplicated in the South after all,[38] at least among diverse ethnic groups motivated more by economics and less by religious fervor. This generalization needs testing in other southern quasi-contractual communities such as Ebenezer, Georgia, Hillsborough Township, South Carolina, New Bern, North Carolina, and Manniktown, Virginia.

By the same token, there is further need for comparative analysis of white ethnicity in the antebellum South. Lawrence Taylor found in his study of the West Sayville, New York, Dutch that, whereas outward ethnic markers of customs, dress, and food have disappeared from the community, ethnicity is firmly ensconced in the minds of the residents through vocation, religion, and voluntary organizations.[39] His Barthian analysis, coupled with sensitivity to both objective and subjective aspects of ethnicity, has resulted in a reevaluation of Dutch ethnicity. The southern white ethnic experience could benefit from the same approach. The process of creating "southerners" from "Purrysburgers" that led eventually to the firestorm of the 1860s most likely occurred in the decades between 1790 and 1830. It was sometime during these decades that the expansive plantation economy of South Carolina and the ideology that accompanied it, unknown to the original colonists of 1732, enveloped the entire township, thereby contributing to an alteration in "community." Just as race and slavery amalgamated the whites of Lunenburg County, Virginia, so also did that institution forge a distinctive southern ideology of community in and around Purrysburg Township.[40] Contrary to conventional wisdom, however, becoming a southerner did not necessarily preclude simultaneous affinity for white ethnic identification as others have suggested.[41] Such identification may have been symbolic or may even have been imputed more to the Purrysburg planters by others than by themselves. Nonetheless, ethnic boundaries persevered up to and beyond the War between the States.

Unfortunately the documentary evidence will not unequivocally support any one answer over others. But if questions remain as to exactly what the process of adaptation was, it is now at least apparent that the general trend among township residents, as it most likely was among other white ethnic groups in the antebellum South, was the transformation of ethnic identity and not its eradication. At least some Purrysburg settlers to the third, fourth, and fifth generation perceived themselves, not solely as South Carolinians, but also as the inheritors of a distinct ethnic heritage.

Old World cultures, as Taylor discovered, could not be merely shrugged off as one might remove a warm winter coat indoors. Culture and cultural assumptions are "worn a good deal closer to the skin."[42] If the ethnic behaviors in Purrysburg Township are at all indicative of regional ethnic adaptation to the constraints placed upon community building and ethnic identification, it would not be inconceivable that the Rebel Gray that faced the Yankee Blue was woven, at least partially, from French, German, Swiss, and Scots-Irish thread. The multistrand network of relationships that emerged in Purrysburg Township speaks more eloquently to the tenacity and creativity of the long since departed immigrants and their progeny than any epitaph etched into the weathered gravestones standing silently through the years along the old river road.

Notes

Preface

1. During the more than two decades I have spent studying and writing about Purrysburg and its inhabitants, I have discovered wide discrepancies in the spelling of the name of the township. It is referred to in various sources as Purrysbourg, Purrysburgh, Purrysburg, Purrysborough, Purrysbourgh, Purysbourgh, Purysbourg, Purysburg, Purrisburgh, Purisburgh, Puresburgh, Priesburg, Parisburg, Parrysburgh, Parysburg, Pourrisburgh, Petersburg, Rarysburg, and Furysburg. At least two different writers have also located the township site in Georgia. Some of the confusion comes from the usual problems associated with handwritten documents. The multiethnic composition of the township also contributed to the multiple spellings—some more derived from the French-speaking sector (Purrysbourg, Purrysbourgh, Purysbourg), some more derived from the Germanic sector (Purrysburgh, Purysburgh, Purrisburgh), and at least one indicative of the English heritage of the officials who sanctioned its creation (Purrysborough). Its location on the sometimes uncertain boundary between South Carolina and Georgia has led to its erroneous placement in the wrong colony on occasion. For example, in the index to the Kemble Papers, "Parisburg" is listed as being in Georgia. See *The Kemble Papers,* vol. 2, *1780–1781,* in *Collections of the New York Historical Society for the Year 1884*, vol. 17 (New York: Printed for the Society, 1885), 462. Finally, it should be noted that different generations of the Purry family in Neuchâtel, Switzerland, have chosen alternate spellings of the surname. Jean Pierre, the founder of the township spelled his name with the double "r." I will take his spelling as the normative one for the surname in this study and will use the suffix "burg" to render "Purrysburg" as the operative spelling of the township.

2. On a subsequent visit to the site, I found a modern street sign marking the route of the Purrysburg–Charleston road, which is still in service and well maintained.

Introduction

1. It can be argued that Sumner Chilton Powell's *Puritan Village: The Formation of a New England Town* (Middletown, Conn.: Wesleyan University Press, 1963) was the first monograph in the new community study–social history genre, but it was with the publication in 1970 of the four key volumes by these authors that the methodology was fully exploited. See John Demos, *A Little Commonwealth: Family Life in Plymouth Colony* (New York: Oxford University Press, 1970); Philip J. Greven Jr., *Four Generations: Population, Land, and Family in Colonial Andover, Massachusetts* (Ithaca, N.Y.: Cornell University Press, 1970); Kenneth A. Lockridge, *A New England Town: The First One Hundred Years, Dedham, Massachusetts, 1636–1736* (New York: W. W. Norton, 1970); and Michael Zuckerman, *Peaceable Kingdoms: New England Towns in the Eighteenth Century* (New York: Alfred A. Knopf, 1970). For a helpful overview of the historiography of the formative years

of the new social history, see Stephanie Grauman Wolf, *Urban Village: Population, Community, and Family Structure in Germantown, Pennsylvania, 1683–1800* (Princeton, N.J.: Princeton University Press, 1976; first Princeton paperback printing, 1980), 3–16.

2. Page Smith, *As a City upon a Hill: The Town in American History* (New York: Alfred A. Knopf, 1966), viii; Thomas Bender, *Community and Social Change in America* (New Brunswick, N.J.: Rutgers University Press, 1978), 71; Bruce Collins, *White Society in the Antebellum South* (New York: Longman, 1985), vii; David J. Russo, *Families and Communities: A New View of American History* (Nashville: American Association for State and Local History, 1974), 255.

3. Darrett B. Rutman and Anita H. Rutman, *A Place in Time: Middlesex County, Virginia, 1650–1750* (New York: W. W. Norton, 1984); Orville Vernon Burton, *In My Father's House Are Many Mansions: Family and Community in Edgefield, South Carolina* (Chapel Hill: University of North Carolina Press, 1985); Robert C. Kenzer, *Kinship and Neighborhood in a Southern Community: Orange County, North Carolina, 1849–1881* (Knoxville: University of Tennessee Press, 1987); Robert D. Mitchell, *Commercialism and Frontier: Perspectives on the Early Shenandoah Valley* (Charlottesville: University Press of Virginia, 1977); Carville V. Earle, *The Evolution of a Tidewater Settlement System: All Hallow's Parish, Maryland, 1650–1783*, Research Paper no. 170 (University of Chicago, Department of Geography, 1975); Richard R. Beeman, *The Evolution of the Southern Backcountry: A Case Study of Lunenburg County, Virginia, 1746–1832* (Philadelphia: University of Pennsylvania Press, 1984); Lois Green Carr and Lorena S. Walsh, "The Planter's Wife: The Experience of White Women in Seventeenth-Century Maryland," *William and Mary Quarterly*, 3rd ser., 34 (October 1977): 542–71; Russell Menard, *Economy and Society in Early Colonial Maryland* (New York: Garland, 1985); Thomas H. Breen, *Tobacco Culture: The Mentality of the Great Tidewater Planters on the Eve of the Revolution* (Princeton, N.J.: Princeton University Press, 1985). There are also edited volumes of special note. Thad W. Tate and David L. Ammerman published a book of highly influential articles that were originally presented at a conference on the Chesapeake in the seventeenth century on 1–2 November 1974. See Tate and Ammerman, eds., *The Chesapeake in the Seventeenth Century: Essays on Anglo-American Society* (Chapel Hill: University of North Carolina Press, 1979). For two of the earliest forays into southern social history, see Aubrey C. Land, "Economic Base and Social Structure: The Northern Chesapeake in the Eighteenth Century," *Journal of Economic History* 25 (December 1965): 639–54, and Lois Green Carr, Aubrey C. Land, and Edward C. Papenfuse, eds., *Law, Society, and Politics in Early Maryland: Proceedings of the First Conference on Maryland History, June 14–15, 1974* (Baltimore: Johns Hopkins University Press, 1977).

4. Note especially in this regard Joyce E. Chaplin, *An Anxious Pursuit: Agricultural Innovation and Modernity in the Lower South, 1730–1815* (Chapel Hill: University of North Carolina Press, 1993); Richard Waterhouse, *A New World Gentry: The Making of a Merchant and Planter Class in South Carolina, 1670–1770* (New York: Garland, 1989); Peter A. Coclanis, *The Shadow of a Dream: Economic Life and Death in the South Carolina Low Country, 1670–1920* (New York: Oxford University Press, 1989); Rachel N. Klein, *Unification of a Slave State: The Rise of the Planter Class in the South Carolina Backcountry, 1776–1808* (Chapel Hill: University of

North Carolina Press, 1990); Stephanie McCurry, *Masters of Small Worlds: Yeoman Households, Gender Relations, and the Political Culture of the Antebellum South Carolina Low Country* (New York: Oxford University Press, 1995); Lawrence S. Rowland, Alexander Moore, and George C. Rogers Jr., *The History of Beaufort County, South Carolina,* vol. 1, *1514–1861* (Columbia: University of South Carolina Press, 1996); Larry E. Hudson Jr., *To Have and to Hold: Slave Work and Family Life in Antebellum South Carolina* (Athens: University of Georgia Press, 1997); Allan Gallay, *The Formation of a Planter Elite: Jonathan Bryan and the Southern Colonial Frontier* (Athens: University of Georgia Press, 1989); Robert Olwell, *Masters, Slaves, and Subjects: The Culture of Power in the South Carolina Low Country, 1740–1790* (Ithaca, N.Y.: Cornell University Press, 1998); Kaylene Hughes, "Populating the Back Country: The Demographic and Social Characteristics of the Colonial South Carolina Frontier, 1730–1760" (Ph.D. dissertation, Florida State University, 1985); Katherine Hurt Richardson, "'As Easy to Build Towns as Draw Schemes . . . ,' Colonial South Carolina Settlement Patterns: Towns on the Frontier" (M.A. thesis, University of South Carolina, 1988); William B. Barr, "Strawberry Ferry and Childsbury Towne: A Socio-Economic Enterprise on the Western Branch of the Cooper River, Saint John's Parish, Berkeley County, South Carolina" (M.A. thesis, University of South Carolina, 1995); George D. Terry, "'Champaign Country': A Social History of an Eighteenth Century Lowcountry Parish in South Carolina, St. John's Berkeley County" (Ph.D. dissertation, University of South Carolina, 1981).

5. Rutman and Rutman, *A Place in Time*, 21. I have used Page Smith's appellation here to describe Beeman's Lunenburg County not because he calls it such (he does not) but because it fits so well Smith's definition of a cumulative community. See Smith, *City upon a Hill*, 17, 30, 32.

6. Christopher Hill, *Society and Puritanism in Pre-Revolutionary England* (New York: Schocken Books, 1964).

7. Smith is one of the few who acknowledged the presence of the contractual community in the South, but as he searches for it in the context of the New England English Puritan culture, he finds it "usually in the form of enclaves, of isolated communities, often the offspring of the covenanted communities of New England." See Smith, *City upon a Hill*, 12. George Lloyd Johnson Jr.'s community study of the Cheraws District of the upper Pee Dee River near what was to have become Queensboro Township is perhaps the research that comes closest to this kind of inquiry. See George Lloyd Johnson Jr., *The Frontier in the Colonial South: South Carolina Backcountry, 1736–1800* (Westport, Conn.: Greenwood Press, 1997).

8. Darrett B. Rutman, "The Social Web: A Prospectus for the Study of Early American Community," 57–123, in William L. O'Neill, ed., *Insights and Parallels: Problems and Issues of American Social History* (Minneapolis: Burgess, 1973), 76–77. Rutman does call for "a great deal of work on many specific communities before generalizations can be attempted." See Rutman, "Social Web," 77. For a closer look at the issue of ethnicity as well as other factors contributing to the identity formation of colonial Americans, see Bernard Bailyn and Philip D. Morgan, eds., *Strangers within the Realm: Cultural Margins of the First British Empire* (Chapel Hill: University of North Carolina Press for the Institute of Early American History and Culture, 1991); Nicholas Canny and Anthony Pagden, eds., *Colonial Identity in the Atlantic World, 1500–1800* (Princeton, N.J.: Princeton University Press, 1987);

Ronald Hoffman, Mechal Sobel, and Fredrika J. Teute, eds., *Through a Glass Darkly: Reflections on Personal Identity in Early America* (Chapel Hill: University of North Carolina Press for the Omhundro Institute of Early American History and Culture, 1997); Michael Zuckerman, ed., *Friends and Neighbors: Group Life in America's First Plural Society* (Philadelphia: Temple University Press, 1982); Aaron Spencer Fogleman, *Hopeful Journeys: German Immigration, Settlement and Political Culture in Colonial America, 1717–1775* (Philadelphia: University of Pennsylvania Press, 1996).

9. Bertrand Van Ruymbeke, "L'émigration huguenote en Caroline du Sud sous le régime des Seigneurs Propriétaires: Étude d'une communauté du Refuge dans une province britannique d'Amérique du Nord (1680–1720)," 2 vols. (Ph.D. dissertation, Université de la Sorbonne-Nouvelle, Paris III, 1995); idem, "The Huguenots of Proprietary South Carolina: Patterns of Migration and Integration," 26–48, in Jack P. Greene, Rosemary Brana-Shute, and Randy J. Sparks, eds., *Money, Trade, and Power: The Evolution of Colonial South Carolina's Plantation Society* (Columbia: University of South Carolina Press, 2001); John F. Bosher, "Huguenot Merchants and the Protestant International in the Seventeenth Century," *William and Mary Quarterly,* 3rd ser., 52 (1995): 77–102; idem, "The Imperial Environment of French Trade with Canada, 1660–1685," *English Historical Review* 108 (1993): 50–82; R. C. Nash, "Huguenot Merchants and the Development of South Carolina's Slave-Plantation and Atlantic Trading Economy, 1680–1775," 208–40, in Bertrand Van Ruymbeke and Randy J. Sparks, eds., *Memory and Identity: The Huguenots in France and the Atlantic Diaspora* (Columbia: University of South Carolina Press, 2003); Patricia D. Beaver and Helen M. Lewis, "Uncovering the Trail of Ethnic Denial: Ethnicity in Appalachia," 51–68, in Patricia D. Beaver and Carole E. Hill, eds., *Cultural Diversity in the U.S. South: Anthropological Contributions to a Region in Transition,* Southern Anthropological Society Proceedings, no. 31 (Athens: University of Georgia Press, 1998), 54–55; see also 2–3; Daniel B. Thorp, *The Moravian Community in Colonial North Carolina: Pluralism on the Southern Frontier* (Knoxville: University of Tennessee Press, 1989), 4, 7, 199; Gallay, *Formation of a Planter Elite*, xv; Mitchell, *Commercialism and Frontier*, x, 239.

10. In using the term *slave society* here, I follow Robert Olwell's characterization of the colonial South Carolina lowcountry as a society whose primary goal at all levels was the maintenance of control over the African American slave population upon whose labor an entire way of life depended. See Olwell, *Masters, Slaves, and Subjects*, 5.

11. It should be noted that the very term *assimilation* as an historical occurrence is laden with quite substantial ideological baggage and has been reinterpreted and subjected to heated debates over the past twenty years. See Russell A. Kazal's excellent historiographical review article "Revisiting Assimilation: The Rise, Fall, and Reappraisal of a Concept in American Ethnic History," *American Historical Review* 100, no. 2 (April 1995): 437–71. For earlier assessments, see Olivier Zunz, "American History and the Changing Meaning of Assimilation," *Journal of American Ethnic History* 4, no. 3 (Spring 1985): 53–72, and Rudolph J. Vecoli, "Return to the Melting Pot: Ethnicity in the United States in the Eighties," *Journal of American Ethnic History* 5, no. 1 (Fall 1985): 7–20.

12. Collins's book is among the more recent in the substantial literature on southern identity. See also among others Wilbur J. Cash, *The Mind of the South* (New York: Alfred A. Knopf, 1941); William R. Taylor, *Cavalier and Yankee: The Old South*

and American National Character (New York: George Braziller, 1961); C. Vann Woodward, *The Burden of Southern History*, rev. ed. (Baton Rouge: Louisiana State University Press, 1968); Peter H. Wood, *Black Majority: Negroes in Colonial South Carolina from 1670 through the Stono Rebellion* (New York: Knopf, 1974); David M. Potter, "The Enigma of the South," *Yale Review* 51 (October 1961): 142–51. Beeman attempts to confront the reality of ethnic diversity in Lunenburg County, Virginia, but, as he accepts the southern white identity thesis and in fact argues its full operation in the county, white ethnic groups are lost very quickly in his analysis. For a social science perspective on this issue, see Beaver and Lewis, "Uncovering the Trail of Ethnic Denial."

13. Duane Meyer's *The Highland Scots of North Carolina, 1732–1776* (Chapel Hill: University of North Carolina Press, 1961) explores the Highland Scots as an immigrant group but appears to assume the existence of a Scottish identity without ever attempting to assess its contours or persistence over time. Daniel B. Thorp's more recent *The Moravian Community in Colonial North Carolina* contains excellent discussions of the persistence of shifting ethnic boundaries, but since his inquiry is limited only to the first twenty years of the Moravian community in North Carolina, he cannot provide longitudinal analysis beyond the first generation. Stephanie Wolf's *Urban Village* perhaps provides a few more glimpses of German ethnic declension—or adaptation (her conclusions are somewhat unclear on this point)—but takes as its case study Germantown, Pennsylvania.

14. Although historians of the South have yet to examine the types of contractual, ethnically diverse communities emphasized here, there is a voluminous theoretical literature on the nature of frontier settlement patterns, community types, and the relationship between large and small settlements. On frontier settlement patterns and the relationship between large and small settlements, see Kenneth E. Lewis, *The American Frontier: An Archeological Study of Settlement Pattern and Process* (New York: Academic Press, 1984); Stanton W. Green and Stephen M. Perlman, eds., *The Archeology of Frontiers and Boundaries* (Orlando: Academic Press, 1985), especially the chapters by Green and Perlman, "Frontiers, Boundaries, and Open Social Systems," 3–13, John Justeson and Steven Hampson, "Closed Models of Open Systems: Boundary Considerations," 15–30, and Patricia E. Ruberton and Peter F. Thorbahn, "Urban Hinterlands as Frontiers of Colonization," 231–49. On community types, see below and Keith S. O. Beavon, *Central Place Theory: A Reinterpretation* (London: Longman, 1977); Patricia E. Rubertone, "Landscape as Artifact: Comments on 'The Archaeological Use of Landscape Treatment in Social, Economic and Ideological Analysis,'" *Historical Archeology* 23, no. 1 (1989): 50–54; Margaret C. Rodman, "Empowering Place: Multilocality and Multivocality," *American Anthropologist* 94, no. 3 (September 1992): 640–56; Patricia D. Beaver, *Rural Communities in the Appalachian South* (Lexington: University of Kentucky Press, 1986). Beaver's reference notes 1–3 on p. 167 annotate her indebtedness to the pioneering work of Durkheim, Tönnies, and Weber, as well as to the more recent models of J. A. Barnes, Elizabeth Bott, J. Clyde Mitchell, and C. J. Calhoun. For social science case studies of community types, see Beaver's studies cited above, Kenneth E. Lewis, *Camden: A Frontier Town in Eighteenth Century South Carolina*, Anthropological Studies, no. 2 (Columbia: Institute for Archeology and Anthropology, University of South Carolina, 1976), and Elmora Messer Matthews, *Neighbor and Kin: Life in a Tennessee Ridge Community* (Nashville: Vanderbilt University Press, 1965). Historians have also worked

with these theoretical constructs to some extent. See Rutman and Rutman, *A Place in Time*, Rutman, "Social Web," Barr, "Strawberry Ferry," and Richardson, "'As Easy to Build Towns'" as examples.

15. For an extended discussion of the conception of ethnicity and the process of measuring it in an historical context, note Arlin C. Migliazzo, introduction to "Ethnic Diversity on the Southern Frontier: A Social History of Purrysburgh, South Carolina, 1732–1792" (Ph.D. dissertation, Washington State University, 1982).

16. Charles S. Dwight, "Address of the President," *Transactions of the Huguenot Society of South Carolina* 44 (1939): 21, hereafter cited as *THSSC*. The monument was ultimately built and dedicated in May 1941.

17. A recent example of the latter tendency is the erroneous placement of the township in the colony of Georgia. See Louis DeVorsey, *The Georgia–South Carolina Boundary* (Athens: University of Georgia Press, 1982), index entry under Purrysburg, *GA*. Whether the placement of the township in Georgia was done to highlight the boundary question or was an oversight by the author, it continues a practice that dates back to the nineteenth century.

18. Arthur Henry Hirsch, *The Huguenots of Colonial South Carolina* (Durham, N.C.: Duke University Press, 1928), 28–29; the Reverend George Howe, *History of the Presbyterian Church in South Carolina*, 2 vols. (Columbia, S.C.: Duffie & Chapman, 1870), 1:210; Henry A. M. Smith, "Purrysburgh," *South Carolina Historical and Genealogical Magazine* 10 (October 1909): 187–89, 194, hereafter cited as *SCHGM*. It must be noted that the Smith article is the most even-handed treatment of the settlement as an ethnically pluralistic whole, but the author still falls victim to the ambiguous use of the "Swiss" designation and carries his story only to the mid-1730s. See also the brief but informative account of the township provided by Robert L. Meriwether, *The Expansion of South Carolina, 1729–1765* (Kingsport, Tenn.: Southern Publishers, 1940), 34–41.

19. Gilbert P. Voigt, "The German and German-Swiss Element in South Carolina, 1732–1752," *Bulletin of the University of South Carolina*, no. 113 (September 1922); idem, "The Germans and German-Swiss in South Carolina, 1732–1765: Their Contribution to the Province," *Proceedings of the South Carolina Historical Association* 5 (1935): 17–25.

20. Harriet Dubose Kershaw Leiding, "Purrysburg: A Swiss-French Settlement of South Carolina, on the Savannah River," *THSSC* 39 (1934): 27–39.

21. Albert B. Faust, *The German Element in the United States*, 2 vols. (New York: Houghton-Mifflin, 1909), 1:217.

22. See the letters of the Reverend Joseph Bugnion to the bishop of London dated 20 June 1733 and 15 July 1733 and the letter of Purrysburg inhabitants to the bishop (no date), Bishop of London—General Correspondence, 1703–69, Fulham Palace Papers, microfilmed copies at the South Caroliniana Library, University of South Carolina, Columbia, South Carolina, hereafter cited as SCL; George W. Williams, "Letters to the Bishop of London from the Commissaries in South Carolina," *South Carolina Historical Magazine* 78 (July 1977): 216–17, 234–35, 240–41, hereafter cited as *SCHM*; J. H. Easterby and Ruth S. Green, eds., *The Colonial Records of South Carolina: The Journal of the Commons House of Assembly*, vols. 1736–50 (Columbia: Historical Commission of South Carolina, 1951–1962), 1736–39: 33–34, 38–39, hereafter cited as Easterby, *JCHA*; Hirsch, *Huguenots of Colonial South Carolina*, 82–83.

23. Jon Butler, *The Huguenots in America: A Refugee People in New World Society* (Cambridge, Mass.: Harvard University Press, 1983).

24. Note especially John Higham, "Hanging Together: Divergent Unities in American History," *Journal of American History* 61 (June 1974): 5–28, and Thomas Bender, "Wholes and Parts: The Need for Synthesis in American History," *Journal of American History* 73 (June 1986): 120–36.

25. Anthony F. C. Wallace, "Foreword," in Lawrence J. Taylor, *Dutchmen on the Bay: The Ethnohistory of a Contractual Community* (Philadelphia: University of Pennsylvania Press, 1983), xi.

26. George A. Hillery Jr., "Definitions of Community: Areas of Agreement," *Rural Sociology* 20 (1955), quoted in Colin Bell and Howard Newby, *Community Studies: An Introductions to the Sociology of the Local Community* (New York: Praeger, 1972), 27.

27. Margaret Stacey, "The Myth of Community Studies," *British Journal of Sociology* 20 (June 1969): 134–47.

28. Jon Butler, *Awash in a Sea of Faith: Christianizing the American People* (Cambridge, Mass.: Harvard University Press, 1990), 5.

29. Kathleen Neils Conzan, Harry S. Stout, E. Brooks Holifield, and Michael Zuckerman, "Forum," *Religion and American Culture: A Journal of Interpretation* 6, no. 2 (Summer 1996): 117.

30. Stout, "Forum," 118.

31. Bradley J. Wood, *This Remote Part of the World: Regional Formation in Lower Cape Fear, North Carolina, 1725–1775* (Columbia: University of South Carolina Press, 2004); see also Norbert Elias, "Towards a Theory of Communities," in Colin Bell and Howard Newby, eds., *The Sociology of Community: A Selection of Readings* (London: Frank Cass and Company, 1974), xxxii–xxxiii; Bell and Newby, "Introduction," in *The Sociology of Community*, xlvii. For some of the most instructive thoughts on network by historians theory, note especially Darrett B. Rutman, "Assessing the Little Communities of Early America," *William and Mary Quarterly*, 3rd ser., 43 (April 1986): 177–78; idem, "Social Web," 57–123; Rutman and Rutman, *A Place in Time*, 12, 27–29; Bender, *Community and Social Change*, 122–23.

32. Although network theoretical assumptions will animate this analysis of Purrysburg Township, there are certainly other perspectives from which to study early America. In a seminal essay from 1977 one of the leading social historians of early America, Michael Zuckerman, suggested that the concept of modernization might provide a useful framework for community based historical inquiry. See Michael Zuckerman, "The Fabrication of Identity in Early America," *William and Mary Quarterly*, 3rd ser., 34, no. 2 (April 1977): 183–214.

33. Bernard Bailyn, *Education and the Forming of American Society: Needs and Opportunities for Study* (Chapel Hill: University of North Carolina Press, 1960); Oscar Handlin, *The Uprooted: The Epic Story of the Great Migrations That Made the American People* (Boston: Little, Brown, 1951).

Chapter One

1. Smith, *City upon a Hill*, 7, 17, 286. Quotation from 6.

2. Portions of this chapter have appeared previously in somewhat different form in my previous publications. See Arlin C. Migliazzo, "A Tarnished Legacy Revisited:

Jean Pierre Purry and the Settlement of the Southern Frontier," *SCHM* 92 (October 1991): 232–52, and idem, ed., *Lands of True and Certain Bounty: The Geographical Theories and Colonization Strategies of Jean Pierre Purry* (Selinsgrove, Pa.: Susquehanna University Press, 2002).

3. The biographical information on Jean Pierre Purry in this chapter is taken from a variety of sources, including Frédéric Alexandre-Marie Jeanneret and J. H. Bonhôte, *Biographie neuchâteloise*, vol. 2 (Le Locle: Courvoisier, 1863), 240–72; Hugues Jéquier, Jaques Henriod, and Monique De Pury, *La Famille Pury* (Neuchâtel: Caisse De Famille Pury, 1972), 22–25, 107 (G XII–XIII); Dr. Auguste Châtelain, "Purrysbourg," *Museé Neuchâtelois*, new ser. 7 (May–June 1920): 84–94, 119–25; Louis-Edouard Roulet, "Jean Pierre Pury: Explorateur (1675–1736)," 237–42 in Michel Schlup, *Biographies neuchâteloises* (Hauterive: Editions Gilles Attinger, 1996); idem, "Jean-Pierre Pury et ses projets de colonies en Afrique du Sud et en Australie," *Musée Neuchâtelois* (1994): 49–63; Carlo Ginzburg, *Latitude, Slaves and the Bible: An Experiment in Microhistory* (abstract), 2000, www.helsinki.fi/collegium/events/Purry.pdf (18 September 2003); C. C. Macknight, "Research Notes on J. P. Purry," unpublished paper, Department of History, Faculty of Arts, Australian National University, Canberra, Australia, 13 July 1993; idem, "Neither Useful nor Profitable: Early Eighteenth Century Ideas about Australia and Its Inhabitants," typescript of a lecture given at the National Library of Australia, 22 September 1993. See also Edward Heawood, *A History of Geographical Discovery in the Seventeenth and Eighteenth Centuries* (London: Cambridge University Press, 1912; reprint, New York: Octagon Books, 1965), 80–81; Louise Jones Dubose, "Palmetto Landmarks: Purrysbourg," transcript of radio broadcast for 21 November 1948, SCL, 1; Kenneth Coleman, *Colonial Georgia: A History* (New York: Charles Scribner's Sons, 1976), 9; Verner W. Crane, *The Southern Frontier, 1670–1732* (Ann Arbor: University of Michigan Press, 1929; first Ann Arbor paper edition, 1956), 283–84, and others as cited.

4. After the death of the Abbot of Orleans in 1694, questions arose as to who had legitimate authority over the canton of Neuchâtel. The Prince of Conti and the Duchess of Nemours advanced rival claims, and both attempted to rule. Matters in Neuchâtel were complicated further when the Hohenzollern family of Prussia claimed authority over the canton in 1707. Local resistance thwarted an attempt by Conti to wrest power from the Prussians in 1709. This political turmoil engulfed members of the Purry family, most of whom (including Jean Pierre Purry's cousins Daniel and Samuel) initially supported Conti's claim. Daniel was was named councilor of state by Conti in 1694. Marie de Nemours, however, refused to accept the appointment, and Daniel was turned out of office. She died in 1707, and the Hohenzollern representative Frederick I won out over no less that twenty-five claimants to suzerainty over the canton. In 1709 Daniel and his son Samuel were ennobled by Frederick, two years after most of the Purrys had switched allegiances to the Prussian family. Although there is no definitive documentary evidence to prove that Jean Pierre Purry was first caught in the political crossfire of 1694 and then reaped the political reward of his relatives' royal about-face in 1709, Roulet finds it difficult to believe that the dates coincide so perfectly by mere happenstance. See Roulet, "Jean-Pierre Pury et ses projets," 52.

5. Roulet, "Pury: Explorateur," 237.

6. Jeanneret and Bonhôte contend that Purry attempted, but failed, to resurrect his commercial interest in the wine industry by exporting Neuchâtel wines to

Holland. See Jeanneret and Bonhôte, *Biographie neuchâteloise*, 251. There is little corroborating evidence to support their acceptance of this endeavor reported in M. E. H. Gaullieur's "Une émigration suisse dans l'Amerique Anglaise au XVIIIme. siècle," *Revue Suisse* (1854): 38 and reproduced nearly word for word by Jeanneret and Bonhôte. Roulet argues that Purry must have spent enough time in the area to have learned the Dutch language because it makes no sense to him that the Swiss-French-speaking Purry would have been put in charge of seventy men if he could not communicate with them. Roulet's conclusion is built on the assumption that the seventy men under him were Dutch, which, because of the use of mercenary soldiers by the company, is somewhat suspect. See Roulet, "Jean-Pierre Pury et ses projets," 53.

7. Purry supposedly had questioned a number of Dutch mariners about the conditions at the Cape of Good Hope and received confirmation that wine grapes would do exceedingly well in that part of the world. His kinsman and civic official Samuel Purry assisted in securing the vines. See Jeanneret and Bonhôte, *Biographie neuchâteloise*, 251.

8. If Jeanneret and Bonhôte (and Gaullieur) are correct regarding Purry's introduction of viniculture in the Cape Colony, this month-long sojourn in southern Africa would be the time when his grape plants would have been planted. They seem to imply that Purry had great success as a cultivator of wine grapes here, though his total time at the Cape amounted to only about two and a half months. It is possible that he was able to cultivate some land with the permission of the company or have employed some persons unknown to do so in his name, but he could not have overseen the enterprise as they infer. It must be noted, however, that if indeed he brought wine grape plants to the colony and they did prosper, such a success would certainly seem to substantiate his theory of climatology.

9. "Advertisement," 3–4, in *A Method for Determining the Best Climate of the Earth on a Principle to Which All Geographers and Historians Have Been Hitherto Strangers in a Memorial Presented to the Governors of the East India Company in Holland for Which the Author Was Obliged to Leave the Country*, by John Peter Purry, anonymous translation from the French (London: privately printed for Peter Cooper, 1744), 3.

10. Macknight did find, however, direct evidence in the form of a letter to the directors of the company from Christophel van Swol, governor general of the Dutch East India Company's Indonesian operation, that Purry was indeed involved with the Reformed congregation as "for some time he has acted in the role of Reader in the French language, being a person connected with the church." See Macknight, "Research Notes," 4, and "Neither Useful nor Profitable," 6. This congregation probably included a number of French Huguenots with whom Purry would have more in common than with Calvinists from other linguistic groups. There were more than thirty French Reformed refugees affiliated with the church by 1721. See Roulet, "Jean-Pierre Pury et ses projets," 55.

11. See Macknight, "Research Notes," 3, and "Neither Useful nor Profitable," 6.

12. Jenneret and Bonhôte, *Biographie neuchâteloise*, 252; Macknight, "Research Notes," 3.

13. For a brief biography of Nuyts's checkered life and career as well as a detailed account of the Dutch discovery of the South Australia coast, see "Pieter Nuyts," *Flinders Ranges Research*, 13 September 2003, www.picknowl.com.au/homepages/

rkfadol/nuyts.htm (25 September 2003). See also Michael Pearson, *Great Southern Land: The Maritime Exploration of Terra Australis* (Canberra: Australian Government Department of the Environment and Heritage, 2005), 36.

14. Geographers had long associated certain degrees of latitude with their own peculiar temperature gradients. Purry's contribution, ultimately mistaken though it was, proceeded from his conviction that earlier theories regarding climate, heat, and the amount of sunlight were erroneous. These false notions probably caused theoreticians to miss completely their true connection and in all likelihood contributed to a way of understanding what we today call climatology that made it impossible for them to uncover the interlinked relationship between sunlight, heat, climate, and soil fertility. Because Purry had traveled so extensively, by the time he arrived at the Dutch East India Company's Batavian station, the disjunction between his own personal observations and regnant scientific wisdom became too obvious for him to deny. See Migliazzo, "A Tarnished Legacy Revisited," 233–34.

15. *Kaffraria* is the English term for the portion of southern Africa claimed but not yet settled by the Dutch north of the Great Kei River and proceeding up the Indian Ocean coastline past present-day Transkei to the Natal region to which Purry turned his attention. The French term he used—*le pais des cafres*—means literally the country of the Bantus. The Bantus had begun their migration southward from West Africa about the time of Christ and had reached southern Africa with their farming and ironworking technologies before the Dutch arrived in the seventeenth century.

16. H. Roy Merrens, "The Physical Environment of Early America: Images and Imagemakers in Colonial South Carolina," *Geographical Review* 59 (October 1969): 536–37; C. P. Summerall, "Address of General C. P. Summerall at the Dedication of the Huguenot Cross at Purrysburg, South Carolina, May 4, 1941," *THSSC* 46 (1941): 38; Crane, *Southern Frontier*, 284; Coleman, *Colonial Georgia*, 9.

17. Purry's decision to approach van Swol was actually his second attempt to convince a high ranking company official of his theory. He had earlier written to "Mr. Director Boddens" regarding the great potential of Kaffraria in southern Africa. Boddens died sometime after Purry first contacted him, and in the period following the director's death, Purry realized that the Terre de Nuyts could have even more productive potential than Kaffraria, hence its inclusion in his communqué to van Swol. The dates and exact content of his correspondence with Boddens are unknown, but it is certainly within the realm of possibility that it was in the context of this relationship that his theories first began to take more specific definition. By the time that he approached Christophel van Swol with his ideas, they had been refined and expanded. The manuscript he sent to van Swol appears not to have survived. From Purry's comments in the preface to his published revision of this manuscript (see following note), we can surmise that the manuscript text Purry prepared for van Swol's consideration was quite a bit longer and more detailed than the *Mémoire* finally published in 1718. We also know that a portion of what he included in the *Mémoire* was new to the *Mémoire* and was intended to answer possible objections to his arguments in the manuscript text assessed by van Swol. For a comprehensive annotated edition of all of Purry's published tracts and memorials on geography and colonization, see Migliazzo, *Lands of True and Certain Bounty.*

18. Upon his return to Europe, a revision of this extensively researched essay, *Mémoire sur le pais des Cafres et la terre de Nuyts par raport à l'utilité que la*

Compagnie des Indes Orientales en pourroit retirer pour son commerce (Amsterdam: Pierre Humbert, 1718), would become his first published tract. It also appeared in Dutch translation. For general background on Purry's attempts to found a colony based on his theory of climates, see Albert B. Saye, "The Genesis of Georgia: Merchants as Well as Ministers," *Georgia Historical Quarterly* 24 (September 1940): 194–95, hereafter cited as *GHQ*; idem, "The Genesis of Georgia Reviewed," *GHQ* 50 (June 1966): 154–55; Milton Ready, "The Georgia Concept: An Eighteenth Century Experiment in Colonization," *GHQ* 55 (Summer 1971): 161; Roger A. Martin, "John J. Zubly Comes to America," *GHQ* 61 (Summer 1977): 125–29; Kenneth Coleman, "The Southern Frontier: Georgia's Founding and the Expansion of South Carolina," *GHQ* 56 (Summer 1972): 166–67.

19. Purry writes that, "when I came out with my *Mémoire* in Batavia, I first attracted public hatred, and in the mind of most people I passed for a man with a wounded brain." See Migliazzo, *Lands of True and Certain Bounty*, 110.

20. Migliazzo, *Lands of True and Certain Bounty*, 111.

21. Jean Pierre Purry, *Second mémoire sur le pais des Cafres et la terre de Nuyts Servant d'éclaircissement aux propositions faites dans le premier, pour l'utilité de la Compagnie des Indes Orientales* (Amsterdam: Pierre Humbert, 1718). This pamphlet was also published in a Dutch edition in 1718.

22. An intriguing footnote to the Dutch East India Company chapter of Purry's life has been the suggestion that satirist Jonathan Swift drew on aspects of his writings as partial inspiration for his famous satire. Swift began *Gulliver's Travels* after the publication of Jean Pierre's memorials to the company and may have been quite conversant with their contents. Lemuel Gulliver was shipwrecked after a violent storm to the northwest of Tasmania (then called Van Diemen's Land)—very close to the Terre de Nuyts. The islands of Lilliput and Blefuscu might have matched St. Peter and St. Francis Islands, both of which are mentioned prominently in both Purry's tracts. Finally, in the second memorial Jean Pierre notes the possibility that giants may live along the Terre de Nuyts. See Pearson, *Great Southern Land*, 36; "History of Ceduna," Winco Eclipse Tours, Inc., http://www.eclipsesafari.com/id30_m.htm (3 August 2003). For Purry's conjectures about the indigenous population of the Terre de Nuyts, see Migliazzo, *Lands of True and Certain Bounty*, 95.

23. Purry may have actually feared for his safety if he remained in Amsterdam after April 1719. The author of the "Advertisment" to the 1744 English translation of the first memorial notes that "Neither this Memorial, nor another which accompanied it, were well receiv'd, insomuch that a Friend of his told him privately, *he had best get out of the Way, for that some Things had been observed in both Papers, which ought not to be made Publick.*" See "Advertisement," in *A Method for Determining the Best Climate of the Earth*, 3. The title page to this translation carries explicit language that makes clear the threat to Purry should he remain. For the full title of this translation see note 9 above.

24. "Advertisement," in *A Method for Determining the Best Climate of the Earth*, 4.

25. Great Britain, Public Records Office, "Transcripts of Records Relating to South Carolina, 1685–1790," hereafter cited as BPRO, South Carolina Department of Archives and History, hereafter cited as SCDAH, 11:128; Jean Pierre Purry, *Memorial Presented to His Grace My Lord the Duke of Newcastle Chamberlain of His Majesty King George, &c., and Secretary of State: Upon the Present Condition of Carolina*

and the Means of Its Amelioration, trans. Charles C. Jones Jr. (Augusta: Privately printed for the translator by J. H. Estill, 1880), 9; Crane, *Southern Frontier*, 284. The timing of and rationale for his appointment as director-general is unclear. See the next paragraph.

26. According to one scholar, by 1719 stock in the company sold for forty times its face value. See Jacqueline Young, *Germans in the Colonial Southeast* (Bonn-Bad Godesberg: Inter Nations, 1977), 9.

27. See Jeanneret and Bonhôte, *Biographie neuchâteloise*, 251. The translation from the French is from Ginzburg, *Latitude, Slaves and the Bible*, 4.

28. Roulet, "Pury: Explorateur," 240.

29. The previously cited studies by C. C. Macknight are especially noteworthy in this regard.

30. Although this interpretation solves some ambiguities in the sources for this period of Purry's life, it should be observed that it does not address all of them. Jeanneret and Bonhôte, again following Gaullieur, note that Purry's "excellent success" with the vineyards in South Africa proceeded from his hard work and care in choosing the best soils, by which they imply that he remained there to tend the vines. It is clear from company records that Purry did not spend even one complete season in Kaffraria. See Jeanneret and Bonhôte, *Biographie neuchâteloise*, 251.

31. Young, *Germans in the Colonial Southeast*, 9–10; Jean Pierre Purry, *Spéculations sur le changes étrangers, contenant le juste rapport de Paris avec les principales places d'Europe, suivant le cours d'Amsterdam* (Paris, 1726).

32. BPRO 11:128–31; *Collections of the South Carolina Historical Society*, 5 vols. (Charleston: South Carolina Historical Society, 1857–1897), 1:272–73, vol. 2:160, hereafter cited as *CSCHS*; Crane, *Southern Frontier*, 284; Coleman, *Colonial Georgia*, 9.

33. BPRO 11:127–31, quotation from 127.

34. See Jean Pierre Purry, *Mémoire Presenté à Sa Gr. My Lord Duc de Newcastle, Chambellan de S. M. le Roi, George & c. & Secretaire d'État: sur l'état présent de la Caroline & sur le moyens de l'améliorer* (London: G. Bowyer, 1724).

35. BPRO 11:13–14.

36. "Complaints against the Lords Proprietors of Carolina," in W. Keith Kavenagh, ed., *Foundations of Colonial America: A Documentary History*, vol. 3 (New York: Chelsea House, 1973), 1796–1801; Charles Christopher Crittenden, "The Surrender of the Charter of Carolina," in Ernest M. Lander Jr. and Robert K. Ackerman, eds., *Perspectives in South Carolina History: The First Three Hundred Years* (Columbia: University of South Carolina Press, 1973), 35–42; M. Eugene Sirmans, *Colonial South Carolina: A Political History, 1663–1763* (Chapel Hill: University of North Carolina Press, 1966), 103–63. For a concise account of the destructive Yamassee conflict, see James H. Merrell, *The Indians' New World: Catawbas and Their Neighbors from European Contact through the Era of Removal* (Chapel Hill: University of North Carolina Press for the Institute of Early American History and Culture, 1989), 65–80; Chapman J. Milling, *Red Carolinians* (Chapel Hill: University of North Carolina Press, 1940), 135–64.

37. Robert M. Weir, *Colonial South Carolina: A History* (Columbia: University of South Carolina Press, 1997), 143–47, 149–50.

38. Meriwether, *Expansion of South Carolina*, 6; Lewis Cecil Gray, *History of Agriculture in the Southern United States to 1860*, vol. 1 (Washington, D.C.: Carnegie Institution of Washington, 1933), 120; Clarence L. Ver Steeg, "Slaves, Slavery, and the Genesis of the Plantation System in South Carolina: An Evolving Social-Economic Mosaic," 103–32 in Clarence L. Ver Steeg, *Origins of a Southern Mosaic: Studies of Early Carolina and Georgia* (Athens: University of Georgia Press, 1975), 117, 120, 131. Carl Bridenbaugh estimates that in 1730 there were 12,000 whites in South Carolina, who constituted a quarter of the total population. In the three lowcountry precincts of the colony there were fifty-three black slaves for every three whites. See Carl Bridenbaugh, *Myths and Realities: Societies of the Colonial South* (New York: Atheneum, 1963), 61. Weir contends that the black population of the province reached 20,000 that same year. See Weir, *Colonial South Carolina*, 145.

39. Kavenagh, *Foundations of Colonial America*, 1796–1801; Meriwether, *Expansion of South Carolina*, 17.

40. Hughes, "Populating the Back Country," vii–viii

41. Sirmans, *Colonial South Carolina*, 129–63.

42. Details for this paragraph and the one previous came from Hughes, "Populating the Back Country," ix–x; Crane, *Southern Frontier*, 219–20, 229, 231, 234; Meriwether, *Expansion of South Carolina*, 17–18, 20. A brief sketch of Barnwell's life appeared in the anonymous article "Barnwell of South Carolina," *SCHGM* 2 (January 1901): 47–50.

43. Crane, *Southern Frontier*,. 282.

44. Crane, *Southern Frontier*, 315.

45. Joshua Gee, *The Trade and Navigation of Great Britain Considered* (London, 1729) quoted in Crane, *Southern Frontier*, 315.

46. The only known English translation of the French original was done by Charles C. Jones Jr. Jones had 250 copies of his translation printed privately for distribution. Subsequent citations of this document will be from the Jones text, copy 220, unless otherwise noted. See Purry, *Memorial to the Duke of Newcastle*.

47. Purry, *Memorial to the Duke of Newcastle*, 12–15. In this pamphlet, Purry used the name "Georgia" for the first time to delineate crown lands south of the Savannah River, thereby apparently becoming the first person to suggest the name. This was probably another incidence of Purry's attempt at subtle diplomacy. By naming these lands after King George II, he may have hoped for special consideration for his own fiefdom in South Carolina. He has been called the entrepreneurial father of Georgia as his settlement plan set the stage for its colonization. See Saye, "Merchants as Well as Ministers," 195; Ready, "Georgia Concept," 161.

48. *CSCHS* 1:196–97, 286; 2:166; BPRO 11:282; Crane, *Southern Frontier*, 285–86. There appears to be some discrepancy between what the Lords Proprietors offered and what Purry thought he accepted. In a letter to the Duke of Newcastle dated 9 July 1725, Purry's agent Jean Vat noted that the proprietors contracted to grant Purry 24,000 acres of land for bringing 600 Swiss to South Carolina. Four years after their arrival the immigrants were to pay yearly fees amounting to 300 pounds sterling. The letter also reiterated that the proprietors agreed to pay passage for the emigrants from England to Charles Town. Finally, Vat wanted some assurance that recent South Carolina legislation promising provisions, arms, and ammunition for

the immigrants for nine months after their arrival would indeed be forthcoming. He had not yet received a response to a petition he presented to the duke for the king in May of 1725 regarding support for the prospective colonists. Vat believed that such assurance of colonial support for the Swiss immigrants would calm the anxieties of those who might decide to leave for the New World and redound to the benefit of the empire. See BPRO 11:314–15.

Comparing Vat's letter to other extant sources creates a significant interpretive problem because of the substantial disparity among the accounts. The problem of which party would be liable for transportation costs might be partially explained by the fact that, although Purry understood the costs of transporting them would be met completely by the Lords Proprietors, they might have considered their obligation met by paying for the costs of transport between England and Charles Town. Purry would then be responsible for costs between the Swiss cantons and England and again between Charles Town and their ultimate destination. The land awards and numbers of immigrants are more difficult issues to resolve. A possible explanation might proceed from the multiple levels of involvement by various parties. At least five different parties (the Lords Proprietors, Lords Commissioners of Trade, Purry, his associates, and Vat) were involved in negotiations by summer 1725. When this fact is coupled with the observation that all the numbers in the sources whether regarding land, money, or people are multiples of 300, confusion could certainly have been possible. Finally, the wording used in the actual written documents might have led to variant readings depending on the perspective of the reader. For example, although Purry was only awarded a 12,000-acre barony for 300 colonists according to one account, he might have reasoned that quadrupling the number of colonists to 1,200 would lead to a quadrupling of land awarded to 48,000 acres, which was his initial request. Similarly, since Vat's letter notes that Purry had agreed to transport 600 colonists for 24,000 acres, he could have surmised that doubling the number of people to 1,200 would logically double his land grant from the proprietors. He may not have recognized that the Lords Proprietors no longer wanted to grant him that much land, no matter how many immigrants he settled in South Carolina, even though both the Duke of Newcastle and the Lords Commissioners of Trade had earlier agreed to this sizable barony. It must be said that, although any of these scenarios are plausible explanations, without further collaborating documentation that does not appear to be available, they are ultimately based on creative conjecture. A later memorial to the Lords Commissioners of Trade and Plantations, dated 24 March 1730 and authored by Purry's son Charles on his father's behalf, however, makes mention of agreements of 27 April 1725 and 1 May 1725 between the elder Purry and the Lords Proprietors that could have resolved the most egregious of the incon-sistencies noted above. The April agreement granted to John Vat 24,000 acres in trust for Purry and "(in consideration of Three Pence Sterling per Annum, per Acre, as a Quit Rent to be paid Them [the proprietors]) to defray the Charges of Transporting from England to South Carolina 600 persons." The May agreement "further granted 12,000 acres more at One Penny per Annum per Acre, and 12,000 Acres more, in consideration of one pepper Corn for the whole 12,000 Acres, on Condition, that the said Purry should, at his own Charges, settle 600 Swiss persons, over and above the first 600." See BPRO 14:77–78. I have been unable to find either these documents or clear reference to them in the extant records, but, if Charles Purry has faithfully reproduced the facts, it renders the rather muddled series of events quite coherent.

49. George Fenwick Jones, "The Secret Diary of Pastor Johann Martin Boltzius," *GHQ* 53 (March 1969): 78; *CSCHS* 3:291; Crane, *Southern Frontier*, 286; For the special functions of the immigration or land agent, see Gilbert P. Voigt, "German and German-Swiss Immigration into South Carolina, 1732–1752," *Bulletin of the University of South Carolina*, no. 113 (September 1922): 18–19. Jones notes that Vat guided the second transport of Salzburg Lutheran émigrés to their new home across the Savannah River at Ebenezer in the mid-1730s. See Jones, "Secret Diary," 78.

50. For a more complete explanation of the problems of the early modern Swiss state, see chap. 2 below.

51. *CSCHS* 3:291.

52. BPRO 12:153–54, 14:77–78; Leiding, "Purrysburg: A Swiss-French Settlement," 28; Dubose, "Landmarks," 2. The quotation is from BPRO 12:153–54.

53. *CSCHS* 1:241; Quotations from BPRO 12:154.

54. *CSCHS* 1:250: Leiding, "Purrysburg: A Swiss-French Settlement," 28.

55. G. Kurz, "Special Investigations by State Archivist (Berne) G. Kurz," in Albert B. Faust, *Lists of Swiss Emigrants in the Eighteenth Century to the American Colonies*, 2 vols. (Washington, D.C.: National Genealogical Society, 1920), 2:1–26, esp. 18; *CSCHS* 1:241.

56. Arthur Henry Hirsch, "Some Phases of the Huguenot-Angelican Rivalries in South Carolina before 1730," *Presbyterian Church Department of History Journal* 13 (1928): 19–20; idem, *Huguenots of Colonial South Carolina*, 149.

57. BPRO 12:85.

58. *CSCHS* 1:241.

59. Roulet, "Pury: Explorateur," 240; Ginzburg, *Latitude, Slaves and the Bible*, 5.

60. Crane, *Southern Frontier*, 287.

61. Hughes, "Populating the Back Country," 4.

62. "A Proposal for Improving and the Better Settling of South Carolina," received by the Board of Trade from Johnson, 7 March 1730, BPRO 14:58–60; "Col. Johnson's Proposal for Better Improving and Settling South Carolina," received by the Board of Trade from Johnson, 18 March 1730, and "Explanation of My Scheme," received by the Board of Trade from Johnson, 30 April 1730. The latter two citations are taken from Richard P. Sherman, *Robert Johnson: Proprietary and Royal Governor of South Carolina* (Columbia: University of South Carolina Press, 1966), 108–9.

63. Report of the Board of Trade to the Privy Council, 26 May 1732, quoted in Sherman, *Robert Johnson*, 116.

64. Easterby, *JCHA*, 1736–39:227, 268, 276, 282–83, 341; "An Act to Provide a Full Supply for Subsisting Poor Protestants," in Kavenagh, *Foundations of Colonial America*, 2141–43; Meriwether, *Expansion of South Carolina*, 21.

65. *South Carolina Gazette*, 25 November 1732, hereafter cited as *SCG*; Chaplin, *Anxious Pursuit*, 38, 158–59.

66. Chaplin, *Anxious Pursuit*, 39.

67. Much of the data for this paragraph and the two following was excerpted from "Instructions to Our Trusty and Well belov'd Robert Johnson, . . . ," BPRO 14:174–77; Thomas Cooper and David J. McCord, *The Statutes at Large of South Carolina*, 10

vols. (Columbia: A. S. Johnston, 1836–1841), 1:430; Smith, "Purrysburgh" 189–90; *CSCHS* 2:122–23, 177–78; 3:306; Sherman, *Robert Johnson*, 108–12; Meriwether, *Expansion of South Carolina*, 19–20; Voigt, "Germans and German-Swiss: Their Contribution to the Province," 17. The quotations are from BPRO 14:176.

68. Alan D. Watson's article, "The Quitrent System in Royal South Carolina," *William and Mary Quarterly,* 3rd ser., 33 (April 1976): 183–211 provides an overview of the policies and problems of the royal quitrent system after the land reform act of November 1731.

69. Katherine Hurt Richardson argues that the South Carolina township plan of settlement most closely resembled similar strategies of Connecticut, New York, and Pennsylvania (i.e., scattered settlement on farms in extensive townships with a nucleated village). British officials, however, specifically mentioned Massachusetts Bay and New Hampshire as precedents for the plan. See Richardson, "'As Easy to Build Towns,'" 22; BPRO 14:174.

70. Ready, "Georgia Concept," 162; see also Saye, "Genesis of Georgia Reviewed," 156–58; Coleman, "Georgia's Founding," 171; *CSCHS* 2:123, 182; Crane, *Southern Frontier*, 287. Purry seems also to have counted among his influential supporters Sir John Percival, first Earl of Egmont. See Betty Wood, *Slavery in Colonial Georgia, 1730–1775* (Athens: University of Georgia Press, 1984), 17.

71. BPRO 14:77–78. Quotation from BPRO 14:5.

72. BPRO 14:112–13, 237–38. Quotations are from 237–38.

73. BPRO 15:103.

74. Quotations are from BPRO 15:62–64 and 115. See also *CSCHS* 2:125, 127, 129, 182–83; Smith, "Purrysburgh," 189. The "Instructions" inaccurately refer to the "forty thousand acres" he was to have received from the Lords Proprietors. See BPRO 15:62, 125.

75. There appears to be some confusion in dating Purry's first arrival in South Carolina. Most sources agree on 1731. Purry himself notes that his party arrived in May of that year. But in a petition by Jean Vat to the president of the Privy Council dated 7 March 1731, Vat says that Purry and his company arrived in 1730. In the Julian calendar used at this time, the days up to and including 24 March would have been reckoned as occurring in the previous year. Hence, the 1730 date is most likely taken to mean 1730/31 because of the calendar disparity. (Likewise, the 1731 date of Vat's petition should be taken as 1731/32). To arrive by May 1731, Purry's party must have left Europe sometime in the late winter—probably early March at the latest. Corroborating evidence clearly points to 1731 as the correct year of their arrival in the Gregorian calendar. See BPRO 15:103; 16:350.

76. It should be noted that there are discrepancies in the records on at least two important points connected with the official launch of the township. Some sources speak about a 40,000-acre grant to Purry by King George II on 1 September. The land was purported to be just outside the township limits. I have been unable to find the original source of this supposed grant. In documents relating both to Purry's abortive first attempt to settle a colony in South Carolina during the proprietary period and his second successful effort (see note 74 above), the 40,000-acre figure is used, but, in the context of negotiations, the number clearly should be 48,000. The king, through the Privy Council in June 1732, did direct Governor Johnson to grant Purry up to

48,000 acres contiguous to the township if he met all the appropriate conditions. As shall become evident below, this sizable grant became the source of major tension. Reference to the 40,000-acre grant in secondary sources also identifiy it as "Swiss Quarters." If the amount of land is discounted, the reference most likely is to both the township proper as well as the six-mile-wide buffer zone surrounding it, both of which were off limits to everyone except Purrysburg settlers.

A second aberration regards the amount Purry was to receive from the South Carolina government for transporting colonists to Purrysburg. Although many sources cite the 600-pound sterling amount, the act ratified by the South Carolina General Assembly on 20 August 1731 gives the figure of 400 pounds sterling.

See BPRO 15:116, 123; 16:350–51; Migliazzo, *Lands of True and Certain Bounty*, 156–58; Rowland, *History of Beaufort County*, 119; Robert Mills, *Statistics of South Carolina* (Charleston: Hurlbut and Lloyd, 1826), 369–70; Purry, *Memorial to the Duke of Newcastle*, 6; Dr. F. Muench, "The Story of Purysburg," *Charleston Sunday News and Courier*, 10 April 1898, 10; Smith, "Purrysburgh," 190–91; Leiding "Purrysburg: A Swiss-French Settlement," 29.

77. Jean Pierre Purry, "*Instruction pour ceux qui auroient dessein d'accompagner le soussigné Jean Pierre Purry en Caroline*," translated as "Proposals by Mr. Peter Purry of Newfchatel . . . ," and published in *Gentleman's Magazine* (August, September, and October, 1732). This translation was included in B. R. Carroll, *Historical Collections of South Carolina*, 2 vols. (New York: Harper & Bros., 1836), 2:121–23. Quotations are taken from the Carroll text.

78. Jean Pierre Purry, "*Description abrégée de l'état présent de la Caroline Meridionale*" translated as "A Description of the Province of South Carolina" and published in *Gentleman's Magazine* (August, September, and October, 1732). This translation was included in B. R. Carroll, *Historical Collections*, 2:124–39 as well as other document collections.

79. Thomas Nairne's *A Letter from South Carolina*, 2nd ed. (London: R. Smith, 1718) provides a helpful nearly contemporaneous view. Notice also the glowing description given by the Reverend Johann Martin Boltzius of the nearby Ebenezer, Georgia settlement after more than fifteen years and much death and privation in the area. See Klaus G. Loewald, Beverly Starika, and Paul S. Taylor, trans. and eds., "Johann Martin Boltzius Answers a Questionnaire on Carolina and Georgia, Part II," *William and Mary Quarterly,* 3rd ser., 15 (April 1958): 236–44. Raymond A. Mohl's article, "'The Grand Fabric of Republicanism,' A Scotsman Describes South Carolina, 1810–1811," *SCHM* 71 (January 1970): 178–79, provides a later account in many ways strikingly similar to Purry's. In John Lambert's journal of his travels in South Carolina in the first decade of the nineteenth century, he spends an entire chapter on the less than salubrious effects of climate and geography, including wind storms, sleet, and hail, the presence of disease and death due to yellow fever, typhus, influenza, and dysentery, and the irritations of temperature and mosquitoes. Still he writes, "Whatever may be the severity of the seasons in South Carolina, at particular times, yet it must be allowed that the climate is, upon the whole, agreeable, and the winters remarkably fine." See John Lambert, *Travels through Lower Canada and the United States of North America in the Years 1806, 1807, and 1808 . . .*, 3 vols. (London: Richard Phillips, 1810), 2:463–94. Quotation from 2:473.

80. It is instructive to note that in the comprehensive enumeration of the potential exports of South Carolina that appears in Purry's *Memorial to the Duke of Newcastle*, nearly all the listed goods except cocoa were produced in some quantity in the colony. For the list, see Migliazzo, *Lands of True and Certain Bounty*, 127.

81. See the Reverend Samuel Urlsperger. *Detailed Reports on the Salzburger Emigrants Who Settled in America . . .*, 18 vols., gen. ed. George Fenwick Jones; vols. 1 and 2, trans. by Herman J. Lacher; vol. 3, trans. and ed. by George Fenwick Jones and Marie Hahn; vols. 4 and 5, trans. and ed. by George Fenwick Jones and Renate Wilson; vol. 6, trans. and ed. by George Fenwick Jones and Renate Wilson; vol. 7, trans. and ed. by George Fenwick Jones and Don Savelle; vol. 8, trans. by Maria Magdalena Hoffman-Loerzer, Renate Wilson, and George Fenwick Jones, ed. by George Fenwick Jones; vol. 9 trans. by Don Savelle, ed. by George Fenwick Jones; vol. 10, trans. Don Savelle and George Fenwick Jones, ed. by George Fenwick Jones; vol. 11, trans. by Eva Pulgram, ed. by George Fenwick Jones; vol. 12, trans. by Irmgard Neuman, ed. by George Fenwick Jones; vols. 13–14, ed. by George Fenwick Jones; vol. 13, trans. by David Roth and George Fenwick Jones; vol. 14, trans. by Eva Pulgram, Magdalena Hoffman-Loerzer, and George Fenwick Jones; vol. 15, trans. and ed. by George Fenwick Jones; vol. 16, ed. by George Fenwick Jones, 1753 trans. by George Fenwick Jones, 1754 trans. by Renate Wilson and George Fenwick Jones; vol. 17 ed. and annotated by George Fenwick Jones, 1759 trans. by David Noble, 1760 trans. by George Fenwick Jones (Athens: University of Georgia Press, 1968–1993); vol. 18, trans. and ed. by George Fenwick Jones and Renate Wilson (Camden, Maine: Picton Press, 1995), 5:292–93. Hereafter cited as *Reports*, with volume and page numbers. More than eighty years later, this was still a common explanation. See François Alexandre Frédéric Duc de La Rochefoucauld Liancourt, *Travels through the United States of North America, the Country of the Iroquois, and Upper Canada, in the Years 1795, 1796, and 1797: With an Authentic Account of Lower Canada*, 2 vols. (London: R. Phillips, 1799), 1:578, and Mohl, "'Grand Fabric of Republicanism,'" 183.

82. Although the "*Description*" and the "*Instruction*" were written in Charles Town in September 1731 after Purry and his small party returned from the township site, there is some uncertainty as to whether the manuscript documents circulated at all at that early date and, if so, in what circles. It is logical to assume that South Carolina authorities (the governor, council, and Commons House) would have been aware of their existence and may have even seen Purry's manuscripts. The documents certainly did not exist in printed form at this time either in the original French or in English translation. (Circumstantial evidence makes it doubtful that Jean Pierre was fluent in English). Their English publication in *Gentleman's Magazine* in 1732 served two functions. First, it signaled the implementation of Johnson's township plan. Second, the pamphlet served to assure the outnumbered white merchants and planters of the lowcountry that new immigrants were on the way. For a concise analysis of the influence of promotional literature in the southern colonies and Purry's traditional role in the genre, see Hugh F. Lefler, "Promotional Literature of the Southern Colonies," *Journal of Southern History* 33 (February 1967): 3–25. Hope Francis Kane's Ph.D. dissertation, "Colonial Promotion and Promotion Literature of Carolina, 1660–1700" (Brown University, 1930), provides the best analysis of the promotional tract in the earlier period.

83. Jeanneret and Bonhôte, *Biographie neuchâteloise*, 252–53. I have been unable

to locate a copy of this "prémiére edition" in the original French.

84. See Jean Pierre Purry, *Description abrégée de l'état présent de la Caroline Meridionale, nouvelle edition, avec des eclaircissemens, les actes des concessions faites à ce suject à l'auteur, tant pour luy que pour ceux qui voudront predre parti avec luy, Et enfin une instruction qui contient les conditions, sous lesquelles on pourra l'accompagner* (Neuchâtel, 1732). To lend even greater credibility to his colonizing efforts, Purry ended a subsequent printing of the nouvelle edition with three attestations to the good progress of the first township inhabitants and to his own exemplary character, as well as an advertisement for his next departure for Purrysburg. The only copy of the new edition in French that I have been able to locate includes these letters of 20 August and 5 October 1733 and a certificate dated 5 August 1733 from male inhabitants of the township verifying the truth of Purry's description of South Carolina published the previous year. Clearly these letters were appended to Purry's "nouvelle edition"of 1732 to persuade others to immigrate to Purrysburg on its founder's return trips to Europe for more recruits.

85. Kurz, "Investigations," 17–18; Muench, "Story of Purysburg," 10; Châtelain, "Purrysbourg," 89; Dr. Adolph Gerber, "The Canton of Basel and the Conditions of Its Inhabitants in the Country Districts," 2:86–217 in Faust, *Lists*, 2:87–88; Faust, *Lists*, 1:iv–viii; idem, "Swiss Immigration to the American Colonies in the Eighteenth Century," *American Historical Review* 22 (1916–1917): 21–43.

86. Agreement between Jean Pierre Purry and James Edward Oglethorpe, 4 December 1731, copy at the Hargrett Rare Book and Manuscript Library, University of Georgia Libraries, Athens, Georgia; Thomas Hart Wilkins, "James Edward Oglethorpe: South Carolina Slaveholder?" *GHQ* 88, no. 1 (Spring 2004): 87–88; idem., "An Economic Interpretation of the Founding of the Colony of Georgia" (M.A. thesis, University of Georgia, 2002), 31; Florence Janson Sherriff, "The Saltzburgers and Purrysburg," *Proceedings of the South Carolina Historical Association* (1963): 15; Coleman, "Georgia's Founding," 171. Both Webb Garrison and Thomas Hart Wilkins argue that Purry negotiated the contract with Oglethorpe to secure his influence and support for the Purrysburg venture. While Purry may have been somewhat fearful that his colonial effort might also be destroyed at the last minute by British authorities as had been his earlier attempt, a more plausible interpretation and one that Garrison offers is that, because trustees could not own land in Georgia, Oglethorpe assured himself of a South Carolina estate with this arrangement. See Webb Garrison, *Oglethorpe's Folly: The Birth of Georgia* (Lakemont, Ga.: Copple House Books, 1982), 44, 169; Wilkins, "James Edward Oglethorpe," 88. Oglethorpe may have provided some undisclosed service to Purry as Viscount Percival, first Earl of Egmont (another Georgia trustee) seems to indicate, but it probably had to do with issues other than actual negotiations with the government for the initial settlement of Purrysburg. See *Diary of Viscount Percival, First Earl of Egmont*, 3 vols. (London: H. M. Stationery Office, 1920–23), 1:286. Quoted in Garrison, *Oglethorpe's Folly*, 229. It should also be noted that this agreement was patently illegal according to the provisions of the township plan passed by the South Carolina Assembly.

87. BPRO 15:103–5. It is instructive to note the ingenious strategy employed by Purry and Vat here. They conveniently fail to mention that the 12,000 acres was only free of quitrent payments in Purry's original proposal, not in the final plan of settlement certified by the Board of Trade. As previously observed, the figure of 48,000 acres

from the 1724–26 affair is also subject to much greater nuancing than is apparent in this petition.

88. BPRO 15:105–7.

89. Ibid., 15:82–83

90. Ibid., 15:113–20.

91. Ibid., 15:84, 121–26; 16:121. The "Additional Instructions" wrongly report at one point in the document that the grant was for 40,000 acres—which number appeared erroneously on at least one previous occasion. See BPRO 15:125. See also *CSCHS* 2:131; Smith, "Purrysburgh," 192. This may have been the point at which Oglethorpe intervened on Purry's behalf. See note 86 above.

92. Smith, "Purrysburgh," 194–95, 201–2; Voigt, "German Immigration," 19.

Chapter Two

1. Menard, *Economy and Society*, 12, 50; Rutman, "Social Web," 68.

2. Note particularly Roger Green's warning against dispersed settlement patterns in Virginia in *Virginia's Cure; or, An Advisive Narrative Concerning Virginia* (London, 1662) in Peter Force, comp., *Tracts . . . Relating Principally to the . . . Colonies*, vol. 3, tract 15, 4–6, as quoted in Rutman, "Social Web," 69.

3. Richardson, "'As Easy to Build Towns,'" 1; McCurry, *Masters of Small Worlds*, 31–34. Quotation is from Barr, "Strawberry Ferry and Childsbury Towne," 2.

4. Chaplin, *Anxious Pursuit*, 38–39, 158–59, 164, 210.

5. Richardson, "'As Easy to Build Towns,'" 1–2, 23–24.

6. Purry, *Memorial to the Duke of Newcastle*, 11. His calculation would more precisely be 33$^1/_3$ degree.

7. It is quite intriguing to recognize that had Purry's climatological prognostications been taken seriously, the site of Purrysburg Township actually may have been quite a bit more salubrious for the immigrants. If we extend by one-third of one degree a line on either side of the thirty-third degree of north latitude westward across South Carolina we discover that Purry's theory would place the coastal region from just south of Charleston to Georgetown in the optimal range. In the interior, the prospective township sites most near this band would include Williamsburg, Orangeburg, Amelia, Sax Gotha, and New Windsor. The coastal region was already yielding substantial wealth to the planter elite, so settlement there was impossible. Of the interior township sites certainly Williamsburg and Orangeburg found substantial success, and the other sites at least had less deleterious effects upon the health of their inhabitants if not conditions more conducive to commercial prosperity.

8. BPRO 14:238; Lawrence Sanders Rowland, "Eighteenth Century Beaufort: A Study of South Carolina's Southern Parishes to 1800" (Ph.D. dissertation, University of South Carolina, 1978), 103; Rowland, *History of Beaufort County*, 119; Gallay, *Formation of a Planter Elite*, 19, 55. Gallay notes that settlers from nearby St. Helena's Parish were particularly warm in their welcome to the Purrysburg immigrants because they fortified St. Helena's defensive establishment without occupying any of its rich alluvial land. See Gallay, *Formation of a Planter Elite*, 19.

9. For the information in this and the following two paragraphs I have relied heavily on Charles F. Kovacik and John J. Winberry, *South Carolina: A Geography* (Boulder, Colo.: Westview, 1987), 18–48; Lewis, *American Frontier*, 33; McCurry, *Masters of Small Worlds*, 22–30; and Chaplin, *Anxious Pursuit*, 145.

10. Mohl, "A Scotsman Describes South Carolina, 1810–1811," 174–75. To give some idea of the relative monetary value of pine barren land, the traveler cites figures that peg the price of tidal swamp land at up to 200 times that of pine barren land. According to Stephanie McCurry's figures, pine barren land was valued at twenty cents per acre in the mid-1820s. See Mohl, "A Scotsman Decribes South Carolina, 1810–1811," 175; McCurry, *Masters of Small Worlds*, 27. When the Duc de la Rochefoucauld Liancourt traveled in the area a decade earlier, he wrote of the pine barrens, "I am not yet tired of these superb forests; but on traversing them, you cannot but regret, that a soil, which bears such trees should not produce any thing else, and that nineteen twentieths of that soil may, perhaps, remain for ever uncultivated in Carolina." See La Rochefoucauld Liancourt, *Travels through the United States of North America*, 1:602–3.

11. Chaplin, *Anxious Pursuit*, 209–10.

12. George Fenwick Jones, *The Georgia Dutch: From the Rhine and Danube to the Savannah, 1733–1783* (Athens: University of Georgia Press, 1992), 22; A. G. Roeber, "The Origin of Whatever Is Not English among Us: The Dutch-Speaking and German-Speaking Peoples of Colonial British America," 220–83, in Bailyn and Morgan, *Strangers within the Realm*, 238–39; Harold Ferken, "The Swiss Background of the Purrysburg Settlers," *THSSC* 39 (1934): 20. Quotation from William Martin, *Switzerland: From Roman Times to the Present,* with additional chapters by Pierre Béguin, trans. Jocasta Innes (New York: Praeger, 1971), 132.

13. Christopher Herold, *The Swiss without Halos* (New York: Columbia University Press, 1948), 10; Georg Thürer, *Free and Swiss: The Story of Switzerland*, adapt. and trans. R. P. Heller and E. Long (London: Oswald Wolff, 1970), 13–14.

14. The friendship pact between France and the Confederation (1777) exposed western Switzerland to possible French domination since Geneva, Basel, the Jura, and Neuchâtel were not included in the Swiss sphere by the Swiss themselves. See Wilhelm Oeschsli, *History of Switzerland, 1499–1914*, trans. Eden and Cedar Paul (Cambridge: Cambridge University Press 1922), 252–53. Note also Hans Kohn, *Nationalism and Liberty: The Swiss Example* (New York: Macmillan, 1956), 7–8; Lina Hug and Richard Stead, *Switzerland* (New York: G. P. Putnam's Sons, 1900), 316; Herold, *The Swiss without Halos*, 19, 134–35.

15. Thürer, *Free and Swiss*, 70.

16. Martin, *Switzerland: From Roman Times*, 132; Oeschsli, *Switzerland, 1499–1914*, 282; Thürer, *Free and Swiss*, 70; Jones, *The Georgia Dutch*, 22–24, quotation from 24.

17. Saturday, 24 November 1764. "We now entered Switzerland. They are a phlegmatic nation. Jacob showed no signs of lively joy at the sight of his country." Thursday, 29 November 1764. "At five I set out and had a pleasant drive to Berne." Jacob rejoiced not a little to find himself in his own capital, within two miles of which he was born." From Frederick A. Pottle, *Boswell on the Grand Tour: Germany and Switzerland, 1764* (New York: McGraw-Hill, 1953), 202, 210–11. Note also the letter from the German translator of Boswell, Dr. Fritz Guttinger of Zurich, to Pottle, 202. See also Kohn, *Nationalism and Liberty*, 7, 19.

18. Henry Cabot Lodge, gen. ed., *The History of Nations*, 25 vols. (Philadelphia: John D. Morris and Company, 1906–1908), 13:327–593, "Switzerland," by Charles Dandliker, rev. and ed. by Elbert Jay Benton, 460, 487–88; Herold, *The Swiss without*

Halos, 154; Oeschsli, *Switzerland, 1499–1914*, 248–49; Thürer, *Free and Swiss*, 69; Walter Sorell, *The Swiss: A Cultural Panorama of Switzerland* (New York: Bobbs-Merrill, 1972), xiii. Quotation from Bernard Bailyn and Philip D. Morgan, "Introduction," 1–31, in Bailyn and Morgan, *Strangers in the Realm*, 20.

19. Although these were the years of greatest exodus, it should be noted that Huguenots fled to London as late as 1745 and established the community of New Bordeaux in South Carolina in 1764. See the anonymous article "An Emigration of Huguenots to South Carolina in 1764," *Proceedings of the Huguenot Society of London* 5 (1894–96): 179–87.

20. The origin of the term *Huguenot* to denote French Calvinists is still somewhat ambiguous, but there are a number of plausible theories. For a good point-counterpoint (Calvinist-Catholic) perspective on the term, see Pastor Tollin, Lic. Dr., "Concerning the Name 'Huguenot,'" *Proceedings of the Huguenot Society of London*, 6 (1898–1901): 325–55, and "Notes and Queries," *Proceedings of the Huguenot Society of London*, 3 (1888–91): 420–21. Janet G. Gray's "The Origin of the Word Huguenot," *Sixteenth Century Journal* 14 (1983): 349–59, is the most comprehensive and synthetic overview.

21. Warren C. Scoville, "The Huguenots and the Diffusion of Technology, II," *Journal of Political Economy* 60 (October 1952): 406; Howe, *History of the Presbyterian Church*, 1:114. For excellent background study of the plight of the French Huguenots and the Piedmontese Waldensians, see Hannah F. Lee, *The Huguenots in France and America*, (Cambridge: J. Owen, 1843; reprint, 2 vols. in 1, Baltimore: Genealogical Publishing, 1973); G. A. Rothrock, *The Huguenots: A Biography of a Minority* (Chicago: Nelson-Hall, 1979); N. M. Sutherland, *The Huguenot Struggle for Recognition* (New Haven, Conn.: Yale University Press, 1980); William Ferguson Colcock, "The Huguenots in Northern Italy," *THSSC* 83 (1978): 52–58; "The Historic Celebration of the Vaudois," *Proceedings of the Huguenot Society of America* 2 (20 April 1888–13 April 1891): 58–65.

22. A. J. Grant, *The Huguenots* (London: T. Butterworth, 1934), 200–202; Reaman, *The Trail of the Huguenots*, 107; Herold, *The Swiss without Halos*, 83; Scoville, "Technology, II," 405–7.

23. Scoville, "Technology, II," 407–10; Dandliker, "Switzerland," 498.

24. Fogleman, *Hopeful Journeys*, 23–25, 28; Gerber, "The Canton of Basel and the Condition of Its Inhabitants," 87–88. In addition to Purry's writing on South Carolina, a number of German speakers published accounts of the province that mentioned Purry's project. See for example the anonymously written *Neue Nachricht Alter und neuer Merckwürdigkeiten* (St. Gall, 1734), 53–55; J.K.L., *Der nunmehro in der Neuen Welt vergnügt und ohne Heimwehe Lebende Schweizer oder Kurtze und eigentliche Beschreibung des gegenwärtigen Zustands der Königlichen Englischen Provenz Carolina. Aus den neulich angekomenen Briefen der alldorten sich befindenden Schweizeren zusamen getragen* (Bern: Johannes Bondeli, 1734), 7, 37–39; *Kurtz-verfaßte Reiß-Beschreibung Eines neulich Auß der in West-Indien gelegenen Landschafft Carolina, In sein Vatterland zuruck gekommenen Lands Angehörigen Samt einem Bericht von disers Lands Art, Natur und Eigenschafften* (Zurich: Bürcklischer, 1738), 5, and Johannes Tobler, "Beschreibung von Carolina (n.p., n.d.)," 3. These documents are part of the microfilmed Schweizerische Landesbibliothek collection

at the South Caroliniana Library. I am indebted to my colleague Professor Elisabeth Buxton for her translations of these German documents and others noted below.

25. Extract of a letter from Governor Johnson to Mr. Hutcheson, 18 November 1732, SCL; Smith, "Purrysburgh," 193–94; Martin, "Zubly Comes to America," 127.

26. There are some discrepancies with regard to the number of these early arrivals. Purry notes that up to 15 December 1732 he transported a total of 152 colonists. Johnson's report of the same date mentions that Purry has arrived with 120 Swiss, 50 of whom were adult males. The governor took care "to furnish them at the Expence of the public of this province with provisions and all sorts of necessarys and those who first arrived are gone to purisburg and expressed great satisfaction at their reception." Johnson's wording here seems to indicate that this group of 120 is not the first to arrive (perhaps alluding to the November transport). See BPRO 16:4–5.

27. Miscellaneous Records, 2D:3–6, "Commissions and Instructions, 1732–1742," hereafter cited as MR, SCDAH. The act of appearing before the provincial governor to swear allegiance to the crown was part of the sometimes nebulous citizenship transfer process in South Carolina. See James H. Kettner, *The Development of American Citizenship, 1608–1870* (Chapel Hill: University of North Carolina Press, 1978), 85–86, 96–97.

28. This is a generalization based upon my examination of extant sources of all types because no separate passenger lists for ships debarking in South Carolina for the relevant years have been found. See A. Harold Lancour, comp., "Passenger Lists of Ships Coming to North America," *Bulletin of the New York Public Library* 41, no. 5 (1937): 389–410.

29. Jean Pierre Purry, *Kurtze jedoch zuverläßige Nachricht von dem gegenwärtigen Zustand und Beschaffenheit de Mittägigen Carolina in America oder West-Indien, Welche Landschaft Georgien genennet wird, aufgesetzt In Charlestown oder Carlstadt von vier glaubwürdigen Schweitzern, und aus der Frantzösischen Sprache anietzo verdeutscht. Welchem eine Nachricht von denen so genannten Wilden, welche in derselben Gegend wohnen, beygefüget ist*, trans. Samuel Benjamin Walthern (Leipzig, 1734). The full title in English is *Short but reliable news of the present-day condition of middle Carolina in America or the West Indies, which is called Georgia, written in Charlestown or Carlstadt, by four credible Swiss, translated into German from the French language. Included is news of the so-called savages who live in the same area.* I am indebted to my colleague Professor Elisabeth Buxton for her translation of the document from the German.

30. Jean Pierre Purry was only the first and most conspicuous of those who contracted with South Carolina authorities to settle immigrants on the frontier. In some ways his success spurred both the colony and other individuals to follow his lead. Two other names associated with contractual communities in colonial South Carolina are Sebastian Zouberbühler and John Jacob Riemensperger. The success of these individuals had much to do with the "lure of sufficient land, low taxes, and exemption from pressing obligations" and a disparity between "their current position and future prospects at home compared with opportunities offered in distant lands," but it took the perseverance of determined individual recruiters such as Purry to make the contracts work—and their efforts were not often appreciated in the Swiss homelands of the immigrants. Riemensperger was expelled from Zurich and exiled from the

Confederation for his attempt to persuade Swiss citizens to settle in South Carolina. Quinche received a reprimand for trying to drum up recruits for South Carolina in Berne. By the 1740s the Confederation prohibited emigration. See *Neue Nachricht*, 54; Hughes, "Populating the Back Country," 72–77; Young, *Germans in the Colonial Southeast*, 11; Faust, *Lists*, 1:9. Quotation from Jones, *Georgia Dutch*, 27. Quotations in this note from Marianne Wokeck, "Harnessing the Lure of the 'Best Poor Man's Country': The Dynamics of German-Speaking Immigration to British North America, 1683–1783," 204–43 in Ida Altman and James Hory, eds., *"To Make America": European Emigration in the Early Modern Period* (Berkeley: University of California Press, 1991), 211.

31. R. W. Kelsey, "Swiss Settlers in South Carolina," *SCHGM* 23 (July 1922): 91; Smith, "Purrysburgh," 201–3; Voigt, "German Immigration," 14–15, 17; Kurz, "Investigations," 25; Howe, *History of the Presbyterian Church*, 1:211; Garrison, *Oglethorpe's Folly*, 111.

32. Daniel Ravenel, "Historical Sketch of the Huguenot Congregations of South Carolina," *THSSC* 7 (1900): 9; Muench, "Story of Purysburg," 10; Sirmans, *Colonial South Carolina*, 168; Roeber, "Whatever Is Not English among Us,"240, note 49.

33. The granting of land in colonial South Carolina was a tedious and often confusing process. See Brent H. Holcomb, introduction to volume 4 of *Petitions for Land from the South Carolina Council Journals*, 7 vols. (Columbia: South Carolina Magazine of Ancestral Research, 1996–1999), n.pag. Hereafter cited as Holcomb, *Petitions for Land*. See also the anonymous article "Granting of Land in Colonial South Carolina," *SCHM* 77 (July 1976): 208–12; Hughes, "Populating the Back Country," 36. For a more detailed discussion of this and related land issues, see Robert K. Ackerman, *South Carolina Colonial Land Policies* (Columbia: University of South Carolina Press, 1977).

34. Eveleigh to Oglethorpe, 28 May 1735, in Mills Lane, ed., *Oglethorpe's Georgia: Colonial Letters, 1733–1743*, 2 vols. (Savannah: Beehive Press, 1975), 1:170; Evarts B. Greene and Virginia Harrington, *American Population before the Federal Census of 1790* (New York: Columbia University Press, 1932; reprint, Glouster, Mass.: Peter Smith, 1966), xxiii.

35. There have always been two serious, but unacknowledged, problems in determining the ethnic and cultural background of the Purrysburg settlers. The first problem is the extreme difficulty in tracing the hundreds of family lines back to their places of origin. To label a family French-Swiss or German-Swiss just because their immediate domicile prior to emigration happened to be Neuchâtel or Berne does not prove Swiss citizenship or cultural heritage. Nor does assigning French Huguenot status to French-speaking Calvinists of Geneva prove that they were actually religious refugees from France. Similar complexities arise when attempting to determine conclusively the homelands of the German speakers called Palatines because of the movement of Swiss families into the Electoral Palatinate and the nearby Kraichagau in the two generations after the Thirty Years' War. Yet assumptions regarding the homelands of the Purrysburg residents are made constantly in the literature. The loose usage of the key geographical terms is the second problem especially as it impringes upon the relationship between the Swiss Confederation and south central Europe. The boundaries of the Palatinate, for example, shift from study to study. Marianne Wokeck includes the canton of Zurich in southwestern Germany—which, of course did not even exist

in the eighteenth century. A. G. Roeber, in *Palatines, Liberty, and Prosperity*, links south German notions of liberty to the Swiss example, though we have already noted that practical liberty was highly problematic there by the eighteenth century. Thomas Brady's *Turning Swiss* uses "South Germany" to describe a region home to German, Swiss, French, Austrian, and Italian cultures. Today the people of this "South Germany" are citizens of six different states. When overlaid with the shifting boundaries of south central European regions and the internal tensions of the Swiss Confederation in the eighteenth century, the "Germanic" cast given to the cantons has further confounded our understanding of the origins of Purrysburg families. In light of the above, I have opted to follow primary source inferential data and reputable secondary evidence that seems to me to have some claim to legitimacy in my assessment of the origins of groups of Purrysburg settlers. I will also endeavor to note potential discrepancies in the literature. I must leave it to family historians and genealogists to supply posterity with the exact places of origin for individual immigrants. See Wokeck, "Harnessing the Lure," 227; A. G. Roeber, *Palatines, Liberty, and Property: German Lutherans in Colonial British America* (Baltimore: Johns Hopkins University Press, 1993), 2; Thomas A. Brady Jr., *Turning Swiss: Cities and Empires, 1450–1550* (Cambridge: Cambridge University Press, 1985), 1, 5

36. George Fenwick Jones, recognized authority on the Salzburg immigration to Georgia, disputes the often cited presence of Salzburg Lutherans in Purrysburg. Jones, however, provides no direct evidence to substantiate his claim. He argues merely that the Reverend Boltzius would have mentioned them in his journal had such a party taken up residence in the township. See Jones, *Georgia Dutch*, 27.

37. Allen D. Candler and Lucian L. Knight, eds., *The Colonial Records of the State of Georgia*, 25 vols., 1–19 and 21–26 (Atlanta: C. P. Byrd, 1904–16), vol. 5: *The Journal of the Earl of Egmont*, 566, hereafter cited as Candler, *CRG*; Voigt, "German Immigration," 8, 15; Smith, "Purrysburgh," 201; Summerall, "Address," 43; Meriwether, *Expansion of South Carolina*, 35–36; Hirsch, *Huguenots of Colonial South Carolina*, 32. The Salzburg Lutheran immigration is an integral part of the story of Purrysburg. For background on this impressive group, see *Collections of the Georgia Historical Society*, 15 vols. (Savannah: Georgia Historical Society, 1840–), 4:11–12, hereafter cited as *CGHS*; the Reverend P. A. Strobel, *The Salzburgers and Their Descendants* (Baltimore: T. Newton Kurtz, 1855; American Culture Series, Ann Arbor: University Microfilms, 1974, reel 573), 25–30, 33–34, 42; G. D. Bernheim, *History of the German Settlements and the Lutheran Church in North and South Carolina* . . . (Philadelphia: Lutheran Book Store, 1872; reprint, Spartanburg, S.C.: Reprint Co., 1972), 35–37; Milton Rubincam, "Historical Background of the Salzburg Emigration to Georgia," *GHQ* 35 (June 1951): 99–115; J. M. Hofer, "The Georgia Salzburgers," *GHQ* 18 (June 1934): 99–117; R. L. Brantley, "The Salzburgers in Georgia," *GHQ* 14 (September 1930): 214–24; C. T. Atkinson, *A History of Germany, 1715–1815* (1908; reprint, New York: Barnes and Noble, 1969), 85–86; Ernest F. Henderson, *A Short History of Germany*, 2 vols. in 1 (New York: MacMillan, 1911), 99–100. For a more detailed account of all of the European ethnic groups that eventually found their way to Purrysburg, see Arlin C. Migliazzo, "Sources of the Purrysburgh Population: The European Context," *THSSC* 87 (1982): 51–63.

38. Unfortunately these problems were not unique to the South Carolina township colonists. Bradford J. Wood discovered similar problems in the concurrent settlement

of the lower Cape Fear region of North Carolina. See Wood, *This Remote Part of the World*, 50–55.

39. BPRO 15:166–69. A resolution of council allowed the surveys to proceed as long as the surveyor general received a warrant from the governor prior to the survey. See BPRO 15:198.

40. BPRO 16:316–23, 347–58, 404–13; 17:8–9, 22–30; *CSCHS* 3:306, 310. Purry probably contributed his share to the confusion by ceding some township land illegally to James Oglethorpe, one of the trustees of the new colony of Georgia and to others as will be seen. As noted previously, Oglethorpe received 3,000 acres of his land in the extreme southern part of Purrysburg. See "Agreement between Purry and Oglethorpe," cited previously, Wilkins, "James Edward Oglethorpe," 87–89, and Garrison, *Oglethorpe's Folly*, 170. Quotation from BPRO 16:319. The intricacies and aberrations of South Carolina's land policies as well as the issues of quitrent payments, the land boom, and Johnson's part in all this are ably examined in Sirmans, *Colonial South Carolina*, 170–82.

41. Besides the royal governor, among the most prominent of these landowners were Colonel Samuel Prioleau, Jonathan Bryan, John Roberts, the Broughton, Middleton, and Bull families, and Savannah merchant Robert Williams. There was also at least one 12,000-acre tract dating from the proprietary period that lay within the township environs. This may have been the basis for Benjamin Whitaker's 1739 challenge to Charles Purry's request that his late father's land fall to him. Acting on behalf of John Roberts (the assignee of former proprietor Lord Carteret), Whitaker was able to block temporarily the transfer of Purry's land to his eldest son. The council also allowed Joseph Edward Flower 500 acres in the township "taking into consideration the Petitioner had been very instrumental in the settling of the said township and he was settled there before his Majesty's Royal Instructions were signified." See Holcomb, *Petitions for Land*, 1:19, 44, 48 (quotation in note), 90, 95, 133, 136, 3:200; Colonial Land Plats, recorded copies, 21 vols., SCDAH 5:2; Royal Land Grants 1731–47, microfilm copies at LGS, 5342, pt. 2, 13, 26–33.

42. Land Grants, Colonial Series, 1731–76, 56 vols. SCDAH. Microfilmed copies were studied at the Library of the Genealogical Society of the Church of Jesus Christ of Latter Day Saints (hereafter cited as LGS) in Salt Lake City, Utah, 1731–47; Summerall, "Address," 42. The Georgia trustees also seem to have been involved in land dealings in and around Purrysburg. Note Candler, *CRG*, 21:62. All quotations are taken from BPRO 17:185–87.

43. Sirmans, *Colonial South Carolina*, 176, 179, 186. See also note 40. For a more complete examination of the problems associated with the land boom of the 1730s, see Weir, *Colonial South Carolina*, 112–15. The problems between Johnson, St. John, and Whitaker go far deeper than just the quitrent law of 1731. In addition to the overview provided by Weir, note BPRO 15:159–69 for some of the other complaints of St. John and Whitaker and BPRO 17:187–89 for Johnson's perspective.

44. BPRO 16:121–22, 153–54, 156–60, 169–70; *CSCHS* 2:137–38, 141, 338; 3:342; Easterby, *JCHA*, 1736–39:205; Lane, *Oglethorpe's Georgia*, 1:74; W. Stitt Robinson, *The Southern Colonial Frontier, 1607–1763* (Albuquerque: University of New Mexico Press, 1979), 168; Sirmans, *Colonial South Carolina*, 186; Meriwether, *Expansion of South Carolina*, 23, 35; Smith, "Purrysburgh," 203; Garrison,

Oglethorpe's Folly, 169. Quotations from BPRO 16:157.

45. Details for this and the subsequent paragraph may be found in BPRO 15:133–34, 16:347–58, 366–67, 384–86. Quotations from *CSCHS* 2:264 and 3:313. See also Charles G. Cordle, ed., "The John Tobler Manuscripts: An Account of German-Swiss Emigrants in South Carolina, 1737," *Journal of Southern History* 5 (February 1939): 95; Hughes, "Populating the Back Country," 14, 26–31; Meriwether, *Expansion of South Carolina*, 21–25; Sirmans, *Colonial South Carolina*, 165, 186. For the merchants' response to Purry and an official, scathing rebuke to the merchants, as well as an assessment of the deplorable treatment of Purry's colonists, see BPRO 16:196, 202–3, 220–22 and 17:70–82.

46. It is important to recognize that, although most of the colonists came from the agricultural, laboring, or small craft sectors of the European population, there were a few highly successful and influential immigrants who followed Purry to South Carolina. He counted on their support and assistance in recruiting others to his colonial venture. Once Purrysburg Township became a reality, Purry appointed these "several Persons of Substance and Prudence" to serve as overseers "to protect advise and assist the rest of this new Colony in Settling the said Township." Because the overseers did their work with no "Salary or Allowance for their trouble and daily Attendance altho they are unavoidably liable to several extraordinary Expences on that Account," Purry petitioned the king's council on their behalf in 1734. He requested that in view of their service they each be granted additional lands, not to exceed 300 acres each, in the six-mile buffer zone surrounding the township on three sides. Because his request was indefinite regarding the amount of land and number of overseers involved, the council appears to have set aside 2,000 acres to reward these men of substance. See BPRO 16:317, 322; 17:28–29, 158. Quotations in this note from BPRO 16:320–21.

47. The following discussion is drawn from an analysis of Colonial Land Plats, SCDAH, and from the microfilmed copies of Royal Land Grants, LGS, as well as other sources as noted.

48. Joseph W. Barnwell and Mabel L. Webber, copiers and arrangers, "St. Helena's Parish Register," *SCHGM* 23 (April 1922): 47, 56, 66, 69; A. S. Salley Jr., *Minutes of the Vestry of St. Helena's Parish, South Carolina, 1726–1812* (Columbia, S.C.: State Company, 1919), 24, 38, 40, 47; *CSCHS* 2:274 and 3:313; Wills of John Pennefather and Isaiah Overy, microfilmed copies of the CWA Transcripts, LGS, 1740–47; Easterby, *JCHA*, 1748:273; Candler, *CRG*, 5:198 and 22, pt. 2:110; George C. Rogers Jr., "The Huguenots of the Old Beaufort District," *THSSC* 85 (1980): 13; Meriwether, *Expansion of South Carolina*, 38; Leiding, "Purrysburg: A Swiss-French Settlement," 31; Royal Land Grants, LGS film, 5342, pt. 2, 481–83; S. Charles Bolton, *Southern Anglicanism: The Church of England in Colonial South Carolina* (Westport, Conn.: Greenwood Press, 1982), 64–65.

49. *Reports* 7:19.

50. Hughes, "Populating the Back Country," 36.

51. Robert Parker of Savannah, grateful for Purrysburg's existence so close to the Georgia town, observed in December 1734 that "when at Purrysburg (to its praise be spoken) only one warrant has been served since its first settling." Although the evidence does not substantiate Parker's rather exaggerated claim, his sentiment does express deep frustration with the time and effort it took to receive legal title to land.

See Parker to the trustees, December 1734, in Lane, *Oglethorpe's Georgia,* 1:74.

52. Holcomb, *Petitions for Land*, 1:132–33.

53. Ibid., 1:21.

54. Here again it is intriguing to note that among the most expeditiously concluded land acquisitions were those of Hector Berenger De Beaufin, perhaps the most wealthy of all Purrysburg's early settlers. One took just over three months and another eight months. Another substantial Purrysburg settler, John Linder, received legal title to one of his claims in just under six months. See Colonial Land Grants (Copy Series), 41:122–24, 193, 233. The Colonial Land Grants (Copy Series), otherwise known in earlier publications as the Township Grants (vols. 41 and 42), provide the bases for these generalizations.

55. In his petition of 24 February 1743/44, Grand included an attestation from his majesty's collector of the customs and former Purrysburg resident and justice of the peace Hector Berenger De Beaufin that Beaufin had in his possession grants for lots and land in Purrysburg, but he did not receive one for Grand's land. Beaufin added, "This I have occasion to remember, because the man being anxious about his grant, made me search for it more than once." Beaufin finally looked over the list of grants in the secretary's office, but only found reference to Grand's town lot (no. 35). Grand went so far as to produce a duplicate of the plat for the council to bolster his case. See Holcomb, *Petitions for Land*, 1:182–83. For Verley's case, see Holcomb, *Petitions for Land*, 1:199.

56. Holcomb, *Petitions for Land*, 3:27–28.

57. The provincial government appears to have forced Purrysburg's early settlers to cast lots to determine who received what land. See Meriwether, *Expansion of South Carolina*, 36.

58. Holcomb, *Petitions for Land*, 1:102.

59. Ibid., 2:197.

60. Ibid., 3:5, 27–28; Meriwether, *Expansion of South Carolina*, 36.

61. The following discussion is based on an analysis of a copy of the survey of "Purysburgh=Town" executed ca. 1765, Map Box 11–10, SCDAH, Special Land Grants, 1731–47, and other sources as noted.

62. Notations on the plat give 213 feet as the length, but if the chain measurement of 3.195 is correct the 210.87 number obtains.

63. Most of the streets appear never to have been named. I have only been able to determine the names of four streets from other sources as they are not marked on this or any other plat of the town. Bay or Front Street "fronted" on the Savannah River and stood between it and the first town lots. Church Street was the next street to the east, obviously named for the town sanctuary located on lot 32. Savannah Street nearly bisected the town east to west at Church Street. The extreme northerly street that separated the town proper from township glebe lands was called Broad North Street. The high road from Charles Town passed through Purrysburg on Church Street.

64. There is some discrepancy as to the number of town lots as well as their size. According to Johnson's township plan, only 250–300 acres were to be set aside for the town proper to be divided into 200 quarter-acre lots. Yet the town plat from 1765 clearly shows 455 one-acre lots. The smallest town lots granted were one-half acre in size, and many received grants for full-acre lots.

65. Eight hundred acres were set aside for the town and its common, as shown in both maps 6 and 7. If the upper limit dimensions of the town proper are used (1.325 × 0.85), Purrysburg would encompass 1.12625 square miles, or roughly 720 acres. If the lower-limit dimensions are used (1.325 × 0.625), the town shrinks to 0.828125 square miles or 530 acres. Because the town narrows gradually from north to south, the common must have somewhat less than 200 acres, though it was supposed to encompass 260 acres. See Smith, "Purrysburgh,"195. I have been unable to determine the location of the town square noted by Richardson and others. See Richardson, "'As Easy to Build Towns,'" 171.

66. Only town lots 57, 289, and 403 along this boundary were unallocated by the end of 1738.

67. Richardson, "'As Easy to Build Towns,'" 23. Lewis argues that this spatial town arrangement, which he calls a row settlement, was a European form often associated with small trading towns. Both Long Bluff and Ninety-Six developed in this manner. See Kenneth E. Lewis, "Functional Variation among Settlements on the South Carolina Frontier: An Archeological Perspective," 251–74 in Stanton W. Green and Stephen M. Perlman, eds., *The Archeology of Frontiers and Boundaries* (Orlando, Fla.: Academic Press, 1985), 266.

68. *CSCHS* 3:305. See also Special Land Grants, 1731–47, LGS.

69. Einar Haugen, "Language and Immigration," 1–36 in Einar Haugen, *The Ecology of Language: Essays by Einar Haugen*, selected and intro. by Anwar S. Dil (Stanford, Calif.: Stanford University Press, 1972), 1–2.

70. Larry Lepionka, "Purrysburg: An Archeological Survey: A Report on the Archeological Investigation of the Colonial Site of Purrysburg, Founded in 1733 by Jean Pierre Purry of Neuchatel" (Beaufort, October 17, 1979), 3; Daniel Elliot, "Archeological Reconnaissance of the Purrysburg Tract, Jasper County, South Carolina" (Garrow & Associates, January 24, 1985), 32; *Reports* 6:53 (third quotation), 8:131, 9:63 (first quotation), 10:16, 22. Lepionka's survey was subsequently published. See *Swiss American Historical Society Newsletter* 16, no. 2 (1980): 18–29.

71. Clara A. Langley, abstracter, *South Carolina Deed Abstracts, 1719–1772*, vol. 1 (Easley, S.C.: Southern Historical Press, 1983), 294. Hereafter volumes in this series will be cited as Langley, *Deed Abstracts* with the requisite volume and page number designations. The quotation is from *Reports* 8:131.

72. The fact that Purrysburg was not granted parish status and hence representation in the Commons House of Assembly until February 1746/7 even though it met the criteria by the mid-1730s illustrates the extent to which colonial leadership conspired to keep political power—and therefore some say in policies that affected them—out of the hands of Purrysburg inhabitants.

73. *Reports* 7:150 (quotation), 170–72.

74. Katie-Prince Ward Esker, comp., *South Carolina Memorials, 1731–1776: Abstracts of Selected Land Records*, vol 2 (New Orleans: Polyanthos, 1977), 136–37, 160; *Reports* 3:201, 4:46, 53, 6:187; Alexandra Morrison Carpenter, "Purrysburg, South Carolina," address presented to the Colonial Dames of Georgia, 13 May 1930, 3. Typescript copy from the library of the Huguenot Society of South Carolina, Charleston, South Carolina.

75. Kurz, "Investigations," 25; letter of Samuel Dyssli quoted in William Greer Albergotti III, *Albergotti Creek: The Chronicles of a Colonial Family of the South*

Carolina Sea Islands (Columbia: R. L. Bryan, 1979), 11.

76. Kurz, "Investigations," 25; Kelsey, "Swiss Settlers," 85–91; Migliazzo, *Lands of True and Certain Bounty*, 160–63

77. *SCG*, 8 September 1739 and 18 October 1742; *CSCHS* 2:295; Jones, *Georgia Dutch*, 64–65.

78. Rogers, "Huguenots of Old Beaufort District," 3, 5; Hirsch, *Huguenots of Colonial South Carolina*, 13.

79. Sirmans, *Colonial South Carolina*, 168.

Chapter Three

1. "A New Voyage to Georgia. By a Young Gentleman. Giving an Account of His Travels to South Carolina, and a Part of North Carolina . . . ," 2nd ed. (London, 1737); reprinted in H. Roy Merrens, ed., *The Colonial South Carolina Scene, 1697–1774* (Columbia: University of South Carolina Press, 1977), 110–21, citation to 111–12.

2. "A New Voyage to Georgia," 120.

3. Russo, *Families and Communities*, 6; Rutman, "Social Web," 77.

4. Rutman and Rutman, *A Place in Time*, 120.

5. As noted in chapter 2, the process of receiving legal title to land was always cumbersome and fraught with irregularities, which is why the list of original Purrysburg landholders in table 2 has been compiled primarily from my examination of the Colonial Land Plats, recorded copies, 1731–1775, 21 volumes, SCDAH, supplemented by the Colonial Land Grants (Copy Series)/Township Grants, Royal Land Grants, and other sources when necessary. While I realize that plats do not legally convey land, I reason that in attempting to build the most comprehensive list possible, there is a greater likelihood that prospective landowners (especially foreign immigrants unfamiliar with the complexities of colonial land policy) would complete the initial process rather than the latter. In addition, by proclamation of Governor Johnson in 1735, no grants in townships were to be conveyed to any person but the one whose name appeared on the original warrant. This proclamation would seem to reinforce my hope that plat records provide the best possible opportunity for a complete list of Purrysburg landholders and their dependents. At the same time, I appreciate the difficulties in using any land records to calculate total population figures as noted by Kaylene Hughes. Nonetheless, extant plat records give us our best chance, and these records, used in conjunction with the other modes of estimating population, will yield highly accurate numbers. See Hughes, "Populating the Back Country,"37–40. Table 2 includes only those original petitioners for land whose success before the governor and council resulting in the platting of land by the surveyor general's office. It does not include those who subsequently purchased land in the township from the original owners. Allocations that appear to be duplicates or are in some other way suspect are noted with an asterisk.

6. Since fifty acres of land was granted to each family member, servant, and slave in the household, it is impossible to determine the number of family members represented by each grant of land as lands granted to households for servants and slaves were not distinguished in the land records. Also, because servants were entitled to fifty acres in their own right after they completed their term of indenture, land records are not an accurate way to determine the total population of the township, since servants could

be counted multiple times. In 1755 the acreage granted to the heads of households was increased from fifty to a hundred acres. See Hughes, "Populating the Back Country," 36.

7. Jéquier et al., *La Famille Pury*, 70 (D[1] XIV); Holcomb, *Petitions for Land* 2:104–5; MR, 2O, pt. 1:288–89; Langley, *Deed Abstracts,* 3:244; Records of Mesne Conveyance (Charleston Deeds), vols. A–ZZZZ, bound volumes, O. T. Wallace County Office Building, Charleston, South Carolina, microfilmed copies, SCDAH, 4H: 173–75, hereafter cited as RMC; *Reports* 5:279, 7:104, 9:91; Jones, *Georgia Dutch*, 120.

8. Hughes, "Populating the Back Country," 53, 55–57.

9. Jeanneret and Bonhôte, *Biographie neuchâteloise*; Certificate for David Giroud from the Commune of Petit Bayard, 26 February 1732, SCL.

10. Harry Alexander Davis, *Some Huguenot Families of South Carolina and Georgia, Supplement No. 3* (Washington, D.C., 1940) Library of the Huguenot Society of South Carolina, 1–51.

11. Harry Alexander Davis, *Some Huguenot Families of South Carolina and Georgia, Supplement No. 2* (Washington, D.C., 1937), Library of the Huguenot Society of South Carolina, 1.

12. "History of the Humbert Family," SCL, 1.

13. Harry Alexander Davis, *The Gindrat Family: A Supplement to Some Huguenot Families of South Carolina and Georgia* (Washington, D.C., 1933); letter of William Greer Albergotti III to Arlin Migliazzo, 4 June 2003, 4.

14. *Yemassee Bluff News,* March 2000, 2; Jones, *The Georgia Dutch*, 120; *Reports* 11:13; Meriwether, *Expansion of South Carolina*, 36 (n. 6), 38.

15. *Yemassee Bluff News,* December 2002, 3.

16. Ibid.

17. Harry Alexander Davis, *Some Huguenot Families of South Carolina and Georgia* (Washington, 1926), 2; Hutson Papers, "LaFitte," South Carolina Historical Society, 1, hereafter cited as SCHS; Sara S. Ervin, "Notes on the History of the Giroud and Allied Families of Purrysburg, South Carolina—Being a Record of the Family for Three Generations before Coming to America and for Four Generations in South Carolina, Up to About the Time of the War between the States," *THSSC* 48 (June 1943): 36.

18. Davis, *Some Families*, 32, 35; "Our Huguenot Ancestors: Their Homes in France," *THSSC* 75 (1970): 95; "Memorial Tablets in the French Protestant (Huguenot) Church in Charleston, South Carolina," and "Alphabetical List of Memorial Tablets," *THSSC* 75 (1970): 72.

19. "An Act For encouraging the Manufacture of Silk in this Province, under the Direction of Mr. John Lewis Poyas, for Seven Years, passed by the General Assembly, 25 March 1738," copy at SCL; "Poyas" genealogical records in the possession of Ms. Carolyn Holbrook, Atlanta, Georgia. Copies xeroxed for the author.

20. Rutman and Rutman, *A Place in Time*, 60.

21. Converse D. Clowse, *Economic Beginnings in Colonial South Carolina, 1670–1736* (Columbia: University of South Carolina Press, 1971), 25. On the problem of faulty cartography, note especially Converse D. Clowse and William Patterson Cumming, "Geographical Misconceptions of the Southeast in the Cartography of the Seventeenth and Eighteenth Centuries," *Journal of Southern History* 4 (November 1938): 476–92.

22. For an instructive overview of family life on the South Carolina colonial frontier, see Hughes, "Populating the Back Country," 120–28.

23. *Reports* 4:198–99, author's parentheses.

24. John Duffy, "Eighteenth Century Carolina Health Conditions," *Journal of Southern History* 28 (August 1952): 289–90; Menard, *Economy and Society*, 140, 144; Darrett B. Rutman and Anita H. Rutman, "Of Agues and Fevers: Malaria in the Early Chesapeake," *William and Mary Quarterly*, 3rd ser., 33 (January 1976): 31. Carr and Walsh claim that the life expectancy for a seventeenth-century Maryland immigrant was forty-three years—70 percent of them expiring before the age of fifty. See Carr and Walsh, "The Planter's Wife," 542.

25. Clowse, *Economic Beginnings*, 31, 33; Coclanis, *Shadow of a Dream*, 32; Kovacik and Winberry, *South Carolina: A Geography*, 32–33; "Report of Sir James Wright on the Condition of the Province of Georgia on 20 September 1773," *CGHS* 3:159. On the connection between climate and disease note especially Lionel Chalmers, *An Account of the Weather and Diseases in South Carolina* (London: Edward and Charles Dilly, 1776) and David Ramsey, *Sketch of the Soil, Climate, Weather, and Disease of South Carolina* (Charleston, S.C.: W. P. Young, 1796). For a more complete treatment of this topic, note Duffy's book *Epidemics in Colonial America* (Baton Rouge: Louisiana State University Press, 1953).

26. Gerald L. Cates, "The Seasoning: Disease and Death among the First Colonists of Georgia," *GHQ* 64 (Summer 1980): 149, 151–54; Clowse, *Economic Beginnings*, 35; Coclanis, *Shadow of a Dream*, 41; Hughes, "Populating the Back Country," 96–99; Rutman and Rutman, "Of Agues and Fevers," 50, 52; Carville V. Earle, "Environment, Disease, and Mortality in Early Virginia," 96–125 in Tate and Ammerman, *The Chesapeake*, 99; George Fenwick Jones, *The Salzburger Saga: Religious Exiles and Other Germans along the Savannah* (Athens: University of Georgia Press, 1984), 109. For extended discussions of disease in South Carolina, see St. Julien Ravenel Childs, *Malaria and Colonization in the Carolina Low Country, 1526–1696* (Baltimore: Johns Hopkins University Press, 1940); idem, "Notes on the History of Public Health in South Carolina, 1670–1800," *Proceedings of the South Carolina Historical Association* (1932): 13–22; Joseph I. Waring, *A History of Medicine in South Carolina, 1670–1825* (Charleston: South Carolina Medical Association, 1964); John Duffy, "Yellow Fever in Colonial Charleston," *SCHGM* 52 (October 1951): 189–97. A common belief at the time held that a sick mother could pass her illness to her nursing child through diseased breast milk. See *Reports* 7:181.

27. Earle, "Environment and Disease," 99–100, 104, 107–8, 112; Hughes, "Populating the Back Country," 97.

28. Coclanis, *Shadow of a Dream*, 41; Hughes, "Populating the Back Country," 97–98.

29. Hughes, "Populating the Back Country," 102.

30. *Reports* 8:330

31. *Reports* 9:192.

32. *Reports* 10:73–74; 18:198.

33. Purrysburg appears to have had some reputation as a site of baths with curative powers, but they also seem to have been ineffectual in restoring health. See *Reports* 11–12:74–75.

34. *Reports* 9:94; Chaplin, *Anxious Pursuit*, 96; Hughes, "Populating the Back Country," 102–3.

35. *Reports* 11–12:13–14.

36. Volume 41 of the Colonial Land Grants (Copy Series)/ Township Grants shows grants to "the heirs of Ulrick Bac," and to Anna Barbara Francke. See also *Reports* 3:208; 4:40 142; Royal Grants, LGS film 5342, pt. 2, 1731–47, 481–83. See also the letter written by Samuel Dyssli to his family and friends in Europe, 3 December 1737, in Kelsey, "Swiss Settlers," 89.

37. *CRG* 21:271; Spencer B. King Jr., *Georgia Voices: A Documentary History to 1872* (Athens: University of Georgia Press, 1966), 13.

38. *Reports* 16:24, 30, 55–56, 190; 17:281.

39. Coleman, *Colonial Georgia*, 34.

40. The Reverend John Ulrick Giessendanner kept a record of deaths among residents of these townships and records only four due to accidents between 1735 and 1760 (two shootings, one trampling, one drowning). Using Giessendanner's data, Kaylene Hughes calculated that 22 percent of deaths of women of childbearing age were attributable to the hazards of pregnancy and childbirth and that 36 percent of deaths were among children under one year of age. See Hughes, "Populating the Back Country," 81, 88, 100.

41. William Stephens, *A Journal of the Proceedings in Georgia*, 2 vols. (Ann Arbor, Mich.: University Microfilms, 1966), 1:392.

42. Gilbert P. Voigt, "Side-Light on Conditions in Certain German Settlements in South Carolina, 1734–1751," *Bulletin of the University of South Carolina*, no. 113 (September 1922): 30. There is some discrepancy regarding this second accident as the Reverend Boltzius has it occurring in early 1739, while Voigt places it in the early 1740s. There is a possibility that there was only one accident in 1739 and all these individuals perished, although this interpretation is highly unlikely from a close reading of all the accounts. See also *Reports* 6:14, 23.

43. *Reports* 8:507; 13–14:36,121; 17:238.

44. *Reports* 13:97; T. W. Lipscomb, ed., *The Colonial Records of South Carolina: The Journal of the Commons House of Assembly, November 12, 1754–September 23, 1755*, vol. 13 (Columbia: University of South Carolina Press, 1986), 29, hereafter cited Lipscomb, *JCHA*, 13. Linder's murder was reported to the Commons House of Assembly in the mid-1750s, but little else is known about the circumstances of his death. John Linder Jr. and John Linder Sr. of Purrysburg were still alive during the Revolutionary War. Perhaps the John Linder killed by Native Americans was the son of John Linder Jr.

45. *Reports* 3:100; 4:142, 162, 192; 5:47; 7:85–86; 10:171; Jones, *The Salzburger Saga*, 17, 40; Jones, *Georgia Dutch*, 120.

46. *Reports* 5:171. Although not named in this account, strong circumstantial evidence from other sources indicates that this was probably Hans Krüsy.

47. *Reports* 5:213–14; 9:29, 34; 13–14:170; 16:50–51. The judge appears to have been Johann Frederick Holzendorf. See *Reports* 5:214, n. 236. Schrempf was the son-in-law of Theobald Kieffer Sr. and his wife. See *Reports* 16:30.

48. Lorena S. Walsh, "'Til Death Us Do Part'": Marriage and Family in Seventeenth Century Maryland," in Tate and Ammerman, *The Chesapeake*, 126–52; Darrett B.

and Anita H. Rutman, "Now-Wives and Sons-in-Law: Parental Death in a Seventeenth Century Virginia County," in 153–82, Tate and Ammerman, *The Chesapeake*.

49. The mortality rate has been named as a specific reason for what otherwise might be seen as hasty marriages on the southern frontier. The promise of land was another. See Jones, *Salzburger Saga*, 25, 28. Orville Vernon Burton found much the same search for security and identity in uncertain surroundings as the motivation for marriage in nineteenth-century Edgefield County, South Carolina. See Burton, *In My Father's House*, 369, n. 116. See also Walsh, "'Til Death,'" 148; Rutman and Rutman, "Parental Death," 169; Coleman, *Colonial Georgia*, 34.

50. Extract of an anonymous letter from Purrysburg, 26 January 1734, in Lane, *Oglethorpe's Georgia*, 1:39–40; *SCG*, 2 March 1734, in "Historical Notes," *SCHGM* 5 (July 1904): 192.

51. "The Giroud Family," typescript, SCL, 2; Holcomb, *Petitions for Land*, 1:67; Langley, *Deed Abstracts*, 3:357, 359; *Reports* 17:55; RMC, 3N:345–47, 4H:173–75, 4P:431–32.

52. Coleman, *Colonial Georgia*, 170; Voigt, "Side-Light," 28–29.

53. On the nature of Swiss ethnicity note especially Uriel Weinreich, *Languages in Contact: Findings and Problems* (New York: Columbia University Press, 1953), 84, 86, 89, 91–92.

54. *Reports* 2:22, 31, 48, 51, 117–18, 143; 4:192, 202; 5:47; 6:221; 7:85–6, n. 20.

55. Information for this and the preceding paragraph was taken from Letter of Anthony Gondy of Charles Town to his brother near Lausanne, 28 May 1733, in Kelsey, "Swiss Settlers," 86; George Fenwick Jones, ed., "Johann Martin Boltzius' Trip to Charleston, October 1742," *SCHM* 82 (April 1981): 90; *Reports* 2:21; 3:260; 5:47, 61, 125, 139; 7:85, 173; 8:39, 167, 178, 182–83, 192, 197, 349; 9:29, 34, 129–30, 242; 10:117–18, 175; Jones, *Georgia Dutch*, 166; Jones, *Salzburger Saga*, 67, 72–73. The Kieffers had one other daughter, Barbara, according to the list of those qualifying before Governor Robert Johnson in December 1732. Although she is not mentioned by name in the available records, there is a possibility that she married Valentin Depp, a Purrysburg shoemaker and brother of Jacob's wife. Depp is referred to as Theobald Sr.'s son-in-law and Schrempf's brother-in-law. See *Reports* 15:17; 16:30; 18:186, 226.

56. *Reports* 2:118.

57. *Reports* 2:31; Voigt, "Side-Light," 21.

58. Weinreich, *Languages in Contact*, 84, 86, 89, 91–92; Kelsey, "Swiss Settlers," 86.

59. RMC, 3E:86; Wills of James Richard, Andrew Greniere (Greigniere), John Garvey, Jacob Barraque, Jonas Pelot, David Humbert, Gideon Mallet, Daniel Mallet, David Mongin, LGS; Deed of Gift Indenture, Nicholas Winkler and Anna Margaritha Winkler; Deed of Gift Indenture, Nicholas Winkler and Nicholas Winkler Jr.; Deed of Gift Indenture, David Saussy Sr. and George and Margaritha Kehl, MR, 2N:453–54; Court of Common Pleas: Judgment Rolls, hereafter cited as CCPJR, *Henry Laurens et al. vs. John Lewis Bourguin and Margaret Chiffelle Bourguin*, Box 64A, no. 319A, SCDAH; Comptroller General Accounts Audited: Revolutionary War Claims, Claim of Jane Donnom Bourguin, SCDAH; Oscar E. Imer to Monsieur le Secretaire de la Societe d'histoire de Charleston, South Carolina, le 18 Octobre 1911, SCHS; "Records Kept by Colonel Isaac Hayne," *SCHGM* 11 (January 1910): 35; "Dupont Genealogy," *THSSC* 76 (1971): 107; Mabel L. Webber, "Extract from the Journal of Mrs. Ann Manigault, 1754–1781," *SCHGM* 21 (January 1920): 10. See also note 56 above.

60. Roeber, *Palatines, Liberty, and Property*, 224.

61. Quotations from Holcomb, *Petitions for Land*, 1:134. See also Langley, *Deed Abstracts*, 3:357; Holcomb, *Petitions for Land*, 1:156.

62. Holcomb, *Petitions for Land*, 1:194, 200; RMC, 3A:385–87, 4V:61–62.

63. Richard David Brooks, "Cattle Ranching in Colonial South Carolina: A Case Study in History and Archeology of the Lazarus/Catherina Brown Cowpen" (M.A. thesis, University of South Carolina, 1988), 25–26. Bradford Wood also found evidence of the passing of estate property to females in the lower Cape Fear region. See Wood, *This Remote Part of the World*, 50.

64. Langley, *Deed Abstracts*, 3:351–52, 359; RMC, 3K:343–44. Quotations from Langley, *Deed Abstracts*, 4:82.

65. Holcomb, *Petitions for Land*, 1:67, 71; RMC, 3E:86; Langley, *Deed Abstracts*, 3:357; RMC, 2N:211–17, 3N:345–47, Brent H. Holcomb, abstracter, *South Carolina Deed Abstracts, 1773–1778: Books F-4 through X-4* (Columbia: South Carolina Magazine of Ancestral Research, 1993), 197, hereafter cited as Holcomb, *Deed Abstracts, 1773–1778*; RMC, 4P:416–18.

66. *Reports* 4:119–20, 219; 5:172, 227; 6:23; 9:29, 34, 46, 264; 13–14:90–91. Quotation from *Reports* 11–12:17–18. The fact that when Jacob sold his Purrysburg town lot in 1742, his daughter Marguerite, not his wife was listed on the deed of conveyance would seem to indicate either that she was not present or that they were on less than amicable terms. See RMC, 3E:86.

67. *Reports* 3:316; 4:119.

68. *Reports* 5:84; Jones, *Salzburger Saga*, 48; Walsh, "'Til Death,'" 138.

69. *Reports* 4:170.

70. *Reports* 4:29; 5:73; 14:87.

71. Rutman, "Social Web," 74; Walsh, "'Til Death,'" 141, 144, 147.

72. *Reports* 5:78–79, 92, 118, 173, 182, 228; 7:108; Jones, *Salzburger Saga*, 99.

73. *Reports* 14:170.

74. *Reports* 15:51.

75. *Reports* 8:167, 178, 182–83, 192.

76. *Reports* 7:85, 228; 8:29–30, 52, 117, 152–53, 174, 178, 315, 353, 359, 401, 406, 410, 491; 18:186. There is some question as to when Valentin moved to Purrysburg to learn his shoemaking trade. See *Reports* 8:29–30, 359.

77. *Reports* 9:47, 270, n. 13.

78. Jones, *Georgia Dutch*, 101; *Reports* 6:25, 174; 7:160; 8:126; 9:242.

79. Langley, *Deed Abstracts*, 4:248.

80. "Abstracts of Records of the Proceedings in the Court of Ordinary, 1764–1771," compiled by Mabel L. Webber and Elizabeth H. Jervey, *SCHGM* 23 (April 1922): 80 and 23 (July 1922): 158; Inventories of Andrew Hendrie, 1763–67, and Margaret Jean Henery (Hendrie), 1772–76, microfilmed copies, LGS.

81. "Abstracts, Court of Ordinary," Webber and Jervey, *SCHGM* 44 (January 1943): 51, and 44 (April 1943): 110, and 44 (July, 1943): 175; Will of David Mongin, CWA Transcripts, 1767–71; Inventories of David Mongin, 1769–71; and Marion (Mary Ann) Mongin, 1771–74, LGS; "Notes Relative to Bourguin and Kelsall," *THSSC* 75 (1970): 214.

82. Philip J. Greven Jr., "Family Structure in Seventeenth-Century Andover, Massachusetts," 136–53, in Michael Gordon, ed., *The American Family in Social-Historical Perspective*, 3rd ed. (New York: St. Martin's Press, 1983), 142–49; Walsh, "'Til

Death,'" 134–35; Demos, *A Little Commonwealth*, 103; Rutman and Rutman, "Parental Death," 164–65. Burton also found remarkably equitable partition of estates in Edgefield County in the mid–nineteenth century. See Burton, *In My Father's House*, 107–8.

83. Colonial Land Plats, 1731–75, SCDAH 17:167–68; Holcomb, *Petitions for Land*, 4:89.

84. MR, 2Y:30.

85. RMC, 4H:173–75, 4L:429, 4P:416–18; Langley, *Deed Abstracts*, 4:212.

86. RMC, 3E:15–17; Langley, *Deed Abstracts*, 4:82.

87. Will of Gideon Mallet, CWA Transcripts, 1767–71; inventory of Gideon Mallet, 1769–71, LGS.

88. H. Roy Merrens, "A View of Coastal South Carolina in 1778: The Journal of Ebenezer Hazard," *SCHM* 73 (October 1972): 188.

89. Rutman and Rutman, *A Place in Time*, 106–7, 113.

90. This observation reinforces Bridenbaugh's contention that "inferior" planters and their families clung closely to their cultural customs and the Rutmans' discovery that, in Middlesex County, Virginia, it was the wealthy who tended to marry outside the local area while others married within. See Bridenbaugh, *Myths and Realities*, 75 and Rutman and Rutman, *A Place in Time*, 157.

91. Demos, *A Little Commonwealth*, 99; Walsh, "'Til Death,'" 137–40.

92. Burton, *In My Father's House*, 105, 116.

Chapter Four

1. Bailyn and Morgan, "Introduction," in *Strangers within the Realm*, 25. A. G. Roeber argues further that for Lutherans and those of the Reformed tradition, "the church operated as a center of cultural life." See Roeber, "Whatever Is Not English among Us," 256.

2. Patricia U. Bonomi, *Under the Cope of Heaven: Religion, Society, and Politics in Colonial America* (New York: Oxford University Press, 1986), esp. 217–18.

3. Erskine Clark, *Our Southern Zion: A History of Calvinism in the South Carolina Low County, 1690–1990* (Tuscaloosa: University of Alabama Press, 1996), 3–4.

4. Smith, *City upon a Hill*, 157; Bender, *Community and Social Change*, 65–66.

5. George C. Rogers Jr., *History of Georgetown County, South Carolina* (Columbia: University of South Carolina Press, 1970), 55, 71, 79; Bridenbaugh, *Myths and Realities*, 97, 116; Rutman and Rutman, *A Place in Time*, 53.

6. Arthur H. Hirsch, Henry A. M. Smith, and Gilbert P. Voigt have been the most productive scholars contributing to our understanding of Purrysburg, but their approaches are either institutional or center on only one of the two major ethnic immigrant groups, obscuring the issue of community and ethnicity by labeling Purrysburg settlers "Swiss." See Hirsch, *Huguenots of Colonial South Carolina*; Smith, "Purrysburgh," 187–219; Gilbert P. Voigt, "Swiss Notes on South Carolina," *SCHGM* 21 (July 1920): 93–104; idem., "The German and German-Swiss Element in South Carolina, 1732–1752"; idem., "Cultural Contributions of German Settlers to South Carolina," *SCHM* 53 (October 1952): 183–89; idem., "Religious Conditions among German-Speaking Settlers in South Carolina, 1732–1774," *SCHM* 56 (April 1955): 59–66.

7. Joseph Henry Dubbs, "History of the Reformed Church, German," 8:214–423, in the Reverend Philip Schaff and others, *The American Church History Series*,

revised ed., 8 vols. (New York: Charles Scribner's Sons, 1882–1910), 8:222–28; the Reverend E. T. Corwin, "History of the Reformed Church, Dutch," 8:1–212, *The American Church History Series*, 8:23; Grant, *The Huguenots*, 14; Reaman, *Trail of the Huguenots*, 48, 63, 65; Howe, *History of the Presbyterian Church* 1:19, 20, 26; Frederick Dalcho, *An Historical Account of the Protestant Episcopal Church in South Carolina from the First Settlement of the Province to the War of the Revolution* (Charleston: E. Thayer, 1820), 147; Hirsch, "Huguenot-Anglican Rivalries," 3; George Fenwick Jones, ed, *Henry Newman's Salzburger Letterbooks* (Athens: University of Georgia Press, 1966), 284–85 and n. 59; Summerall, "Address," 41. Scottish Calvinist John Knox is known to have identified himself with the French Huguenots during his two-year preaching assignment in Dieppe. On the other hand, attempts to unite German Lutherans and German Reformed, while successful elsewhere, failed in South Carolina as late as 1787. See Reaman, *Trail of the Huguenots*, 87; Dubbs, "Reformed Church, German," 18–19.

8. Corwin, "Reformed Church, Dutch," 8:24; Howe, *History of the Presbyterian Church*, 1:218, 255, 266, 312.

9. *Reports* 4:197, n. 218; Voigt, "German Immigration," 8. Disputing the findings of other scholars such as Robert Meriwether, George Fenwick Jones contends that there were no Salzburg Pietists resident at Purrysburg, but his evidence is circumstantial. Even the journals of Boltzius and Gronau indicate the presence of Evangelical Lutherans in the township. See Jones, *Georgia Dutch*, 27; *Reports* 4:197.

10. In contradistinction to the rancorous relationship between the Lutherans and Reformed of Purrysburg and Ebenezer, Laura Becker found their intercourse quite free of contumely in Reading, Pennsylvania. She does err, however, when generalizing about the universality of such harmonious relationships. See Laura L. Becker, "Diversity and Its Significance in an Eighteenth Century Pennsylvania Town," 196–221, in Zuckerman, *Friends and Neighbors*, 205.

11. *Reports* 3, supplement, trans. and ed. by W. H. Brown, 278–79; Jones, *Letterbooks*, 38, n. 13, 284–85; Strobel, *Salzburgers and Their Descendants*, 250. The antagonism of the Pietists for Calvinists which found its way to America was not an isolated phenomenon in southern American religious history. See Walter Brownlow Posey, *Religious Strife on the Southern Frontier* (Baton Rouge: Louisiana State University Press, 1965) and Michael Kraus, *Intercolonial Aspects of American Culture on the Eve of the Revolution with Special Reference to the Northern Towns* (New York: Columbia University Press, 1928), 65, in this regard. At the same time it should be noted that the Pietist renewal movement deeply affected not only Lutheran but also the Reformed and Free Church expressions of Christianity after the late seventeenth century. Mainstream German Lutheran Pietism centered at Halle in Prussia and given its distinctive tenor by Philip Jakob Spener and August Hermann Francke, deeply touched a number of prominent religious leaders of the era such as Count Zinzendorf, George Whitefield, and John Wesley. See Roeber, "Whatever Is Not English among Us," 220, 246–47.

12. *Reports* 9:136.

13. Ibid., 14:60.

14. Arthur Lyon Cross, *The Anglican Episcopate and the American Colonies* (New York: Longmans, Green, 1902), 46, 48; Thomas Cooper and David J. McCord, eds., The *Statutes at Large of South Carolina*, 10 vols. (Columbia: A. S. Johnston, 1836–1841), 2:232, quoted in Clarence L. Ver Steeg, "Internal Politics in Proprietary

Carolina: An Emerging Political Mosaic," 30–68, in idem., *Origins of a Southern Mosaic*, 42; see also 43 and 47.

15. Bolton, *Southern Anglicanism*, 140–41; Waterhouse, *New World Gentry*, 128–29, Sirmans, *Colonial South Carolina*, 97–98; Elmer D. Johnson and Kathleen Lewis Sloan, eds., *South Carolina: A Documentary Profile of the Palmetto State* (Columbia: University of South Carolina Press, 1971), 61–62.

16. Thorp, *The Moravian Community in Colonial North Carolina*, 157–61, quotation from 160.

17. Cooper and McCord, *Statutes at Large*, 2:282–94; Bolton, *Southern Anglicanism*, 31, 47–48, 90; Hirsch, "Huguenot-Anglican Rivalries," 14–16; George C. Rogers, Jr., *Church and State in Eighteenth-Century South Carolina* (Charleston: Dalcho Historical Society, 1959), 14, 16–17. The polity of the Huguenot Church followed the presbyterial format and was administered in accordance with the principles of *Le discipline ecclésiastique des Églises Reformées de France.* Note Hirsch, *Huguenots of Colonial South Carolina*, 48. Notable with regard to language and liturgy is the comparison between British and Dutch imperial policy pertaining to refugee Huguenots. In British America language could be retained but not the Reformed liturgy. In the Dutch Cape Colony, however, the use of the French language in worship was proscribed, but because of the status of the Dutch Reformed Church, Reformed liturgical practice was encouraged although Huguenots could not maintain their own churches. They were merged with the Dutch Reformed congregations. See Captain W. H. Hinde, R. E., "The Huguenot Settlement at the Cape of Good Hope," *Proceedings of the Huguenot Society of London* 5 (1894–96): 205–21.

18. The Huguenot Church of Charles Town adhered to the liturgy introduced by the Reformed churches in the principalities of Neuchâtel and Velangen in 1713 with subsequent editions of the liturgy published in 1737 and 1772. See Ravenel, "Historical Sketch," 65, and Hirsch, *Huguenots of Colonial South Carolina*, 50.

19. Quotation from Williams, "Letters to the Bishop of London," *SCHM* 78 (April 1977): 147; see also Bolton, *Southern Anglicanism*, 155; Hirsch, *Huguenots of Colonial South Carolina*, 75–76, 134.

20. Robert M. Kingdon, *Geneva and the Consolidation of the French Protestant Movement, 1564–1572: A Contribution to the History of Congregationalism, Presbyterianism, and Calvinist Resistance Theory* (Geneva: Librairie Droz, 1967), 37.

21. Bolton, *Southern Anglicanism*, 4, 28, 151–52: Clark, *Southern Zion*, 46; Sirmans, *Colonial South Carolina*, 98. By 1700, Dissenting congregations outnumbered Anglican churches in South Carolina by three to one. The power of the Dissenters was so great that, while they could not block the Church Act of 1706, they did force Anglican church construction and ministerial salaries to be funded from import duties and a tax on slaves, not from parish taxes. See Bonomi, *Under the Cope of Heaven*, 49.

22. The Reverend Albert M. Shipp, *The History of Methodism in South Carolina* (Nashville: Southern Methodist Publishing House, 1884; reprint, Spartanburg, S.C.: Reprint Company, 1972), 43; Howe, *History of the Presbyterian Church*, 1:210; Muench, "Story of Purysburg," 10; Dalcho, *History of the Episcopal Church*, 386. Hirsch states categorically that Bugnion was born and raised in France, but the evidence is less than compelling. He may have here fallen victim to some of the same erroneous assumptions that plagued Faust's confident assertion that Bugnion was

German and Bolton's more recent contention that Bugnion was affiliated with the German Reformed denomination. See Hirsch, *Huguenots of Colonial South Carolina*, 96, n. 24, and Bolton, *Southern Anglicanism*, 169. Lutheran residents of Purrysburg called Bugnion the "French student of theology that was their (meaning the French Reformed) preacher," The context of this quotation would seem to indicate that Bugnion was a Reformed theologian. See *Reports* 1:64, author's parenthesis.

23. Bugnion to the Bishop of London, 20 June 1733, Bishop of London—General Correspondence, 1703–69, Fulham Palace Papers, microfilmed copies at SCL.

24. Williams, "Letters to the Bishop of London," *SCHM* 78 (April 1977): 147 and 78 (July 1977): 216–17; Bernheim, *History of The German Settlements*, 96; Extract of anonymous letter from Purrysburg, 26 January 1734, in Lane, *Oglethorpe's Georgia*, 1:39; *Reports* 1:64.

25. Bugnion to the bishop of London, 15 July 1733, Bishop of London—General Correspondence, SCL; Young, *Germans in the Colonial Southeast*, 11; Williams, "Letters to the Bishop of London," *SCHM* 78 (July 1977): 217, 234–35, 240–41; Deed of Mortgage, Joseph Bugnion to William Cattey and George Austin, SCHS; RMC, R:135–36, 408, 412; Easterby, *JCHA*, 1736–39:33–34, 38–39, 618; Hirsch, *Huguenots of Colonial South Carolina*, 64–66; Dalcho, *History of the Episcopal Church*, 433; petition of "Les habitants de Purrysbourg," no date, Bishop of London—General Correspondence, SCL.

26. Dalcho, *History of the Episcopal Church*, 386; Robinson, *Southern Colonial Frontier*, 229. On Chiffelle's failure to learn German, see *Reports* 4:197, 206; 5:115, and Jones, *Salzburger Saga*, 84–85. Quotations from *Reports* 2:26.

27. In a petition of 5 November 1754, Chiffelle applied for 400 acres of land in Purrysburg based on his headright of three children, one servant, and four slaves for whom he had not yet received land. In January 1755 he noted that he had four children. Chiffelle and his sister were also platted town lots 115 and 58 in joint ownership on 6 and 9 September 1736, respectively. A John Lewis Cheffele (Scheffley) was platted 450 acres in Purrysburg Township on 3 January 1735 and also town lot 119 on 23 April 1736. See Holcomb, *Petitions for Land*, 4:89; Lipscomb, *JCHA*, 13:44; Colonial Land Plats, SCDAH 9:384–86.

28. *Reports* 2:98–99, 103; Rogers, *Georgetown County*, 80. Quotation from *Reports* 5:253.

29. Quotations from *Reports* 4:13, 26, 181; 5:108. See also *Reports* 4:197, 206; Easterby, *JCHA*, 1736–39:212, 219; Voigt, "German Immigration," 11.

30. Stephens, *Journal of the Proceedings*, 2:396. Mary Musgrove was of Indian descent and with her husband ran a trading post near Ebenezer. See E. Merton Coulter, "Mary Musgrove: Queen of the Creeks," *GHQ* 11(March 1927): 1–30. It should be noted that even the Reverend Boltzius, easily Chiffelle's most vocal critic, married those who were not resident in his neighborhood. See, for example, *Reports* 13:133. Other sources for this paragraph and the one following will be listed in the subsequent three notes.

31. Quotation from *Reports* 4:35.

32. It is intriguing to note Wesley's description of Purrysburg in the wake of the Hopkey-Williamson affair. There is no previous indication that he had visited the township before his Charles Town journey to confer with Commissary Garden about

Chiffelle. Wesley wrote of the place where Hopkey was married: "Mr. Belinger . . . sent a negro lad with me [on Friday, who conducted me safe] to Purrysburg [in the evening; a town the most without the appearance of a town I ever saw, with no form or comliness or regularity]. Oh, how hath God stretched over this place 'the lines of confusion and the stones of emptiness!' Alas, for those whose lives were here vilely cast away through oppression, through divers plagues and troubles! O earth! how long wilt thou hide blood? How long wilt thou cover thy slain?" See Nehemiah Curnock, ed., *The Journal of the Rev. John Wesley, A.M.*, standard ed. 8 vols. (New York: Eaton and Mains, 1909–16), 1:352. As editor of the minister's journal, Curnock added to Wesley's account of the township by noting speciously, "It is said that Purrysburg was the first place in the province to introduce slavery. This crime against humanity and other irregularities, ecclesiastical and moral, among which the unlawful marriage of Miss Sophy was prominent, explain Wesley's strong feeling about the place." See Curnock, *Journal of Wesley*, 1:352, n. 1.

33. Candler, *CRG*, 5:60–61; Stephens, *Journal of the Proceedings*, 1:40, 45, 48; 2:396; *Reports* 3:241, 247; 4:34–35; 9:238; 18:205–6, 219; William D. Smyth, "Travellers in South Carolina in the Early Eighteenth Century," *SCHM* 79 (April 1978): 124; David T. Morgan, "John Wesley's Sojourn in Georgia Revisited," *GHQ* 64 (Fall 1980): 256–57; Coleman, *Colonial Georgia*, 148–49; Cross, *Anglican Episcopate*, 50; Curnock, *Journal of Wesley*, 1:327–30, 333–39. For a concise account of the dilemmas faced by immigrant pastors, see Bonomi, *Under the Cope of Heaven*, 39–41. Her account of the Anglican clergy is particularly germane to understanding the complexity of assessing religious life in the colonial South. See Bonomi, *Under the Cope of Heaven*, 41–50.

34. *Reports* 4:197.

35. Chiffelle's petition was in no way out of order. According to legislation, once a township included 100 heads of household, it was eligible for status as a parish and to send representatives to the Commons House. Purrysburg obviously satisfied this stipulation by the time of Chiffelle's petition.

36. Cooper and McCord, *Statutes at Large*, 3:668–69; Sherriff, "The Saltzburgers and Purrysburg," 15; Robinson, *Southern Colonial Frontier*, 229; History Committee, St. Helena's Episcopal Church, Beaufort, South Carolina, *The History of the Parish Church of St. Helena, Beaufort, South Carolina* (Columbia: R. L. Bryan for St. Helena's Episcopal Church, 1991), 52; Bolton, *Southern Anglicanism*, 140; Waterhouse, *A New World Gentry*, 128; Howe, *History of the Presbyterian Church*, 1:21; Sirmans, *Colonial South Carolina*, 98; Dalcho, *History of the Episcopal Church*, 385.

37. Barnwell and Webber, "St. Helena's Parish Register," *SCHGM* 23 (January 1922): 24, and *SCHGM* 23 (April 1922): 106; History Committee, *History of the Parish Church of St. Helena*, 74; Dalcho, *History of the Episcopal Church*, 379.

38. *Reports* 2:23; 5:108, 135 n.143, 146–47, and 276. Quotation from *Reports* 5:146.

39. Stephens, *Journal of the Proceedings*, 2:186; Oglethorpe to the trustees, 10 June 1743, in Candler, *CRG* 24:31–32 and "Petition to General Oglethorpe from the German and French of Savannah," 24:33–36; *Reports* 5:276; Jones, *Salzburger Saga*, 83–85; Jones, *Georgia Dutch*, 83; Howe, *History of the Presbyterian Church*, 1:578; Davis, *Fledgling Province*, 19; Coleman, *Colonial Georgia*, 158. Two of the twenty-seven who signed the 10 June 1743 reimbursement request, Jean Pierre Breton and

J. (Jeremiah) O. Valloton, had moved from Purrysburg. See Jones, *Georgia Dutch*, 83.

40. *Reports* 17:281.

41. Colonial Land Plats, SCDAH 4:173; 9:386–87.

42. Because no church building existed until 1738, the Reverend Bugnion must have held services in his home on town lot number 5 or at the home of another township settler. The Reverend Chiffelle's home became the place of worship in 1737 and served as such until St. Peter's Church was completed the following year.

43. Unfortunately the register and other records for St. Peter's Parish have been lost, and there are few other documents extant from which Purrysburg church officers from the colonial period can be determined. In December 1754 David Humbert and Melchior Leichtensteiger are noted as churchwardens in the Commons House Journal. A parish pastoral call letter of 1 March 1759 gives the most complete listing of church officers for the parish. The signatories are Gabriel Ravot and David Saussy, churchwardens, and David Giroud, John Bourquin Imer, John Burke, Solon Kealt, Isaac Brabant, and Melchior Auchensteiger (Leichtensteiger), vestrymen. It is unknown why only six vestrymen rather than the full complement of seven signed the letter. See Lipscomb, *JCHA,* 13:27; Agnes Beville Tedcastle, submitter, "Call Letter" in "A Pastor for the Parish of St. Peter, Purrysburg, South Carolina," *THSSC* 28 (1923): 43. Only one officer can be identified from other records. In a deed of conveyance from August 1765, Daniel Marett is designated as a sexton. An officer or employee of the church under the vestry and churchwardens, the sexton cared for church property. The sexton might also be in charge of digging graves or ringing the bell for services. RMC, 3E:17–20. No other reference to any named church officer has been located. The one reference in the journals of the Reverend Boltzius to the Purrysburg church officers noted, not surprisingly, that there are nothing but "abominations among the sextons and simple people and the preacher is no pastor of his flock." See *Reports* 5:279.

44. Sources for this paragraph in addition to the ones noted include Cooper and McCord, *Statutes at Large*, 3:669; *Reports* 5:108; RMC, 3H:494–95, 3M:289–90, 3O:476–78, 3P:338–40; Plat of "Purysburgh=Town" ca. 1765 and "Purrysbourg Township" plat, n.d., SCDAH; Smith, "Purrysburgh," 206. Quotation from Terry W. Lipscomb, ed., *The Colonial Records of South Carolina: The Journal of the Commons House of Assembly, October 6, 1757–January 24, 1761*, Parts 1 and 2 (Columbia: SCDAH, 1996), 302, hereafter cited Lipscomb, *JCHA,* 1 and 2; Henry L. Beck, "Purrysburg as It Is Today," *THSSC* 39 (1934): 42; Summerall, "Address," 43.

45. Quotations from Lipscomb, *JCHA,* 13:44; Holcomb, *Petitions for Land*, 4:88.

46. RMC, 2P:442–43; *Reports* 5:28; Bond, MR, 2L pt. 2:370; Inventory of the Reverend Henry Chiffelle, 1758–61, LGS.

47. *Reports* 1:64, 78, 95, 115; 2:6, 26, 89, 95, 98, 156, 162, 199, 217–18; 3:23, 27, 54, 115, 239; 4:xiii, 20–21, 26, 181, 194, 197–98, 202, 206, 219; 5:26, 115, 139–40, 210–11, 216, 296; 8:162, 411; 9:29, 42, 70, 79, 86, 192; 10:98; 13:106, 127; 14:6, 34, 60, 114; 16:72; 17:254; Young, *Germans in the Colonial Southeast*, 11.

48. *Reports* 2:124; 3:19, 27, 39, 54, 116, 247; 4:13, 53, 79, 164, 219, 224, 229; 5:171–72, 279; 6:268; Bernheim, *German Settlements*, 193. Quotation from *Reports* 8:251.

49. *Reports* 8:276; 18:131. Quotation from *Reports* 16:171.

50. *Reports* 6:82–83; 8:530; Jones, *Georgia Dutch*, 245.

51. *Reports* 5:115, 155, 296; 6:268, 300; 8:420, 440–41, 487; 13:76, n. 9; Jones,

Georgia Dutch, 106. The ties to Ebenezer grew so close over the colonial era that representatives from at least four Purrysburg families, the Franckes, Kieffers, Metsgers, and Winklers, settled permanently in the Georgia Lutheran town. See Strobel, *Salzburgers and Their Descendants*, 180–81. Note also Carpenter, "Purrysburg, South Carolina," 5.

52. *Reports* 18:186, 226 (quotation).

53. It seems that at least French was still spoken in the township in the 1760s. In a court case filed against Imer by one of his parishioners in January 1768 to recover money loaned to the minister, Imer noted in French that he promised to pay the debt. French was also used to date a bill of sale for pew number 16 in the Purrysburg Anglican Church in 1767. Though the extent of usage cannot be accurately determined, the fact of its usage on legal documents argues for the continued viability of the French language at the township. See CCPJR, *Margaret Henery (Hendrie) vs. Abraham Imer*, SCDAH; RMC, 3H:494–95.

54. Himeli to Imer, 25 February and 3 April 1759 in Tedcastle, "A Pastor for the Parish of St. Peter," 38–41; "Call Letter," in ibid., 43; *Reports* 17:281. It is intriguing to note that the protocol of the meeting of the Neuveville Board of the Freemen which released Imer from his responsibilities was addressed to "Burgomaster Chiffelle, Chairman." See "Excerpt from the Protocol Drawn Up at a Meeting of the Board of the Freemen of Neuveville, 16 October 1759," in Tedcastle, "A Pastor for the Parish of St. Peter, Purrysburg," 37.

55. "Excerpt from the Protocol Drawn Up at a Meeting of the Board of the Freemen of Neuveville," 37–38.

56. Quoted in Grace Fox Perry, "The Lost Settlement of Purrysburg, Part 2," *Charleston News and Courier*, 1 April 1956, 3-C.

57. Grace Fox Perry, *Moving Finger of Jasper* (Ridgeland, S.C.: Confederate Centennial Committee, 1947), 11; *Reports* 17:281 (final quotation).

58. "Mr Woodmason's Account of South Carolina, North Carolina, Georgia, . . . , 1766," quoted in Hirsch, *Huguenots of Colonial South Carolina*, 88; "Woodmason's Account," quoted in *The History of the Parish Church of St. Helena*, 14; Robinson, *Southern Colonial Frontier*, 229; Award to Jane Imer, MR, 3S:284–85. Stümpel was a German and a former officer in Frederick the Great's army. After some problematic decisions on his part, he succeeded in bringing a large contingent of German speakers to settle at Hard Labor Creek in Londonderry Township in the 1760s. See Young, *Germans in the Colonial Southeast*, 28.

59. RMC, 3D:271, 4G:275–81, 376–81, 4W:45–50; Award to Jane Imer, MR, 3S:284–85; Inventory of Abraham Imer, 1763–67, LGS. See also Holcomb, *Deed Abstracts, 1773–1778*, 215; Tedcastle, "A Pastor for the Parish of St. Peter," 38–41.

60. The wording of this "Bond for performance of Covenants" includes what appears to be a hybrid English-French term (*Tenements Heriditaiments* [*sic*], meaning, roughly, inherited property). This is the only French terminology used in the document and may have been inserted to include any property in the Swiss Confederation Imer retained or had passed on to his children living there, thus further securing this covenant by effectively placing a lien on inherited property of Imer's children by his first wife. Within four months of this bond, Imer had married Ann and together they sold the 334-acre parcel in Purrysburg to Champernoun Williamson, but neither his marriage or the land transaction appears to have brought him much financial return or security. This marriage and/or the financial and legal maneuvering around it may

have precipitated or accelerated Imer's conflict with his Purrysburg congregation. See RMC, 3B:437–40.

61. Quoted in Perry, *Moving Finger of Jasper*, 16.

62. Muench, "Story of Purysburg," 10; Dalcho, *History of the Episcopal Church*, 386.

63. American historian of religion Jon Butler might argue for understanding the phenomenon as a series of regional and idiosyncratic religious revivals, or "awakenings," but his revisionist interpretation does not diminish the extent of religious enthusiasm, which both energized and sustained colonial evangelicalism. He does, however, contend that the *effects* of the revivals were rather modest. See Jon Butler, "Enthusiasm Described and Decried: The Great Awakening as Interpretive Fiction," *Journal of American History* 69 (1982): 305–25. My interpretation follows more closely Patricia U. Bonomi's analysis that finds eighteenth-century American colonists progressively more influenced by religious perspectives, especially with regard to politics, throughout the colonial period. See Bonomi, *Under the Cope of Heaven*. Thomas J. Little's, "'Adding to the Church Such as Shall Be Saved': The Growth and Influence of Evangelicalism in Colonial South Carolina," 363–82, in Greene, *Money, Trade, and Power* also speaks to the dynamic religious effects of the evangelical movement upon South Carolina from the 1740s into the nineteenth century.

64. David T. Morgan, "The Great Awakening in South Carolina, 1740–1775," *South Atlantic Quarterly* 70 (1971): 595–96; Clarke, *Our Southern Zion*, 77.

65. Much of this early scholarship argued that South Carolinians remained relatively unaffected by the Great Awakening if compared to the revivalist fervor sweeping other colonies. Although George Whitefield visited South Carolina on three separate occasions, the contention was that he failed to have any widespread impact in the province. Part of Whitefield's failure was attributed to his much publicized and acrimonious disagreements with the Anglican commissary of South Carolina, the Reverend Alexander Garden, as well as the controversial behavior of Whitefield's most noted South Carolina convert, the mystical Hugh Bryan. For examples of scholarship in this genre, note especially David T. Morgan Jr., "George Whitefield and the Great Awakening in the Carolinas and Georgia, 1739–1740," *GHQ* 54 (Winter 1970): 517–39; idem., "The Consequences of George Whitefield's Ministry in the Carolinas and Georgia, 1739–1740," *GHQ* 55 (Spring 1971): 62–82; William Howland Kenney III, "George Whitefield, Dissenter Priest of the Great Awakening, 1739–1741," *William and Mary Quarterly,* 3rd ser., 26 (January 1969): 75–93; idem., "Alexander Garden and George Whitefield: The Significance of Revivalism in South Carolina, 1738–1741," *SCHM* 71 (January 1970): 1–16. Note also Butler, "Enthusiasm Described and Decried," 311; Candler, *CRG,* 4, supplement: 75; and Sirmans, *Colonial South Carolina*, 231. For a general overview of religion in the region written from this interpretive perspective, see especially Donald G. Mathews, *Religion in the Old South* (Chicago: University of Chicago Press, 1977). Alan Heimert's *Religion and the American Mind from the Great Awakening to the Revolution* (Cambridge, Mass.: Harvard University Press, 1966) also downplays the impact of the Awakening in the colonial South.

66. Robert M. Calhoon, *Evangelicals and Conservatives in the Early South, 1740–1861* (Columbia: University of South Carolina Press, 1988); Alan Gallay, "The Origins of Slaveholders' Paternalism: George Whitefield, the Bryan Family, and the Great Awakening in South Carolina," *Journal of Southern History* 53, no. 3 (August 1987): 367–94; idem., *The Formation of a Planter Elite*, Klein, *Unification of a Slave*

State; McCurry, *Masters of Small Worlds*; Olwell, *Masters, Slaves, and Subjects*; Waterhouse, *A New World Gentry.*

67. The Reverend John P. Lockwood, *Memorials of the Life of Peter Böhler, Bishop of the Church of the United Brethren* (London: Wesleyan Conference Office, 1868), 96–97, 117–19; idem., *The Western Pioneers; or, Memorials of the Lives and Labours of the Rev. Richard Boardman and the Rev. Joseph Pilmoor* (London: Wesleyan Conference Office, 1881), 163, 167; J. Taylor Hamilton, "A History of the Unitas Fratrum or Moravian Church in the United States of America," 425–508, in vol. 8 of *The American Church History Series*, 440; Shipp, *History of Methodism*, 89, 110, 130, 133 (Pilmoor quotation), 215; Howe, *History of the Presbyterian Church*, 1:226, 317, 468; Bonomi, *Under the Cope of Heaven*, 77; *Reports* 9:209, 219; *Georgia Gazette*, 17 January and 21 February 1765. Quotations regarding Ettewein from George F. Jones, ed., "Report of Mr. Ettwein's Journey to Georgia and South Carolina, 1765," *SCHM* 91 (October 1990): 251.

68. On the surface it might appear unlikely that the archbishop of Canterbury would take such an interest in evangelizing slaves in the remote colony, but if we take into consideration the high regard in which John Wesley held the Moravians with whom he traveled to Georgia, the commissioning of this group for the Carolina mission field might not seem so far fetched.

69. The mistrust was particularly acute between Lutherans and Moravians, as demonstrated by the entries in Boltzius's journal after Kieffer had related this incident to him. See *Reports* 5:241–42, 296.

70. Sources for this and the preceding paragraph are letter of P. Böhler to a magistrate of New York on the occasion of his sentencing, 25 January 1743, quoted in Lockwood, *Life of Böhler*, 117–19. See also Hamilton, "History of the Unitas Fratrum," 440; Lockwood, *Memorials of Boardman and Pilmoor*, 163; idem, *Life of Böhler*, 95–97; Voigt, "Germans and German-Swiss: Their Contribution to the Province," 25; First and third quotations from Lockwood, *Life of Böhler,* 95. Second quotation from *Reports* 5:296. Nehemiah Curnock, the editor of the Reverend John Wesley's journals, attributed to Wesley a comment asserting that slavery first appeared in South Carolina at Purrysburg. Although the attribution is questionable and the statement patently false, the circumstances surrounding the commissioning of the Moravian missionaries to Purrysburg by Dr. Potter, the archbishop of Canterbury, and their insistence upon making the township the center of their ministrations would seem to imply that Wesley or another person of similar reputation assumed the prevalence of slavery in the township and communicated that sentiment openly. See note 32 above.

71. *Reports* 7:19 (quotation); Jones, *Salzburger Saga*, 81.

72. Agnes Beville Tedcastle, submitter, "Testimonial Granted to Honorable Jonas Pelot, of Neuveville Switzerland," *THSSC* 36 (1931): 60–62; idem., "A Pastor for the Parish of St. Peter," 44; Coy K. Johnston, *Two Centuries of Lawtonville Baptists, 1775–1975* (Columbia: State Printing Company, 1974), 5; Little, "'Adding to the Church,'" 376; Rowland, "Eighteenth Century Beaufort," 198–99. There appears to be some discrepancy with regard to the organization of Euhaw Baptist Church. While Johnston places its founding in the 1740s, the Lowcountry Council's publication *Historic Resources* contends that 1751 is the correct date. The discrepancy proceeds from the fact that the Euhaw church was technically organized earlier, as a daughter church of First Baptist Church of Charles Town, but was not officially

declared autonomous from it until the ordination of Pelot. See Lowcountry Council of Governments, *Historic Resources of the Lowcountry: A Regional Survey of Beaufort County, South Carolina, Colleton County, South Carolina, Hampton County, South Carolina, Jasper County, South Carolina* (Columbia: SCDAH, 1979), 171; Little, "'Adding to the Church,'" 376.

73. Johnston, *Two Centuries of Lawtonville Baptists*, 2–3, 5–6; RMC, 2B:60–61, 3M:289–90, 3P:338–40; Holcomb, *Petitions for Land*, 3:5, 27–28; Little, "'Adding to the Church,'" 370, 375 . It is worth noting that the other Purrysburg resident who played a significant role in the religious life of the later colonial South, the Reverend Zubly, witnessed the sale of Pelot's town lot. See RMC, 3P:338–40.

74. Voigt, "Germans and German Swiss: Their Contribution to the Province," 25. Zubly has been the subject of numerous studies since the middle of the twentieth century. Much of his writing has also been published. Note especially Roger A. Martin, *John J. Zubly, Colonial Georgia Minister* (New York: Arno Press, 1982), Randall M. Miller, ed., *"A Warm and Zealous Sprit": John J. Zubly and the American Revolution: A Selection of His Writings* (Macon, Ga.: Mercer University Press, 1982), and Janice Louise Seaman, "John Joachim Zubly: Voice for Liberty and Principle" (thesis, University of South Carolina, 1982), for the most recent book length contributions to the literature.

75. There is some confusion as to the year the Zubly family arrived in South Carolina. Most sources cite the year 1726, but one German account indicates that David Zubly may have left as late as 1736. See *Kurtz-verfaßte Reiß-Beschreibung Eines neulich Auß der in West-Indien gelegenen Landschafft Carolina*, 3–4. Since Zubly appears to have been traveling alone according to this source, he may have actually made a trip back to St. Gall, and the traveler who wrote this description of Zubly's trip to South Carolina met him on his return to South Carolina.

76. Shortly after Zubly's ordination, his father sent him an original drawing that represented the ascent of Elijah to heaven from 2 Kings 2. He added his best wishes for his son's successful ministry and concluded with a verse in German: *So wünschet denn aus liebem Herz,* (With a loving heart he wishes) / *Und zeichnet auch mit Liebeshand,* (With a loving hand he signs [the drawing]) / *Der des Besitzers Vater ist,* (The one who is the father of the [new] owner) / *Und David Zübli wird genannt.* (Who is called David Zubly)—*Gemacht in Purrysbourg, South Carolina in Granville County, Anno Dommini 1745*. See Joseph Henry Dubbs, *History of the Reformed Church, German*, 8:214–423, in *The American Church History Series*, 8:297–98.

77. Zubly and Mühlenberg had known each other since the early 1750s. The information for this and the preceding three paragraphs came from Candler, *CRG*, 24:364; Holcomb, *Petitions for Land*, 4:88–89; *Reports* 14:153; 17:209; Will of David Zubly, 1757–63; Will of Jacob Waldburger, 1767–1771; Inventory of Margeret Jean Henery (Hendrie), 1772–76; RMC, 3P:338–40; Webber and Jervey, "Abstracts of the Court of Ordinary," *SCHGM* 42 (October 1941): 198; Lilla Mills Hawes, ed., *The Journal of the Reverend John Joachim Zubly A.M., D.D. March 5, 1770 through June 22, 1781* (Savannah: Georgia Historical Society, 1989), ix–xvi, 1, and nn. 41–42, 46, 9–10, 14–15, 24–26, 30–32, 65–66, 69–72, 74, 97; Voigt, "Swiss Notes," 98; Martin, "Zubly Comes to America," 131, 135; Theodore G. Tappert and John W. Doberstein, trans., *The Journals of Henry Melchior Mühlenberg*, 3 vols. (Philadelphia: Evangelical Lutheran Ministerium of Pennsylvania and Adjacent States and Mühlenberg Press, 1942), 2:595, 610, 663; Merrens, "A View of South Carolina," 188; Marjorie Daniel,

"John Joachim Zubly—Georgia Pamphleteer of the Revolution," *GHQ* 19 (March 1935): 6–7; Howe, *History of the Presbyterian Church*, 1:255, 266, 312, 376; Dubbs, "Reformed Church, German," 297–303, 338; Gallay, *Formation of a Planter Elite*, 125. The first quotation is from *Reports* 9:223; the second is from Tappert and Doberstein, *Journals of Mühlenberg*, 2:663.

In his entry for 27 October 1774, Mühlenberg noted that Zubly had hoped he would stay in his home, but the Lutheran did not want to give any credence to the suspicion that he was Reformed, so Zubly made other arrangements for him. Perhaps enlightened as to the difficulties facing his friend, the next day Zubly encouraged Mühlenberg to invite the Ebenezer pastors to visit him privately when he traveled upriver to the town rather than lodge with either of them initially. Mühlenberg apparently did not let his concern stop him from taking coffee with the Zublys in November or from accompanying Zubly to the latter's church in February 1775—perhaps because the congregation comprised both Reformed and Lutheran communicants. See Tappert and Doberstein, *Journals of Mühlenberg*, 2:595–96, 601, 682.

78. *Reports* 17:167 (first quotation), 259 (second quotation).

79. *Reports* 17:209, 281 (quotations).

80. Bonomi, *Under the Cope of Heaven*, 92, 125; Butler, *Awash in a Sea of Faith*, 177; idem., "Enthusiasm Described and Decried," 313.

81. The petition presented to the House has been lost, but the copy addressed to the Honorable Daniel DeSaussure and members of the Senate dated 7 February 1789 bears the signatures of Hezekiah Roberts, Jacob Winkler, Daniel Giroud, Philip A. Mayer, [illegible] Mayer, Conrade Hover, Jns. L. Miruff [Kireff?], George Enos, John B. Jones, George Fisher, Jacob Strobhart, Melchior Humbert, Abraham Bininger, Nicholas Winkler, Wm. Laurence, James Roberts, and Lewis Giroud, *General Assembly Papers*, SCDAH

82. The Constitution of 1778 allowed the formation of a church by any fifteen adult male Protestants of at least twenty-one years of age. It also permitted any church to petition the legislature to receive incorporation, which then gave it the right to own and control property of a religious nature. See Jerome J. Nadelhaft, *The Disorders of War: The Revolution in South Carolina* (Orono: University of Maine at Orono Press, 1981), 38. Quotation from Michael E. Stevens, ed., and Christine M. Allen, asst. ed., *The State Records of South Carolina: Journals of the House of Representatives, 1789–1790* (Columbia: University of South Carolina Press, 1984), 55, hereafter cited as *JHR* 1789–90.

83. *JHR* 1789–90:55.

84. *General Assembly Papers*, SCDAH; *JHR* 1789–90:55, 137, 145–46, 169, 182, 187, 247.

85. Bonomi, *Under the Cope of Heaven*, 218; Little, "'Adding to the Church,'" 368. American historians of religion freely acknowledge the power of the local environment to force Old World religious normative practices and doctrines to prove their value or be refashioned. Hence, the religious life of immigrants had to be created, not inherited from European traditions, even though their origins were in the Old World homelands. See Butler, *Awash in a Sea of Faith*, 5–6; Bonomi, *Under the Cope of Heaven*, 221.

86. Although Calhoon nuances the general consensus that southern evangelicals and conservatives confronted each other as adversaries between 1740 and 1775 and

became independent collaborators in the revolutionary and early national periods, he nonetheless agrees with the essential contours of the consensus. He does argue that the antagonism in the late colonial period was not as adversarial as some observers have noted. See Calhoon, *Evangelicals and Conservatives*, 9–10.

87. For examples of these arguments, see Leigh Eric Schmidt, "'The Grand Prophet,' Hugh Bryan: Early Evangelicalism's Challenge to the Establishment and Slavery in the Colonial South," *SCHM* 87 (1986): 238–50; Harvey H. Jackson, "The Carolina Connection: Jonathan Bryan, His Brothers, and the Founding of Georgia, 1733–1752," *GHQ* 68 (Summer 1984): 147–72; Gallay, *The Formation of a Planter Elite*; idem., "The Origins of Slaveholder's Paternalism." The research of these scholars forms the basis for much of what follows regarding the Bryan family.

88. *Reports* 6:93–94

89. *Reports* 9:86.

90. *Reports* 11:32–34. There is some confusion with regard to the reverend's baptism of slave children of Purrysburg masters. This boy's baptism may have been the first of two such services, the second occurring between late March 1747 and April of 1751. If there were two baptisms, the identities of the masters of the second slave boy are not revealed. See Loewald, "Questionnaire, II," 246.

91. *Reports* 8:33.

92. Gallay, *Formation of a Planter Elite*, 165.

93. Bailyn, *Education and the Forming of American Society*, 15–18, 22, 25–28; Sirmans, *Colonial South Carolina*, 232; Walsh, "'Til Death,'" 148–50; Rutman and Rutman, *A Place in Time*, 69–70; Rogers, *Georgetown County*, 91–92; Burton, *In My Father's House*, 80–81; Bridenbaugh, *Myths and Realities*, 100–104.

94. It is granted that A. G. Roeber correctly maintains that the theology of German-speaking Lutherans, Reformed, and Moravians emphasized education, but so did that of the French-speaking Reformed. The fact that more Purrysburg German speakers seem to have gained access to some education than French speakers has more to do with the greater sustained financial support for the Salzburg Pietist émigrés in Ebenezer than any lack of interest on the part of the French speakers of the township. See Roeber, "The Dutch-Speaking and German-Speaking Peoples," 271.

95. In other areas of settlement in South Carolina, the French Huguenots and their descendants placed a premium on education although they did not create any distinct educational movement in the colony. See Hirsch, *Huguenots of Colonial South Carolina*, 153–54, 156, 158–59.

96. *Reports* 1:79, 96; 2:89; 4:142; Coleman, *Colonial Georgia*, 154.

97. Unlike nearly every other southern community, Purrysburg appears to have had no provision to care for its orphans in the early years. This apparent lack of concern can be attributed to the political machinations of South Carolina authorities rather than to a lack of humanitarian impulses on the part of the Purrysburg settlers. Since in southern towns the parish was charged with primary responsibility for orphan and poor relief, the unwillingness of provincial lowcountry legislators to confer parish status upon the township until 1746/7 left care uneven and haphazard because of the poverty of most township residents in the early years. See Jones, *Salzburger Saga*, 112. On provisions for orphans in other southern areas, see Rutman and Rutman, "Now-Wives," 161; idem., *A Place in Time*, 196; Rogers, *Georgetown County*, 72.

98. *Reports* 2:141, 148, 170, 199, 218; 3:116, 188–89, 239; 4:9; 5:296; 17:281;

RMC, 3H:89–90; Langley, *Deed Abstracts*, 3:110, 359–60; Perry, *Moving Finger of Jasper*, 11–12 (quotations); Lockwood, *Life of Böhler*, 96–97; Voigt, "Side-Light," 28; *Gazette of the State of Georgia*, 13 May 1790.

99. *Reports* 2:166. Quotation from *Reports* 2:148.

100. *Reports* 9:195–96.

101. The sources for this and the previous paragraph (excluding the quotations) are George Fenwick Jones, contributor, "Two Salzburger Letters from George Whitefield and Theobald Kiefer II," *GHQ* 62 (Spring 1978): 54; Coleman, *Colonial Georgia*, 161–62; *Reports* 4:4, 6, 31–32, 54, 77, 79–80, 142, 170, 180, 192, 202, 219, 229; 5:10, 15, 34, 82, 98, 114, 140, 162, 190, 213–14, 227, 300; 6:119; 7:73, 199, 216; 9:29, 195–96; 13:127, 133; 14:80; 18:131; Jones, *Georgia Dutch*, 166, 260. For a good description of the Ebenezer orphanage, note especially Lothar L. Tresp, "The Salzburger Orphanage at Ebenezer in Colonial Georgia," *Americana-Austriaca, Beitrage zur Amerikakunde* 3 (1974): 190–234. The Reverend George Whitefield helped raise money for the Ebenezer orphanage. See *Reports* 9:102.

102. Jones to Lydes, 18 September 1740, in Lane, *Oglethorpe's Georgia*, 2:482; King, *Georgia Voices*, 27; Coleman, *Colonial Georgia*, 168. For a more detailed analysis of the Bethesda orphanage, see Neil J. O'Connell, O.F.M., "George Whitefield and Bethesda Orphan House, I," *GHQ* 54 (Spring 1970): 41–62; idem., "George Whitefield and Bethesda Orphan House, II," *GHQ* 54 (Summer 1970): 183–208; Morgan, "Whitefield's Ministry in the Carolinas and Georgia," 62–82; Thomas P. Haviland, "Of Franklin, Whitefield, and the Orphan," *GHQ* 29 (December 1945): 211–16; Erwin C. Surrency, "Whitefield, Habersham, and the Bethesda Orphanage," *GHQ* 34 (June 1950): 87–105. For a contemporary account of life at the orphanage, see Lilla Mills Hawes, ed., "A Description of Whitefield's Bethesda: Samuel Fayrweather to Thomas Prince and Thomas Foxcroft," *GHQ* 45 (December 1961): 363–66.

103. *The Journals of George Whitefield*, 21 March 1746, quoted in Shipp, *History of Methodism*, 110.

104. Candler, *CRG*, 9:378, 398. On Whitefield's unsuccessful attempts to found a college in Georgia, see Mollie C. Davis, "Whitefield's Attempt to Establish a College in Georgia," *GHQ* 55 (Winter 1971): 459–70; and idem., "The Countess of Huntingdon and Whitefield's Bethesda," *GHQ* 56 (Spring 1972): 72–82.

105. Mitchell, *Commercialism and Frontier*, 105; Wolf, *Urban Village*, 147–48, 150; Zuckerman, "Introduction,"in *Friends and Neighbors*, 23; Bonomi, *Under the Cope of Heaven*, 87.

106. Patricia Bonomi notes a number of factors that contributed to church involvement in the colonial era, including geography and family tradition. Ironically one of the key factors, community cohesion, bore an inverse relationship to churchgoing for the initial generation of Purrysburg settlers. See Bonomi, *Under the Cope of Heaven*, 87. Quotation from Bailyn and Morgan, *Strangers within the Realm*, 256.

107. Zuckerman, "Introduction," in *Friends and Neighbors*, 23.

108. Roeber found this adaptation among Reformed Germans outside Pennsylvania, many of whom did as the descendants of the German speakers of Purrysburg did —they moved to English Presbyterianism. Bailyn and Morgan notice the same tendency. Laura L. Becker discovered that in multicultural Reading, Pennsylvania, the French Huguenot and Dutch minorities attended the German Reformed Church. See Roeber, "Dutch-Speaking and German-Speaking Peoples," 249; Bailyn and Morgan, *Strangers within the Realm*, 249; and Becker, "Diversity and Its Significance," 197.

109. Frederik Barth, *Ethnic Groups and Boundaries* (Boston: Little, Brown, 1969).

110. Gallay, *Formation of a Planter Elite*, 165.

Chapter Five

1. Wolf, *Germantown*, 155–56. I have borrowed the terms in quotation marks from Wolf. She notes the same process at work in even more homogenous communities such as Germantown, Pennsylvania (157).

2. *Reports* 1:108.

3. Eveleigh to Oglethorpe, 28 May 1735, in Lane, *Oglethorpe's Georgia*, 1:170, author's parenthesis.

4. Jones, *Newman's Letter Books*, 135, 177, 218; *Reports* 2:6, 62; 3:218, 231, 245; 4:35, 68, 117; 5:36, 78, 137–38, 165, 241, 253; Klaus G. Loewald, Beverly Starika, and Paul S. Taylor, trans. and eds., "Johann Martin Boltzius Answers a Questionnaire on Carolina and Georgia," *William and Mary Quarterly,* 3rd ser., 14 (April 1957): 249, 261; *SCG*, 18 August 1739; Meriwether, *Expansion of South Carolina*, 37.

5. *Reports* 2:105, 143, 166, 172, 184, 197, 218; 3:116, 239, 261; 4:29, 68, 142, 198–99, 218; 5:85–86, 171, 182, 196, 279; 6:28, 166; 7:104; Commissioners of Forfeited Estates: Claims on Estates; *Estate of John Buche vs. John Linder Jr.,* SCDAH; *SCG*, 8 September 1739 and 11 June 1741; Meriwether, *Expansion of South Carolina*, 38–39; "Notes Relative to Bourguin and Kelsall," 214; CCPJR (87A, 63A); Tedcastle, "Testimonial Granted to Honorable Jonas Pélot of Neuveville, Switzerland," 61; Stephens, *Journal of the Proceedings*, 1:458; Lane, *Oglethorpe's Georgia*, 1:77; Candler, *CRG*, 22, pt. 2:447.

6. Lewis, *Camden: A Frontier Town*; idem., *The American Frontier*; Hughes, "Populating the Back Country"; Barr, "Strawberry Ferry"; Joseph A. Ernst and H. Roy Merrens, "'Camden's turrets pierce the skies!': The Urban Process in the Southern Colonies during the Eighteenth Century," *William and Mary Quarterly,* 3rd ser., 30 (October 1973): 555, 557.

7. On the urban and economic processes at work in the southern colonies, note the following early specialized studies: Leila Sellers, *Charleston Business on the Eve of the American Revolution* (Chapel Hill: University of North Carolina Press, 1934); Oscar H. Darter, *Colonial Fredericksburg and Neighborhood in Perspective* (New York: Twayne, 1957); James H. Soltow, *The Economic Role of Williamsburg* (Williamsburg: Colonial Williamsburg, distributed by the University Press of Virginia, 1965); Rogers, *History of Georgetown County.*

8. Richardson, "'As Easy to Build Towns,'" 9; Barr, "Strawberry Ferry," 4, 13; Kenneth E. Lewis, "Functional Variation among Settlements on the South Carolina Frontier: An Archeological Perspective," 251–74, in Green and Perlman *Archeology of Frontiers*, 257; Mitchell, *Commercialism and Frontier*, 8; Lewis, *American Frontier*, 22

9. "The Journal of Peter Gordon," 3–37, in Trevor Reese, ed., *Our First Visit to America: Early Reports from the Colony of Georgia, 1732–1740* (Savannah: Beehive Press, 1974), 35.

10. "Testimony of Peter Shepard, Patron" (to the South Carolina Commons House of Assembly), as quoted in DeVorsey, *The Georgia–South Carolina Boundary*, 57.

11. Easterby, *JCHA*, 1736–39:150–51.

12. Ibid., 1736–39:101.

13. "A New Voyage to Georgia," 111–12. Quotation from Christie to Oglethorpe,

14 December 1734, in Lane, *Oglethorpe's Georgia*, 1:69. There is also reference to a law passed sometime in the mid-1730s (perhaps 1735) to cut a road through Smith's Ferry to Purrysburg. See "The Public to John Hammerton, Esq.," Inventories, 1732–1746, microfilmed copies, LGS.

14. R. Nicholas Olsberg, ed., *The Colonial Records of South Carolina: The Journal of the Commons House of Assembly, 23 April 1750–31 August 1751*, vol. 10 (Columbia: University of South Carolina Press, 1974), 61, 182–83, 335, hereafter cited as Olsberg, *JCHA,* 10.

15. Quotations from Terry W. Lipscomb, ed., *The Colonial Records of South Carolina: The Journal of the Commons House of Assembly, November 21, 1752–September 6, 1754*, vol. 12 (Columbia: University of South Carolina Press, 1983), 130 (author's parenthetical phrase), hereafter cited as Lipscomb, *JCHA,* 12, see also 131; idem. *JCHA,* 13:144.

16. Until the 1750s there were no roads in upper St. Peter's Parish above Purrysburg except for Native American paths. See Johnston, *Lawtonville Baptists*, xiv; Kilgo, *Pipe Creek*, 11.

17. Easterby *JCHA,* 1736–39:367; 1742–44:437; 1749–50:377, 444, 452; Terry W. Lipscomb, ed., *The Colonial Records of South Carolina: The Journal of the Commons House of Assembly, November 20, 1755–July 6, 1757*, vol. 14 (Columbia: University of South Carolina Press, 1989), 73, hereafter cited as Lipscomb, *JCHA,* 14; Christie to Oglethorpe, 14 December 1734, in Lane, *Oglethorpe's Georgia*, 1:69; Candler, *CRG,* 15:212–14; Adele Stanton Edwards, ed., *Journal of the Privy Council, 1783–1789* (Columbia: University of South Carolina Press, 1971), 125, 171; Sirmans, *Colonial South Carolina*, 251. On the commissioners and the vital need to keep the roads open, see Candler, *CRG,* 16:180, and Lothar L. Tresp, trans. and annotater, "September 1748 in Georgia, from the Diary of John Martin Boltzius," *GHQ* 47 (September 1963): 321. The requirement to keep the roads passable—such as the stipulation that residents of Hilton Head Island help maintain the Purrysburg road though it was thirty miles distant—could work a significant hardship on the colonists. See Lipscomb, *JCHA*, 14:73.

18. The fact that Charles and Jermyn were blood relatives of colonial leaders in Georgia and South Carolina certainly did not hurt their chances of securing a positive ruling on any matter brought before provincial gentry leadership. Their brother was Sir James Wright, royal governor of Georgia; and their father, South Carolina chief justice Robert Wright. The Wrights also pioneered tidal rice culture technology in the region. See Rowland, *History of Beaufort County*, 179.

19. Quotations from Lipscomb, *JCHA,* 1 and 2:266. See also Lawrence S. Rowland, "The Purrysburg Swiss in the Beaufort District," *THSSC* 98 (1993): 23, and Rowland, Moore, and Rogers, *History of Beaufort County*, 179.

20. Lipscomb, *JCHA,* 1 and 2:266.

21. The Rochester Ferry was also known as Screven's Ferry, and the Rochester Causeway as Union Causeway. It remained the principal lowcountry Savannah River crossing well into the mid–nineteenth century. Lipscomb, *JCHA*, 1 and 2:267; Lawrence S. Rowland, "Alone on the River: The Rise and Fall of the Savannah River Rice Plantations of St. Peter's Parish, South Carolina," *SCHM* 88 (1987): 126; Rowland, "The Purrysburg Swiss," 23.

22. William Edwin Hemphill, Wylma Ann Wates, and R. Nicholas Olsberg, eds.,

The State Records of South Carolina: Journals of the General Assembly and House of Representatives, 1776–1780 (Columbia: University of South Carolina Press, 1970), 102; hereafter cited as *JGAHR*.

23. *JGAHR* 102, 110–11.

24. Lowcountry Council, *Historic Resources*, 178–79. Although the road to the ferry was to be completed by the fall of 1770, inhabitants of St. Peter's Parish petitioned the Georgia Commons House of Assembly over impaired access to Savannah because Hugh Kennedy fenced his land on the Georgia side of the Savannah River at the ferry crossing. The petitioners asked that the road leading from the ferry be declared a public road so commercial exchange between South Carolina and Savannah could be expedited. See Candler, *CRG*, 15:212–14.

25. Hawes, *Journal of Zubly*, 1, n. 46; Archibald Campbell, Esquire, Lieutenant Colonel, *Journal of an Expedition against the Rebels of Georgia in North America . . .*, edited and with an introduction by Colin Campbell (Darien, Ga.: Ashantilly Press, 1981): 42; Jones, "Boltzius' Trip to Charleston," 88, n. 5; Candler, *CRG*, 14:426; 15:115–16, 131, 274–75; 26:180; Harold E. Davis, *The Fledgling Province: Social and Cultural Life in Colonial Georgia, 1733–1776* (Chapel Hill: University of North Carolina Press, 1976), 51.

26. Frank H. Norton, ed., *The Hugh Finlay Journal: Colonial Postal History, 1773–1774* (Brooklyn: Mercantile Library Association, 1867; reprint, Columbus, Ohio: U.S. Philatelic Classics Society, 1975), 60.

27. RMC 4V:310–11.

28. Ted Ruddock, ed., *Travels in the Colonies in 1773–1775 Described in the Letters of William Mylne (1734–1790)* (Athens: University of Georgia Press, 1993), 26.

29. Eveleigh to Oglethorpe, 28 May 1735, in Lane, *Oglethorpe's Georgia*, 1:170; Loewald, "Questionnaire, II," 243. On the cosmopolitan aspects of colonial towns see Darter, *Colonial Fredericksburg*, passim.

30. *A Map of South Carolina and a Part of Georgia*, from the surveys of William Bull, William DeBrahm, and John Stuart (Charing Cross, 1780), SCHS; Hughes, *Populating the Back Country*, 106.

31. Marvin T. Smith, "100% Archeological Survey of the Purrysburg Tract, Jasper County, South Carolina" (Garrow and Associates, June 10, 1985), 16; Elliot, "Archeological Reconnaissance of the Purrysburg Tract, 51; Michael B. Trinkley, "An Archeological Overview of the South Carolina Woodland Period: It's the Same Old Riddle," 73–89, in Albert C. Goodyear III and Glen T. Hanson, eds., *Studies in South Carolina Archeology: Essays in Honor of Robert L. Stephenson*, Anthropological Studies 9, Occasional Papers of the South Carolina Institute of Archeology and Anthropology (Columbia: University of South Carolina, 1989), 73.

32. Luigi Castiglioni, *Luigi Castiglioni's Viaggio: Travels in the United States of North America, 1785–1787*, trans. and ed. by Antonio Pace with Natural History Commentary and *Luigi Castiglioni's Botanical Observations*, trans. by Antonio Pace and ed. by Joseph and Nesta Ewan (Syracuse, N.Y.: Syracuse University Press, 1983), 123; Lambert, *Travels through Lower Canada*, 27–28. Lambert makes special note of the efforts of Purrysburg settlers to preserve the artifacts. See Lambert, *Travels through Lower Canada*, 28.

33. Lowcountry Council, *Historic Resources*, 175; Larry E. Ivers, *Colonial Forts of South Carolina, 1670–1775* (Columbia: University of South Carolina Press, 1970),

48–50; David G. Anderson, "The Mississippian in South Carolina," 101–32, in Goodyear and Hanson, *Studies in South Carolina Archeology*, 107.

34. Clarence L. Ver Steeg, "Slaves, Slavery, and the Genesis of the Plantation System in South Carolina: An Evolving Social-Economic Mosaic," 103–32, in Ver Steeg, *Southern Mosaic*, 109; Gary L. Hewitt, "The State in the Planter's Service: Politics and the Emergence of a Plantation Economy in South Carolina," 49–73, in Greene, *Money, Trade, and Power*, 50–58; Clowse, *Economic Beginnings*, 236; George Fenwick Jones, "Commissary Von Reck's Report on Georgia," *GHQ* 47 (March 1963): 105; Philip M. Brown, "Early Indian Trade in the Development of South Carolina: Politics, Economics, and Social Mobility during the Proprietary Period, 1670–1719," *SCHM* 76 (July 1975): 118, 123; David H. Corkran, *The Carolina Indian Frontier* (Columbia: University of South Carolina Press, 1970), 1, 4, 8–9, 20. Quotation from Christie to Oglethorpe, 14 December 1734, in Lane, *Oglethorpe's Georgia*, 1:68. Along with other frontier settlements, colonial Camden also participated extensively in the Indian trade. See Lewis, *Camden: A Frontier Town*, xv.

35. Easterby, *JCHA*, 1736–39:150–51; Parker to Mr. Hucks, 24 December 1734, in Lane, *Oglethorpe's Georgia*, 1:79. This issue may have been one of the reasons for the eventual overthrow of the trustees. See Randall M. Miller, "The Failure of the Colony of Georgia under the Trustees," *GHQ* 53 (1969): 1–17.

36. Jones, *Georgia Dutch*, 260; *Reports* 7:20; 14:87; 16:55.

37. Ivers, *Colonial Forts of South Carolina*, 48–50; Candler, *CRG*, 4, supplement: 122; Beaufin to Simond, 23 January 1734, in Lane, *Oglethorpe's Georgia*, 1:37; Easterby, *JCHA*, 1736–39:369; Loewald, "Questionnaire, II," 245; *Reports* 2:5; 4:50; 6:193, 8:123, 378; Jones, *Salzburger Saga*, 74. For a more comprehensive discussion of the sentry towns, see Meriwether, *Expansion of South Carolina*, 10.

38. William L. McDowell Jr., ed., *Colonial Records of South Carolina: Documents Relating to Indian Affairs, May 21, 1750–August 7, 1754*, vol. 1 (Columbia: South Carolina Archives Department, 1958), 79; Ivers, *Colonial Forts of South Carolina*, 16; Abel Doysié, ed., "Journal of a French Traveller in the Colonies, 1765, I," *American Historical Review* 26 (July 1921): 736; William L. McDowell Jr., ed., *Colonial Records of South Carolina: Documents Relating to Indian Affairs, 1754–1765*, vol. 2 (Columbia: University of South Carolina Press, 1970), 506; Lipscomb, *JCHA*, 12:315; idem., *JCHA*, 13:29. For a more detailed examination of Indian-white relations in colonial South Carolina, note especially James Adair, *The History of the American Indians Particularly Those Nations Adjoining to the Mississippi, East and West-Florida, Georgia, South and North Carolina and Virginia* (London: Edward and Charles Dilly, 1775; reprint, New York: Johnson Reprint Corporation, 1968); John R. Swanton, *The Indians of the Southeastern United States* (Washington, D.C.: Government Printing Office, 1946); Charles M. Hudson, *The Southeastern Indians* (Knoxville: University of Tennessee Press, 1976); Milling, *Red Carolinians*.

39. *Reports* 8:108.

40. Holcomb, *Petitions for Land*, 3:5.

41. Jones, "Von Reck's Report," 104; idem., trans. and ed., "Johann Martin Boltzius Reports on Georgia," *GHQ* 47 (June 1963): 218; *Reports* 2:5.

42. Frank J. Klingberg, "The Indian Frontier in South Carolina as Seen by the Society for the Propagations of the Gospel Missionaries," *Journal of Southern History* 5 (November 1939): 490; Ivers, *Colonial Forts*, 36; Thomas Eyre to Robert Eyre, 4 December 1740, in Lane, *Oglethorpe's Georgia*, 2:504; *Reports* 2:5; 3:241, 247, 314.

43. Lewis, *Camden: A Frontier Town*, 13–14.

44. First quotation from Bolton, *Southern Anglicanism*, 140; second from Sirmans, *Colonial South Carolina*, 97. See also BPRO 14:174–77; Waterhouse, *New World Gentry*, 128; Hughes, "Populating the Back Country," 134–35.

45. Some of the town lot plats and grants are missing dates, but the breakdown of dated lots in the 1730s are 1733—fifty-five, 1734/35—fourteen, 1736—sixty, 1737—thirty-six, 1738—four.

46. A prime example of these irregularities can be seen in the fact that, while at least 103 town lots were claimed in Purrysburg between 1735 and 1738, a total of only 101 petitions for land in the township are extant for the entire period from 1735 to 1756. See Holcomb, *Petitions for Land*.

47. Both Meriwether and Rowland concur that Purrysburg boasted at least 100 homes and perhaps 450 inhabitants by 1736. See Meriwether, *Expansion of South Carolina*, 35; Rowland, "The Purrysburg Swiss," 22. H. A. M. Smith cites Frederick Dalcho's figure of close to 100 dwellings by 1735. See Smith, "Purrysburgh," 207.

48. Waterhouse, *New World Gentry*, 157.

49. Quotations from Easterby, *JCHA*, 1746–47:57. See also, Easterby, *JCHA*, 1746–47:197; Jones, "Boltzius' Trip to Charlestown," 98; Voigt, "Side-Light," 40.

50. BPRO 14:176; Cooper and McCord, *Statutes at Large* 3:669; Kovacik and Winberry, *South Carolina: A Geography*, 8.

51. Dale was finally seated on 31 March 1749, nearly seventeen years after the founding of Purrysburg Township. He served until his death on 16 September 1750. No record of a writ to fill his seat has been found. Peter Timothy served from 1751 to 1754. Egerton Leigh succeeded him in 1754 and served the parish until 1760. In 1757 St. Peter's Parish was granted a second representative to the Commons House. Samuel Carne was elected to serve as the second representative from 1757 to 1760. See *JCHA*, 1748, 1749, 1751–52, 1752–54, 1754–55, 1755–57, 1757–60.

52. Easterby, *JCHA*, 1748:8, 19, 137, 148, 161, 165; and 1749–50:8–10; Rogers, "Huguenots of Old Beaufort," 7; Mary Bondurant Warren, comp., "South Carolina Jury Lists, 1718 through 1753," *Heritage Papers* (1977): 27, 30, 33, 36, 60, 71, 80, 84, 101, 106, 116, 120–22, 127, 129–30; Ge Lee Corley Hendrix and Morn McKoy Lindsay, comps., *The Jury Lists of South Carolina, 1778–1779* (published privately, 1976), 62, 64–65; Robert M. Weir, ed., "Muster Roles of the South Carolina Granville and Colleton County Regiments of Militia, 1756," *SCHM* 70 (October 1971): 231; Rowland, "Eighteenth Century Beaufort," 236. On the universal practice of electing elites to office, see Rutman and Rutman, *A Place in Time*, 145; Rogers, *Georgetown County*, 56, 76–77; Bernard Bailyn, "Politics and Social Structure in Virginia," 193–214, in T. H. Breen, ed., *Shaping Southern Society: The Colonial Experience* (New York: Oxford University Press, 1976), 194. "Deference or Defiance in Eighteenth Century America? A Round Table," *Journal of American History* 85 (June 1998): 13–97, provides a variety of more contemporary perspectives on the deference question in colonial America.

53. Gregorie, *Records of the Court of Chancery*, 17.

54. Holcomb, *Petitions for Land*, 1:22.

55. Albergotti, *Albergotti Creek*, 9, 11. Quotations from 11.

56. Details for this and the preceding paragraph came from Robert Olwell, "Practical Justice: The Justice of the Peace, the Slave Court, and Local Authority in Mid-Eighteenth Century South Carolina," 256–77, in Greene, *Money, Trade, and*

Power, 256–57, 261–62, 265, 271; idem., *Masters, Slaves, and Subjects*, 72–73; Waterhouse, *New World Gentry*, 126.

57. Olwell, "Practical Justice,"262–63. Quotation from 263.

58. Olwell, "Practical Justice," 262, 265.

59. See chapter 7 for Purrysburg military officers and their ranks.

Chapter Six

1. David L. Coon, *The Development of Market Agriculture in South Carolina, 1670–1785* (New York: Garland, 1989), 106–7, 117–18, 120–21, 146.

2. Ibid., 270.

3. Chaplin, *Anxious Pursuit*, 164.

4. Journal of the Georgia Trustees, 24 May 1733, quoted in Jones, *Georgia Dutch*, 33.

5. Merrens, *The Colonial South Carolina Scene*, 121.

6. E. Merton Coulter, ed., *The Journal of Peter Gordon, 1732–1735* (Athens: University of Georgia Press, 1963), 40–41, 64; Francis Moore, *A Voyage to Georgia, Begun in the Year 1735 (1735–1736)*, 81–156, in Reese, *Our First Visit to Georgia*, 104; Martin, "Zubly Comes to America," 128; quotations from George Fenwick Jones, ed., "Von Reck's Second Report from Georgia," *William and Mary Quarterly,* 3rd ser., 22 (April 1965): 321; Beaufin to Simond, 23 January 1734, in Lane, *Oglethorpe's Georgia*, 1:37; *Reports* 6:155.

7. Quotation from Parker to the trustees from Savannah, Georgia, December 1734, in Lane, *Oglethorpe's Georgia*, 1:75–76. See also ibid., 1:74; Parker to Mr. Hucks, 24 December 1734, 1:76–77, and Noble Jones to the trustees, 1 July 1735, 1:202–7.

8. Quotation from Causton to the trustees, 16 January 1736, in Lane, *Oglethorpe's Georgia*, 1:100; Moore, *Voyage to Georgia*, 110.

9. Lane, *Oglethorpe's Georgia*: Joseph Fitzwalter to Oglethorpe, 16 January 1735, 1:87–88; from James Horner, 27 January 1735, 1:117; Eveleigh to Oglethorpe, 28 May 1735, 1:169; Amatis to the trustees, 30 June 1735, 1:199, and 5 July 1735, 1:214; Martha Causton to the trustees, 16 January 1738, 2:326; Stephens, *Journal of the Proceedings*, 1:225–26; Easterby, *JCHA,* 1749–50:381–82; Candler, *CRG,* 26:143; Coleman, *Colonial Georgia*, 115. For analyses of the Georgia silk enterprise, note especially Pauline Tyson Stephens, "The Silk Industry in Georgia," *Georgia Review* 7 (Spring 1953): 39–49; Marguerite B. Hamer, "The Foundations and Failure of the Silk Industry in Provincial Georgia," *North Carolina Historical Review* 12 (April 1935): 125–48; Mary Thomas McKinstry, "Silk Culture in the Colony of Georgia," *GHQ* 14 (September 1930): 225–35; James W. Holland, "The Beginning of Public Agricultural Experimentation in America," *Agricultural History* 12 (July 1938): 271–98; W. Calvin Smith, "Utopia's Last Chance? The Georgia Silk Boomlet of 1751," *GHQ* 59 (Spring 1975): 25–37.

10. Candler, *CRG,* 9:18–20, 26; 21:117; 22, pt. 1:97; 22, pt. 2:447; Gawin L. Corbin, "The First List of Pew Holders of Christ-Church, Savannah," *GHQ* 50 (March 1966): 80; *Journal of Thomas Causton, Esq.*, 243–77, in Reese, *Our First Visit to Georgia*, 258; Stephens, *Journal of the Proceedings*, 1:293, n. 71, 458; Eveleigh to Verelst, 24 March 1736, in Lane, *Oglethorpe's Georgia*, 1:255; *Reports* 8:145; 14:123; 16:55–56; 18:200, and n. 4; Davis, *Fledgling Province*, 102, 150–52.

11. Jones, *Newman's Letterbooks*, 193, 536, 541, 581; *Reports* 1:64; 2:159, 181; 3:50.

12. *Reports* 8:445.

13. *Reports* 2:6, 26–27, 71, 88, 104–5, 141, 165, 170, 195, 217, 220; 3:14, 16, 136, 138, 140–42, 152, 162, 166, 241, 253; 5:25–26, 119, 156; 7:214; Loewald, "Questionnaire," 248. Quotation from *Reports* 10:59.

14. Rhys Isaac, *The Transformation of Virginia, 1740–1790* (Chapel Hill: University of North Carolina Press for the Institute of Early American History and Culture, 1982), 46–52.

15. *Reports* 4:68 (quotations), 115. Holzendorf appears to have left the township by the early 1740s, after some land troubles, to develop a plantation and practice medicine at Frederica down the Savannah River. See *Reports* 8:150; Jones, *Salzburger Saga*, 45. One Ebenezer settler, Mr. Zant, who enlisted in the military during King George's War, made a special trip to Purrysburg to be bled just before his deployment in May 1740. See *Reports* 7:107.

16. *Reports* 7:149–50. The year before Ebenezer physician Christian Ernst Thilo visited Purrysburg to provide medicines for the ill missionaries Schulius and Böhler. The medicine had no effect on Schulius, who died in mid-July. Böhler recovered. See *Reports* 6:172.

17. Davis, *Some Huguenot Families, Supplement No. 3*, 2; *Reports* 8:329–30 (quotations).

18. *Reports* 8:330 (quotation), 332; Jones, *Salzburger Saga*, 47–48.

19. *Reports* 8:467 (quotations), 494.

20. Ibid., 9:27 (quotation) and 270, n. 23.

21. Ibid., 7:54; 8:366 (quotation); Jones, *Salzburger Saga*, 71–72.

22. *Reports* 8:371–74, 376–77, 405, 458.

23. Ibid., 8; 430, 455–56; 9:269 and n. 16.

24. Ibid., 8:431, 455, 473–74 (first quotation), 481, 493, 511–12 (second quotation); 9:21, 269, and n. 15; Jones, *Salzburger Saga*, 69.

25. *Reports* 8:190.

26. Ibid., 8:431–32.

27. Ibid., 8:458.

28. Ibid., 8:493–94, 512 (first quotation); 9:21 (second quotation); Jones, *Salzburger Saga*, 72.

29. *Reports* 8:532.

30. Ibid., 10:73–74 (first quotation); 18:198 (second quotation). A salivation was a procedure that stimulated the production of saliva in the mouth by the application of a mercury precipitation such as calumel. See *Reports* 18:198, n. 3.

31. Ibid., 6:23, 66; 9:94; 12:74–75; 13:102–3; 17:261; Jones, *Georgia Dutch*, 239. The Purrysburg midwife probably saved the life of Mrs. Hernberger. See Jones, *Georgia Dutch*, 239. There is some evidence to indicate that the Bourguin family was actually of Roman Catholic heritage. If true, it would help explain the almost visceral distrust Boltzuis exhibited toward Dr. Bourguin since Salzburg Lutherans maintained a greater animoisty toward Roman Catholics than for Reformed Protestants. It should also be noted that if Purry knowingly allowed a Catholic family to join his colony, he violated the terms with British authorities as Purrysburg was to be populated exclusively by Protestants. See below, chapter 7, note 7.

32. In addition to other references cited, the sources for this and the following three paragraphs are: *Reports* 2:62, 89, 172, 184, 187, 197, 199; 3:23, 216, 231, 244–45, 253; 4:65, 123; 5:196, 242, 244, 253–54, 279, 292–93; 6:28, 194, 231; 7:199, 205, 212, 221–22 (quotation), 270; 8:15, 29, 50, 488, 493–94, 507; 9:67, 103,

107; 18:29, 35; Jones, *Salzburger Saga*, 48–49, 62–63; idem., *Georgia Dutch*, 226.

33. According to a report in 1749 this rice stamp was able to process a thousand pounds of grain in twenty-four hours. See *Reports* 13:134.

34. The Kieffers also reduced their price for this boat from twenty-one pounds, eight shillings sterling. See *Reports* 18:29.

35. Jones, *Newman's Letterbooks*, 135, 177, 190, 218, 220, 587; *Reports* 4:35; 5:70; 8:108.

36. Candler, *CRG*, 25:334 and 26:53; Voigt, "Side-Light," 29; *Reports* 4:29, 75, 170, 181, 196, 218; 5:86, 253; 7:147, 169, 239; 8:50, 124, 349; 9:34, 162, 243; 11:7; 13:7, 12, 60; 14:50, 99, 137; 16:50–51; Jones, *Salzburger Saga*, 59; Jones, *Georgia Dutch*, 228. It is unclear whether the purchase of the blacksmith tools went through because the next year Boltzius wrote, "Some time ago we had an opportunity to have a German smith from Carolina . . . but he moved to Purrysburg because we could not arrange for his redemption." See *Reports* 6:166. The millstones for the gristmill may have been purchased from Charles Purry, who had some on his property in Purrysburg. See *Reports* 6:173.

37. *Reports* 12:70 (first quotation), 81–82. For a more detailed discussion of the Ebenezer mills see George Fenwick Jones, "The Salzburger Mills: Georgia's First Successful Enterprises," *Yearbook of German-American Studies* 23 (1988): 105–17.

38. This was not an uncommon occurrence in colonial America. See Kraus, *Intercolonial Aspects of American Culture*, 37.

39. See *Reports* 4:196 for an example of these tendencies.

40. The Reverend Boltzius, in his inimitable style, put quite a different twist on the search for work, writing in 1741 that Purrysburg settlers "make many unnecessary trips in process of earning a living. Their desire to get rich corrupts body and soul." See *Reports* 8:162.

41. Ibid., 3:116; 4:10–12, 75, 201 (quotation); 5:170–71, 241, 253; 8:507; Davis, *Fledgling Province*, 96.

42. Loewald, "Questionnaire, II," 243.

43. *Reports* 6:185.

44. Ibid., 6:100, 112, 164, 316 (second quotation); 9:80 (first quotation); Jones, *Salzburger Saga*, 23, 54. Before receiving counterfeit bills, Boltzius believed "making money is quite harmless." See *Reports* 9:80.

45. *Reports* 7:180–81; 8:485 (quotation).

46. Ibid., 8:512–13; 18:30 (quotation).

47. Ibid., 8:75, 106, 309, 378, 392, 394; 9:59, 67, 79; 10:13–14; 15:180; 18:4; Holcomb, *Petitions for Land*, 1:168.

48. *Reports* 7:150.

49. *SCG*, 9–16 November 1734, quoted in Smith, "Purrysburgh," 201.

50. Quoted in Smith, "Purrysburgh," 203–4; Holcomb, *Petitions for Land*, 1:45, 133, 136.

51. *Reports* 7:150.

52. Loewald, "Questionnaire," 248.

53. *Reports* 7:150.

54. Holcomb, *Petitions for Land*, 1:21, 35, 96, 131, 149, 154, 168, 173, 183; 3:5, 27–28, 42–43, 54–55, 64, 160–61; 4:67, 91, 100, 148–49.

55. *Reports* 2:203, 211, 219; 3:199, 258; 4:6, 48, 154, 172; 5:218; Jones, *Salzburger Saga*, 76.

56. *Reports* 4:194 (first quotation), 206; 5:108, 273; 6:104 (second quotation).

57. Ibid., 6:40; see also ibid., 6:48.

58. Ibid., 7:278.

59. Ibid., 8:332.

60. Loewald, "Questionnaire," 246.

61. Davis, *Fledgling Province*, 42.

62. These are the two earliest bill of sale records for Purrysburg landholders, and both are written in French. See RMC, 3A:213–15, 3D:432–33; Langley, *Deed Abstracts*, 3:203, 277.

63. Langley, *Deed Abstracts*, 2:154; 3:357–58; RMC, S:390–91, 4Q:89.

64. Langley, *Deed Abstracts*, 1:365–66; 2:1, 350, RMC, 2P:442–43.

65. RMC, 3E:86, 3H:26–28, 3T:41, 4O:200–204; Langley, *Deeds Abstracts*, 2:90; 3:357, 371.

66. Candler, *CRG*, 5:658; *Reports* 2:124, 141; 3:19, 23, 27, 39, 54–55, 99–100, 109, 116, 207–8, 236, 260, 289; 4:13, 31, 53, 57, 67, 161, 197–98, 213, 215–16, 218, 219 (and n. 244), 220, 222, 224, 229; 5:6, 29, 34, 42–44, 47, 53, 82, 84–85, 114, 139–40, 171–2, 232, 290; Jones, *Salzburger Saga*, 99.

67. Sources for this paragraph as well as the preceding three are *Reports* 3:180; 6:100, 173; 7:212; 8:366, 371–72, 376, 431, 455, 458; Jones, *Salzburger Saga*, 69; Stephens, *Journal of the Proceedings*, 1:458; Candler, *CRG*, 4, supplement: 200–202; 5:566, 586; 23:323; Lane, *Oglethorpe's Georgia*, Fitzwalter to Oglethorpe, 16 January 1735, 1:87–88 and Oglethorpe to the trustees, 18 May 1736, 1:267; Eveleigh to Verelst, 9 August 1736, in Candler, *CRG*, 21:206.

68. Details from this and the previous paragraph came from the following sources: Letter from a citizen of Berne, 4 February 1735, quoted in Carpenter, "Purysburg, South Carolina," 3; *Reports* 2:147, 169; 3:58, 97, 104, 106 (quotation), 115, 261; 4:123, 126; 5:36, 78, 137–38, 165, 173, 182, 242–43; 7:256; 8:108, 131, 144, 268–69; 14:35, 102–3; 18:100–101; Jones, *Salzburger Saga*, 23; Strobel, *Salzburgers and Their Descendants*, 102.

69. Kelsey, "Swiss Settlers," 86.

70. *Journal of Causton*, 263, 273.

71. Stephens, *Journal of the Proceedings*, 1:45, 48; Smyth, "Travellers in South Carolina," 124; Morgan, "Wesley's Sojourn Revisited," 253–62; Coleman, *Colonial Georgia*, 148–49.

72. *Reports* 6:171. Runaways commonly had two major routes of escape through the Beaufort District. One was via the channels and waterways of the sea islands, and the other was through the pine barrens. If runaways took the latter route, the only viable Savannah River crossings were Purrysburg and Palachuccola. See Rowland, *History of Beaufort County*, 131.

73. Stephens, *Journal of the Proceedings*, 1:238, 243–44, 297–98; Candler, *CRG*, 25:440; *Reports* 13:122, 125; 14:40.

74. There are conflicting accounts of the exploits of this suspicious character. See *Reports* 9:247–49; Jones, *Salzburger Saga*, 77–78, idem., *Georgia Dutch*, 162–63. Quotation from *Reports* 9:248.

75. *Reports* 3:254–55; 5:42–44 and n. 45, 149, 211.

76. Ibid., 2:90; 3:122–23.

77. Quotations from *Reports* 3:19 and 23; see also 115.

78. Richard M. Jellison, "Antecedents of the South Carolina Currency Acts of 1736 and 1746," *William and Mary Quarterly,* 3rd ser., 16 (October 1959): 563; *SCG*, 18 August 1739. See also Candler, *CRG,* 21:179–80. Charles Purry removed to Beaufort/Port Royal, and Montaigut to Savannah. Another Purrysburg shopkeeper, Daniel Choupard, left for St. Michael's Parish, probably also in the first decade of settlement because of similar problems. See Webber and Jervey, "Abstracts of the Court of Ordinary," *SCHGM* 43 (1942): 179.

79. This party probably included Jacob Keiffer, who supported Charles Purry's efforts to resolve a dispute with provincial authorities regarding payment of passage expenses from Europe to South Carolina for the Purrysburg settlers. See *Reports* 8:276, 285, 352, 367.

80. Holcomb, *Petitions for Land*, 1:139–40, 166–67, 200; 2:117, 252; 3:23 (first quotation), 28 (second quotation), 46, 72, 217; 4:88–89, 93. Smith notes that Holzendorf arrived in Purrysburg from Brandenburg with two servants, but their identities are unknown. See Smith, "Purrysburgh," 198. In April 1743 Ring received a second grant at Acton. See Jones, *Georgia Dutch*, 93.

81. Stephens, *Journal of the Proceedings*, 1:412; Causton to Oglethorpe, 7 July 1735, in Lane, *Oglethorpe's Georgia*, 1:215, 218; Jones, *Georgia Dutch*, 51, 93, 163; *Reports* 4:123, 170; 6:14, 166; 7:85; 8:163; 15:9; Clowse, *Economic Beginnings*, 52.

82. Will of Thomas Newall, CWA transcripts, 1732–37, LGS; *Reports* 4:181; Inventories of J. P. Purry, 1736–39, and Isaac Bonijoe, 1739–43, LGS; Dobree to the trustees, February 1737, in Lane, *Oglethorpe's Georgia*, 1:302; Stephens to the trustees, 31 December 1741, in Candler, *CRG,* 13:190–91.

83. In chronological sequence, the one enumeration from 1735 to 1739 was for two blacks (Robert Williams). The three from 1740 to 1749 were for four (Peter Delmestre), five (the Reverend J. J. Zubly), and two (Peter Mallett). The fourteen from 1750 to 1756 were for eight (the Reverend Francis Pelot), fourteen (Henry Desaussure), one (Isaac Brabant), two (Jonas Pelot), six (Caspar Morganshaller [Gaspar Morgantaller]), seven (Drury Dunn), seventeen (David Mongin), three (David Giroud), seven (William Elbert), four (the Reverend Henry Chiffelle), eight (David Rumpf), four (Jacob Strouper [Stroubhart]), three (George Strouper [Stroubhart]), and five (John Linder). The figures were gleaned from an analysis of the four volumes of Holcomb, *Petitions for Land.*

Other sources add a few more details regarding township residents of the slaveholding class prior to 1760. The *South Carolina Gazette* identified Peter Delmestre, who advertised "one negro wench for monthly hire" in the 11 June 1741 issue, and John Rodolf Grant, who in the 18 October 1742 issue offered "A plantation containing 350 Acres choice rice and corn land in Purrysburg Township fronting Savannah River . . . with a good dwelling house and other commodious buildings thereon also some choice cattle and a good negro slave." The Kieffer family owned three slaves sometime before May 1741. See *Reports* 8:192. Ulisse Antoine Albergotti owned at least eight slaves in late 1738. See Langley, *Deed Abstracts*, 2:1. A survey of extant wills and inventories for Purrysburg landholders from 1733 to 1760 reveals that a few others owned slaves. Founder Jean Pierre Purry (six), Isaac Bonijoe (five), John Pennefather (unknown number), and Abraham Ehrhardt (unknown number) were also slaveholders in this early period. See tables 5 and 6—especially table 6, Aggregate Estate Values and Slave Ownership and the following discussion of estate values—for more details on wills and inventories of Purrysburg landholders.

84. *Reports* 7:227

85. Ibid., 278.

86. Ibid., 9:196.

87. Ibid., 8:192, 238, 378; 11:7, 32, 34; 14:100; 18:29; Jones, *Salzburger Saga*, 70.

88. Quotations taken from Stephens, *Journal of the Proceedings*, 1:412 and *Reports* 7:194, respectively.

89. Loewald, "Questionnaire," 235.

90. RMC, S:390, 3D:432–33; Langley, *Deed Abstracts*, 2:1; 3:357–58. John Chevillette may have also owned land, or at least resided on land, outside Purrysburg while still holding title to land in the township. The *South Carolina Gazette* carried a notice in the 22 November 1735 issue of the sale of the Hampstead plantation five miles from Charles Town. Prospective buyers were instructed to see John Chevillet at the plantation.

91. *Reports* 6:318; Davis, *Some Huguenot Families, Supplement No. 3*, 7–8. A few Purrysburg settlers had already moved away in the 1730s, some through marriage to residents of Ebenezer and others, such as Samuel Augsperger (Ausbourger), who left for Frederica in the mid-1730s, to find work. See Jones, *Georgia Dutch*, 64–65. The Reverend Boltzius reported in early 1743 after another flooding of low-lying township land that "other people from Purrysburg have had to abandon such land for this reason, and some of those have moved to a bountiful region near Port Royal where, however, they do not get their own land but to a certain extent are vassals of some prominent gentlemen in London, to whom this barony belongs." Unfortunately Boltzius fails to provide names either of the Purrysburg expatriates or the "gentlemen in London." See *Reports* 10:14. The Purrysburg cobbler John Jacob Reck may have been one of those who removed temporarily to the Port Royal area. See *Reports* 9:103; 18:4.

92. RMC, 2P:174–79, 180–85, 2Q:297–98, 2Y:600–602, 2Z:198–207; Langley, *Deed Abstracts*, 3:317. See also the master list of those platted land in the township (table 2).

93. Esker, *South Carolina Memorials*, 2:160.

94. Langley, *Deed Abstracts*, 3:43, 110, 352; Esker, *South Carolina Memorials*, 2:136–37.

95. RMC, 2X:309–16; Langley, *Deed Abstracts*, 3:147.

96. RMC, 2S:313–18.

97. Ibid., 2 H:104–14, 2N:211–17. The 9 June 1763 issue of the *Georgia Gazette* carried the following advertisement: "Dr. Henry Lewis Bourguin gives notice of opening a shop in Mrs. Campbell's house near the church in Savannah where he will practice physick and surgery." He also sold candy, spices, and sugar in addition to medicines.

98. The M. H. and D. B. Floyd Papers, collection no. 1308, box 37, folder 463, Georgia Historical Society; Davis, *Some Huguenot Families, Supplement No. 3*, 3, 9–11, 18–19.

99. Richard Hofstadter, *America at 1750: A Social Portrait* (New York: Random House / Vintage Books, 1973), 163–67; Robert M. Weir, *"A Most Important Epocha":*

The Coming of the Revolution in South Carolina (Columbia: University of South Carolina Press, 1970), 4; Sirmans, *Colonial South Carolina*, 226–27; Alice Hanson Jones, *Wealth of a Nation to Be: The American Colonies on the Eve of the Revolution* (New York: Columbia University Press, 1980), 113, 341, 358, 445; Weir, *Colonial South Carolina*, 141.

100. Weir, *Colonial South Carolina*, 146, 149, 150–51, 160; Russell R. Menard, "Slavery, Economic Growth, and Revolutionary Ideology in the South Carolina Lowcountry," 244–74, in Ronald Hoffman, John J. McCusker, Russell R. Menard, and Peter J. Albert, *The Economy of Early America: The Revolutionary Period, 1763–1790* (Charlottesville: University Press of Virginia for the United States Capitol Historical Society, 1988), 250–51, 257–58.

101. Chestnutt, "South Carolina's Expansion," iii–iv.

102. *Georgia Gazette*, 24 August 1768.

103. The following discussion is based on a comparative analysis of wills and inventories for those granted land in Purrysburg Township drawn from microfilmed copies of CWA Transcripts and handwritten inventory duplicates, LGS. Individual documents are as follows: Wills: T. Newall, J. Pennefather, J. Richard, I. Overy, D. Godet, A. Greniere, A. Erhardt, D. Zubly, P. Lafitte, J. Barraque, Jonas Pelot, J. Stroubhar(t), A. Jindra, F. G. Ravot, D. Humbert, J. Waldburger, G. Mallet, D. Mongin, M. J. Henery (Hendrie), John Pelot, T. Camber, D. Mallet, F. Erhardt; Inventories: J. P. Purry, W. Staples, I. Bonijoe, J. Detrick, A. Chardonnet, A. Grenier(e), H. Girardin, M. Roro (Rorere), H. Chiffelle, H. Desaussure, A. Imer, A. Hendrie, J. Dupont, L. Quinch, H. Jeanerett, A. Walser, J. Barraque, Jonas Pelot, J. Stroubhar(t), A. Jindra, D. Humbert, J. Waldburger, G. Mallet, D. Mongin, M. A. Mongin, M. J. Henery (Hendrie), John Pelot, T. Camber, D. Mallet, H. Meuron.

104. Littlefield, *Rice and Slaves*, 8–9, 175–76; *Georgia Gazette*, 25 April 1765, 10 June 1767, 4 April 1770, 31 May 1775. The 31 May 1775 issue describes the filed upper teeth and forehead "country marks" of the Vauchier's slave January.

105. For a history of ranching in South Carolina from its genesis to the Yamassee War, see John S. Otto, "The Origins of Cattle-Ranching in Colonial South Carolina, 1670–1715." *SCHM* 87 (April 1986): 117–24. For developments after 1715, see Brooks, "Cattle-Ranching in Colonial South Carolina."

106. John J. McCusker and Russell R. Menard, *The Economy of British America, 1607–1789* (Chapel Hill: University of North Carolina Press for the Institute of Early American History and Culture, 1985), 184. There were obviously bottlenecks in this exchange. In 1746 the attempt to increase the number of horses at the township ran into the inelasticity of supply. There were plenty of mares, but since a single well-off resident had the only stallion, he charged thirty shillings sterling for stud service—a price too exorbitant for small livestock ranchers to pay at the time. See *Reports* 18:30.

107. Candler, *CRG*, 6:445; 8:289–90, 453, 595; Coleman and Ready, *CRG*, 27:91, 98; 28:pt. 1, 319, 368; McCusker and Menard, *Economy of British America*, 182; Menard, "Slavery, Economic Growth, and Revolutionary Ideology," 260–61.

108. The following discussion is based on an analysis of the RMC volumes, Langley, *Deed Abstracts*, and Holcomb, *Deed Abstracts*.

109. RMC, 3A:582–87, 3B:328–30, 4P:416–21.

110. Ibid., 3B:154–57, 3D:276–77, 334, 3P:66–68, 4F:40–44; Langley, *Deed Abstracts*, 3:244, 266, 275, 357; Holcomb, *Deed Abstracts, 1773–1778*, 197.

111. Weir noted the tendency among pre-Revolutionary planters to be involved in a rather wide variety of commercial endeavors. See Weir, *Colonial South Carolina*, 153.

112. *Georgia Gazette*, 9 May 1765.

113. RMC, 3Y:324–28, 3Z:311, 315; Holcomb, *Deed Abstracts, 1773–1778*, 43, 53.

114. RMC, 3E:379, 3K:344–46, 3N:347–50; Langley, *Deed Abstracts*, 3:299, 324. To secure his bond, Pendarvis transferred two more tracts of land to Leichtensteiger totaling 850 acres. See RMC, 3W:207–9.

115. RMC, 2P:174–79, 180–85, 2Y:187–204, 2Z:172–74, 3C:379–92, 3X:59–60, 3Z:115–116, 4E:60–61.

116. "The Giroud Family," 2, SCL; Holcomb, *Petitions for Land*, 3:112. For some reason, Giroud did not request fifty acres for himself.

117. Both Marguerite and Ann were widows of the original grantees of these lots (John Henry Deroche and Pierre Fourqueran, respectively). See RMC, 3E:86, and Langley, *Deed Abstracts*, 2:357.

118. RMC, 3T:41.

119. MR, 2O, pt. 1:288–89.

120. Holcomb, *Petitions for Land*, 3:112.

121. Overcrowding in the retail trade in the wake of the French and Indian War, coupled with the lure of massive profits in plantation agriculture, may have helped push Giroud toward extensive land acquisitions in the 1760s. See Weir, *Colonial South Carolina*, 164–65.

122. Langley, *Deed Abstracts*, 3:357; RMC, 3B:154–62.

123. RMC, 3N:341–43, 3O:262–64, 525–28, 3Q:154–57, 3S:224–26, 413, 3Y:363, 4R:143–48, 4V:306–8, 4W:307; Langley, *Deed Abstracts*, 4:94. It should also be noted that Giroud must have resold lot number 10 to the Deroche family at some point because in June 1766 Purrysburg cordwainer Abraham Deroche sold it back to Giroud. The deed of sale to the Deroche family has been lost. See Langley, *Deed Abstracts*, 3:311

124. The following discussion is based on an analysis of bills of sale, deeds, and bonds involving Adrian Mayer from May 1762 to September 1777. Sources were the volumes of the RMC, Holcomb, *Deed Abstracts, 1773–1778*, and Langley, *Deed Abstracts*, 3. See Holcomb, *Petitions for Land,* 4:240–41 for Mayer's first request for land in Purrysburg.

125. McCusker and Menard, *Economy of British America*, 182; Menard, "Slavery, Economic Growth, and Revolutionary Ideology," 261.

126. Hendrix and Lindsay, *Jury Lists of South Carolina*, 62.

127. Rowland, "Alone on the River, 129.

128. *Georgia Gazette*, 2 August 1764.

129. Ibid., 1 August 1765.

130. Ibid., 12 January 1774. On the intricacies of tidal rice culture, see Sam B. Hilliard, "The Tidewater Rice Plantation: An Ingenious Adaptation to Nature," *Geoscience and Man* 12 (20 June 1975): 57–66.

131. Journal of Archibald Simpson, quoted in Howe, *History of the Presbyterian Church*, 1:317.

132. Inventory of Jacob Stroubhart, 1765–69; Bond, J. L. Borguin to Henry Chiffelle, MR, 2L, pt. 2:370; Bill of Sale, George Strobhart (Stroubhart) to John Strobhart

(Stroubhart), MR, 2P:18; Bill of Sale, George Strobhart (Stroubhart) to David Unseld and Rodolph Strotreaker of Georgia, MR, 2O, pt. 2:331–32; Bill of Sale, David Geroud (Giroud) to Sutcliffe and Co., MR, 2S:526; Bond, Thomas Newall and Nathan Russell to John Burguin (Bourguin), George Hooper, and David Alexander, MR, 2W:349; Benjamin Guerard to J. Hartsone, John Bush (Buche), James Brown, and Charles Dupont, MR, 2U:152–53.

133. The following discussion is based on an analysis of the Judgment Rolls of the Court of Common Pleas involving Purrysburg settlers, SCDAH and other sources as noted.

134. Webber and Jervey, "Abstracts of the Court of Ordinary," *SCHGM* 23 (April 1922): 80; (July 1922): 158; 24 (July 1923): 106 (quotation); 25 (July 1924): 146–47; 27 (April 1926): 91; 40 (October 1939): 138.

135. Ibid., 44 (April 1943): 112–13.

136. Ibid., 44 (January 1943): 51, (April 1943): 107, 110, (July 1943): 175; Gregorie, *Records of the Court of Chancery*, 589.

137. Coon, *Development of Market Agriculture*, 117; Chaplin, *Anxious Pursuit*, 161.

138. Chaplin, *Anxious Pursuit*, 161–63.

139. Ibid., 160; Hamer, "Failure of the Silk Industry," 140.

140. Migliazzo, *Lands of True and Certain Bounty*, 128.

141. Ibid., 141, 143–44, 153; Robert C. Haywood, "Mercantilism and South Carolina Agriculture, 1700–1763," *SCHM* 60 (January 1959): 21. The Swiss had been long noted for their expertise in sericulture. See Dandliker, "Switzerland," 428–29 and Scoville, "Technology, II," 407–8.

142. *SCG,* 29, January 1731/2, 5 February 1731/2, l6 September, 2 December 1732 and 5 May 1733; Meriwether, *Expansion of South Carolina*, 37; Hirsch, *Huguenots of Colonial South Carolina*, 198.

143. *SCG*, 4 December 1736, 15 February 1739/40, 1 April 1745, 19 September 1755; Easterby, *JCHA,* 1736–39:562; 1742–44:552; 1744–45:191, 460; Chaplin, *Anxious Pursuit*, 160; Hirsch, *Huguenots of Colonial South Carolina*, 198, 200; Meriwether, *Expansion of South Carolina*, 37; Gray, *History of American Agriculture*, 1:185–86; [R. and J. Dodsley], *A Description of South Carolina* (Pall Mall, 1761), in Carroll, *Collections,* 2:236–37; *CGHS* 4:9. Quotation from Merrens, *The Colonial South Carolina Scene*, 173.

144. *SCG*, 23 December 1732, 21 July 1733, 9 November 1734, 15 February 1739, 30 April 1741, 3 April 1742; Easterby, *JCHA,* 1736–39:336–37, 344–45, 353, 395, 423, 464–65, 658, 843; "An Act for encouraging the Manufacture of Silk," SCL; Smith, "Purrysburgh," 189; Hirsch, *Huguenots of Colonial South Carolina*, 199–200; Meriwether, *Expansion of South Carolina*, 37; Gray, *History of American Agriculture*, 1:185; Haywood, "Mercantilism," 22.

145. *Reports* 14:43; 18:201; Jones, *Georgia Dutch*, 221–22; Lane, *Oglethorpe's Georgia*, 1:70; Candler, *CRG*, 26:93, 143.

146. *Reports* 8:181, 509; Jones, *Georgia Dutch*, 221.

147. *Reports* 18:4 (quotation), 30.

148. Lane, *Oglethorpe's Georgia*, 2:326. On the commercial accomplishments and contributions of the Salzburgers to the silk enterprise, note especially, Hester Walton Newton, "The Agricultural Activities of the Salzburgers in Colonial Georgia," *GHQ* 18 (September 1934): 248–63, and idem, "The Industrial and Social Influences of the

Salzburgers of Colonial Georgia," *GHQ* 18 (December 1934): 335–53.

149. Quotations from *Reports* 9:101. See also Hamer, "Failure of the Silk Industry," 139.

150. *Reports* 18:40; Hamer, "Failure of the Silk Industry," 139.

151. *Reports* 11:7; 13:26; 14:124; Hamer, "Failure of the Silk Industry," 139.

152. It should be noted that the industry in Purrysburg suffered a relapse in 1754 either because of an affliction visited upon the silkworms or because of the deaths of important practitioners there. See *Reports* 16:188.

153. In 1751 Boltzius downplayed Purrysburg's role in the industry by reporting that "a little silk has been made in Purrysburg." See Loewald, "Boltzius Answers a Questionnaire," 261.

154. Quotation from *Reports* 17:39; Coleman and Ready, *CRG* 28, pt. 1:126. See also Hamer, "Failure of the Silk Industry," 139. Hamer found that in 1756 South Carolina shipped at least 1,525 pounds of silk to Savannah. Ebenezer sent 1,232 pounds, and Savannah residents produced 1,024.

155. *Reports* 17:158. It is unclear what caused the poor output of silk in 1748/9, 1754, or 1760. Mulberry leaves were susceptible to frost damage and red ants indigenous to the region could destroy silkworm eggs and larvae. See Tresp, "August, 1748," 212, 215.

156. Jones, "Ettewein's Journey," 259.

157. *SCG*, 27 April 1767, *South Carolina Gazette and Country Journal*, 12 May 1767, hereafter cited as *SCGCJ*; Easterby, *JCHA*, 1742–44:509, 552; Candler, *CRG*, 24:319–20, 343; 25:502–03; 26:99, 136, 291; Coleman, *Colonial Georgia*, 114; Meriwether, *Expansion of South Carolina*, 37. Purrysburg settlers were less than satisfied at times with the prices paid by Georgia merchants. See Candler, *CRG*, 26:219.

158. *SCG*, 27 April 1767; *SCGCJ*, 12 May 1767, 8 July 1767; Daniel Benoît, *Les frères Gibert: Deux pasteurs de Désert et du Refuge, (1728–1817)* (Toulouse, 1889), 210–11; Brooke Hindle, *The Pursuit of Science in Revolutionary America, 1735–1789* (Chapel Hill: University of North Carolina Press, 1956), 201; Dr. J. M. Lesesne, "An Address by Dr. J. M. Lesesne at the 208th Anniversary Of the Arrival of the French Huguenots at New Bordeaux," *Transactions of the McCormick County Historical Society* 1 (1971–1972): 33; Hirsch, *Huguenots of Colonial South Carolina*, 201; idem, "French Influence on American Agriculture in the Colonial Period with Special Reference to the Southern Provinces," *Agricultural History* 4 (January 1930): 6–7; Anne C. Gibert, *Pierre Gibert, Esq. the Devoted Huguenot: A History of the French Settlement of New Bordeaux, South Carolina* (privately published, 1976) 31; Meriwether, *Expansion of South Carolina*, 254.

159. *SCGCJ*, 14 January 1772; J. Rion McKissick, "Some Observations of Travelers on South Carolina, 1820–1860," *Proceedings of the South Carolina Historical Association* 2 (1932): 48; Hindle, *Pursuit of Science*, 200; Meriweather, *Expansion of South Carolina*, 37; Gibert, *Pierre Gibert*, 31; Perry, "Lost Settlement," *News and Courier*, 1 April 1956. Robert Mills's letter quoted in Elliot, "Archeological Reconnaissance of the Purrysburg Tract," 14.

160. McCurry, *Masters of Small Worlds*, 96.

161. Van Ruymbeke, "L'émigration huguenote"; idem, "Huguenots of Proprietary South Carolina"; Bosher, "Huguenot Merchants and the Protestant International";

idem, "The Imperial Environment of French Trade with Canada"; Nash, "Huguenot Merchants."

162. Jon Butler's recent essay "The Huguenots and the American Immigrant Experience," 194–207, in Van Ruymbeke and Sparks, *Memory and Identity,* speaks of both the assimilation of the Huguenots and also their ability to shape their American identity as well as the American immigration experience.

163. Littlefield, *Rice and Slaves*, 134; Wood, *Black Majority*, 177–78.

164. CWA Will Transcripts: Jacob Barraque, Abraham Jindra, Gideon Mallet, Francis Gabriel Ravot, Jacob Stroubhart; inventory of Margaret Jean Henery (Hendrie), 1772–76; Bill of Sale, Hannah Mayerhoffer to Lewis Winkler and Melchior Pholker, MR, 2P:143; Deed of Gift, Margaret Henrieu (Henriod) to David Saussy, MR, 2P:414; CCPJR, (57A, 23A), (64A, 319A).

165. Nash, "Huguenot Merchants," 219.

166. Hughes, "Populating the Back Country," 113.

167. Ship mills looked somewhat like a paddlewheel ship. The paddle was turned by the river's current, which powered the gear that turned the millstones. Because it could rise and fall with the river, it was quite an efficient design. See *Reports* 13:63.

168. Lepionka, "Purrysburg: An Archeological Survey," 5; Lowcountry Council, *Historic Resources*, 183. See also the article by Rob Dewig, "Ancient Brick-Lined Pit a So Carolina Historical Mystery," which originally appeared in the 21 May 2001 edition of Beaufort's *Carolina Morning News*. Viewed online at http://farshores/acarwell.html (3 August 2003).

169. Lepionka, "Purrysburg: An Archeological Survey," 9.

Chapter Seven

1. Bailyn and Morgan, "Introduction," in *Strangers within the Realm*, 25–26.

2. Gallay, *Formation of a Planter Elite*, 19; Hughes, "Populating the Back Country," 24.

3. Beaufin to Simond, 23 January 1734, in Lane, *Oglethorpe's Georgia*, 1:38; Meriwether, *Expansion of South Carolina*, 35; Hughes, "Populating the Back Country," 19–20.

4. Hughes, Populating the Back Country," 20–21; John W. Gordon, *South Carolina and the American Revolution: A Battlefield History* (Columbia: University of South Carolina Press, 2003), 11.

5. Other commissions were granted in 1734, but the names of the recipients are illegible. Two commissions for lieutenant and ensign were granted to unknown Purrysburg men on 29 July 1741. Lieutenant Lafitte became colonel of the Granville County Regiment in place of Hugh Bryan on 25 April 1742. See Inventories, 1732–1746, "The Public to John Hammerton, Esq.," SCDAH; Voigt, "Germans and German-Swiss: Their Contribution to the Province," 22.

6. "A New Voyage to Georgia," 112, 120.

7. "Letter from Carolina . . . ," trans. Fanny Bandelier, 538–39, in "Notes and Comment," *Catholic Historical Review* 4 (January 1919): 539.

8. Quotation from Easterby, *JCHA*, 1742–44:261–62, 268; see also Sumerall, "Address," 43. Even with such preparation South Carolinians remained doubtful that the colony could successfully repel an enemy attack. See Weir, "*A Most Important Epocha*," 3.

9. Larry E. Ivers, *British Drums on the Southern Frontier: The Military Colonization of Georgia, 1733–1749* (Chapel Hill: University of North Carolina Press, 1974), 13.

10. Beaufin to Simond, 23 January 1734, in Lane, *Oglethorpe's Georgia*, 1:38; Eveleigh to Oglethorpe, 28 May 1735, in Lane, *Oglethorpe's Georgia*, 1:170.

11. The major source for these events is Francis Moore, "A Voyage to Georgia, Begun in the year 1735" (1735–36), (1744), 81–156, in Reese, *Our First Visit to America*. Note especially 107–8, 130–31, 136, 140–42, 145, 149–51. See also Lane, *Oglethorpe's Georgia*, 1: Oglethorpe to the trustees, 27 February 1736, 240–41; Oglethorpe to Broughton, 28 March 1736, 259; Anonymous letter, 12 April 1736, 261–62; Oglethorpe to the trustees, 18 May 1736, 267; Jones, "Von Reck's Second Report," 327–29; Ivers, *British Drums*, 60–63; *Reports* 4:28–29.

12. Stephens, *Journal of the Proceedings*, 2:130; Easterby, *JCHA*, 1739–41:76–77, 158; Ver Steeg, "Slaves, Slavery, and the Genesis of the Plantation System in South Carolina," 107; Wood, *Black Majority*, 319; Ivers, *British Drums*, 88; Hughes, "Populating the Back Country," 24. Voigt notes that John Frederick Holzendorf played an active role in quelling the revolt. See Voigt, "Germans and German-Swiss: Their Contribution to the Province," 22.

13. *Reports* 5:85; Oglethorpe to Bull, in Easterby, *JCHA*, 1739–41:160; Voigt, "Germans and German-Swiss: Their Contribution to the Province," 22.

14. "Report of the Committee Appointed by the General Assembly of South Carolina in 1740 on the St. Augustine Expedition under General Oglethorpe," *CSCHS* 4:74–75; Easterby, *JCHA*, 1739–41:230, and Oglethorpe to Bull, 24 June 1740, *JCHA*, 1741–42:123 (quotation); Voigt, "Germans and German-Swiss: Their Contribution to the Province," 22; Hughes, "Populating the Back Country," 80.

15. "Report of the Committee," *CSCHS* 4:154; Stephens, *Journal of the Proceedings*, 2:348 (quotation), 350, 354, 368, 370; Ivers, *British Drums*, 101; Gallay, *Formation of a Planter Elite*, 25–28. For a broader examination of the southern experience during the war, see Norman W. Caldwell, "The Southern Frontier during King George's War," *Journal of Southern History* 7 (February 1941): 37–54.

16. *Reports* 7:57, 107–8 (quotation).

17. *Reports* 7:6, 93–94, 107–8, 111, 117, 130, 166; Jones, *Georgia Dutch*, 276; Robert M. Weir, "Harmony We Were Famous For: An Interpretation of Pre Revolutionary South Carolina Politics," 421–46, in Stanley M. Katz and John M. Murrin, eds., *Colonial America: Essays in Politics and Social Development*, 3rd ed. (New York: Alfred A. Knopf, 1983).

18. "An Attempt Towards an Estimate of the Value of South Carolina for the Right Honourable the Lords Commissioners for Trade and Plantations, by James Glen, Esq. Governour, 1751," 177–91, in Merrens, *The Colonial South Carolina Scene*, 179.

19. Olsberg, *JCHA*, 10:447–49.

20. Weir, "Muster Rolls," 23; Meriwether, *Expansion of South Carolina*, 39.

21. Lipscomb, *JCHA*, 12:315; ibid., 13:29; Ivers, *Colonial Forts*, 16.

22. Military service records at the SCDAH indicate that the following men with land in Purrysburg township took part in the Fort Prince George Expedition under Singleton and MacPherson: John Burguin (Bourquin), John Bucche (Buche), George Delabere (deserted), Jacob Gosman (Gasman), John Lastinger, Adrian Mayer, John Henry Mayerhoffer, Andrew Pence, Abraham Ravow (Ravot), Lenard Reynowan

(Reynower), James Rhod, Abraham Vaucher, John Walser, and Lewis Winckler. Colonel John Chevillette also participated in the expedition. See also Sirmans, *Colonial South Carolina*, 315. Robert M. Weir places the Cherokee War in a broader context by viewing it as one of many related issues in the 1760s that challenged gentry authority in the colony. See Weir, "The Cherokee War and the Indirect Challenge to the Carolina Gentry," chap. 11, in *Colonial South Carolina*, 265–89. For an excellent analysis of the issues and consequences of the Cherokee War, note especially Milling, *Red Carolinians*, 266–331, and Hughes, "Populating the Back Country," 143–49.

23. Young, *Germans in the Colonial Southeast*, 25. The refugees may have been housed in forts built specifically for them in Purrysburg and other refugee destinations. See Ivers, *Colonial Forts*, 18.

24. Hughes, "Populating the Back Country," 152.

25. The South Carolina Association antedated the general American Continental Association created by the First Continental Congress and also had a much broader purpose. See Edward McCrady, *The History of South Carolina in the Revolution, 1775–1780* (New York: Macmillan, 1902; reissued 1969), 3, 5 and Christopher Ward, *The War of the Revolution*, 2 vols. (New York: Macmillan, 1952), 1:18.

26. "Historical Notes," *SCHGM* 7 (April 1906): 106. Other members of the Second Provincial Congress from St. Peter's were Colonel Stephen Bull, William Williamson, Thomas Middleton (son of William), and William Brisbane. See William Edwin Hemphill, ed., and Wylma Ann Wates, asst. ed., *The State Records of South Carolina: Extracts from the Journals of the Provincial Congresses of South Carolina, 1775–1776* (Columbia: South Carolina Archives Department, 1960), 5, 75, 130–31. See also William Moultrie, *Memoirs of the American Revolution*, 2 vols. (New York: David Longworth, 1802; reprint, in one volume, New York: Arno Press, 1968), 1:44. Former Purrysburg residents or their direct descendants served on other committees: Daniel Desaussure for St. Helena's and David Zubly for Ninety-Six District. Zubly was the grandson of original Purrysburg landholder David and son of the Reverend John Joachim Zubly. The Zubly family still held land in the township. See will of David Zubly, CWA transcripts, 1757–63, LGS; Moultrie, *Memoirs*, 1:43, 45.

27. "Journal of the Council of Safety," *CSCHS* 3: Laurens to Committee for St. Helena's, 9 January 1776, 161; Quotation from Laurens to Committee for St. Peter's, 10 January 1776, 163.

28. Laurens to Committee for St. Peter's, 19 January 1776, 197–98. See also Laurens to Bull, 19 January 1776, 197; Laurens to Committee at Beaufort, 199. All references from "Journal of the Council," *CSCHS* 3.

29. Council entry, 22 December 1775, 108; Laurens to Bull, 19 January 1776, 197; Laurens to Committee for St. Peter's, 19 January 1776, 197–98 (quotations). All references from "Journal of the Council," *CSCHS* 3, author's parenthesis.

30. George C. Rogers Jr., "Aedanus Burke, Nathaniel Greene, Anthony Wayne, and the British Merchants of Charleston," *SCHM* 67 (April 1966): 74.

31. Council entry, 13 July 1775, "Journal of the Council," *CSCHS* 2:37.

32. Laurens to Bull, 25 January 1776, 216; Laurens to the Provincial Congress at Savannah, 24 January, 1776, 218–19; Laurens to Committee for St. Helena's, 27 January 1776, 227–28. All citations from "Journal of the Council," *CSCHS* 3.

33. Lee to Armstrong, 15 August 1776, *Charles Lee Letterbook*, SCL.

34. Campbell, *Journal of an Expedition*, vii, ix–x, xii–xiv; Henry Lumpkin, *From*

Savannah to Yorktown: The American Revolution in the South (Columbia: University of South Carolina Press, 1981), 27–29; John Richard Alden, *The South in the Revolution, 1763–1789* (Baton Rouge: Louisiana State University Press, 1957), 232–33, 235; Doyce B. Nunis Jr., "Colonel Archibald Campbell's March From Savannah to Augusta, 1779," *GHQ* 45 (September 1967): 275–76; Gallay, *Formation of a Planter Elite*, 156.

35. Quotation from Lumpkin, *From Savannah to Yorktown*, 29.

36. The Orderly Book of Benjamin Lincoln, 3 January 1779. Quoted by permission of the Huntington Library, San Marino, California, hereafter cited as Lincoln, Orderly Book.

37. The Benjamin Lincoln Papers, 13 reels (Boston: Massachusetts Historical Society, 1967), reel 3, Lincoln to Laurens, 4 January 1779. Hereafter cited as BLP no. 2 or no. 3; Lincoln, Orderly Book, 4, 6, and 10 January 1779; Moultrie, *Memoirs*, 1:321; Campbell, *Journal of an Expedition*, xv; Grimke Order Book, 4 and 10 January 1779, SCHS; John S. Pancake, *This Destructive War: The British Campaign in the Carolinas, 1780–1782* (Tuscaloosa: University of Alabama Press, 1985), 32; Lumpkin, *From Savannah to Yorktown*, 30; McCrady, *South Carolina in the Revolution, 1775–1780*, 330, 332, 343; "Records of the Regiments of the South Carolina Line, Continental Establishment," *SCHGM* 5 (April 1904): 83.

38. BLP no. 3: Lincoln to Laurens, 4 January 1779.

39. Ibid., no. 3: Lincoln to Walton, 15 January 1779; Lincoln to Lowndes, 21, 24, and 26 January 1779; Lincoln to Rutledge, 19 February 1779. Lincoln was not alone in his assessment of the militia's capabilities. George Washington and Lincoln's successor Nathaniel Greene had similar complaints. See Pancake, *This Destructive War*, 52. For a somewhat more complimentary perspective on the role of the provincial militia in the Revolution see the revisionist article by Robert C. Pugh, "The Revolutionary Militia in the Southern Campaign, 1780–1781," *William and Mary Quarterly*, 3rd ser., 14 (April 1957): 154–75.

40. BLP no. 3: Lincoln to Lowndes, 15 January 1779.

41. Ibid.: Lincoln to Lowndes, 4 February 1779; Lincoln to Washington, 7 February 1779; Lincoln to President of Congress, 12 February 1779.

42. See the cases for the following dates in 1779 in BLP no. 3:7–11, 13–14, 20, 23, 25–26, 30 January; 1–3, 5, 8–9 February; 15–17, 19, 22 March; Pancake, *This Destructive War*, 47.

43. BLP no. 3: Court Martial of Baswell Brown, 14 January 1779, author's parenthesis.

44. Grimke Order Book, 17 January 1779; see also Lincoln, Orderly Book, 17 January 1779.

45. Grimke Order Book, 24 February 1779; see also Lincoln, Orderly Book, 24 February 1779.

46. Grimke Order Book, First entry, undated but before 4 January 1779, probably 3 January 1779; see also Lincoln, Orderly Book, 3 January 1779.

47. Grimke Order Book, 4 and 10 January 1779.

48. Lincoln, Orderly Book, 5 January 1779.

49. Ibid., 30 January 1779.

50. Grimke Order Book, 5 and 30 January 1779; BLP no. 3: Lincoln to Rutledge, 17 February 1779; Lincoln to Rutledge, 23 February 1779.

51. Flagrant disregard of orders was probably one of the reasons that Lincoln introduced compulsory "exercises, maneuvers, and discipline" characteristic of the "main army" four days later. Troops were ordered to exercise daily from 6:30 to 8:30 in the morning and from 4:00 to 6:00 in the evening. See Lincoln, Orderly Book, 3 February 1779.

52. BLP no. 3: Lincoln to Elbert, 25 January 1779.

53. There were specific rum allotments for certain contingents of the forces sta-tioned at Purrysburg (officers, artilleryman, sailors). This discretionary treatment may have generated ill will and contentiousness in the camp. See BLP no. 3: Lincoln to Bee, 17 March 1779 and 8 April 1779; Grimke Order Book, 24 and 27 January 1779.

54. Grimke Order Book, 18 February 1779; Candler, *CRG*, 13:748 and 14:169.

55. Moultrie, *Memoirs*, 1:275–76, quoted in Campbell, *Journal of an Expedition*, 118.

56. BLP no. 3: Lincoln to Washington, 7 February 1779.

57. Ibid., no. 3: Lincoln to Washington, 5 January 1779.

58. Ibid., no. 2: Drayton to Lincoln, 25 December 1778; BLP no. 3: Lincoln to Drayton, 12 and 20 January and 1 and 7 February 1779; Lincoln to Lowndes, 12 and 28 January 1779; Lincoln to Elbert 27 January 1779; Lincoln to Ashe, 30 January 1779.

59. BLP no. 3: Lincoln to Elbert, 31 January 1779; Lincoln to Valentine, 20 January 1779.

60. BLP no. 2: Extract from the minutes of Congress, 30 November 1778.

61. Regarding the filing and processing of these claims, see Helen Craig Carson, "Notes and News from the Archives: Accounts Audited of Claims Growing out of the Revolution," SCHM 75 (July 1974): 201–4.

62. The following discussion is drawn from examination of the Comptroller General Accounts Audited: Revolutionary War Claims for the Winkler family, the Stroubharts, David Wanderly, David Saussy, David Mongin, Abraham Ravot, Abraham Binninger, Jane Donnam Bourguin, John Baptiste Bourguin, John Lewis Bourguin, John L., David, and Benjamin Buche, Philip Christian, Abraham and Henry Gindrat, Gideon Mallett, Cornelius Dupont, David Giroud, and Mr. Gasman, SCDAH. The monetary values in the following paragraphs as well as in table 10 are in pounds sterling unless otherwise noted.

63. Note Eugene R. Fingerhut's article "Uses and Abuses of the American Loyalists' Claims: A Critique of Quantitative Analysis," *William and Mary Quarterly,* 3rd ser., 25 (April 1968): 245–58, on the pitfalls of overusing this type of data to make generalizations concerning economic and social life in the Revolutionary era.

64. Beeman, *Evolution of the Southern Backcountry*, 170.

65. BLP no. 3: "An Account of Provisions Purchased by Peter Mallett in South Carolina for the Use of Northern Troops," 2 February 1779; Mallett to Lincoln 4 February 1779; Drayton to Lincoln, 13 March 1779; McHugo to Lincoln, 20 March and 21 April 1779.

66. Kilgo, *Pipe Creek*, 23.

67. BLP no. 3: Lincoln to Bee, 16 April 1779.

68. BLP no. 3: "Deposition of Robert McGinnis," 12 January 1779; Lincoln to Rutledge, 23 February 1779; Campbell, *Journal of an Expedition*, xii, 39–41, 45,

49; Moultrie, *Memoirs*, 1:262, 264, cited in Campbell, *Journal of an Expedition*, 114; Pancake, *This Destructive War*, 32–33; Lumpkin, *From Savannah to Yorktown*, 29–30.

69. Pancake, *This Destructive War*, 33; Lumpkin, *From Savannah to Yorktown*, 30.

70. BLP no. 3: Lincoln to Rutledge, 4 March 1779; Lincoln to Jay, 7 March 1779; Rutherford to Lincoln, 24 March 1779; Grimke Order Book, 28 February 1779 and following and Court of Inquiry at Purrysburg, 13 March 1779; Lincoln, Orderly Book, 9 March 1779 and 19 March 1779. For a detailed analysis of the defeat and contemporary accounts of the battle, see William E. Coxe, ed., "Brigadier General John Ashe's Defeat in the Battle of Brier Creek," *GHQ* 57 (Summer 1973): 295–302, and "Journals of Lieut. Col. Stephen Kemble," 1–247, in *Collections of the New York Historical Society for the Year 1883*, vol. 16, *The Kemble Papers*, vol. 1, *1773–1789* (New York: printed for the Society, 1884), 175–76. See also C. F. W. Coker, ed., "Journal of John Graham, South Carolina Militia, 1779," *Military Collector and Historian*, 19 (Summer 1967): 47; Lumpkin, *From Savannah to Yorktown*, 30–31; Pancake, *This Destructive War*, 33.

71. Campbell, *Journal of an Expedition*, 74.

72. BLP no. 3: "Council of War at Purrysburg," 4 and 5 March 1779.

73. Ibid., no. 3: White to Lincoln, 2 and 6 January 1779; Lincoln to Mulligan 19 March 1779; Campbell, *Journal of an Expedition*, xv. White had under his command the galleys *Congress* and *Lee* and other naval vessels, including a powder sloop saved after the fall of Savannah.

74. BLP no. 3: Melven to Lincoln, 13 February 1779; Lincoln to Mulligan, 19 March 1779; Lincoln to Rutledge, 22 March 1779; Lincoln to Bee, 24 March 1779; Drayton to Lincoln, 24 March 1779; Lincoln to Jay, 2 April 1779; Carpenter, "Purrysburg, South Carolina," 5; Summerall, "Address," 43.

75. Pinckney to Lincoln, 26 March 1779, SCL; BLP no. 3: Winson to Lincoln, 27 April 1779; Gordon, *South Carolina and the Revolution*, 64–65. George C. Rogers Jr. contends that the Huguenots of St. Peter's Parish, Purrysburg, provided an important bulwark against British intentions in the state. See Rogers, "Huguenots of the Old Beaufort District," 11.

76. BLP no. 3: Lincoln to Lowndes, 10 February 1779; "Lincoln's Instructions to General Rutherford," 10 February 1779; Lincoln to Bull, 26 March 1779; Lincoln to Rutledge, 1 April 1779.

77. Pinckney to Lincoln, 26 March 1779, SCL.

78. BLP no. 3: Lincoln to Saunders, 5 April 1779.

79. Ibid., no. 3: Lincoln to Armstrong, 5 April 1779.

80. Campbell, *Journal of an Expedition*, 33–34. Campbell misidentifies General Lincoln as the officer "parading 1000 Continental troops within 800 yards of the ferry." Lincoln did not arrive at the Purrysburg post until 3 January. The commander may have been General Howe drilling the soldiers, perhaps to keep up morale. The estimate of 1,000 Continentals is probably somewhat high considering the crushing defeat just inflicted upon American forces under Howe at Savannah.

81. BLP no. 3: Cater to J. L. Bourguin, 21 January 1779.

82. Ibid., no. 3: Stafford to Lincoln, 21 February 1779.

83. Ibid., no. 3: Lincoln to Ashe, 3 March 1779.

84. Ibid., no. 3: Pinckney to Lincoln, 30 March 1779.

85. Ibid., no. 3: Dillon to J. L. Bourguin, (no date) April 1779.

86. Ibid., no. 3: Moultrie to Lincoln, 24 April 1779; Coker, "Journal of John Graham," 42; Corkran, *Indian Frontier*, 69. For the role of the Catawba Indians in the Revolution, see Douglas Summers Brown, *The Catawba Indians: The People of the River* (Columbia: University of South Carolina Press, 1966), 252–80, and Charles M. Hudson, *The Catawba Nation* (Athens: University of Georgia Press, 1970), 51, 110–11.

87. BLP no. 3: Lincoln to Lovell, 12 April 1779.

88. Ibid., no. 3: Lincoln to Bull, 13 April 1779; Lincoln to Moultrie, 22 April 1779; Lincoln to Rutledge, 23 April 1779.

89. Sources for this and the following paragraph are BLP no. 3: Moultrie to Lincoln, 29 April, 30 April 1:00 P.M. and 8:00 P.M., and 5 May 1779; Lincoln to Moultrie, 30 April, 2 and 6 May 1779; Lincoln to Rutledge, 2 May 1779; Lincoln to Mayson, 9 May 1779; Lincoln to Walton, 10 May 1779; Lincoln to Jay, 4 June 1779; Cooper and McCord, *Statutes at Large*, 8:150, quoted in Howe, *History of the Presbyterian Church*, 1:479; Kenneth Coleman, *The American Revolution in Georgia, 1763–1789* (Athens: University of Georgia Press, 1958), 128; Russell F. Weigley, *The Partisan War: The South Carolina Campaign of 1780–1782* (Columbia: University of South Carolina Press, 1970), 13; Pancake, *This Destructive War*, 34, 60, 63, 65–66; Lumpkin, *From Savannah to Yorktown*, 31–40; Gordon, *South Carolina and the American Revolution*, 67–69.

90. Bernhard A. Uhlendorf, ed. and trans., "Diary of Captain Johann Hinrichs, 104–317, in *The Siege of Charleston, With An Account of the Province of South Carolina: Diaries and Letters of Hessian Officers . . .* (Ann Arbor: University of Michigan Press, 1938), 180–81, n. 2. See also Gordon, *South Carolina and the American Revolution*, 69.

91. Uhlendorf, "Diary of Hinrichs," 179.

92. John Shy, "British Strategy for Pacifying the Southern Colonies, 1778–1781," 155–73, in Crow and Tise, eds., *Southern Experience*, 158–59 and passim. Note also Paul H. Smith, *Loyalists and Redcoats: A Study in British Revolutionary Policy* (Chapel Hill: University of North Carolina Press, 1964); Pancake, *This Destructive* War, 33, 244; Robert McCluer Calhoon, *The Loyalists in Revolutionary America, 1760–1781* (New York: Harcourt Brace Jovanovich, 1965); Weigley, *Partisan War*, 8–9, 244.

93. One hundred thirty-seven skirmishes, battles, or military actions took place in South Carolina over the course of the war. Of these, 103 were fought between patriot and loyalist South Carolina factions. South Carolinians made up at least part of the military force of either or both sides in twenty other engagements. Ninety-Six District alone accounted for nearly one-third of the total number of battles. See Francisco de Miranda, *The New Democracy in America: Travels of Francisco de Miranda in the United States, 1783–1784*, ed. John S. Ezell and trans. Judson P. Wood (Norman: University of Oklahoma Press, 1963), 24.

94. Nadelhaft, *Disorders of War* graphically details the destruction of the war. Note especially 61–62, 66, 73, 80. See also "Diary of Hinrichs, 179–81; Coker, "Journal of John Graham," 43–44.

95. BLP no. 3: Lincoln to Williamson, 1 May 1779.
96. "Diary of Hinrichs," 151.

Chapter Eight

1. Klien, *Unification of a Slave State*, 305.

2. Charles Gregg Singer, *South Carolina in the Confederation* (Philadelphia: University of Pennsylvania Press, 1941), 13–15; Beeman, *Evolution of the Backcountry*, 158.

3. Nadelhaft, *Disorders of War*, 62, 129.

4. J. L. Bourquin Jr. to Joachim Hartstone, 14 March 1787, quoted in Olwell, *Masters, Slaves, and Subjects*, 279.

5. David Saussy received reimbursement for a variety of requisitioned supplies, and John Morgandollar's (Morgantaller) wagon was borrowed. Captains John L. Buche and Jacob Winkler of the township took part in the operation. See Governor's Message, no. 459, 1786–1788, SCDAH; Comptroller General Accounts Audited, David Saussy and John Morgandollar, SCDAH. Quotation from *The Gazette of the State of Georgia*, 26 April 1787, hereafter cited as *GSG*.

6. *GSG*, 26 April 1787.

7. Governor's Message, no. 459, 1786–1788, SCDAH.

8. Sources for these first two paragraphs are Nadelhaft, *Disorders of War*, 77–79, 87–88, 105–42, 216. Edward McCrady, *The History of South Carolina in the Revolution, 1780–1783* (New York: Macmillan, 1902), 555–69; Jerome Nadelhaft, "Ending South Carolina's War: Two 1782 Agreements Favoring the Planters," *SCHM* 80 (January 1979): 50. Ella Pettit Levett, "Loyalism in Charlestown, 1761–1784," *Proceedings of the South Carolina Historical Society* 6 (1936): 15; General Assembly Papers, 3 December 1792, SCDAH.

9. Jean Baptiste Bourguin died in late 1783 in his midnineties, having lived for more than fifty years in Purrysburg. His obituary ran in South Carolina and Georgia newspapers. See *South Carolina Weekly Gazette*, 20 January 1784, quoted in "Notes Relative to Bourguin and Kelsall," *THSSC* 75 (1970): 214; *GSG*, 4 December 1783.

10. Commissioners of Forfeited Estates—Claims on Estates: *John Linder, Sr. vs. David Saussy, George Keal, Thomas Cooper, John B. Bourguin, Samuel Stirk; John Linder, Jr. vs. Estate of John Buche, Estate of Adrian Mayer, John Stroubhart, Capt. Thomas Budd, Thomas Cooper*, SCDAH.

11. Commissioners of Forfeited Estates—Claims on Estates: *J. L. Bourguin vs. John Linder, Sr. and John Linder, Jr.*, SCDAH.

12. Commissioners of Forfeited Estates—Sales at Jacksonburg, Pocotaligo, and Charleston, SCDAH; Holcomb, *Deed Abstracts, 1783–1788*, 56; Michael E. Stevens, ed, *The State Records of South Carolina: Journals of the House of Representatives, 1792–1794* (Columbia: University of South Carolina Press, 1988), 73, hereafter cited as Stevens, *JHR*, 1792–94.

13. Holcomb, *Deed Abstracts, 1783–1788*, 134, 142, 280–81, 308; *GSG*, 10 April 1788; Court of Chancery Papers, Bundle 1788–1799, no. 2, *John D. Mongin v. Joseph Fickling*, SCDAH.

14. Court of Chancery Papers, Bundle 1788–1799, no. 9, *Powell, Hopton & Co. vs. Lewis B. Keall, executor of David Keall*; Holcomb, *Deed Abstracts, 1783–1788*, 411.

15. John Lewis Bourguin also served as administrator of Mary Ann's estate as her "nearest friend." See Court of Ordinary Records, 1771–1775, cited in "Notes Relative to Bourguin and Kelsall," 214.

16. The preceding discussion of the administration and disbursement of David Mongin's estate is taken from the Court of Chancery Papers, Bundle 1788–1799, no. 10, *Jane Godfrey vs. William Mongin, executor of David Mongin*, SCDAH and other sources as noted.

17. MR, 2U:152–53; Edwards, *Journals of the Privy Council*, 125, 171.

18. General Assembly Papers, 1787, SCDAH.

19. Michael E. Stevens, ed. and Christine M. Allen, asst. ed., *The State Records of South Carolina: Journals of the House of Representatives, 1791* (Columbia: University of South Carolina Press, 1985), 97–98, hereafter cited as Stevens and Allen, *JHR*, 1791; General Assembly Papers, 25 June 1791.

20. Stevens, *JHR*, 1792–94:510.

21. William Bartram, *Travels through North and South Carolina, Georgia, East and West Florida* (Charlottesville: University Press of Virginia; 1980 facsimile of the 1792 edition), 28; Merrens, "Journal of Hazard,"177, 187–89; Davis, *Fledgling Province*, 45; "Journal of Simpson," quoted in Howe, *History of the Presbyterian Church*, 1:468; Archibald Henderson, *Washington's Southern Tour, 1791* (Boston: Houghton Mifflin, 1923), 203, 205–6 (quotation); *GSG*, 12 May 1791; Lowcountry Council, *Historic Resources*, 172; Perry, *Moving Finger of Jasper*, 13; John and Janet Stegeman, "President Washington at Mulberry Grove," *GHQ* 61 (Winter 1977): 342; Carpenter, "Purrysburg, South Carolina," 6; Shipp, *History of Methodism*, 214–15.

22. Castiglioni, *Viaggio*, 123, 125; La Rochefoucauld Liancourt, *Travels through the United States of America*, 602–3; John Melish, *Travels through the United States of America in the Years 1806 and 1807, and 1809, 1810, and 1811 . . .*, 2 vols. (Philadelphia: Printed by G. Palmer for J. Melish, 1815), 1:23, 280, 290; Ruby A. Rahn, *River Highway for Trade: The Savannah* (Savannah: U.S. Corps of Engineers, 1968), 41; John Davis, *Travels of Four Years and a Half in the United States of America during 1798, 1799, 1800, 1801, and 1802*, with an introduction and notes by A. J. Morrison (New York: Henry Holt, 1909), 66–67; Lambert, *Travels through Lower Canada and the United States of North America*, 3:27–29.

23. Ruby Rahn lists Purrysburg as one of the first of the Savannah River landings to become well-known along with Ebenezer, Abercorn, Mt. Pleasant, Sisters Ferry, Hudson's Ferry, and Silver Bluff. See Rahn, *River Highway*, 11–12.

24. *The Daily Georgian*, 10 May 1824, 24 June 1824; *Savannah Georgian*, 5–7, 9–10 January 1826, 20 July 1826; *Savannah Daily Georgian*, 16 April 1827; Rahn, *River Highway*, 27.

25. *The Daily Georgian*, 24 June 1824; *Savannah Republican*, 3 November 1825, 7 December 1825; *Savannah Georgian*, 5–7, 9–10 January 1826, 18, 20 July 1826, 17 August 1826, 27 October 1826, 8 November 1826; *Savannah Daily Georgian*, 16 April 1827; *The Georgian*, 25 November 1829.

26. Lambert, *Travels through Lower Canada and the United States of North America*, 3:1–2, 20–22, 25–27 (quotation).

27. Ibid., 3:27.

28. Ibid., 3:27–28.

29. Ibid., 3:28–29.

30. Ibid., 3:29–30.

31. Ibid., 3:30.

32. Ibid., 3:61.

33. Perry, "The Lost Settlement of Purrysburg." Quotation from Perry, *Moving Finger of Jasper*, 15.

34. Election managers for Purrysburg from 1791 to 1846:1791—Joachim Hartstone and Peter Porcher Jr. (Stevens and Allen, *JHR*, 1791:439; 1793—Peter Porcher and Captain John Jones (Stevens, *JHR*, 1792–94:446–48; 1836—W. N. Hurdy and A. A. Bush (General Assembly Papers, 21 December 1836); 1837—W. W. Harder and A. A. Bush (General Assembly Papers, December 1837); 1843—Augustus Bush and John Middleton (General Assembly Papers, 19 December 1843); 1844—Hezekiah Strobhart, Christopher L. Cook, John Middleton, and Augustus Bush—New River and Purrysburg (General Assembly Papers, 16 December 1844; 1846—Christopher Cook, Hezekiah Strobhart, and Washington Pelotte (General Assembly Papers, 24 November 1846).

35. In addition to references already cited, sources for this and the previous paragraph are Rowland, "Eighteenth Century Beaufort," 346; *U.S. Gazetteer* cited in the Floyd Papers, CGHS; Richard Xavier Evans, "Robert Mills' Letter on South Carolina, 1804," *SCHGM* 39 (July 1938): 111–12; General Assembly Papers, petition of 15 November 1822; "Population Schedules of the First Census of the United States, 1790: Rhode Island, South Carolina, Vermont, Virginia, and 1840 Census of Pensioners for Revolutionary or Military Services" (Washington, D.C.: National Archives and Records Service—General Services Administration, 1960); "1824 Tax Returns," SCDAH.

36. MR, 3Y:145–46; Samuel Gaillard Stoney, ed., "The Autobiography of William John Grayson," *SCHGM* 49 (January 1948): 29–30; Perry, *Moving Finger of Jasper*, 43–44. Adam Rothman of Georgetown University has recently argued that some slaves, such as this informant, betrayed fellow slaves out of antagonism, prudence, or a hope of reward. See Adam Rothman, "'Servile Deceit' and the Limits of Slave Resistance in the United States." Paper delivered at the Southern Historical Association Meeting, 5 November 2004, Memphis, Tennessee. The reason for this conspirator's change of heart is unknown.

37. *The Royal Georgia Gazette*, 15 March 1781; *GSG*, 22 May 1783, 29 May 1783, 11 March 1784; *Columbian Museum and Savannah Advertiser*, 28 April 1797, 5 October 1798; *The Republican and Savannah Evening Ledger*, 26 February 1811. John Stroubhar's knowledge of his slaves' country of origin and the description of Cupper's slave as having "a yellowish complexion" bear further witness that township landholders, like other South Carolina slave owners, recognized differences between African tribal/ethnic groups. See Littlefield, *Rice and Slaves*, 8–9.

38. Barnwell and Webber, "St. Helena's Parish Register," *SCHGM* 23 (January 1922): 24; History Committee, *Parish Church of St. Helena*, 53; Dalcho, *History of the Protestant Episcopal Church*, 386, 465–573.

39. This may have been the same John Beck who petitioned the South Carolina legislature to be allowed to run a stage line from Charleston to Savannah using his ferry as "the present route is thought extremely inconvenient by reason of water passage from Savannah to Purrysburg being twenty-four miles distance and the passage rather difficult in the winter season." See General Assembly Papers, n.d., SCDAH.

40. Robert Adams to Dr. Buist, 1807, quoted in Beck, "Purrysburg as It Is Today," 43–44; Howe, *History of the Presbyterian Church*, 1:578; Johnston, *Two Centuries of Lawtonville Baptists*, 18. On the revivals of the early nineteenth century, see John B. Boles, *The Great Revival, 1787–1805* (Lexington: University Press of Kentucky, 1972); Klien, *Unification of a Slave State*, 282; the Reverend William M. Baker, *The Life and Labours of the Rev. Daniel Baker, D. D.: Pastor and Evangelist* (Philadelphia: William S. and Alfred Martien, 1858), 155–67; History Committee, *Parish Church of St. Helena*, 99–105.

41. *GSG*, 13 May 1790.

42. Court of Chancery Papers, Bundle 1788–1799, no. 10, *Jane Godfrey vs. William Mongin, executor of David Mongin.*

43. General Assembly of South Carolina Free School Reports (Reports of the Commissioners of Free Schools, 1818–1863, SCDAH.

44. Rahn, *River Highway*, 42. Johnson published two maps of North and South Carolina in 1862. One was a cooperative effort with a colleague named Browning showing "Purisburg," and another published in New York contained both a "Perrysburg"and a "Purysburg." See "Johnson's Map of North and South Carolina," A. J. Johnson (New York, 1862). Supporting the erroneous contention that there was no town of Purrysburg by the 1830s is the fact that neither "Purrysburg" nor any variant appears on the 1839 "Map of the Southern States" drawn and enlarged by Stiles, Sherman, and Smith. See also the land plat for John P. Raymond, 25 April 1852, library of the Huguenot Society of South Carolina.

45. Lowcountry Council, *Historic Resources*, 174; Perry, *Moving Finger of Jasper*, 13–14, 62–63. The Purrysburg jugwell was first mentioned in an 1862 letter Bostick wrote. See Lowcountry Council, *Historic Resources*, 183; Lepionka, "Purrysburg: An Archeological Survey," 5.

46. John Bennett Walters, *Merchant of Terror: General Sherman and Total War* (Indianapolis: Bobbs-Merrill, 1973), 74; see also 68, 82.

47. Walters, *Merchant of Terror*, 82–83; John G. Barrett, *Sherman's March through the Carolinas* (Chapel Hill: University of North Carolina Press, 1956), 39. On officer sentiment with regard to the South Carolina campaign, see Major General H. W. Halleck to Major General W. T. Sherman, 18 December 1864, and Sherman's reply to Halleck, 24 December 1864, both in General William T. Sherman, *Personal Memoirs of Gen. W. T. Sherman*, 3rd ed., rev. and corrected, 2 vols. (New York: Charles L. Webster and Company, 1890), 2:222–23, 226–28; Walters, *Merchant of Terror*, 188. On the thoughts of the enlisted men, see Captain David Power Conyngham, *Sherman's March through the South with Sketches and Incidents of the Campaign* (New York: Sheldon and Company, 1865), 310–11; Walters, *Merchant of Terror*, 188; Sherman, *Personal Memoirs*, 2:254.

48. Quotations from Sherman, *Personal Memoirs*, 2:239–40. See also Walters, *Merchant of Terror*, 185; Barrett, *Sherman's March*, 40–41; Conyngham, *Sherman's March*, 301–3.

49. Barrett, *Sherman's March*, 36–37; William Greer Albergotti III, "Purrysburg—Not Death but Murder," *THSSC* 108 (2004): 107–8.

50. Barrett, *Sherman's March*, 45–46 (quotation); Walters, *Merchant of Terror*, 186–87.

51. Walters, *Merchant of Terror*, 185, 187; Albergotti, "Not Death but Murder," 108.

52. Sherman, *Personal Memoirs*, 2:241 (quotation); Barrett, *Sherman's March*, 46. Many have argued that the town of Purrysburg disappeared long before the outbreak of war, but it was still a viable entity until February 1865. Size did not equate with viability as a contemporary description of nearby Hardeeville makes clear. See Joseph LeConte, *'Ware Sherman? A Journal of Three Months' Personal Experience in the Last Days of the Confederacy; with an Introductory Reminiscence by His Daughter Caroline LeConte* (Berkeley: University of California Press, 1937), 4. See also Albergotti, *Albergotti Creek*, 77.

53. Conyngham, *Sherman's March*, 310–11.

54. Ibid., 310.

55. Walters, *Merchant of Terror*, 192–204; Barrett, *Sherman's March*, 52–56, LeConte, *'Ware Sherman?*, 81.

56. Perry, *Moving Finger of Jasper*, 14.

57. Perry, "The Lost Settlement of Purrysburg," 3-C; Perry, *Moving Finger of Jasper*, 14; Lowcountry Council, *Historic Resources*, quoting Pierre Robert's 1879 article on Purrysburg in the *Hampton Guardian*; "Map of the State of South Carolina" issued by the Department of Agriculture of South Carolina, 1883, SCDAH.

58. Muench, "Story of Purysburg," 10.

59. Rowland notes that Purry was poisoned by the slave, but Glen's proclamation said that Purry "was forced by violence from his house and then strangled, stabbed in the breast with a knife and thrown into a creek, his body having been found with several marks of violence upon it four foot deep in the water and about thirty-three pounds of small shot tied up in bags and made fast to different parts of it." See MR 2K:77–78; Rowland, *History of Beaufort County*, 120.

60. Inventory of Lewis Quinche, 21 April 1764.

61. *The Republican and Savannah Evening Ledger*, 19 February 1811; Rogers, "Beaufort," 11–14; Rowland, *History of Beaufort County*, 120, 190; Lowcountry Council, *Historic Resources*, 26, 59; Perry, *Moving Finger of Jasper*, 8, 19, 24, 33, 42–43, 45–46, 59–60, 124, 128, 142, 166–67; *Yemassee Bluff News*, 23 May 2006.

62. *GSG*, 29 May 1783, 25 September 1783, 4 and 11 December 1783, 11 March 1784; *Columbian Museum and Savannah Advertiser*, 13 April 1798; Hawes, *Journal of Zubly*, 1, n. 41, 74; *Columbian Museum and Savannah Daily Gazette*, 10 April 1817; *The Republican and Savannah Evening Ledger*, 19 February 1811, 1 September 1812, 17 December 1812 (quotation); Muench, "Story of Purysburg," 10. The last of the original 1730s settlers to expire appears to have been Mrs. Agnes Parker (maiden name unknown), who had moved to Savannah. She was nearly eighty years old when she died in October 1792. See *The Georgia Gazette*, 25 October 1792.

63. Such an attitude toward community solidarity was not unknown even after significant political and social upheaval. The Rutmans discovered a similar response by Middlesex County neighbors following Bacon's Rebellion, and the Poughkeepsie community acted likewise in the wake of the Revolution. See Rutman and Rutman, *A Place in Time*, 86, 92; Jonathan Clark, "The Problem of Allegiance in Revolutionary Poughkeepsie," 285–317, in David Hall, John M. Murrin, and Thad Tate, eds., *Saints and Revolutionaries: Essays in Early American History* (New York: W. W. Norton, 1984).

Conclusion

1. Bender, *Community and Social Change*, 7.

2. Beaver, *Rural Communities in the Appalachian South*, 1. George Fenwick Jones is the latest of many historians who have labeled the township a "failure." See Jones, introduction to *Reports* 8:iii.

3. Rutman and Rutman, *A Place in Time*, 22; Rutman, "Social Web," 58–60.

4. Bender, *Community and Social Change*, 7.

5. Ibid., 7, 122.

6. Earle, "Evolution of a Tidewater Settlement System," 6.

7. Rutman and Rutman, *A Place in Time*, 120.

8. Richard Beeman discovered the same phenomenon operating in Lunenburg County, Virginia, at roughly the same time. See Beeman, *Evolution of the Southern Backcountry*, 11, 13.

9. The terms *commercial community* and *commercial agricultural community* are taken from Darrett Rutman's discussion and his quotation of Jackson Turner Main in "Social Web," 80–81. My labeling of Charles Town as a commercial community and Purrysburg as a commercial agricultural community is my own construction.

10. Rogers, *History of Georgetown County*, 218.

11. Bender, *Community and Social Change*, 70.

12. Bailyn and Morgan, *Strangers within the Realm*, 27.

13. Wsevolod W. Isajiw, "Definitions of Ethnicity," *Ethnicity* 1 (1974): 111. Social scientists have also been found guilty on this count. See Raymond E. Wolfinger, "The Development and Persistence of Ethnic Voting," *American Political Science Review* 59 (December 1965): 896–908. Note Michael Parenti's critical rejoinder "Ethnic Politics and the Persistence of Ethnic Identification," *American Political Science Review* 61 (September 1967): 717–26.

14. Isajiw, "Definitions of Ethnicity," 112.

15. George De Vos, "Ethnic Pluralism: Conflict and Accommodation," in George De Vos and Lola Romanucci-Ross, eds., *Ethnic Identity: Cultural Continuities and Change* (Palo Alto, Calif.: Mayfield, 1976), 17; Barth, *Ethnic Groups and Boundaries*, 11; Andrew Greeley, *Ethnicity in the United States: A Preliminary Reconnaissance* (New York: John Wiley and Sons, 1974), 291; idem, "Ethnicity as an Influence on Behavior," in Otto Feinstein, ed., *Ethnic Groups in the City: Culture, Institutions, and Power* (Lexington, Mass.: D. C. Heath; Heath Lexington Books, 1971), 4; Joe R. Feagin, *Racial and Ethnic Relations* (Englewood Cliffs, N.J.: Prentice-Hall, 1978), 9; Richard Kolm, "Ethnicity in Society and Community," in *Ethnic Groups*, 65.

16. Maldwyn A. Jones, *American Immigration* (Chicago: University of Chicago Press, 1960), 51. Jon Butler's monograph on the Huguenots comes close to the same conclusion.

17. Carl N. Degler, *Out of Our Past: The Forces That Shaped Modern America*, rev. ed. (New York: Harper and Row, 1970), 296.

18. Isajiw, "Definitions of Ethnicity," 115.

19. George De Vos and Lola Romanucci-Ross, "Preface," in *Ethnic Identity*, vi; De Vos, "Ethnic Pluralism," 17; Sister Francis Jerome Woods, C.D.P., *Cultural Values of American Ethnic Groups* (New York: Harper and Brothers., 1956), 12; Daniel Bell, "Ethnicity and Social Change," in Nathan Glazer and Daniel P. Moynihan, eds.,

Ethnicity: Theory and Practice (Cambridge, Mass.: Harvard University Press, 1975), 153, 159.

20. Amy Chua, *World on Fire: How Exporting Free Market Democracy Breeds Ethnic Hatred and Global Instability* (New York: Anchor Books, 2004); note especially 14–15, 69, 72, 120–21, 185, 217, 236, 290.

21. Abner Cohen, "Introduction," in Abner Cohen, ed., *Urban Ethnicity* (London: Tavistock Publications, 1974), x; William G. Lockwood, "Introduction," in William G. Lockwood, ed., *Beyond Ethnic Boundaries: New Approaches in the Anthropology of Ethnicity*, Michigan Discussions in Anthropology, vol. 7 (Ann Arbor: University of Michigan Department of Anthropology, 1984), 3–4.

22. Isajiw, "Definitions of Ethnicity," 122.

23. David Schneider from *American Kinship*, cited in Talcott Parsons, "Some Theoretical Considerations on the Nature and Trends of Change in Ethnicity," in Glazer and Moynihan, *Ethnicity: Theory and Practice*, 65; Glazer and Moynihan, *Ethnicity: Theory and Practice*, 18.

24. Handlin, *The Uprooted*, 194.

25. Gordon Allport, cited in Donald L. Horowitz, "Ethnic Identity," in *Ethnicity: Theory and Practice*, 120.

26. Greeley, *Ethnicity in the U.S.*, 297; De Vos, "Ethnic Pluralism," 8, 15–16; Isajiw, "Definitions of Ethnicity," 121.

27. Schneider, cited in Parsons, "Theoretical Considerations," 66; Bell, "Ethnicity and Social Change," 171. See also Herbert J. Gans, "Symbolic Ethnicity: The Future of Ethnic Groups and Cultures in America," *Ethnic and Racial Studies* 2 (January 1979): 1–20.

28. "Journal of Rev. Joseph Pilmoor," quoted in Shipp, *History of Methodism*, 130. On the disappearance of French Huguenot ethnicity by the Revolutionary era, see Hirsch, *Huguenots of Colonial South Carolina*, 261.

29. Rowland, "Eighteenth Century Beaufort," 328–29.

30. General Assembly Papers, "Petition of the Presbyterian Congregation in the Town of Purysburg, St. Peter's Parish, 7 February 1789; *Yemassee Bluff News*, 23 May 2006; Perry, *Moving Finger of Jasper,* 15; Emory L. Jarrott and Robert L. Bass, transcribers, "Transcription of Epitaphs and Inscriptions, Strobhar Cemetery, Jasper County, South Carolina, Savannah River–Oakatee, Purrysburgh Section," 29 December 1976, SCL. Note also the Dupont cemetery inscriptions in the same document.

31. Jane H. Pease and William H. Pease, *A Family of Women: The Carolina Petigrus in Peace and War* (Chapel Hill: University of North Carolina Press, 1999), 9, 11–12 (quotation); Lowcountry Council, *Historic Resources*, 174.

32. Rowland, "Alone on the River," 134; Jane and William Pease, *Family of Women*, 12–13, 15–16, 18, 21.

33. Petigru's laudatory remarks read in part: "Though the Huguenots have been scattered far and wide and given proof in every clime of the power that abides with sincere religious faith, nowhere, it is believed, have they been more conspicuous,—and nowhere has the sentiment of honor so characteristic of their race, been cherished with more devotion than in South Carolina." CSCHS 2:16.

34. Rogers, "Huguenots of the Old Beaufort District," 3; Amy E. Friedlander, "Carolina Huguenots: A Study in Cultural Pluralism in the Low Country, 1679–1768"

(Ph.D. dissertation, Emory University 1979). Marjorie Stratford Mendenhall in her 1940 Ph.D. dissertation argued that ethnic characteristics of the white immigrants to South Carolina contributed to the vitality and commercial success of the young state between 1790 and 1860. See Marjorie Stratford Mendenhall, "A History of Agriculture in South Carolina, 1790–1860" (Ph.D. dissertation, University of North Carolina, 1940), 1.

35. Weinreich, *Languages in Contact*, 84, 92, 97.

36. Joyner, *Down by the Riverside*, xx–xxii. Joyner also notes the difficulty in assessing the importance or direction of linguistic change. See 203. Smith found much the same mutuality in the creolization of white and black cultures in Georgia. See Julia Floyd Smith, *Slavery and Rice Culture in Low Country Georgia, 1750–1860* (Knoxville: University of Tennessee Press, 1985), 181–82.

37. William G. Lockwood, "An Exploratory Comparison of Language and Religion as Criteria of Ethnic Affiliation," 85–86, in Lockwood, *Beyond Ethnic Boundaries*, 85–98.

38. Johnson's study of the settlement of the Cheraws District of the upper Pee Dee is perhaps illustrative on this point.

39. Taylor, *Dutchmen by the Bay*, 20, 22, 37–38, 41–42.

40. Collins, *White Society*, x, 11, 182; Beeman, *Evolution of the Southern Backcountry*, 13.

41. Note especially Beeman, *Evolution of the Southern Backcountry*, 139. Collins's implicit argument is that since such a high percentage of southerners in 1860 had been born in the Deep South (92.7 percent, in the case of South Carolina), this fact in effect meant that they were ethnically uniform and "Southernism . . . flourished amidst a uniformity in ethnic mix." See Collins, *White Society*, 187.

42. I am indebted to Lawrence Taylor for this excellent analogy. See Taylor, *Dutchmen by the Bay*, 30.

Bibliography

Archival and Genealogical Sources

The Georgia Historical Society, Savannah, Georgia

The M. H. and D. B. Floyd Papers.

Hargrett Rare Book and Manuscript Library, University of Georgia, Athens, Georgia

Agreement between Jean Pierre Purry and James Edward Oglethorpe, 4 December 1731. Copy of the French original and English translation.

The Huntington Library, San Marino, California

The Orderly Book of General Benjamin Lincoln, HM 659, microfilmed copy.

John Ford Bell Library, University of Minnesota, Minneapolis, Minnesota

Novissima et perfectissima Africae descripto (Carel Allard, 1696).

Library of the Genealogical Society, Church of Jesus Christ of Latter-Day Saints, Salt Lake City, Utah

South Carolina Land Grants, Colonial Series, 1731–76, 56 volumes, microfilmed copies.

South Carolina Inventories of Estates, 1736–82, microfilmed copies.

South Carolina Miscellaneous Records, Main Series, 1671–1973, 153 volumes, microfilmed copies.

South Carolina Wills, 1736–1782, microfilmed copies of CWA Transcripts.

Library of the Huguenot Society of South Carolina, Charleston, South Carolina

Davis, Harry Alexander. *Some Huguenot Families of South Carolina and Georgia.* N.p., 1926.

———. *The Gindrat Family: A Supplement to Some Huguenot Families of South Carolina and Georgia*. Washington, D.C., 1933.

———. *Some Huguenot Families of South Carolina and Georgia, Supplement No.* 2. Washington, D.C., 1937.

———. *Some Huguenot Families of South Carolina and Georgia, Supplement No.* 3. Washington, D.C., 1940.

Land Plat for John P. Raymond, 25 April 1852.

Typescript copy of Alexandra Morrison Carpenter, "Purrysburg, South Carolina." Address presented to the Colonial Dames of Georgia, 13 May 1930.

Massachusetts Historical Society, Boston, Massachusetts

Benjamin Lincoln Papers. Microfilm, 13 reels.

National Library of Australia, Canberra, Australia

Bellin, Jacques. *Carte réduite des terres australes*. Paris: Chez Didot, 1753.

Bowen, Emanuel. *A Complete Map of the Southern Continent,* 1744.

O. T. Wallace County Office Building, Charleston, South Carolina

Records of Mesne Conveyance (Charleston Deeds).

South Carolina Department of Archives and History, Columbia, South Carolina

Colonial Land Grants (Copy Series). Vols. 41 and 42. Also known as the Township Grants.

Colonial Land Plats, recorded copies, 1731–75, 21 volumes.
Commissioners of Forfeited Estates: Claims on Estates.
Commissioners of Forfeited Estates: Sales of Estates.
Comptroller General Accounts Audited: Revolutionary War Claims.
Court of Chancery Papers, Bundle 1788–99.
Court of Common Pleas: Judgment Rolls.
General Assembly Papers.
General Assembly of South Carolina Free School Reports (Reports of the Commissioners of Free Schools), 1818–63.
Governor's Message, no. 459, 1786–88.
"Map of the State of South Carolina." Department of Agriculture of South Carolina, 1883.
Military Service Records: Fort Prince George Expedition, October 1759–January 1760.
Miscellaneous Records, Main Series, 1671–1973, 153 volumes.
Purrysbourg Township Plat, n.d., Map Case 5–14. (Digital image, Tillinghast copy —Series S213187).
Purrysburgh Township Plat (Hugh Bryan's map of 1735), Verticle File 4–3. (Digital image, Tillinghast copy—Series S213187).
Purysburgh=Town Plat, ca. 1765, Map Box 11-10. (Digital copy—Series S213187).
Records of Mesne Conveyance (Charleston Deeds), microfilmed copies.
Tax Returns, 1824.
Transcripts of Records Relating to South Carolina in the British Public Records Office, 1685–1790.

South Carolina Historical Society, Charleston, South Carolina
Deed of Gift and Mortgage, the Reverend Joseph Bugnion.
Grimke Order Book.
Hutson Papers, "LaFitte."
Map of South Carolina and a Part of Georgia from the surveys of William Bull, William De Brahm, and John Stuart. Charing Cross, 1780.
Map of South Carolina and a Part of Georgia from the survey of William De Brahm, 1757.
Map showing the subdivisions of Col. Pury's Barony, ca. 1735.
Oscar E. Imer to Monsieur le Secrétaire de la Société d'histoire de Charleston, South Carolina, 18 October 1911.

South Caroliniana Library, University of South Carolina, Columbia, South Carolina
"An Act For encouraging the Manufacture of Silk in this Province, under the Direction of Mr. John Lewis Poyas, for Seven Years, passed by the General Assembly," 11 March 1737/8, copy.
Certificate for David Giroud from the Commune of Petit Bayard, 26 February 1732.
Charles Lee Letterbook.
Extract of a letter, Johnson to Hutcheson, 18 November 1732.
Emory L. Jarrott and Robert L. Bass, transcribers, "Transcriptions of Epitaphs and Inscriptions, Strobhar and Dupont Cemetaries, Jaspar County, SC Savannah River—Oakatee, Purrysburg Section, 29 December 1976.
Fulham Palace Papers: Bishop of London—General Correspondence, 1709–69, microfilm copies.

"The Giroud Family," typescript.
History of the Humbert Family.
"Palmetto Landmarks: Purrysburg." Transcript of radio broadcast by Louise Jones Dubose, 21 November 1948.
Pinckney (Colonel Charles C.) to Benjamin Lincoln, 26 March 1779.
Schweizerische Landesbibliothek, thermofax copies.

Personal Correspondence

William Greer Albergotti III to Arlin C. Migliazzo, 8 December 2002 and 4 June 2003.
Carolyn Holbrook to Arlin C. Migliazzo on the Poyas family, 2 March 2000.

Published Primary Sources

Bandelier, Fanny, trans. "Letter from Carolina." *Catholic Historical Review* 4 (January 1919): 538–39.
Barnwell, Joseph W., and Mabel L. Webber. "St Helena's Parish Register." *South Carolina Historical and Genealogical Magazine* 23 (January 1922): 8–25; (April 1922): 46–71; and (July 1922): 102–51.
Bartram, William. *Travels through North and South Carolina, Georgia, East and West Florida.* Charlottesville: University Press of Virginia, 1980; facsimile of the 1792 edition.
Campbell, Lieutenant Colonel Archibald, Esq. *Journal of an Expedition against the Rebels of Georgia in North America . . .*, edited and introduced by Colin Campbell. Darien, Ga.: Ashantilly Press, 1981.
Candler, Allen D., and Lucien L. Knight, eds. *The Colonial Records of the State of Georgia.* 25 vols (1–19 and 21–26). Atlanta: C. P. Byrd, 1904–16.
Carroll, B. R., ed. *Historical Collections of South Carolina.* 2 vols. New York: Harper and Brothers, 1836.
Cartography Associates. *David Rumsey Map Collection.* http://www.davidrumsey.com (7 November 2005).
Castiglioni, Luigi. *Luigi Castiglioni's Viaggio: Travels in the United States of North America, 1785–1787,* trans. and ed. by Antonio Pace with natural history commentary and *Luigi Castiglioni's Botanical Observations*, trans. by Antonio Pace and ed. by Joseph and Nesta Ewan. Syracuse, N.Y.: Syracuse University Press, 1983.
Coker, C. F. W., ed. "Journal of John Graham, South Carolina Militia, 1779." *Military Collector and Historian* 19 (Summer 1967): 35–47.
Coleman, Kenneth, ed. "Agricultural Practices in Georgia's First Decade." *Agricultural History* 33 (October 1959): 196–99.
Coleman, Kenneth, and Milton Ready, eds. *The Colonial Records of the State of Georgia.* Vols. 27–28, pt. 1. Athens: University of Georgia Press, 1976–77.
Collections of the Georgia Historical Society. 15 vols. Savannah: Georgia Historical Society, 1840–.
Collections of the New York Historical Society for the Year 1883. Vol. 16. New York: Printed for the Society, 1884.
Collections of the New York Historical Society for the Year 1884. Vol. 17. New York: Printed for the Society, 1885.
Collections of the South Carolina Historical Society. 5 vols. Charleston: South Carolina Historical Society, 1857–97.

Conyngham, Captain David Power. *Sherman's March through the South with Sketches and Incidents of the Campaign*. New York: Sheldon and Company, 1865.

Cooper, Thomas, and David J. McCord, eds. *The Statutes at Large of South Carolina*. 10 vols. Columbia: A. S. Johnston, 1836–1841.

Corbin, Gawin L. "The First List of Pew Holders of Christ-Church, Savannah." *Georgia Historical Quarterly* 50 (March 1966): 74–86.

Cordle, Charles G., ed. "The John Tobler Manuscripts: An Account of German-Swiss Emigrants in South Carolina, 1737." *Journal of Southern History* 5 (February 1939): 83–97.

Coulter, E. Merton, ed. *The Journal of Peter Gordon, 1732–1735*. Athens: University of Georgia Press, 1963.

Cox, William E., ed. "Brigadier General John Ashe's Defeat in the Battle of Brier Creek." *Georgia Historical Quarterly* 57 (Summer 1973): 295–302.

Cross, Jack L., ed. "The Letters of Thomas Pinckney, 1775–1780." *South Carolina Historical Magazine* 58 (July 1957): 145–62.

Curnock, Nehemiah, ed. *The Journal of the Rev. John Wesley, A.M.*, standard ed., 8 vols. New York: Eaton and Mains, 1909–16.

Davis, John. *Travels of Four Years and a Half in the United States of America during 1798, 1799, 1800, 1801, and 1802*. With an introduction and notes by A. J. Morrison. New York: Henry Holt, 1909.

de Miranda, Francisco. *The New Democracy in America: Travels of Francisco de Miranda in the United States, 1783–1784*. Edited by John S. Ezell. Translated by Judson P. Wood. Norman: University of Oklahoma Press, 1963.

Diary of Viscount Percival, First Earl of Egmont. 3 vols. London: H.M. Stationery Office, 1920–23.

Doysié, Abel, ed. "Journal of a French Traveler in the Colonies, 1765, I." *American Historical Review* 26 (July 1921): 726–47.

"Dupont Genealogy," *Transactions of the Huguenot Society of South Carolina* 76 (1971): 106–7.

Easterby, J. H., and Ruth S. Green, eds. *The Colonial Records of South Carolina: The Journal of the Commons House of Assembly*. Vols. 1736–50. Columbia: Historical Commission of South Carolina, 1951–62.

Edwards, Adele Stanton, ed. *Journals of the Privy Council, 1783–1789*. Columbia: University of South Carolina Press, 1971.

Esker, Katie-Prince Ward, comp. *South Carolina Memorials, 1731–1776: Abstracts of Selected Land Records*. Vol. 2. New Orleans: Polyanthos, 1977.

Evans, Richard Xavier. "Robert Mills' Letter on South Carolina, 1804," *South Carolina Historical and Genealogical Magazine* 39 (July 1938): 110–17.

Faust, Albert B. *Lists of Swiss Emigrants in the Eighteenth Century to the American Colonies*. 2 vols. Washington, D.C.: National Genealogical Society, 1920.

Gee, Joshua. *The Trade and Navigation of Great Britain Considered*. London, 1729.

Green, Roger. *Virginia's Cure; or, An Advisive Narrative Concerning Virginia*. London, 1662. Reprinted as tract 15 in Peter Force, comp., *Tracts . . . Relating Principally to the . . . Colonies*. (Washington, D.C.: P. Force, 1844), 3:4–6.

Gregorie, Anne King, ed. *Records of the Court of Chancery of South Carolina, 1671–1779*. Washington, D.C.: American Historical Association, 1950.

Hawes, Lilla Mills, ed. "A Description of Whitefield's Bethesda: Samuel Fayrweather to Thomas Prince and Thomas Foxcroft." *Georgia Historical Quarterly* 45 (December 1961): 363–66.

———, ed. *The Journal of the Reverend John Joachim Zubly A.M., D.D. March 5, 1770 through June 22, 1781*. Savannah: Georgia Historical Society, 1989.

Hemphill, William Edwin, ed., and Wylma A. Wates, asst. ed. *The State Records of South Carolina: Extracts of the Journals of the Provincial Congresses of South Carolina, 1775–1776*. Columbia: South Carolina Archives Department, 1960.

Hemphill, William Edwin, Wylma A. Wates, and R. Nicholas Olsberg, eds. *The State Records of South Carolina: Journals of the General Assembly and House of Representatives, 1776–1780*. Columbia: University of South Carolina Press, 1970.

Hendrix, Ge Lee Corley, and Morn McKoy Lindsay, comps. *The Jury Lists of South Carolina, 1778–1779*. Privately published, 1976.

Holcomb, Brent H. *Petitions for Land from the South Carolina Council Journals*. 7 vols. Columbia: South Carolina Magazine of Ancestral Research, 1996–99.

———, abstracter. *South Carolina Deed Abstracts, 1773–1778 Books F-4 through X-4*. Columbia: South Carolina Magazine of Ancestral Research, 1993.

Jéquier, Hugues, Jaques Henriod, and Monique De Pury. *La Famille Pury*. Neuchâtel: Caisse De Famille Pury, 1972.

Johnson, Elmer O., and Kathleen Lewis Sloan, comps. and eds. *A Documentary Profile of the Palmetto State*. Columbia: University of South Carolina Press, 1971.

Jones, George Fenwick, contributor. "Two Salzburger Letters from George Whitefield and Theobald Kiefer II." *Georgia Historical Quarterly* 62 (Spring 1978): 50–57.

———, ed. *Henry Newman's Salzburger Letterbooks*. Athens: University of Georgia Press, 1966.

———, ed. "Johann Martin Boltzius' Trip to Charleston, October 1742." *South Carolina Historical Magazine* 82 (April 1981): 87–110.

———, ed. "Report of Mr. Ettwein's Journey to Georgia and South Carolina, 1765." *South Carolina Historical Magazine* 91 (October 1990): 247–60.

———, ed. "The Secret Diary of Pastor Johann Martin Boltzius." *Georgia Historical Quarterly* 53 (March 1969): 78–110.

———, ed. "Von Reck's Second Report from Georgia." *William and Mary Quarterly*, 3rd ser., 22 (April 1965): 319–33.

———, trans. "Commissary Von Reck's Report on Georgia." *Georgia Historical Quarterly* 47 (March 1963): 95–110.

———, trans. and annotator. "John Martin Boltzius Reports on Georgia." *Georgia Historical Quarterly* 47 (June 1963): 216–19.

Kavenagh, W. Keith, ed. *Foundations of Colonial America: A Documentary History*. Vol. 3. New York: Chelsea House, 1973.

King, Spencer B., Jr. *Georgia Voices: A Documentary History to 1872*. Athens: University of Georgia Press, 1966.

Lambert, John. *Travels through Lower Canada and the United States of North America in the Years 1806, 1807, and 1808. . . .* 3 vols. London: Richard Phillips, 1810.

Lancour, A. Harold, comp. "Passenger Lists of Ships Coming to North America." *Bulletin of the New York Public Library* 41, no. 5 (1937): 389–410.

Lane, Mills, ed. *General Oglethorpe's Georgia: Colonial Letters, 1733–1743*. 2 vols. Savannah, Ga.: Beehive Press, 1975.

Langley, Clara A., abstracter. *South Carolina Deed Abstracts, 1719–1772*. 4 vols.

Easley, S.C.: Southern Historical Press, 1983–84.

La Rochefoucauld Liancourt, François Alexandre Frédéric, duc de. *Travels through the United States of North America, the Country of the Iroquois, and Upper Canada, in the Years 1795, 1796, and 1797: With an Authentic Account of Lower Canada.* 2 vols. London: R. Phillips, 1799.

LeConte, Joseph. *'Ware Sherman? A Journal of Three Month's Personal Experience in the Last Days of the Confederacy; with an introductory reminiscence by His Daughter Caroline LeConte.* Berkeley: University of California Press, 1937.

Lipscomb, Terry W., ed. *The Colonial Records of South Carolina: The Journal of the Commons House of Assembly, November 21, 1752–September 6, 1754.* Vol. 12. Columbia: University of South Carolina Press, 1983.

———, ed. *The Colonial Records of South Carolina: The Journal of the Commons House of Assembly, November 12, 1754–September 23, 1755.* Vol. 13. Columbia: University of South Carolina Press, 1986.

———, ed. *The Colonial Records of South Carolina: The Journal of the Commons House of Assembly, November 20, 1755–July 6, 1757.* Vol. 14. Columbia: University of South Carolina Press, 1989.

———, ed. *The Colonial Records of South Carolina: The Journal of the Commons House of Assembly, October 6, 1757–January 24, 1761.* Parts 1 and 2. Columbia: South Carolina Department of Archives and History, 1996.

Loewald, Klaus G., Beverly Starika, and Paul S. Taylor, trans. and eds. "Johann Martin Boltzius Answers a Questionnaire on Carolina and Georgia." *William and Mary Quarterly,* 3rd ser., 14 (April 1957): 218–61.

———, trans. and eds. "Johann Martin Boltzius Answers a Questionnaire on Carolina and Georgia, Part II." *William and Mary Quarterly,* 3rd ser., 15 (April 1958): 228–52.

McDowell, William L., Jr., ed. *Colonial Records of South Carolina: Documents Relating to Indian Affairs, May 21, 1750–August 7, 1754.* Vol 1. Columbia: South Carolina Archives Department, 1958.

———. *Colonial Records of South Carolina: Documents Relating to Indian Affairs, 1754–1765.* Vol. 2. Columbia: University of South Carolina Press, 1970.

McKissick, J. Rion. "Some Observations of Travelers on South Carolina, 1820–1860." *Proceedings of the South Carolina Historical Association* 2 (1932): 44–51.

Melish, John. *Travels through the United States of America in the Years 1806 and 1807, and 1809, 1810, and 1811. . . .* 2 vols. Philadelphia: Printed by G. Palmer for John Melish, 1815.

Merrens, H. Roy. "A View of Coastal South Carolina in 1778: The Journal of Ebenezer Hazard." *South Carolina Historical Magazine* 73 (October 1972): 177–93.

———, ed. *The Colonial South Carolina Scene: Contemporary Views, 1697–1774,* tricentennial edition, no. 7. Columbia: University of South Carolina Press, 1977.

Migliazzo, Arlin C., ed. *Lands of True and Certain Bounty: The Geographical Theories and Colonization Strategies of Jean Pierre Purry.* Translations by Pierrette C. Christianne-Louvrien and 'BioDun J. Ogundayo. Selinsgrove, Pa.: Susquehanna University Press, 2002.

Miller, Randall M., ed. *"A Warm and Zealous Spirit": John J. Zubly and the American Revolution: A Selection of His Writings.* Macon, Ga.: Mercer University Press, 1982.

Mills, Robert. *Atlas of the State of South Carolina*. Baltimore: F. Lucas Jr., 1825.

Mohl, Raymond A. "'The Grand Fabric of Republicanism': A Scotsman Describes South Carolina, 1810–1811." *South Carolina Historical Magazine* 71 (January 1970): 178–79.

Moultrie, William. *Memoirs of the American Revolution*. 2 vols. New York: David Longworth, 1802. Reprint, in one volume, New York: Arno Press, 1968.

Nairne, Thomas. *A Letter from South Carolina*. 2nd. ed. London: R. Smith, 1718.

Norton, Frank H., ed. *The Hugh Finlay Journal: Colonial Postal History, 1773–1774*. Brooklyn: Mercantile Library Association, 1867. Reprint, Columbus, Ohio: U.S. Philatelic Classics Society, 1975.

Nunis, Doyce B., Jr. "Colonel Archibald Campbell's March from Savannah to Augusta, 1779," *Georgia Historical Quarterly* 45 (September 1967): 275–86.

Olsberg, R. Nicholas, ed. *The Colonial Records of South Carolina: The Journal of the Commons House of Assembly 23 April 1750–31 August 1751*. Vol. 10. Columbia: University of South Carolina Press, 1974.

"Population Schedules of the First Census of the United States, 1790: Rhode Island, South Carolina, Vermont, Virginia, and 1840 Census of Pensioners for Revolutionary or Military Service." Washington, D.C.: National Archives and Records Service—General Services Administration, 1960. Microfilmed copy.

Pottle, Frederick A. *Boswell on the Grand Tour: Germany and Switzerland, 1764*. New York: McGraw-Hill, 1953.

Purry, Jean Pierre. *Description abrégée de l'état présent de la Caroline Meridionale, nouvelle edition, avec des eclaircissemens, les actes des concessions faites à ce suject à l'auteur, tant pour luy que pour ceux qui voudront predre parti avec luy, Et enfin une instruction qui contient les conditions, sous lesquelles on pourra l'accompagner*. Neuchâtel: Privately published, 1732.

———. *Kurtze jedoch zuverläßige Nachricht von dem gegenwärtigen Zustand und Beschaffenheit de Mittägigen Carolina in America oder West-Indien, Welche Landschaft Georgien genennet wird, aufgesetzt In Charlestown oder Carlstadt von vier glaubwürdigen Schweitzern, und aus der Frantzösischen Sprache anietzo verdeutscht. Welchem eine Nachricht von denen so genannten Wilden, welche in derselben Gegend wohnen, beygefüget ist,* trans. Samuel Benjamin Walthern. Leipzig, 1734.

———. *Mémoire Presenté à Sa Gr. My Lord Duc de Newcastle, Chambellan de S. M. le Roi, George & c. & Secretaire d'État: sur l'état présent de la Caroline & sur le moyens de l'améliorer*. London: G. Bowyer, 1724.

———. *Mémoire sur le pais des Cafres et la terre de Nuyts par raport à l'utilité que la Compagnie des Indes Orientales en pourroit retirer pour son commerce*. Amsterdam: Pierre Humbert, 1718.

———. *Memorial Presented to His Grace My Lord the Duke of Newcastle Chamberlain of His Majesty King George, &c., and Secretary of State: Upon the Present Condition of Carolina and the Means of Its Amelioration*. Translated by Charles C. Jones Jr. Augusta: Privately printed for the translator by J. H. Estill, 1880.

———. *A Method for Determining the Best Climate of the Earth on a Principle to Which All Geographers and Historians Have Been Hitherto Strangers in a Memorial Presented to the Governors of the East India Company in Holland for Which the Author Was Obliged to Leave the Country*. Anonymous translation from the

French. London: Privately printed for Peter Cooper, 1744.

———. *Second mémoire sur le pais des Cafres et la terre de Nuyts Servant d'éclaircissement aux propositions faites dans le premier, pour l'utilité de la Compagnie des Indes Orientales*. Amsterdam: Pierre Humbert, 1718.

———. *Spéculations sur le changes étrangers, contenant le juste rapport de Paris avec les principales places d'Europe,suivant le cours d'Amsterdam*. Paris, 1726.

"Records Kept by Colonel Isaac Hayne." *South Carolina Historical and Genealogical Magazine* 11 (January 1910): 27–38.

"Records of the Regiments of the South Carolina Line, Continental Establishment." *South Carolina Historical and Genealogical Magazine* 5 (April 1904): 82–89.

Reese, Trevor, ed. *Our First Visit to America: Early Reports from the Colony of Georgia, 1732–1740*. Savannah, Ga.: Beehive Press, 1974.

Ruddock, Ted, ed. *Travels in the Colonies in 1773–1775 Described in the Letters of William Mylne*. Athens: University of Georgia Press, 1993.

Salley, A. S., Jr. *Minutes of the Vestry of St. Helena's Parish, South Carolina, 1726–1812*. Columbia, S.C.: State Company, 1919.

Sherman, General William T. *Personal Memoirs of Gen. W. T. Sherman,* 3rd ed., revised and corrected. 2 vols. New York: Charles L. Webster and Company, 1890.

Stephens, William. *A Journal of the Proceedings in Georgia*. 2 vols. Ann Arbor, Mich.: University Microfilms, 1966.

Stevens, Michael E., ed. *The State Records of South Carolina: Journals of the House of Representatives, 1792–1794*. Columbia: University of South Carolina Press, 1988.

———. *The State Records of South Carolina: Journals of the House of Representatives, 1791*. Columbia: University of South Carolina Press, 1985.

———, ed., and Christine M. Allen, asst. ed. *The State Records of South Carolina: Journals of the House of Representatives, 1789–1790*. Columbia: University of South Carolina Press, 1984.

Stoney, Samuel Gaillard, ed. "The Autobiography of William John Grayson." *South Carolina Historical and Genealogical Magazine* 49 (January 1948): 22–40.

Tappert, Theodore G., and John W. Doberstein, trans. *The Journals of Henry Melchior Mühlenberg*. 3 vols. Philadelphia: Evangelical Lutheran Ministerium of Pennsylvania and Adjacent States and Mühlenberg Press, 1942.

Tedcastle, Agnes Beville, submitter. "A Pastor for the Parish of St. Peter, Purrysburg, South Carolina." *Transactions of the Huguenot Society of South Carolina* 28 (1923): 37–44.

———, submitter. "Testimonial Granted to Honorable Jonas Pelot, of Neuveville, Switzerland." *Transactions of the Huguenot Society of South Carolina* 36 (1931): 60–62.

Tresp, Lothar, trans. and annotator. "September, 1748 in Georgia, from the Diary of John Martin Boltzius." *Georgia Historical Quarterly* 47 (September 1963): 320–32.

Uhlendorf, Bernhard Alexander, ed. and trans. *The Seige of Charleston, with an Account of the Province of South Carolina: Diaries and Letters of Hessian Officers*. Ann Arbor: University of Michigan Press, 1938.

Urlsperger, Rev. Samuel. *Detailed Reports on the Salzburger Emigrants Who Settled in America. . . .* Gen. ed. George Fenwick Jones. Vols. 1 and 2 trans. by Herman J.

Lacher. Vol. 3 trans. and ed. by George Fenwick Jones and Marie Hahn. Vols. 4 and 5 trans. and ed. by George Fenwick Jones and Renate Wilson. Vol. 6 trans. and ed. by George Fenwick Jones and Renate Wilson. Vol. 7 trans. and ed. by George Fenwick Jones and Don Savelle. Vol. 8 trans. by Maria Magdalena Hoffman-Loerzer, Renate Wilson, and George Fenwick Jones, ed. by George Fenwick Jones. Vol 9 trans. by Don Savelle, ed. by George Fenwick Jones. Vol. 10 trans. Don Savelle and George Fenwick Jones, ed. by George Fenwick Jones. Vol. 11 trans. by Eva Pulgram, ed. by George Fenwick Jones. Vol. 12 trans. by Irmgard Neuman, ed. by George Fenwick Jones. Vols. 13 and 14 ed. by George Fenwick Jones, vol. 13 trans. by David Roth and George Fenwick Jones, vol. 14 trans. by Eva Pulgram, Magdalena Hoffman-Loerzer, and George Fenwick Jones. Vol. 15 trans. and ed. by George Fenwick Jones. Vol 16 ed. by George Fenwick Jones, 1753 trans. by George Fenwick Jones, 1754 trans. by Renate Wilson and George Fenwick Jones. Vol 17 ed. and annotated by George Fenwick Jones, 1759 trans. by David Noble, 1760 trans. by George Fenwick Jones. Athens: University of Georgia Press, 1968–1993. Vol. 18 trans. and ed. by George Fenwick Jones and Renate Wilson. Camden, Me.: Picton Press, 1995.

Warren, Mary Bondurant, comp. "South Carolina Jury Lists, 1718 through 1753." *Heritage Papers* (1977).

Webber, Mabel L., ed. "Extract from the Journal of Mrs. Ann Manigault, 1754–1781." *South Carolina Historical and Genealogical Magazine* 21 (January 1920): 10–23.

Webber, Mabel L., and Elizabeth H. Jervey, eds. "Abstracts of the Records of the Proceedings in the Court of Ordinary." *South Carolina Historical and Genealogical Magazine* 23 (April 1922): 77–83, (July 1922): 158–61; 24 (July 1923): 101–15; 25 (July 1924): 143–47; 27 (April 1926): 91–94; 40 (October 1939): 137–41; 42 (October 1941): 194–98; 44 (January 1943): 43–51, (April 1943): 107–15, (July 1943): 173–83.

Weir, Robert M., ed. "The Muster Roles of the South Carolina Granville and Colleton County Regiments of Militia, 1756." *South Carolina Historical Magazine* 70 (October 1971): 226–39.

Williams, George C. "Letters to the Bishop of London from the Commissaries in South Carolina." *South Carolina Historical Magazine* 78 (January 1977): 1–31, (April 1977): 120–47, (July 1977): 213–42.

Books and Monographs

Ackerman, Robert K. *South Carolina Colonial Land Policies*. Columbia: University of South Carolina Press, 1977.

Adair, James. *The History of the American Indian Particularly Those Nations Adjoining the Mississippi, East and West Florida, Georgia, South and North Carolina, and Virginia*. London: Edward and Charles Dilly, 1775. Reprint, New York: Johnson Reprint Corporation, 1968.

Albergotti, William Greer, III. *Albergotti Creek: The Chronicles of a Colonial Family of the South Carolina Sea Islands*. Columbia, S.C.: R. L. Bryan Company, 1979.

Alden, John Richard. *The South in the Revolution, 1763–1789*. Baton Rouge: Louisiana State University Press, 1959.

Altman, Ida, and James Hory, eds. *"To Make America": European Emigration in the*

Early Modern Period. Berkeley: University of California Press, 1991.
Ardener, Edwin, ed. *Social Anthropology and Language*. London: Tavistock Publications, 1971.
Aries, Philippe. *L'enfant et la vie familiale sous l'Ancien Régime*. Paris: Plon, 1960.
Atkinson, C. T. *A History of Germany, 1715–1815*. 1908. Reprint, New York: Barnes and Noble, 1969.
Bailyn, Bernard. *Education and the Forming of American Society*. New York: W. W. Norton, 1972.
Bailyn, Bernard, and Philip D. Morgan, eds. *Strangers within the Realm: Cultural Margins of the First British Empire*. Chapel Hill: University of North Carolina Press for the Institute of Early American History and Culture, 1991.
Baker, Rev. William M. *The Life and Labours of the Rev. Daniel Baker, D.D.: Pastor and Evangelist*. Philadelphia: William S. and Alfred Martien, 1858.
Barrett, John G. *Sherman's March through the Carolinas*. Chapel Hill: University of North Carolina Press, 1956.
Barth, Frederik. *Ethnic Groups and Boundaries*. Boston: Little, Brown, 1969.
Beaver, Patricia D. *Rural Communities in the Appalachian South*. Lexington: University of Kentucky Press, 1986.
Beaver, Patricia D., and Carol E. Hill, eds. *Cultural Diversity in the U.S. South: Anthropological Contributions to a Region in Transition*. Southern Anthropological Society Proceedings, no. 31. Athens, Ga.: University of Georgia Press, 1998.
Beavon, Keith S. O. *Central Place Theory: A Reinterpretation*. London: Longman, 1977.
Beeman, Richard R. *The Evolution of the Southern Backcountry: A Case Study of Lunenburg County, Virginia, 1746–1832*. Philadelphia: University of Pennsylvania Press, 1984.
Bell, Colin, and Howard Newby. *Community Studies: An Introduction to the Sociology of the Local Community*. New York: Praeger, 1972.
———, eds. *The Sociology of Community: A Selection of Readings*. London: Frank Cass and Company, 1974.
Bender, Thomas. *Community and Social Change in America*. New Brunswick, N.J.: Rutgers University Press, 1978.
Benoît, Daniel. *Les frères Gibert: Deux pasteurs de Désert et du Refuge, (1728–1817)*. Toulouse, 1889.
Bernheim, G. D. *History of the German Settlements and of the Lutheran Church in North and South Carolina*. . . . Philadelphia: Lutheran Book Store, 1872. Reprint, Spartanburg, S.C.: Reprint Company, 1972.
Billington, Ray Allen. *The Protestant Crusade, 1800–1860: A Study of the Origins of American Nativism*. New York: Macmillan, 1938.
Bloch, Marc L. B. *La société féodale: La formation des liens de dependence*. Paris: A. Michel, 1939.
———. *La société féodale: Les classes et le gouvernement des homes*. Paris: A. Frichel, 1940.
Boles, John B. *The Great Revival, 1787–1805*. Lexington: University Press of Kentucky, 1972.
Bolton, S. Charles. *Southern Anglicanism: The Church of England in Colonial South Carolina*. Westport, Conn.: Greenwood Press, 1982.

Bonomi, Patricia U. *Under the Cope of Heaven: Religion, Society, and Politics in Colonial America*. New York: Oxford University Press, 1986.

Brown, Douglas Summers. *The Catawba Indians: The People of the River*. Columbia: University of South Carolina Press, 1966.

Brady, Thomas A., Jr. *Turning Swiss: Cities and Empires, 1450–1550*. Cambridge: Cambridge University Press, 1985.

Braudel, Fernand. *La Méditerranée et le monde mediterranéen à l'époque de Philippe II*. Paris: Colin, 1949.

Breen, Thomas H., ed. *Shaping Southern Society: The Colonial Experience*. New York: Oxford University Press, 1976.

———. *Tobacco Culture: The Mentality of the Great Tidewater Planters on the Eve of the Revolution*. Princeton, N.J.: Princeton University Press, 1985.

Bridenbaugh, Carl. *Myths and Realities: Societies of the Colonial South*. New York: Atheneum, 1963.

Burton, Orville Vernon. *In My Father's House Are Many Mansions: Family and Community in Edgefield, South Carolina*. Chapel Hill: University of North Carolina Press, 1985.

Butler, Jon. *Awash in a Sea of Faith: Christianizing the American People*. Cambridge, Mass.: Harvard University Press, 1990.

———. *Huguenots in America: A Refugee People in New World Society*. Cambridge, Mass.: Harvard University Press, 1983.

Calhoon, Robert M. *Evangelicals and Conservatives in the Early South, 1740–1861*. Columbia: University of South Carolina Press, 1988.

Calhoon, Robert McCluer. *The Loyalists in Revolutionary America, 1760–1781*. New York: Harcourt Brace Jovanovich, 1965.

Canny, Nicholas, and Anthony Pagden, eds. *Colonial Identity in the Atlantic World, 1500–1800*. Princeton, N.J.: Princeton University Press, 1987.

Carr, Lois Green, Aubrey C. Land, and Edward C. Papenfuse, eds. *Law, Society, and Politics in Early Maryland: Proceedings of the First Conference on Maryland History, June 14–15, 1974*. Baltimore: Johns Hopkins University Press, 1977.

Cash, Wilbur J. *The Mind of the South*. New York: Alfred A. Knopf, 1941.

Chalmers, Lionel. *An Account of the Weather and Diseases of South Carolina*. London: Edward and Charles Dilly, 1776.

Chaplin, Joyce E. *An Anxious Pursuit: Agricultural Innovation and Modernity in the Lower South, 1730–1815*. Chapel Hill: University of North Carolina Press, 1993.

Childs, St. Julien Ravenel. *Malaria and Colonization in the Carolina Low Country, 1526–1696*. Baltimore: Johns Hopkins University Press, 1940.

Chua, Amy. *World on Fire: How Exporting Free Market Democracy Breeds Ethnic Hatred and Global Instability*. New York: Anchor Books, 2004.

Clark, Erskine. *Our Southern Zion: A History of Calvinism in the South Carolina Low Country, 1690–1990*. Tuscaloosa: University of Alabama Press, 1996.

Clowse, Converse D. *Economic Beginnings in Colonial South Carolina, 1670–1730*. Columbia: University of South Carolina Press, 1971.

Coclanis, Peter A. *The Shadow of a Dream: Economic Life and Death in the South Carolina Low Country, 1670–1920*. New York: Oxford University Press, 1989.

Cohen, Abner. *Two-Dimensional Man: An Essay on the Anthropology of Power and*

Symbolism in Complex Society. Berkeley: University of California Press, 1974.

———, ed. *Urban Ethnicity*. London: Tavistock, 1974.

Coleman, Kenneth. *The American Revolution in Georgia*. Athens: University of Georgia Press, 1958.

———. *Colonial Georgia: A History*. New York: Charles Scribner's Sons, 1967.

Collins, Bruce. *White Society in the Antebellum South*. New York: Longman, 1985.

Coon, David L. *The Development of Market Agriculture in South Carolina, 1670–1785*. New York: Garland, 1989.

Corkran, David H. *The Carolina Indian Frontier*. Columbia: University of South Carolina Press, 1970.

Crane, Verner W. *The Southern Frontier, 1670–1732*. Ann Arbor: University of Michigan Press, 1929. First Ann Arbor paper edition, 1956.

Cross, Arthur Lyon. *The Anglican Episcopate and the American Colonies*. New York: Longmans, Green, 1902.

Crow, Jeffrey J., and Larry E. Tise, eds. *The Southern Experience in the American Revolution*. Chapel Hill: University of North Carolina Press, 1978.

Dalcho, Frederick. *An Historical Account of the Protestant Episcopal Church in South Carolina from the First Settlement of the Province to the War of the Revolution*. Charleston: E. Thayer, 1820.

Darter, Oscar H. *Colonial Fredericksburg and Neighborhood in Perspective*. New York: Twayne, 1957.

Davis, Harold E. *The Fledgling Province: Social and Cultural Life in Colonial Georgia, 1733–1776*. Chapel Hill: University of North Carolina Press, 1976.

Degler, Carl N. *Out of Our Past: The Forces That Shaped Modern America*. Rev. ed. New York: Harper and Row, 1970.

Demos, John. *A Little Commonwealth: Family Life in Plymouth Colony*. New York: Oxford University Press, 1970.

DeVorsey, Louis. *The Georgia–South Carolina Boundary*. Athens: University of Georgia Press, 1982.

De Vos, George, and Lola Romanucci-Ross, eds. *Ethnic Identity: Cultural Continuities and Change*. Palo Alto, Calif.: Mayfield, 1975.

Duffy, John. *Epidemics in Colonial America*. Baton Rouge: Louisiana State University Press, 1953.

Earle, Carville V. *The Evolution of a Tidewater Settlement System: All Hallow's Parish, Maryland, 1650–1783*. Research Paper no. 170. Chicago: University of Chicago, Department of Geography, 1975.

Faust, Albert B. *The German Element in the United States*. 2 vols. New York: Houghton, Mifflin, 1909.

Feagin, Joe R. *Racial and Ethnic Relations*. Englewood Cliffs, N.J.: Prentice Hall, 1978.

Febvre, Lucien P. V. *La terre et l'evolution humaine: Introduction geographique à l'histoire*. 2nd ed. Paris: Renaissance du livre, 1922.

Feinstein, Otto, ed. *Ethnic Groups in the City: Culture, Institutions, and Power*. Lexington, Mass.: Heath Lexington, 1971.

Fischer, David Hackett. *Historians' Fallacies: Toward a Logic of Historical Thought*. New York: Harper and Row, 1970.

Fogleman, Aaron Spencer. *Hopeful Journeys: German Immigration, Settlement and Political Culture in Colonial America, 1717–1775*. Philadelphia: University of Pennsylvania Press, 1996.

Gallay, Alan. *The Formation of the Planter Elite: Jonathan Bryan and the Southern Colonial Frontier*. Athens: University of Georgia Press, 1989.

Garrison, Webb. *Oglethorpe's Folly: The Birth of Georgia*. Lakemont, Ga.: Copple House Books, 1982.

Genovese, Eugene D. *The Political Economy of Slavery: Studies in the Economy and Society of the Slave South*. New York: Pantheon Books, 1965.

———. *Roll Jordan Roll: The World the Slaves Made*. New York: Pantheon Books, 1974.

Gibert, Anne C. *Pierre Gibert, Esq., the Devoted Huguenot: A History of the French Settlement of New Bordeaux, South Carolina*. Privately published, 1976.

Glazer, Nathan, and Daniel Patrick Moynihan. *Ethnicity: Theory and Practice*. Cambridge, Mass.: Harvard University Press, 1975.

Goodyear, Albert C., III, and Glen T. Hanson, eds. *Studies in South Carolina Archeology: Essays in Honor of Robert L. Stephenson*. Anthropological Studies, no 9. Occasional Papers of the South Carolina Institute of Archeology and Anthropology. Columbia: University of South Carolina Press, 1989.

Gordon, John W. *South Carolina and the American Revolution: A Battlefield History*. Columbia: University of South Carolina Press, 2003.

Gordon, Michael, ed. *The American Family in Social-Historical Perspective*. 3rd ed. New York: St. Martin's Press, 1983.

Gordon, Milton M. *Assimilation in American Life: The Role of Race, Religion and National Origins*. New York: Oxford University Press, 1964.

Grant, A. J. *The Huguenots*. London: T. Butterworth, 1934.

Gray, Lewis Cecil. *History of Agriculture in the Southern United States to 1860*. Vol. 1. Washington, D.C.: Carnegie Institution of Washington, 1933.

Greeley, Andrew. *Ethnicity in the United States: A Preliminary Reconnaissance*. New York: John Wiley and Sons, 1974.

———. *Why Can't They Be Like Us?* New York: E. P. Dutton, 1971.

Green, Stanton W., and Stephen M. Perlman, eds. *The Archeology of Frontiers and Boundaries*. Orlando, Fla.: Academic Press, 1985.

Greene, Evarts B., and Virginia D. Harrington. *American Population before the Federal Census of 1790*. New York: Columbia University Press, 1932. Reprint, Glouster, Mass.: Peter Smith, 1966.

Greene, Jack P., Rosemary Brana-Shute, and Randy J. Sparks, eds. *Money, Trade, and Power: The Evolution of Colonial South Carolina's Plantation Society*. Columbia: University of South Carolina Press, 2001.

Greven, Philip J., Jr. *Four Generations: Population, Land, and Family in Colonial Andover, Massachusetts*. Ithaca, N.Y.: Cornell University Press, 1970.

Grimm, Harold J. *The Reformation Era, 1500–1650*. 2nd ed. New York: Macmillan, 1973.

Hall, David, John M. Murrin, and Thad Tate, eds. *Saints and Revolutionaries: Essays on Early American History*. New York: W. W. Norton, 1984.

Handlin, Oscar. *Boston's Immigrants, 1790–1865: A Study of Acculturation*. Rev. ed. Cambridge, Mass.: Harvard University Press, 1959.

———. *Race and Nationality in American Life*. Boston: Little, Brown, 1957.

———. *The Uprooted: The Epic Story of the Great Migrations That Made the American People*. Boston: Little, Brown, 1951.

Hansen, Marcus Lee. *The Immigrant in American History*. Cambridge, Mass.: Harvard University Press, 1940.

Haugen, Einar. *The Ecology of Language: Essays by Einar Haugen*. Selected and introduced by Anwar S. Dil. Stanford, Calif.: Stanford University Press, 1972.

Heawood, Edward. *A History of Geographical Discovery in the Seventeenth and Eighteenth Centuries*. London: Cambridge University Press, 1912. Reprint, New York: Octagon Books, 1965.

Heimert, Alan. *Religion and the American Mind from the Great Awakening to the Revolution*. Cambridge, Mass.: Harvard University Press, 1966.

Henderson, Archibald. *Washington's Southern Tour, 1791*. Boston: Houghton Mifflin, 1923.

Henderson, Ernest F. *A Short History of Germany*. 2 vols in 1. New York: Macmillan, 1911.

Herold, J. Christopher. *The Swiss without Halos*. New York: Columbia University Press, 1948.

Higgins, W. Robert, ed. *The Revolutionary War in the South—Power, Conflict, and Leadership: Essays in Honor of John Richard Alden*. Durham, N.C.: Duke University Press, 1979.

Higham, John. *Strangers in the Land*. New York: Atheneum, 1963.

———. *Writing American History: Essays on Modern Scholarship*. Bloomington: Indiana University Press, 1970; Midland Book Edition, 1972.

Hill, Christopher. *Society and Puritanism in Pre-Revolutionary England*. New York: Schocken Books, 1964.

Hindle, Brooke. *The Pursuit of Science in Revolutionary America, 1735–1789*. Chapel Hill: University of North Carolina Press, 1956.

Hirsch, Arthur Henry. *The Huguenots of Colonial South Carolina*. Durham, N.C.: Duke University Press, 1928.

History Committee, St. Helena's Episcopal Church, Beaufort, South Carolina. *The History of the Parish Church of St. Helena, Beaufort, South Carolina*. Columbia, S.C.: R. L. Bryan Company, 1991.

Hoffman, Ronald, Mechal Sobel, and Fredrika J. Teute, eds. *Through a Glass Darkly: Reflections on Personal Identity in Early America*. Chapel Hill: University of North Carolina Press for the Omohundro Institute of Early American History and Culture, 1997.

Hoffman, Ronald, John J. McCusker, Russell R. Menard, and Peter J. Albert, eds. *The Economy of Early America: The Revolutionary Period, 1763–1790*. Charlottesville: University Press of Virginia for the United States Capitol Historical Society, 1988.

Hofstadter, Richard. *America at 1750: A Social Portrait*. New York: Random House, 1971; Vintage Books edition, 1973.

———. *The Progressive Historians: Turner, Beard, and Parrington*. Chicago: University of Chicago Press, 1968.

Holloman, Regina E., and Serghei A. Arutiunov, eds. *Perspectives on Ethnicity*. The Hague: Mouton, 1978.

Howe, Rev. George. *History of the Presbyterian Church in South Carolina*. 2 vols.

Columbia, S.C.: Duffie and Chapman, 1870.

Hudson, Charles M. *The Catawba Nation*. Athens: University of Georgia Press, 1970.

———. *The Southeastern Indians*. Knoxville: University of Tennessee Press, 1976.

Hug, Lina, and Richard Stead. *Switzerland*. New York: G. P. Putnam's Sons, 1900.

Isaac, Rhys. *The Transformation of Virginia, 1740–1790*. Chapel Hill: University of North Carolina Press for the Institute of Early American History and Culture, 1982.

Ivers Larry E. *British Drums on the Southern Frontier: The Military Colonization of Georgia, 1733–1749*. Chapel Hill: University of North Carolina Press, 1974.

———. *Colonial Forts of South Carolina, 1670–1775*. Columbia: University of South Carolina Press, 1970.

Jeanneret, Frédéric Alexandre-Marie, and J. H. Bonhôte, *Biographie neuchâteloise*. 2 vols. Le Locle: Courvoisier, 1863.

Johnson, George Lloyd, Jr. *The Frontier in the Colonial South: South Carolina Backcountry, 1736–1800*. Westport, Conn.: Greenwood Press, 1997.

Johnston, Coy K. *Two Centuries of Lawtonville Baptists, 1775–1975*. Columbia: State Printing Company, 1974.

Jones, Alice Hanson. *Wealth of a Nation to Be: The American Colonies on the Eve of the Revolution*. New York: Columbia University Press, 1980.

Jones, Charles C., Jr. *History of Savannah, Georgia from Its Settlement to the Close of the Eighteenth Century*. Syracuse, N.Y.: D. Mason and Company, 1890.

Jones, George Fenwick. *The Georgia Dutch: From the Rhine and Danube to the Savannah, 1733–1783*. Athens.: University of Georgia Press, 1992.

———. *The Salzburger Saga: Religious Exiles and Other Germans along the Savannah*. Athens: University of Georgia Press, 1984.

Jones, Maldwyn Allen. *American Immigration*. Chicago: University of Chicago Press, 1960.

Joyner, Charles W. *Down by the Riverside: A South Carolina Slave Community*. Chicago: University of Chicago Press, 1984.

Katz, Stanley M., and John M. Murrin, eds. *Colonial America: Essays in Politics and Social Development*. 3rd ed. New York: Alfred A. Knopf, 1983.

Kenzer, Robert C. *Kinship and Neighborhood in a Southern Community: Orange County, North Carolina, 1849–1881*. Knoxville: University of Tennessee Press, 1985.

Kettner, James H. *The Development of American Citizenship, 1608–1870*. Chapel Hill: University of North Carolina Press, 1978.

Kingdon, Robert M. *Geneva and the Consolidation of the French Protestant Movement, 1564–1572: A Contribution to the History of Congregationalism, Presbyterianism, and Calvinist Resistance Theory*. Geneva: Librairie Droz, 1967.

Klein Rachael N. *Unification of a Slave State: The Rise of the Planter Class in the South Carolina Backcountry, 1776–1808*. Chapel Hill: University of North Carolina Press, 1990.

Kohn, Hans. *Nationalism and Liberty: The Swiss Example*. New York: Macmillan, 1956.

Kovacik, Charles L., and John J. Winberry. *South Carolina: A Geography*. Boulder, Colo.: Westview, 1987.

Kraus, Michael. *Intercolonial Aspects of American Culture on the Eve of the Revolution with Special Reference to the Northern Towns*. New York: Columbia University Press, 1928.

Lander, Ernest M., Jr., and Robert K. Ackerman, eds. *Perspectives in South Carolina History: The First Three Hundred Years*. Columbia: University of South Carolina Press, 1973.

Laslett, Peter. *The World We Have Lost: England before the Industrial Revolution*. London: Methuen, 1965.

Lee, Hannah F. *The Huguenots in France and America*. Cambridge: J. Owen, 1843. Reprint, 2 vols in 1. Baltimore: Genealogical Publishing, 1973.

Lewis, Kenneth E. *The American Frontier: An Archeological Study of Settlement Pattern and Process*. New York: Academic Press, 1984.

———. *Camden: A Frontier Town in Eighteenth Century South Carolina*. Anthropological Studies, no. 2. Columbia: Institute for Archeology and Anthropology, University of South Carolina, 1976.

Littlefield, Daniel C. *Rice and Slaves: Ethnicity and the Slave Trade in Colonial South Carolina*. Baton Rouge: Louisiana State University Press, 1981.

Lockridge, Kenneth A. *A New England Town: The First One Hundred Years, Dedham, Massachusetts, 1636–1736*. New York: W. W. Norton, 1970.

Lockwood, Rev. John P. *Memorials of the Life of Peter Böhler, Bishop of the Church of the United Brethren*. London: Wesleyan Conference Office, 1868.

———. *The Western Pioneers; or, Memorials of the Lives and Labours of the Rev. Richard Boardman and the Rev. Joseph Pilmoor*. London: Wesleyan Conference Office, 1881.

Lockwood, William G., ed. *Beyond Ethnic Boundaries: New Approaches in the Anthropology of Ethnicity*. Michigan Discussions in Anthropology, vol. 7. Ann Arbor: University of Michigan Department of Anthropology, 1984.

Lodge, Henry Cabot, gen. ed. *The History of Nations*. 25 vols. Philadelphia: John D. Morris & Co., 1906–1908. Vol. 13, pp. 327–593: "Switzerland," by Charles Dandliker, revised and edited by Elbert J. Benton.

Lowcountry Council of Governments. *Historic Resources of the Lowcountry: A Regional Survey of Beaufort County, South Carolina, Colleton County, South Carolina, Hampton County, South Carolina, Jasper County, South Carolina*. Columbia: South Carolina Department of Archives and History, 1979.

Lumpkin, Henry. *From Savannah to Yorktown: The American Revolution in the South*. Columbia: University of South Carolina Press, 1981.

McCrady, Edward. *The History of South Carolina in the Revolution, 1775–1780*. New York: Macmillan, 1901. Reprint, New York: Russell and Russell, 1969.

———. *The History of South Carolina in the Revolution, 1780–1783*. New York: Macmillan, 1902.

McCurry, Stephanie. *Masters of Small Worlds: Yeoman Households, Gender Relations, and the Political Culture of the Antebellum South Carolina Low Country*. New York: Oxford University Press, 1995.

McCusker, John J., and Russell R. Menard. *The Economy of British America, 1607–1789*. Chapel Hill: University of North Carolina Press for the Institute of Early American History and Culture, 1985.

Malin, James C. *The Grassland of North America: Prolegomena to Its History*. Lawrence: Kans.: privately printed, 1947.

Martin, Roger A. *John J. Zubly, Colonial Georgia Minister*. New York: Arno Press, 1982.

Martin, William. *Switzerland: From Roman Times to the Present*. With additional chapters by Pierre Béguin. Translated by Jocasta Innes. New York: Praeger, 1971.

Mathews, Donald G. *Religion in the Old South*. Chicago: University of Chicago Press, 1977.

Matthews, Elmora Messer. *Neighbor and Kin: Life in a Tennessee Ridge Community*. Nashville: Vanderbilt University Press, 1965.

Menard, Russell. *Economy and Society in Early Colonial Maryland*. New York: Garland, 1985.

Meriwether, Robert L. *The Expansion of South Carolina, 1729–1765*. Kingsport, Tenn.: Southern Publishers, 1940.

Merrell, James H. *The Indians' New World: Catawbas and Their Neighbors from European Contact through the Era of Removal*. Chapel Hill: University of North Carolina Press for the Institute of Early American History and Culture, 1989.

Meyer, Duane. *The Highland Scots of North Carolina, 1732–1776*. Chapel Hill: University of North Carolina Press, 1961.

Milling, Chapman J. *Red Carolinians*. Chapel Hill: University of North Carolina Press, 1940.

Mills, Robert. *Statistics of South Carolina*. Charleston: Hurlbut and Lloyd, 1826.

Mitchell, Robert D. *Commercialism and Frontier: Perspectives on the Early Shenandoah Valley*. Charlottesville: University Press of Virginia, 1977.

Nadelhaft, Jerome J. *The Disorders of War: The Revolution in South Carolina*. Orono: University of Maine at Orono Press, 1981.

Nash, Gary. *Red, White, and Black: The Peoples of Early America*. Englewood Cliffs, N.J.: Prentice-Hall, 1974.

Oechsli, Wilhelm. *History of Switzerland, 1499–1914*. Translated by Eden and Cedar Paul. Cambridge: Cambridge University Press, 1922.

Olwell, Robert. *Masters, Slaves, and Subjects: The Culture of Power in the South Carolina Low Country, 1740–1790*. Ithaca, N.Y.: Cornell University Press, 1998.

O'Neill, William L., ed. *Insights and Parallels: Problems and Issues in American Social History*. Minneapolis: Burgess, 1973.

Pancake, John S. *This Destructive War: The British Campaign in the Carolinas, 1780–1782*. Tuscaloosa: University of Alabama Press, 1985.

Pearson, Michael. *Great Southern Land: The Maritime Exploration of Terra Australis*. Canberra: Australian Government Department of the Environment and Heritage, 2005.

Pease, Jane H., and William H. *A Family of Women: The Carolina Petigrus in Peace and War*. Chapel Hill: University of North Carolina Press, 1999.

Perry, Grace Fox. *Moving Finger of Jasper*. Ridgeland, S.C.: Confederate Centennial Committee, 1947.

Pirenne, Henri. *Economic and Social History of Medieval Europe*. Translated by I. E. Clegg. New York: Harcourt, Brace, 1937.

Powell, Sumner Chilton. *Puritan Village: The Formation of a New England Town*. Middletown, Conn.: Wesleyan University Press, 1963.

Posey, Walter Brownlow. *Religious Strife on the Southern Frontier*. Baton Rouge: Louisiana State University Press, 1965.

Rahn, Ruby A. *River Highways for Trade: The Savannah*. Savannah, Ga.: U.S. Corps of Engineers, 1968.

Ramsey, David. *Sketch of the Soil, Climate, Weather, and Disease of South Carolina*. Charleston, S.C.: W. P. Young, 1796.

Reaman, G. Elmore. *The Trail of the Huguenots in Europe, the United States, South Africa, and Canada*. Baltimore: Genealogical Publishing, 1966.

Robinson, W. Stitt. *The Southern Colonial Frontier, 1607–1763*. Albuquerque: University of New Mexico Press, 1979.

Roeber, A. G. *Palatines, Liberty, and Property: German Lutherans in Colonial British America*. Baltimore: Johns Hopkins University Press, 1993.

Rogers, George C., Jr. *Church and State in Eighteenth-Century South Carolina*. Charleston, S.C.: Dalcho Historical Society, 1959.

———. *The History of Georgetown County, South Carolina*. Columbia: University of South Carolina Press 1970.

Rothrock, G. A. *The Huguenots: A Biography of a Minority*. Chicago: Nelson-Hall, 1979.

Rowland, Lawrence S., Alexander Moore, and George C. Rogers Jr. *The History of Beaufort County, South Carolina*. Vol. 1, 1514–1861. Columbia: University of South Carolina Press, 1996.

Russo, David J. *Families and Communities: A New View of American History*. Nashville: American Association of State and Local History, 1974.

Rutman, Darrett B., and Anita H. Rutman. *A Place in Time: Middlesex County, Virginia, 1650–1750*. New York: W. W. Norton, 1984.

Schaff, Rev. Philip, Rt. Rev. Henry C. Potter, Rev. Samuel M. Jackson, and others, gen. eds. *The American Church History Series*. Rev. ed. 8 vols. New York: Charles Scribner's Sons, 1882–1910.

Schlup, Michel. *Biographies neuchâteloises*. Vol. 1. Hauterive: Editions Gilles Attinger, 1996.

Schrag, Peter. *The Decline of the WASP*. New York: Simon and Shuster, 1971.

Sellers, Leila. *Charleston Business on the Eve of the American Revolution*. Chapel Hill: University of North Carolina Press, 1934.

Sherman, Richard P. *Robert Johnson: Proprietary and Royal Governor of South Carolina*. Columbia: University of South Carolina Press, 1966.

Shipp, Rev. Albert M. *The History of Methodism in South Carolina*. Nashville: Southern Methodist Publishing House, 1884. Reprint, Spartanburg, S.C.: Reprint Company, 1972.

Singer, Charles Gregg. *South Carolina in the Confederation*. Philadelphia: University of Pennsylvania Press, 1941.

Sirmans, M. Eugene. *Colonial South Carolina: A Political History, 1663–1763*. Chapel Hill: University of North Carolina Press, 1966.

Smith, Julia Floyd. *Slavery and Rice Culture in Low Country Georgia, 1750–1860*. Knoxville: University of Tennessee Press, 1985.

Smith, Page. *As a City upon a Hill: The Town in American History*. New York: Alfred A. Knopf, 1970.

Smith, Paul H. *Loyalists and Redcoats: A Study in British Revolutionary Policy*. Chapel Hill: University of North Carolina Press, 1964.

Soltow, James H. *The Economic Role of Williamsburg*. Williamsburg: Colonial Williamsburg, distributed by the University Press of Virginia. 1965.

Sorell, Walter. *The Swiss: A Cultural Panorama of Switzerland*. New York: Bobbs-Merrill, 1972.

Stapleton, Rev. Ammon. *Memorials of the Huguenots in America with Special Reference to Their Emigration to Pennsylvania*. Carlisle, Pa.: Huguenot Publishing, 1901.

Strobel, Rev. P. A. *The Salzburgers and Their Descendants*. Baltimore: T. Newton Kurtz, 1855. Reproduced on reel 573, American Cultural Series (Ann Arbor, Mich.: University Microfilms, 1974).

Sutherland, N. M. *The Huguenot Struggle for Recognition*. New Haven, Conn.: Yale University Press, 1980.

Swanton, John R. *The Indians of the Southeastern United States*. Washington, D.C.: Government Printing Office, 1946.

Tate, Thad W., and David L. Ammerman, eds. *The Chesapeake in the Seventeenth-Century: Essays on Anglo-American Society*. Chapel Hill: University of North Carolina Press, 1979.

Taylor, Lawrence J. *Dutchmen on the Bay: The Ethnohistory of a Contractual Community*. Philadelphia: University of Pennsylvania Press, 1983.

Taylor, William R. *Cavalier and Yankee: The Old South and American National Character*. New York: George Braziller, 1961.

Thernstrom, Stephan. *Poverty and Progress: Social Mobility in a Nineteenth Century City*. Cambridge, Mass.: Harvard University Press, 1964.

Thorp, Daniel B. *The Moravian Community in Colonial North Carolina: Pluralism on the Southern Frontier*. Knoxville: University of Tennessee Press, 1989.

Thürer, Georg. *Free and Swiss: The Story of Switzerland*. Adapted and translated by R. P. Heller and E. Long. London: Oswald Wolff, 1970.

Van Ruymbeke, Bertrand, and Randy J. Sparks, eds. *Memory and Identity: The Huguenots in France and the Atlantic Diaspora*. Columbia: University of South Carolina Press, 2003.

Ver Steeg, Clarence. *Origins of a Southern Mosaic: Studies of Early Carolina and Georgia*. Athens: University of Georgia Press, 1975.

Wallace, Anthony F. C. *The Death and the Rebirth of the Seneca*. New York: Alfred A. Knopf, 1970.

Walters, John Bennett. *Merchant of Terror: General Sherman and Total War*. Indianapolis: Bobbs-Merrill, 1973.

Ward, Christopher. *The War of the Revolution*. 2 vols. New York: Macmillan, 1952.

Waring, Joseph I. *A History of Medicine in South Carolina, 1670–1825*. Charleston: South Carolina Medical Association, 1964.

Waterhouse, Richard. *A New World Gentry: The Making of a Merchant and a Planter Class in South Carolina, 1670–1770*. New York: Garland, 1989.

Weigley, Russell F. *The Partisan War: The South Carolina Campaign of 1780–1782*. Columbia: University of South Carolina Press, 1970.

Weinreich, Uriel. *Languages in Contact: Findings and Problems*. New York: Columbia University Press, 1953.

Weir, Robert M. *"A Most Important Epocha": The Coming of the Revolution in South Carolina*. Columbia: University of South Carolina Press, 1970.

———. *Colonial South Carolina: A History*. Columbia: University of South Carolina Press, 1997.

Wolf, Stephanie Grauman. *Urban Village: Population, Community, and Family*

Structure in Germantown, Pennsylvania, 1683–1800. Princeton, N.J.: Princeton University Press, 1976; first Princeton paperback printing, 1980.

Wood, Betty. *Slavery in Colonial Georgia, 1730–1775*. Athens: University of Georgia Press, 1984.

Wood, Bradford J. *This Remote Part of the World: Regional Formation in Lower Cape Fear, North Carolina, 1725–1775*. Columbia: University of South Carolina Press, 2005

Wood, Peter H. *Black Majority: Negroes in Colonial South Carolina from 1670 through the Stono Rebellion*. New York: Alfred A. Knopf, 1974.

Woods, Sister Frances Jerome, C.D.P. *Cultural Values of American Ethnic Groups*. New York: Harper and Brothers, 1956.

Woodward, C. Vann. *The Burden of Southern History*. Rev. ed. Baton Rouge: Louisiana State University Press, 1968.

Young, Jacqueline. *Germans in the Colonial Southeast*. Bonn-Bad Godesberg: Inter Nations, 1977.

Michael Zuckerman. *Peaceable Kingdoms: New England Towns in the Eighteenth Century*. New York: Alfred A. Knopf, 1970.

———, ed. *Friends and Neighbors: Group Life in America's First Plural Society*. Philadelphia: Temple University Press, 1982.

Secondary Sources: Journal Literature, Dissertations, Internet, and Other Materials

Albergotti, William Greer, III. "Purysburg—Not Death but Murder." *Transactions of the Huguenot Society of South Carolina* 108 (2004): 106–13.

Axtell, James. "The Ethnohistory of Early America: A Review Essay." *William and Mary Quarterly*, 3rd ser., 35 (January 1978): 110–44.

"Barnwell of South Carolina." *South Carolina Historical and Genealogical Magazine* 2 (January 1901): 46–88.

Barr, William B. "Strawberry Ferry and Childsbury Towne: A Socio-Economic Enterprise on the Western Branch of the Cooper River, Saint Johns's Parish, Berkeley County, South Carolina." M.A. thesis, University of South Carolina, 1995.

Beck, Henry L. "Purrysburg as It Is Today." *Transactions of the Huguenot Society of South Carolina* 39 (1934): 40–44.

Bender, Thomas. "Wholes and Parts: The Need for Synthesis in American History." *Journal of American History* 73 (June 1986): 120–36.

Bosher, John F. "Huguenot Merchants and the Protestant International in the Seventeenth Century." *William and Mary Quarterly*, 3rd ser., 52 (1995): 77–102.

———. "The Imperial Environment of French Trade with Canada, 1660–1685." *English Historical Review* 108 (1993): 50–82.

Brantley, R. L. "The Salzburgers in Georgia." *Georgia Historical Quarterly* 14 (September 1930): 214–24.

Brooks, Richard David. "Cattle Ranching in Colonial South Carolina: A Case Study in History and Archeology of the Lazarus/Catherina Brown Cowpen." M.A. thesis, University of South Carolina, 1988.

Brown, Philip M. "Early Indian Trade in the Development of South Carolina: Politics, Economics, and Social Mobility during the Proprietary Period, 1670–1719." *South Carolina Historical Magazine* 76 (July 1975): 118–28.

Butler, Jon. "Enthusiasm Described and Decried: The Great Awakening as Interpretive Fiction." *Journal of American History* 69 (1982): 305–25.

Caldwell, Norman W. "The Southern Frontier during King George's War." *Journal of Southern History* 7 (February 1941): 37–54.

Carr, Lois Green, and Lorena S. Walsh. "The Planter's Wife: The Experience of White Women in Seventeenth-Century Maryland." *William and Mary Quarterly,* 3rd ser., 34 (October 1977): 542–71.

Carson, Helen Craig. "Notes and News from the Archives: Accounts Audited of Claims Growing out of the Revolution." *South Carolina Historical Magazine* 75 (July 1974): 201–4.

Cates, Gerald L. "The Seasoning: Disease and Death among the First Colonists of Georgia." *Georgia Historical Quarterly* 64 (Summer 1980): 146–58.

Châtelain, Dr. Auguste. "Purrysburg." *Musée Neuchâtelois,* new series 7 (May–June 1920): 84–94, 121–25.

Chestnutt, David Rogers. "South Carolina's Expansion into Georgia, 1720–1765." Ph.D. dissertation, University of Georgia, 1973.

Childs, St. Julien Ravenel. "Notes on the History of Public Health in South Carolina, 1670–1800." *Proceedings of the South Carolina Historical Association* (1932): 13–22.

Clowse, Converse D., and William Patterson Cumming. "Geographical Misconceptions of the Southeast in the Cartography of the Seventeenth and Eighteenth Centuries." *Journal of Southern History* 4 (November 1938): 476–92.

Colcock, William Ferguson. "The Huguenots in Northern Italy." *Transactions of the Huguenot Society of South Carolina* 83 (1978): 52–58.

Coleman, Kenneth. "The Southern Frontier: Georgia's Founding and the Expansion of South Carolina." *Georgia Historical Quarterly* 56 (Summer 1972): 163–74.

Columbian Museum and Savannah Advertiser.

Columbian Museum and Savannah Daily Gazette.

Conzan, Kathleen Neils, Harry S. Stout, E. Brooks Holifield, and Michael Zuckerman. "Forum." *Religion and American Culture: A Journal of Interpretation* 6, no. 2 (Summer 1996): 107–29.

Coulter, E. Merton. "Mary Musgrove, 'Queen of the Creeks': A Chapter of Early Georgia Troubles." *Georgia Historical Quarterly* 11 (March 1927): 1–30.

Daily Georgian.

Daniel, Marjorie. "John Joachim Zubly: Georgia Pamphleteer of the Revolution." *Georgia Historical Quarterly* 19 (March 1935): 1–16.

Davis, Mollie C. "The Countess of Huntingdon and Whitefield's Bethseda." *Georgia Historical Quarterly* 56 (Spring 1972): 72–82.

———. "Whitefield's Attempt to Establish a College in Georgia." *Georgia Historical Quarterly* 55 (Winter 1971): 459–47.

"Deference or Defiance in Eighteenth Century America: A Round Table." *Journal of American History* 85 (June 1998): 13–97.

Dewig, Rob. "Ancient Brick-Lined Pit a So Carolina Historical Mystery." *Carolina Morning News.* 21 May 2001. Accessed online at http://www./farshores.org/acarwell/html, 3 August 2003.

Duffy, John. "Eighteenth Century Carolina Health Conditions." *Journal of Southern History* 28 (August 1952): 289–302.

———. "Yellow Fever in Colonial Charleston." *South Carolina Historical and Genealogical Magazine* 52 (October 1951): 189–97.

Dunn, Richard S. "The Social History of Early New England." *American Quarterly* 24 (December 1972): 661–79.

Dwight, Charles S. "Address of the President." *Transactions of the Huguenot Society of South Carolina* 44 (1939): 20–21.

Elliot, Daniel. "Archeological Reconnaissance of the Purrysburg Tract, Jasper County, South Carolina." Garrow and Associates, 24 January 1985.

"An Emigration of Huguenots to South Carolina in 1764." *Proceedings of the Huguenot Society of London* 5 (1894–96): 179–87.

Ernst, Joseph A., and H. Roy Merrens. "'Camden's turrets pierce the skies!': The Urban Process in the Southern Colonies during the Eighteenth Century." *William and Mary Quarterly,* 3rd ser., 30 (October 1973): 549–74.

Ervin, Sara S. "Notes on the History of the Giroud and Allied Families of Purrysburg, South Carolina—Being a Record of the Family for Three Generations before Coming to America and for Four Generations in South Carolina, Up to About the Time of the War between the States." *Transactions of the Huguenot Society of South Carolina* 48 (June 1943): 36–42.

Faust, Albert B. "Swiss Emigration to the American Colonies in the Eighteenth Century." *American Historical Review* 22 (1916–1917): 21–44.

Ferken, Harold. "The Swiss Background of the Purrysburg Settlers." *Transactions of the Huguenot Society of South Carolina* 39 (1934): 20–26.

Fingerhut, Eugene R. "Uses and Abuses of the American Loyalists' Claims: A Critique of Quantitative Analysis." *William and Mary Quarterly,* 3rd ser., 25 (April 1968): 245–58.

Friedlander, Amy E. "Carolina Huguenots: A Study in Cultural Pluralism in the Low Country, 1679–1768." Ph.D. dissertation, Emory University, 1979.

Gallay, Alan. "The Origins of Slaveholders' Paternalism: George Whitefield, the Bryan Family, and the Great Awakening in South Carolina." *Journal of Southern History* 53, no. 3 (August 1987): 367–94.

Gans, Herbert J. "Symbolic Ethnicity: The Future of Ethnic Groups and Cultures in America." *Ethnic and Racial Studies* 2 (January 1979): 1–20.

The Gazette of the State of Georgia

Georgia Gazette.

Ginzburg, Carlo. *Latitude, Slaves and the Bible: An Experiment in Microhistory* (abstract). 2000. www.helsinki.fi/collegium/events/Purry.pdf (18 September 2003).

"Granting of Land in Colonial South Carolina." *South Carolina Historical Magazine* 77 (July 1976): 208–12.

Gray, Janet G. "The Origin of the Word Huguenot." *Sixteenth Century Journal* 14 (1983): 349–59.

Hamer, Marguerite B. "The Foundations and Failure of the Silk Industry in Provincial Georgia." *North Carolina Historical Review* 12 (April 1935): 125–48.

Haviland, Thomas P. "Of Franklin, Whitefield, and the Orphan." *Georgia Historical Quarterly* 29 (December 1945): 211–16.

Haywood, Robert C. "Mercantilism and South Carolina Agriculture, 1700–1763." *South Carolina Historical Magazine* 60 (January 1959): 15–27.

Higham, John. "Hanging Together: Divergent Unities in American History." *Journal of American History* 61 (June 1974): 5–28.

Hillery, George A., Jr. "Definitions of a Community: Areas of Agreement." *Rural Sociology* 20 (1955): 111–23.

Hilliard, Sam B. "The Tidewater Rice Plantation: An Ingenious Adaptation to Nature." *Geoscience and Man* 12 (20 June 1975): 57–66.

Hinde, Captain W. H., R. E. "The Huguenot Settlement at the Cape of Good Hope." *Proceedings of the Huguenot Society of London* 5 (1894–1895): 205–21.

Hirsch, Arthur Henry. "French Influence on American Agriculture in the Colonial Period with Special Reference to Southern Provinces." *Agricultural History* 4 (January 1930): 1–9.

———. "Some Phases of the Huguenot-Anglican Rivalries in South Carolina before 1730." *Presbyterian Church Department of History Journal* 13 (1928): 2–22.

"The Historic Celebration of the Vaudois." *Proceedings of the Huguenot Society in America* 2 (20 April 1888–13 April 1891): 58–65.

"Historical Notes." *South Carolina Historical and Genealogical Magazine* 5 (July 1904): 189–93 and 7 (April 1906): 106.

"History of Ceduna." Winco Eclipse Tours, Inc. www.eclipsesafari.com/id30_m.htm (3 August 2003).

Hofer, J. M. "The Georgia Salzburgers." *Georgia Historical Quarterly* 18 (June 1934): 99–117.

Holland, James W. "The Beginning of Public Agricultural Experimentation in America." *Agricultural History* 12 (July 1938): 271–98.

Hughes, Kaylene. "Populating the Back Country: The Demographic and Social Characteristics of the Colonial South Carolina Frontier." Ph.D. dissertation, Florida State University, 1985.

Isajiw, Wsevolod W. "Definitions of Ethnicity." *Ethnicity* 1 (1974): 111–24.

Jackson, Harvey H. "The Carolina Connection: Jonathan Bryan, His Brothers, and the Founding of Georgia, 1733–1752." *Georgia Historical Quarterly* 68 (Summer 1984): 147–72.

Jellison, Richard M. "Antecedents of the South Carolina Currency Acts of 1736 and 1746." *William and Mary Quarterly,* 3rd ser., 16 (October 1959): 556–67.

Johnson, A. J. "Johnson's Map of North and South Carolina." New York, 1862.

Jones, George F. "Compilation of Lists of German-Speaking Settlers of Purrysburg." *South Carolina Historical Magazine* 92 (October 1991): 253–68.

———. "The Salzburger Mills: Georgia's First Successful Enterprises." *Yearbook of German-American Studies* 23 (1988): 105–17.

Kane, Hope Francis. "Colonial Promotion and Promotion Literature of Carolina, 1660–1700." Ph.D. dissertation, Brown University, 1930.

Kazal, Russell A. "Revisting Assimilation: The Rise, Fall, and Reappraisal of a Concept in American Ethnic History." *American Historical Review* 100, no. 2 (April 1995): 437–71.

Kelsey, R. W. "Swiss Settlers in South Carolina." *South Carolina Historical and Genealogical Magazine* 23, no. 3 (July 1922): 85–91.

Kenney, William Howland, III. "Alexander Garden and George Whitefield: The Significance of Revivalism in South Carolina, 1738–1741." *South Carolina Historical Magazine* 71 (January 1970): 1–16.

———. "George Whitefield, Dissenter Priest of the Great Awakening, 1739–1741." *William and Mary Quarterly,* 3rd ser., 26 (January 1969): 75–93.

Klingberg, Frank J. "The Indian Frontier in South Carolina as Seen by the Society for the Propagation of the Gospel Missionaries." *Journal of Southern History* 5 (November 1939): 479–500.

Land, Aubrey C. "Economic Base and Social Structure: The Northern Chesapeake in the Eighteenth Century." *Journal of Economic History* 25 (December 1965): 639–54.

Lefler, Hugh T. "Promotional Literature of the Southern Colonies." *Journal of Southern History* 33 (February 1967): 3–25.

Leiding, Harriet Dubose Kershaw. "Purrysburg: A Swiss-French Settlement of South Carolina, on the Savannah River." *Transactions of the Huguenot Society of South* Carolina 39 (1934): 27–39.

Lepionka, Larry. "Purrysburg, an Archeological Survey: A Report on the Archeological Investigation of the Colonial Site of Purrysburg, Founded in 1733 by Jean Pierry Purry of Neuchatel." Beaufort, October 17, 1979; subsequently published in the *Swiss American Historical Society Newsletter* 16, no. 2 (1980): 18–29.

Lesesne, Dr. J. M. "An Address by Dr. J. M. Lesesne at the 208th Anniversary of the Arrival of the French Huguenots at New Bordeaux." *Transactions of the McCormick County Historical Society* 1 (1971–1972): 30–36.

Levett, Ella Pettit. "Loyalism in Charlestown, 1761–1784." *Proceedings of the South Carolina Historical Society* 6 (1936): 3–17.

Lieberson, Stanley. "A Societal Theory of Race and Ethnic Relations." *American Sociological Review* 26 (December 1961): 902–10.

McKinstry, Mary Thomas. "Silk Culture in the Colony of Georgia." *Georgia Historical Quarterly* 14 (September 1930): 225–35.

Macknight, C. C. "Neither Useful nor Profitable: Early Eighteenth Century Ideas about Australia and Its Inhabitants." Typescript of a lecture given at the National Library of Australia, 22 September 1993.

———. "Research Notes on J. P. Purry." Unpublished paper, Department of History, Faculty of Arts, Australian National University, Canberra, Australia, 13 July 1993.

Malin, James C. "The Turnover of Farm Population in Kansas." *Kansas Historical Quarterly* 4 (November 1935): 339–72.

Martin, Roger A. "John J. Zubly Comes to America." *Georgia Historical Quarterly* 61 (Summer 1977): 125–39.

"Memorial Tablets in the French Protestant (Huguenot) Church in Charleston, South Carolina" and "Alphabetical List of Memorial Tablets." *Transactions of the Huguenot Society of South Carolina* 75 (1970): 49–93.

Mendenhall, Marjorie Stratford. "A History of Agriculture in South Carolina, 1790–1860." Ph.D. dissertation, University of North Carolina, 1940.

Merrens, H. Roy. "The Physical Environment of Early America: Images and Image-makers in Colonial South Carolina." *Geographical Review* 59 (October 1969): 530–56.

Migliazzo, Arlin C. "British Mercantile Theory and French Huguenot Labor: The Wine and Silk Industries in Colonial South Carolina." Unpublished seminar paper, Department of History, Washington State University, 29 January 1980.

———. "The Burdens of Intimacy: Family Life on the Southern Frontier, 1732–1773."

Social Science Perspectives Journal: Proceedings of the 1986 Seattle Conference [final paper] (1986): 1–16.

———. "Ethnic Diversity on the Southern Frontier: A Social History of Purrysburgh, South Carolina, 1732–1792." Ph.D. dissertation, Washington State University, 1982.

———. "Sources of the Purrysburgh Population: The European Context." *Transactions of the Huguenot Society of South Carolina* 87 (1982): 51–63.

———. "A Tarnished Legacy Revisted: Jean Pierre Purry and the Settlement of the Southern Frontier. 1718–1736." *South Carolina Historical Magazine* 92 (October 1991): 232–52.

———. "'To Serve and to Protect': Purrysburg Township, South Carolina and the Defense of the Southern Colonial Frontier." Paper presented at the Southern Historical Association Meeting, 4 November 2005, Memphis.

Miller, Randall M. "The Failure of the Colony of Georgia under the Trustees." *Georgia Historical Quarterly* 53 (March 1969): 1–17.

Morgan, David T., Jr. "The Consequences of George Whitefield's Ministry in the Carolinas and Georgia, 1739–1740." *Georgia Historical Quarterly* 55 (Spring 1971): 62–82.

———. "George Whitefield and the Great Awakening in the Carolinas and Georgia, 1739–1740." *Georgia Historical Quarterly* 54 (Winter 1970): 517–39.

———. "The Great Awakening in South Carolina, 1740–1775." *South Atlantic Quarterly* 70 (1971): 595–606.

———. "John Wesley's Sojourn in Georgia Revisited." *Georgia Historical Quarterly* 64 (Fall 1980): 253–62.

Muench, Dr. F. "The Story of Purrysburg." *Charleston Sunday News and Courier,* 10 April 1898, 10.

Nadelhaft, Jerome. "Ending South Carolina's War: Two 1782 Agreements Favoring the Planters." *South Carolina Historical Magazine* 80 (January 1979): 50–64.

Newton, Hester Walton. "The Agricultural Activities of the Salzburgers in Colonial Georgia." *Georgia Historical Quarterly* 18 (September 1934): 248–63.

———. "The Industrial and Social Influences of the Salzburgers in Colonial Georgia." *Georgia Historical Quarterly* 18 (December 1934): 335–53.

"Notes and Queries." *Proceedings of the Huguenot Society of London* 3 (1888–91): 420–21.

"Notes Relative to Bourguin and Kelsall." *Transactions of the Huguenot Society of South Carolina* 75 (1970): 214–15.

O'Connell, Neil J., O.F.M. "George Whitefield and Bethesda Orphan House." *Georgia Historical Quarterly* 54 (Spring 1970): 41–62 and 54 (Summer 1970): 183–208.

Otto, John S. "The Origins of Cattle-Ranching in Colonial South Carolina, 1670–1715." *South Carolina Historical Magazine* 87 (April 1986): 117–24.

"Our Huguenot Ancestors: Their Homes in France." *Transactions of the Huguenot Society of South Carolina* 75 (1970): 94–98.

Parenti, Michael. "Ethnic Politics and the Persistence of Ethnic Identification." *American Political Science Review* 61 (September 1967): 717–26.

Perry, Grace Fox. "The Lost Settlement of Purrysburg, Part 2." *Charleston News and Courier,* 1 April 1956 3-C. Copy at the Library of the Huguenot Society of South Carolina.

"Pieter Nuyts." *Flinders Ranges Research*. 13 September 2003. www.picknowl.com.

au/homepages/rkfadol/nuyts.htm (25 September 2003).

Potter, David M. "The Enigma of the South." *Yale Review* 51 (October 1961): 142–51.

Pugh, Robert C. "The Revolutionary Militia in the Southern Campaign, 1780–1781." *William and Mary Quarterly,* 3rd ser., 14 (April 1957): 154–75.

Ravenel, Daniel. "Historical Sketch of the Huguenot Congregations of South Carolina." *Transactions of the Huguenot Society of South Carolina* 7 (1900): 7–74.

Ready, Milton. "The Georgia Concept: An Eighteenth Century Experiment in Colonization." *Georgia Historical Quarterly* 55 (Summer 1971): 157–72.

Republican and Savannah Evening Ledger.

Richardson, Katherine Hurt. "'As Easy to Build Towns as Draw Schemes . . .' Colonial South Carolina Settlement Patterns: Towns on the Frontier." M.A. thesis, University of South Carolina, 1988.

Rodman, Margaret C. "Empowering Place: Multilocality and Multivocality." *American Anthropologist* 94, no. 3 (September 1992): 640–56.

Rogers, George C., Jr. "Aedanus Burke, Nathaniel Greene, Anthony Wayne, and the British Merchants of Charleston." *South Carolina Historical Magazine* 67 (April 1966): 74–83.

———. "The Huguenots of the Old Beaufort District." *Transactions of the Huguenot Society of South Carolina* 85 (1980): 1–14.

Rothman, Adam. "'Servile Deceit' and the Limits of Slave Resistance in the United States." Paper presented at the Southern Historical Association Meeting, 5 November 2004, Memphis, Tenn.

Roulet, Louis-Edouard. "Jean-Pierre Pury et Ses Projets de Colonies en Afrique du Sud et en Australie," *Musée Neuchâtelois* (1994): 49–63.

Rowland, Lawrence S. "Alone on the River: The Rise and Fall of the Savannah River Rice Plantations of St. Peter's Parish, South Carolina." *South Carolina Historical Magazine* 88 (1987): 121–50.

———. "Eighteenth Century Beaufort: A Study of South Carolina's Southern Parishes to 1800." Ph.D. dissertation, University of South Carolina, 1978.

———. "The Purrysburg Swiss in the Beaufort District." *Transactions of the Huguenot Society of South Carolina* 98 (1993): 20–26.

Royal Georgia Gazette.

Rubertone, Patricia E. "Landscape as Artifact: Comments on 'The Archeological Use of Landscape Treatment in Social Economic and Ideological Analysis.'" *Historical Archeology* 23, no. 1 (1989): 50–54.

Rubincam, Milton. "Historical Background of the Salzburger Emigration to Georgia." *Georgia Historical Quarterly* 35 (June 1951): 99–115.

Rutman, Darret B. "Assessing the Little Communities of Early America." *William and Mary Quarterly,* 3rd ser., 43 (April 1986): 163–78.

Rutman, Darret B., and Anita H. Rutman. "Of Agues and Fevers: Malaria in the Early Chesapeake." *William and Mary Quarterly,* 3rd ser., 33 (January 1976): 31–60.

Savannah Georgian.

Savannah Republican.

Saye, Albert B. "The Genesis of Georgia: Merchants as Well as Ministers." *Georgia Historical Quarterly* 24 (September 1940): 191–201.

———. "The Genesis of Georgia Reviewed." *Georgia Historical Quarterly* 50 (June 1966): 153–61.

Schmidt, Leigh Eric. "'The Grand Prophet,' Hugh Bryan: Early Evangelicalism's Challenge to the Establishment and Slavery in the Colonial South." *South Carolina Historical Magazine* 87 (1986): 238–50.

Scoville, Warren C. "The Huguenots and the Diffusion of Technology, II." *Journal of Political Economy* 60 (October 1952): 392–411.

Seaman, Janice Louise. "John Joachim Zubly: Voice for Liberty and Principle." M.A. thesis, University of South Carolina, 1982.

Sherriff, Florence Janson. "The Saltzburgers and Purrysburg." *Proceedings of the South Carolina Historical Association* (1963): 12–22.

Smith, Henry A. M. "Purrysburgh." *South Carolina Historical and Genealogical Magazine* 10 (October 1909): 187–219.

Smith, Marvin T. "100% Archeological Survey of the Purrysburg Tract, Jasper County, South Carolina." Garrow and Associates, 10 June 1985.

Smith, W. Calvin. "Utopia's Last Chance? The Georgia Silk Boomlet of 1751." *Georgia Historical Quarterly* 59 (Spring 1975): 25–37.

Smyth, William D. "Travellers in South Carolina in the Early Eighteenth Century." *South Carolina Historical Magazine* 79 (April 1978): 113–25.

South Carolina Gazette.

South Carolina Gazette and Country Journal.

South Carolina Weekly Gazette.

Stacey, Margaret. "The Myth of Community Studies." *British Journal of Sociology* 20 (June 1969): 134–47.

Stegeman, John, and Janet Stegeman. "President Washington at Mulberry Grove." *Georgia Historical Quarterly* 61 (Winter 1977): 342–46.

Stephens, Pauline Tyson. "The Silk Industry in Georgia." *Georgia Review* 7 (Spring 1953): 39–49.

Summerall, C. P. "Address of General C. P. Summerall at the Dedication of the Huguenot Cross at Purrysburg, South Carolina, May 4, 1941." *Transactions of the Huguenot Society of South Carolina* 46 (1941): 38–44.

Surrency, Erwin C. "Whitefield, Habersham, and the Bethesda Orphanage." *Georgia Historical Quarterly* 34 (June 1950): 87–105.

Terry, George D. "'Champaign Country': A Social History of an Eighteenth Century Lowcountry Parish in South Carolina, St. John's Berkeley County." Ph.D. dissertation, University of South Carolina, 1981.

Tollin, Pastor, Lic. Dr. "Concerning the Name 'Huguenot.'" *Proceedings of the Huguenot Society of London* 6 (1898–1901): 325–55.

Tresp, Lothar L. "The Salzburger Orphanage at Ebenezer in Colonial Georgia." *Americana-Austriaca, Beitrage zur Amerikakunde* 3 (1974): 190–234.

Van Ruymbeke, Bertrand. "L'émigration huguenote en Caroline du Sud sous le régime des Seigneurs Propriétaires: Étude d'une communauté du Refuge dans une province britannique d'Amerique du Nord (1680–1720)." 2 vols. Ph.D. dissertation, Université de la Sorbonne–Nouvelle, Paris III, 1995.

Vecoli, Rudolph J. "Return to the Melting Pot: Ethnicity in the United States in the Eighties." *Journal of American Ethnic History* 5, no.1 (Fall 1985): 7–20.

Vincent, Joan. "The Structuring of Ethnicity." *Human Organization* 33 (Winter 1974): 375–79.

Voigt, Gilbert P. "Cultural Contributions of German Settlers to South Carolina." *South Carolina Historical Magazine* 53 (October 1952): 183–89.

———. "The German and German-Swiss Element in South Carolina, 1732–1752." *Bulletin of the University of South Carolina,* no. 113 (September 1922).

———. "The Germans and German-Swiss in South Carolina, 1732–1765: Their Contribution to the Province." *Proceedings of the South Carolina Historical Association* 5 (1935): 17–25.

———. "Religious Conditions among German-Speaking Settlers in South Carolina 1732–1774." *South Carolina Historical Magazine* 56 (April 1955): 59–66.

———. "Swiss Notes on South Carolina." *South Carolina Historical and Genealogical Magazine* 21 (July 1920): 93–104.

Watson, Alan D. "The Quitrent System in Royal South Carolina." *William and Mary Quarterly,* 3rd ser., 33 (April 1976): 183–211.

Wilkins, Thomas Hart. "An Economic Interpretation of the Founding of the Colony of Georgia." M.A. thesis, University of Georgia, 2002.

———. "James Edward Oglethorpe." *Georgia Historical Quarterly* 88, no. 1 (Spring 2004): 85–94.

Wolfinger, Raymond E. "The Development and Persistence of Ethnic Voting." *American Political Science Review* 59 (December 1965): 896–908.

Yemassee Bluff News.

Zuckerman, Michael. "The Fabrication of Identity in Early America." *William and Mary Quarterly,* 3rd ser., 34, no. 2 (April 1977): 183–214.

Zunz, Oliver. "American History and the Changing Meaning of Assimilation." *Journal of American Ethnic History* 4, no. 3 (Spring 1985): 53–72.

Index

Proper names are indexed according to their most common usage. Variant spellings found in extant sources are enclosed in parentheses.

About the Author

Arlin C. Migliazzo is a professor of history at Whitworth College in Spokane, Washington, where he has also served as department chair and director of faculty development. He is a former Fulbright/Hays Scholar in American Studies and the editor of *Teaching as an Act of Faith: Theory and Practice in Church-Related Higher Education* and *Lands of True and Certain Bounty: The Geographical Theories and Colonization Strategies of Jean Pierre Purry.*